Biophysical
Science

EUGENE ACKERMAN

Consultant, Section of Biophysics
Mayo Clinic

Associate Professor of Biophysics
Mayo Foundation

Rochester, Minnesota

Biophysical Science

PRENTICE-HALL INTERNATIONAL

London

1962

Library of Congress Catalog Card Number 62-11880

Printed in the United States of America

07715-C

182296

Preface

This book presents an introduction to many of the topics which are presently considered part of biophysics. Biophysics deals with biological problems; accordingly, the various chapters have been grouped by the type of problem described rather than by the methodology employed. The mathematical level required has been limited, in most cases, to elementary calculus.

As a separate discipline, biophysics is a recent addition to the sub-divisions of natural science. Until the mid-nineteenth century, it was quite common for investigators to be natural scientists contributing to many diverse fields. A well-known scientist who exemplified this wide range of interest was Hermann von Helmholtz, who was trained as a medical doctor and practiced medicine. He not only conducted histological studies of the eye and ear, but also worked on theories of vision and hearing. In addition to being an excellent biologist, Helmholtz was an outstanding physicist. He developed acoustic instrumentation which he used for frequency analyses of speech and music. His contributions to thermodynamics are emphasized by the term *Helmholtz free energy*. His name is associated with a law in geometrical optics as well as with a differential equation for sinusoidal waves.

With the growth of factual knowledge, it became more difficult for a person to do significant work in both the physical and biological sciences. Within each division of natural science, large numbers of subdivisions appeared; each small field had its own textbooks, its own theories, and its own part of human knowledge.

However, there is a group of problems for which extreme specialization is not desirable. Many of the problems of biophysics fall into this category, and require a knowledge of several specialized fields. For example, a complete background for the study of vision must include geometrical optics, spectroscopy, quantum biochemistry, physiology, psychology, neurophysiology, and electronics.

A certain group of research topics, all of which involve both biology and advanced physics, have come to be called biophysics. However, there is no general agreement concerning the topics properly belonging to this field. Those included here are the author's choice and emphasize his interests. They do include most of the fields generally assigned to biophysics.

Biophysics has become a field that is important for all physicists to study. For the prospective college teacher, it presents a variety of examples which can make general physics more interesting and of greater direct personal appeal. Accordingly, students from biological and premedical curricula will learn more physics in a general course taught by an instructor well versed in biophysics. Similarly, the industrial physicist will find that a biophysics course will broaden his appreciation of the applications of physics.

Biophysics is likewise a valuable course for seniors or graduate students majoring in biological sciences or medicine. Representing a different approach to topics they may study in other courses, biophysics can make an important contribution to a well-rounded training in biology. The premedical student will find that a biophysics course will help him to understand normal and abnormal physiology and will make electromedical apparatus more useful to him.

Another group for which a biophysics course may be useful is that of electrical engineers. The field of medical electronics has grown almost concurrently with the growth of biophysics.

Each of these different types of readers will have different backgrounds and preparations, so background material from physics and biology is introduced at appropriate points. Such background material will give the reader an appreciation of the importance of both physics and biology. Biophysics is as unsuited to people who know no biology as to those who know no physics.

In terms of the nature of the material covered, biophysics is certainly closer to conventional biology than to traditional physics. Nonetheless, most physics majors can equip themselves, by extra reading, with sufficient biological knowledge to understand all the topics of biophysics. However, certain students majoring in the biological sciences must accept on faith the conclusions of many mathematical proofs. In terms of methodology, as opposed to content, biophysics is closer to physics than to biology.

To develop a branch of natural science as a logical structure, it is desirable to describe the behavior of highly organized systems in terms of the properties of simpler systems. This is not always feasible and in some cases cannot be followed at all. For example, in physics one discusses electric currents before attempting to present electronic conduction bands in metals. In this text we have tried to start from more general topics with which all varieties of readers will be intuitively familiar, and proceed to simpler but more abstract ideas. Thus, Part A on special sensory systems includes a chapter on vision and the eye; the neural aspects of vision are presented in a chapter following discussion of nerve activity; the molecular actions which convert light into nerve impulses form the basis of a chapter in Part D which deals with molecular biology; finally, the eye as a coding mechanism is discussed in a chapter on information theory located in Part E. Specialized physical instruments, necessary for these and other studies, are discussed in the last part of the text.

All of the areas of the text taken together comprise biophysics. Within each area a careful selection has been made from a variety of topics all of which are part of biophysics. The topics included in this text were chosen not only for their relative importance, but also for their suitability for presentation in a one-year course for students with a variety of backgrounds. Other possible topics are included in the discussion questions at the end of each section of the text.

It is the author's hope that the reader of this book will gain an insight into the nature of the topics included in biophysics, recognizing the attempt to quantify and develop biological problems in terms of physical models wherever this is practical. The reader should become acquainted both with the biological basis of the various areas of biophysics and also with the essential role of mathematical analysis in most biophysical problems.

The author wishes to thank his many students and friends, all of whom have had such a profound influence on the material in this text. It is not possible to name all who have helped, but special mention is made of those who contributed an extra amount of their time and ideas. They are: Dr. A. Anthony and Dr. G. K. Strother of the Pennsylvania State University; Dr. A. A. Benson of the University of California; Dr. K. N. Ogle, Dr. A. L. Orvis, and Dr. C. M. Gambill of the Mayo Clinic; and Dr. A. S. Brill of Yale University. The permission of numerous publishers and authors to reprint their figures is also gratefully acknowledged. Without secretarial help, this text would never have been completed; special thanks are due

Miss Frances Fogle (Pennsylvania State University) and Miss Lorette Hentges (Mayo Clinic) for their part in making this text a reality.

Eugene Ackerman

Rochester, Minnesota

Contents

A. Special Sensory Systems

1. Sound and the Ear   3

1. Hearing, 3;   *2. Acoustics,* 5;   *3. Hearing Tests,* 10;   *4. Anatomy and Action of the Ear,* 19

2. Light and the Eye   27

1. Vision, 27;   *2. Optics,* 29;   *3. Anatomy of the Eye,* 34; *4. Thresholds and Acuity,* 43

3. Special Uses of Hearing and Vision   52

1. Introduction, 52;   *2. Echo-Location in Bats,* 53;   *3. Echo-Location in Other Animals,* 58;   *4. Sense of Direction in Bees and Ants,* 59;   *5. Migration and Homing,* 61

B. Nerve and Muscle

4. The Conduction of Impulses by Nerves   69

1. The Role of the Nervous System, 69;   *2. A Brief Glance at Electricity,* 72;   *3. Anatomy and Histology of Neurons,* 74;   *4. The Spike Potential,* 78;   *5. Synaptic Conduction,* 83

5. Electrical Potentials of the Brain   88

1. Electroencephalography, 88; 2. The Central Nervous System, 89; 3. Feedback Loops and the Nervous System, 92; 4. The Electroencephalographic Patterns, 96; 5. Abnormal Electroencephalographic Patterns, 100; 6. Summary, 102

6. Neural Mechanisms of Hearing   104

1. Place and Telephone Theories, 104; 2. Cochlear Mechanism of Neural Excitation, 108; 3. Arm Analogs and Neural Sharpening, 111; 4. Cortical Representation, 113; 5. Summary of Hearing, 117

7. Neural Aspects of Vision   119

1. Color Discrimination, 119; 2. Cellular Mechanisms, 124; 3. Direct Neural Measurements, 129; 4. Neural Sharpening and Analyses, 131; 5. Cortical Representation, 133; 6. Summary of Vision, 135

8. Muscles   137

1. Introduction, 137; 2. Anatomy, 138; 3. Physical Changes During Muscular Contraction, 141; 4. Muscle Chemistry, 147; 5. Electron-Microscope Studies of Muscles, 151; 6. Summary, 154

9. Mechanical and Electrical Character of the Heart Beat   157

1. Role of the Vertebrate Circulatory System, 157; 2. Blood Pressures and Velocities, 158; 3. The Vertebrate Heart, 161; 4. The Heart Sequence, 163; 5. Electrocardiography, 168; 6. Physics of Dipoles, 171; 7. Vector Electrocardiography, 175; 8. Summary, 177

C. Physical Microbiology

10. Cellular Events Produced by Ionizing Radiations   185

1. Ionizing Radiation as a Biological Tool, 185; 2. Dosage, 187; 3. Mitosis and Meiosis, 189; 4. Visible Cellular Effects, 191; 5. Genetic Effects, 196; 6. Evolution, Mutation and Fall-out, 200; 7. Summary, 201

Contents

11. The Absorption of Electromagnetic and Ultrasonic Energy   204

1. Role of Nonionizing Radiation, 204; 2. Electrical Impedances, 205; 3. Biological Impedance, 208; 4. Ultrasonics, 213; 5. Nondestructive Effects of Ultrasound, 214; 6. Diathermy, 217; 7. Summary, 218

12. Destructive Effects of High Intensity Ultrasound   220

1. High Intensity Ultrasound, 220; 2. Cavitation, 222; 3. Biological Cells and Cavitation, 224; 4. Cellular Fragilities and Resonances, 226; 5. Neurosurgery with Ultrasound, 230

13. Mechanical Resonances of Biological Cells   233

1. Experimental Basis, 233; 2. Interfacial-Tension Model, 236; 3. Gelatinous-Shell Model, 240; 4. More Exact Treatments, 242; 5. Summary, 244

14. Structure of Viruses   246

1. Introduction, 246; 2. Phage Studies Using Bacteriological Methods, 248; 3. Virus Studies Using Physical Methods, 251; 4. Physical Biochemistry of Viruses, 254; 5. Phage Genetics, 256; 6. Summary, 260

D. Molecular Biology

15. X-ray Analyses of Proteins and Nucleic Acids   267

1. Protoplasm, 267; 2. Proteins, 271; 3. Nucleic Acids, 277; 4. X-ray Diffraction, 280; 5. Protein Structure, 286; 6. Nucleic Acid Structure, 292; 7. Summary, 296

16. Molecular Action of Ionizing Radiations   299

1. Introduction, 299; 2. Polymers, Proteins, and DNA, 300; 3. Radiation Damage to Synthetic High Polymers, 302; 4. Target Theory, 305; 5. Inactivation of Dried Protein Films, 307; 6. Indirect Effects on Proteins and Nucleic Acids, 311; 7. Summary, 313

17. Enzyme Kinetics of Hydrolytic Reactions   315

1. Introduction, 315; 2. Enzymes, 318; 3. Michaelis-Menten Kinetics of Hydrolases, 320; 4. Action of Inhibitors, 327

18. Enzymes: Kinetics of Oxidations   332

1. Catalase, 332; 2. Peroxidase, 341; 3. Biological Oxidations, 344; 4. Oxidative Phosphorylation, 346; 5. Summary of Enzyme Kinetics, 349

19. Molecular Basis of Vision   351

1. Color Vision and Photopigments, 351; 2. Rhodopsin, 352; 3. Other Photopigments, 357; 4. The Origin of the Neural Spike, 358

20. Photosynthesis   360

1. Introduction, 360; 2. A Little Plant Histology, 361; 3. Basic Chemistry of Photosynthesis, 364; 4. The Path of Carbon in Photosynthesis, 368; 5. The Photosynthetic Pigments, 370; 6. The Light Reaction, 373; 7. Summary, 377

E. Thermodynamics and Transport Systems

21. Thermodynamics and Biology   385

1. The Role of Thermodynamics in Biology, 385; 2. The Laws of Thermodynamics, 386; 3. Other Thermodynamic Functions, 390; 4. Equilibrium Constants, 392; 5. Reactions of Catalase, 396

22. Thermodynamics of Enzyme Reactions   401

1. Collision Theory of Reactions, 401; 2. Collision Theory Applied to Enzyme Reactions, 406; 3. Absolute Rate Theory, 408; 4. Denaturation Studies, 412; 5. Diffusion Studies, 415; 6. Summary, 417

23. Diffusion, Permeability and Active Transport   419

1. Introduction, 419; 2. Diffusion Equations, 421; 3. The Diffusion of Oxygen into Cells, 426; 4. Permeability of Red Blood Cells, 429; 5. Active Transport, 432; 6. Summary, 435

24. The Molecular Basis of Nerve Conduction   437

1. Donnan Membrane Potentials, 437; 2. Quasi-Static Analogs, 440; 3. Biochemical Extractions, 443; 4. Clamped Nerve Experiments, 446; 5. Summary, 457

25. Information Theory and Biology   460

1. Languages, 460; *2. Information Theory — General Discussion,* 461; *3. Information and Sensory Perception,* 467; *4. Information Theory and Protein Structure,* 471; *5. The Coding of Genetic Information,* 474; *6. Summary,* 475

F. Specialized Instrumentation

26. Absorption Spectrophotometry   481

1. Role of Absorption Spectrophotometry in Biology, 481; *2. Units and Symbols of Absorption,* 484; *3. Spectrophotometers,* 488; *4. Flow Systems,* 495; *5. Split-Beam and Dual-Beam Spectrophotometers,* 496

27. Quantum Mechanical Basis of Molecular Spectra   501

1. Introduction, 501; *2. An Elementary Approach to Quantum Mechanics,* 502; *3. Molecular Spectra — Rotational and Vibrational Bands,* 509; *4. Electronic Levels of Atoms and Molecules,* 516

28. Magnetic Measurements   525

1. Magnetic Effects in Biology, 525; *2. Paramagnetism and Diamagnetism,* 526; *3. Static Measurement Techniques,* 528; *4. Resonance Measurements,* 531; *5. Limitations and Applications of Magnetic Measurements,* 534

29. Microscopy   537

1. Types of Microscopes, 537; *2. The Bright-Field Light Microscope,* 538; *3. The Dark-Field Microscope,* 542; *4. Phase-Contrast Microscopy,* 544; *5. Interference-Contrast Microscopy,* 545; *6. The Polarizing Microscope,* 548; *7. Ultraviolet and X-ray Microscopes,* 550; *8. The Electron Microscope,* 551

30. Tracer Techniques   557

1. Introduction, 557; *2. Radioactive Tracers,* 558; *3. C^{14},* 563; *4. I^{131},* 565; *5. P^{32},* 566; *6. Stable Isotopes,* 567; *7. N^{15},* 568; *8. Summary,* 570

31. Electronic Computers

571

1. Need for High Speed Computation, 571; *2. Analog and Digital Computers,* 572; *3. A Bone–Density Analog Computer,* 573; *4. Curve Fitters,* 577; *5. Digital Computers,* 580

Appendices

A.   *Auditory Acoustics,* 589
B.   *Geometrical Optics,* 595
C.   *Electrical Terminology (Used in Chapters 4 through 7),* 605
D.   *Ionizing Radiations,* 610

Index

615

A

Special Sensory Systems

Introduction to Part A

The first two chapters were chosen as biophysical topics, the ideas of which are intuitively familiar to a wide group of potential readers. These two chapters on "Sound and the Ear" and "Light and the Eye" emphasize basic concepts such as the physical nature of the stimuli and the anatomical character of the receptors. The ideas of Chapters 1 and 2 are extended in Chapter 3, "Special Uses of Sensory Systems," to unique applications of auditory and visual information by several animal species —uses which man can duplicate only with electronic equipment.

Sensory systems form links between the central nervous system and the external world. Biophysicists study not only hearing and vision, but also other sensory systems such as taste, proprioception, and balance. However, the special senses of hearing and vision appear more appropriate for textbook material since they have been studied in greater detail.

Ultimately, a discussion of hearing must involve such complex concepts as nerve mechanisms and information theory. These are presented in later chapters, following more general developments, namely, in Chapter 6, Part B, and Chapter 25, Part E. Likewise, additional topics in the field of vision are included in Chapter 7, Part B, Chapter 19, Part D, and Chapter 25, Part E.

I

I

Sound and the Ear

I. Hearing

The study of hearing is one of the oldest fields in biophysics. The reception and analysis of sound by the human ear has interested men who studied either physics or biology and has appealed especially to persons having a background in both the physical and biological sciences. The hearing mechanisms form one of the major sensory systems through which animals are stimulated by their environment. Vertebrates, in particular, have complicated sensory receptor systems which analyze incident sound waves for tone, quality, and loudness.

Man relies on visual information when he wants accuracy such as is required in recording scientific data. However, in communicating daily with the people around him, man relies principally on hearing. As a result of this major role of hearing in social intercourse, persons with a hearing deficiency suffer more social disapproval than do those with visual deficiencies. Hearing is important not only for communicating with other persons, but also for avoiding many dangers such as being struck by an automobile. In addition, we learn to recognize certain living creatures and many types of events by their noises, for example, the cat's meow and the telephone's ring. Human emotions, too, are

3

influenced by the sense of hearing.   Many of our forms of entertainment
—concerts, theatre, movies, radio, and even television—depend upon
our sense of hearing.

Hearing can be studied from many different points of view.   Physicists have learned how sound waves are generated and how they are
transmitted.   Anatomists have probed into the structure of the ear on a
gross level and also on a microscopic level.   They have traced the pathways by which auditory nerve impulses travel from the ear to the brain.
Psychologists, physiologists, and physicists all have studied the thresholds
of sensitivity of the hearing system and the way in which we understand
speech.   Most of these groups, and especially biophysicists, have been
interested in the manner in which the hearing organ operates, how
sounds are analyzed, how they are converted into nervous impulses and
then separated according to pitch, quality, and loudness.   In this
chapter and in Chapter 6, "Neural Mechanisms of Hearing," an attempt
has been made to synthesize all of these different avenues of approach,
while emphasizing those parts of each which have the greatest interest
to the biophysicist.

The first careful study of the ear and attempt to relate its structure
to hearing was carried out by Helmholtz.   Before that period, various
theories of hearing existed, but few have had more significance than one
which has survived in our colloquial speech.   This was the idea that the
ears were connected to a common hollow region within the head where
the sound was somehow stored.   If, so this theory went, we were not
careful, the sound would go in one ear (through the storage chamber)
and out the other.

Since the middle of the last century, hearing has been the subject of
many scientific investigations.   The nature of these studies was radically
altered around 1930 by the introduction of electronic techniques.
These techniques have completely changed the study of hearing; they
have dramatically influenced the interpretation of all phases of hearing
from pure acoustics to the final analyses of sounds within the brain.   So
complete is the dependence on electronic techniques today, that it is
hard to remember that Helmholtz and Lord Rayleigh could do acoustic
experiments successfully without electronic instrumentation.

Hearing is the response to mechanical, vibratory stimuli.   Not all
such stimuli evoke the sensations of hearing.   The sound must be loud
enough to be heard and also be of a suitable pitch.   The latter condition
is physically equivalent to saying the vibration must be within the
audible frequency range.   Vibrations outside of this frequency range
may be detected by human sensory systems other than hearing.   At
frequencies too low to be heard, vibrations are perceived through the
sense of touch; much greater amplitudes are needed for touch than are

needed for hearing. Frequencies higher than the audible range are not sensed until the energy becomes so great as to cause local heat and pain. Between these two extremes lie the frequencies to which the ear is sensitive. The exact frequency range depends on the person; it is influenced by his age and by the environment.

All vertebrates have a hearing apparatus homologous to our ear, although the frequency ranges to which they respond are varied. Many other animals such as insects are sensitive to vibratory energy over a wide range of frequencies, but their receptors are different, and the mechanisms involved in their response may be different. Even the single-celled animal, paramecium, can respond to vibratory energy in some fashion. Thus, there are many different types of sensory systems excited by vibratory mechanical energy. One of these, namely the human hearing apparatus, has been chosen for presentation in this chapter and in its sequel, Chapter 6, in Section B.

2. Acoustics

The physical aspects of sound transmission and the vibration of the ear are a subdivision of acoustics. The latter, in turn, is a branch of physical mechanics. In order to read with understanding journal articles dealing with the ear and hearing, it is very helpful to be familiar with the terminology of acoustics and with the electro-acoustic analogs often used. The various acoustic terms useful in describing studies of hearing are defined and discussed briefly in Appendix A, entitled "Auditory Acoustics." In contrast, this section of this chapter contains only a few of the acoustic terms used most frequently in studies of the ear and hearing.

Perhaps most familiar is the term *frequency* which describes how many times a second the sound pattern is repeated. The simplest possible case is one in which the *sound pressure, p,* can be described by an equation such as

$$p = p_0 \sin 2\pi\nu t \tag{1}$$

where p_0 is the acoustic pressure amplitude, t is the time, and ν is the frequency. This is referred to as a *pure tone.* The latter term is applicable since tone (or pitch) is the sensation associated with frequency. Most sounds consist of a mixture of frequencies which gives the sound its characteristic quality and timbre. A tuning fork comes close to producing a pure tone. One can come even closer by using an electronic oscillator and loudspeaker.

Any complex tone can be represented as a sum of simpler pure tones.

This is known as a Fourier representation. In many cases, only a finite or a discrete set of frequencies is necessary; then, we refer to the representation as a Fourier series. Speech and the character of musical instruments are determined by the frequencies present and their relative amplitudes. In the most general case, the sound is represented by an amplitude distribution which is a continuous function of frequency. This amplitude function is called a Fourier transform. The amplitude distribution for a sound "ee" is shown in Figure 1.

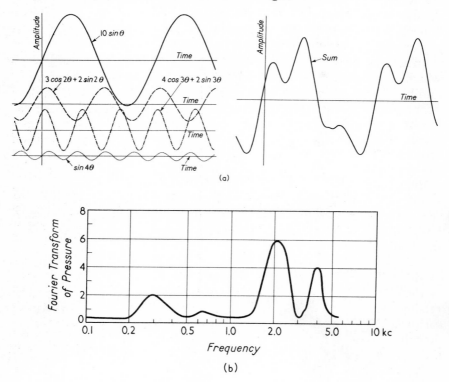

Figure I. (a) Fourier Series. The complex wave form labeled "sum" can be formed by adding relative amounts of four pure tones shown. (b) Fourier transform (or spectrum). The spectrum of the sound "ee" has the general form shown. The Fourier transform is a complex number; only its absolute value is shown.

A term closely related to frequency is *wavelength*, λ. This is the distance between the two nearest wavefronts with the same displacement and particle velocity in a plane sound field. If one knows the frequency and the velocity of sound propagation c, the wavelength may be determined by the relationship

$$\lambda = \frac{c}{\nu} \tag{2}$$

The wavelength is important in discussing diffraction, a phenomenon common to all wave-motion. Diffraction patterns are significant when the wavelength is comparable to the object the sound wave encounters. At shorter wavelengths, specular reflection and shadows are produced, whereas at longer wavelengths, the wave is transmitted as though the object were not there.

In air, a low tone of frequency 35 cps has a wavelength of about 10 m, which is comparable in size to a house. At the other end of the human audible range, a frequency of 9×10^3 cps (9 kc) has a wavelength of about 3 cm which is small compared to a person's head. Thus, the lowest audible frequencies will be diffracted around a house; in other words, the sound waves at these lowest frequencies will appear to bend around most obstacles. This makes it difficult to localize the source of the very low frequency tones below 100 cps. Conversely, the highest audible frequencies will form sharp shadows around small objects; the source of a 5–10 kc tone is easy to locate. At frequencies around 1 kc, the wavelength is comparable to the head. The diffraction pattern has the effect of increasing the amplitudes at the ear above those in the incident wave.

This increased amplitude makes the sounds near 1 kc seem extra loud.[1] The loudness is not simply determined by the particle velocity v or the displacement in the incident wave. Rather, the loudness is most readily related to another physical characteristic, the *sound pressure amplitude*. The latter and not the particle velocity or displacement is actually measured in most acoustic experiments. The sound pressure p is defined as the difference between the average (or equilibrium) pressure P_0 and the instantaneous total pressure, P; that is,

$$p = P - P_0 \tag{3}$$

Diagrammatically, one may represent this as shown in Figure 2. The acoustic pressure p is a scalar which will vary with both position and time.

Two waves of the same amplitude but traveling in opposite directions give rise to what is known as a *standing wave pattern*. Under some conditions, the wavelengths correspond to the characteristic dimensions of

---

[1] Other effects discussed later in the chapter also contribute to the increased loudness of sounds at 1–3 kc.

a physical system, and the phenomenon of *resonance* arises. This is illustrated in Figures 3 and 4 for strings and organ pipes. Note that in each case a series of characteristic (eigen) frequencies exists. Vibrations at these frequencies are particularly easy to excite. The lowest possible frequency is called the *fundamental frequency* or *first harmonic*. The next highest frequency is called the *first overtone*. If it is an integral multiple of the fundamental, it is called a harmonic. For example, an overtone five times the fundamental is the fifth harmonic. The standing wave pattern in the outer ear is discussed further in Section 4.

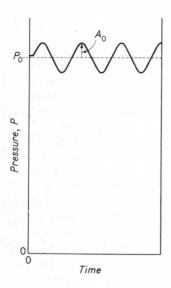

Figure 2. The dotted line shows the average pressure P_0 and the solid line indicates the absolute pressure P. The difference between P_0 and P is the acoustic pressure p. The maximum of p is A_0, the acoustic pressure amplitude. The figure is drawn for a pure tone showing simple harmonic dependence of p on time. In general, the form of p is more complex. An rms value of p can be specified but not an amplitude for a complex wave form.

It was noted above that the loudness of a given pure tone is determined primarily by the sound pressure amplitude. Often, another physical term, intensity, is associated with loudness. Intensity is the energy transmitted across a unit area per unit time. In practice, intensity is difficult to measure and not too useful as a concept for studies of hearing. For a plane wave, the intensity Υ is related to the pressure by

$$\Upsilon = \frac{\bar{p}^2}{\rho c} \qquad (4)$$

where $\bar{p}$ is the root mean square (rms) acoustic pressure, ρ is the density of the air, and c is the wave velocity. For other wave shapes, the expression is more complex (although the term ρc always appears). The intensity for a given value of $\bar{p}$ varies with the temperature, since ρc also varies. Loudness depends only on $\bar{p}$, not on the temperature.

Instead of presenting data in terms of the rms sound pressure amplitudes, it is customary to use the sound pressure level L. This is defined by

$$L = 20 \log \left(\frac{p}{p_0}\right) \text{ db} \qquad (5)$$

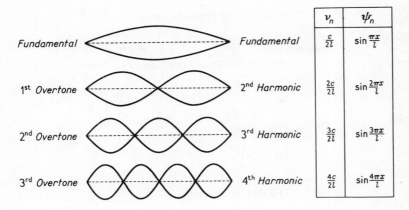

		ν_n	ψ_n
Fundamental	Fundamental	$\frac{c}{2l}$	$\sin\frac{\pi x}{l}$
1st Overtone	2nd Harmonic	$\frac{2c}{2l}$	$\sin\frac{2\pi x}{l}$
2nd Overtone	3rd Harmonic	$\frac{3c}{2l}$	$\sin\frac{3\pi x}{l}$
3rd Overtone	4th Harmonic	$\frac{4c}{2l}$	$\sin\frac{4\pi x}{l}$

Figure 3. Resonances of strings. The characteristic or resonant frequency is ω_n and the characteristic or eigenfunction is ψ_n. The displacement can be described by

$$y = \sum A_n \psi_n e^{\pm j\omega_n}$$

where the A_n 's are the amplitudes. The wave velocity

$$c = \sqrt{\frac{T}{\epsilon}}$$

where T is the tension and ϵ is the mass per unit length.

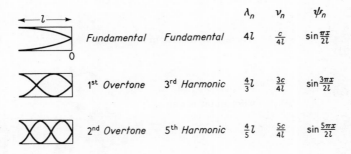

			λ_n	ν_n	ψ_n
	Fundamental	Fundamental	$4l$	$\frac{c}{4l}$	$\sin\frac{\pi x}{2l}$
	1st Overtone	3rd Harmonic	$\frac{4}{3}l$	$\frac{3c}{4l}$	$\sin\frac{3\pi x}{2l}$
	2nd Overtone	5th Harmonic	$\frac{4}{5}l$	$\frac{5c}{4l}$	$\sin\frac{5\pi x}{2l}$

Figure 4. Particle velocity for various overtones of a closed-end organ pipe. See Figure 3 for definition of the symbols. When the particle velocity has a node, the acoustic pressure has an anti-node, and conversely. The external ear canal resembles a closed-end organ pipe with a fundamental around 3 kc.

TABLE I

Various Sound Pressure Levels

Dynes/cm²	SPL	
	160 db	
10,000.00		Mechanical damage to human eardrum
	140	Pain threshold
		Jet motor
	120	Discomfort threshold
100.00		
		Riveter (peak values)
		Damage to human hearing after prolonged exposure
	100	Average factory
		Subway car
		Automobile
	80	Class lecture
1.00		Loud radio
	60	Typical office
		Conversational speech
	40	Average living room
0.01		
	20	Very quiet room
0.0002	0	Threshold of hearing

In air it is customary to use for p_0 the arbitrary value 2×10^{-4} dynes/cm². The 20 in the definition of decibels (db) arose out of historical reasons; from the properties of logarithms, one might equally well write this as

$$L = 10 \log \left(\frac{p^2}{p_0^2}\right) \tag{6}$$

or, for a plane wave,

$$L = 10 \log \left(\frac{\Upsilon}{\Upsilon_0}\right) \tag{7}$$

The latter is actually the original definition of a decibel. However, Υ depends on temperature, the medium, and the wave shape, so that the sound pressure level defined by Equation 5 is really a more convenient quantity.

The use of a logarithmic unit is helpful in plotting graphs, and to some extent loudness is proportional to the sound pressure level at fixed frequency. The logarithmic unit makes it possible to compare two sound pressure levels without knowing the absolute value of either. It also makes it appear as if many acoustic measurements were more precise than they actually are. The table on page 10 gives the sound pressure level of several common sounds, as well as the sound pressure amplitude p.

In addition to decibels, persons working in psycho-acoustics have used many exotic units such as phons[2] and sones.[3] The purpose of these has been to bring the numbers measured into a closer correspondence with the psychological sensation of loudness. These units all depend on experiments on groups of people and are accordingly difficult to interpret either in terms of any direct physical significance or even in terms of their application to an individual.

In this section, the physical quantities *important in hearing* have been introduced, and their application to a study of hearing has been indicated. The measurement of the typical values of these quantities, significant in human hearing, has given rise to a variety of types of tests. They are discussed in the following section.

3. Hearing Tests

There are various ways of studying hearing. Tests on humans which do not involve any surgical techniques are discussed in this section. Clinically, the most widely employed tests measure the threshold of hearing. The observed thresholds are then compared with the normal threshold. The simplest of these tests uses pure tones. However, the

[2] The loudness level of a sound measured in phons is defined as the sound pressure level of a 1 kc pure tone which sounds equally loud to the average observer.

[3] The loudness of a sound may be measured in sones. A loudness of 1 sone is identical to a loudness level of 40 phons. The loudness of other sounds is measured in sones by subjective comparison to a 1 sone loudness. Ideally, the loudness in sones should be linearly related to the loudness level in phons. No such simple relationship exists.

exact sound pressure levels of the normal thresholds seem to be rather difficult to determine. The graph in Figure 5 shows the results of several investigations. These emphasize that the threshold depends to

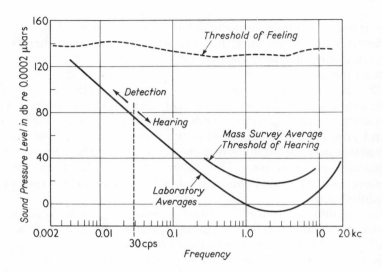

Figure 5. Pure tone thresholds. Note that the laboratory averages with trained, selected personnel are consistently lower than the mass survey averages. Recent studies at The Pennsylvania State University by Professor J. Corso and his associates gave mass survey values between the two curves shown. Notice that the threshold of feeling is not near the threshold of hearing at either 30 cps or 20 kc. The latter are limits of hearing in the sense that people can no longer distinguish tones outside of these limits. After J. C. R. Licklider, in *Handbook of Experimental Psychology*, S. S. Stevens, ed. (New York: John Wiley & Sons, Inc., 1951).

some extent on who measures it. Notice that the ordinate is in decibels; thus a difference of 20 db means a factor of 10 in the sound pressure. All the curves show the same general shape with a minimum threshold, that is maximum sensitivity, in the frequency range from 1–4 kc. When the tests are conducted under controlled laboratory conditions, with carefully screened young people, the thresholds are lower than those found in mass surveys.

There exist various types of limits of hearing, none of which are very precise. These limits include a minimum pressure threshold and an upper pressure limit at each frequency, as well as a highest and a lowest frequency limit at which one can hear. Of these, the threshold sound pressure level is most precise, but even it is a statistical limit. If an individual is presented with an acoustic pressure close to his threshold, he will hear the tone sometimes and not at other times. It is customary in tests of this nature to choose the halfway point where the subject hears the tone 50 per cent of the time as the limit of hearing.

The upper limit of hearing is an even less clear concept. As the sound pressure level is raised towards 110 db, one becomes aware of feeling the sound in the external ear. At a still higher sound pressure level, perhaps 130 db, one begins to experience pain. If the sound pressure level is raised to 145 db, the pain becomes very severe. It has been shown in accidents due to carelessness that at sound pressure levels of about 155–160 db the human eardrum is ruptured. (The eardrum will eventually heal.)

It is instructive to convert these sound pressure levels for eardrum rupture to actual sound pressures. Recall that the sound pressure level is defined by

$$L = 20 \log_{10} (p/p_0)$$

where
$$p_0 = 0.0002 \text{ dynes/cm}^2$$

If
$$L = 160 \text{ db}$$

then
$$\log_{10} p/p_0 = 8$$

or
$$p/p_0 = 10^8$$

Hence
$$p = 2 \times 10^4 \text{ dynes/cm}^2$$

This is the root mean square acoustic pressure. The acoustic pressure amplitude will be the $\sqrt{2}$ times greater for a pure tone. This gives an acoustic pressure amplitude A_0 of

$$A_0 \doteq 3 \times 10^4 \text{ dynes/cm}^2$$

The average atmospheric pressure is about 10^6 dynes/cm², so that 160 db may also be written

$$A_0 \doteq 0.03 \text{ atm}$$

The sound pressure level at which the eardrum is ruptured puts an upper limit on the loudness which one can hear. The low frequency limit to hearing is due to a different type of phenomenon. It used to be stated that the upper and the lower frequency limits of hearing were at the frequencies where the thresholds of pain and hearing crossed. At the low frequency end of the human hearing range, this does not seem to be the case. Rather, the limit at about 30 cps is due to the inability to identify tones or direction of frequency change.

In the audible range, a person recognizes the direction in which a frequency change occurs, provided it is sufficiently great. For example, if the frequency is lowered from, say, 1,000 cps to 500 cps, the listener hears a decrease in frequency of one octave. (A frequency ratio of 2 is called an octave in music.) Below about 30 cps, the listener cannot really distinguish tones or tell whether the frequency is being raised, lowered, or held constant. If the frequency is lowered to, say, 1 cps, the tone identified is not the applied sound frequency but rather something in the neighborhood of 1,000 cps.

Likewise, at high frequencies a point is reached above which a person can no longer distinguish tones. In addition, the threshold sound pressure rises very sharply. This latter effect limits experiments at the high frequency end of the spectrum. The exact frequency range in which this sharp rise occurs varies widely from individual to individual. For one graduate student who worked in the Pennsylvania State University Acoustics Laboratory, this sharp rise occurred around 25 kc. He could tell that 23 kc was higher in pitch than 22 kc. The author's ears failed to respond to reasonable sound pressure levels if these were above 17 kc in frequency, whereas his wife did not hear above 6 kc.

The highest frequency which normal humans hear varies by a factor of more than three.[4] This may seem large, but it is small compared to the variations in the pure tone thresholds. Variations from one individual to another may be as high as 40 db within the normal range of hearing. These numbers, when translated into actual acoustic pressures, represent a pressure ratio of a hundredfold, truly an enormous variation.

In an ordinary room, the lowest sound pressure levels one can hear are limited by the ambient noise. In a very quiet room, where all the ambient noise is below the hearing threshold, the physiological noise level is approximately at the threshold of hearing. This physiological noise is due to a variety of causes: the pulse in the ear, the muscles contracting, breathing, and any motion of the joints. Physiological noise is effective only at those frequencies where the ear is most sensitive; that is, the range 1–4 kc.

Most sounds come to the ear from the air. Some, such as a few of the physiological noises, are transmitted by bone conduction. The entire structure of the middle and inner ear discriminates strongly in favor of airborne vibration as opposed to bone conduction. However, a sufficiently strong signal can be conducted by the bone. The bone conduction threshold can be observed by blocking the ears[5] or by applying a vibrator directly to the head. The sound pressure levels necessary for hearing by bone conduction are about 40 db higher than by air conduction, and the threshold curve is much flatter.

[4] Eight kc to higher than 25 kc.
[5] This may raise the threshold.

The pure tone hearing threshold tests described above depend on the accuracy of the apparatus and the technique of the operator, as well as on the hearing of the person being tested.   By suitable calibrating techniques, the equipment can be standardized so that the sound pressure levels are accurately known to within 1 db (that is, about ± 10 per cent in the actual sound pressure).   It is difficult to improve on this by more than a factor of 2.   The effect of the operator is harder to remove.   He must present successively lower and then higher sound pressure levels to the subject.   If he starts far above the threshold, the subject becomes familiar with the tone and will distinguish it at lower sound pressure levels than if the operator started below the threshold. The operator must cross and recross the threshold until, in his judgment, he has found a stable value.

One very ingenious attempt to remove the effect of the operator was introduced by von Békèsy.   His audiometer includes the person being tested as part of a feedback loop in an automatic control device designed to keep the sound pressure level at the ear close to the threshold.   The system is illustrated in block diagram form in Figure 6.   The output

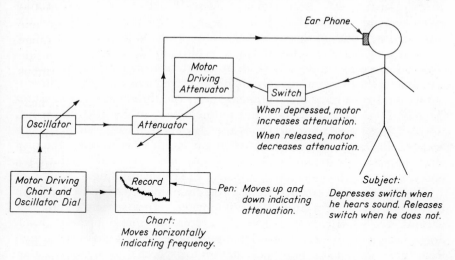

Figure 6. Block diagram of the Békèsy audiometer which records the threshold of hearing without influence of any operator other than the subject.

of an oscillator is fed through a variable attenuator to the earphones. The subject is given a switch which he depresses when he hears the tone and releases when he does not.   The switch is connected to a reversible motor which drives the variable attenuator in such a fashion that the sound pressure level increases with the switch released and decreases with the switch depressed. The entire setup then hunts for the threshold, continuously crossing and recrossing it. A recording pen is attached to the variable attenuator. The pen writes on a calibrated chart, recording the instantaneous setting of the attenuator. Another motor drives both the chart and the oscillator so that a record is obtained of threshold level versus frequency. This level is recorded without any effect of the examiner.

The Békèsy audiometer is very successful in limiting the role of any operator other than the subject. It also gives a continuous record of threshold versus frequency instead of values only at discrete points. It presents the threshold curve directly in a graphical form. However, it has several disadvantages. It is slower than an audiometer operated at discrete frequencies by an experienced technician. It is impossible with the Békèsy audiometer to distinguish between losses in a certain frequency range and apparent losses due to extraneous physiological noises such as swallowing. Using the discrete frequency audiometer, the operator crosses and recrosses the threshold, thereby eliminating the effect of extraneous physiological noises. Finally, the Békèsy audiometer depends on the skill of the subject and his understanding of the instructions. Both of these will vary from person to person, introducing a nonhearing variable into the apparent threshold.

An ideal compromise would be an instrument similar to the Békèsy audiometer but operating only at discrete frequencies. If the instrument could remain at one frequency until the threshold stays constant for, say, 15 seconds and then shift automatically to the next frequency, it would encompass most of the advantages of both the discrete frequency and the Békèsy audiometer. Unfortunately, this becomes so complex electronically that the author knows of only one audiometer of this type, and it takes a skilled electronic engineer to keep it running.

The information obtained from a speech audiometer is different from that found by using a pure tone audiometer. In a speech audiometer various test words are presented at a constant sound pressure level. Some persons who have appreciable pure tone hearing losses at certain frequencies do not show any hearing loss for speech. Conversely, other people, with normal pure tone thresholds, have marked speech hearing deficiencies. The problem of recognition of speech is much more complex than hearing a pure tone. Understanding speech involves the function of several parts of the brain. Actually, speech can still be understood if any two continuous octaves of the audible spectrum are presented and the rest of the energy filtered out. The quality of the speech will be altered, but it is still understandable. (Even up to 50 per cent of every syllable or word can be removed. The remainder when compressed to eliminate the blank times is still understandable.)

The speech threshold measures a person's ability to participate in a conversation or listen to a lecture. It depends as much on the functional condition of the brain as it does on the action of the ear. In contrast, the pure tone threshold indicates to a greater extent the action of the ear itself.

As people grow older, the pure tone thresholds are raised, particularly at higher frequencies. For people of all ages, these thresholds are raised by exposure to loud noises. The latter effect is reversible if only occasional exposures occur but is quite irreversible after years of continuous exposure. It is not worth while here to go into the details of current estimates on criteria for levels at which, say, 5 per cent of the persons will be appreciably deafened after years of exposure. The currently accepted levels are lower than those which exist in many factories today.

The relationship of pleasure to audible frequency range is very complicated. In these days of high fidelity, stereophonic sound, and extended frequency ranges, one might guess that the greater the frequency range, the more pleasing. This does not seem to be the case. Older people find hearing aids which correct their high frequency losses make music sound harsh and unpleasant but that flat response amplifiers increase their satisfaction in listening to music. In other words, what the listener is used to hearing is enjoyable.

Other types of information can be gleaned from experiments similar to those used to obtain the pure tone threshold curves. One test is to ask the subject to match in loudness tones of different frequencies. On the basis of these results, equal loudness curves can be drawn. They are illustrated in Figure 7. The lowest is the threshold curve itself. As the sound pressure level is raised, the equal loudness curves tend to flatten out, approaching straight lines by the time the sound pressure level at 1 kc has reached 100 db.

Another test is to ask the subject to choose just noticeable differences in loudness. A change of this nature is sometimes referred to as a difference limen, abbreviated DL. When the sound pressure level is 60 db or more above the threshold of hearing the DL is of the order of 0.5 db[6] throughout most of the auditory range. At lower sound pressure levels, the DL's are greater. At 30 db above threshold they are about 1 db; they are as large as 6 db near threshold.

Similarly, difference limens, or just noticeable differences, exist as the frequency is varied. At very low frequencies, a 0.5 cps change is detectable. In the middle frequency range (around 1 kc), the normal person can notice a 3 cps change. At the very high frequency end of the audible range, changes greater than 25 cps are necessary before a

---

[6] That is to say, it is between 0.25 and 1.0 db.

change of pitch is noticed. These difference limens for frequency
change are not independent of the sound pressure level. As the latter
is lowered, the size of the difference limen for frequency changes increases.

The presence of these finite steps, dignified by the term difference
limens, resembles the phenomena well known in many phases of
chemistry and physics, usually grouped under the classification quantum

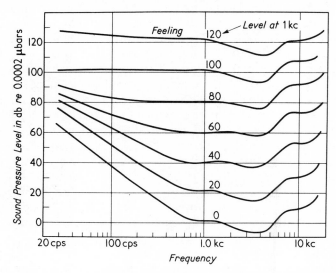

Figure. 7. Equal loudness contours after the American Standards Association (1936). There is no general agreement on
the exact shape of these curves, but the general flattening at
higher sound pressure levels is always observed. After J. C. R.
Licklider, in *Handbook of Experimental Psychology*, S. S. Stevens,
ed. (New York: John Wiley & Sons, Inc., 1951).

mechanics. Similarly, pure tone thresholds measured on individuals at
very low frequencies suggest some type of quantum effect. Quantum
effects do occur in acoustics, but the physical quanta of sound energy,
known as *phonons*, are far too small to associate them in any way with
hearing. Just as does the photon, the phonon has an energy, E, such that

$$E = h\nu$$

where h is Planck's constant and ν is the frequency. A straightforward
calculation will show the reader that, even at the threshold of hearing,
a huge number of phonons must be reaching the ear each second, or
even each cycle. This number is so large that the phonon cannot be
responsible for the quantization observed in hearing studies.

The hearing tests described in this section give no direct clues to the location of the organs responsible for the effects observed. These hearing tests are simple in that they do not necessitate surgery or putting electrodes into people. By contrast, the studies described in the next section and in Chapter 6 allow one to determine whether the effects are mechanical or nervous and to gain insight into the mechanism of hearing.

4. Anatomy and Action of the Ear

The ear is the organ of hearing. Sound waves impinge on the ear which couples them to the endings of the sensory nerve associated with hearing. It is customary to divide the mammalian ear into three major divisions: the outer ear, the middle ear, and the inner ear. The outer and the middle ear are filled with air; their primary purpose seems to be to conduct sound to the inner ear. The inner ear consists of several parts, some of which are concerned with balance, and one of which is part of the hearing apparatus. Although anatomically the inner ear is one organ and is served by one cranial nerve, only the cochlear portion of the inner ear is associated with hearing.

The incident sound waves in the air surrounding the head enter the outer ear first. This consists of three parts, an *external auricle* (or pinna), a narrow tube called the *external auditory meatus*, and the *tympanic membrane* (or eardrum). These are illustrated in Figure 8. The auricles are almost vestigial in humans and play a very minor role in the phenomenon of hearing. In most mammals, the pinnae are large and can be raised, lowered, and rotated. In this way they can be used to help locate the origin of a given sound. In rodents, and some other mammals also, the auricle is at times laid down across the opening to the meatus to give some protection against very loud sounds.

In humans, the external auditory meatus (or ear canal) is somewhat circular in cross section and more or less a straight tube. In an average adult, it is about 1.04 ml in volume and about 2.7 cm long. As in many other biological

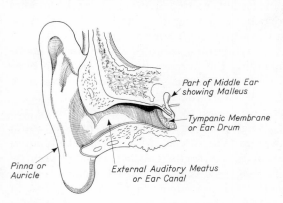

Figure 8. The outer ear. After A. J. Carlson and V. Johnson, *The Machinery of the Body* (Chicago: The University of Chicago Press, 1941).

measurements, variations of ± 10 per cent from the mean are quite usual but variations as great as ± 20 per cent are rare. The meatus is terminated by a thick fibrous membrane called the tympanum or tympanic membrane. Along the edges of the membrane are glands which secrete a waxlike substance called cerumen. This forms a protective coating. In cases of irritation, an excess of this wax is secreted, often causing a temporary loss of hearing.

The external auditory meatus may be thought of somewhat as a closed-end organ pipe. The tympanum at the end of the meatus is relatively stiff. Here, the particle velocity should be a minimum and the acoustic pressure a maximum. The opening to the air should be just the opposite, a pressure node and particle velocity antinode. The diagram in Figure 4 shows that the external auditory meatus at resonance is a quarter wavelength long. At this frequency, about 3 kc, there will be a maximum acoustic pressure delivered to the inner ear for a given incident pressure. This resonance corresponds to the minimum in the pure tone threshold curve. Studies with probe tubes attached to microphones show that the maximum pressure amplification in the ear canal is about 10 db. This is not sufficient to account for the threshold minimum from 1–4 kc but definitely contributes to it.

At the base of the external auditory meatus is the tympanic membrane. In humans it is oval in shape, about 66 mm^2 in area and about 0.1 mm thick. It couples the vibration of the air molecules in the outer ear to the small bones of the middle ear. At extreme intensities the tympanic membrane is a nonlinear device; that is, it produces harmonics and subharmonics of the frequencies exciting it. These nonlinear effects however are only important at very high sound pressure levels. In some mammalian species, the tympanum vibrates as an elastic membrane. In other species including the human, the motion of the tympanum is more like that of a rotating piston. The mode of vibration of the tympanum was studied in detail by von Békèsy.

Various techniques have been used to observe the motion of the tympanum. The simplest is to glue a long light stick to the tympanum and observe the motion of the end of the stick. Most of these techniques are useful *only* at low frequencies; the results can be extended only by extrapolation. Tests of this type show that the particle velocity of the tympanum is of the same order of magnitude as that in a plane wave in air. Applying this result to 0 db, the approximate threshold at 1 kc, one finds for the particle velocity v

$$v = \frac{p}{\rho c}$$

$$v \doteq 5 \times 10^{-6} \text{ cm/sec}$$

or for the displacement ξ

$$\xi = \frac{v}{2\pi\nu} \doteq 10^{-9} \text{ cm} = 0.1 \text{ Å}$$

This displacement is smaller than an atomic radius!

The tympanic membrane forms the outer boundary of the middle ear. The latter is an air-filled space in the temporal bone; this space is referred to as the *tympanic cavity*.   It has a volume of about 1 ml and an irregular shape.   Within this cavity are three small bones or *ossicles*, which are

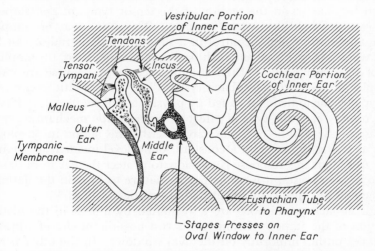

Figure 9. The middle ear which is filled with air is connected by two membranes called windows to the fluid-filled canals of the inner ear.   The eustachian tube connecting it with the pharynx is even smaller in diameter than is indicated here. Modified from *Life: An Introduction to Biology* by G. G. Simpson, C. S. P. Hendrigh, and L. H. Tiffany, © 1957, by Harcourt, Brace & World, Inc.

named according to their shapes.   These are the *malleus* (hammer), the *incus* (anvil), and the *stapes* (stirrup).   They are illustrated in Figure 9.   The general purpose of these bones seems to be to help match acoustic properties of the air and the inner ear.   The ossicles act as a mechanical transformer and increase the fraction of the incident energy available to excite the mechanisms of the inner ear.

The bones of the middle ear are so pivoted that they are particularly insensitive to vibrations of the head and to bone-conducted sound waves. One action of the ossicles is to amplify the acoustic pressure of vibrations transmitted from the air via the tympanum, while at the same time discriminating against vibrations reaching them via the skull. This insensitivity of the ossicles to bone conduction, as well as the symmetry of the vocal cords, restricts most of the hearing of one's own voice to sound transmitted in the air from the mouth around to the ears. (This can be demonstrated by covering one's ears while talking and noting the changes in loudness and quality.)

The ossicles are believed to have an additional function besides impedance matching. This is to decrease the amount of energy fed into the inner ear at high sound levels. Part of this is thought to be accomplished by changes in the tension of the tensor tympani and stapedius muscles which hold the ossicles in place. The action may be compared to the automatic volume control in a superheterodyne radio. In both cases, when a large signal enters the system and is detected, the amplification of an earlier portion of the system is decreased. These are specific examples of so-called "feedback systems" or "automatic control," as this type of phenomenon is called by physicists and engineers. (Physiologists usually call this type of effect a "homeostatic mechanism.") In the case of the middle ear, one may describe this action in teleological terms as trying to maintain a constant sound level incident to the inner ear. Although this response is too slow to protect the ear from damage due to sudden noises, it is of the proper nature to explain the flattening of the equal loudness contours at high intensities.

High signal transmissions are also limited by a shift in the mode of vibration of the stapes. In one of its two possible modes of vibration, the stapes pushes uniformly on the oval window. In the other it rocks in such a fashion that it causes a negligible net displacement of the oval window. The latter type of motion is believed more important at higher intensities. Both the variable coupling and the two possible modes of vibration are nonlinear effects. Both contribute to harmonic generation as well as to amplitude distortion.

In physical form the outermost ossicle, the malleus, is pressed against the tympanic membrane. The innermost one, the stapes, pushes against a membrane called the *oval window* which separates the air-filled middle ear from the liquid-filled channels of the inner ear. The oval window forms one end of one of these channels, the *scala vestibuli*. Another channel, the *scala tympani*, also ends in a membrane separating it from the middle ear. This second membrane is called the *round window*.

The effective area of the tympanum in a human is about 0.66 cm² of which perhaps 0.55 cm² is in contact with the malleus. The force F_m on the malleus, due to the acoustic wave, equals the product of the pressure, p_t, on the tympanum times the area of contact. That is,

$$F_m = 0.55\, p_t$$

Models indicate that the ossicles have a theoretical mechanical advantage of 1.3. Therefore, the force on the stapes F_s would be given by

$$F_s = 1.3F_m$$

if friction were absent. Likewise, the pressure p_w, exerted by the stapes on the oval window, which it contacts for 0.032 cm², can be computed from

$$p_w = F_s/0.032$$

Solving for the pressure amplification,

$$A = \frac{p_w}{p_t}$$

one finds a theoretical value, in the absence of friction, of twenty-two-fold. Actual measurements carried out by von Békèsy have shown that the correct value is

$$A = 17x$$

The latter number is a 25 db gain in acoustic pressure. This value is believed valid throughout most of the auditory range although it is based on extrapolations from low frequencies and high sound pressures.

Since the middle ear is filled with air, any difference in pressure on the two sides of the tympanic membrane will tend to displace the membrane. Small differences in pressure at frequencies to which the cochlea responds cause the vibrations of the tympanic membrane during normal hearing. In contrast, large slow changes in pressure, due to atmospheric variations or altitude changes, could distort the shape and position of the tympanic membrane. To avoid this distortion, a connection is necessary between the middle ear and the ambient air; but this connection must be unable to transmit changes that take place in less than a tenth of a second. A small narrow tube will do exactly this. Such a tube does connect the middle ear with the pharynx; it is called the *eustachian tube*.

The soft walls of the eustachian tube are easily collapsed by an excess pressure outside the tube. This leads to a very unpleasant feeling often experienced when descending in an airplane. Swallowing, chewing gum, or attempting to blow with the mouth and nose held shut, all open the eustachian tube permitting the equalization of the pressure outside and within the middle ear.

The outer and the middle ear together produce a maximum pressure amplification of about 35 db. They tend to reduce the hearing of sounds that are conducted through the bones, to make one insensitive to one's own voice except inasmuch as it is heard through air conduction outside the head, and also to act as an automatic control unit. None of

these are essential for hearing, although all are desired effects.   It is
possible to hear without a tympanic membrane and without ossicles.
There is a hearing loss under these conditions, but this loss is comparable to the variations in the normal range of hearing thresholds.
However, the two windows to the inner ear, one of which is driven much
more than the other by the incident wave, are necessary for hearing.

The inner ear consists of several portions all having two common fluids,
and all served by the eighth cranial nerve.   Only the cochlear portion
of the inner ear is associated with hearing.   Grossly, the *cochlea* is a

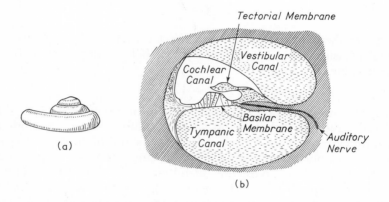

Figure 10. (a) The cochlea or inner ear removed from the bone.
(b) Cross section through one turn of the cochlea.   The tympanic and vestibular canals are filled with perilymph and the
cochlear canal with endolymph.   After A. J. Carlson and V.
Johnson, *The Machinery of the Body* (Chicago: The University
of Chicago Press, 1941).

spiral; in the human there are two and a half complete turns.   Around
this spiral run three parallel, fluid-filled ducts.   These are illustrated in
Figures 10 and 11.   The fluid in the tympanic and vestibular ducts is
called the *perilymph*.   These two ducts (or *scalae*) are connected at the
apex of the spiral through a small duct called the *helicotrema*.   Somewhat
sandwiched between these two ducts is the *cochlear duct* (or *scala media*).
It is filled with a fluid, similar to that of the other two, called the
endolymph.   The endolymph and perilymph are anatomically and
electrically separated from each other.   Between the cochlear duct and
the vestibular duct is a very thin fibrous membrane known as *Reisner's
membrane*.   Between the cochlear duct and the tympanic duct is a thicker
membrane called the *basilar membrane*.   The basilar membrane gets

progressively broader and thicker as one proceeds toward the apex of the spiral.

The basilar membrane is the seat of the *organ of Corti*, shown in detail in Figure 11. This organ contains the nerve endings. Thus one may think of the organ of Corti as a neuromechanical transducer. (A transducer is a device which converts one form of energy to another form.)

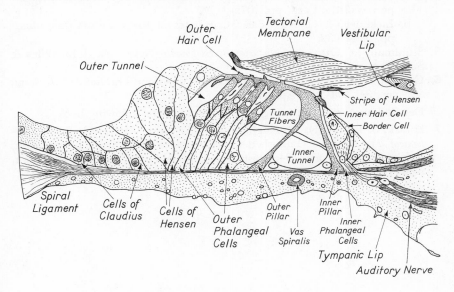

Figure 11. Histology of the organ of Corti. After A. A. Maximow and W. Bloom, *Textbook of Histology* (Philadelphia: W. B. Saunders Company, 1957).

Histologists have studied the organ of Corti in great detail. It seems as if almost every cell has its own name. The diagram in Figure 11 shows many of these. It includes Claudine cells, Hensen cells, inner and outer hair cells, and the tectorial membrane. It is believed that the bending of the hair cells in some way excites the nerve endings which are located in the organ of Corti.

The action of the inner ear intimately involves the nervous system. The details are deferred to Chapter 6 which follows chapters on the conduction of impulses by nerves and the electrical potentials of the central nervous system.

REFERENCES

1. Hunter, J. L., *Acoustics* (Englewood Cliffs, New Jersey: Prentice-Hall, Inc., 1957).

2. Beranek, L. L., *Acoustic Measurements* (New York: John Wiley & Sons, Inc., 1949).

3. Wever, E. G., and Merle Lawrence, *Physiological Acoustics* (Princeton, New Jersey: Princeton University Press, 1954).

4. Stevens, S. S., ed., *Handbook of Experimental Psychology* (New York: John Wiley & Sons, Inc., 1951).

    a. von Békèsy, Georg, and W. A. Rosenblith, "The Mechanical Properties of the Ear," pp. 1075–1115.

    b. Licklider, J. C. R., "Basic Correlates of the Auditory Stimulus," pp. 985–1039.

5. Stuhlman, Jr., Otto, *An Introduction to Biophysics* (New York: John Wiley & Sons, Inc., 1943).

6. Corso, J. F., "Age and Sex Differences in Pure-Tone Thresholds," *J. Acous. Soc. Am.*, **31**, 498–507 (April 1959).

Detailed anatomical drawings can be found in the following book:

7. Polyak, S. L., Gladys McHugh, and D. K. Judd, *The Human Ear in Anatomical Transparencies* (Published under auspices of Sonotone Corporation, Elmsford, New York, 1946, distributed by T. H. McKenna, New York, New York).

2

Light and the Eye

I. Vision

In many aspects of human life, vision is far more important than any other sensation. History, legal agreements, and knowledge of the universe are all recorded in a written form. Without vision these would be of little value. In most measurements in physics, it is customary to base sensitive, precise observations on visual data. In mechanics, the position of a pointer on a balance, length on a meter stick, and pressure are all measured visually. Even in acoustics, precise data are usually based on the readings of electrical meters. This latter is the direct result of the prominent role played by electronics in acoustics. (Similar statements can be made about all other branches of physics.) In chemistry and in the biological sciences, electronic tools have also come to be widely used measuring devices. Today, in almost all of natural science, the reading of electrical meters is an important means of gathering data. However, even before the advent of electronics, the data of the biologist and the chemist, just as those of the physicist, were based primarily on what he could measure by visual means.

Vision plays other roles in life besides data gathering. Many of our aesthetic pleasures come from objects which are viewed. The preliminary part of the mating procedure in humans is based on visual stimulation. Furthermore, vision acts to protect man from many dangers such as those which beset him in crossing a street, driving a car, or climbing the stairs. For other types of activity, vision is not necessary but nonetheless plays an important role in normal human beings; most outstanding of these is the sense of balance. Finally, it should be noted that human beings use visual cues more frequently than any other type of sensory information.

Vision depends on light. During most of the evolutionary development of animals, light came primarily from the sun. It is only in recent times that artificial lighting has been used. Since, in their development, all animals were exposed to similar physical light stimuli, it is not surprising that all animals have similar visual ranges. This uniformity contrasts sharply with the spread of the frequency ranges of hearing which vary by more than an order of magnitude from one species to another.

It is necessary to understand something about the physical character of visible light to have an appreciation of the phenomena of vision. Light may be discussed, depending on the problem under consideration, from three different avenues of approach. The first of these, and historically the oldest, is called geometrical optics. It applies to many problems in optics which can be solved by treating light as if it were propagated as bundles of rays, each normal to the wave front. Most of geometrical optics dealing with lenses can be discussed from this point of view. The optical properties of the eye as a focusing lens system are most simply described by geometrical optics.

The second approach to the study of light places its emphasis on wave aspects. Light waves are electromagnetic in character; the properties of the waves are used to describe the transmission of light through a medium. In particular, the wave theories are useful in discussing such phenomena as diffraction, interference, polarization, and resolving power. The wave theories are also useful in discussions of visual acuity and color vision.

From the point of view of physics, the most basic approach to a study of light is that of quantum mechanics. It is used in problems dealing with the emission or absorption of light. In the quantum theory, light is considered to be made of packets (or quanta) of energy called photons. The probability of finding a photon at a given place can be described by a mathematical form called a wave function. This quantum view of light is necessary for studies of visual thresholds described in this chapter and for the discussions in Chapter 19 of the absorption of light on a molecular scale.

The next section of this chapter presents several of the physical phenomena of light which apply directly to vision. These include the three avenues of approach outlined above, namely, geometrical optics, electromagnetic waves, and the quantum theory of light. This is followed by Section 3, on the anatomy of the human eye. The optical properties of the eye considered as a thick lens, as well as visual defects, are included in that section. Biophysicists have also been interested in visual thresholds and in measurements of visual acuity; these are discussed in the final section of this chapter.

Many aspects of vision will be deferred to later chapters. For example, color vision and the neural mechanisms making vision possible are described in Chapter 7 which follows other chapters on the operation of the nervous system. The properties of the retinal pigments which absorb light are easier to understand following a study of enzymes. The visual pigments are discussed in Chapter 19, Part D. Finally, Chapter 25, on information theory, contains a section which includes visual information.

2. Optics

A. Geometrical Optics

Many properties of lens and mirror systems can be treated by regarding light as bundles of rays each of which moves at right angles to the wavefront. This approach is utilized in this section in the discussion of the properties of thick lenses. These properties are applied to the eye in subsection B of Section 3.

From the point of view of geometrical optics, the most important property of a medium is the velocity at which light is propagated. In free space, the velocity of light is usually designated by the symbol c, and in cgs units, it has the value

$$c = 3 \times 10^{10} \text{ cm/sec}$$

It is customary to specify the velocity v in any other medium by the index of refraction, n. This is a dimensionless number defined by the ratio

$$n = \frac{c}{v} \tag{1}$$

(Strictly speaking, n is always the index of refraction referred to the velocity of light in free space. However, one may also use the relative index of refraction n_{12} between any two media, where n_{12} is defined by

$$n_{12} = \frac{v_2}{v_1}) \tag{2}$$

The use of geometrical optics to describe the properties of thick lenses is outlined in Appendix B. The details will not be pursued here. Rather, it is hoped that readers interested in geometrical optics will turn to this appendix where the behavior of light at surfaces of refraction (lenses) is discussed.

In the eye, the luminous energy passes through a series of curved surfaces of refraction. All of these surfaces may be approximated by sections of spheres whose centers lie on a common line. This general case has been shown to be mathematically equivalent to a single thick lens, which separates two media of different indices of refraction. It is not possible to relate the image and object distances by as simple an expression as that for a thin lens, such as Equation 10 of Appendix B.

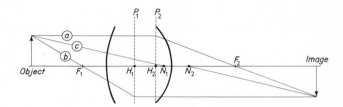

Figure 1. A thick lens immersed in different media on its two sides. F_1 and F_2 are focal points. Note that F_1 does not equal F_2. The principal points are H_1 and H_2, and the nodal points are N_1 and N_2. Rays a, b, and c are drawn as in Figures B-6 and B-7 of Appendix B.

However, six cardinal points completely specify the lens action. These consist of two focal points, two principal points, and two nodal points. This general case is illustrated in Figure 1. The cardinal points are defined in Figure 1; they will be used in the next section to describe the eye.

The strength of a lens (or its power), L, is defined as the reciprocal of the focal length f measured from the corresponding principal plane; that is

$$L = \frac{1}{f} \tag{3}$$

When f is measured in meters, L will be expressed in diopters. A lens with a shorter focal length can produce a real image for closer objects than a lens with a longer focal length. Thus, the lens produces a greater algebraic change in curvature of an incident light front. In this sense, a lens of shorter focal length is indeed stronger. In any case, increasing the radius of curvature of a converging surface will increase the focal length and decrease the lens strength.   In a system of a series of spherical surfaces, such as is found in the eye, the forward and backward focal lengths will be different.

B. Light as an Electromagnetic Wave

Although many actions of lens systems may be adequately described by geometrical optics, others cannot be.   In the last chapter, reference was made to the phenomena of diffraction and interference.   Diffraction refers to the fact that a wave will not behave as a bundle of rays, especially

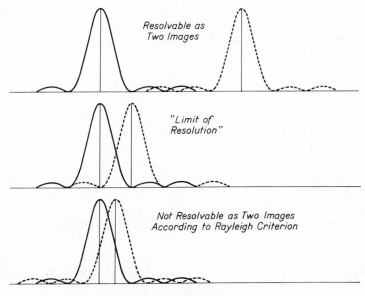

Figure 2. Dual Diffraction Patterns.

in the neighborhood of objects comparable in linear dimensions to the wavelengths of the light.   (See Chapter 1 for a definition of wavelength.) In discussing sound, it was noted that the wavelengths of many audible sounds were comparable to the sizes of rooms and buildings.   Thus, speech sound waves are diffracted by (or bent around) the furniture and other objects.   The wavelength of visible light is much smaller than most common objects; hence, diffraction effects are not a usual part of everyday experience.   However, experiments with slits, fine wires, small spheres, and so forth show that diffraction effects do occur.   For similar reasons, interference effects in the form of standing waves are familiar in sound experiments but demand special equipment in order to be demonstrated for light.   These and many other experiments make

it impossible to avoid the conclusion that light is a wave motion represented to a sufficient approximation by rays only in limited circumstances. The limitations are sufficiently broad to allow the use of
geometrical optics in many visual problems.

The wave nature of light has two very important consequences for the
sensation of vision. The first is that there is a theoretical limit to the
resolution of any lens system, including the eye; that is, there is a minimum separation of two points whose images are resolvable. Figure 2
shows the diffraction patterns of the light originating from two point
light sources. If one computes the dimensions of the diffraction patterns
of the light originating at the two points and asks that the central
maximum of one coincide with the first minimum of the second, one
finds that the angular separation θ of the lines from the lens center to
the two points is given by

$$\theta = \frac{1.22\lambda}{a} \tag{4}$$

where λ is the wavelength of the light and a is the radius of the aperture
of the lens. It is often assumed that this is about the minimum separation
at which two points can be distinguished. The reciprocal of θ in minutes
of arc is called the resolving power. Actually, trained microscopists
and spectroscopists resolve slightly smaller angles than the one computed
by the formula above. (This formula was first developed by Lord
Rayleigh; it is often called the Rayleigh criterion.)

In addition to its use in predicting resolving power, the wave nature
of light is necessary to discuss color vision. If light of a narrow wavelength band is present, it is said to be monochromatic; that is, it gives
the sensation of a single color. Only about one octave (that is, a factor
of two in the frequency) is visible to humans. In wavelength terms,
the visible spectrum runs from about 760 $m\mu$ (red) down to about
380 $m\mu$ (violet), although the exact limits quoted by different experi-
menters vary. One octave seems a narrow band when compared with
the sense of hearing where musical tones are audible in at least nine
octaves. The resolution of different wavelengths by the eye is much
poorer than the sharp tone discrimination of the ear. Combinations of
different wavelengths of light produce complex color sensations because
the eye does not analyze frequencies in any fashion analogous to that of
the ear.

Light waves are not elastic disturbances. A number of different
types of experiments have left no doubt that light waves are electromagnetic waves. Two of these experiments will be mentioned here.
First, one can compute on theoretical grounds that an electromagnetic
wave should be transverse and have a velocity which can be determined

by electrostatic and magnetic measurements. Polarization experiments confirm that light waves are transverse. Optically determined values of the velocity of light, c, agree with those predicted for electromagnetic waves to better than one part in a million.

Further evidence that light consists of electromagnetic waves is its continuity with radiation produced by other methods. Using techniques which overlap at their wavelength limits, one may produce radio waves, microwaves (radar), heat waves (infrared), light waves, ultraviolet rays, X rays, and γ rays. Thus, all of these are part of the same basic phenomenon: electromagnetic waves. No explicit use will be made of the electromagnetic properties of light waves in the chapters on the eye or on vision in this text.

C. Light as Photons

The electromagnetic wave theory correctly describes the transmission of light, but a number of other effects are impossible to understand without the quantum theory. These include the characteristic spectra of atoms, the absorption spectra of atoms and molecules, the photoelectric effect, black-body radiation, and the failure of the equipartition of energy for electrons in a metal and for the vibrations of diatomic gases at room temperatures. All of these and many other phenomena have been explained only in the terms of quantum mechanics. Quantum mechanics teaches that energy comes in packets or quanta. The probability of finding the packet at a given place is determined by the square of the amplitude of a wave function. In particular, for electromagnetic waves, the quantum theory states that energy E comes in photons each having the energy

$$E = \frac{hc}{\lambda} \tag{5}$$

where h is Planck's constant, which is about 6.6×10^{-27} erg·sec, c is the velocity of light, and λ is the wavelength. The relative probability of finding a photon at a given place is essentially identical to the intensity computed on the basis of the electromagnetic wave theory. Strictly speaking, a measured quantity has been specified by a probability, but experimentally these two are indistinguishable.

The photon nature of light is important in describing the threshold of vision. It is likewise necessary, in Chapter 19, where vision is discussed on the molecular level. In the latter case one may ask: How many photons react with a molecule; how do the photons change the sensitive molecules; and how are the resulting small bursts of energy transduced to neural impulses? Unfortunately, it will appear that one cannot give a complete answer. Nonetheless, the language of photons and of quantum mechanics is the only one in which these topics are discussed. The reader with a background in biology, or even an undergraduate physics major, may feel that this topic of quantum mechanics has been introduced too lightly, but only the concepts of quantum mechanics which are needed for a discussion of vision have been included above.

Quantum mechanics is necessary for an understanding of characteristic spectra. Accordingly, quantum theory is discussed more thoroughly in Chapter 27. Even there, the author must make several statements which are foreign to everyday experience and certainly are not proved in this text. It is hoped that, in spite of this, the reader will at least gain a feeling of what quantum mechanics is and how it is used, even though he may be completely unable to manipulate it.

3. Anatomy of the Eye

A. Gross Anatomy

The gross anatomies of all the vertebrate eyes are very similar. For simplicity, numerical values will be given only for the human eye. The human eyeball is roughly a sphere approximately 2.4 cm in diameter. It is supported in a special socket in the cranium. The orientation of the eyeball is controlled by six sets of muscles. These rotate the eyeball quite freely because the socket is well lubricated. The muscles are controlled by three pairs of nerves. The relative tensions in the muscles are signals which might be used by the brain to determine the location of the object viewed.[1] Many binocular judgments of distance, size, and orientation could be "computed" by the central nervous system from data on the relative tensions of these muscles.

The external covering of the eyeball is made up of three spherical layers, as shown in Figure 3. The outermost is the *sclera*. It is a white fibrous coat commonly called the "white of the eye." At the very front portion of the eye, the sclera leads into the cornea, a clear transparent structure which admits light into the eye. The human cornea is about 12 mm in diameter and has a radius of curvature of about 8 mm. A major part of the refractive power occurs at the cornea.

On top of the sclera is another thin layer called the *choroid layer*. It contains the blood vessels and a pigmented substance. The choroid layer does not continue all the way around to the cornea, as is shown in Figure 3.

---

[1] The evidence as to whether or not this information is actually used by humans is quite controversial.

The third and innermost layer of the eyeball is the *retina*.   The active photoreceptors, called *rods* and *cones*, are located in the retina.   It is convenient to divide the retina into ten layers.   Light must pass through

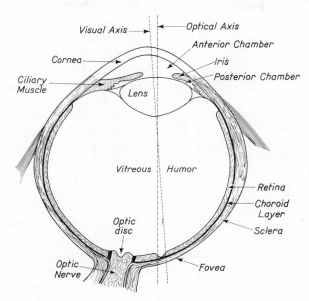

Figure 3. The eye.   After A. A. Maximow and W. Bloom, *Textbook of Histology* (Philadelphia: W. B. Saunders Company, 1957).

eight of these before reaching the rods and cones located in the ninth layer.

Slightly displaced from the intersection of the optic axis of the eye with the retina is a yellow spot known as the *fovea centralis* (the *macula lutea*).   It is a slight depression on the surface of the retina.   The active elements in the fovea are all cones; they are very closely packed.   For maximum acuity, the eye is directed so that the image falls on the fovea.

Somewhat on the nasal side of the fovea is the optic disk.   Here the optic nerve pierces through the sclera, the choroid layer, and the retina; in the center of the optic nerve are a vein and an artery.   From this disk, nerve fibers and blood vessels branch out over the surface of the retina.   Objects focused on this disk cannot be seen since there are no rods or cones in it.   Thus, this disk is referred to as the blind spot. One may put two marks on a piece of paper as indicated in Figure 4, cover one eye, and fixate one of the marks.   If one then alternately moves his head toward and away from the paper, the other mark will

disappear when its image falls on the blind spot.   In Figure 4, the   ×ˌ
the . , and the   : disappear at different distances.

Within the eye there are additional, optically important structures.

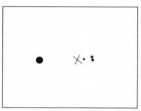

Figure 4. Pattern to observe the blind spot in the
eye.   Fixate the right eye
on the large dot and bring
the face very close to the
figure.   Now slowly move
the face away while keep-
ing the right eye fixated on
the large dot.   The other
symbols will disappear and
then reappear as their
images cross the blind spot
on the retina.

One of these is the *iris*, which acts as a light
diaphragm.   In bright light, the iris has a minimum opening.   This is desirable for several
reasons.   A smaller opening means fewer light
photons enter the eye, thereby decreasing the
"overloading" of the retinal system.   In addition, it improves the validity of the approximation which is made in the discussion of
spherical lenses, namely, that just a small
section of a sphere is used.[2]   Thus, a small iris
opening limits such distortions as spherical
aberration, field curvature, and coma associated with finite sections of spheres.   Finally,
a small iris opening increases the depth of
focus.   The reason for this can be seen from a
simple ray diagram, such as is shown in
Figure 5.   At night, maximum acuity and
depth of focus are less important than maximum sensitivity.   At this time the iris is opened
to its widest.

Another optically significant structure within
the eye is the *crystalline lens*.   In spite of its name, this is actually a cellular
structure.   The rear face is curved more sharply than the front.   The
eye accommodates to objects at different distances by changing the curvature of the front face of this lens.   When the object is farther away, a
weaker lens is needed to focus the image on the retina than when the
object is closer.   Hence, for more distant objects, the lens must be
flatter, whereas, for closer objects, it must become more curved.

The shape of the crystalline lens is controlled by a ring of muscles
surrounding the lens.   These are called the *ciliary muscles*.   Most
physiologists believe that the lens is normally held in a strained position
by the ciliary fibers.   These fibers hold the lens in a flattened condition
suitable for viewing distant objects.   When the ciliary muscle contracts,
it moves the base of the fibers forward permitting the lens to relax into
a more curved shape.   When the muscle relaxes, the lens is again placed
under tension.

The space between the lens and the retina is filled with the *vitreous
humor*, a jelly-like mass of material traversed by fibrils.   Staining

[2] See Appendix B.

techniques indicate that the vitreous humor does contain some sort of structure. Optically, the vitreous humor is indistinguishable from the

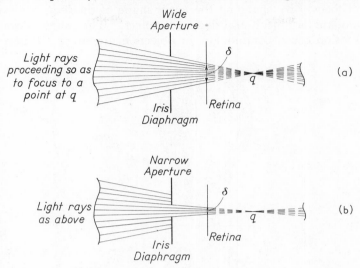

Figure 5. Effect of aperture on depth of focus. A point focused at q will appear as a circle of diameter δ on the retina. As shown in (a), if the aperture of the iris diaphragm is wide, the diameter of δ will be large; hence, one image will blur into the next unless q is very close to the retina. Thus, increasing the aperture decreases the depth of focus. As shown in (b), a narrower aperture increases the depth of focus but decreases the luminous energy reaching the retina.

aqueous humor which fills the space in the eyeball between the cornea and the crystalline lens. The aqueous humor, as its name implies, is a water-like solution containing the normal solutes of a body fluid.

B. Geometrical Optics of the Eye

Light enters the eye through the transparent cornea. It then passes through the aqueous humor, through the crystalline lens, and into the vitreous humor. It is received on the photosensitive retina, where there must be an image in focus if the object is to be seen clearly. The dimensions, radii of curvatures, distances apart, and positions of the six cardinal points are shown in Figure 6 for a schematic eye.

The greatest part of the refractive power of the eye occurs at the cornea.   Individuals lacking a lens can still see, but their vision is much less sharp than that of a normal person because the image on the retina is out of focus.   By changing the exact shape of the lens, the eye can accommodate for objects at different distances.   The young person with normal vision can accommodate for objects nearer than 250 mm.   An

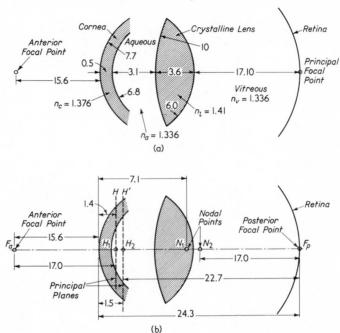

Figure 6. Optical properties of the eye.   All distances shown are mm.   The values are averages and will vary from individual to individual.   These drawings, not to scale, show Ogle's modification of Gullstrand's schematic eye.   Notice that although the lens of the eye appears to be strong in air, it is much weaker *in situ* since the difference in index of refraction between the lens and the surrounding media is much smaller. After K. N. Ogle, *Optics, An Introduction for Ophthalmologists* (Springfield, Ill.: C. C. Thomas, 1961).

object distance of 250 mm corresponds to about 16 focal lengths. Accordingly, to compensate for the change in image distance as the object is moved from about 16 focal lengths to infinity, the effective posterior focal length of the eye must change about 6 per cent.   In terms of the radius of curvature of the crystalline lens, this corresponds to a change of around 20 per cent.   The posterior focal length of the average human eye from the second principal point H' to the posterior focal point $+F$ is 2.2 cm. Thus, the eye has a strength of about 48 diopters.

If the eye is stronger than this, images of distant objects will be focused in front of the retina. Such an eye is called *near-sighted* or *myopic* because near objects will be focused on the retina. This ocular defect can be corrected by placing a negative (diverging) lens in front of the eye. "Normal" vision is the ability to focus on the retina images of objects more than 25 cm away.

If the refractive power of the eye is too weak, the image will be formed behind the retina, and positive lenses are needed for correction. Such eyes are called *hyperopic* or *far-sighted*. By and large, it is not possible to design a corrective positive lens for objects at all distances and so bifocals or trifocals are necessary.

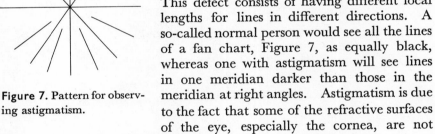

Figure 7. Pattern for observing astigmatism.

Another frequent defect, which can be corrected by glasses, is called astigmatism. This defect consists of having different focal lengths for lines in different directions. A so-called normal person would see all the lines of a fan chart, Figure 7, as equally black, whereas one with astigmatism will see lines in one meridian darker than those in the meridian at right angles. Astigmatism is due to the fact that some of the refractive surfaces of the eye, especially the cornea, are not spherical but have different curvatures in two meridians.

To recapitulate, the eye lends itself to a description in the terms of geometrical optics. The eye is a system of spherical surfaces separated by media of different indices of refraction. Optically, it can be described in terms of six cardinal points. The common defects easily corrected by glasses can also be described in the language of geometrical optics.

C. Histology of the Eye

Each gross structure of the eye can be described on a microscopic scale. This is the role of histology. The evidence from histology, in turn, forms part of the basis of the biophysics of vision. Without a knowledge of the histology of the retina, there can be no neural interpretation of vision, such as is discussed in Chapter 7. Likewise, the parts of the eye, referred to in subsection B, can be described in terms of their histological structures.

Light enters the eye through the cornea, whose microscopic structure is shown in Figure 8. First, the light passes through an outer layer of epithelial cells. These cells are separated by a thin membrane from an inner fibrous layer which in thickness comprises most of the cornea. These fibers are very similar to the fibers in the sclera. Those in the cornea are unique in that they are arranged in an orderly fashion. It appears that it is this orderliness of the fibers of the cornea that is responsible for its transparency as contrasted with the opacity of the sclera. Inside the fibrous layer of the cornea is another very thin limiting membrane and finally a lining of cells called endothelial cells.

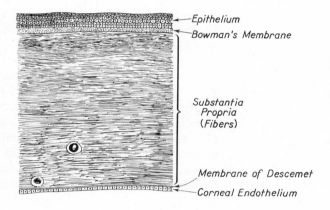

Figure 8. Histology of the cornea. After Schaffer, in A. A. Maximow and W. Bloom, *Textbook of Histology* (Philadelphia: W. B. Saunders Company, 1957).

As noted previously, the shape of the cornea is responsible for the major refraction of the eye. Any large irregularities or abrasions would reduce the acuity of vision. The usefulness of the eye depends on keeping the cornea clear and transparent. If a large object approaches the cornea, the eyelids are closed by a reflex action. Smaller particles are removed by blinking and through tear formation. The outer epithelial layer of the cornea is very highly innervated; the nerves terminate in bare nerve endings. Any slight disturbance stimulates these endings, resulting eventually in the blinking reflex. All persons normally blink quite frequently; this cleans and moistens the outer surface of the cornea which otherwise would become dehydrated and lose its transparency.

It always appears surprising when one first encounters the idea that light can pass through several layers of cells and fibers and still retain its original form.   If these layers are arranged in a sufficiently orderly fashion, there is relatively little scattering or absorption of light as it passes through the tissue.

The so-called "crystalline lens" is also a cellular structure.   The cells are long hexagonal columns.   Most of the cell nuclei are grouped in a restricted region of the lens which is not active in vision.   A typical cross section of a lens is shown schematically in Figure 9.

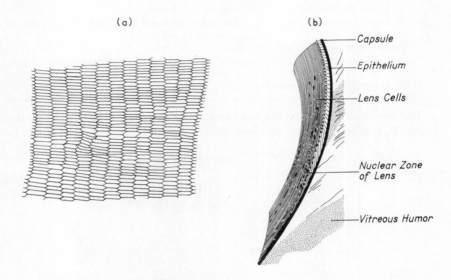

Figure 9. Histology of the lens.   (a) Frontal section through the equator of the lens showing the regular arrangement of the cells.   (b) Transverse section through the lens.   After Schaffer, in A. A. Maximow and W. Bloom, *Textbook of Histology* (Philadelphia: W. B. Saunders Company, 1957).

The last cellular structure of the eye, through which incoming light must pass, is the retina.   Here, the active photoreceptors are located. There are two types of receptors, called rods and cones.   Although not customary, it is technically correct to refer to these rods and cones as transducers.   These transducers convert light energy into electrical impulses which travel along the nerve fibers.   As noted earlier, the retina may be divided into 10 layers.   These are diagrammed in Figure 10.   Starting from the outermost layer, away from the light, one can list the layers shown in Table I.

TABLE 1
Layers of the Retina

	Layer	Function or Structure
Path of Light	1. Pigmented epithelium	absorbs light, limits reflection
	2. Rods and cones	the photoreceptors
	3. Outer limiting membrane	
	4. Outer nuclear layer	cell bodies of rods and cones
	5. Outer plexiform layer	synapses between processes from rods and cones and cells of layer 6
	6. Inner nuclear layer	neuron cell bodies
	7. Inner plexiform layer	synapses between processes from cells of layers 6 and 8
	8. Layer of ganglion cells	neuron cell bodies
	9. Optic nerve fibers	also some blood vessels, connective tissue, and so forth
	10. Inner limiting membrane	

The neurons in the retina are similar to those in other parts of the nervous system. Their detailed form and action are discussed in

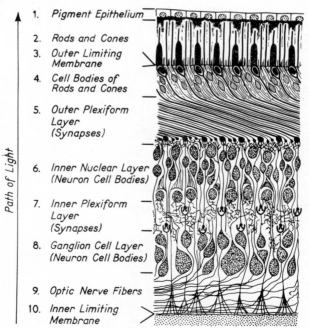

Figure 10. Histology of the retina. After A. A. Maximow and W. Bloom, *Textbook of Histology* (Philadelphia: W. B. Saunders Company, 1957).

Chapter 4. For the purposes of this chapter, one should note that the neurons are the functional units of the nervous system. Each consists essentially of a cell body, a long process called an axon, and shorter processes called dendrites. The rod and cone cell bodies are similar to neuron cell bodies except that they are attached to photoreceptors in lieu of axons.

It should be emphasized that light goes through layers 10, 9, 8, 7, 6, 5, 4, 3 before being useful for vision in layer 2. The arrangement of two layers of neuron cell bodies, with their connections to the rod and cone cell bodies, as well as almost innumerable connections between neuron cell bodies, is indeed complex. To those who have looked behind the front panels of an electronic digital computer, the retinal structure suggests strongly that the output of the rods and cones is analyzed in a computerlike fashion by these layers of nerve cell bodies. And indeed, it will be shown in Chapter 7 that electrophysiological evidence supports this suggestion.

Within the layers of nerve cell bodies, a number of different types of cells have been discovered. In discussing the mechanism of color vision, it is important to include these different types. A discussion of their forms will be deferred until Chapter 7.

4. Thresholds and Acuity

In this section, three different types of measures of the sensitivity of the eye are discussed. The first is the quantum threshold, that is, the minimum number of photons necessary to elicit a sensory response. The second is the relative sensitivity of the eye to light of varying wavelengths. The last measure, the acuity, represents the keenness of vision and is measured by the minimum separation of two objects that can just be discriminated as two and not one.

A. Quantum Thresholds

Vision occurs when light is absorbed by the photosensitive rods and cones. At the threshold of vision, only a minimum of light is necessary. The absorption of light is best described in terms of quantum theory. A natural question then is: How many photons must be absorbed by a visual receptor (rod or cone) for the subject to see a flash of light? This problem was first investigated in detail by the biophysicist S. Hecht.

His first approach was to use light of wavelengths to which the eye was most sensitive and to expose the eye to short flashes. The eyes were dark-adapted to make their sensitivity a maximum. The number of photons striking the cornea for a just noticeable flash was measured.

The number was reduced by the fraction (about $\frac{4}{5}$) which he found to be absorbed in the eye. The final number, then, should be the minimum or number of photons necessary for threshold vision. At least it would be if this number were much larger than one, in which case all pulses could be considered as having equal numbers of photons. Otherwise, the entire data would have to receive a probability-type interpretation.

Early estimates based on this method indicated that about 150 photons were necessary at the cornea, and about 30 of these reached the retina for a just visible flash. As this number was redetermined during the 1920's and 1930's, it decreased steadily from 30 down to one or two. This small number violates the original basis of the determinations because the number of photons in a light pulse, the number absorbed along the way, and even the fraction absorbed in the retina of those which get there, are subject to probability considerations. In general, one cannot measure these probabilities separately. However, the average number of photons b absorbed by a single receptor of the retina will be proportional to the intensity I, provided the eye does not move; that is,

$$b = kI \qquad (6)$$

The proportionality constant k will vary with many factors including the size of the test patch, the pupil opening, the wavelength, and the length of the flash. It is clearly desirable to carry out an experiment to measure the threshold number of photons independently of k. The following mathematical manipulations indicate how to design an experiment which satisfies this criterion.

The number of photons absorbed by a photoreceptor in the retina during a given flash is an integer. It may have any positive value, or it may be zero. However, the average number of photons need not be an integer but will have a definite value b. The probability P that m photons will be absorbed during a flash by the photoreceptor will be given by the Poisson probability distribution, namely:

$$P(m) = \frac{e^{-b}b^m}{m!} \qquad (7)$$

Vision will occur if some given integral number n or more photons are absorbed during the exposure. The probability P_n that n or more photons will be absorbed in a flash is given by

$$P_n = \sum_{m=n}^{\infty} P(m) = 1 - \sum_{0}^{n-1} P(m) \qquad (8)$$

Now, one may plot computed values for P_n against log b, giving curves such as those shown in Figure 11. Notice that each of these has a different slope. Although the value of b is not known, the value of the intensity I can be measured. Therefore, a plot of the fraction of number of correct responses when the light was perceived by the subject against the log I should have the same shape as one of the curves shown in Figure 11. By adding an arbitrary constant to log I, it should be possible to show that the experimental points correspond best to one value of n.

This experiment satisfies the criterion of not needing to measure the constant k in Equation 6 and gives unique data for the determination for any individual value of the integer n in Equation 8. The value for this constant for some human subjects indicates that n is as high as eight. For other subjects, consistent values as low as one or two have

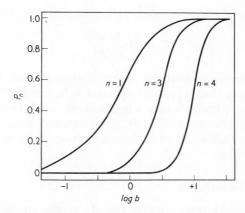

Figure 11. P_n versus log b for quantum threshold calculation. In this graph, P_n is the Poisson distribution probability for n or more events occurring, and b is the average number of events occurring.

been found for the number of photons necessary to elicit a visual response. In spite of these individual variations, the human data support the idea that the quantum threshold n is a very low number. Most of these measurements are for rod vision, but there is nothing to indicate that the threshold number of photons absorbed is different for cones.

For the human eye, it is impossible to determine whether the response measured is that of a single receptor. It is possible in experiments using invertebrate eyes, such as those of the king crab, *limulus*. These eyes have only rod-like receptors called *ommatidia*. There is one receptor per nerve fiber. For threshold experiments, the eye, with the optic nerve attached, is removed from the animal. The nerve is then dissected until only one nerve fiber remains intact. It then becomes possible to measure electrically the response of only one receptor.   Such experiments indicate either one or two photons are necessary to initiate an electrical response in the nerve fiber.   Most investigators today use the number one; that is, one photon *absorbed* in the receptor, one response.   (Note that this is very different from the statement, one photon reaching the receptor, one response.)

This quantum threshold seems surprisingly small since one photon has so little energy.   It is instructive to compute the size of a photon of visible light.   Applying Equation 5 to the energy E of a photon of green light, wavelength about 5,000 Å, one finds that

$$E \doteq 4 \times 10^{-12} \text{ ergs}$$

In terms of a mole of photons (often called an einstein), this becomes

$$E \doteq 40 \, \frac{\text{kcal}}{\text{mole}}$$

Readers familiar with chemical thermodynamics will recognize that these numbers imply that a photon of green light can break only a small number of molecular bonds when it is absorbed.   It is indeed impressive that such a small change can alter the electrical state of the photo-receptor in such a fashion as to initiate a nervous pulse which results in the sensation of vision.

B. Luminosity Thresholds

The above-mentioned sensitivity is based on the number of photons absorbed.   This absorption is the result of the action of certain photo-sensitive pigments found in the rods and cones of the retina.   The relative fraction of light that reaches the rods and cones and is absorbed varies markedly with wavelength.   It is convenient to separate the effect of wavelength from the numerous other factors altering threshold intensities.   To do this, a set of threshold data is taken, varying only the wavelength.   The entire set is multiplied by a normalizing constant chosen to reduce the minimum threshold to an arbitrary value.   The reciprocal of the normalized threshold is known as the *relative luminosity*. Relative luminosity curves have been measured both for dark-adapted eyes and for light-adapted eyes.   Vision under conditions of dark adaptation is called *scotopic*, whereas vision with light-adapted eyes is called *photopic*.

In either case, one may interpret the thresholds as the intensity at which a response is obtained 50 per cent of the time.   For short flashes, less than 10 milliseconds, the product of the intensity and exposure length determines the observed threshold, whereas for long exposures, say more than 50 milliseconds, only the intensity is important. The exact size of the test patch used becomes very important if it is two minutes of arc or less. With very small test patches, the exact location of the test patch very markedly affects the shape of the relative luminosity versus wavelength curve. For larger test patches, threshold curves are obtained which do not depend specifically on the particular area on the retina which is illuminated.

The general shape of the relative luminosity curves for photopic and scotopic vision is shown in Figure 12. Owing to the definition of

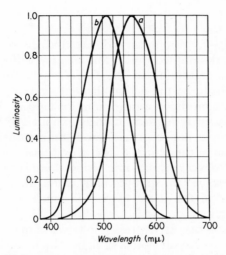

Figure 12. Relative luminosity curves. The curve for the dark-adapted eye is labeled *b* and for the light-adapted eye, *a*. After Committee on Colorimetry, The Optical Society of America, *The Science of Color* (New York: Thomas Y. Crowell Company, 1953), p. 225.

relative luminosity, the absolute height of the curves does not have any significance. Much greater intensities are needed for photopic vision than for scotopic vision. (This difference is part of everyday experience. After the lights are turned off at night a room looks totally dark, but gradually one can see more and more objects in it.) Luminosity threshold measurements are not easy to perform. More than half an hour is necessary for dark adaptation. Care must be taken to illuminate the same area of the retina, and many other precautions must be observed as well. However, the relative luminosity curves do lead to reproducible results.

The separation of the maximum points of the scotopic and the photopic curves can be interpreted as an indication that luminosity depends on at least two types of receptors. The simplest interpretation might be to assign scotopic vision to the rods and photopic vision to the cones. This choice would be indicated by the fact that the scotopic sensitivity is greater in the periphery where there are more rods, whereas the photopic response is greatest in the fovea where there are no rods. However, this separation of function is definitely oversimplified; the rods appear to be active in both dark-adapted and light-adapted eyes, whereas the cones are active only in light-adapted eyes.

C. Acuity

Studies of the acuity of vision also indicate that the rods are the active elements in the dark-adapted eye. The acuity of the eye adapted to scotopic vision is a minimum at the fovea where there are no rods. Thus, the rods seem to be the active elements in scotopic vision. The acuity of scotopic vision shows a maximum for light at the retinal region where the rod density is highest, namely, about 20° from the fovea. Acuity under scotopic conditions is lower than under photopic conditions in any region of the retina. The neural basis for this is discussed in Chapter 7. However, in photopic vision there is a sharp maximum in the ability to resolve two spots of light when the images fall on the fovea. The acuity in the foveal region is much greater than in the remainder of the retina.

The acuity of vision may be expressed in terms of the minimum angular separation of two equidistant points of light which can just be resolved. The angular separation θ between two points, when expressed in radians, is approximately equal to the distance between the points divided by the distance from the eye, provided θ is less than 0.1. The angle θ will also be equal to the separation of the two images on the retina divided by the distance from the second nodal point. From Equation 4, one can calculate a minimum value of θ, according to the Rayleigh criterion, for green light ($\lambda = 5 \times 10^{-5}$ cm) and an iris diameter of about 0.5 cm. Rounding off to one significant figure, the limit, according to this criterion, would be

$$\theta_R \doteq 1 \times 10^{-4} \text{ radians} \doteq 0.03 \text{ minutes of arc}$$

This is a theoretical lower limit for the resolution of two points of light.

Experiments have shown that most people cannot resolve two points of light if their separation is as small as 5×10^{-4} radians. Persons with the most acute vision can resolve an angular separation of about 2×10^{-4} radians under optimum conditions. Because this is higher than the Rayleigh criterion, it seems that visual resolution must be limited by other factors such as scattering, spherical aberration, and the separation of the receptors in the retina.

In the center of the fovea where the resolution is greatest, the cones are separated by about two microns from center to center. In order to resolve two points of light as separate images, it must be necessary to excite at least two cones while leaving one in between unexcited. Thus, the images on the retina would have to be separated at least four microns from center to center. If it were necessary to have two cones unexcited between the images of the two spots, this number would be increased to six microns. The maximum resolution observed of 2×10^{-4} radians corresponds to a separation between the image centers on the retina of five microns. In other words, the discrete structure of the retinal receptors could be responsible for the lower limit of resolution for persons with the most acute vision.

The psychophysical processes of recognizing shapes are very complex. However, a minimum requirement for small objects is that the angular separation of their different parts be larger than the limit of resolution. At 25 cm from the eye, an angle of 5×10^{-4} radians would correspond to about 100 microns. This is about the length of a *Paramecium caudatum* which should accordingly be recognized as having a rod shape at that distance. In contrast, the smaller species, *Paramecium aurelia*, would have to be brought closer to the eye before its shape could be recognized by the unaided eye, even under ideal conditions of lighting.

In a camera, resolution in white light is often limited by chromatic aberration, that is, the different wavelengths focus at different planes. The resolution can be improved to some extent by using a system of positive and negative lenses made of different types of glass.[3] The index of refraction of each will vary in a different fashion with wavelength. By a proper choice, a combination can be made which has a positive focal length that is almost independent of wavelength throughout the visible region.

Chromatic aberration in the eye is minimized by limiting the wavelengths of light to which the eye will respond. A bare retina from which the vitreous humor has been removed will respond far into the ultraviolet. However, in the intact eye, the cornea absorbs most energy at wavelengths shorter than 3,000 Å. Accordingly, energy at these wavelengths does not contribute to vision although it can produce corneal damage.

The crystalline lens has a very sharp cutoff at about 3,800 Å. Persons without this lens cannot accommodate to different object distances, lack acuity, but can see objects using ultraviolet radiations only. They have

----

[3] These are called achromatic lenses.

a sensation of violet when viewing ultraviolet. Persons with a lens do not receive any appreciable energy at the retina at wavelengths shorter than about 3,800 Å. Thus, the lens (and cornea) limit the photons reaching the retina to wavelengths greater than 3,800 Å.

On the long wavelength side, the water molecules in the cornea and aqueous humor eventually absorb most of the energy at wavelengths longer than 12,000 Å. However, the eye pigments become very insensitive to light above 7,000 Å, and are almost unresponsive above 8,000 Å. Technically, to find the long wavelength limit, one should go to such high intensities that the eye is heated but not badly burned; this experiment is rarely performed.

Thus, the filter action of the lens and cornea, plus the response characteristic of the optically active pigments in the photoreceptors tend to restrict the wavelength band, thereby reducing chromatic aberration. In addition, the greatest acuity occurs in photopic vision at the fovea. In this region, there are only cones which probably do not respond to blue light. In this region also is a yellow pigment believed by many to further eliminate the blue end of the spectrum. Accordingly, the acuity at the fovea is greatest not only for objects viewed with monochromatic green light, but also for those seen in white light.

REFERENCES

1. Stuhlman, Otto, Jr., *Introduction to Biophysics* (New York: John Wiley & Sons, Inc., 1943).
2. Stevens, S. S., ed., *Handbook of Experimental Psychology* (New York: John Wiley & Sons, Inc., 1951).
   a. Judd, D. B., "Basic Correlates of the Visual Stimulus," pp. 811–867.
   b. Graham, C. H., "Visual Perception," pp. 868–920.
3. Glasser, Otto, ed., *Medical Physics* (Chicago, Illinois: Year Book Publishers, Inc., 1944) Vol. 1.
   a. Luckiesh, Matthew, and F. K. Moss, "Light, Vision, and Seeing," pp. 672–684.
   b. Sheard, Charles, "Optics: Ophthalmic, With Applications to Physiologic Optics," pp. 830–869.

For a more thorough discussion of optics at an intermediate physics level, see:

4. Robertson, J. K., *Introduction to Physical Optics*. 2nd ed. (New York: D. Van Nostrand, 1935).

For a more complete discussion of histology of the eye, see:

5. Maximow, A. A., and William Bloom, *Textbook of Histology* (Philadelphia: W. B. Saunders Company), any recent edition.

For a presentation from the point of view of medical physiology, see:

6. Best, C. H., and N. B. Taylor, *Physiological Basis of Medical Practice.* 7th ed. (Baltimore: Williams & Wilkins Company, 1961).
7. Ogle, K. N., *Optics: An Introduction for Ophthalmologists* (Springfield, Illinois: Charles C. Thomas, 1961).

3

Special Uses of Hearing and Vision

I. Introduction

Biophysicists have, in one fashion or another, been interested in many sensory systems including hearing, vision, olfaction, taste, touch, temperature, pain, proprioception, and time. All are contained in the human body. There is no reason to suppose that some living organisms could not be sensitive to types of stimuli other than those to which humans respond, such as magnetic fields or even neutron beams. All experiments to date, however, tend to confirm that the types of sensory mechanisms active in humans are the only important ones in other living organisms. The differences which do exist involve quantitative aspects such as the frequency range of hearing, the wavelength band of vision, and the particular chemicals to which an organism responds. It is conceivable, nonetheless, that the failure to find other sensory systems may reflect our ignorance rather than their nonexistence.

In spite of our inability to detect basically different systems, there are many novel ways in which the known sensations are used. For example, certain types of plants "compute" the average length of sunlight per day to find out when to flower, or when to shed their leaves. Others use the length of night, and still others the average light-to-darkness ratio. Another example is the sense of time, which is poor in most humans. Certain animals, for example, cockroaches, have a much more highly developed sense of time than man does.

In some phenomena, such as bird homing, it is not well understood just what sensory cues or information the animal does use. In others, particularly echo-location, an understanding was developed only after physical analogs had been constructed. Before this, it was beyond human conception to design the proper experiments, even though these experiments could have been readily carried out. To put it in a some-what different fashion, human intuition is often a poor guide to experi-mental design. Someone must not only develop the proper ideas but also be persuasive enough to interest his peers.

In the following section, the ability of bats to use echo-location in flight, in capturing prey, and in avoiding obstacles is set forth. Many years ago a few persons, perhaps by chance, hit on the correct solution to how a bat senses its surroundings, but these solutions were discarded by their contemporaries as absurd. Pasteur said that chance favors the mind prepared by study and experimentation. We might add, it also favors the man who lives in an age in which his contemporaries are like-wise prepared.

Besides bats, other mammals and some birds use echo-location. These are also discussed in this chapter. Bees use sensory information for direction-finding and homing; this involves time and orientation senses, and also perhaps the ability to detect polarized light. Making a beeline for home is discussed in Section 4. The concluding section of this chapter deals with bird navigation and homing.

2. Echo-Location in Bats

In many families of bats, the sense of vision is poorly developed, hence the colloquial expression, "blind as a bat." It has been shown by direct experimentation that bats fly, hunt, and avoid obstacles, as well when blindfolded as when their eyes are open. Anatomically, the visual portion of the bat brain is very poorly developed, whereas the acoustic or auditory portion makes up a major part of the brain. This suggests that they sense their surroundings through auditory stimuli. Indeed, deafened bats, or ones with their ears covered over, cannot fly well, avoid obstacles, or hunt in the same fashion as normal bats. Covering the bat's mouth (and nose) also interferes in a like manner with its flight.   Many experiments have shown that bats navigate, sense their surroundings, and hunt by a process known as echo-location.

Echo-location has been used for many years to determine the depth of the ocean.   During World War II, two practical applications of echo-location were developed.   Systems using electromagnetic echoes are called radar, whereas those employing acoustic echoes are named sonar. In either case, a pulse of energy is sent out, reflected from an object, and the returning echo is detected.   By measuring the time for the echo to return, one can compute the object distance.   For radar, if the object is at a distance d of 60 km, the pulse will return in the time t necessary to travel $2d$ or. 120 km.   That is

$$t = \frac{2d}{c} = \frac{120 \text{ km}}{3 \times 10^5 \text{ km/sec}} = 0.4 \text{ millisecond}$$

The echo will be weaker than the original pulse emitted.   To detect the echo, the original pulse must have stopped before the echo returns. Thus, very short pulses are necessary.   To aid in distinguishing the echo from noise, among other reasons, the original pulse is emitted at a carrier frequency which is high compared to the reciprocal of the pulse length. For radar, frequencies of 10^9 to 3×10^{10} cps are used.

An echo-location system like that described above will determine distance but not shape.   To find the latter, it is necessary to emit many pulses, each one in a slightly different direction.   These echoes must all occur before the object has moved very far.   Thus, a high pulse-repetition rate is needed to find detail.   By contrast, a low rate is needed to find distant objects.

Finally, to be useful for determining distance and shape, there must be some way of rapidly displaying the echoes as a function of direction and time of return because there is not time to do a paper-and-pencil calculation for most uses of echo-location.   A similar rapid sensing of shape and motion occurs when watching the wheel of a moving car. One does not see that each point on the wheel describes a curve of complex form and then figure out that the wheel is turning; rather, one perceives this directly.   Therefore, any successful echo-location system must reveal directly the shape, size, and distance of the objects.   Human brains do not do this with echoes.   Therefore, radar and sonar equipment display their results after electronic computation.   The bat brain apparently makes a similar calculation directly.

Radar works well in air but is useless under water since the electromagnetic waves are rapidly absorbed.   Sonar, although less effective than radar in air, can be used to locate objects under water.   The speed of sound in water is only 1.5 km/sec, so much longer pulses can be used for sonar; to limit sound absorption, much lower frequencies are employed, usually around 3×10^4 cps.

Griffin and Galambos showed in 1941 that bats use a sonar type of echo-location. Since then, Griffin and his associates have studied echo-location in bats in great detail. The bats emit and detect airborne sound pulses; these travel at the speed of sound, 0.34 km/sec. A bat can use comparatively long pulse lengths and still recognize close objects. The pulse lengths used by an individual bat may vary from around 1 millisecond to 5 milliseconds. The lower limit allows a bat to distinguish echoes from objects as close as 15 cm (6 inches). Other species of bats with poorer acoustic orientation use pulses of 10 to 100 milliseconds.

To be effective, the wavelength of the sounds in the bat's pulse must be of the order of the linear size of the smallest objects the bat chases. The wavelength λ is equal to the velocity of sound divided by the frequency. The latter is easier to measure electronically. The frequency of the sound which the bat emits varies during the pulse by a factor of close to two. The highest frequency in some species is around 100 kc, where the wavelength λ of sound in air is about 0.3 cm. Appreciable echoes should occur until the diameter of the object is about $\lambda/2$, in this case, about 0.05 cm (20 mils). Behavioral experiments with wire grids show that such bats are extremely successful in avoiding wires 0.3 cm in diameter but cannot detect wires 0.025 cm in diameter. The shape of the pulse is shown in Figure 1.

The role of the frequency changes during the sound pulse is not known. One possibility is that it is used to indicate size, the lower frequencies being reflected less by small objects than the higher ones. The directivity pattern of the sound emitted by the bat also changes during the pulse in such a manner as to support this hypothesis. The higher frequencies are concentrated into a narrower beam, favoring their reflection from smaller objects directly ahead of the bat.

Another possibility is that the bat uses its own particular frequency variations to distinguish its echoes from those of other bats close by or from surrounding noises. Bats must be very skillful at distinguishing their own pulses from others because they navigate well in the presence of thousands of other bats in dark caves with hard reflecting walls. They are also able to detect their own pulses from loud noises. Attempts at "jamming" bat sonar, with broad-band noise, have so far failed. The sound pressure level (see Chapter 1) near the bat's mouth is about 120 db, that is, about 175 dynes/cm². Even broad-band noise signals at these sound pressure levels in the bat's frequency range have failed to jam the bat's sonar, although the echoes are very weak compared to the over-all noise levels.

It is interesting to compare the physical characteristics of a bat with radar and sonar equipment. The table on page 57 lists some data for radar and sonar systems of World War II, and the insectivorous bat, *Eptesicus fuscus*. It is clear that the bat compares favorably with the **sonar** and radar systems.

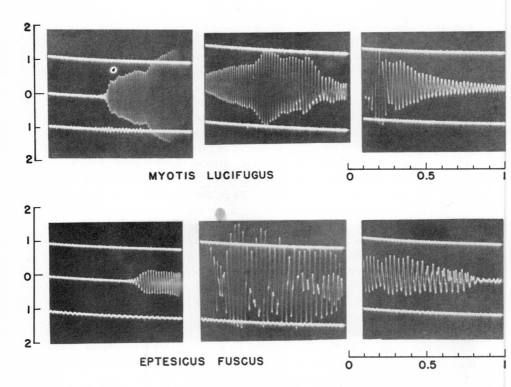

Figure 1. Photographs of oscilloscope traces of the sound pressure pulses emitted by two different species of bats. The time markers are in milliseconds. After D. R. Griffin, *Listening in the Dark* (New Haven, Connecticut: Yale University Press, 1958).

The bat is superior to the radar and sonar systems in some respects. When the insect-hunting bat is far above the ground it emits only long pulses at a comparatively slow repetition rate, that is, 50 millisecond pulses, five times per second. As it approaches its prey, the pulse length shortens to two milliseconds and the repetition rate increases to 200 per second. This makes maximum use of its available facilities.

TABLE I

Echo-Location Comparisons

| | Radar Systems | | Sonar System QCS/T | Bat (*Eptesicus fuscus*) |
	SCR-268 (ground-based)	AN/AB-10 (air-borne)		
Wavelength (cm)	150	3.2	5–13	0.4–2
Approximate total weight (kg)	13,000	58	about 100	0.014
Peak power output (watts)	75,000	10,000	600	10^{-4}
Minimum detectable echo power (watts)	10^{-13}	10^{-13}	?	10^{-16} to 10^{-14}
Target detected	Airplanes	Airplanes	Submarines	Insects
Size of target (m²)	3–5	3–5	10	10^{-4}
Working range for target (km)	150	80	2.5	10^{-1}
Length of emitted pulse ($2d$) (meters)	1,800	240	100–300	1–5

The bat is far inferior to radar and sonar in other respects, particularly in its ability to distinguish shapes. Bats apparently could not distinguish solid objects in the shape of a cross from others in the shape of a circle, although all were large compared to the minimum sizes the bat detected. Furthermore, insectivorous bats will chase pebbles thrown into the air just as readily as they pursue moths.

Various families of bats differ in their anatomy and their use of echolocation. There is no simple relationship between the range of hearing and the pulses used. All bats can hear from 30 cps to 100 kc or higher according to electrophysiological data. However, the largest bats depend on visual information and lack a "sonar" system. Certain Central American bats emit very high frequency pulses; these are pure tone pulses, in the range of 80–120 kc, and of comparatively low intensity. Other bats use pulses whose frequencies decrease to as low as 20 kc. One species, *Rousettus aegyptiens*, the Egyptian tomb bat, emits a pulse whose frequency goes from 100 kc to 6.5 kc each pulse. Some types of bats emit their pulses through their mouths, others through their nostrils, and still others can use either. Many species of bats have specially shaped external ears which act as directional receiving horns, and others have bizarre nose forms which act as horns for the emitted signal. Figure 2 shows an insectivorous bat.

Before the development of radar and sonar, it was hard to guess how bats navigated. The present knowledge followed the construction of these physical analogs. Moreover, the pulses of the bats can be detected, analyzed, and displayed only by modern acoustic and electronic techniques. In order to discover the details of bat navigation, Griffin and his associates had to be prepared to apply modern physical techniques.

Figure 2. Photograph of a flying bat, after Edgerton. After Griffin, D. R., *Listening in the Dark* (New Haven, Connecticut: Yale University Press, 1958).

3. Echo-Location in Other Animals

Because bats use echo-location, one might wonder if other animals can also use this type of information. The answer is a strong affirmative; the number of animals known to use echo-location has grown rapidly since 1945. The list includes birds that live in dark caves, marine animals, and, to a limited extent, humans. It is not inconceivable that certain deep-sea fish also use some form of echo-location.

Among birds, two types have been shown to use auditory clues when flying in dark caves. One of these is the oilbird of the valley of Caripe, in Venezuela, named *Steatornis caripensis*. These birds, when flying in the light, use their visual system to sense their surroundings. In the dark, either at night or far within their caves, they emit clicks of 1 to 1.5 millisecond duration with frequencies in the neighborhood of 7 kc. This is lower than most bat sound pulses. However, bird hearing is, in general, limited to the same range as human hearing, in contrast to small mammals most of which can hear frequencies as high as 100 kc. Thus, it is physiologically reasonable that the oilbirds should use lower frequencies than the bats. It seems physically reasonable also because the oilbird, being much larger, is concerned with larger objects (and therefore does not need short wavelengths).

Certain swiftlets (*Collecalic brevirostris unicolor*) also live in caves. Although studied in less detail than the oilbird, it has been found that the cave-dwelling swiftlets emit sharp clicks when flying in the dark. The ability of the swiftlet to fly in the light is only slightly impaired if either its eyes or ears are covered. It becomes quite helpless when both are masked. No studies have been made of the frequencies of its clicks.

Marine mammals, such as porpoises and small whales, have hearing ranges which extend well above 100 kc. Their hearing has been shown by conditioning experiments to be extremely sensitive. All of this group of animals emit short sound pulses. Only the pulses from porpoises have been studied in detail. They emit more and shorter pulses when hunting for fish. Experiments have shown that porpoises use these pulses for echo-location both in navigating and in locating food.

Other animals are thought to use echo-location, although the evidence is less certain. For example, deep-sea fish emit light flashes and certain electrical fish send out weak electrical impulses. It is quite possible that both of these are also used for echo-location of some type.[1]

There is also some evidence that blind humans use the echoes of their footsteps to sense their closeness to objects. Attempts have been made to extend this sense electronically to give details of size, shape, and hardness. These have all failed because the added information gained was less than that lost by wearing earphones or interfering with the normal hearing of sound.

4. Sense of Direction in Bees and Ants

Besides echo-location, other sensory information is used in ways which are unique to limited groups of animals. In this section, the sense of direction in bees and ants is briefly considered. Humans possess a sense of direction and use many different types of clues as guides such as knowledge of the terrain, the stars, the compass, road signs, and mile posts. Most of these are unavailable to bees and ants; nonetheless, they proceed straight from their homes to a food source and back again. This is the biological source of the colloquial expression "made a beeline."

There is no doubt that, when ants follow the trails of other ants, they use olfactory senses as a guide to direction. Likewise, they also can use

[1] Many of these electrical fish can detect electrical impulses with sensory receptors, known as the lateral line organs. To some degree, these electrical receptors represent a type of sensory system not found in humans. Although all sensory receptors respond to electrical stimulation, humans have none that are specialized for this type of stimulus.

some sort of kinesthetic sense. However, if the trail is completely obliterated, the ants still proceed directly to their homes.

The ants apparently can sense the angle of the sun's rays and use this information to determine directions. If ants are imprisoned while returning to their nests and kept for a period of hours in a darkened container, they start off in the wrong direction when released. The direction chosen makes the same angle with the rays of the sun as did the correct path at the time of their initial imprisonment.

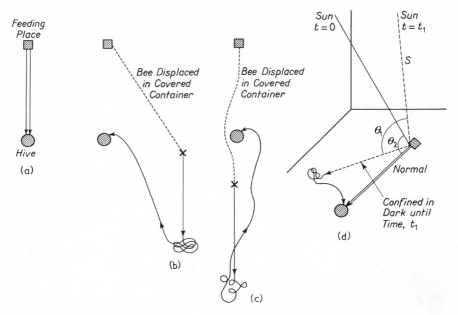

Figure 3. Flight patterns of bees returning to their hive from a feeding place. Sketch (a) shows the normal flight pattern. The flight patterns of bees displaced from their feeding places are diagrammed in sketches (b) and (c). The change in pattern when the bee is confined is illustrated in sketch (d).

Similar experiments have been conducted with bees. They, too, will proceed in the wrong direction after release following imprisonment in the dark. After flying in the wrong direction the distance to where their hives should have been, they "recognize an error" and fly in a random fashion over a very small area. Finally using some other sense, perhaps memory of the surroundings, they fly straight to their hives. This is illustrated in Figure 3a.

If a bee is moved in a darkened container from its feeding place and released shortly thereafter, it makes a beeline in the direction its hive would have been had it not been moved. Arriving at the wrong site, it circles and eventually travels in a fairly straight line to its hive. This is diagrammed in Figure 3b.

Not only can bees find their way to the hive by the angle with the rays of the sun, but they also communicate to other bees the location of a new source of food in terms of this angle. When a bee finds such a source, it goes through a complicated dance pattern on the side of the hive. The amplitude of the pattern communicates the time of flight and the predominant angle with the vertical reveals the angle between the flight path and the sun's rays.

Bees and other insects have vision extending into the ultraviolet; this portion of the sun's spectrum is useful to insects but not to mammals. There are reports that bees can sense not only the direction of the sun's rays but also their polarization. Other reports indicate that the apparent ability to sense polarization is misleading. (It should be noted there is a small polarization effect in human vision which can be just barely demonstrated by psychophysical tests.) Whether or not the bees use the angle of polarization, their precision in comparing their flight path with the angle of the sun's rays is far beyond anything humans can do without the help of physical instrumentation.

5. Migration and Homing

Although insects use the angle of the sun's rays to return to their homes, they have other sensory information which allows them to "home" if their angle computations have led them astray. Other animals such as bats, fish, turtles, and pigeons also exhibit homing tendencies. It is most likely that bats do not use any form of visual clues. Some evidence indicates that fish and turtles, as do insects, use the sun in homing. One type of fish, the bass, probably has an internal clock and avoids the errors made by ants and bees when imprisoned in the dark.

Certain pigeons have been selected and bred for their ability to home. These birds may be taken hundreds of miles from their nests in containers which are completely covered so that they cannot see the surroundings. Even though the pigeons have never been in that location before, many are able to follow a very straight line to their nest. (However, they must be trained over increasingly large distances starting with about 25 miles, before the longest flights are possible.)

Various theories have attempted to relate the pigeon's homing to a combination of hypothetical senses. One of these postulated an extreme ability to detect the angle of the sun and combine it with a very precise internal "clock" to find direction.   Another, based on the behavior of untrained birds in new territories, ascribed homing to flying in random circles until some feature of the terrain was recognized.   A third theory assigned homing to an ability to detect the vertical component of the earth's magnetic field and the Coriolis force (experienced by bodies moving at an angle to the earth's axis of rotation).   None of these has ever been conclusively disproved.   However, experiments to verify any of these theories have all been inconclusive.

It is the author's guess that pigeons use strictly visual clues of a very ordinary kind in homing.   If this is true, pigeons must be unique in their ability to see a limited number of features of the skyline from a long distance.   Not only must they be able to see these features, but they must also possess the ability to learn these features well enough to orient themselves, even if released at a long distance from their origin. This guess has been strongly conditioned by experiments on bird migration.

Birds migrate as far as 15,000 km over territory they have never seen before and yet manage to return to their own nesting areas of a kilometer or so in radius.   They thus have a tremendous precision of migration. It is possible that most are led on their initial flights by other birds who have flown the "course" before, but nonetheless they must either be born with or acquire a tremendous store of visual memory with which to compare their surroundings.   This visual memory must be very precise to keep them on course for 8,000 miles.   At the same time, it cannot be too precise or rigid, lest the birds be confused by changes in the terrain which occur from year to year.   The large number of birds killed by flying into radio towers and monuments for many years after their construction attest to the fact that birds only observe a limited number of features of their terrain and discard other information.   Likewise, the ability of various species to migrate at night indicates that the position of the sun is at best only one of the visual clues used during migration.

Man is born with comparatively little information inherited at a conscious level.   By analogy, one might suspect, therefore, that birds had to acquire their knowledge of the terrain on the first migration or two. However, very few people could learn so many landmarks so quickly; by analogy again, this type of learning would also seem unlikely for birds. Perhaps a better comparison than a human is a self-controlled (that is, internal radar controlled) airplane which can fly from the west coast of the United States to the east coast and land on the proper runway with only a few feet margin of error.   Such planes have been built with a radar memory of the terrain imprinted on their magnetic tapes.   The same problems of precision while ignoring fine details affect the self-controlled plane and the migrating bird.

At least one European plover, hatched from its egg in isolation from all other birds, developed with a memory of the terrain over which its species migrated. This bird, at the start of the fall season, became extremely restless in captivity but made no consistent attempt to fly in any given direction. When it was placed in the Paris Planetarium with the proper skyline and the proper orientation of stars for that time of year, the bird attempted to fly along the migration course characteristic of its species. It simulated flight southward to the Mediterranean shore, then turned eastward and simulated flight around the Mediterranean to Africa. By simulated day it used the skyline to navigate, and on simulated clear nights it used the position of the stars. A built-in "clock" (time sense) enabled the bird to "compute" the proper position of the stars at that time of night for the Mediterranean shore at that season of year.

There is nothing to indicate that similar built-in, inherited memories exist in all migratory birds. Nor is there any reason to guess whether or not some inherit their memories and others acquire them on their first flights. (Migration experiments do give one reason to doubt the carry-over of learning experiments from birds to man.) Birds use their visual sensations in migrating in a very special way which man is not adapted to emulate, except through his artifacts such as the "migrating" airplane.

REFERENCES

A large portion of the material in this chapter was based on the experimental work of D. R. Griffin and his co-workers. A pleasant review of this work, on a high, technical level, but written in an entertaining fashion, is his book:

1. Griffin, D. R., *Listening in the Dark: The Acoustic Orientation of Bats and Men* (New Haven, Connecticut: Yale University Press, 1958). This book contains 386 pages of text as well as 467 references, which are pertinent to the present chapter.

Two shorter articles are in *Scientific American*:

2. Griffin, D. R., "Bird Sonar" **190**: 78–83 (March 1954).
3. Griffin, D. R., "More About Bat 'Radar'" **199**: 40–44 (Jan. 1958).

The homing of bees and ants is discussed in:

4. Fraenkel, G. S., and D. L. Gunn, *Orientation of Animals: Kinesis, Taxes and Compass Reactions* (New York, N.Y.: Oxford University Press, 1940).
5. von Frisch, Karl, *Dancing Bees: An Account of the Life and Senses of the Honey Bee*. Translated by Dora Ilse (London, England: Methuen and Company, Ltd., 1954).

6. Baylor, E. R., and F. E. Smith, *Polarized Light and Bees* (Unpublished data).
7. de Vries, Hessel, and J. W. Kuiper, "Optics of the Insect Eye," *Ann. New York Acad. Sc.* **74**: 196–203 (1958).

The homing and navigation of birds are discussed in:

8. Matthews, G. V. T., *Bird Navigation* (New York: Cambridge University Press, 1955).
9. Griffin, D. R., and C. G. Gross, book review of G. V. T. Matthews' *Bird Navigation.* *Quart. Rev. Biol.* **32**: 278–279 (1957).
10. Yeagley, Henry L., "A Preliminary Study of a Physical Basis of Bird Navigation," *J. Appl. Physiol.* **18**: 1035–1063 (Dec. 1947).
11. Sauer, E. G. F., "Celestial Navigation by Birds," *Scientific Am.* **199**: 42–47 (Aug. 1958).

Homing in fish is discussed by:

12. Hasler, A. D., et al., "Sun Orientation and Homing in Fishes," *Limnology Oceanography* **3**: 353–361 (1958).

The following two articles also deal with subjects related to those in this chapter. Both are in *Reviews of Modern Physics*, Vol. 31 (1959).

13. Schmitt, O. H., "Biological Transducers and Coding," pp. 492–503.
14. Bullock, T. H., "Initiation of Nerve Impulses in Receptor and Central Neurons," pp. 504–514.

DISCUSSION QUESTIONS—PART A

The following topics are suitable for student reports, term papers, or library examinations in connection with Part A of this text. It is assumed the student will answer the questions with the help of adequate library facilities.

1. Besides vision and hearing, biophysicists have been active in studies of taste and olfaction. What is the present state of knowledge in these fields?

2. Insects as well as mammals sense vibrations and sound. Describe the receptor organs, the threshold versus frequency curves, and the equipment necessary to measure vibration and sound thresholds for insects.

3. Invertebrates respond to light when it falls upon special sensory organs. Describe briefly the simple and compound eyes of insects and the "eye-spot" of Euglena. How is visual acuity possible in the compound eye?

4. Discuss the evidence concerning any possible role of polarized light in the vision of man, vertebrates, and insects.

5. At various times, it has been reported that animals could in some way sense or respond to magnetic fields. Review critically the evidence for such a magnetic sense.

6. Ants communicate and sense direction, in part, by the odor of certain specific chemical compounds which they secrete. These compounds are referred to by various names as pheromones, ectohormones, and chemical releasers. Describe the evidence for such compounds.

7. Describe in detail the methods for observing the motion of the eardrum (tympanic membrane) and of the ossicles of the middle ear.

8. Develop the mathematical theory of the Helmholz resonator. How was this type of resonator used to analyze speech?

9. Békèsy audiometers are discussed in Chapter 1. Draw up ideal specifications for such an audiometer and compare them with those of a commercially available model.

10. The theory of lenses discussed in Chapter 2 uses the infinitesimal approximation of small angles

$$\sin \theta \doteq \theta$$

Derive third order equivalent formulas and discuss in terms of these formulas: spherical aberration, coma, field curvature, astigmatism, and image distortion. What is the importance of these various effects for the eye?

11. Compare the pulses emitted by several species of bats in terms of sound pressure level, sound frequency, pulse length, and repetition rate. Relate these to the physical structure of the ears, nose, and mouth of the particular species and to their feeding habits.

12. Describe in considerable detail the experiments indicating that bees can sense the angle of the sun's rays.

B

Nerve and Muscle

Introduction to Part B

The following six chapters are devoted to biophysical studies of nerves and muscles and to the interpretation of other phenomena in terms of the properties of these two tissues. The first chapter of this part (Chapter 4) contains a discussion of the conduction of information by nerve fibers in the form of electrical impulses. Several concepts of basic electrical theory, needed in various chapters throughout the text, are summarized in Appendix C; it is hoped that readers unfamiliar with these terms will read that appendix.

In Chapter 5, "Electrical Potentials of the Brain," the so-called "electroencephalographic waves" are described. Their interpretation and relationship to nerve impulse conduction is also discussed. Chapters 6 and 7 discuss the neural mechanisms associated with hearing and vision, respectively. The ideas presented in Chapters 1 through 5 are used in these two chapters about the neural aspects of hearing and vision.

The physical and chemical nature of muscular contraction forms the basis for Chapter 8. Some biochemical concepts, presented more fully in later chapters, are introduced in order to restrict the discussion of muscles to Chapter 8. Finally, the last chapter in Part B, "Mechanical and Electrical Character of the Heart Beat," applies many of the ideas presented in Chapters 4 and 8 to the mammalian heart.

The molecular description of the action of nerve axons is deferred to Chapter 24 following discussions of thermodynamics and active transport.

4

The Conduction of Impulses by Nerves

1. The Role of the Nervous System

The nervous system is composed of units called neurons which transmit information in the form of electrical pulses from one place within the organism to another.   This action is essential for the rapid responses of animals to external stimuli.   Animals respond more rapidly than plants do to conditions outside themselves.   For instance, certain plants have flowers which are open only in bright sunlight, and deciduous trees shed their leaves during the fall season.   However, these are comparatively slow responses involving time intervals from minutes to days.   In contrast, the responses of a motorist to a red light or of a fly to an approaching swatter are both very much quicker.   These rapid responses of animals timed in milliseconds or, at most, seconds are mediated by the nervous system.

The rapid coordinations and responses of animals strongly suggest that the nervous system must transmit information in an electrical or magnetic form.   One might reach this conclusion without detailed

69

knowledge of the structure and properties of the neurons. Studies of nerves have shown that they consist of bundles of long processes called *axons* or nerve fibers. The axons are each a part of an individual neuron. Along the nerve fiber, the information is coded and transmitted in the form of an "all-or-none" or "on-off" electrical pulse called an *action potential* or *spike potential*.

On a teleological basis, the problems of the nervous system are similar to those of transmitting telephone messages over long distances. Either there must be many parallel low frequency channels, or fewer high frequency channels, each modulated by many separate signals. The living organisms which respond rapidly to external stimuli (that is, animals) have varying numbers of parallel low frequency electrical channels. The number of channels increases with the complexity of the animal. Along each of these channels (nerve fibers), information is transmitted by electrical pulses, referred to as action (or spike) potentials. The individual channel, with its energy supply and its connections, is called a *neuron*.[1] Its distinguishing features involve the biological generation and transmission of electrical potentials.

The earliest experiments which could be called bioelectrical occurred toward the end of the eighteenth century. Galvani put two dissimilar metals into a frog's leg muscle and observed a twitch. He correctly associated the response with electricity but assumed that the electricity was generated within the muscle by a vital process. Volta proved that Galvani's electricity was not of biological origin; the existence of true biological potential generators was not discovered for almost another century. Today, it is known that all nerve fibers, in fact, probably all cell membranes, are charged electrically. The membrane charges, as well as the spike potentials, are so small that they could not be observed with the instrumentation of Galvani and Volta. The field of bioelectricity is a fertile one for the application of electronic gadgeteering and physical instrumentation; it has attracted many persons with a background in physics who welcomed a challenging biological problem to which they could apply their previous training. A major application of bioelectricity is the study of the conduction of impulses by nerves.

Animals possess other mechanisms, besides the bioelectrical properties of the nervous system, for transmitting information from one part to another. These other systems are called *endocrine*; they involve the internal secretion of certain chemicals called *hormones*. The hormones alter metabolic rates, dilation of blood vessels, and secretory rates at

---

[1] Some giant invertebrate fibers are fusion products of several embryonic neurons.

specific target organs.   Similarly, when information is transmitted from one neuron to another, there is often a chemical intermediate.   The process differs from the endocrine system only in the length of time involved.   The hormones act, in general, over a period of hours or days, whereas the transmission from one neuron to the next takes only milliseconds.   Some hormones act faster so that there is no sharp dividing line between the hormones and the neuro-chemical transmitters. Plants also possess chemical transmitters.   The distinguishing feature of higher animals is their nervous system, which transmits information far more rapidly than the endocrine systems do.

Biophysicists have studied both the nervous and the endocrine systems. Both lend themselves to the application of complex physical techniques, and both can be analyzed by the type of reasoning common to physics and electronics.   This is particularly true of the interactions between groups of neurons, of interactions between groups of endocrine glands, and also of the neuron-endocrine interactions.   In all of these, "feedback" loops exist in which the effect produced alters the behavior of the neurons or endocrine glands producing these effects.   Physicists and electrical engineers refer to these types of control mechanisms as "negative feedback"; physiologists have called many of them "homeostatic" mechanisms because they tend to keep the state of the organism constant.

In this text, only the actions of the nervous system are discussed.   It is the aim of this chapter to present, in so far as possible, a picture of the physical properties of nervous tissues and a description of how nerve fibers conduct spike potentials.   Because each reader will have a different background, an attempt has been made first to present the fundamentals of electricity.   A more detailed discussion of electrical terminology can be found in Appendix C.   The electricity section of this chapter is followed by a brief description of certain salient features of the vertebrate neuron.   Details of the physical characteristics of the action potential are then presented.   The final section of this chapter deals with conduction from one neuron to the next, called *synaptic transmission*.

Many aspects of the nervous system are discussed in other chapters. Chapter 5 describes the electrical potentials of the brain and contains a discussion of feedback mechanisms.   Chapters 6 and 7 deal with the neural aspects of vision and hearing.   Chapter 8 includes the stimulation of muscles by nerves, and Chapter 9 the neural control of the heart rate. Perhaps most important of all, from the point of view of the biophysicist, the molecular basis of the action potential is discussed in Chapter 24. A knowledge of the material in Part D (molecular biology) and the other chapters of Part E (thermodynamics and transport systems), makes that chapter much easier to understand.

2. A Brief Glance at Electricity

Physicists consider all matter to be made up of neutral atoms, which, in turn, are made up of positively and negatively charged particles. Although large chunks of matter are electrically neutral, on a subatomic scale, many particles have a net charge. In a liquid or a crystal, there are often ions or groups of atoms which are likewise charged. For instance, NaCl splits into Na^+ and Cl^- ions in a water solution. In an NaCl crystal, the sites are occupied by Na^+ and Cl^- ions. Even water has measurable H^+ and OH^- concentrations. Thus, on an atomic or molecular scale, charges frequently do not balance out even though a volume containing many molecules is approximately electrically neutral.

Likewise, when a metal is placed in a liquid, or when two dissimilar metals are placed in contact, the two faces of the surfaces of discontinuity become charged. The "dry" cell and storage battery are examples of two metals in a liquid. Unlike charges are separated at the metal-liquid interfaces. If two dissimilar metals are used, the charge separation will be unequal; charges will flow when these two metals are connected by an external conductor. The thermocouple is an example of a practical use of the charge separation at the junction of two metals.

If charge is not allowed to flow after equilibrium has been established, the actual charge separation is very small in each of the cases above; the net charge separation is negligible compared to a coulomb. This leads one to suspect that although matter is approximately neutral, in no case do the charges balance out to the last electron. Biological cells and parts of cells are not exceptions. The net charge on any cell measured in coulombs is infinitesimal, but measured in the units of the charge on an electron e, it is appreciable. The neurons are distinguished from most other cells in that they are specialized to transmit changes in their surface potential rapidly. (Muscle fibers are similar to neurons in this respect.)

The flow of electrical *charge* is known as *electrical current*. Currents are measured in units called amperes. Early investigators of bioelectrical phenomena regarded the current as the fundamental event in the conduction of impulses by neurons. Hence, they referred to these as action currents.

Considerable experimental evidence, however, supports the *electrical potential* changes as being uniquely a property of the neuron membrane. In any case, the potential is the parameter actually measured in most experiments. The *electrical potential difference* between two points is defined in elementary physics as the energy received by a unit charge when it is carried between these two points. Thus, it is a potential energy per unit charge. Electrical potential is usually measured in volts.

Qualitatively, one may think of the potential as similar to an electrical pressure or force driving positive charges to regions of lower potential (and negative ones in the opposite direction). The ratio of the potential difference to the current flowing through a conductor is called the *resistance R*. For many substances, R is a constant independent of the current. In these cases, one can easily analyze direct-current circuits, such as those shown in Figure 1.

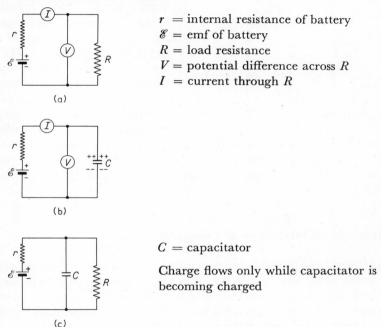

r = internal resistance of battery
$\mathscr{E}$ = emf of battery
R = load resistance
V = potential difference across R
I = current through R

(a)

(b)

C = capacitator

Charge flows only while capacitator is becoming charged

(c)

Figure I. (a) Direct current circuit. (b) Direct current circuit with capacitor. (c) Simplified circuit representing a resting axon (see Chapter 24).

Most bioelectrical phenomena involve changes which occur quite rapidly in time. As stated in the first chapter, events with complex time dependence can be analyzed in terms of simple harmonic changes (alternations) at one frequency. In electricity, a-c circuits are more complex than d-c inasmuch as elements other than resistances can impede the flow of an alternating current. In an a-c circuit of fixed frequency, the ratio of the potential to the current is called the *impedance*. The ratio of the component of the potential in phase with the current, to the current, is called the resistance, whereas the ratio of the out-of-phase component of the potential to the current is the *reactance*. Reactances arise due to *capacitors*, C, which do not pass direct current, and *inductors*, L, which do not impede a direct current.   An a-c circuit is illustrated in Figure 2.   Inductors are not as frequently encountered in

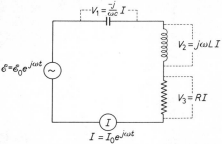

biological systems as are capacitors.   Most biological membranes act as capacitors in an equivalent electrical circuit.   As such, they may be charged, maintaining a fixed potential difference between their two sides, or they may conduct a rapid change in potential.   These ideas are applied directly to neurons in Section 4 of this chapter.

Figure 2. An a-c series circuit.   Note in the symbolism used that $\mathscr{E}$, $\mathscr{E}_0$, I, I_0, V_1, V_2, V_3 are all complex numbers and e is base of natural logarithms.

In addition, most membranes can generate a potential difference between their two sides, thereby expending chemical energy.   Such a generator is called an *electromotive force* or *emf*.   These generator properties of neuron and muscle membranes are discussed in this chapter and in Chapter 8, as well as in Chapters 23 and 24.

3. Anatomy and Histology of Neurons

The functional unit of the nervous system is called the *neuron*.   It consists of a nerve *cell body*, small processes called *dendrites*, and one large process called an *axon*.[2]   Outside of the central nervous system, many of the larger axons are surrounded by a thick, fatty *myelin sheath*.   The sheath is interrupted somewhat periodically at the *nodes of Ranvier*. Along the side of the sheath are satellite cells called *Schwann cells*.   Some axons are more than a meter long.   A diagram of such a neuron is presented in Figure 3.   Smaller axons, although not as thickly myelinated, are always surrounded by a lipid layer, as well as by extremely small satellite cells.

The neuron[3] is a single cell.   The dimensions of the cell body, of its nucleus, and of the diameters of the axons and dendrites are all typical of other cells, ranging for vertebrates from $1-100$ μ.   The length of the axon is the outstanding exception, being far longer than typical cellular

---

[2] Some authors use axon and dendrite to indicate direction of transmission. In this text, axon and nerve fiber are used as synonyms.   Some neurons have the cell body in the middle of the nerve fiber rather than at one end.

[3] The satellite cells along the myelinated fibers are actually separate cells but are considered part of the neuron, nonetheless.

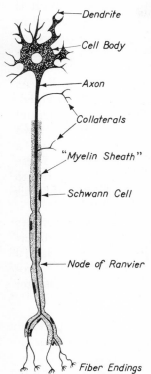

Dendrite

Cell Body

Axon

Collaterals

"Myelin Sheath"

Schwann Cell

Node of Ranvier

Fiber Endings

Figure 3. Diagram of a large myelinated axon. Dark-staining material in cell body is called *Nissl substance*. In some neurons, the axon is off to one side of the cell body; in others the cell body is in the middle of the axon. In both of these types the dendrites are attached directly to the axon; that is, both extreme ends of the axon appear similar. After A. A. Maximow and W. Bloom, *Textbook of Histology* (Philadelphia: W. B. Saunders Company, 1957).

dimensions. For example, the neurons that control the muscles in the finger have their cell bodies in the spinal cord, whereas their axons run the entire length of the arm. In the elephant and giraffe, the lengths of some of the axons are as great as 3 or 4 meters.

The axons are grouped together in bundles called *nerves*. Each nerve consists of a large number of axons of various sizes carrying impulses in their respective physiologically important direction. Just as the axons are grouped in nerves, the nerve cell bodies usually occur in compact clusters known as *ganglia*. In vertebrates, the ganglia within the central nervous system are referred to as *nuclei* (which is a confusing term). The axon bundles are called *fiber tracts* within the central nervous system.

Connections between two neurons are called *synapses*. These occur between the branched ends of axons, dendrites, and collaterals of different neurons. Other axons end at receptors, such as the hair cells of the organ of Corti in the ear. Still others terminate at controlled targets, as the motor end plates of a muscle fiber, for example.

In vertebrates, the nervous system is organized into a central nervous system and peripheral nerves and ganglia. Throughout the entire system, the basic element is the neuron. There is nothing inherent in the axon to control the direction in which it conducts. This is a property of the synapse only. In general, a peripheral nerve will contain both sensory (or afferent) axons which conduct toward the central nervous system, and motor (or efferent) axons which conduct away from it.

The sensory axons conduct impulses from the receptors to the nerve cell bodies. Along vertebrate, afferent pathways extending from receptors to the cerebral cortex, the axons conduct toward the cell bodies. In these, there is always at least one cell body in a ganglion outside of the central nervous system. For example, the sensory pathways entering the spinal cord have their first cell body in ganglia at the dorsal roots of the spinal cord, just out-side the spinal column.   In these ganglia, synapses occur; the axons entering the spinal cord are those of the second neuron.

In efferent pathways leading to muscles, glands, and other target organs, the axon conducts impulses from the nerve cell body.   These pathways may be conveniently divided into the voluntary motor path-ways and the autonomic systems.   The voluntary motor pathways have all their cell bodies within the central nervous system.   For example, the cell bodies for the axons which control the toe muscles are within the spinal cord.

In contrast to the voluntary pathways, the autonomic pathways almost always have a synapse and cell body outside the central nervous system. The autonomic system is divided into two parts on a functional and anatomical basis.   Those pathways leaving the spinal cord in the nerves between the thoracic and lumbar vertebrae comprise the thoracolumbar division, or sympathetic system.   The other part of the autonomic system, with pathways which leave the central nervous system via the sacral region of the spinal column or the cranium itself, is called the craniosacral division, or parasympathetic system.   Most organs are supplied by the craniosacral division as well as the thoracolumbar division.

The thoracolumbar division, in most of its activities, prepares an animal for "fight or flight."   The effects of stimulation of the thoraco-lumbar system include accelerating heart and respiratory rates, sup-pressing digestion, increasing blood flow to striated muscles, increasing blood pressure, and decreasing blood flow to the skin and smooth muscle.   In general, stimulation of the craniosacral system produces effects which are opposite to those produced by the thoracolumbar division.

Although the neurons within the central nervous system look similar to those without, they are different in many respects.   If a nerve fiber is injured within the central nervous system, the entire neuron degener-ates.   On the contrary, if a peripheral nerve is severed, the fibers will regrow out of the old nerve trunk from the central ends.   Another difference is the sensitivity to oxygen.   If a neuron within the central nervous system (of an adult) is deprived of oxygen for a short period of time, it will be irreversibly destroyed.   In contrast, axons outside the central nervous system will continue to conduct impulses for more than an hour in the absence of oxygen.   This is in part due to the difference between the sensitivity of the nerve cell bodies and the axons.   These differences hold for the larger axons which are heavily myelinated outside the central nervous system, as well as for the smaller, less myelin-ated axons.

The neuron cell bodies are, in several ways, similar to the secretory cells of endocrine glands. The dark-staining material within the nerve cell body, known as *Nissl substance*, has been shown to be chemically and morphologically identical (in electron micrographs) to cellular organelles, known as ribosomes and Golgi bodies. The ribosomes are associated with protein synthesis, and the Golgi bodies with secretion. The nerve cell body appears to "secrete" the axon and dendrites. The metabolic rate and the protein synthesis in the nerve cell body are both greatest when the axon is being formed or replaced after injury and are at a minimum in normal adults. By contrast, the axon appears to lack ribosomes and the ability to synthesize proteins. One may consider the nerve cell body to be an intracellular secreting cell, whereas endocrine gland cells produce extracellular secretions.

The axons do not possess the organelles necessary for protein synthesis. They do contain mitochondria, which are intracellular organelles associated with metabolism. No qualitative differences are known between the metabolism of axons and that of other animal cells.

The axons are surrounded by myelin sheaths and satellite cells. It is not known if these are important in providing the proper chemical media for axon metabolism. However, it is quite well established that for all axons—vertebrate and invertebrate, so-called "myelinated" and "unmyelinated," large and small—for all of these, the satellite cells extend out and coil around the axon forming a double lipid layer known as myelin. In the larger vertebrate axons, outside of the central nervous system, such as those diagrammed in Figure 3, the satellite cells, called Schwann cells, have processes which are wrapped many times around the axons. In these, the myelin sheath is very easily visible.

Where the processes from two neighboring Schwann cells meet, the myelin layer is much thinner and is pierced by canals about 300 Å in diameter. This region is known as a node of Ranvier. The so-called nonmyelinated fibers appear to have similar "canals" through their myelin sheaths all along the axon. Thus, their axons are in more or less continuous chemical contact with the intercellular fluids. In contrast, the large myelinated fibers appear to communicate chemically with the intercellular fluids only at the nodes. The possible electrical significance of the myelin sheaths is discussed in the next section.

At the end of the neural fibers, the surface layer appears in the electron microscope to contain small vesicles. It is believed that these are filled with the chemical carriers active in synaptic transmission. This idea will be referred to again in Section 5 of this chapter. These tiny vesicles are so small that they cannot be conveniently observed except in the electron microscope.

As a vertebrate, man's greatest interest has been in vertebrate nerves.

However, certain invertebrate axons are easier to work with because of their greater diameter. The maximum diameter of the vertebrate axon is about 20 microns. By contrast, squids have axons larger than 200 μ in diameter; these are visible to the unaided eye. Insects, too, sometimes have large axons; the cockroach has some as large as 50 μ. The extreme size of the squid axon has made it of especial interest and importance in all studies of the conduction of impulses by nervous tissues. The synapses of the large invertebrate neurons have also proved convenient to study. The material in this chapter and in Chapter 24 is based in part on studies of invertebrate axons.

4. The Spike Potential

An electrode placed on the crushed end of a nerve bundle is in contact with the interior of the axons of this nerve. The potential is negative relative to the medium surrounding the axons. This potential, in normal axons, ranges from 50 to 100 mv. It is comparable in size to the contact potentials and polarization potentials which can occur at electrodes. However, when these artifacts are reduced to the microvolt range, the true resting potential of the nerve axon remains. Diagrammatically, the axon may be represented, as in Figure 4, by an insulator shaped as a cylindrical shell. The inner and outer faces of the shell are charged. The hollow shell is filled with one conducting medium (cytoplasm) and immersed in another (intercellular fluid). This picture applies to all axons except the thickly myelinated ones, which will be discussed further later in this section.

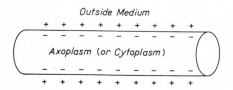

Figure 4. Diagrammatic representation of resting axon. This figure is an alternate way of expressing the information in Figure 1(c).

The existence of these potentials across the extremely thin axon membrane indicates the ability of these membranes to withstand very high electrical field strengths. Dry air breaks down at 3×10^6 v/m. Many insulators (including corrosion on spark plugs) raise the field strength necessary for breakdown of air as high as 10^8 v/m. At the surfaces of many biological cells, including neurons, it appears that high field strengths of about 10^8 v/m occur. These are in such small regions that numbers for air prove misleading. The cell membranes are more nearly analogous to the junctions between two dissimilar metals. At the latter, field strengths as high as 5×10^9 v/m are known without sparking or breakdown of any sort. Thus, it is not too surprising that the neuron membrane can withstand field strengths at which dry air breaks down.

When the axon is stimulated, its surface potential changes in a characteristic fashion to an action potential or a spike potential. (The latter name arose from the appearance of these impulses on the screen of a cathode ray oscilloscope.) Axons may be stimulated by any of a wide variety of means. Electrical pulses of various shapes, heat, cold, chemical changes, and mechanical pressures all lead to the same

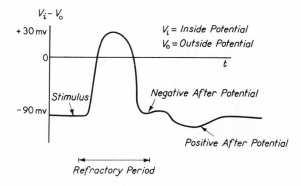

Figure 5. Diagrammatic representation of the time course of the spike potential at a fixed point along the axon. During the refractory period, another impulse cannot be started. The threshold for stimulation is lowered during the negative after potential and raised during the positive after potential. The magnitude and duration of these effects is characteristic of the particular nerve fiber.

phenomena. The local membrane polarization disappears, reverses in polarity very quickly, then returns to normal over a series of "bumps." The spike potential formed in this fashion travels down the axon in both directions from the point of stimulation. (Owing to the nature of the synapses, only one of these directions is usually effective when an intact nerve is stimulated.) The time dependence of the potential at one spot is shown in Figure 5. The corresponding distributions of charges along the axon cylinder at a given time are shown in Figure 6.

In laboratory experiments, spike potentials are usually excited by electrical stimuli because they are easier to control in time, space, and strength than are any other type of stimuli. For very weak stimuli, a local response occurs which is similar to, but smaller than, the spike potential. As the stimulus is increased, a certain threshold is reached where a transmitted spike potential is generated. The spike potential then travels along the axon at a characteristic velocity.

The spike potential is an all-or-none response. Either there is a transmitted spike or there is not. If the spike is present, its height and shape are independent of the stimulus strength. The neuron acts in a similar manner to a flip-flop electronic circuit such as used in counters and in digital computers. That is to say, the neuron is either in the conducting or nonconducting state; nothing is transmitted in between. This analogy seems so strong that it is hard to avoid describing the computer in anthropomorphic terms and the nervous system in terms of a digital computer.

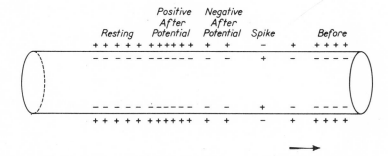

Figure 6. Space distribution of charges along an axon conducting a spike potential. Arrow shows direction in which spike is moving.

If an axon is cut, and the two pieces insulated electrically, no impulse travels from one part to the other. However, if the two are connected by a metallic conductor, or a salt bridge, the spike potential crosses readily from one part of the axon to the other. This emphasizes the essentially electrical nature of the action potential. These spike potentials occur in tissues, which are fluid-like media. Currents in fluids are carried by ions, therefore it is appropriate to consider the resting potential as well as the spike potential as due to ionic distributions.

While the spike potential is present at the axon, another one cannot be started. By contrast, several subthreshold stimuli may be summed to give a response if they come close enough together in time. During the positive after-potential, the threshold is increased. The lengths of time for these potentials and the rate of conduction of the spike potentials led to the classification of vertebrate axons presented in the table on page 81.

Particular attention should be called to the giant squid axon. From

TABLE I

Properties of Axon and Fiber-like Cells

Property	Units	Vertebrate axon type			Fiber or filament type		
		A	B	C	Skeletal muscle	Squid axon	Nitella
		Myelinated					
Diameter	μ	10–20	3	1	10	200	200
Conduction velocity	m/sec	50–160	3–15	0.7–2.3	3	20	0.01
Absolute refractory period	msec	0.4–1.0	0.12	2.0	5	1	1,000
-After potential							
Size	per cent of spike	3–5	None	3–5	None*	None	?
Duration	msec	12–20	None	50–80	None*	None	?
+After potential							
Size	per cent of spike	0.2	1.5–4.0	1.5	10	5	?
Duration	msec	40–60	100–300	300–1,000	500	5–15	?
Resting potential	mv	90	90	90	90	70	100
Spike height	mv	140	140	140	140	90	100

* Strictly speaking, this is wrong; see Chapter 8.

a comparative point of view, it is a huge axon.   It is possible to shove all sorts of electrodes and shafts inside this axon.   Experiments with squid axons confirm that the resting potential and the spike potential depend only on the membrane, not on the bulk of the axoplasm.   This is in accord with the charge distribution shown in Figures 2 and 4.   Similar experiments have shown that this pattern is valid also for all other axons, for muscle fibers, and for many long algal cells.

The local response has the same form as the spike potential shown in Figures 4 and 7a.   A small depolarization applied externally results in a flow of ions, so that a greater depolarization of the membrane occurs.

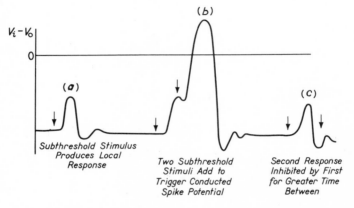

Figure 7. Temporal summation of subthreshold responses.

Figure 7b shows a second subthreshold stimulus following closely after a first one.   These add and give rise to a conducted spike potential. Figure 7c illustrates two stimuli slightly further apart in time.   In this case, the first local response inhibits the second one.

Both the local responses and the conducted spike potential involve a flow of ions.   In the initial or resting condition, the K^+ concentration inside the fiber is greater than that outside and the Na^+ less than that outside.   The ions are maintained with this distribution at the expense of metabolic energy.   The spike potential does not merely result in a depolarization of the axon membrane, since the potential actually reverses in sign.   Rather, measurements of the complex impedance Z, per unit surface area, have shown that ionic conduction increases both during the regenerative phase of the spike and again during the recovery.

Tracer experiments and others described in Chapter 24 have shown that Na^+ flows into the axon during the regenerative phase and K^+ flows out during the recovery phase.   This may be summarized by the diagram shown in Figure 8.   This entire process is an active one, so that the spike potential is not attenuated as it travels along the axon but, rather, is built up anew at each spot along the way.

The velocity at which a spike potential travels along a fiber is limited by the diameter of the fiber.   Larger diameters correspond to larger velocities.   In the large "myelinated" vertebrate fibers, the spike travels at a rate in excess of that predicted from the axon diameter.   It

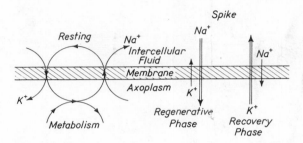

Figure 8. Ion movements across axon surface.   After A. L. Hodgkin and R. D. Keynes, "Active Transport in Nerve," J. Physiol. 128: 28 (1955).

is believed that the regenerative and recovery phases described above occur only at the nodes.   In between, the spike is simply conducted, the entire segment acting as a single conductor.   The spike potential thus is attenuated between the nodes and restored to its characteristic height at the nodes.

The myelin sheaths of the "nonmyelinated" axons may act primarily as electrical insulation between fibers.   This limits the probability that a spike potential along one axon will stimulate its neighbor.   Muscle fibers have similar spike potentials but lack myelin insulation.   In the muscle, unlike the nerve, it may be desirable for one fiber to stimulate other parallel ones, although this has never been demonstrated to occur.

5. Synaptic Conduction

Along the axon, the information is transmitted as an electrical spike potential.   This transmitted spike is maintained at a constant height by renewal and amplification, either continuously or at certain nodes. There are thus two symbols for coding transmitted information: either a spike or its absence.   In other words, all neural information is coded as binary digits.   (See Chapter 25.)

The axon transmits equally well in either direction, but in the intact

animal it is only used in one direction.   This limitation is imposed by
the synapses between neurons and by their junctions with the sensory
receptors.[4]   Similar limitations exist for muscle fibers which conduct
spike potentials in either direction along the fiber but are only stimulated
in life at the junction between the nerve terminals and the muscle.   At

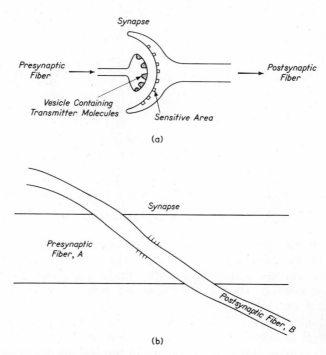

Figure 9. (a) Chemical transmission.   The incoming spike releases packets of molecules which diffuse across synapse to
produce local excitation at sensitive areas.   Diagrammatic
representation. (b) Electrical transmission. With suitable
geometry, a large field strength can be created in synapse by a
spike potential on fiber *A*, thereby exciting *B*.   The geometry
and synaptic rectification prohibits conduction in the other
direction.   Diagrammatic representation.

this point, the muscle fiber has a special structure called an *end plate*.
The neuromuscular junction is homologous to the synapses between
neurons; much of our knowledge of neural synaptic conduction is based
on studies of the neuromuscular junction.   Accordingly, the term

---

[4] Synapses are probably not polarized in some invertebrates.

"synaptic conduction" is interpreted in this section to include the transmission of spike potentials from nerve to muscle.

Two different modes of synaptic conduction occur: electrical and chemical. These are illustrated in Figure 9. The electrical conduction may be very rare; it has been demonstrated positively only for the "giant synapse" in the crayfish. At this synapse, impulses travel electrically from one axon to another with negligible time delay. Conduction can occur only in one direction. Similar giant synapses in the squid, however, exhibit appreciable time delay and no electrical transfer of charge. Conduction across the squid giant synapses, just as across all vertebrate synapses studied, is mediated by a specific chemical.

There is no reason to believe that the same chemical is involved at all the synapses lacking direct electrical transfer. On the contrary, there is considerable evidence to indicate that different substances act at different synapses. Most nerve fiber terminals are so small that it is impossible to make direct observations and hence, determine the transmitter substance. As a result of the small size, only very small amounts of the transmitting chemicals are necessary. At the neuromuscular junction in vertebrates about 10^{-18} moles of acetylcholine (ACh) produce a spike potential. ACh is the only synaptic transmitter substance which has been definitely confirmed.

In chemical transmission, the substance, as ACh, is released when a spike potential reaches the appropriate nerve fiber terminal. It then diffuses across the synapse. This distance is of the order of a micron or two, and diffusion can occur in a millisecond or two. The diffusing substance is then absorbed at the receiving terminal or motor end plate, where it changes the ionic permeability of the membrane. Finally, the absorbed molecules are enzymatically destroyed.

Experiments with vertebrate motor end plates have shown that the area sensitive to ACh is extremely small; it is confined specifically to the outer surface of the motor end plate nearest to the nerve endings. This outer surface may be regarded as a chemoreceptor. Furthermore, these studies showed that ACh does not produce a depolarization of the membrane but increases its permeability to all small cations such as Li^+, Na^+, and K^+. Finally, the ACh is destroyed by a specific protein catalyst, acetylcholinesterase, located in the end plate.

The response across the synapse is a local response. The spike potential may originate near there as in the case of vertebrate muscle fibers and giant synapses in squid. In contrast, in sensory neurons (whose axon runs towards the cell body) the spike is formed at the distal end of the axon where several fiber terminals join together. In motor neurons, where the local response occurs in dendrites, the transmitted spike potential is formed at or past the nerve cell body.

One spike potential on a presynaptic fiber may excite one spike potential on the postsynaptic fiber. In some cases, a spike on any one of several different presynaptic fibers may excite a spike on a given postsynaptic fiber. At other synapses, one spike on a presynaptic fiber will produce only a local subthreshold response. In this case, there exists the possibility of adding subthreshold responses from several synapses to produce a spike potential. Thus, the neuron can act as an adder. Likewise, two, three, or more local responses in a short time at one synapse may be necessary to produce a transmitted impulse. Then the synapse is acting as a "divider." If several terminals from one neuron cell synapse with differing time delays at the same second neuron, then the original spike could be "multiplied."

Neurons can likewise subtract. This is possible because not all postsynaptic membranes are similar. For instance, ACh produces a spike potential at motor end plates but inhibits heart muscles. (This inhibitory effect of the ACh secreted by the vagus nerve endings in the heart led to its original discovery.) At inhibitory junctions, the transmitter substance increases the permeability to K^+ and larger cations but does not alter the Na^+ or Li^+ permeability. The net result is a change in the transmembrane potential and an increase in the local response necessary at other synapses to start a transmitted spike. This produces, effectively, subtraction of the impulses from two different incoming neurons.

At the synapses, then, the arithmetic processes of addition, subtraction, multiplication, and division can occur. Because the local responses exhibit a complex time pattern, the calculus operations of integration and differentiation can also be produced. However, the neurons are not as simple as electronic circuits, and the various numerical processes are also much more complex. This situation may be described in mathematical terms by saying the system is nonlinear. For example, a dividing synapse, if presented with three impulses, may transmit one; but seven will be necessary for two transmitted spikes and 14 or more will be needed for three transmitted spikes.

In addition, the synaptic conduction is altered by slow potential fluctuations which are small compared to the membrane potentials and by changes in the ionic content of the intracellular fluid. Aside from the direct effects of K^+ and Na^+, the Ca^{++} and Mg^{++} and particularly their ratio alter the synaptic conduction. At the neuromuscular junction, it has been shown that ACh is released in packets of the order of 1,000 molecules from small vesicles in the nerve endings. The probability of a given packet entering the intercellular fluid is a function of the Ca^{++}/Mg^{++} ratio.

To summarize this section, transsynaptic conduction usually occurs in one direction. It may be mediated by electrical charge conduction or special chemical transmitters.   The latter alter the permeability of the surface of the second neuron (or the muscle fiber) at specific receptor spots.   Depending on the receptor, and perhaps on the chemical nature of the transmitter, this may result in stimulation or inhibition. All manner of arithmetic and calculus operations can occur at synapses between neurons.   The behavior is similar to that in digital computers but far more complex.

REFERENCES

1. Maximow, A. A., and William Bloom, *A Textbook of Histology* 4th ed. (Philadelphia: W. B. Saunders Company, 1942).
2. Glasser, Otto, ed., *Medical Physics* (Chicago, Illinois: Year Book Publishers, Inc.).
   a. Beutner, R., "Bioelectricity," (1944) Vol. I, pp. 35–88.
   b. Curtis, H. J., and K. S. Cole, "Nervous System: Excitation and Propagation of Nerve," (1950) Vol. II, pp. 584–595.
   c. Rashevsky, N., "Nervous System: Mathematical Theory of Its Functions," (1950) Vol. II, pp. 595–603.
3. Barron, E. S. G., ed., *Modern Trends in Physiology and Biochemistry* (New York: Academic Press, Inc., 1952).
   a. Grundfest, H., "Mechanisms and Properties of Biological Potentials," pp. 193–228.
4. Stevens, S. S., ed., *Handbook of Experimental Psychology* (New York: John Wiley & Sons, Inc., 1951).
   a. Brink, Frank, Jr., "Excitation and Conduction in the Neuron," pp. 50–93.
   b. ——— "Synaptic Mechanisms," pp. 94–120.
5. *Reviews of Modern Physics*, Vol. 31 (1959).
   a. Schmitt, F. O., "Molecular Organization of the Nerve Fiber," pp. 455–465.
   b. Katz, Bernard, "Nature of the Nerve Impulse," pp. 466–474.
   c. ——— "Mechanisms of Synaptic Transmission," pp. 524–531.

5

Electrical Potentials of the Brain

I. Electroencephalography

Electroencephalography is a study (or graphing) of the electrical potentials on the surface of the head. In terms of its derivation, electroencephalography (electro + encephalon + ography) could refer to any electrical potentials of the head. Actually, it is restricted to those potentials, other than neuron spikes, that are associated with the brain's action. At the outer surface of the scalp, these electroencephalographic (eeg)[1] potentials are small compared to the potentials due to the heartbeat and are comparable to the potentials associated with the motion of the muscles controlling the eye, jaw, neck, and so on. The small

[1] Throughout this chapter, the abbreviation "eeg" will be used as an adjective or noun as appropriate, to refer either to these potentials, to the recording apparatus, or to the graphic record of these potentials as a function of time. The eeg potentials arise from the action of nervous tissue. The student will find it profitable to have read thoroughly the preceding chapter before starting this one. A knowledge of that material is presupposed in this chapter.

eeg potentials can be observed only with electronic amplifiers which discriminate both against other potentials of physiological origin and against electrical noise.

The characteristic form of the eeg pattern has been used clinically and experimentally. Various types of epilepsy have typical eeg patterns which are useful for diagnosis and occasionally in treatment. Brain tumors likewise may be located from an eeg if the tumor is sufficiently close to the brain's surface. Many brain injuries can be diagnosed from alterations in the patterns of the potentials near the injury. Behavioral experiments use eeg patterns to indicate alarm reactions, sensory responses, and so forth.

From the viewpoint of this text, the more significant application of these so-called "brain waves" is that they may indicate the operation of the central nervous system. Many theories have been proposed, based on the form of these brain potentials. To date, none of these theories has been altogether successful. The eeg potentials are a building block which may eventually lead to an understanding of the function of the brain.

The potentials associated with brain activity may be as large as 100 microvolts on the human scalp; these can be observed electronically. In laboratory animals, it is more difficult, if not impossible, to measure eeg potentials outside the skull. Small electrodes inserted through the skull onto the surface of the brain indicate potentials similar to those found on the human scalp. In other studies, electrodes are inserted into the interior of the brain. Potentials measured within the brain, with electrodes so large (diameter 0.01 mm or greater) that they respond to some type of average of the activity of many cells, are also referred to as eeg potentials. The instrument used to record the potentials is called an *electroencephalograph* and the record an *electroencephalogram*.

2. The Central Nervous System

The eeg potentials result from the action of the central nervous system. To aid in discussing these brain potentials, an outline of the anatomy of the central nervous system is given in this section. In Section 3 of this chapter, some of the actions of the central nervous system are interpreted by analogy with electronic feedback networks.

The central nervous system, as is the case with all other nervous tissue, is made up of neurons. Some carry information into the central nervous system; these are sensory or afferent neurons. Others carry spike potentials out of the central nervous system and are called motor or efferent neurons. The great majority of the units within the central nervous system start and end there; these are called interneurons. Thus, many neurons form links between other neurons. As was pointed out in the last chapter, one neuron may receive impulses from several neurons, and it may excite or inhibit more than one other neuron. Each neuron follows an all-or-none law; that is, it either is or is not conducting a spike potential. This assemblage of neurons connecting with other neurons is very similar in form to a complex digital computer whose units are in one of two possible states.

In addition to the spike potentials, there are also more diffuse changes in electrical potential in various areas of the brain. These may also play an important role in the central nervous system function, for example, by altering the synaptic transmission from one neuron to the next. These diffuse, slower potential changes are analogous to what one might expect to find in an analog computer. They indicate the difficulty of trying to use any electronic model for the central nervous system.

The vertebrate central nervous system is easily divided into two major parts: the brain and the spinal cord. Both are surrounded by three membranes, or meninges, which serve to protect the central nervous system from injury. Between the various meninges are layers of cerebrospinal fluid which cushion the central nervous system from shock. There are also fluid-filled chambers within the central nervous system itself: four ventricles in the brain and the central canal in the spinal cord. All four ventricles and the spinal canal are interconnected.

Various nerves leave (or enter) the central nervous system. Along the spinal cord, a pair of nerves passes between each pair of vertebrae. These supply sensory, motor, and autonomic fibers to all parts of the body other than the head. In addition, 12 pairs of nerves originate in the brain itself.

The spinal cord and brain consist of white matter and gray matter. The white color is due to the myelin around the large nerve fibers; the white matter is made up of fiber tracts. The gray matter contains most of the cell bodies. Some of these are arranged in compact volumes referred to as nuclei. Many nuclei can be associated with specific functions or actions, such as control of respiration, or conducting impulses from muscular proprioceptors, and so forth. However, the over-all action of the nervous system, particularly with respect to subjective phenomena as thinking or memory, is still in the realm of speculation.

Figure 1 shows the structure of a medial section through the human brain. The portion of the brain joining the spinal column is called the *brain stem*. In lower vertebrates, as fishes, there are two small bumps

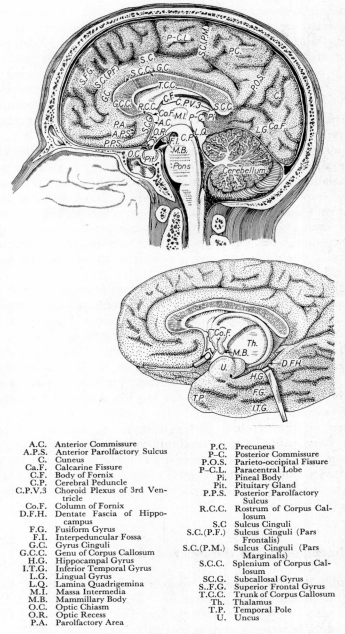

A.C.	Anterior Commissure	P.C.	Precuneus
A.P.S.	Anterior Parolfactory Sulcus	P–C.	Posterior Commissure
C.	Cuneus	P.O.S.	Parieto-occipital Fissure
Ca.F.	Calcarine Fissure	P–C.L.	Paracentral Lobe
C.F.	Body of Fornix	Pi.	Pineal Body
C.P.	Cerebral Peduncle	Pit.	Pituitary Gland
C.P.V.3	Choroid Plexus of 3rd Ventricle	P.P.S.	Posterior Parolfactory Sulcus
Co.F.	Column of Fornix	R.C.C.	Rostrum of Corpus Callosum
D.F.H.	Dentate Fascia of Hippocampus		
		S.C	Sulcus Cinguli
F.G.	Fusiform Gyrus	S.C.(P.F.)	Sulcus Cinguli (Pars Frontalis)
F.I.	Interpeduncular Fossa		
G.C.	Gyrus Cinguli	S.C.(P.M.)	Sulcus Cinguli (Pars Marginalis)
G.C.C.	Genu of Corpus Callosum		
H.G.	Hippocampal Gyrus	S.C.C.	Splenium of Corpus Callosum
I.T.G.	Inferior Temporal Gyrus		
L.G.	Lingual Gyrus	SC.G.	Subcallosal Gyrus
L.Q.	Lamina Quadrigemina	S..F.G.	Superior Frontal Gyrus
M.I.	Massa Intermedia	T.C.C.	Trunk of Corpus Callosum
M.B.	Mammillary Body	Th.	Thalamus
O.C.	Optic Chiasm	T.P.	Temporal Pole
O.R.	Optic Recess	U.	Uncus
P.A.	Parolfactory Area		

Figure 1. Medial aspects of the human brain. Copyright *The CIBA Collection of Medical Illustrations* by Frank H. Netter, M.D., Vol. 1, "The Nervous System," 1953.

called the *cerebral hemispheres* near the olfactory area. In mammals, and to the greatest extent in man, these cerebral hemispheres are a major part of the brain. The cerebral cortex which covers the hemispheres is so folded around and over the brain stem in mammals that the eeg potentials on the skull are related to the cerebral cortex only, and probably only to the outermost layers of the cerebral cortex. (By placing electrodes within the brain, eeg potentials can be measured as a function of the part of the brain nearest the electrodes, rather than of the outer layers of the cortex.)

The portion of the brain stem connected directly to the cerebral cortex is called the *thalamus*. The sensory pathways all have synapses in the thalamus. Certain thalamic regions are believed associated with emotional responses. Thus, if an electrode is placed in the appropriate spot in a rat's thalamus, it will pull a lever to shock itself in preference to eating food. Other areas in the thalamus produce just the opposite effect when stimulated. It appears proper to consider all mammals, and possibly all vertebrates, as having emotions homologous to ours and represented by thalamic centers.

Thought, memory, conscious sensations, and conscious motor activity are all associated with the cerebral cortex. The cerebrum is attached to the thalamus. In the relative size and complexity of his cerebral cortex, man is unique among the animals. As illustrated in Figure 2, certain areas can be associated with specific functions. However, the role of many areas of the cerebral cortex is not known, nor is it known how man analyzes, or thinks, or remembers. Because it reflects, in some sense, the activity of this part of the brain, the eeg has attracted the interest of many investigators.

However, if the cerebral cortex is removed, similar eeg patterns remain. Even fishes, whose cerebral cortices are negligible, possess typical eeg patterns similar to man's. The eeg is a vertebrate phenomenon; insect ganglia do not exhibit comparable potentials. The eeg must, in some way, be related to the structure and function of the vertebrate central nervous system.

3. Feedback Loops and the Nervous System

It is possible that the eeg potentials reflect, in some manner, feedback loops within the central nervous system. Whether or not this is the case is a moot point, but there is no doubt that feedback loops are important in all coordinated animals and, in particular, in the over-all action of the nervous system. The basic elements of a feedback loop are shown in Figure 3. They consist of (a) a quantity being controlled, such as the temperature of a room; (b) a method of sensing this quantity such as a thermostat; and (c) an active mechanism whose rate can be varied by the sensing element to effect the control (in this example, an oil furnace). If the control opposes changes, the loop is said to have a negative feedback. Similar negative feedback loops are common in electronics. One such frequent use is to keep an amplifier's gain constant in spite of changes in supply voltages and tube characteristics. Feedback loops can also

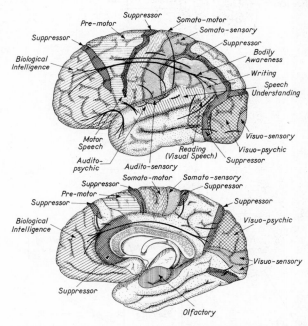

Figure 2. Functions of the human cerebral cortex. Copyright *The CIBA Collection of Medical Illustrations* by Frank H. Netter, M.D., Vol. 1, "The Nervous System," 1953.

maintain the output of a power supply at a constant voltage or vary an amplifier's gain to keep its output constant. The latter is illustrated in Figure 3b.

Instead of just one room, it is sometimes desired to regulate independently the temperature of several rooms. Individual thermostats may control dampers in the hot air lines to their respective rooms and a complex system must coordinate the results of the various thermostats to control the furnace. Complex, interlocking loops also occur in the nervous system.

The thermostat operates only in an on-off, that is, all-or-none, manner. If, instead of the thermostat, one uses a thermocouple, or

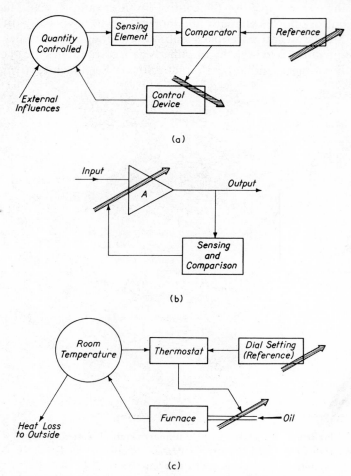

(a)

(b)

(c)

Figure 3. (a) General scheme of negative feedback control loop (servomechanism). Large cross-hatched arrows indicate variable elements. (b) Block diagram of negative feedback loop to keep amplifier output constant. Such amplifiers can be used to present subjects with speech of constant (average) sound pressure level. (c) Negative feedback control loop used to regulate room temperature. In practice, an additional loop is used to keep furnace below some set temperature.

thermistor bridge circuit, it is possible to obtain a voltage proportional to the error in temperature from the 68°F at which the system is set.

This error signal may be amplified and used to vary continuously the rate of flow of oil to the furnace. In this case, the further from 68°F the greater the change in heating rate.

Instead of negative feedback, one may have positive feedback. Then any small change will be added to and amplified by the controlling element. Positive feedback is used in electronic oscillators. It is also active at the membrane of nerve fibers. If their potential is slightly decreased by external means, the membrane senses this and alters its permeability to augment the decrease. Most feedback loops which

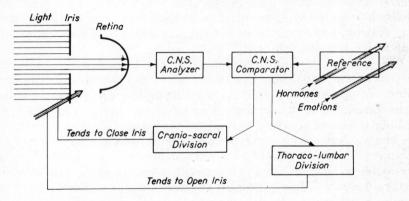

Figure 4. Feedback control loop regulating iris opening.

have been studied, and which involve more than one neuron, are of the negative variety.

For example, the iris diaphragm of the eye (see Chapter 2) is controlled by nerve fibers of both the craniosacral and thoracolumbar divisions of the autonomic nervous system. Its negative feedback loop is shown in Figure 4. Light enters the eye through the iris diaphragm and is converted to neural impulses in the retina. Some place in the retina or brain both the total neural impulses and the maximum per area of the retina are "computed." These are each "compared" to built-in values and the nerve fibers to the iris are activated in such a fashion as to decrease the differences; that is, negative feedback occurs. The built-in comparison value can be varied just as the thermostat setting. Both the emotional state of the individual and the hormonal balance in the blood alter the control values for the iris feedback loop. Exactly how this process occurs within the brain is not fully understood, although it is known that certain areas and fiber tracts are involved, and others are not.

A very impressive use of multiple negative feedback loops occurs in the control of voluntary muscular action.   When a person wills to write his name with a pen or to scratch his back, many negative feedback loops are active.   The person does not consider how to move each muscle fiber or how to tense one muscle and relax its opponent.   Rather, his nervous system, at a level below consciousness, finds the deviation from the desired location and controls the muscles to reduce this deviation.   If the action can be seen, feedback loops involving the visual system are the most important (to humans).   There are, in addition, sense organelles within every muscle called proprioceptors, which send signals to the central nervous system "describing" the tension in that muscle.   The feedback loops involving proprioceptors are important for back-scratching, walking, and many other activities in which one does not see the limb which is controlled.

The presence of many coordinated negative feedback loops in the nervous system is analogous to a large electronic or mechanical computer. Moreover, the fact that neurons obey an all-or-none principle makes them correspond to the elements of an electronic digital computer.   An additional feature common to many of the giant electronic "brains" is a scanning device which sweeps continuously over the elements of the "memory."   If this type of phenomenon occurs in the brain, it seems reasonable to look for it in the integrated potentials at the surface of the cerebral cortex.   These potentials are called eegs; the remainder of the chapter is devoted to their description, analysis, and applications.

4. The Electroencephalographic Patterns

Changing electrical potentials are always found on the surface of the brain of a living vertebrate; that is, an eeg pattern can always be found. This indicates that the nerve fibers in the central nervous system are never at rest.   By way of contrast, the nerves to a relaxed or anesthetized limb may be completely inactive for long periods.   The continual activity of the central nervous system might indicate some type of scanning system or, perhaps, the storage of memory in neural feedback loops.   However, neither of these is supported by direct experimental evidence.

The potentials in an adult human between the surface of the cortex and a neutral region, such as an ear lobe, are as large as 10 mv.   They change more slowly than the sharp spike potentials of individual neurons. The eeg potentials represent an average of the changes in a large number of neurons.   By and large, the potentials travel over the surface of the cortex, so that, for a distance of a few millimeters, there is a time difference in the eeg pattern rather than a major difference in form.

Because the eeg patterns vary from one area of the brain to another, many studies use eight to 12 electrodes on each half, or as many as 24 on the entire cortical area. Figure 5 shows a typical electrode arrangement. The form of the eeg from the human scalp is not very different from that on the surface of the cortex; accordingly, most human studies

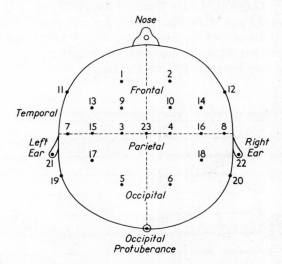

Figure 5. Electrode arrangement on scalp is indicated by dots. The differences between pairs of these electrodes are recorded to obtain graphic records such as shown in Figures 6 and 7.

use the potentials on the outside of the scalp. These are smaller by a factor of 100, that is, up to 10 mv on the cortex but 100 μv or less on the scalp. This large difference is caused by the high electrical resistance of the bone. The eeg potentials outside the meninges are the same as those on the cortex itself.

The eeg patterns are normally observed with oscilloscopes or recorded with pen galvanometers on moving paper. The exact form observed depends on the equipment used. Most eeg equipment responds to signals from 1–100 cps, although there are potentials outside of this frequency range. One of the most striking features of a graphic eeg record is that there appear to be pronounced frequencies present, as shown in Figure 6.

However, if the eeg voltages are fed into frequency analyzers of conventional types, no sharply delineated frequencies are found. Instead, there is a continuous spread of energy from zero to 100 cps per second, albeit with peaks in certain frequency regions. This continuous spectrum is in sharp contrast to the visually recognized discrete frequencies.

Electronic studies, using autocorrelators, have revealed that emphasized frequencies do occur. These frequencies are not maintained for many periods, so that they do not give sharp peaks on a frequency analyzer.

The characteristic eeg rhythms of humans are classified by size, shape, and frequency. The most outstanding normal pattern is the so-called "α-rhythm." These waves are between 8 and 13 cps. They are more sinusoidal and regular than the other types of waves. On the surface of the scalp, the α-waves are about 20 μv or less in amplitude. They are usually present in adult humans, especially in the occipital and parietal areas (see Figure 5 for the location of these areas). However,

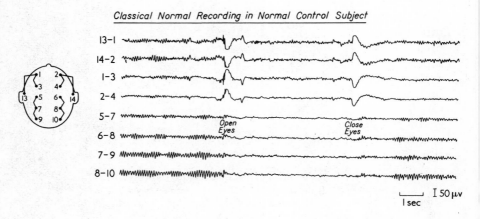

Figure 6. Normal eeg patterns illustrating abolition of the α-rhythm with eyes open. If eyes remained open for longer period of time, the α-rhythm would build up again. Original figure of R. G. Bickford, M.D., Mayo Clinic.

many normal adults completely lack α-waves both on the scalp and on the cortex.

Besides the α-rhythm, there are so-called "β-waves" in the frequency range of 14–50 cps. They are always present in normal adults. The β-waves are smaller in amplitude than the α-waves and are usually spindle shaped. In some adults, there are large voltage (50–100 μv), slow ($\frac{1}{2}$–4 cps) δ-waves, as well as slightly faster θ-waves in the frequency range 5–7 cps. Both the δ- and the θ-waves are often associated with abnormalities.

Although the eeg patterns are not the same for all normal adults, they do vary with the activity of the central nervous system. The most studied example is the α-rhythm, which occurs predominantly in the occipital region where vision is projected on the surface of the cortex. If the eye is suddenly focused on a bright image, the α-rhythm is abolished leaving only higher frequency, low voltage waves in the eeg pattern. With continued concentration, the α-rhythm returns. The α-rhythm is also altered by blinking. With the eyes closed, it is slower than with the eyes open.

Similarly, the eeg pattern is altered by anesthesia and by sleep. With anesthesia, the α-rhythm tends to build up and then later to disappear. As one falls asleep the eeg pattern changes dramatically. During the drifting-off stage, the α-rhythm tends to disappear. (In individuals lacking an α-rhythm when awake, one appears during the drifting-off stage.) As the α-rhythm disappears, 4–6 cps waves appear. In the next stage, 14–16 cps spikes with the spindle shape of β-waves appear; this is the "dream" stage. With full sleep, very slow $\frac{1}{2}$–3 cps waves predominate. A sudden stimulus produces an 8–14 cps (α-wave) burst superimposed on the slow waves.

Eeg patterns not only are dependent on the state of awareness and optical activity, but they also vary considerably during development. On the scalp of a year-old baby, there appear the first orderly eeg rhythms. These are occasional bursts of 4–8 cps, especially in the occipital area. By four years of age, 7–8 cps appear. At nine years of age, the frontal and parietal waves are slower than in adults, and 9–10 cps rhythms are more common in the occipital region. Even at 14 years of age, when people in many parts of the world are supporting themselves and reproducing, childish forms are found in the eeg. By 19, however, all the records are adult in form.

There can be no question that the eeg provides real clues as to the mental state and activity. It varies with age, with sleep, and anesthesia, and with shutting the eyelids. Eeg changes associated with certain abnormal states are well known and used clinically. They are discussed in Section 5. Likewise, eeg records are used routinely in behavioral experiments to indicate alarm reactions, conditioning, and so forth. None of these answer the fundamental question of the function and origin of the eeg potentials.

In spite of many experiments, the role of the eeg potentials is still obscure. The simplest hypothesis would seem to be that they represent some type of scanning by the brain of impulses coming in on the sensory neurons and of information within the brain. This hypothesis is simplest to one who has worked with large digital computers. The experimental data either supporting or refuting this hypothesis are very weak.

Perhaps the place to start studying the role of the eeg potentials is in discovering their origin. Here, the experimental data are conflicting.

Some people have found that a small part of the cortex, when isolated from the remainder of the brain, will continue to produce eeg rhythms. Others have claimed, on the basis of their experiments, that large areas or all of the cortex must remain intact to produce normal eeg rhythms. Still others believe, again on the basis of experiments, that the eeg patterns involve closed neuron circuits which include both the cerebral cortex and the thalamus.

The scanning hypothesis cannot explain how some normal persons can lack the α-rhythm which is so predominant in most others. Furthermore, there is no simple explanation of the variation of the spatial distribution from one head to another. Again, the speed or frequency of the α-rhythm does not relate to any known sensory, motor, or thought process of the majority of normal persons. (See, however, the discussion of epilepsy in the next section.) The theories that include the thalamus as part of the feedback loop are difficult to reconcile with the absence of changes of the eeg on the scalp of persons with thalamic tumors. The lack of any definite cellular knowledge regarding the origin of the eeg makes it extremely hard to interpret.

5. Abnormal Electroencephalographic Patterns

Clinically, abnormal eeg patterns are used to localize brain tumors and to study epilepsy. Although various investigators have reported a relationship between psychological disturbances and eeg patterns, these seem so uncertain that they will not be discussed further here. Both the tumor and epilepsy patterns have been intensively studied, and the results not only are clinically useful but they serve to emphasize our inability to directly relate brain activity and eeg patterns.

The most reliable method of detecting brain tumors is the so-called "pneumoencephalograph." In this method, the fluid spaces of the brain and spinal cord are drained, the fluid being replaced with air. X-ray photographs are then taken. The contrast in X-ray opacity between the brain and air is large (although between brain and fluid it is negligible). A tumor is discovered from a distortion of the ventricles. This method of diagnosis has a definite mortality rate, it is extremely painful, and it fails to reveal small tumors.

By contrast, the eeg can show a brain tumor two years before the pneumoencephalograph does, is not painful, and has a zero mortality rate. Its use is limited by its complexity and the volumes of records which must be analyzed, and by its failure to show tumors below the surface of the cerebral cortex. Using 24 electrodes, as shown in Figure 5, there are 276 possible pairs. If eight pairs are recorded at one time, for five minutes per set, a total of about four hours is necessary. By making judicious choices, this time can be reduced to an hour, but a great many paper recordings must be closely scrutinized.

On analyzing these records, four types of abnormalities associated with brain tumors are found. These are: a δ-rhythm; a θ-rhythm; high voltage single spikes or multiple spikes at 10–20 cps; and episodic or continuously enhanced α-rhythms. None of these abnormal rhythms are due to tumor tissue which is always silent, but the abnormalities are most pronounced in the part of the brain nearest the tumor. The eeg changes are most useful in localizing abnormal growths along the surface of the cerebral cortex, but there are no major changes in the eeg pattern

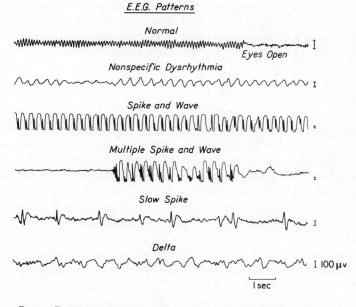

Figure 7. The various abnormal eeg patterns each have specific clinical implications. For example, the "spike and wave" is characteristic of petit mal seizures. Original figure of R. G. Bickford, M.D., Mayo Clinic.

on the scalp because of tumors along the brain stem. Bilateral differences in the eeg patterns also help locate cerebral tumors.

Another clinical use of eeg patterns is for studies of epilepsy. In general terms, an epileptic seizure is an uncontrolled hyperexcitability and spontaneous discharge of part of the central nervous system. If the discharge occurs in motor areas of the cerebral cortex, the person has a violent seizure with muscular spasms followed by unconsciousness. This is called a *grand mal* seizure. In other persons, the sensory areas of the cortex are hyperexcited, producing sensory illusions such as buzzing in the ear, spots of light, or nausea, followed by unconsciousness. Illusions followed by unconsciousness are called *petit mal* seizures. Another type of epileptic seizure is called *psychomotor*, an attack in which the person has sensory illusions followed by inappropriate automatic actions and then amnesia. All three types have characteristic eeg patterns, such as those shown in Figure 7. For a given patient, these eeg abnormalities are more constant than the exact nature of the seizure. All are characterized by large, low frequency waves.

One might be tempted to conclude that the size of the eeg indicated the degree of nervous activity. However, there are also electrically silent seizures in which the normal potentials are markedly decreased. The eeg is nonetheless useful in determining the type of epilepsy, choosing the treatment, and following the patient's progress.

6. Summary

The eeg patterns are tantalizing in that they seem to be intimately associated with the over-all action of the brain. They are useful for clinical purposes, just as a patient's temperature may be of interest to a physician with no knowledge of temperature control mechanisms on the cellular level. The fundamental question of interest to the biophysicist is: In what way are the eeg patterns related to the actions of the neurons of the brain? This question has not been answered.

It may be that extending measurements to lower frequencies, small regions of the brain, and so forth, may provide more clues. It seems more probable that what is needed are new ideas concerning the interpretation of the data and the planning of additional experiments.

REFERENCES

The form and action of the central nervous system are described in many texts. The following were used in writing this chapter.

1. Best, C. H., and N. B. Taylor, *The Physiological Basis of Medical Practice*, 7th ed., 1961 (Baltimore, Maryland: Williams & Wilkins Company).
2. Ranson, S. W., and S. L. Clark, *The Anatomy of the Nervous System: Its Development and Function*, 10th ed., 1959 (Philadelphia: W. B. Saunders Company).

3. Netter, F. H., *Nervous System* CIBA Collection of Medical Illustrations, CIBA Pharmaceutical Products, Inc. (Summit, New Jersey, 1953)

A popular book describing electroencephalography is:

4. Walter, W. G., *The Living Brain* (New York: W. W. Norton & Company, Inc., 1953).

Somewhat more technical discussions can be found in:

5. Gibbs, F. A., "Electro-encephalography," *Medical Physics*, Otto Glasser, ed. (Chicago, Illinois: Year Book Publishers, Inc., 1944) Vol. 1, pp. 361–371.
6. Kaada, B. R., "Electrical Activity of the Brain," *Ann. Rev. Physiol.* **15**: 39–62 (1953). (This includes 265 references.)

Clinical uses are discussed in the text edited by:

7. Shedlovsky, Theodore, ed., *Electrochemistry in Biology and Medicine* (New York: John Wiley & Sons, Inc., 1955).
   a. Bagchi, B. K., "Preoperative Electroencephalographic Localization of Brain Tumors," pp. 331–351.
   b. Jasper, H. H., "Electrical Signs of Epileptic Discharge," pp. 352–359.

Journal References: Biophysical experiments using brain potentials can be found in many recent journals including the *J. Acoustical Soc. Am., Am. J. Physiol., Biophysics* (USSR).

6

Neural Mechanisms of Hearing

I. Place and Telephone Theories

Hearing may be approached from various viewpoints. Some of these have been so completely studied it is unlikely that in 50 years our concepts will have changed appreciably. These aspects of hearing were presented in Chapter 1. They included the nature of sound transmission through the atmosphere, and the gross anatomy and the histology of the ear. Similarly, the role of the outer and middle portions of the ear as pressure amplifiers and mechanical transformers is quite well established. As was discussed in Chapter 1, a maximum amplification of about 35 db can be obtained.

Other aspects of hearing are far less well understood. Specifically, the conversion of acoustic energy to neural spikes in the inner ear and the analysis of these spikes in the central nervous system are current areas of research. They are discussed in the present chapter. It is assumed that the reader is familiar with the material in Chapter 1 on "Sound and the Ear," as well as in Chapters 4 and 5 on the "Conduction of Impulses by Nerves," and the "Electrical Potentials of the Brain."

The physicist regards the inner ear as a transducer, that is, as a device which converts one form of energy into another. The inner ear converts mechanical energy into electrical spikes on nerve fibers. It was only in the 1940's that a reasonable understanding of this action was developed. Before considering the modern studies, the ideas firmly believed not very many years ago will be briefly examined. Two general types of theories were developed: the resonator theory, and the telephone theory. Although neither can be supported any longer, the theories were both very successful in one sense. Each correlated many of the known facts and inspired scientists to carry out further experiments. Then, additional studies showed that neither theory was correct and led to the present concepts of cochlear action.

The resonator theory was developed by Helmholtz. He had studied musical instruments and found that they all resonated. Moreover, he

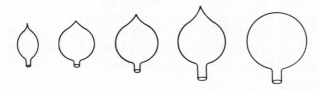

Figure 1. Helmholtz resonators. The exact shape and symmetry are not important. The resonant frequency depends on the volume of the cavity and the cross sectional area and length of the neck. Some glass Christmas tree ornaments make excellent Helmholtz resonators.

carried out frequency analyses of sound with specially built resonators. They are still known as Helmhòltz resonators. Their form is shown in Figure 1. The resonant frequency depended on the geometrical properties of the resonator. By using a series of these, Helmholtz could analyze the harmonics (that is, overtones) in a piano note and could even analyze some of the frequency components of speech. Helmholtz resonators were widely used until the advent of electronic analyzers. The latter are more convenient and much more precise but in all cases depend on an electrical resonant circuit.

Helmholtz knew only mechanical resonators and so he looked for these in the cochlea. The most promising structure seemed to be the basilar membrane. This membrane separates the central cochlear duct from the tympanic duct. The basilar membrane supports the organ of Corti with its histologically complex structure and many nerve endings. The basilar membrane has a fiber-like character, and it gets broader and thicker as it proceeds along the spiral to the apex. This resembles the general form of a piano, a collection of strings going from short, thin strings at the high end to thick, long strings at the low end.   Accordingly, the resonator theory postulated that the basilar membrane was made up of resonant fibers held under tension as piano wires.   These fibers were very sharply tuned and resulted in a mechanical analysis of incoming sounds in much the same fashion as the Helmholtz resonators.   Each fiber of the basilar membrane was supposed to activate a nerve fiber. Thus, pitch would be detected by the particular fiber most strongly activated, loudness (or sound pressure level) by the amplitude of the fiber motion, and quality by the relative amplitudes of various fibers.

The resonator theory can be disproved in a number of ways.   One objection, not too serious, is that a sharply tuned resonator is hard to excite; also it continues to vibrate long after the excitation has ceased. It is impossible to design mechanical resonators whose sharpness would permit the pitch discrimination possessed by many people and which would also permit the time resolution necessary to understand speech. If pitch discrimination is partly a function of the nervous system, then the resonators need not be so sharp.   However, this inclusion of the central nervous system destroys the beautiful simplicity of the resonator theory.

The most direct tests of the resonator theory were carried out by Békèsy.   He measured the width of the basilar membrane of human ears and found it changed only by a factor of a hundredfold, whereas the thickness varied by a factor much less than 100.   If this membrane were made up of resonant fibers similar to piano wires, the frequency of resonance f_r should be given by the expression

$$f_r = \frac{1}{2L}\sqrt{\frac{T}{\rho_1}}$$

where T is the tension, ρ_1 is the mass per unit length, and L is the length.   Because audible frequencies vary from 30 to 20,000 cps, that is, by a factor of almost 10^3, $T/\rho_1 L^2$ would have to vary by 5×10^5. Békèsy's measurements of tensions showed that 5×10^5 was at least a factor of 20 too great.   His measurements depended on modern technology and could not have been made at a much earlier date.

With this knowledge that the resonator theory is clearly wrong, it is possible to find other pieces of information also tending to contradict the resonator idea.   For instance, no one has ever actually found fibers in the basilar membrane which were independent of and ran directly across the membrane.

An alternative hypothesis of hearing was the telephone theory. Rayleigh and many other scientists of his day were very impressed with the telephone, which acted as a transducer changing sound energy into electrical energy and then back to sound energy at another point.   They also knew that the cochlea acted as a transducer changing sound energy to electrical energy, but, without electronic gadgets, they knew nothing of the form of this electrical energy. They reasoned that the cochlea acted as a microphone, transmitting along the nerve fibers a signal whose form was that of the incoming pressure wave. In one of its variations, the theory suggested that only the nerve fibers nearest the windows to the middle ear were stimulated by weak sounds but that the entire cochlea was activated by loud sounds.

If the proponents of this theory had had more electronic instruments available, they might have found additional evidence which could have been misinterpreted to support the telephone theory. In one experiment an electrode is placed at or near the cochlea. Definite electrical potentials are discovered which do reproduce the form of the applied pressure wave. These potentials are called cochlear potentials or cochlear microphonics; they are small in magnitude, perhaps no bigger than 100 μv, but they definitely exist in the cochlea and not in the measuring equipment. These cochlear microphonics were discovered in the 1930's by Wever and Bray. Another experiment follows the auditory pathways into the brain stem. If an electrode is placed in these areas, a signal is picked up which is an integrated response of many nerve fibers. This electrical potential reproduces the form of the applied sound pressure, provided the frequency is below 3–4 kc. (Above 4 kc a submultiple of the applied frequency is usually present.)

Several lines of evidence show that the telephone theory cannot be valid over most of the audible range. The most unequivocal of these is that an individual nerve fiber cannot conduct more than 1,000 spikes per second. This limitation occurs because there is a period of 1 millisecond or more following a spike during which time another cannot be generated. The occurrence of 1,000 spikes per second would not allow the nerve fiber to reproduce a sound wave of 1,000 cps. As shown in Figure 2, many spikes are necessary per cycle. Thus, the telephone theory cannot be valid above about 60 cps. Moreover, whereas the integrated spikes in the fiber tracts in the brain stem do reproduce the form of the pressure wave, the potentials on the surface of the cerebral cortex fail to follow above 200 cps.

In addition to the impossibility of individual axons acting as telephone lines, the telephone theory is refuted by a large body of experimental evidence favoring a place theory of hearing. In other words, different frequencies *are* represented at different places along the basilar membrane of the cochlea, albeit not analyzed by a resonator mechanism. For instance, lesions can often be observed in the inner ears of deafened persons. (In order to observe this, the person's hearing had to be tested in the hospital immediately before death. Then the ear had to be removed within an hour after death.) In cases in which specific frequencies were missing in the person's hearing, lesions occurred at corresponding regions along the basilar membrane (as predicted by the resonator theory!). The cochlear microphonics show maxima along the basilar membrane (again at the place indicated by the resonator theory!). Finally, if the basilar membrane of an experimental animal is destroyed

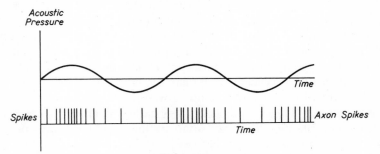

Figure 2. This illustrates that to reproduce a sine wave many spikes per cycle are necessary. Even the 15 per cycle illustrated integrates at best to a crude sine wave.

in a narrow region, it is found by both behavioral and electrical studies that the animal cannot hear in the corresponding frequency region.

Thus, neither the resonator theory nor the telephone theory can be maintained in the light of present knowledge of the ear and the nervous system. Although the resonator theory is anatomically unsound, a spatial localization of frequencies along the basilar membrane does occur. Likewise, although the telephone theory per se cannot be maintained, its prediction of the form of the integrated nerve potentials in the brain stem is reasonably accurate.

2. Cochlear Mechanism of Neural Excitation

Present theories incorporate all of the positive evidence presented in the last section. Needless to say, these theories are somewhat more complex. At least 12 different variations exist around the basic hydrodynamic theory proposed originally by Békèsy. He showed that, in addition to the compressional waves traditionally treated in acoustics, there could also exist certain slow hydrodynamic waves in a structure such as the cochlea. These waves bear certain similarities to surface waves on a large body of water or interfacial tension waves at an oil-water interface. (Note, "bear certain similarities" does not mean "identical to!") These hydrodynamic waves are in a dispersive medium, that is, one in which the wave velocity is a function of the frequency. In such a medium, one may have a piling up of the waves to maxima in certain regions. This phenomenon can be observed in the build up and decrease of surface waves on the ocean. It is also a familiar idea used repeatedly in quantum theory.

The various mathematical analyses of the cochlea, using this type of model, are beyond the scope of this text but should be studied by readers with sufficient mathematical preparation. Békèsy demonstrated

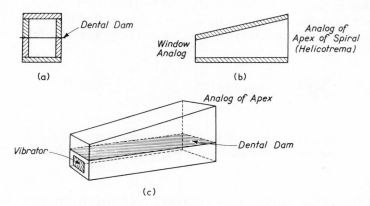

Figure 3. Békèsy's hydrodynamic analog of cochlea. (a) Transverse cross section. This shows two channels separated by dental dam. (b) Longitudinal cross section. This shows increase in width from "window" to "apex." (c) Perspective view. The two end windows as well as the partition are of dental dam.

that these hydrodynamic waves existed not only in the cochlea but also in simple models which are satisfying substitutes for a mathematical analysis. For the simplest model, he used two rigid walls (microscope slides) resting on a solid surface and covered with dental dam (rubber sheet). A slightly more refined system is shown in Figure 3, where two channels and two windows are included. At low frequencies, the actual motion of the dental dam can be observed. There is a maximum region for each frequency; this maximum is more or less independent of the shape of the channels and varies only slightly for major changes of the thickness or tension of the elastic membrane or of the dimensions of the channel. It is important that one window be driven and the other free. The model emphasizes the biological utility of the hydrodynamic waves whose maxima do not depend on exact physical dimensions. There is a maximum shearing force across the membrane at the maximum in amplitude.   The general shape of these maxima is shown in Figure 4.

Experiments with intact and excised ears in humans and laboratory rodents, at low frequency and high intensity, showed similar maxima. For a given sound pressure level, the lower the frequency, the greater is the displacement.   These measurements, when extrapolated to the limit of audibility at 1,000 cps, show that the *maximum* displacements of the basilar membrane may be smaller than a nuclear radius, 10^{-12} cm.

Both the theoretical analyses and the model experiments agree that all that is essential for the maxima of hydrodynamic waves, separated according to frequency, are rigid walls, two parallel tubes separated by an elastic membrane, and two windows, one driven and the other "open"

High Frequency Maximum   Low Frequency Maximum

Figure 4. Maxima of the displacement of the rubber dam for the model in Figure 3. Lower frequencies have maxima nearer the windows.

to the air of the middle ear.   The maxima of these hydrodynamic waves give only a crude place localization of different tones.   The maxima are narrow enough to account for the experiments with lesions and cochlear potentials but are far too broad to explain pitch discrimination by themselves.   One must invoke a neural mechanism for the extremely sharp pitch discrimination which the human ear can perform.   This pattern is discussed further in Section 3.

The over-all action of the cochlea is, then, to convert (transduce) a hydrodynamic wave into electrical spikes on nerve axons.   In an attempt to find the details of how this occurred, Békèsy and his co-workers studied the electrical properties of the cochlea.   Although the over-all goal of describing the cochlear mechanism of neural excitation is still incomplete, many interesting facts have been uncovered.   They have shown that in the intact animal the tympanic and vestibular ducts act as an electrical shield around the cochlear duct.   The fluid in the tympanic and vestibular ducts is a good conductor.   It is, however, electrically insulated from the cochlear duct by the basilar membrane and Reisner's membrane.   Thus, the basilar membrane plays an important role both as the elastic membrane for mechanical vibrations and also as an electrical insulator.   In a phonograph cable, it is necessary to surround the inner conductor with an insulator, which in turn is covered by a second conductor.   The outer conductor is called a shield and is maintained at ground potential. It greatly reduces the pick-up of unwanted signals by the central conductor. In a similar manner, the fluid in the vestibular and tympanic ducts is at body potential and shields the central conductor.

With sufficiently sensitive equipment, it can be shown that many shielded cables have a d-c potential between the inner conductor and the shield. A similar d-c potential exists across the basilar membrane. It can also be shown that any shielded cable acts as a microphone converting alternating pressures into electrical signals. Many people believe the cochlear potentials are of a similar nature, that is, unwanted electrical signals resulting from mechanical vibrations. These are called *microphonics* when they occur in an electronic circuit. By analogy, the cochlear potentials are referred to as microphonics.

Whether the cochlear potential plays any role other than that of a microphonic is not known. The cochlear potential is absent in some deaf cats which lack hair cells; it may be associated with the hair cells in some fashion. Most investigators feel that the hair cells are intimately associated with initiating the nerve potential. Similar hair cells are found at the nerve endings in the inner ear associated with balance and acceleration. The exact manner in which the electrical impulses in the nerve fibers are initiated is not known. (Nor, for that matter, is it known for most sensory nerve endings.)

The description to this point includes most of the outstanding features of the known actions of the cochlear portion of the inner ear. It appears necessary to assign to the nervous system both the acuity of tonal discrimination and also the reconstitution of the individual nerve impulses, to have the integrated form of the original pressure wave.

3. Arm Analogs and Neural Sharpening

The exact mechanism by which the nervous system carries out an extremely sharp frequency analysis is not known. However, it is a familiar fact that the nervous system does sharpen many types of stimuli. Thus, when a bright spot is focused on the retina, the sensitivity of the eye to surrounding areas is decreased. In bright light, this has the advantage of eliminating the effect of stray light. Similarly, if two compass points are pressed against the skin of the forearm at distances greater than about 2.5 cm apart, two sensations are received. At around 2.5 cm the two sensations weaken each other, whereas, at still closer distances, the two sensations add to each other. In the latter case, the person feels the stimulus midway between the two actual compass points. This is illustrated in Figure 5.

Another interesting case is the location of two click-like stimuli on opposite sides of the finger. For long time delays between the two, separate clicks are felt. If the time delay is decreased, the second click

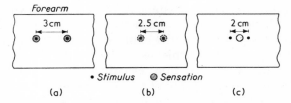

Figure 5. Neural sharpening and funnelling when two compass points are pressed on the arm. For large separation, separate sensations result. Medium separation sensations tend to suppress each other. Small separation sensations add and are located in a "sharpened" area.

is no longer felt. As the time interval approaches zero, a single sensation is felt which approaches midway between the two stimuli and has a larger apparent area. The results of an experiment of this nature are shown in Figure 6. This same type of phenomenon occurs when one locates a sound by the difference in the times of its arrival at the two ears. This addition of more than one stimulus into a single, stronger sensation is called "funnelling" by Békèsy and his co-workers.

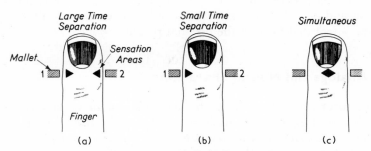

Figure 6. Neural funnelling when the forefinger is struck with two small mallets (clicks). (a) With large time separation, both "clicks" are sensed. (b) With small time separation, only the first is sensed. (c) Simultaneous clicks add to common larger sensation half way between the two stimuli.

These sharpening and locating effects which occur in the senses of touch and sight as well as hearing are very interesting. They emphasize that the nervous system does act as a complex computer with a great deal of feedback. They also emphasize that many of the types of neural action essential for hearing also occur in other senses. It has indeed been possible for Békèsy to make an enlarged cochlear model, using the forearm for a sensing organ. Most of the phenomena of hearing are reproduced by this model.

The model consists of a series of resonant vibrators of varying frequency running along the arm. When these are electrically driven, several neighboring ones respond, the central one most strongly. The person senses the resonant frequency at a much more sharply located spot than is indicated by the behavior of the vibrators. Phenomena of masking, beats, harmonic distortion, and sharp frequency and intensity discrimination are all shown by this "analog" of the ear. Thus, there can be no doubt that the nervous system, in some fashion, does sharpen neural impulses. Likewise, funnelling can be demonstrated for the arm analog. Just how the nervous system goes about sharpening and funnelling is not known.

The arm models of the ear demonstrate that nonlinear and harmonic distortion occurs in the nervous system, as well as in the tympanic membrane and middle ear. It is quite probable that a similar distortion also occurs within the inner ear. This is indicated by the cochlear potentials. However, because the cochlear and neural potentials are so difficult to separate, it is not certain whether distortion actually occurs within the cochlea.

The arm models strongly support the idea that pitch discrimination is, to a large degree, a function of the central nervous system. The details of this action are not known yet. Nonetheless, many experiments with vertebrates, and even invertebrates, have shown that the central nervous system can carry out complex actions such as "sensation sharpening," "amplitude analysis," and "funnelling." Anatomical and electrical studies of the central nervous system emphasize the possibilities of such computerlike actions.

4. Cortical Representation

The spike potentials generated in the basilar membrane of the cochlea travel along the fibers of the acoustic nerve. As has been stated, most sensory nerve cell bodies are located in compact groups called *ganglia*. The acoustic nerve, however, has a diffuse set of cell bodies spread out along its path through the spiral bony partition which supports the cochlea. These nerve cell bodies are called the *spiral ganglion*. The pulses in the second set of axons in the acoustic nerve enter the brain. The acoustic nerve is the eighth one (counting from the front end) to enter the brain; it is often called the *eighth cranial nerve*. As shown in Figure 7, several additional synapses occur within the brain stem. Some of the pulses cross over to the opposite half of the brain stem so

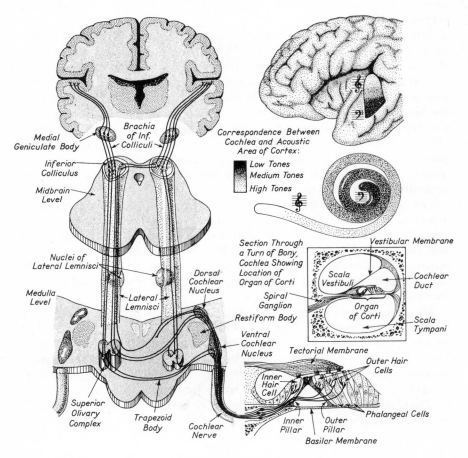

Figure 7. Auditory pathways of the central nervous system. Copyright *The CIBA Collection of Medical Illustrations,* by Frank H. Netter, M.D., Vol. I, "The Nervous System," 1953.

that those starting at either ear are represented in both halves of the brain. Finally, at least in unconscious animals, the pulses are conducted to specific areas on the surface of the temporal lobes of the cerebral hemisphere. This latter projection is believed to be necessary for conscious hearing.

In humans and other primates, this auditory area on the temporal lobe of the cerebral cortex is buried deep in one of the folds of the cortex and is hard to study.   In other mammals, the cerebral projection is on or nearer the exposed portions of the cortex.   In these latter animals, there are always two and, in some animals, three areas where responses appear (in the unconscious animal) when the ear is stimulated. Each of these areas is connected to both ears.   Within each cerebral projection area, specific smaller areas correspond to specific spots along the basilar membrane.

A detailed examination of the acoustic pathway shows that several neurons are involved.   The first is located in the spiral ganglion within the inner ear.   The nerve fibers leaving this ganglion join those from the vestibular portion of the ear to form the eighth cranial nerve.   Within the brain, the vestibular and auditory fibers separate.   Those from the cochlea go to one of two nuclei in the lower brain stem known as the *dorsal* and *ventral cochlear nuclei*.   Some fibers leaving these have synapses with other neurons associated with reflex actions and balance.   Others go to synapses in another nucleus in the lower brain stem called the *superior olivary complex*.   Some fibers synapse in the superior olivary complex on the same side, others on the opposite side of the brain, and still others pass through without interruption, joining fibers from the superior olivary complexes and passing up the brain stem.   In the nuclei of the *lateral lemniscus* farther along the brain stem, some of the auditory fibers end, and others pass through uninterrupted.

In the midbrain level, some of the auditory fibers end at synapses in the *inferior colliculus*.   From here, some fibers cross over to synapses in the opposite inferior colliculus.   All of the fibers of the auditory tract have synapses in another nucleus of the midbrain, the *medial geniculate body*.   Fibers of these neurons finally reach the auditory areas of the cerebral cortex.

The groups of nerve fibers in the brain stem "fire" in such a fashion as to reconstitute the original sound wave, or at least almost do so. Where this synchronization starts is not known.   Wever has proposed that it occurs in the cochlea, that in some fashion the nerve fibers fire in volleys to reproduce the over-all form of the incident pressure wave. The manner in which this could occur is shown in Figure 8, for 15 nerve fibers.   Observe that none fires too often, but that there is a certain over-all synchrony.   This effect need not occur in the cochlea.   It could just as well originate at the first or even second synapse.   This semisynchronous action is called the volley theory.   It states, in its simplest form, that below some frequency, say 100 cps, the number of nerve fibers excited varies with the instantaneous pressure.   From 300 to 3,000 cps, the volley-type effect reproduces the form of the incident sound wave, whereas above 3,000 cps it cannot follow, but reproduces submultiples of the stimulus frequency. Somehow the brain is thought to carry out a frequency analysis on the over-all electrical signal. In other words, the ear carries out a crude frequency analysis in terms of exciting preferentially certain nerve fibers. The central nervous system then carries out a finer frequency analysis.

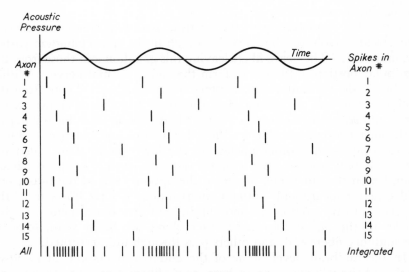

Figure 8. Illustration of the volley principle which allows axons to fire once per cycle and still reproduce the shape of the sound wave.

Although it is clear that the detailed frequency analysis occurs by sharpening within the central nervous system, it is by no means understood exactly how or where this takes place. Part of the difficulty is in distinguishing neural impulses from cochlear potentials. For example, if a click is presented to the ear, two types of electrical potentials result. The first, essentially simultaneous with the click, is the cochlear potential. It remains even if the acoustic nerve is destroyed. The second is the true nerve potential; it occurs after a slight time delay and is abolished if the acoustic nerve is not functioning. For acoustic signals other than clicks, it is difficult to distinguish between these two types of potentials. Accordingly, most studies of the neural responses have been carried out past the first synapse in the diffuse spiral ganglion and usually have been restricted to the central nervous system. This has made it impossible to determine at what level detailed frequency analysis occurs.

5. Summary of Hearing

Biophysical approaches to the sensation of hearing have been discussed in Chapters 1 and 3 as well as in this one. The material in Chapter 1 dealt with the physical parameters of sound important for hearing and with the anatomical characteristics of the ear, both on a gross level and also as revealed by histology. All of these are very important parts of man's knowledge of hearing. These topics in Chapter 1 are all well known and have been firmly established for many years. Although detailed studies may slightly modify them, the contents of Chapter 1 probably will not be dramatically altered. Certain peripheral studies, such as those of the mechanical behavior of the eardrum and ossicles at higher sound pressure levels, will undoubtedly supplement the present picture of the physical properties of the anatomical structure of the ear.

The ideas presented in Chapter 3 on the uses of pulses of sound for echo-location by bats, porpoises, and birds are of more recent origin. The first significant studies in this direction date back only to 1940. Nonetheless, the ideas presented there are all so well supported by experimental evidence that it appears unlikely that they will be significantly altered in the near future. It does seem more probable that echo-location will be recognized as an important factor in other species.

The material in this chapter deals with the most important biophysical aspects of hearing, namely the conversion of sound waves to neural impulses and their analysis within the central nervous system. Although these topics are central to the biophysics of hearing, large gaps still remain in our understanding. Basically, the uncertainties are similar to those discussed in Chapter 5. It is in this general area that significant, major advances may be anticipated.

REFERENCES

1. Wever, E. G., and Merle Lawrence, *Physiological Acoustics* (Princeton, New Jersey: Princeton University Press, 1954).
2. von Békèsy, Georg, and W. A. Rosenblith, "The Mechanical Properties of the Ear," in *Handbook of Experimental Psychology*, S. S. Stevens, ed., (New York: John Wiley & Sons, Inc., 1951) pp. 1075–1115.
3. Articles in *J. Acous. Soc. Am.* by Georg von Békèsy pertinent to this chapter include:
   a. 1949, **21**, pp. 233–245. "The Vibration of the Cochlear Partition in Anatomical Preparations and in Models of the Inner Ear."
   b. 1949, **21**, pp. 245–254. "On the Resonance Curve and Decay Period at Various Points on the Cochlear Partition."
   c. 1953, **25**, 770–785. "Description of Some Mechanical Properties of the Organ of Corti."

d. 1953, **25**, pp. 786–790. "Shearing Microphonics Produced by Vibrations Near the Inner and Outer Hair Cells."

e. 1957, **29**, pp. 489–501. "Sensations on the Skin Similar to Directional Hearing, Beats, and Harmonics in the Ear."

f. 1958, **30**, pp. 399–412. "Funnelling in the Nervous System and Its Role in Loudness and Sensation Intensity on the Skin."

g. 1959, **31**, pp. 338–349. "Synchronism of Neural Discharges and Their Demultiplication in Pitch Perception on the Skin and in Hearing."

4. Other articles in *J. Acous. Soc. Am.*:

a. 1951, **23**, pp. 637–645. Fletcher, Harvey, "On the Dynamics of the Cochlea."

b. 1959, **31**, pp. 356–364. Goldstein, M. H., Jr., N. Y-S. Kiang, and R. M. Brown, "Responses of the Auditory Cortex to Repetitive Acoustic Stimuli."

7

Neural Aspects of Vision

I. Color Discrimination

The anatomical and physical features of the eye were described in Chapter 2. That chapter was terminated without a discussion of color discrimination because the latter depends on the action of nerve cells and the central nervous system. In this chapter, the neural mechanisms necessary for vision will be examined in more detail. To review briefly, the retina acts as a "photoneural" transducer converting incoming electromagnetic energy to spike potentials on nerve fibers. The potentials travel along the optic nerve, enter the central nervous system, and eventually reach specific areas of the cerebral cortex. The information is "analyzed" at a series of synapses, both within the retina and within the central nervous system proper. Out of this analysis there are, in some way, created the sensations of color, acuity, brightness, shape, and so forth. (It is assumed that the reader will be familiar with the ideas of Chapters 2, 4, and 5 before studying this one.)

One step in the over-all process of vision, the photomolecular reactions in the rod and cone cells of the retina, is of extreme importance to an understanding of vision. At the same time, it is not necessary to understand these reactions before discussing the neural aspects of vision.

Accordingly, the molecular reactions are deferred to Chapter 19.

A fundamental test of any theory of the neural aspects of vision is the explanation of color discrimination. The subjective sensations of color are familiar to most humans. However, at the lowest intensities where objects are barely visible to the dark-adapted eye, there is no sensation of color. At light intensities which are just slightly greater than this, colors begin to be sensed.

The sensation of color is a complex function of the wavelengths of light reaching the eye. Just how complex this function is has been emphasized by a set of experiments referred to at the end of Section 4. However, when a large patch of light of the same wavelength is presented to the eye, it is identified as a single color.

A light consisting of a very narrow wavelength band is called *monochromatic*. The other extreme, equal intensities at all wavelengths, is called *white*. The sensation of white can be evoked by many compositions simpler than uniform intensity throughout the visible spectrum. Certain pairs of colored lights, such as blue and yellow, appear white when mixed in equal proportions. The pairs of colors producing white are called *complementary*. Sets of three colors, such as red, green, and blue, as well as sets of four or more colors, also give a sensation of white. Likewise, varied groups of colored lights can produce any given color sensation.

Psychophysicists distinguish several different qualities of sensations associated with color vision. These include *luminosity* (or luminous intensity), *hue*, and *saturation*. Luminosity[1] is defined as a "measure of the flux of luminous energy per unit solid angle emitted by a source." The luminous energy is in turn "an evaluation of radiant energy in terms of its ability to produce brightness."

A colored light, as well as a given luminosity or brightness, will always have a certain hue[2] which is defined as "the quality of a sensation according to which an observer is aware of differences of wavelength of radiant energy." A given colored light may not be a pure hue but may be mixed with white light. This is measured by the saturation[3] which is the "quality of sensation by which an observer is aware of different purities of any one dominant wavelength." For example, pink represents a mixture of red and white; it is said to be less saturated than a pure red color. Hue and saturation taken together constitute *chromaticity*.

It has been known for many years that sets of three stimuli existed,

---

[1] Quoted from: Committee on Colorimetry, The Optical Society of America, *The Science of Color.* (New York: Thomas Y. Crowell Company, 1953.)

[2] *Ibid.*

[3] *Ibid.*

so that by choosing the proper amounts of these, one could match the chromaticity of a given light in terms of the sensation it evoked in the average observer.   If the amounts of each of the three standards are indicated by x, y, and z respectively, then one may represent symbolically a light A, by

$$A = x_A + y_A + z_A$$

and a light B, by

$$B = x_B + y_B + z_B$$

If one now adds equal amounts of A and B to form a new light C, which may be represented as

$$C = x_C + y_C + z_C$$

then it is found that

$$x_A + x_B = x_C \qquad y_A + y_B = y_C \quad \text{and} \quad z_A + z_B = z_C$$

In general, any algebraic combination of colored lights is matched by the corresponding algebraic combination of the amounts of the standards matching these lights.

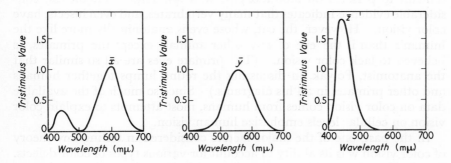

Figure I. Standard C.I.E. tristimulus values of unit energy for indicated wavelengths.   After Committee on Colorimetry, The Optical Society of America, *The Science of Color* (New York: Thomas Y. Crowell Company, 1953) pp. 242–243.

In order to standardize the description of chromaticity, the International Congress on Illumination agreed on three artificial standards. These were chosen so that a monochromatic light at any wavelength in the visible spectrum is matched by an average observer by the amounts $\bar{x}_\lambda$, $\bar{y}_\lambda$, $\bar{z}_\lambda$ shown in Figure 1.   The curve $\bar{y}_\lambda$ has the same shape as the average photopic luminosity curve; it gives the luminosity of a given light.   The curves were normalized so that a white light (of equal spectral density at all wavelengths) is matched by equal amounts of the three standards.   Symbolically, this last may be stated as[4]

$$\int_{380\ m\mu}^{780\ m\mu} \bar{x}_\lambda\, d\lambda = \int_{380\ m\mu}^{780\ m\mu} \bar{y}_\lambda\, d\lambda = \int_{380\ m\mu}^{780\ m\mu} \bar{z}_\lambda\, d\lambda$$

Any colored light can be analyzed spectrophotometrically to give its spectral density E_λ.   This is defined so that the total energy E is given by

$$E = \int_0^\infty E_\lambda\, d\lambda \qquad \left(\text{or in other words}\quad E_\lambda = \frac{dE}{d\lambda} \right)$$

Many spectral densities E_λ will give the same sensation.   To specify the sensation, three numbers, X, Y, Z, are needed; in terms of the artificial standards above

$$X = \int \bar{x}_\lambda E_\lambda\, d\lambda \qquad Y = \int \bar{y}_\lambda E_\lambda\, d\lambda \quad \text{and} \quad Z = \int \bar{z}_\lambda E_\lambda\, d\lambda$$

where all three integrals are evaluated from 380 mμ to 780 mμ.

These color-matching experiments are based on human response. Because they require subjective information, similar experiments are difficult to perform on laboratory or wild animals.   Nonetheless, considerable evidence indicates that many vertebrates, and even insects, have color vision.   However, the cat, whose eye is anatomically more like the human's than is the eye of any other animals except the primates, is believed to lack color vision.   (The primate eyes are all so similar that the anatomist, Polyak, in discussing the retina lumps together humans and other primates in all his diagrams.)   Since so much of the available data on color vision comes from humans, most attempts to explain color vision on cellular levels emphasize human vision.

In the past, one of the major factors considered in testing any theory of color vision was its ability to account for various types of color defects. People whose color vision is normal are called *trichromats* since they need three colored lights to match the hues.   Those needing only two colored lights are called *dichromats* and those with no color distinctions, *monochromats*.

Four different types of dichromasy are known.   Persons with two of these distinguish only blue and yellow.   In this category, the group *protanopes* identifies red and blue-green colors as gray and has low luminosity sensitivity in the red.   In contrast, the *deuteranopes* have a normal luminosity sensitivity in the red but identify greens and purple reds as gray.   The other two types of dichromats distinguish red and

---

[4] These integrals are usually written as extending over the wavelength range from zero to infinity.   However, $\bar{x}_\lambda$, $\bar{y}_\lambda$, and $\bar{z}_\lambda$ are zero at all wavelengths outside of the range 380 mμ to 780mμ.

green but not blue. In this category, the *tritanopes* see purplish blue and greenish yellow as gray, whereas the *tetartanopes* see all blue and yellow as gray.

Several types of monochromasy exist. In one type, called *cone blindness*, only rods are present in the retina. This type of monochromats show a loss of acuity; they retain the scotopic luminosity curve only. This strongly supports the connection between the rods and the scotopic vision.

To further complicate matters, there are various inbetween deficiencies, such as protanomalous trichromasy, in which the red and blue-green sensitivities are markedly less than normal, but all three colors are necessary for matching hues. Almost any combination the reader can imagine is known to occur in humans.

Two general types of theories of color vision have been maintained in the past. One of these, the *tricolor theory*, was supported historically by Young, Helmholtz, and Maxwell. The other type of theory, the *opponents* or *antagonist theory*, has appealed to many psychologists; its many variations are each associated with a person's name such as Hering, Ladd-Franklin, or Adams. The scheme presented in this text is essentially that developed by the biophysicist, Talbot, who emphasized that both theories have some elements of truth. His detailed picture makes more use of the specific structures of the retina than do most of the other theories.

Briefly, the tricolor theories assumed that there were in the retina three pigments, B, G, and R, having maximum absorptions in the blue, green, and red regions respectively. These pigments were postulated to exist in separate receptors which sent impulses to the brain producing responses B', G', and R'. According to this theory, the brain "computed" yellow and white from G' and R' at high luminosities and white from B' at low luminosities. The original forms of the tricolor theory had difficulties with several types of color blindness and with white-black vision. Even the best refinements failed to use the detailed neuron structure of the retina. This last oversimplification seems most misleading. (See Figure 10, Chapter 2, page 42.)

In contrast to the tricolor theories, which attempted to assign a minimum of types of retinal actions, the antagonist (or opponents) theories regarded the retina as the basis of considerably more complex actions. The opponents theories postulated that there were six retinal responses which occurred in antagonistic pairs. Excitation leading to any single response was supposed to suppress the action of the other member of the pair. These six retinal responses were identified as blue-yellow, red-green, and black-white. Various forms of the opponents theories had less trouble explaining black-white vision and several forms of color blindness than did the tricolor theories. Most of the opponents theories attempted to assign retinal distinctions to three different photosensitive pigments or did not specify in any detail how the retina actually produced these responses. The theory discussed in the next section presents a model which includes both a tricolor mechanism in the rods and cones and also an antagonist mechanism, which it assigns to the neurons of the retina. As in all antagonist theories, it assumes that the brain carries out or duplicates the antagonistic action when it receives different impulses from the two eyes or contradictory signals from one eye.

2. Cellular Mechanisms

The tricolor and antagonist theories were originally based almost exclusively on psychophysical evidence. There is considerable other information available in terms of which any theory of vision must ultimately stand or fall. The evidence from histology, electrophysiology, biochemistry, and communication must all be included before a theory of vision can be considered complete. The scheme described in the following pages was developed by Talbot in an attempt to synthesize these diverse lines of evidence into a model which would be convenient both to use and to form a basis for designing additional experiments. It is used in this text as a convenient scheme in terms of which many different types of phenomena may be described.

Talbot started with the idea that any proposed scheme of color vision must contain at least three different color receptors, although only two types, the rods and the cones, are known. Talbot assumed that the receptors included two types of cones indicated by δ and ι in Figure 2, as well as rods indicated by ρ. These are connected to cell bodies labeled a for rods and b for the cones. (The letters on these and the other cell bodies discussed are those assigned by Polyak in his book, *The Retina*.)

The three types of receptors, δ, ι, and ρ, are assumed to have different absorption spectra. The receptor ρ is postulated to contain the pigment rhodopsin (visual purple) whose spectral absorption peak is in the blue-green at 497 mμ; this type of receptor is used for blue vision in this theory. The cone ι is assumed to have iodopsin whose spectrum has an absorption peak near the green at 562 mμ. (Actually, Talbot desires ι to represent red, so he has had to add a contribution from ρ and δ labeled dz in the figure.) The third receptor δ is a green-absorbing cone of exact nature unspecified. Talbot suggests this might be a modified form of rhodopsin, "daylight rhodopsin." The necessity of this δ cone for which there is neither histological nor biochemical evidence is the greatest weakness of this model. Nonetheless, a minimum of three photosensitive pigments is needed for any type of theory of color vision.

Axons from the cell bodies *a* and *b* synapse with processes from neuron cell bodies in the next layer of the retina. The latter neurons are called *bipolar* cells. Several different types can be distinguished called *d, e, f, h, i, k,* and *l*. The *d* cells are large; they are connected to several rods

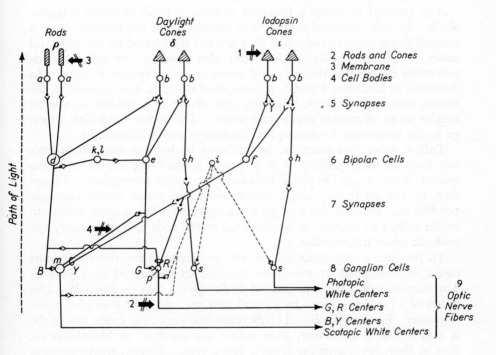

Figure 2. Simplified form of Talbot's scheme for assigning function to the known histological elements of the retina. Letters refer to known cell types. Numbers on right refer to retinal layers described in Chapter 2. Arrows with numbers show locations of deficiencies hypothesized to explain four types of color blindness. After S. A. Talbot, "Retinal Color Mechanism," *J. Optical Soc. Am.* **41**: 936 (1951).

and at least one cone. The *e* and *f* cells are smaller, each connected to several cones. The *h* cells are midget bipolars which synapse with only one neuron on the side toward the brain. The *i* cells are called *centrifugal amacrine bipolars* for they synapse only with the ganglion cells of the eighth retinal layer. The k and l types are *lateral amacrine* cells synapsing with the other bipolars of the same layer.

The cell bodies of the innermost layer of neurons in the retina are called *ganglion cells*. Three identified types are used in Talbot's model. The largest are the m cells which synapse with fibers from d, e, and f bipolars. The middle-sized p cells also synapse, albeit in a different fashion, with fibers from d, e, and f. Finally, the smallest cell bodies, labeled s, synapse only with one h bipolar.

Any attempt to assign a function to each of these elements is guesswork. In this proposed model, it is assumed that the neurons have a natural firing period even when they are not stimulated by the rods and cones. The cell bodies of the latter also produce the spike action-potentials even when the rods and cones are not exposed to light. As discussed in Chapters 4 and 5, a network of neurons, such as exist in the retina, can add, subtract, multiply, and divide in a fashion somewhat similar to an electronic digital computer. The action potentials which go to the brain may be a complex function of the incident light.

Talbot states that since the h-s pathway is the only one which does not become more diffuse as it proceeds toward the central nervous system, it can carry the detail necessary for acuity perception. Therefore, he assigns it the role of black and white vision under photopic conditions. Because the d-m pathway represents the largest, easiest to excite cells, and because it is connected to the rods ρ, it must carry the scotopic white information.

To produce antagonistic effects, the responses of the three receptors could be combined at successive neurons as illustrated in Figure 2. The responses of ρ and δ are added at d to give a blue response B. The spikes of ι (as reproduced by f) and of d are added at p to give a red response. Because the B and G fibers synapse very close to the side of the m and p cells respectively, their spikes are assumed to be inhibitory, that is, they slow down the natural firing rate. Yellow, made up from G and R, would then accelerate m, whereas R would accelerate p. Thus, Talbot has an antagonist theory whereby white and black are antagonistic at the ganglion cell s, blue and yellow at the ganglion cell m, and green and red at the ganglion cell p.

In order to decrease a firing rate, m and p must have a normal firing rate regulated by feedback loops set up through the k and l bipolars. Similarly, in order to suppress the effects of glare and scattering within the eye and to decrease firing during prolonged stimulation, fibers such as those of the i type cell must be present. Neural sharpening can also be produced by i, k, and l cells.

Anatomically, Talbot's model is quite successful in assigning a role to almost all of the histologically distinct neuron types in the retina.

He does not assign a role to the n, o, and r ganglion cells of Polyak and has to assume two types of cones, although there is no direct evidence for the latter. The model is successful in using three basic photosensitive pigments which are acted on in a positive manner as demanded by the tricolor stimulus theories of Young and Helmholtz. It also has all the advantages of the opponents theories in having B-Y, R-G, W-S antagonists in the response of the retinal nerves. One must assume, as do other opponents theories, similar antagonistic actions in the central nervous system in analyzing conflicting information.

In addition to the histological and psychophysical evidence strongly supporting this model, several other types of detailed subjective information can be correlated using the theory of color vision outlined above. In particular, the evidence for the role of the rods in blue color vision, experiments with test patches of color on light-adapted eyes, kinetic experiments, and abnormal vision will be discussed.

The role of the rods in scotopic vision is agreed upon quite generally. The absorption curve of the pigment rhodopsin in the rods is similar to the scotopic luminosity curve, and many indirect lines of evidence support the role of the rods in scotopic vision. The connection between the rods and blue vision is supported by subjective observation. For example, green and blue appear brighter peripherally where there are more rods, whereas yellow and red are brighter at the fovea. Similar support comes from studies of the narrow range of intensities between the scotopic threshold and the threshold at which color is identified. Subjects usually experience a sensation of gray in this achromatic range. The size of achromatic range is greater for red than for blue. Because the rods alone are stimulated in the achromatic range, this suggests that the rods ρ are intimately connected with blue vision.

Other types of data concerning the thresholds for color vision come from studies using light-adapted eyes and narrow test patches illuminating $1°$ or $2°$ of the visual field. Many variations have been tried using eyes adapted to various colored lights and using the same or other colored lights as test patches. Other experiments have presented test patches in different parts of the visual field. All of the experiments indicate at least six characteristic absorption curves. Attempts to assign these curves to different receptors implies six pigments. No evidence from either histology or biochemistry can be interpreted to make six pigments a reasonable number. By contrast, the scheme diagrammed in Figure 2 is in accord with at least six spectra if the experiments are really fatiguing the neural elements as well as the receptors. If one admits different fatigue curves for cell types ρ, δ, ι, d, e, f, h, m, and p, one can predict that there may be a very large number of absorption curves for light-adapted eyes under varying conditions.

Similar experiments, using much smaller test fields, show that in the photopic eye the central 20′ of the fovea lacks blue, and the central 15′ lacks both blue and yellow. This is to be expected from the model under discussion for the fovea contains no rods. In the absence of rods, there would also be no d or m type cells. At 570 mμ, a wavelength in the yellow, the central 15′ of the fovea give a gray sensation. This supports the antagonistic roles of green and red used in the model at the p type cells. (Note that yellow would normally be sensed by the m type cells, supposedly missing from the fovea.)

Time measurements have fascinated many biophysicists. In the eye, one can measure kinetic curves of recovery rate to bright illuminations of various durations. At least four different time constants can be found by these experiments. For short flashes of 0.02–0.10 sec, there is a very rapid recovery. For longer exposures, there is an after image for 0.5 to 5 sec, a recovery of the cone threshold from 20 to 200 sec, and a recovery of the rod threshold (dark adaptation) between 4 and 40 minutes. Talbot's model with three receptors, k, l, and i cells, all contributing to the time constants, predicts the existence of several kinetic curves, more so than the above experiments reveal.

Additional kinetic constants can be found from stimulating the eye by means other than light. A wide variety of stimuli, such as magnetic fields of 60 cps, electrical stimuli, and excess pressure, all produce visual sensations. In the dark-adapted eye, the sensation is reported to be blue, corresponding to the fact that the large fibers of the d-m system are easiest to stimulate. In a series of experiments, eyes were light-adapted and then the electrical threshold stimulus needed to elicit a light sensation was determined. Under these conditions, a series of kinetic recovery curves is obtained which are more rapid than the times for recovery of rod and cone vision. Hence, the neurons themselves must be stimulated. A final conclusion from these experiments is that fatiguing or blocking does occur at the neural level within the retina, so that the 1° and 2° test patch experiments are not exclusively measurements of dye spectra.

Concerning abnormal vision, Figure 2 has arrows or numbers marked for the structures suggested missing in (1) protanopia (the ι cones), (2) deuteranopia (the p cell fiber to the optic nerve), (3) tritanopia (the rods), and (4) tetartanopia (the yellow connections from e and f to d). The detailed account will not be reviewed here. Suffice it to point out that, with a complex system of this nature, plus duplicate mechanisms within the central nervous system, there is almost no end of types of color blindness possible. The theory of vision outlined in Figure 2 can account for any known or conceivable type of color blindness.

In the present section, the results of subjective experiments on color discrimination have been developed around a single cellular model based on histological findings and the actions of neurons. This model has helped to organize and combine the experimental data obtained from a variety of approaches using many techniques. It is useful in that it orders past knowledge about the visual mechanisms in a form that is easy to remember; it will be used in succeeding sections to describe evidence from electrical measurements of spike potentials, as well as to interpret neural sharpening and analyses.

3. Direct Neural Measurements

Measurements of neural spike potentials were made by Hartline and his co-workers who recorded impulses from the optic nerves of limulus and vertebrate eyes. The eye of the king crab, limulus, is particularly simple because it consists of many individual rodlike receptors called *ommatidia*. Each of these receptors is connected to an individual nerve fiber. When the nerve is dissected until just one fiber remains intact, a slow natural

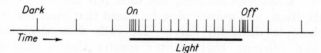

Figure 3. Diagrammatic representation of response of a single limulus ommatidium. The vertical lines represent spike potentials. Solid horizontal line represents light on. Note dark rate, on-burst, steady rate in light, off-burst, and return to dark rate. After H. K. Hartline, H. G. Wagner, and F. Ratliff, "Inhibition in the Eye of *Limulus*," *J. Gen. Physiol.* **39**: 651 (1956); H. K. Hartline and F. Ratliff, "Inhibitory Interaction of Receptor Units in the Eye of *Limulus*," *J. Gen. Physiol.* **40**: 357 (1957).

firing rate is observed in the dark. This is illustrated in Figure 3. If a threshold stimulus is applied to this single ommatidium, an extra spike is observed. If light stimuli considerably above threshold are used, the response is somewhat more complicated as is also shown in Figure 3. Initially, there is a very rapid (transient) burst of spikes as the light is turned on. This is followed by a slower steady-state "firing" rate far faster than the dark rate. The steady-state rate is a function of the intensity of the light stimulus. When the stimulus is removed (that is, the light is turned off), there is another transient burst of spikes, followed by a gradual return to the dark rate. There is no reason to doubt that individual retinal rods and cones of vertebrates would follow this same pattern.

Another type of experiment carried out by Hartline and his co-workers involved the vertebrate eye. These experiments were more difficult to perform and also much more difficult to interpret in a quantitative fashion. Nonetheless, the results molded the thinking of everyone who has worked in the field of vision since then. In these experiments, the vertebrate eye was removed with the optic nerve intact. The nerve was dissected until just one fiber remained. Through many experiments, a variety of types of fibers were found. All showed a spontaneous, rhythmic background firing. Some increased this rate on stimulation; more of them were almost completely "silent" during intense stimulation showing a strong "on" and a strong "off" burst of spike potentials. In other words, these experiments produced just the results expected from the model in Figure 2. (Or maybe one should reverse this, since the experiments came first.)

Another method of obtaining electrophysiological data is to remove the cornea, lens, and vitreous humor of an intact eye. Electrodes are passed over the surface of the retina until the response is that of a single nerve fiber. Granit, in Sweden, has used this method in detail. In snakes, rats, frogs, and guinea pigs, he found that most fibers gave the normal photopic threshold curve. He calls these *dominators*. Other fibers giving different, characteristic spectra Granit calls *modulators*. In most animals, Granit found three, sometimes four modulators, whose spectra differed from the photopic threshold curve.

Granit's data show very clearly the need for an inhibition mechanism during continuous illumination. The animal data are hard to interpret in terms of human vision owing to controversies over whether the animals really see colors as separate sensations. Moreover, Granit's criterion for observing antagonistic effects was very weak. These experiments with exposed retinas do provide evidence for a mechanism such as that provided by the *i* cells in Talbot's model.

In summary, then, the direct neural measurements indicate that vertebrate nerve fibers of the optic nerve show more response when a light intensity changes than during continuous illumination; in many cases, the rate of spike formation is depressed or abolished during strong illumination. This is in direct contrast to the response of individual receptors whose rate is apparently increased on direct stimulation. Complex neural interaction (that is, computation) is an important part of retinal function. In this respect, the retina acts like a part of the brain. The retina is a subdivision of the brain in terms of its embryological formation. It further resembles the brain in giving rise to electrical potentials, which are similar in some ways to the electroencephalographic potentials.

4. Neural Sharpening and Analyses

Inhibition in the retina can be demonstrated in other ways. One of the more striking is the process called *neural sharpening*. Similar effects in hearing were discussed in the last chapter. Sharpening within the retina was demonstrated directly in the experiments of Hartline and co-workers with limulus eyes. The nerve fibers from the ommatidia go through a complex *plexus*, not clearly understood anatomically, in which the various fibers apparently synapse with one another. If two receptors are stimulated instead of one, as described in Section 3, their

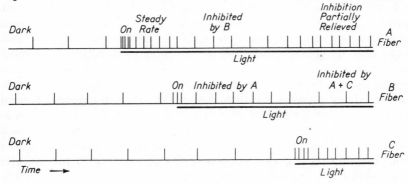

Figure 4. Diagrammatic representation of three ommatidia. *A* and *C* are so far separated that there is no mutual interaction. However, both *A* and *C* interact with *B*. After H. K. Hartline, H. G. Wagner, and F. Ratliff, "Inhibition in the Eye of *Limulus*," *J. Gen. Physiol.* **39**: 651 (1956); H. K. Hartline and F. Ratliff, "Inhibitory Interaction of Receptor Units in the Eye of *Limulus*" *J. Gen. Physiol.* **40**: 357 (1957).

responses can be shown to be interrelated. These relationships exist at the ommatidia themselves but are abolished if the nerve fibers are dissected free (that is, removed from the plexus) from the ommatidia to the points of observation (and cut thereafter). Thus, the interrelationships depend on the neural plexus. As a result, the stimulation of one ommatidium raises the threshold and decreases the steady-state firing rate of the second ommatidium used. These effects are reciprocal and are important only for very close neighbors.

The response of an individual receptor, then, depends on the state of stimulation of its neighbors (or more correctly, on the firing rate of its neighbors). For example, one may choose three receptors, *A*, *B*, and *C*, such that *A* and *B* inhibit each other and *B* and *C* inhibit each other but *A* and *C* are too far apart to have an appreciable mutual effect. The results of this experiment are illustrated in Figure 4. If one stimulates A and observes a firing rate, it can be reduced by simultaneously stimulating B. If now C is also stimulated, the firing rate of B will be reduced, thereby permitting the rate of A to rise toward its original value. Thus, the response of any receptor, although affected directly only by its neighbors, depends in a complicated manner on the responses of all the other receptors.

Similar mutual inhibitions have been observed in vertebrate eyes between the receptors exciting one ganglion cell. It is tempting to hypothesize that in the limulus these mutual interactions are the result of direct interfiber synapses, but in the human retina they are mediated by h and k type cells. This mutual inhibition of neighboring receptors serves to increase acuity by decreasing the effects of glare and of scattering within the eye. It also makes the threshold much higher near a bright object. Thus, gradations at the edge of a bright light appear much sharper to the eye than to a series of independent photocells.

Sharpening effects of this type are well known in psychophysical studies. They support the idea that neighboring receptors do inhibit each other. Psychophysical evidence, however, cannot clarify whether these effects in human vision occur at the receptors themselves or at the first set of neurons with which the rod and cone fibers synapse. It is even possible that a major portion of the sharpening in human vision occurs within the central nervous system.

A different type of neural analysis has been demonstrated by Land and his associates. They found that, although the description given previously in this chapter for color discrimination was valid for large patches of color or for one or two colors in the visual field, it was very misleading for color vision as it normally occurs. To show this, they used two photographic slides, one exposed in the short wavelength region of visible light and the other in the long wavelength region. When these were used simultaneously but illuminated with two different broad bands of light, the natural color sensations were reproduced. Similar experiments with narrow bands of light (that is, monochromatic lights) produced about two-thirds of the possible colors. The effective colors depended only on the per cent of the maximum (or average) of each light transmitted and not on their absolute intensities. It further depended on a random (or gaussian) distribution of small patches of colors such as occur in the normal visual field.

These results can be brought into accord with the model in Figure 2 by very slightly modifying the assumptions made. One notes in that model that although three receptors are excited, essentially two *ratios* are used for color vision under photoptic conditions. These are the ratios of the responses of the m and p type cells to that of the s type cells. It is clear that only the two ratios can be important and not the absolute rates of firing of m and p, or else color sensation would (on this model) vary rapidly with light intensity. For specific color sensations, these ratios must be compared with standards. For large patches of light of the same color, these standards must exist within the nervous system.

To reconcile the model with Land's experiments, it is necessary to assume that with small randomly distributed patches of colors, the nervous system computes an average value for each ratio and then compares the ratios to this average rather than to absolute standards. Teleologically, this would be desirable because it permits one to distinguish colors independently of the exact spectrum of the lighting used— clouds in the sky, and so on. The model of Figure 2, with this added assumption, predicts correctly that two broad bands of light, illuminating two slides, should be able to produce all possible color sensations. Two narrower bands cannot excite as many different values for the ratios of the responses of the m and p cells to the response of the s cells, and hence cannot simulate all colors.

This interpretation emphasizes that the model of Figure 2 uses three types of receptors and is thereby a tricolor model. However, the data from these three are analyzed as one absolute value, used for acuity and brightness sensations, and as two ratios used for color sensations. One might well ask if the added assumption is valid. Although more experiments are necessary to answer this question, it may be noted that at any rate the assumption of average standards instead of absolute ones is, a priori, no more unreasonable than the possibility of neural sharpening. (As recently as 1950 the latter was considered unlikely.)

Another question one might raise is whether the nervous system uses the same standards for the m/s and p/s ratios throughout the visual field. Land's experiments show that people identify colors correctly with three different pairs of broad bands of light in three different parts of the visual field. Teleologically, this also is desirable because it allows one to recognize colors as the same, some of which are in direct sunlight and others in shade.

Whether the model of Figure 2 continues to prove useful, or needs to be drastically revised, the experiments described in this section indicate that the nervous system carries out many complex, computer-like actions. As with most actions of this nature, the exact neural mechanisms are not well understood even though the evidence for their occurrence is very strong.

5. Cortical Representation

The complex series of synapses of the visual pathway through the central nervous system is shown in Figure 5. It should be noted that responses from either eye for a given area in the visual field eventually

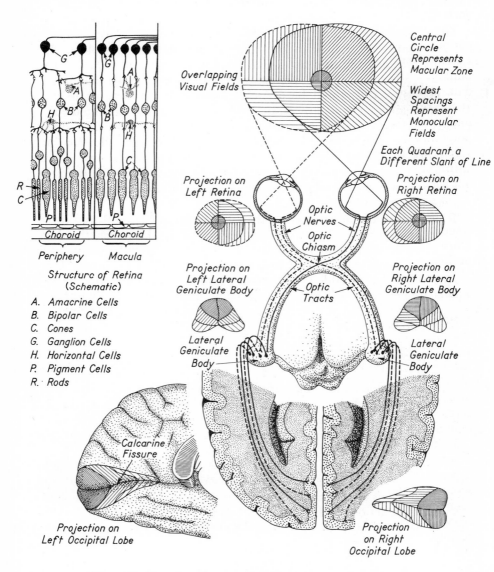

Figure 5. Neural pathways of vision in the central nervous system. Copyright *The CIBA Collection of Medical Illustrations,* by Frank H. Netter, M.D., Vol. 1, "The Nervous System," 1953.

appear (or are "projected onto") the occipital lobe of the cerebral cortex opposite to the half of the visual field containing the object. Further, the area of maximum acuity around the fovea occupies a major portion of the surface of the cortex.

The stimuli are not simply transmitted through the synapses. At various points in the midbrain, auxiliary fibers lead off to autonomic systems, such as the feedback loops controlling the iris, and to tear, blinking, and sudden withdrawal centers. Moreover, a great deal of data processing may occur at these synapses. For example, potentials at the retina follow a light blinking 1,000 times per second, those in the midbrain barely follow 100 times per second, whereas the cortical potentials can at most follow 10 per second. The potentials on the surface of the occipital lobe occur first locally and then spread over the entire cortex. Under the action of anesthesia, the local potentials do not spread as far.

No one yet knows the exact role of these potentials or their relationship to conscious sensations. The complexity of the synapses and responses of the visual pathway cannot but fill us with awe and wonder. Unraveling the clues to the role of the various parts is a challenging problem.

6. Summary of Vision

Vision can be studied from many different points of view. In Chapter 2, the physical properties of light waves and optical systems necessary for vision were discussed. Likewise, the gross anatomy and histology of the vertebrate eye were described. These topics all are within the realm of definitive, quantitative knowledge unlikely to change in the near future. In Chapter 3, novel uses of vision in homing and navigation of birds and bees were discussed. These uses depend critically on the actions of the central nervous system.

In this chapter, the neural aspects of vision were organized around a model, illustrated by Figure 2. Many phenomena of vision can be described in terms of this model, such as color vision, photopic and scotopic vision, all experiments supporting a tricolor theory, all experiments supporting an antagonist theory, kinetic data, coding in the optic nerve and retinal potentials. The model uses most of the known histological structures (as well as one unknown one, the "daylight rod" δ). The model can be modified to bring it into accord with the experiments by Land and his associates. This model also can explain all varieties of visual defects. Nonetheless, one must expect that as more data are gathered and new types of experiments are designed, the model must eventually yield to a more sophisticated one.

REFERENCES

1. Judd, D. B., "Basic Correlates of the Visual Stimulus," *Handbook of Experimental Psychology*, S. S. Stevens, ed. (New York: John Wiley & Sons, Inc., 1951), pp. 811–867.
2. Polyak, Stephen, *Retina: The Anatomy and the Histology of the Retina in Man, Ape, and Monkey, Including the Consideration of Visual Function, the History of Physiological Optics, and the Histological Laboratory Technique* (Chicago, Illinois: University of Chicago Press, 1941).
3. Talbot, S. A., "Recent Concepts of Retinal Color Mechanisms," *J. Opt. Soc. Am.* **41**: 895–941 (1951).
4. Hartline, H. K., and F. Ratliff, "Inhibitory Interaction of Receptor Units in the Eye of Limulus," *J. Gen. Physiol.* **40**: 357–376 (1957).
5. Land, E. H., "Experiments in Color Vision," *Scientific Am.* **200**: 84–99 (May 1959).

8

Muscles

I. Introduction

A very general property of all living matter is the ability it has to alter its size or shape by contracting or expanding a given region of its body. In most of the higher animals, certain cells or groups of cells are specialized to contract or relax, thereby changing the position and shape of the animal. Other similar groups of cells contract and relax to pump fluids (blood) through the animal, force food through the digestive tract, and so forth. Aggregates of these specialized contractile cells are called *muscle tissues*, or simply *muscles*. All other forms of protoplasm exhibit a contractility similar to that of muscles, but the latter are specialized to emphasize this property of contractility. Thus, contractility is trivially obvious in human muscles but can also be demonstrated in all living cells.

Muscles have been of interest to biophysicists for many years; their study will probably remain one of the fields of biophysical research for years to come. Most of the earlier studies on muscles were part of a larger field called *biomechanics*. This field was explored primarily by workers who, because of their backgrounds and training, labeled themselves physiologists and anatomists. Today, biomechanics per se has passed out of the fields of active research except for experiments on specialized topics such as body resonances and tissue elasticity. These topics are part of biophysics (although they are not described in this text).

Starting some time in the 1920's, muscles were studied as biochemical complexes. At the same time, biophysicists related the heat changes which occurred in muscles to a mixture of chemical and mechanical effects. These studies markedly influenced the direction of biochemical research as a whole and still form part of the basis for current models of oxidative mechanisms in protoplasm.

A slight refinement in the above-mentioned biochemical and thermal studies involves the use of extraction techniques. The muscles are ground up; certain compounds, for example, myosin, are extracted and purified; and then their properties are studied. It is believed that the nature of the contractile process should be related to the properties of the chemical constituents of muscles.

Recent advances in research on the contractile process in muscles have come about through the use of highly specialized physical instrumentation and by the introduction of the ideas and concepts of molecular structure and form. Thus, muscle studies are increasingly falling within the scope of biophysics and biophysical chemistry. For example, the enzyme reactions and the optical density changes in living muscle have been followed by using specially constructed spectrophotometers. Likewise, microelectrode techniques have made it possible to observe the magnitude and form of the electrical surface potentials, as well as the action potential spikes which precede contraction. Perhaps most important of all, a special physical tool, the electron microscope, has been used to extend the range of observation to smaller size pieces of muscle than can be seen with the light microscope. The interpretation of electron micrographs of muscles has dramatically altered the acceptable models of muscular contraction, at the same time emphasizing the need for further studies of protein structure before muscular contraction can be understood on a molecular level.

2. Anatomy

Muscles are found in all of the more advanced animals, both invertebrate and vertebrate. All are transducers converting chemical energy into electrical energy, heat energy, and useful mechanical energy. Muscles appear in a variety of sizes and shapes; they differ in the forces they can exert and in their speed of action. In this chapter, only vertebrate muscles will be discussed.

Anatomically, muscles can be classified in many ways, in terms of function, of innervation, of body location, of embryological development, and of histology. The histologic classification is the most widely used and probably the least ambiguous. Histologically, one can distinguish, in the vertebrates, two types of muscles: striated and smooth. Striated muscle, when viewed under the microscope, appears to have alternate dark and light bands distributed in a regular pattern across long fibers. Smooth muscle consists of shorter fibers with no striations.

Striated muscles form a large portion of our meat diet. If one examines a piece of steak, one notes there are large bundles or subdivisions of the muscle. The entire muscle is surrounded by a sheath of connective tissue. Between the large bundles comprising the muscle run connective tissues, blood vessels, and nerves. Each large bundle is then divided into smaller bundles, and each of these is finally subdivided

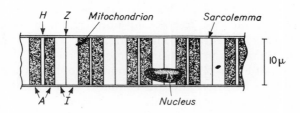

Figure I. Diagram of striated muscle fiber. Each fiber contains many nuclei and mitochondria. In general, the fiber is not as straight as shown in the diagram. The different bands are characterized as follows. The *A* Band stains dark and is anisotropic (birefringent); it is also called the *Q* disc. The *I* Band stains less and is isotropic; it is also called the *J* disc. The *Z* disc, in middle of *I* band, stains darkly. The *H* zone is the less stained region in middle of *A* band.

into "muscle fibers." The major portion of the striated muscle is made up of these fibers, 10–100 μ in diameter, and of lengths that reach 100 cm or more in the larger vertebrates. A piece of the fiber under high magnification would look something like Figure 1. Each fiber is crossed by a number of bands, each with its own name.

The ends of the fibers of many striated muscles are attached to tendons. Throughout the length of the muscle fiber run still smaller fibers called *myofibrils*. These possess the same characteristic striations of the original muscle fibers. For reasons not at all understood, the corresponding bands of adjacent myofibrils are lined up with one another, thereby causing the striation of the entire muscle fiber. Besides the fibrils, a striated muscle fiber contains several other organelles and is surrounded by a special membrane called the *sarcolemma*. (The prefixes myo- and sarco- both are used widely to identify muscle and muscle-like structures.) The organelles include small bodies associated with oxidative mechanisms known as *mitochondria*, as well as many nuclei. Thus, one may regard the striated muscle fiber as a single, polynuclear cell, but the entire concept of cell becomes rather meaningless in this connection.

Three types of striated muscles are known: (1) the skeletal muscles which form long, unbranched fibers with the nuclei distributed just inside the outer edge of the fiber, (2) special muscles of the face and head region, which are made up of branched fibers with cell nuclei located just inside the outer edge of the fiber, and (3) cardiac muscle in which the nuclei are at the center of the fiber cross section and in which all of the fibers branch to such an extent that very few ends can be found. In addition, cardiac muscle has intercalated discs which occur between the cell nuclei and divide the fibers into units resembling cells. This chapter emphasizes vertebrate skeletal muscles. Chapter 9 describes various aspects of the action of cardiac muscle.

As can be seen in Figure 1, there are a number of bands present along the striated muscle fiber. They are common to all striated muscles. The bands which stain dark are also birefringent; that is, they split unpolarized light into two beams. Any such substance also transmits light at a velocity which depends on the angle between the plane of polarization and the fiber axis. This birefringence is believed to be due to the lining up of large protein macromolecules, but the exact molecular basis is not well understood in the muscle striations. The birefringent bands are labeled *A*, for anisotropic, that is, index of refraction depends on direction of the incident light.

By contrast, the less heavily stained bands have no polarizing properties. They are labeled *I*, for isotropic. In many ways, the *I* bands are harder to understand than the *A* bands, for it is believed that the protein molecules are oriented in both.

In the center of the *I* band is a darker staining disc called the *Z* disc. In the center of the *A* band is a lighter staining region called the *H* zone. Because the cell concept is not too helpful in discussing muscle fibers, the repeating unit is called a *sarcomere*. It is chosen to run from one *Z* disc to the next. A sarcomere may include no nuclei, or one, or even more than one; it is in no sense of the word a cell.

Vertebrate muscles which are not striated are called smooth because they are not made up of bundles of small groups of fibers. Smooth muscles, by contrast to striated ones, consist of short spindle-shaped cells of isotropic material. The cells usually are 15–20 μ long, though some reach a length of 500 μ. A diagram of a typical smooth muscle cell is shown in Figure 2.   The maximum cell thickness at the center of the spindle is usually about 6 μ.

Intact striated muscles rarely contract more than a small fraction of their original length.   Smooth muscles, in contrast, change their length manyfold.   This large change is believed to be due to a slipping of one smooth muscle cell over another.   In all cases of muscular contraction, little if any change of volume occurs.

Muscles are sometimes classified by criteria other than histological ones.   In terms of function and innervation, muscles are separated into voluntary and involuntary.   For an objective definition, those muscles under direct control of the frontal gyrus of the cerebral hemisphere might be called *voluntary*.   By and large, striated muscles are voluntary and smooth muscles are involuntary, but this is not a hard and fast rule.   Certain smooth muscles are under conscious voluntary control in some individuals and not in others.   Likewise, very few individuals can voluntarily control all of their striated muscles.

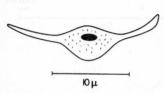

Figure 2. A smooth muscle cell.

10 μ

Muscles may be classified by their kinetic properties.   In terms of speed of response, smooth muscles such as bladder and uterine muscles often take several seconds to contract.   Striated muscle, in contrast, usually contracts rapidly, often reaching its maximum response in a few milliseconds.   Within the same animal, faster muscles are usually paler and slower ones are usually darker.   (The chicken is a particularly good example of this.   The wing muscles work rapidly and are pale, whereas the slower leg muscles are dark.)   This color is more closely associated with an oxygen-storing protein called *myoglobin* than it is with the histological structure.   In the next section, the kinetics of the contraction of striated skeletal muscles are described.

3. Physical Changes during Muscular Contraction

A. Changes of Tension and Length

When a muscle is stimulated it twitches.   If the muscle is held at constant length, it develops a force, whereas if it is weighted down it contracts and does work.   The two simplest situations to study are constant length (*isometric*) and constant force (*isotonic*).   To eliminate the nervous control, it is possible to remove the muscle from the animal body or to cut the nerve fibers.

If one stimulates an excised muscle by means of an electrical shock (or a mechanical impulse, or heat, cold, and so on), a twitch occurs. If the stimuli are spaced a long time apart, the muscle relaxes to its original

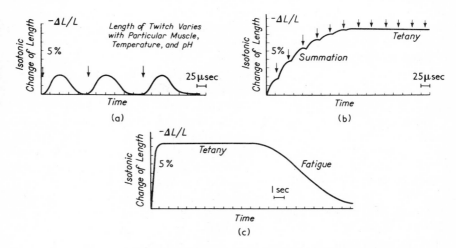

Figure 3. Curves of contraction. (a) Occasional stimulation shows twitches. Arrows indicate stimuli. (b) Frequent stimulation leads to summation. (c) Prolonged tetany leads to fatigue. Note the difference in the time scale as compared to (a) and (b). After S. Cooper and J. C. Eccles, *J. Physiol.* **69**: 377 (1930).

length between twitches, and a contraction curve is obtained of the shape shown in Figure 3a, for isotonic contractions. If the stimulus is repeated before relaxation occurs, summation is observed as shown in Figure 3b. With still more rapidly repeated stimulation, a smooth contraction curve results such as shown in Figure 3c. The steady contraction is called *tetany*. All muscles will eventually fatigue and fail to contract, even though stimulated. This type of fatigue probably never occurs in the healthy intact animal, as the nervous system undergoes fatigue before the muscles do.

Curves illustrating the strength of isometric and isotonic contractions are shown in Figures 4a and 4b, in terms of effect of length on tension developed in isometric contraction and of load on shortening produced during isotonic contraction. Only in isotonic contraction is work done. It is easy to show that the maximum work is done at half the maximum load for muscles for which the straight line relationship of Figure 4a is valid. The straight line can be described by

$$\Delta L = \Delta L_{\text{max}} \left(1 - \frac{F}{F_{\text{max}}}\right)$$

where ΔL is the contraction and F is the load. The work W done on the load is

$$W = F\Delta L_{\text{max}} \left(1 - \frac{F}{F_{\text{max}}}\right)$$

This work W is a maximum when

$$\frac{dW}{dF} = 0 \quad \text{that is, when} \quad F = \tfrac{1}{2} F_{\text{max}}$$

Striated muscles, in general, can develop large forces against a given load but even in tetany can contract only a small amount. In the

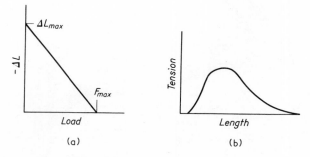

Figure 4. (a) Isotonic contraction. Change in length is plotted as a function of load for a muscle supporting a fixed load (isotonic). The straight line is an approximation only. (b) Isometric tension. Maximum tension developed is plotted as a function of length for a muscle held at various fixed lengths (isometric).

vertebrate body, the skeletal muscles all develop far larger forces than the loads they move. However, the load moves more than the muscle contracts. This is accomplished by the lever action of the muscles and bones with the joints serving as pivots. As shown in Figure 5, the mechanical advantage is considerably less than one, that is, force of the muscle is much greater than load, and the muscle motion is much less than load motion.

To study muscular contraction, it would appear desirable to work with single muscle fibers. However, these are difficult to obtain and few people have succeeded in preparing them. Most experiments have been done on whole muscle.

B. Interaction with the Nervous System

In the intact animal, the muscle contracts following stimulation by the nervous system.   The incoming impulses in the nerve fibers are called electrical spike potentials; similar spike potentials travel along the

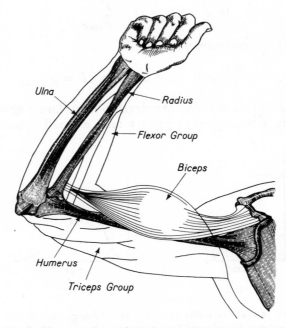

Figure 5. The muscles and the bones of the arm.   The lower arm acts as a lever pivoted at the elbow.   The biceps, which applies force to the lever, is attached to the radius near the elbow.   The load is applied to this lever at the wrist.   Therefore, the theoretical mechanical advantage (TMA) is about 0.1.   Muscles moving most limbs have TMA's of 0.05 to 0.4. Adapted from THE WORLD BOOK ENCYCLOPEDIA with permission © 1961 by Field Enterprises Educational Corporation.   All rights reserved.

muscle fibers.   The interactions of the nerve and muscle fibers and the magnitude and form of the electrical potentials across the sarcolemma are important physical characteristics of muscle.

Each muscle fiber is separately innervated.   Each has at its end a special structure called the *muscle end plate*, near which one or more nerve fibers also end.   The nerve and muscle endings, together with the space between them, is called the *myoneural junction*.   When a spike potential reaches the nerve endings, the latter secrete a special chemical substance,

probably acetylcholine, which is probably also important in the transmission of impulses across synapses between nerves. (Acetylcholine and its
action are described more completely in Chapter 4.) The released acetylcholine diffuses across the myoneural junction (which is of the order of a
few tenths of a micron) and stimulates the formation of a spike potential
in the muscle fiber. The acetylcholine is rapidly destroyed by a protein
catalyst, cholinesterase, present in the muscle end plate. Under certain
conditions, the myoneural junction acts as a "computer," putting out a
number of muscle spike potentials different from the number of incoming
nerve spike potentials.

The muscle fiber membrane is polarized, just as is the axon membrane
discussed in Chapter 4. An action spike potential, similar to that in

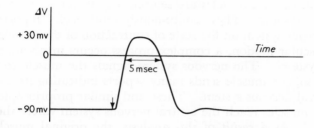

Figure 6. Spike potential of striated muscle. V is the potential difference inside minus that outside the sarcolemma.
The arrow indicates application of stimulus. In cardiac
muscle, the peak of the crest of the action potential lasts much
longer.

nerves, is the first result of stimulation of a muscle fiber, whether the
stimulus be the physiological one from the nervous system or an artificial one, that is, electrical, mechanical, or heat. A typical muscle
spike potential is shown in Figure 6. The action potential differs from
that in nerves only in the duration of the peak, which lasts much longer
in muscle than in nerve.

Originally, the muscle potentials were recorded by means of so-called
"bipolar" or "differentiating" electrodes which measured the potential
difference between two neighboring spots on the muscle. These gave
no possibility of measuring a resting or d-c potential, nor any certainty of
the size of the cellular potentials. These electrodes have been replaced
by microelectrodes made by drawing out a capillary glass tube to a
diameter of less than 1 μ. The tiny capillaries may be inserted through
the wall of a single muscle fiber without damaging the fiber. With such
probes, it is possible to measure both the resting potential and the action

potential of skeletal muscle fibers. An additional difficulty is that the muscle fiber moves during contraction. Provision must be made to permit the microelectrode to move with the fiber. When this is done, consistent records can be obtained of the potentials across the sarcolemma of single muscle fibers.

The spike potential always precedes contraction. After the crest of the spike has passed, the membrane potential starts to return to normal. At this time, the rate of heat production increases. A fraction of a millisecond later, there is a slight relaxation, and then the mechanical contraction of the twitch starts. How the spike potential "signals" the muscle fiber to begin the chemical changes necessary for a twitch is completely unknown. Nonetheless, the spike always precedes a twitch and somehow all the myofibrils do contract simultaneously.

Within all skeletal muscles are sensing organs known as *proprioceptors* or *pacinian corpuscles*. These continuously send back "reports" to the central nervous system on the state of contraction of the muscle. Thus, in any muscular motion, a complex process occurs involving multiloop feedback systems. The nervous system signals the muscle to contract. As it does so, the muscle sends many reports indicating its contraction to the central nervous system. These and similar proprioceptor reports from other muscles reach the central nervous system where they are all "analyzed." As a result of this analysis, the original muscle is "instructed" or controlled to contract faster or slower so as to achieve the desired location. This process has appealed to servomechanism experts who have carried out quite detailed analyses of muscular contraction. Although such analyses can never supply new facts, they have made it possible to understand qualitatively the organizing principles of the muscle-nervous system relationship.

The problem of muscular fatigue also appears to involve the nervous system. A denervated muscle can be held in tetany by repeated stimulation until it tires. However, if the motor nerve causing a muscle to contract is stimulated, it can be shown that the myoneural junction fatigues before the muscle does. Similarly, if the entire normal animal is stimulated (for example, by poking it with a hot soldering iron), it can be shown that fatigue sets in at the synapses in the central nervous system before the myoneural junction has fatigued.

C. Heat Production

Besides studying forces, work, and electrical changes, several biophysicists have followed a quite different approach, namely the measurement of the heat produced by resting and contracting muscles. Muscles produce extra heat when they are working; the extra heat accompanies the conversion of chemical energy to mechanical work. These heat measurements are based essentially on temperature measurements. They are difficult because the maximum temperature rise associated with a muscle twitch is only 0.003°C, and the heat is developed very rapidly. A. V. Hill refined his techniques to the point that he could resolve a few millionths of a degree change in a few milliseconds.

Hill's experiments showed there were three different types of heat production occurring during muscular contraction. The first, called *resting heat,* is associated with metabolism in the resting muscle. The second type of heat production, *initial heat,* accompanies actual contraction and relaxation. The third general type is called *recovery heat;* it is liberated for 20–30 min following activity.

The resting heat is an indication of continuous metabolism in the muscle. It can be altered by stretching the muscle as well as by changes in ionic strength in the surrounding fluids. It is not a constant or simple quantity.

When a muscle contracts and then relaxes, the second type of heat production overrides the resting heat production. This initial heat consists of several components. While the muscle contracts, it develops a "maintenance heat" which starts just after the spike potential passes and continues until relaxation. Some of this maintenance heat is actually produced before contraction occurs. There is, in addition, a "heat of shortening." Under isotonic conditions when the muscle lengthens, a heat of relaxation is measured equal to the work done by the load.

These heat changes attracted the interest of many investigators. However, they are difficult to interpret. There is no simple relationship between the work done and the extra heat produced. The reasons for the rise in heat production before contraction and the dependence of resting heat on muscle length are still not understood. This basic lack of understanding emphasizes the incompleteness of current molecular models of muscular activity.

4. Muscle Chemistry

In the previous section, the various physical changes accompanying muscular contraction were presented. These all involve molecular changes and the conversion of chemical free energy to other forms of energy. Accordingly, it is appropriate to examine the chemical constituents of muscle. These include the types of molecules active during contraction and relaxation. The chemical transformations necessary for energy production are also indicated.

There are more water molecules within the muscle, and indeed within

the myofibril, than any other type of molecule. Present theories do not
assign any specific role to these water molecules, aside from forming a
medium through which the contractile molecules act and also through
which the energy-carrying molecules diffuse. The various organelles
within the muscle, for example, nuclei and mitochondria, have the same
composition as those of other cells. The ionic concentration within
the muscle fibers is similar to that within nerve fibers described in
Chapter 4. The one unique component, outside of the myofibrils, is
the protein *myoglobin*. This is a red pigment similar to the hemoglobin
of red blood cells except that myoglobin has about one-fourth the molecular weight and only one iron atom per molecule (hemoglobin has four
iron atoms per molecule). Myoglobin is generally believed to act as a
storage for oxygen within the muscle fiber.

The myofibrils contain unique molecules not found in other tissues.
Three proteins, myosin, actin, and tropomyosin, are all found in high
concentrations. All three are members of a general class of proteins
called *globulins*, when classified in terms of their solubilities. (Proteins
are condensation polymers formed from small monomers known as
amino acids. The structure of proteins, including those in muscle, is
discussed more fully in Chapter 15.) The actin is similar to many other
globulins in that it can exist in either a globular (sphere-like) form or a
fibrillar form. Small changes in the ionic strength, pH, or temperature
can convert some globulins reversibly from the fibrillar to the globular
form. (In the fibrillar form, they are believed to be arranged in a
helical structure described in Chapter 15.)

The striking physical changes which take place as myosin and actin
shift from one form to the other suggest that they might be the molecules
actually responsible for contraction. Present evidence, discussed more
fully in Section 6, supports the conclusion that these three proteins form
the contractile elements. However, the premise that they change from
globular to fibrillar form appears to be completely fallacious. Rather,
it appears that myosin, actin, and tropomyosin are always in the fibrillar
form in intact muscles. They are formed into thin filaments, visible
only with the electron microscope. These filaments are believed to
develop the actual contractile forces.

The proteins, myosin, actin, and tropomyosin are large molecules
organized into filaments that are long on an atomic scale. When the
myofibril contracts and relaxes, it uses chemical energy which is derived
from a much smaller molecule called *adenosine triphosphate,* or *ATP*. This
small molecule is the source of immediately available chemical energy
for chemical syntheses, for muscular contraction, and for the active
transport of ions and metabolites across cell membranes. A wide
variety of systems within all vertebrate cells can use ATP as a source of

energy. When this happens, the molecule ATP is split into *adenosine diphosphate*, *ADP*, and inorganic phosphate Ⓟ. Symbolically, one may write this as

$$ATP \rightleftharpoons ADP + Ⓟ + energy$$

(Readers without previous knowledge of biochemistry should not allow themselves to be dismayed by this jargon of letters like ATP and ADP. Many people who use them don't know the structural formula represented by these symbols; all one needs to know is the stoichiometric formula written above. The physical forms of ATP and ADP must be very important for their actions, but no one yet has succeeded in relating these concepts. The molecule ATP is made up of one molecule of the purine, adenine; one molecule of the pentose sugar, ribose; and three phosphate groups joined by pyrophosphate bonds. Its structural formula is shown below, but the reader unfamiliar with biochemistry is advised to stick to the symbol ATP rather than trying to remember the structure.

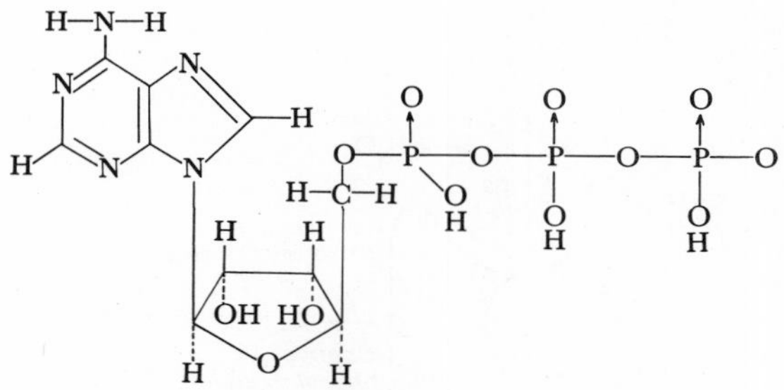

Adenine plus ribose forms the molecule *adenosine*. Adenosine plus one phosphate condenses to *adenylic acid* or *adenosine monophosphate*, *AMP*. The latter plus another phosphate condenses to ADP. Energy is released when ATP is split to ADP and when ADP is split to AMP and Ⓟ.)

There seems to be no doubt, from a large variety of experiments, that ATP is the source of energy used in muscular contraction. Just how this occurs is not clear. For instance, ATP might be split before the muscle contracts or just as it contracts. An alternative possibility is that the muscle proteins store energy which is used during the twitch and then is slowly built up again from ATP during recovery. ATP might form a complex with the muscle proteins. Recent experiments indicate that several intermediates must exist between ATP and the contractile proteins.

Some of the evidence for the direct interaction of ATP comes from experiments with purified myosin and with actin and myosin. If solutions of these proteins in the globular form are mixed with ATP, they form fibers. In the fibrillar form, ATP causes actin-myosin fibers to contract. Moreover, ATP is split in this process because the protein myosin acts as an enzyme catalyzing the splitting of ATP into ADP plus phosphate. Furthermore, if frogs' muscles are soaked in 50 per cent glycerol for months to remove the smaller molecules and then ATP is added, the muscles contract. These brief summaries of many detailed experiments can be interpreted to indicate the role of ATP in muscular contraction, or they may all be artifacts or physiologically unimportant

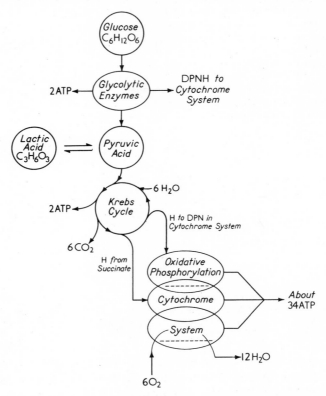

Figure 7. Major steps in the oxidation of glucose. The input consists of glucose and oxygen. Water and CO_2 are formed and energy is stored as ATP, the form used in muscular contraction. Krebs cycle and cytochrome system enzymes are in the mitochondria; glycolytic enzymes are not in the mitochondria.

facts. Direct, spectrophotometric measurements support the latter view, that ATP does not react with the contractile elements. All that is certain is that protein changes occur when the muscle contracts and that ATP is used up to supply the energy for this process.

The steps in the synthesis of ATP from ADP and (P) at the expense of other forms of chemical energy are more clearly understood. This process is a result of the oxidation of many substrates, most of the free energy liberated being used to form ATP. Figure 7 shows several of the major groups of steps in the use of glucose to form ATP. In the absence of oxygen, or in the presence of limited amounts of oxygen, the process stops at lactic acid, as is the case in an active muscle. After activity, the muscle slowly oxidizes the lactic acid the rest of the way to CO_2 and water. These processes are not unique to muscle but occur in all vertebrate cells.

Another important compound in muscles is *creatine*. Just as ADP can be phosphorylated to store energy, creatine can be made to store energy in the form of a phosphate compound, *creatine phosphate*. In the muscle, there is a dynamic balance between the creatine–creatine phosphate system and the ATP–ADP system. Thus, creatine-phosphate acts as a storage depot whose energy can be utilized about as readily as that of ATP.

Chemical studies have revealed many of the basic energy transformations that accompany the changes from relaxed-muscle + glucose + oxygen to contracted-muscle + CO_2 + water. Inherently, however, these methods cannot describe the molecular details of the actual mechanical changes which occur in the active muscle.

5. Electron-Microscope Studies of Muscles

In Section 2, the structure of striated muscles was discussed. In the present section, this discussion will be further amplified to include observations made by electron microscopy and by X-ray diffraction. As was noted earlier, each striated muscle can be broken down into large bundles of small groups of single muscle fibers. Each muscle fiber is some $10–100 \mu$ in diameter and is very long, perhaps as long as the entire muscle. The muscle fiber contains nuclei, mitochondria, and other formed elements as well as myofibrils.

The myofibrils are about 1μ in diameter and may have lengths comparable to that of the entire muscle fiber. Each myofibril is striated with the same bands as the entire muscle fiber. The myofibrils consist of units similar to that shown in Figure 8 which start with the Z disc or membrane and contain one-half of an I band, an A band with a H zone in the middle, one-half of the next I band, and then another Z disc.

Electron-microscope techniques have shown that the myofibrils, in turn, are made up of smaller filaments of two types, thick and thin. The thick ones are about 100 Å (that is, 0.01μ) in diameter and about 2μ

(that is, 20,000 Å) long, whereas the thin ones are about 50 Å in diameter and 1.5 μ long. These filaments also possess a periodicity or striation, but it is only about 400 Å long, a distance that is short compared to the striations on the myofibril. (Indeed, the entire filament is comparable in length to one "unit" along the myofibril.) The dimensions and periodicities of the filaments have been measured independently by X-ray diffraction and by electron-microscope techniques. The two types of data agree well when changes due to dehydration (necessary for electron microscopy but not X-ray diffraction) are included in the calculated results.

At one time, X-ray studies of the form of the filaments were interpreted to show that the general arrangement of amino acids within the proteins changed from a so-called "α form" to a "β form" during contraction (see Chapter 15). Subsequent studies have shown that this

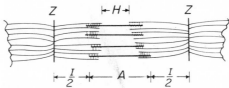

Figure 8. Sliding model of myofibrillar structure. The distance from one Z disc (or membrane) to the next is one myofibrillar unit. During contraction the thick and thin filaments keep the same length but intermesh more completely. The thick filaments are myosin. The thin one contains actin and presumably also tropomyosin. After H. E. Huxley and J. Hanson, "Structure of cross-striated myofibrils," *Biochim. Biophys. Acta* **23**: 229 (1957).

interpretation was wrong; the form of the filaments remains unchanged during contraction. The filaments are made up of helical protein chains but with a nonintegral number of amino acid residues per turn. The entire structure repeats about every 400 Å. Theories which assign muscular shortening to a change in the length or form of the protein molecules all have difficulties explaining these data from electron microscopy and X-ray diffraction, which show that the protein molecules do not change in shape or form during contraction.

Modern electron-microscope techniques permit the determination of still more details of the structure of the myofibrils. It is possible to make electron micrographs of the "ultra structure" of the muscle without dispersing or homogenizing it in any way. For these studies, the muscle is first fixed to harden the protein elements. Then it is "stained" with a heavy metal to increase contrast in the electron microscope. Next, it is filled with, and imbedded in, a plastic such as butyl methacrylate.

Finally, it is cut into sections a few hundred angstroms thick. When these sections are examined in the electron microscope, most are cut at such angles to the myofibrils that they are useless for analysis, but a few will be either at right angles to the myofibrils or along the myofibril. (A great deal of judgment is necessary to discard most of the sections as useless.)

These studies have been interpreted to show that the I bands consist of thin filaments joined by a membrane at their centers (the Z disc). The H zone consists only of thick fibers and the A band is a region of overlap between the thick and thin filaments. These are arranged in a regular array with a definite number of thin filaments surrounding a thick one, varying from two in the flight muscles of insects to six in some vertebrate muscles. Between the thick and thin filaments, there appears to be a series of bridges spaced about 50 or 60 Å apart.

The length of the A band, with the H zone in its center, is then the length of the thick filament as shown in Figure 8. When a muscle (or a myofibril) contracts, the length of the A band remains constant. This implies that the thick filaments do not change in length. Extraction studies have shown that the thick filaments consist entirely of myosin and that they probably contain all the myosin. Chemical studies combined with electron microscopy have shown that the thin filaments contain actin and another protein, presumably tropomyosin.

When the muscle fiber contracts, both the I band and the H zone are shortened. The decrease in length of both these regions is comparable. Therefore, as is shown in Figure 8, the length of the thin filaments also must remain unchanged on contraction. The interpretation of the electron micrographs, then, is that the thin filaments somehow slide in between the thick ones as the muscle contracts.

Just how the thick filaments slide along the thin filaments is a matter of speculation. One might imagine that it takes an ATP molecule to open each bridge between thick and thin filaments and that these then moved in some sort of ratchet fashion in finite steps. The rate of splitting of ATP by myosin and the number of ATP molecules used per twitch both make this finite jump-type motion possible. Again, one might suppose that small kinks appear along the thin filaments and that these move along one bridge at a time. No doubt the reader can construct a few other speculative models himself.

Even if one accepts completely the interpretation of the electron micrographs presented above, there still remain several questions at the molecular level, concerning the mechanism of muscular contraction. It is not known how the muscle action potential triggers the contraction process, although it is known that the action potential always precedes contraction. It is not clear how the numerous filaments all move in a coordinated manner. The details of the coupling, from the free energy released by splitting ATP to the mechanical energy expended by the muscle, are all unknown.

6. Summary

Muscles are the contractile elements of animals. They act as transducers converting chemical energy into mechanical energy. Muscles in vertebrates can be classified according to function and to morphology. Of the various types, the striated muscles, usually associated with voluntary motion, have been studied in greatest detail. Their efficiency, the tensions developed at constant length, and the shortening produced with various loads have all been measured and are well known for many different muscles.

Each striated muscle consists of bundles of small groups of individual muscle fibers. These fibers make up the muscle. The single, striated muscle fiber, about 10 μ in diameter, is surrounded by a single membrane electrically polarized in a fashion similar to that of a nerve fiber. The initial step in the contraction process is an action or spike potential, very similar to that of nerve fibers. This spike potential is normally initiated at the muscle end plate but can also be produced by the same types of stimuli which affect nerve fibers.

Within the striated muscle fiber are many nuclei, mitochondria, microsomes, and so forth, as well as long myofibrils having the same striations as the muscle fiber. The myofibrils contain two types of filaments which in turn are composed of helical fibers of the proteins myosin, actin, and tropomyosin. The two types of filaments appear to overlap in electron micrographs of extended muscles; they intermesh more completely in similar electron micrographs of contracted muscles. The changes during contraction are brought about at the expense of chemical energy stored as ATP.

The energy of ATP is released when the latter is split into its components, ADP and phosphate. This splitting is catalyzed by enzymes called ATP-ases. The protein, myosin, is an ATP-ase, but it may not be active in this fashion in intact myofibrils. The molecular details of how the energy is transferred from ATP to mechanical contractions are not known. The details are not clear on the behavior of the protein filaments within the myofibril as contraction is occurring. The concentration of ATP is "buffered" by the creatine–creatine phosphate system. The net loss of organic phosphate (that is, ATP and creatine phosphate) is restored by the oxidation of glucose. Oxidations in muscles follow the same pathways as in other tissues.

Thus, the basic physical parameters of the gross phenomena associated with muscular contraction are well known, and many of the chemical mechanisms are similar to those in other tissues. In contrast, the molecular description of muscular contraction is an active research area. The ideas involved demand a knowledge of active transport (see Chapter 19) to understand the membrane action, enzyme kinetics (see Chapters 17 and 18) to describe the synthesis and use of ATP, and protein structure (see Chapter 15) to describe the filaments and their behavior during contraction.

REFERENCES

There are many books which deal only with the contraction of striated muscles. Most physiology, biochemistry, and anatomy texts have at least a chapter on this subject. The following list is neither complete nor exhaustive but contains a limited number of references which the author feels to be especially useful to readers wishing to pursue this subject more thoroughly.

1. Best, C. H., and N. B. Taylor, *The Physiological Basis of Medical Practice* 7th ed. (Baltimore, Maryland: The Williams & Wilkins Company, 1961).
2. Heilbrunn, L. V., *An Outline of General Physiology* (Philadelphia: W. B. Saunders Company, 1952).
3. Szent-Györgi, Albert, *Chemistry of Muscular Contraction* 2nd ed. (New York: Academic Press, Inc., 1951).
4. Butler, J. A. V., and J. T. Randall, eds., *Progress in Biophysics and Biophysical Chemistry* (London, England: Pergamon Press, Ltd., 1954) Vol. 4.
    a. Wilkie, D. R., "Facts and Theories About Muscle," pp. 288–324.
    b. Weber, H. H., and Hildegard Portzehl, "The Transference of the Muscle Energy in the Contraction Cycle," pp. 60–111.
5. Ramsey, R. W., "Muscle: Physics," *Medical Physics*, Otto Glasser, ed. (Chicago, Illinois: Year Book Publishers, Inc., 1944) Vol. 1, pp. 784–798.
6. Morales, M. F., Jean Botts, J. J. Blum, and T. L. Hill, "Elementary Processes in Muscle Action: An Examination of Current Concepts," *Physiol. Rev.* **35**: 475–505 (July 1955).
7. Gaebler, O. H., ed., *Enzymes: Units of Biological Structure and Function* (New York: Academic Press, 1956).
    a. Mommaerts, W. F. H. M., "The Actomyosin System and Its Participation in Organized Enzyme Reactions," pp. 317–324.
    b. Morales, M. F., "Is Energy Transferred From ATP to Myosin at the Moment That ATP Is Split?" pp. 325–336.
8. Huxley, H. E., "The Contraction of Muscle," *Scientific Am.* **199**: 66–82 (Nov. 1958).
9. Huxley, A. F., "Muscle Structure and Theories of Contraction," *Progress in Biophysics and Biophysical Chemistry*, J. A. V. Butler and B. Katz, eds. (New York: Pergamon Press, 1957) Vol. 7, pp. 255–318.

10. Whitelock, O. v. S., ed., "Second Conference on Physicochemical Mechanism of Nerve Activity and Second Conference on Muscular Contraction," (Monograph) *Ann. New York Acad. Sc.* **81**: 215–510 (1959).

9

Mechanical and Electrical Character of the Heartbeat

I. Role of the Vertebrate Circulatory System

All vertebrates possess a closed circulatory system. The blood which circulates through this system is a suspension of various types of single cells in a viscous solution of proteins and inorganic salts. The blood is pumped; that is, it is forced to flow through the closed circulatory system. The organ which does the pumping is called the *heart*.

The circulatory system in vertebrates carries oxygen from special exchange organs (lungs or gills) to the other tissues. It also transports carbon dioxide from the tissues back to the lungs or gills. In some amphibia, the skin also serves as an auxiliary gas exchanger. In any case, the blood flows through a special exchange organ in which very thin, moist walls separate the blood from the external environment.

Besides dissolved gases, foods and metabolic waste products are also carried by the blood. The endocrine secretions likewise are transported from gland to target organ by the blood stream. Finally, the blood contains antitoxins and phagocytic cells which help protect the organism from external invaders.

The vertebrate circulatory system, then, is a major internal transportation line for chemical substances. The vessels into which the heart pumps blood are named *arteries*. These branch into smaller and smaller arteries; the smallest are called *arterioles*. The arterioles empty into the *capillaries*. Here, most of the exchanges occur between the blood and the surrounding tissues. The capillaries join to form *venules*, which in turn join to form larger and larger veins leading back to the heart. The circulatory system is not completely closed, however. Some fluid leaves the capillaries, passing into the tissue spaces; it is then called *lymph*. The lymph filters back slowly through several nodes, finally entering the venous portion of the circulatory system.

2. Blood Pressures and Velocities

Before the action of the heart is examined, the flow of the blood through the arteries and veins will be discussed briefly. The flow of the blood can be described in terms of its linear velocity v and its pressure p. The velocity v is, in general, a function both of time and of the point in space at which it is measured. The pressure p is the force per unit area of the fluid. It is a scalar quantity; that is, p is independent of the orientation of the areas used to define it. The zero point for pressure is somewhat arbitrary. So-called "gauge pressure" is the difference between the absolute pressure and the atmospheric pressure. Absolute pressure is measured relative to a zero of no net external forces on the system.

Pressure is a stress and has the dimensions of force per unit area. In the mks system it is measured in newtons/m². Instead of absolute units, pressure is often measured in terms of the height of a column of liquid which it will support. Thus, it may be measured in terms of meters of mercury or meters of water. Some convenient reference numbers to remember are:

$$1 \text{ atmosphere} = 1.0 \times 10^5 \text{ newtons/m}^2$$
$$1 \text{ meter of H}_2\text{O} = 9.8 \times 10^3 \text{ newtons/m}^2$$
$$1 \text{ meter of Hg} = 1.33 \times 10^5 \text{ newtons/m}^2$$

Any convenient height units may be used. The most frequent ones in describing the circulatory system are mm of Hg.

Besides pressure and velocity, another fundamental property of a fluid is its density ρ. For all purposes in this chapter, the blood may be considered as incompressible. Its density is approximately that of water.

A fluid like the blood may possess both kinetic and potential energy. The kinetic energy per unit volume T is

$$T = \tfrac{1}{2}\rho v^2$$

The potential energy per unit volume V results from both the pressure on the fluid,[1] and its height h above the earth. In physics texts, it is shown that, for an incompressible fluid

$$V = \rho g h + p$$

The total energy per unit volume H then is

$$H = p + \rho g h + \tfrac{1}{2}\rho v^2 \tag{1}$$

Bernoulli's equation states that H is a constant. It is true only for nonviscous liquids. In general, the variation of H gives the change in energy per unit volume. The blood loses energy for each cycle in the capillaries. The heart, in pumping, increases the energy per unit volume of blood as the latter passes through the heart. Thus, the heart might be called a chemicomechanical transducer.

When an incompressible fluid flows through a closed system, either the volume flow rate Q (volume per unit time) must be constant at all points or the volume of the system must change. To a first approximation, the average volume of the circulatory system remains constant. Accordingly, the average volume flow rate will usually be the same at all points in the circulatory system. (There are a number of conditions under which more, or fewer, blood vessels are open. For instance, during activity, the blood flow to the muscles increases as more capillaries are open. Similarly, the swelling of erectile tissue is due to expansion of blood sinuses resulting from decreased arteriolar resistance.)

The variation of blood velocity v in a mammal is diagrammed in Figure 1. Although the arteries and veins are much larger than the capillaries, there are so many capillaries that the total cross-sectional area of the tubes open to the blood is much greater than in the larger vessels. Accordingly, the linear velocity of the blood in the capillaries is smaller than in the arteries and veins. The pulsations in the arteries are possible because the walls are elastic and stretch from the force of each heartbeat.

In a similar manner, one may diagrammatically represent the pressure variations. These are shown in Figure 2. The maximum arterial pressure is called the *systolic pressure*, and the minimum arterial pressure is called the *diastolic pressure*. The pressure falls by the time the blood

---

[1] Purists will no doubt object to calling p a form of potential energy per unit volume, but this is satisfactory for discussions of the circulatory system.

reaches the capillaries, and the pressure fluctuations are smoothed out. As the blood enters the venous system, the pressure is still lower. Just before the blood enters the heart, the gauge pressure is negative; because

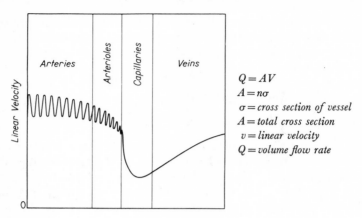

$$Q = AV$$
$$A = n\sigma$$
$$\sigma = cross \ section \ of \ vessel$$
$$A = total \ cross \ section$$
$$v = linear \ velocity$$
$$Q = volume \ flow \ rate$$

Figure 1. Linear velocity of the blood.   Since the volume flow rate, Q, remains approximately constant throughout the circulatory system, a low linear velocity, v, means a large cross section A.   In the capillaries, the vessel cross sections, σ, are small, but the number in parallel, n, is so large that A is greater in the capillaries than in the arterioles or veins.   After C. H. Best and N. B. Taylor, *The Physiological Basis of Medical Practice*, 7th ed.   (Baltimore, Md.: Williams and Wilkins Company, 1961).

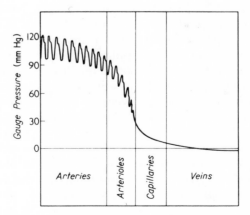

Figure 2. Variation of blood pressure at fixed time.   Values shown are gauge pressure in a normal, adult human.

this pressure is very small, it is conveniently measured in mm of water. In a normal adult human, the venous gauge pressure at the heart is about -40 mm of H_2O.

The arteries and veins have similar flow rates but very different pressures. Accordingly, both have about the same diameter (0.5–12.5 mm i.d.), but the arterial walls are thick and elastic, whereas the venous walls are very thin. The larger pressures in the arteries make reverse flow unlikely; valves limit reverse flow in the veins.

The capillaries are the location of most exchanges of gases, metabolites, and metabolic products. They are thin walled and small in diameter. A red blood cell, 8μ in diameter, distorts the shape of the capillary as it passes through. At the capillary walls, the excess gauge pressure, osmotic forces, and active transport all combine to promote exchanges between the blood stream and the surrounding tissues.

3. The Vertebrate Heart

In warm-blooded vertebrates, the heart keeps pumping for the entire life of the organism. If the heart stops even for a short time, the animal dies. This continuous activity is regulated by both the nervous and the endocrine systems. However, even without these regulatory influences, the heart maintains its rhythmic beat. In cold-blooded animals, the temperature also influences the heart rate. At close to freezing temperatures, their heart rate slows almost to zero.

The heart of the cold-blooded vertebrates is simpler than the mammalian heart. Most fishes and amphibians have a heart made up of a series of chambers as shown in Figure 3. The first, which receives the blood from the veins, is called the *sinus venosus*. It is the pacemaker and originates the heartbeat.

The reptilian heart, also shown in Figure 3, is more specialized. Instead of one auricle, there are two. One receives blood from the lungs only and the other from the remainder of the body. This system is more efficient in aerating the blood than is that of the amphibians and fishes. The sinus venosus does not exist as a separate chamber, but its homolog persists as a sino-auricular (s-a) node on the wall of the auricle serving the body proper.

The mammalian heart is illustrated in diagrammatic form in Figure 4. It consists of four chambers: two auricles and two ventricles. The blood from all the body except the lungs enters the right auricle. It is forced from there into the right ventricle, then into the lungs and back to the left auricle. From there it is forced into the left ventricle and finally through the aorta to all arteries of the body except those going to the

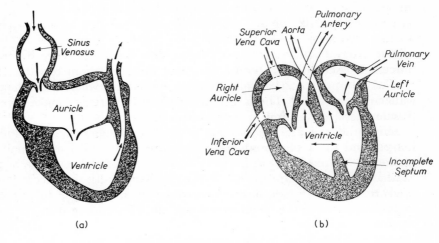

Figure 3. Diagrams of fish and reptile hearts.   (a) Fish heart.
The muscular walls develop successively higher pressures in the
sinus venosus, auricle, and finally ventricle.   (b) Reptile heart.
Note the incomplete septum allowing mixing of blood from
both auricles within the ventricle.

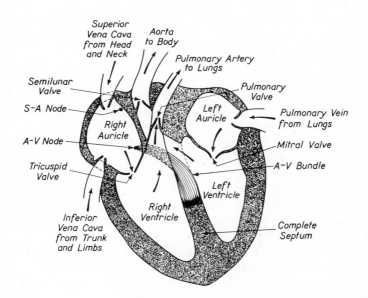

Figure 4. Diagram of the human heart.   Arrows show direction of blood flow.

lungs.   Thus, the blood in a complete circuit goes through the heart twice, once through the left side and once through the right side.   This system is highly efficient in supplying oxygen and removing carbon dioxide, for all the blood passes through the lungs on each trip around the circulatory system.

The walls of the heart consist primarily of muscle tissue.   As in all other striated muscles, the fiber membranes are normally polarized, the inside being 90 mv negative relative to the outside.   Just before contraction occurs, an action current passes over the membrane, reversing its polarity for a short period of time.   The form and nature of these action currents are similar to those of nerve fibers discussed in Chapter 4. The large mass of fibers contracting simultaneously in the heart effectively acts as a large number of electric cells, all in parallel, and each with a high internal impedance.   Although the net current from each fiber is small, the current from the entire muscle is appreciable, giving rise to measurable potential changes on the body surface.

4. The Heart Sequence

A. Over-all Sequence

The mammalian heart pumps blood with uniform sequence which repeats each beat.   First the auricles contract, forcing blood through the auriculoventricular (a-v) valves into the ventricles.   Then the ventricles contract.   This shuts the a-v valves and opens the semilunar and pulmonary valves.   As the ventricles continue to contract, blood is forced into the aorta and pulmonary arteries.   Finally, as the ventricles relax, the semilunar and pulmonary valves close.   The entire sequence is presented in more detail in Figure 5, which shows, with a common time base, the auricular pressure, the ventricular pressure, the aortic pressure, and the ventricular volume for a human heart.   Also, on the same base are shown the electrocardiograph (ekg) record and the sonograph record of a microphone placed against the chest.   Heart pressures have been measured directly in both man and animals.   The ventricular volumes have been found by X-ray techniques.

From the diagram, it is clear that the blood flows from the ventricle into the aorta only during a small part of the cycle.   While this is happening, the ventricular volume falls to a minimum value, but the pressure remains close to its maximum.   Likewise, an examination of the figure shows that the valves open and shut as the direction of the pressure difference across them changes.   The sonograph obtained by putting a broad-band microphone on the chest is strikingly different from what a

person hears through a stethoscope.   The two can be made quite similar
by differentiating the sonograph output twice.

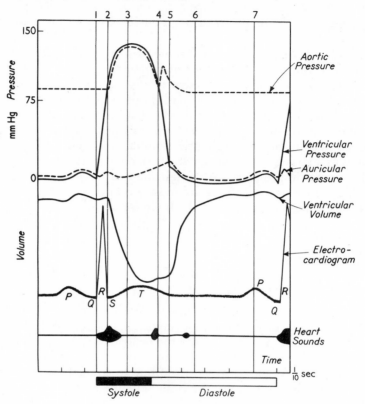

Figure 5. Pressure sequences in the left side of the heart.   The
significance of the vertical lines is as follows: 1. the mitral valve
closes; 2. the semilunar valve opens; 3. the systolic pressure
reaches a maximum; 4. the semilunar valve closes; 5. the mitral
valve opens; 6. end of heart sound; and 7. the auricle starts to
contract.   After C. H. Best and N. B. Taylor, *The Physiological
Basis of Medical Practice*, 7th ed.   (Baltimore, Md.: Williams
and Wilkins Company, 1961).

B. Electrical Events

The heart pulses rhythmically and with a definite sequence.   The beat
is initiated at the sino-auricular (s-a) node, shown in Figure 4.   The
node acts in a fashion similar to a relaxation oscillator putting out an
electrical pulse (about every $\frac{1}{78}$ of a minute in man).   This pulse spreads

in all directions as an electrochemical impulse over the surface of the auricle, causing the muscle fibers to contract. When two pulses reach the opposite side of the auricle from two directions, they annihilate each other because the contracted muscle will not conduct another impulse.

Besides causing the auricle to contract, the electrochemical pulse, originating at the s-a node, also stimulates the auriculo-ventricular (a-v) node (see Figure 4). This node, after a short time delay of about 0.1 sec or slightly less, puts out a new electrical pulse which is conducted down a special group of fibers called the *a-v bundle*, diagrammatically illustrated in Figure 4. These fibers terminate in the central muscular wall between the two ventricles. From these terminals, the pulse spreads over the walls of the ventricles causing them to contract.

The s-a node resembles a free-running electronic multivibrator controlling a second multivibrator, the a-v node, which in turn controls a third multivibrator, the ventricle itself. Many factors suggest this analogy. The fundamental rate of the s-a node can be varied by two different sets of nerves which act to speed or slow the rate of firing of the s-a node. This is analogous to tuning either the resistance or the capacity of a free-running multivibrator.

In some cases, the s-a node fails. Then the a-v node takes over control of the heart. The auricular contraction is no longer properly synchronized with the ventricular action, but this is by no means fatal. The a-v node behaves as an electrical multivibrator synchronized by pulses from the s-a node. When free-running, it has a slower firing rate (about 50 beats per min in man).

If the a-v node also fails, the heart neither stops, nor does the animal die. Rather, the auricular and ventricular walls take over control directly. Their free-running rate is still slower (about 30 beats per min in man). The ventricles and auricles are then completely independent in their times of contractions. On the average, the auricular beat then interferes with, rather than promotes, circulation.

The cardiac muscle fibers, like skeletal-muscle and nerve fibers, have a resting potential around 90 mv, the outside being positive relative to the inside. As in skeletal-muscle and nerve fibers, the action potentials are about 120 mv; that is, the outside is 30 mv negative relative to the inside at the peak of the spike. All three types of fibers are also similar in that the concentration of potassium ions is much higher within the cell than in the surrounding medium, whereas the sodium ion concentrations are just the reverse.

The cardiac muscle fibers differ markedly from skeletal muscle and nerve fibers in the kinetics of the recovery to the resting potential. In the largest mammalian nerve axons, this takes a fraction of a millisecond. In smaller nerve axons and skeletal muscle fibers, the recovery period is

2–5 msec.   By contrast, some cardiac muscle fibers take as long as 200 msec to recover their resting potential.   This period of time is comparable to the period of contraction of the ventricle.

A closely related property is the recovery of the normal low net permeability to potassium ions.   When the resting potential of a voltage-clamped squid axon is suddenly decreased, the net permeability to potassium ions rises rapidly and then falls.   The cardiac muscle cells, in contrast, do not recover their original impermeability to potassium until after the membrane potential returns to its original value.

Like nerve and skeletal muscle, cardiac muscle exhibits a so-called "positive after potential," during which time the resting potential is greater in magnitude, around 100 mv instead of 90 mv, the outside being positive relative to the inside.   The after potential may last close to 500 msec before it is completely abolished.   (The U-wave of the electrocardiogram appears about at the height of the positive after potential. The U-wave is very small; it barely shows on the diagram in Figure 5.)

The exact roles played by potassium and sodium ions in the resting and action potentials of cardiac muscle are not known.   Nonetheless, all experiments indicate that, except for time constants, and perhaps some absolute values, the electrical behavior of cardiac muscle is very similar to that of squid axons discussed in Chapters 4 and 24.

C. Energy

Each time the heart beats, it converts chemical energy into hydrodynamic energy.   The rate of work, that is, power, expended by the heart varies with the activity of the organism.   At rest, both the heart output per beat and the number of beats per minute are comparatively low.   During strenuous exertion, both increase.   The work done at each beat is of two types, kinetic and potential (compare Equation 1, p. 159).   Because the aorta is on the same level as the heart, the potential energy is purely hydrostatic.   Thus, from Equation 1, the work per milliliter is

$$H = \tfrac{1}{2}\rho v^2 + p \tag{2}$$

If q is the volume per stroke, then the work w per stroke is

$$w = q\,H = \tfrac{1}{2}\rho q \overline{v^2} + \bar{p}q \tag{3}$$

where the bar indicates average values.

Of even greater interest is the power Π developed by the heart.   To find this, one must replace the stroke volume q by the volume rate of flow Q (also called the heart output).   Including the contribution of both halves of the heart leads to the expression

$$\Pi = \bar{p}_R Q + \bar{p}_L Q + \tfrac{1}{2}\rho \overline{v_R^2} Q + \tfrac{1}{2}\rho \overline{v_L^2} Q \tag{4}$$

The subscripts refer to the right and left halves. Because the system is closed, Q is the same for both.

Equation 4 is exact and involves no approximations. It is the hydro-dynamic power delivered by the heart. For humans, one may simplify Equation 4 by several approximations. The velocities in the aorta and pulmonary artery are about the same, whereas the aortic pressure is sixfold greater. Hence, one may write

$$\Pi \doteq \tfrac{7}{6} p_L Q + \rho \overline{v_L^2} Q \tag{5}$$

Because blood leaves the ventricles during only a small part of each cycle (see Figure 5), the mean square velocity $\overline{v^2}$ will be very different from the square of the average velocity $(\bar{v})^2$. For humans, it has been found that

$$\overline{v^2} = 3.5(\bar{v})^2$$

The average volume velocity Q must be equal to the cross section A of the aorta times the average linear velocity v, that is

$$\bar{v} = \frac{Q}{A}$$

Substituting these into Equation 5 leads to the following formula for the power developed by the human heart

$$\Pi \doteq \tfrac{7}{6} p_L Q + \frac{3.5\rho Q^3}{A^2} \tag{6}$$

It is instructive to substitute a few numbers in this formula. Some typical human values are

At rest	*Active*	*Both*
p = 100 mm of Hg	p = 100 mm of Hg	A = 0.81 cm²
Q = 3.5 l/min	Q = 35 l/min	ρ = 1 gm/ml

Converting to mks units and substituting in Equation 6 gives

	At rest	*Active*		
$\tfrac{7}{6} p_L Q$	1.0 w	10 w	—	"hydrostatic" power
$\dfrac{3.5\rho Q^3}{A^2}$	0.13 w	130 w	—	"kinetic" power
Π	1.1 w	140 w	—	total heart power

It should be noted that for the human at rest the kinetic energy delivered to the blood is negligible, whereas during vigorous exercise it is the major type of hydrodynamic energy.

5. Electrocardiography

Every time the heart beats, electrical potential changes occur within it. These potentials spread to the surface of the body. Electrodes at almost any pair of points on the surface of the body will show potential differences related in time to the heartbeat. A record of these potential differences is called an *electrocardiogram*; the recording equipment is an *electrocardiograph*. The recording equipment and the records are often indicated by the abbreviations ekg or ecg.

Electrical changes at the surface of the heart were first demonstrated in 1856. Electrocardiography, the science of measuring the associated potentials, did not really develop until physical instrumentation made possible the detection of these small potentials. The first big step was the application of the string galvanometer to electrocardiography in 1903. This was the work of Einthoven, whose ideas dominated the field for many years. Today, all electrocardiographs depend on the action of electronic amplifiers. In this field, as is the case in so many others, the rapid advances have resulted from the widespread application of electronic techniques. The electrocardiogram is used in many clinical diagnoses of heart ailments. It is widely used because of its convenience and also because of the large amount of information which can be obtained without any surgical procedures or any discomfort to the patient.

The electrocardiogram is a record of electrical potential differences at the surface of the body. The heart, however, is not the only source of potentials at the body surface; it is necessary to distinguish between those potentials due to the heart and those originating from other organs. Every muscle within the body undergoes potential changes as its fibers contract. The magnitude of the action potentials for all nerves and all muscle fibers is about 120 mv. The motion of any skeletal muscle can give rise to body-surface potential differences comparable to the ekg potentials. To limit this source of distortion, the ekg is often recorded with the patient lying down.

In addition to potentials of muscular origin, there are also d-c body surface potentials. These exist between the two hands, the hands and the feet, and so forth, and may be as large as 0.1 mv. These potentials can be eliminated by suitable electronic design of the recording apparatus. (It is interesting to note parenthetically that the origin of these d-c potentials is not well understood. The d-c potential between the two arms of many women shows a sharp maximum on one day during the middle of the menstrual cycle. At one time, it was believed that these were associated with ovulation, but the correlation is very poor.)

The ekg potentials can be observed between almost any pair of points on the surface of the human body. If the two points are reasonably separated, the maximum potential difference observed is of the order of 1.0 mv. The ekg has the same period as the heart. Traditionally, three wires were attached to the subject, one to each arm, and the third to the left leg. The ekg was then recorded between the members of each of the three resulting pairs of leads.

Whether the electrocardiogram is recorded between two points on the surface of the body or between one point and a neutral electrode, it

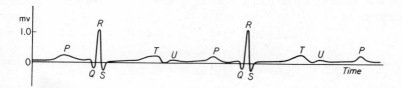

Figure 6. A typical ekg. *P* wave precedes auricular contraction and *QRS* complex is associated with ventricular contraction. Exact height of wave depends on lead used.

always has the shape shown in Figure 6. The neutral electrode can be formed by immersing the subject in a tub of water and placing the electrode far from the body. Provided low resistance electrodes are used, the curve will always have the general shape shown.

The various bumps on the ekg are called *waves*. The P-wave occurs just before auricular contraction. The QRS-complex is associated with the start of ventricular contraction, and the T-wave occurs at the end of ventricular contraction. The amplitude of the ekg waves is shown in the table on page 170. In addition, a smaller U-wave follows the T-wave after ventricular relaxation.

Most frequently, electrodes are placed on both arms and on the left foot, and quite commonly are also placed on the back and on the chest. The ekg's are usually described in terms of *leads*, which means the potential difference between two points. This is confusing terminology because two wires, each ordinarily called a lead, are necessary for one ekg lead.

TABLE I

Normal Human Electrocardiogram Patterns

EKG interval	Amplitude in millivolts	Duration in seconds	Relationship to heart cycle (Figure 5)
P	0.1	0.008	Precedes auricular contraction by about 0.02 sec
P–Q	0.0	0.15–0.20	A–V delay time
Q	0.1	0.04–0.08	
R	1.0	0.04–0.08	Precedes ventricular contraction
S	0.1		
S–T	0.0	0.1 –0.25	Ventricular ejection
T	0.1	0.1	Follows ventricular relaxation
T–P	0.0	0.3	Diastole

In ekg terminology, the potential differences in the three leads are numbered as

$$\text{Lead I} : V_I = V_L - V_R$$
$$\text{Lead II} : V_{II} = V_F - V_R$$
$$\text{Lead III}: V_{III} = V_F - V_L$$

$$(7)$$

where L, R, and F refer to the left arm, right arm, and foot, respectively, and the potentials with the three subscripts refer to the values between these points and a neutral electrode. Elementary algebra reduces these three equations to

$$V_{II} = V_{III} + V_I \qquad (8)$$

that is, if any two of the three "standard" leads are measured the third is thereby determined. This seems trivial, and probably did also to Einthoven, who first pointed it out, but physiologists have dignified Equation 8 by the name "Einthoven's law."

In the following sections of this chapter, the heart is approximated by an equivalent dipole. This equivalent dipole is constant for the QRS-complex and is similar for the P- and T-waves. On the cellular level, the heart cannot be regarded as a mere dipole. It was noted in the last section that at the start of every heartbeat, an electrical spike potential originates at the s-a node and spreads out in all directions over the auricle. Thereafter, the a-v node emits a pulse which travels as a spike potential down the Purkinje fibers of the auriculoventricular bundle of His to initiate a contraction of the muscle fibers of the septum between the two ventricles. The spike potential travels down around the septum and then up the outer sides of the ventricles. In every region, the appearance of the spike potential is followed by a contraction. The spread of the spike potential over the ventricle takes about 60 msec. As it starts down the interventricular septum, the Q-wave appears on the electrocardiogram recorded at the surface of the body. The R-wave coincides roughly with the spike reaching the bottom (apex) of the heart and starting up the outer ventricular walls. The S-wave appears as the spike potential reaches the top of the ventricle.

6. Physics of Dipoles

Einthoven stated that if the three lead voltages given in Equation 7 were represented as vectors directed along the sides of an equilateral triangle, all three could be represented as the projections of a single vector on this triangle. As is seen in Figure 7, this follows for any set of voltages.

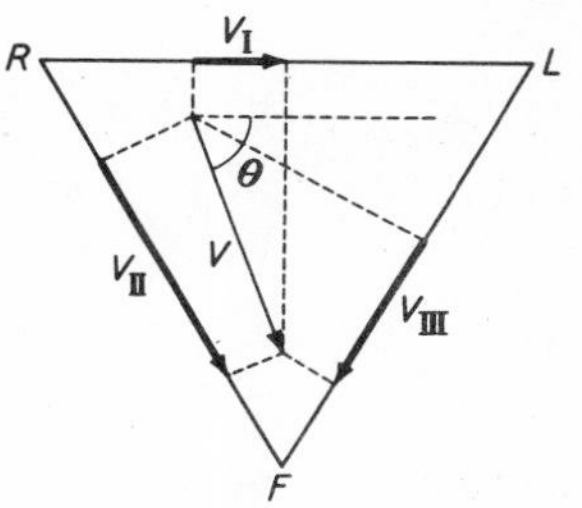

Although this procedure can be carried out for any three points, it has significance only if the resulting vector V indicates or is related to the axis of the heart. The use of an equilateral triangle is based on the assumption that the three points chosen are electrically equidistant from the heart. If this is the case, one should find that

$$V_C = \tfrac{1}{3}(V_L + V_R + V_F) = 0 \qquad (9)$$

Figure 7. Einthoven's triangle. From the figure it can be shown that $V_I = V \cos \theta$; $V_{II} = V \cos (60° - \theta)$ $= \tfrac{1}{2}V \cos \theta + \tfrac{1}{2}\sqrt{2}V \sin \theta$; $V_{III} = V \cos (120° - \theta) =$ $-\tfrac{1}{2}V \cos \theta + \tfrac{1}{2}\sqrt{2}V \sin \theta$; $\therefore V_{II} = V_{III} + V_I.$

Albeit this is hard to test because "neutral" electrodes are never truly neutral, the preceding condition is approximately satisfied. However, it is far from exact.

To obtain three-dimensional information, a fourth electrode is placed on the back or chest. Its voltage, relative to a neutral electrode, is designated by V_B. The ekg "lead" voltage V_{IV} is given by

$$V_{IV} = V_B - V_C$$

where V_C is an approximately neutral lead formed as above. V_{IV} tends to show up heart abnormalities in front or back of the midline of the heart, whereas the first three ekg leads tend to de-emphasize this type of abnormality.

To develop a more precise picture of the basis of the electrocardiogram, it is helpful to be familiar with electrical theory of a more advanced nature. This theory of current sources in a conducting medium is presented in this section. Those whose mathematical background does not include differential equations are advised to omit the remainder of this section and to accept certain statements in the next section as a matter of faith.

The heart behaves as a group of current sources in a finite conducting medium.   A current source is an emf whose internal resistance is much

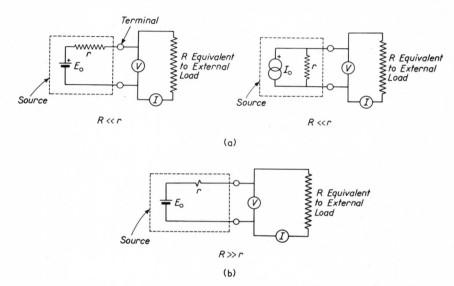

Figure 8. (a) Current source. Two equivalent forms are shown.   In either case, if $r \gg R$, the current source approximations can be made, namely,

$$I \doteq I_0 \equiv E_0/r$$
$$V \doteq RI_0$$

Thus V and I are determined by I_0 and the load.   (b) Voltage source.   If $r \ll R$, the voltage source approximations can be made, namely,

$$I \doteq E_0/R$$
$$V \doteq E_0$$

Thus V and I are determined by E_0 and the load.

greater than the external load.   Thus, the external current will remain constant no matter how the external load is varied.   A current source is illustrated in Figure 8.   (A voltage source is one in which the internal resistance is so low that the terminal voltage will remain constant as the external load resistance is varied.)   The tissues surrounding the heart are electrically similar and comparatively low in impedance.   Because the heart muscle may be regarded as a group of current sources, the potential between any two external points will be the sum of the potentials due to each of the current sources acting independently. (This superposition theorem is not true for voltage sources.)

The potential due to a group of current sources in an infinite conducting medium can be used to find an approximation to the currents

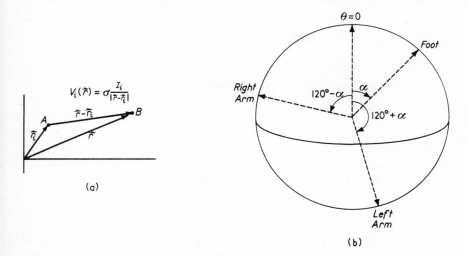

Figure 9. (a) Vector relationship for finding potential V_i due to current source I_i at A. (b) Geometrical relationship between heart dipole along $\theta = 0$ and arms and foot. This diagram is used in deriving the equations on page 175.

produced in the body by the heart. For convenience, the two terminals in Figure 8 will be treated as two sources, one positive and the other negative. Let the location of the ith current source be denoted by the vector distance $\vec{r_i}$ from the origin of the coordinate system as shown in Figure 9. Then the current due to this source, considered by itself, will spread throughout the medium giving rise to a potential $V_i(r)$ at the point $\vec{r}$ from the origin. Because there are no net charges in the medium, the potential V_i must obey the Laplacian equation

$$\nabla^2 V_i = 0$$

(This is shown in any electricity and magnetism text.)

Because the tissues have a finite conductivity γ there will be a current density $\vec{J_i}$ throughout the medium originating from the ith current source

$$\vec{J_i} = \gamma \vec{\nabla} V_i$$

This is a special case of Ohm's law. The unique solution choosing $V = 0$ at infinity is

$$V(r) = \sum_{i=1}^{n} \frac{I_i}{\gamma|\vec{r} - \vec{r}_i|}$$

This may be expanded in a series in $1/r$. Expanding, one obtains

$$V(r) = \frac{1}{\gamma r}\sum I_i + \frac{1}{\gamma r^3}(\sum I_i \vec{r}_i) \cdot \vec{r} + \frac{1}{2\gamma r^5}\sum I_i [3(\vec{r}_i \cdot \vec{r})^2 - (\vec{r} \cdot \vec{r})^2] + \cdots$$

Because no net charge enters or leaves the heart, the first sum is zero. The second sum is called the dipole moment, $\vec{p}$; that is

$$\vec{p} = \sum_{i}^{n} I_i \vec{r}_i$$

A first approximation to the potential due to current sources in an infinite conducting medium is to replace them by an equivalent dipole $\vec{p}$. The potential at r (referred to $V = 0$ at infinity) is

$$V(r) \doteq \frac{\vec{p} \cdot \vec{r}}{\gamma r^3}$$

The preceding expression was obtained for an infinite medium. If one restricts the heart to a sphere of radius R, a somewhat more complex expression is necessary. Consider the equivalent dipole $\vec{p}$ located at the center of a sphere and oriented along the $\theta = 0$ axis of the sphere. In this case

$$\vec{p} \cdot \vec{r} = pr \cos \theta$$

At small values of r, the potential must approach that of a dipole in an infinite medium, namely

$$V \to \frac{p \cos \theta}{\gamma r^2} \qquad \text{as} \qquad r \to 0$$

whereas at the surface, the radial current must be zero, so that

$$\frac{\partial V}{\partial r} = 0 \qquad \text{at} \qquad r = R$$

The unique solution to this approximation is

$$V = \frac{p \cos \theta}{\gamma} \left(\frac{1}{r^2} + \frac{2r}{R^3} \right)$$

which, at the surface of the sphere, reduces to

$$V(R) = \frac{3p \cos \theta}{\gamma R^2} \tag{10}$$

This is clearly only an approximation but is useful in describing the electrocardiogram.

Equation 10 may be applied directly to the standard ekg leads. If the line to the foot makes an angle a with the heart vector, then the right arm is located at $\theta = a + 120°$ and the left at $\theta = a - 120°$ as shown in Figure 9. Therefore, the three voltages, V_L, V_R, and V_F, should be

$$V_L = \frac{3P}{\gamma} \frac{\cos (a - 120°)}{R^2}$$

$$V_R = \frac{3P}{\gamma} \frac{\cos (a + 120°)}{R^2}$$

$$V_F = \frac{3P}{\gamma} \frac{\cos a}{R^2}$$

The three lead voltages may be found by the appropriate differences, and the validity of Equations 8 and 9 can be noted. Thus, the Einthoven triangle is as valid as the spherical approximation with a dipole current source.

Clearly, the representation as a dipole is misleading and at best an approximation. The standard ekg leads are not necessarily the best ones. Various attempts to improve these are discussed in Section 8. Nonetheless, the four or five leads (including both chest and back) have been used for most clinical and diagnostic purposes.

7. Vector Electrocardiography

In attempts to increase the information obtained from the electro-cardiogram, various schemes have been developed. The most success-ful, called *vectorcardiography*, records the magnitude, location, and spatial orientation of the equivalent heart dipole as a function of time. As has been pointed out, the physical relationship between the equivalent dipole and the cellular events in the heart is not in any way obvious. The abnormalities producing a given change in the heart potentials cannot be logically related to the change in many instances. In spite of the inability to logically interpret the vector electrocardiogram, it can still form a powerful diagnostic tool for clinical work. The equiva-lent dipole is referred to as the heart vector. The rationale behind these systems is presented in this section.

Calculations, confirmed by model experiments, show that the use of the four standard ekg leads could give rise to very erroneous interpreta-tions of the location and orientation of the heart vector for hearts as eccentric[2] as those occurring in normal humans. When one adds to this the effects of the nonspherical shape of the human body, it seems very reasonable that the use of the four standard leads loses a great deal of the available information.

An integral part of vector electrocardiography is the equivalent dipole or heart vector. The discussion in the last section illustrated that a net dipole is the first approximation to any distribution of current sources whose net sum is zero. There are an infinite number of distributions which have the same vector dipole as a first approximation. It is in no way obvious that the heart should be well represented by the dipole approximation. Two different types of experiments, which have shown that this approximation is almost as good as the experimental data, are discussed in the following paragraphs.

Let the heart vector be denoted by $\vec{p}$. It is conventional to represent this as a sum of three vectors directed along the cartesian axes. One may write

$$p = p_x \vec{i} + p_y \vec{j} + p_z \vec{k}$$

where the subscripts refer to the scalar components of $\vec{p}$, and $\vec{i}, \vec{j}$, and $\vec{k}$ are unit vectors directed along the x, y, and z axes. Then at any point on the periphery, the voltage V (relative to ground) may be written as a linear sum of the three components of the heart vector; that is to say

$$V = \alpha p_x + \beta p_x + \eta p_z$$

In general, the three constants α, β, η will depend on the location of the dipole, the location of the observation point, and the shape of the torso. The three quantities α, β, η will be constant for the entire QRS-complex if the heart can be represented as a dipole.

If V is measured at four points, one may write four equations

$$V_1 = \alpha_1 p_x + \beta_1 p_y + \eta_1 p_z$$
$$V_2 = \alpha_2 p_x + \beta_2 p_y + \eta_2 p_z$$
$$V_3 = \alpha_3 p_x + \beta_3 p_y + \eta_3 p_z$$
$$V_4 = \alpha_4 p_x + \beta_4 p_y + \eta_4 p_z$$

These may be regarded as four nonhomogeneous, linear equations in the three unknowns p_x, p_y, and p_z. For most sets of the (α, β, η)'s and the V's, there are no consistent solutions for p_x, p_y, and p_z. If, however, the heart vector is a good approximation, the fourth equation should be a linear combination of the first three. This, then, is a simple, unambiguous test of the dipole approximation.

Measurements on humans in which four pairs of wires are used, that is, four independent leads, have shown that the QRS-complex can be

[2] Eccentric here means displaced from the vertical and horizontal center of the torso.

fitted very well by an equivalent dipole for a variety of different sets of points. The P- and T-waves of the ekg definitely cannot be described by the same dipole. Moreover, although the error in fitting V_4 with a linear combination of V_1, V_2, and V_3 is small, it is definitely larger than experimental error.

Another test of the dipole approximation is that of mirror images. For the central dipole in a sphere, discussed in Section 7, the equator of the sphere is a zero potential line. Any two points equidistant from the equator will have potentials which are equal in magnitude but opposite in sign. They are called *mirror points*. For the human torso (or indeed even for a cylinder with an eccentric dipole), the zero potential line is not an anatomically or geometrically obvious feature. Nonetheless, it could be located by finding mirror images if (and only if) the dipole approximation is a good one. Experiments have revealed the existence of a mirror point for the QRS-complex at any arbitrary point on the torso. This also confirms the validity of the dipole approximation. The data are good enough to show the best mirror points are not perfect mirror points. However, the errors are too small to compute a meaningful quadrupole moment.

In practice, the heart vector can be found by two different methods. If one wishes to determine the position of the heart vector in an individual, a lengthy series of determinations of mirror points is sufficient. The other alternative is to use a combination of a series of leads that allows one to compute magnitude and direction of the heart vector without knowing its location. Only the latter seems practical for any clinical purpose.

Several persons have set up systems of linear combinations of five to 16 points of contact with the torso. The aim is to arrive at a set of points which is independent of the exact body shape or the location of the heart but which reveals the direction and magnitude of the heart vector. These "orthogonal" systems have been increasingly successful in recent years.

The success of an equivalent dipole representation of the QRS-complex seems both fortuitous and unfortunate. It implies that the ekg information obtainable from separate parts of the heart is very slight. The validity of the dipole approximation implies that one can measure an average which reflects solely the properties of the heart, but one cannot distinguish individual regions within the heart.

8. Summary

The heart is a large mass of muscle which pumps blood through the vertebrate circulatory system.   Its physical activity may be described in terms of the velocities and pressures acquired by the blood at various points of the circulatory system and also in terms of the power expended. The heart not only does work but also contains tissues which produce periodic beats in a fashion similar to that of a series of electronic multivibrators.   The firing rate of the normal control element, the s-a node, can be increased or decreased both by the nervous system and by certain hormones.

Like the fibers of all striated muscle, the heart fibers are traversed by a spike potential before contraction.   These spike potentials appear as current sources immersed in the surrounding fluid.   The resulting body surface potentials are called *electrocardiographic potentials*.   These are of such a form that the heart may be well approximated by a single dipole. Systems to find the orientation and magnitude of best equivalent dipole are called *vectorcardiography*.   Although clinically useful and challenging to the imagination of the physicist, the equivalent heart dipole seems to lack any basic relationship to the heart itself.

REFERENCES

1. The following monograph is very complete and well worth reading by anyone wishing to pursue the subject in detail.   A large part of the material in this chapter is based on it.

Whitelock, O. v. S., ed., "The Electrophysiology of the Heart," *Ann. New York Acad. Sc.* **65**: 653–1145 (Aug. 1957).

2. Best, C. H., and N. B. Taylor, *The Physiological Basis of Medical Practice* (Baltimore, Maryland: Williams & Wilkins Company), 7th ed., 1961.

Read the chapters on the heart and circulatory system.

3. Glasser, Otto, ed., *Medical Physics* (Chicago, Illinois: Year Book Publishers, Inc., 1950) Vol. 2.

    a. Hamilton, W. F., "Circulatory System: Arterial Pulse," pp. 186–188.

    b. King, A. L., "Circulatory System: Arterial Pulse; Wave Velocity," pp. 188–191.

    c. Hamilton, W. F., "Circulatory System: Heart Output," pp. 191–194.

    d. Landowne, M., and L. N. Katz, "Circulatory System: Heart; Work and Failure," pp. 194–206.

    e. Green, H. D., "Circulatory System: Methods," pp. 208–222.

    f. Nickerson, J. L., "Circulatory System: Methods; Ballistocardiograph," pp. 222–225.

    g. Jochim, K. E., "Circulatory System: Methods; Electromagnetic Flowmeter," pp. 225–228.

    h. Green, H. D., "Circulatory System: Physical Principles," pp. 228–251.

4. Johnston, F. D., "Electrocardiography," *Medical Physics*, Otto Glasser, ed. (Chicago, Illinois: Year Book Publishers, Inc., 1944) Vol. 1, pp. 352–361.
5. Schmitt, O. H., and Ernst Simonson, "The Present Status of Vector-cardiography," *Arch. Int. Med.* **96**: 574–590 (Nov. 1955).

DISCUSSION QUESTIONS—PART B

1. The cell wall of the alga *Nitella* conducts spike potentials similar to those found in nerve and muscle fibers. Describe the equipment necessary to test the dependence of spike height on K^+ concentration. What are the results of such experiments?

2. Some of the evidence for the activity of acetylcholine in nerves is based on studies of the electrical eels. Describe the electrical organ of *Torpedo*, in the terminology of anatomy, histology, electricity, and biochemistry.

3. The terms "spatial summation" and "temporal summation" are used to describe some of the phenomena called "synaptic computation" in Chapter 4. What is the experimental evidence which shows that these occur?

4. Describe how one can show that at the giant synapse in the crayfish, transsynaptic conduction is a purely electrical phenomena, whereas in the human spinal cord it is mediated by special transmitter substances.

5. The compound GABA, gamma aminobutyric acid, has been found to occur in large amounts in the central nervous system and to inhibit transsynaptic conduction. What is the evidence for its action? What is the relationship of GABA to the computation-like functions of the nervous system?

6. The feedback loops controlling the iris have been studied anatomically and from the point of view of a servomechanism. Describe both in more detail than given in the text. Most servomechanisms can be stimulated at their characteristic frequency and caused to oscillate. How was it demonstrated that iris control can be caused to oscillate in a similar fashion?

7. What is an autocorrelator? What is the relationship between the autocorrelation function and the Fourier transform? Use this to demonstrate why the autocorrelator is useful for electroencephalographic studies.

8. What special precautions must be taken in constructing electroencephalographic amplifiers? Describe a practical electronic circuit for such an amplifier and analyze its action.

9. Various mathematical theories have been proposed to describe the motion of the cochlea. Describe the essential features of the theory developed by Fletcher. Be sure to note all approximations which have been made.

10. What is known about the lateral line organs of fish?

11. Many moths have only a limited number of nerve fibers associated with their hearing organs. What is the evidence that only these fibers are active? How might one try to reconcile this with the moth's ability to avoid bats?

12. Describe a recent experiment using arm analogs of the cochlea to study hearing.

13. One method of studying visual systems is to "drive" the eye with a flashing light. Describe the ability to follow as a function of frequency of: the retinal potentials; the potentials in the optic nerve; the nerve potentials in the midbrain; and the cortical potentials.

14. Sketch the anatomical features of the visual system of *limulus*. Describe in more detail the type of experiment summarized in Figure 4 of Chapter 7. Include descriptions of the light source, light-intensity measurements, preparation of nerve fibers, measuring equipment, and conclusions reached.

15. The electrical potentials of the eyeball are sometimes referred to as electroretinograms. Describe the magnitude of the potentials obtained and their time dependence. Illustrate their use with a detailed description of one experiment depending on electroretinograms.

16. The experiments of Land on color vision in a heterochromatic field are reviewed briefly in Chapter 7. Expand this discussion, emphasizing its significance for theories of color vision.

17. Ramsey has used single muscle fibers for studies of their mechanical properties. How does he prepare these fibers? Compare his results with those for whole, excised muscles.

18. The various types of heat produced during muscular contraction are described briefly in Chapter 8. Expand on this description; include equipment necessary to make the measurements, the type of raw data obtained, and their interpretation.

19. Contrast the resting and action potentials of various forms of skeletal muscle, cardiac muscle, of nerves, and of the alga *Nitella*. Include magnitude of the potentials, time course of the spike, and dependence on ionic concentrations.

20. Illustrate the changes in the thick and thin filaments during muscular contraction in terms of the model of A. F. Huxley. Show what type of electron-microscope pictures would be expected for longitudinal sections, for transverse sections at various points along the myofibrillar unit, and for several oblique sections.

21. Ballistocardiography consists of measuring the reaction of the body to the thrust of the heart on the blood. How are ballistocardiographs constructed? What does a typical record look like? How is it related to the electrocardiogram?

22. The heart rate is controlled by two sets of nerves. These in turn are activated by centers in the central nervous system in response to impulses from certain pressure-sensitive and O_2/CO_2-sensitive organs. Fill in the anatomical details to the extent they are known. Represent the over-all system, in block diagram form, as interlocking negative feedback loops.

23. Abnormalities in the electrocardiogram are used to diagnose many heart disorders.   What are several types of pathological conditions which alter the electrocardiogram?   How is the electrocardiogram changed?

24. Pressure pulses are transmitted along the arterial walls for each heartbeat.   These travel at a much greater rate than the blood.   Outline the theory describing this transmission in tubes with viscoelastic walls and filled with an ideal fluid.

25. Newtonian fluids have coefficients of viscosity which are independent of fluid velocity in streamline flow.   Describe the experiments which show that blood is non-newtonian.   Characterize its viscosity.

C

Physical Microbiology

Introduction to Part C

This section of the text deals with the physical properties of cells and groups of cells as revealed by various biophysical studies. The first chapter of Part C, Chapter 10, describes cellular events produced by ionizing radiations. This topic is continued in Part D, Chapter 16, "Molecular Action of Ionizing Radiations." Some scientists consider the material in these two chapters as synonymous with biophysics, whereas others feel that the effects of ionizing radiations should not even be considered as part of biophysics. The emphasis, in Chapter 10, has been placed on the use of ionizing radiations to study the fundamental properties of biological systems.

Not all radiations are damaging. In Chapter 11, the physical properties of cells and of groups of cells revealed by nondestructive electromagnetic and ultrasonic irradiation are discussed. This is followed by two chapters dealing with the effects of high intensity ultrasound; the second of these two, Chapter 13, illustrates one of the areas in which advanced mathematical training is helpful.

The last chapter of Part C is a description of the physico-chemical properties of virus particles. Such particles lie between biological cells and molecules in their complexity and in their physical and chemical properties. The discussion of virus particles is intermediate between the other topics of Part C and the contents of Part D.

IO

Cellular Events Produced by Ionizing Radiations

I. Ionizing Radiation as a Biological Tool

Possible radioactive fallout from tests of atomic bombs is an international concern; all nations realize that radiation from fallout has deleterious effects on human beings. Such radiation damage is unique neither to fallout nor to humans. A number of different types of radiations give rise to similar changes in all living systems. These effects result from ionizations occurring within the living cells. Radiations producing ionization include alpha, beta, and gamma rays; neutrons; protons; deuterons; and X rays. Similar cellular changes can also be produced by ultraviolet irradiation.

A number of complicated responses follow the exposure of the human body, or for that matter, of any vertebrate or higher plant, to ionizing radiations. These responses may be divided into two types: somatic or body effects which occur in the individual, and genetic effects which are transmitted to future generations. The somatic responses in humans include such phenomena as loss of hair; skin disorders; dysfunction of the systems manufacturing blood cells; complete destruction of certain tissues; and induction of malignant growths. The entire subject of somatic responses to ionizing radiations is very complex; empirical knowledge extends beyond that which can be explained in terms of the basic cellular events. No attempt is made in this text to describe the details of the responses of complex organisms to ionizing radiation. Rather, in this chapter, the cellular events are emphasized. These in turn can be described in terms of molecular phenomena, the presentation of which comprises Chapter 16. Genetic effects, in contrast to the somatic ones, occur originally in only one cell, even in higher plants and animals. These genetic effects are also discussed in this chapter.

Ionizing radiations are destructive to living cells. In most cases, this

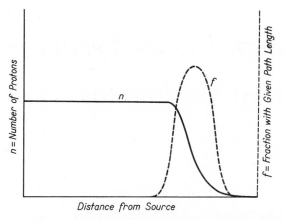

Figure 1. The attenuation of a proton beam passing through tissue.

destruction is undesirable to humans. However, in controlled laboratory experiments, the effect of ionizing radiations can be used to study the organization of the biological cell. In particular, the effects of ionizing radiation are useful for studies of cellular division and of genetics. The use of ionizing radiation as a tool to study biological systems is emphasized in this text.

The various types of ionizing radiations and related subatomic particles are summarized in Appendix D, for the benefit of those unfamiliar with atomic physics. It is sufficient here to note that all these types produce ionization along their path. The heavier ones follow a straight path of definite length; the uniformity of this path length is illustrated by the graph in Figure 1. The lighter ionizing radiations cannot be described in terms of a definite path length, because the path lengths of the individual particles are widely varied. It is possible to determine a maximum distance of penetration such that the remaining energy is less than 1 per cent of the incident energy (or one may determine the distance at which the radiation has decreased to less than background).

It is often of greater biological importance to express the ionization than to detail the path length. The ionization is expressed in terms of dosage, but there is no generally accepted set of units. Instead, various dosage units are used. These are described in the following section.

2. Dosage

The effects of several different types of radiation can be described in terms of the ionization they produce. Historically, the oldest unit used to measure dosage was defined in terms of the ionization produced in air. This unit is called the *roentgen* and is abbreviated r. It is defined for X rays and γ rays as: "The roentgen ($1r$) is the quantity of X or gamma radiation . . . producing 1 esu of ions of either sign per 0.01293 gm of air." This mass of air, 0.01293 gm, occupies one ml at 0°C and 760 mm of Hg pressure. An alternate form is that $1r$ is the quantity of X or gamma radiation which loses 83.4 ergs/gm of air.[1]

To extend this definition to other types of radiation the following units have sometimes been used:

1 *rep* = (roentgen equivalent physical)—quantity of radiation, of any type, producing energy losses of 83.4 ergs/gm in water (or tissue).

1 *rem* = (roentgen equivalent man)—quantity of radiation, of any type, producing effects in man equivalent to $1r$ of X or gamma radiation. This unit depends on the specific effect in man used as the criterion.

1 *reb* = (roentgen equivalent biological)—same as rem except animals or plants may be used instead of man. Accordingly this is also an equivocal definition.

1 *rad* = quantity of radiation of any type producing energy losses of 100 ergs/gm of absorbing material. (For X and γ rays, $1r$ is between 1 rad and 1 rep.)

[1] The figure of 83 ergs/gm can be found by using the average energy loss of 32.5 electron-volts per ion pair in breaking a bond. This average value appears constant for all substances, although it is far above the dissociation energy of most bonds. The extra energy appears as kinetic energy of the ions formed and electronic excitation within the ions formed.

1 *nvt* = thermal neutron flux per cm^2 times time in seconds.

1 *Mdw/ct* = 3 × 10^{17} nvt.

1 pile unit = 10^{17} nvt plus associated gammas and fast neutrons.

These units are all used in the literature. The *r* was originally defined for X rays and is too firmly imbedded in medical terminology to be completely discarded. It would appear far more desirable to express dosage either in terms of energy loss per gram without extra symbols or in terms of the number of particles and their energy. The list of different dosage units is included here because they are all used to describe experiments in biophysics.

The ratio of the rem to the *r* is sometimes called the relative biological effectiveness, abbreviated *RBE*. The accompanying table gives some RBE factors. It should be repeated that these values will vary widely depending on the criterion used.

TABLE I

Some RBE Factors

Radiation	RBE
X	1
gamma	1
1.0 Mev beta particle	1
0.1 Mev beta particle	1.08
Thermal neutron	2–5
1.0 Mev proton	8.5
0.1 Mev proton	10
Fast neutron	10
5 Mev alpha	15
1 Mev alpha	20

Various committees have set up maximum permissible doses for persons working near radiation. The maximum permissible dose is defined as the highest level at which the probability of producing harmful somatic effects is so low that it cannot be measured. Over the course of years, various maximum permissible doses have been chosen. As more knowledge has been obtained, these have decreased steadily. Thus, from 1935 to 1947, an accumulated dose of 0.1 rem per day was considered permissible. This was then lowered to a maximum of 0.3 rem per week. In 1957, the maximum permissible dose was further lowered to 5 rem per year for each year over eighteen years of age. Even these levels might produce appreciable genetic damage and might give rise to malignant tumors. It seems likely that the maximum permissible doses will be further lowered in the future. These values are for whole-body irradiation of radiation workers. Levels for the entire population are set at one tenth those of radiation workers, on the assumption that genetic changes as well as somatic ones would be undetectable.

By 1960, radiation doses to the entire population included about 4 rem in thirty years from background, about 5 rem in thirty years from medical and dental sources, and about 0.3 rem from 1946–1959 from fall-out. The last-mentioned number will continue to increase. A further discussion of fall-out is included in Section 6.

3. Mitosis and Meiosis

Many of the abnormal cellular events resulting from ionization become apparent as a result of cellular division. To appreciate the significance of these alterations, it is necessary to be acquainted with the normal mechanisms of cell division. In most cells, this occurs in a series of characteristic steps called *mitosis*. This is modified in the formation of the cells of sexual reproduction (the sperm and egg cells) into a homologous series of steps referred to as *meiosis*. The major exceptions to the more or less universal nature of mitosis and meiosis are the bacteria which do not possess a clearly defined nucleus and divide in a less organized fashion.

Figure 2 illustrates the process of mitosis. The chromosomes within the cell nucleus are believed to carry most of the genetic information of the cell, controlling its form, metabolism, and function. However, as shown in Figure 2a, the chromosomes do not exist as such in the nucleus during most of the cell life. Rather, during the period between divisions they appear broken up into heavily staining birefringent granules called *chromatin material*. This portion of the cell life between divisions is called *interphase*.

As the cell prepares to divide, the chromatin material is organized into long filaments which pull together to form chromosomes. These are double filaments at this point in mitosis, which is called *prophase*. Simultaneously, a spindle starts to form, the nuclear membrane starts to dissolve, and the nucleoli disappear. This stage is shown in Figure 2b.

In the next stage, *metaphase*, the chromosomes attach at a specific point, the centromere (also called kinetochore), to the spindle, and line up at the center of the cell. As shown in Figure 2c, the nuclear membrane is completely gone.

The chromosomes then each pull apart into two separate fibers and follow the spindles to the cell centers. In the absence of a spindle (which results from certain types of irradiation), the chromosomes do not divide. The forces causing the chromosomes to adhere to the spindle at the centromere, to separate, and to migrate are not at all understood. The observed phenomena known as *anaphase* are shown in Figure 2d. Note that each half of the cell now has the same number and types of chromosomes as the original one in Figure 2b.

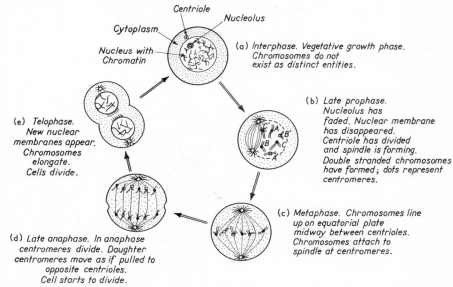

Figure 2. Diagrammatic outline of mitotic cycle. Each cell starts with two homologous chromosomes, distinguished in the diagram by showing their centromeres as dots and squares. Modified from *Life: An Introduction to Biology* by G. G. Simpson, C. S. P. Hendrigh, and L. H. Tiffany, © 1957, by Harcourt, Brace & World, Inc.

Finally, as illustrated in Figure 2e, new nuclear membranes form and the cell pinches in two during the final stage called *telophase*. If no spindle forms, each cell ends up with about half the original number of chromosomes and eventually dies. In normal mitosis, by contrast, one ends up with two duplicates of the original cell. These duplicates are sometimes referred to as daughter cells.

In the normal cells, the chromosomes occur as pairs. The two members of the pair have similar shapes and are believed to control the same characteristics. If the two members of the pair are not identical, one will be *dominant* for each character and the other *recessive*; the cell and the individual usually reflect only the dominant character. However, one chromosome will not be dominant for all the characteristics it controls.   During mitosis, each chromosome is split and, therefore, the daughter cells have the same character as the original cell.

During meiosis, however, the two homologous chromosomes line up together, entwine about one another, and then separate along the spindle to opposite poles.   Thus, the egg and sperm cells end up with half the number of chromosomes as the normal body cells.   This division is not completely random because each egg or sperm cell contains one member of each pair of chromosomes.   When the sperm fertilizes the egg cell, the normal number is re-formed.   Figure 3 illustrates diagrammatically the chromosome changes in meiosis.

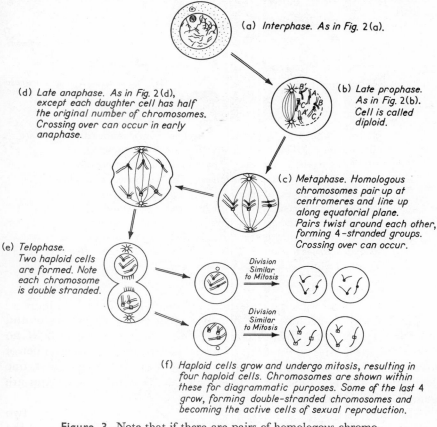

(a) *Interphase. As in Fig. 2(a).*

(d) *Late anaphase. As in Fig. 2(d), except each daughter cell has half the original number of chromosomes. Crossing over can occur in early anaphase.*

(b) *Late prophase. As in Fig. 2(b). Cell is called diploid.*

(c) *Metaphase. Homologous chromosomes pair up at centromeres and line up along equatorial plane. Pairs twist around each other, forming 4-stranded groups. Crossing over can occur.*

(e) *Telophase. Two haploid cells are formed. Note each chromosome is double stranded.*

Division Similar to Mitosis

Division Similar to Mitosis

(f) *Haploid cells grow and undergo mitosis, resulting in four haploid cells. Chromosomes are shown within these for diagrammatic purposes. Some of the last* 4 *grow, forming double-stranded chromosomes and becoming the active cells of sexual reproduction.*

Figure 3. Note that if there are pairs of homologous chromosomes, the cell is called diploid, whereas if there are only half this number of chromosomes, the cell is called haploid. For discussion of crossovers, see Figure 4.   Modified from *Life: An Introduction to Biology* by G. G. Simpsom, C. S. P. Hendrigh, and L. H. Tiffany, © 1957, by Harcourt, Brace & World, Inc.

By and large, the different characteristics are segregated during meiosis according to the member of the homologous pair on which they are located. However, occasionally pieces of the chromosomes break off during meiosis. The broken pieces then rejoin the same homologous pair, but often a part of chromosome A will join the remainder of A′ and vice versa. This breaking and re-forming is known as crossing over. This is hard to observe in animals which reproduce slowly, such as the large mammals, because crossing over is a rare event. However, in fruit flies, wasps, microorganisms, and viruses, the rate of reproduction is so large that the frequencies of crossing over between two loci can be accurately measured. Figure 4 shows a possible crossing over during meiosis.

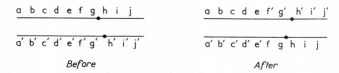

Before   After

Figure 4. One type of crossover. Letters show locations along chromosomes. This is schematic only; most chromosomes are not straight lines and are always twisted when crossovers occur. Dot indicates centromere. For instance, a might represent blue eyes, a′ brown; and g might represent tall, g′ short. Then the offspring with no crossover would always have blue eyes and be tall. With the crossovers shown, blue eyes can occur with short. After H. J. Mueller, Chapter 7 in *Radiation Biology*, Vol. 1, Part 1, A. Hollaender, ed., (New York: McGraw-Hill Book Company, Inc., 1954).

One action of all ionizing radiation and ultraviolet light is to increase the frequency of crossing over of parts of homologous chromosomes. Far from being undesirable, this is a beneficial effect increasing the minor variations within the population. Ultraviolet irradiation strongly favors crossing over as opposed to other genetic changes to be discussed. Radiation-induced crossovers have increased man's knowledge of genetic mechanisms.

4. Visible Cellular Effects

The cellular changes resulting from ionizing radiation are essentially independent of the type of irradiation, provided similar ionization occurs.

The visible cellular effects of irradiation may be divided into two types: those concerned with mitosis (or lack thereof) and those producing degeneration, often leading to cellular death. The sensitivity to irradiation varies markedly from one cell to another. By and large, the cells of higher animals and plants are more sensitive than those of the lower ones. Also, faster growing cells are altered by lower doses of irradiation than more mature cells.

The most sensitive part of most cells is the nucleus. Direct hits in a very narrow region can alter the mitotic figures or the progress of mitosis. This has been demonstrated most convincingly by Zirkle and Bloom and their co-workers, who have used pinpoint beams of protons and ultraviolet (uv) photons on single cells. They exposed single cells of different types to these microbeam radiations. The beam cross section was of the order of 8 μ in diameter. The apparatus was arranged so that the area exposed could be located simultaneously with an optical microscope, and also so that the cell could be followed after irradiation. The entire progress was recorded on a motion picture film, with intervals of several seconds between pictures.

At low doses, no cytological changes were observed when the beam passed through the cytoplasm only. However, when the same types of cells were irradiated with the proton or uv beam passing through the nucleus, the process of mitosis was often altered. If irradiation occurred during the resting phase, when distinct chromosomes cannot be observed, a variety of abnormal effects were produced during the next mitosis, including broken chromosomes, pairs of chromosomes stuck together, and uneven division of chromosomes. During mitosis, when one particular region of the chromosome, the centromere, was hit by as few as a dozen protons, the chromosome no longer lined up with the others. Eventually, it was forced into one of the two daughter cells forming either an auxiliary nucleus or a lobe of the existing one. Higher doses were needed on any other part of the chromosomes to alter mitosis, although these doses were small compared to those necessary to produce damage when used on the cytoplasm only. Several abnormal mitoses are shown in Figures 5–7.

During mitosis, a spindle of fine threads forms and appears to pull the chromosomes apart. Irradiation of the spindle or cytoplasm by protons had little or no effect on the spindle. However, irradiation of any part of the cytoplasm with doses of uv photons several times those used on chromosomes did alter the spindle. The arrangement of the chromosomes was changed; they split into two groups of chromosomes instead of each pair splitting in two.

The nonmitotic visible cellular changes observed are much less pronounced. In extreme cases of high doses to single cells, the cell

membrane is damaged.   Most of the subcellular structures, such as mitochondria, neurofibrils, and myofibrils remain unaltered at doses which
lead eventually to cellular death.

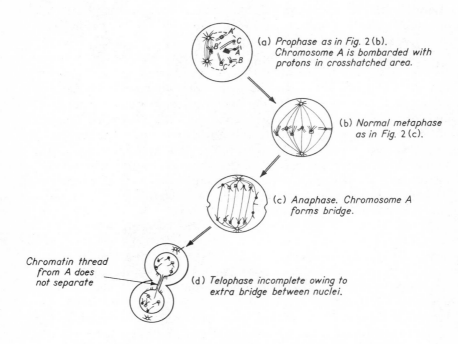

(a) *Prophase as in Fig. 2(b).*
    Chromosome A is bombarded with
    protons in crosshatched area.

(b) *Normal metaphase*
    as in Fig. 2(c).

(c) *Anaphase. Chromosome A*
    forms bridge.

Chromatin thread
from A does
not separate

(d) *Telophase incomplete owing to*
    extra bridge between nuclei.

Figure 5. Diagrammatic representation of results when microbeam of ionizing radiation strikes prophase chromosome.
Similar results are obtained due to irradiation during metaphase.

   The cells of muscle divide only occasionally and those of the adult
vertebrate nervous system not at all.   Cytological changes in these types
of cells are very hard to demonstrate at reasonable doses of ionizing
radiation.   In contrast, cells of most epithelial tissues (covering layers
such as skin) are continually dividing, as are those responsible for
forming erythrocytes (red blood cells) and leucocytes (white blood cells).
These rapidly dividing cells are sensitive to all types of ionizing radiations.
Malignant tumor cells also divide rapidly; treatment with heavy doses
of radiation tends to stop this process.   (It also probably induces changes
in the nuclei of surrounding cells which may lead to new types of
malignant growths.)

Most of the effects on rapidly dividing cells are associated with alterations in the chromosomal material or spindle. The microbeam experiments of Zirkle and co-workers indicate that chromosomal changes are extremely local. This suggests they are direct effects associated with a sensitive volume. Dosage studies likewise show that only a single

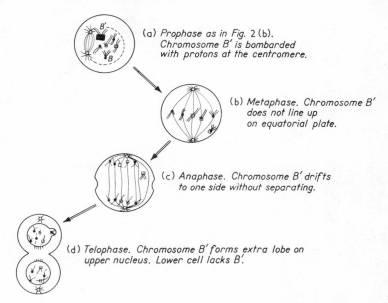

(a) *Prophase as in Fig. 2 (b).*
Chromosome B′ is bombarded
with protons at the centromere.

(b) *Metaphase. Chromosome B′*
does not line up
on equatorial plate.

(c) *Anaphase. Chromosome B′ drifts*
to one side without separating.

(d) *Telophase. Chromosome B′ forms extra lobe on*
upper nucleus. Lower cell lacks B′.

Figure 6. Diagrammatic representation of abnormality resulting from bombarding centromere of one chromosome with ionizing radiation. Similar results are obtained if the centromere is irradiated during metaphase. The reader is reminded that the chromosome shapes and numbers are purely diagrammatic.

ionization is necessary in this critical volume. In contrast, the changes induced by uv photons in the spindle were not direct effects; they could be induced by irradiation of any part of the cytoplasm. Thus, both direct and indirect effects are important.

There are several exceptions to the rule that rapidly dividing cells are more sensitive to ionizing radiations than are other cells. Some types of rapidly growing tumors are quite insensitive, whereas lymphocytes which divide only occasionally are among the most sensitive. The reasons for these differences are not known.

In all cases tested, a decrease of oxygen tends to decrease the effect of the ionizing radiation. Furthermore, certain substances such as the amino acid cysteine, which tend to react with free radicals formed in the irradiation of water, limit the cellular damage of ionizing radiations. Both the oxygen effect and that of the protective agents can be inter-

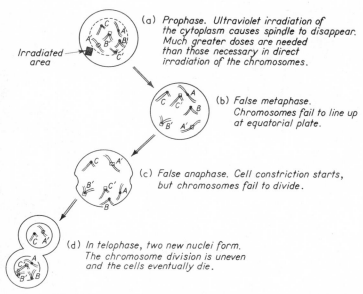

Irradiated area →

(a) *Prophase. Ultraviolet irradiation of the cytoplasm causes spindle to disappear. Much greater doses are needed than those necessary in direct irradiation of the chromosomes.*

(b) *False metaphase. Chromosomes fail to line up at equatorial plate.*

(c) *False anaphase. Cell constriction starts, but chromosomes fail to divide.*

(d) *In telophase, two new nuclei form. The chromosome division is uneven and the cells eventually die.*

Figure 7. Diagrammatic representation of abnormal cellular division resulting from cytoplasmic irradiation with ultraviolet photons. All spots in the cytoplasm are equally sensitive.

preted to support the role of free radicals such as O_2H and OH as the primary elements in the cellular action of ionizing radiation. However, they can be equally well interpreted as altering the products formed by the direct interaction of the ionizing radiation with the chemical constituents of the cells (see Chapter 16).

5. Genetic Effects

At dosage levels producing little or no visible cellular damage, it is still possible to alter the genetic material of the cell so that the progeny will be different. This is true whether one uses simple one-celled plants and animals, or complex organisms such as the mammals and the higher plants. In every case, these genetic effects occur within a single cell and may be classed as cellular events. Just like the visible changes produced in cells, the genetic effects are not very different for X rays, gamma rays, beta rays, protons, and so on.   Even neutrons and ultra-violet irradiation give rise to qualitatively similar genetic effects, although comparing their dosages in terms of ion pairs is not very meaningful. Genetic changes are explained in terms of alterations of one or more chromosomes.

Specific places along the chromosomes are associated with final body characteristics such as height, eye color, and number of fingers.   These spots are called *genes*.   Along each chromosome there are a large number of such genes.   However, along a homologous pair of chromosomes, the homologous genes control the same characteristics.   Thus, in a human, with 24 pairs of chromosomes per body cell, each pair controls a given set of characteristics.   In a highly inbred population, both chromosomes of the pair will usually be the same, but in normal populations the two chromosomes usually will contain many different genes.   The dominant gene will determine the body characteristic.   The recessive gene, though not altering body form, may be transmitted genetically.

It was discovered first with the mold neurospera that each gene apparently controlled one enzyme.   (Enzymes are biological catalysts of a protein nature which control the rate of most chemical and physical processes in living cells.   They are discussed more fully in Chapters 17 and 18.)   This idea led to the hypothesis of a one gene–one enzyme relationship.   Because the idea of the gene was a somewhat fuzzy one, genes are now often defined biochemically as the part of a chromosome associated with a given enzyme.

Further studies of crossovers, particularly in neurospera and viruses, but also in the fruit fly, drosophila, have shown that even this definition of the gene—that is, the part of the chromosome associated with one enzyme—may be misleading.   Each enzyme is a protein made up of amino acids; changes in very small regions along a chromosome, perhaps in pieces 20 Å long, can alter one amino acid in an enzyme.   However, it is not customary to call this small piece a gene.

When any of these tiny regions along the chromosome is altered, the genetic character transmitted will be changed.   Such changes are referred to as mutations.   Most mutations are recessive; that is, they are carried along and reproduced in the chromosomes without changing the body form until descendants occur in which both chromosomes have this mutation.   Most mutations are also lethal; that is, the progeny, both of whose chromosomes have this mutation, either fail to form as embryos or else do not reach maturity.   A few mutations, perhaps one in 10,000, are desirable in that they lead to a characteristic favoring the survival of the species.

The frequency of mutation in bacteria, paramecia, fruit flies, neurospera, mice, and man is increased by exposure to ionizing radiations.   This produces breaks in the chromosomes which come together

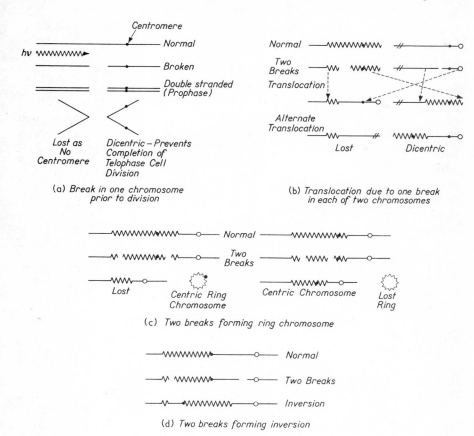

Figure 8. Breaks in chromosomes.   Shapes are diagrammatic only and have *no* physical significance.   Broken ends are not similar to normal chromosome ends but act sticky.   They tend to recombine with other broken ends.   The site of the break is always altered no matter how recombination occurs.   After H. J. Mueller, Chapter 7 in *Radiation Biology*, Vol. 1, Part 1, A. Hollaender, ed., (New York: McGraw-Hill Book Company, Inc., 1954).

(recombine) in many fashions, some very bizarre.   Some types of breaks observed with fruit flies are shown in Figure 8.   Ionizing radiations may also damage or alter chromosomes without actually breaking them.

Instead of trying to use the word "gene" in discussing radiation damage, many investigators now describe their results in new terms like cistron, recon, and muton. The cistron is based on experiments in the so-called "cis" and "trans" configurations. The trans configuration corresponds to having two mutations, one on each member of a pair of chromosomes. If no normal offspring are formed, the two mutations are said to be noncomplementary.

The cis configuration consists of both mutations on the same chromosome and a normal (that is, a so-called "wild-type") chromosome for the other member of the homologous pair. The cis configuration forms a control. In order to be able to use this analysis, the cis configuration must correspond to normal individuals. This shows that both mutations are recessive when compared to the normal. If, in addition, the trans configuration showed the two mutations to be noncomplementary, then they must block the same function. Under these circumstances, the two mutations are said to be in the same *cistron*. Each cistron in turn is made up of smaller chromosomal regions defined in terms of crossover frequency.

By studying relative crossover frequencies for different mutations, and from a knowledge of the chromosome length, one can estimate the minimum separation for crossing over. The unit of length for this minimum separation is called the *recon*.

Likewise, the critical length of the chromosome which must be altered for a mutation to occur is called the *muton*. Experiments with viruses support the idea that the muton and recon are both about 20 Å long, although the recon is probably shorter than the muton. These results are in accord with the view that genetic mutations induced by ionizing radiation occur due to ionizations in a small critical volume.

Studies of the variation of mutation rate with dosage for higher animals have been interpreted in terms of the critical volume target theory. These data led to a volume whose diameter lay between 70 and 80 Å. At one time, when the gene was believed to be a structural unit, these figures were discarded as being a factor of 100 to 1,000 times too small. All theory suggested that if the critical volume differed from the gene, it should be larger because of the influence of ionizations in the water (nucleoplasm) surrounding the chromosome. This point of view is presented in Reference 2 at the end of this chapter. It represented the views commonly held in 1952.

It is now apparent that the best estimates of the critical volume, a sphere about 60 Å in diameter, are larger than the recon or the muton. Thus, apparently, chromosomes are sensitive both to direct hits and to ones very close by but are not altered by ionizations more than about 3 mμ (30 Å) away.

6. Evolution, Mutation, and Fall-Out

The rate of mutation of all living systems is increased by ionizing radiation. One may wonder, then, if it is not possible to speed up the process of evolution by artificially producing mutations by ionizing radiation. This has been done successfully with fruit flies within the laboratory. It is important not to generalize too quickly however, for most of the mutations occurred in highly inbred lines and brought them closer to the wild-type fruit fly outside the laboratory. Further, they were adapting to an environment (the laboratory) different from that which had controlled their evolution. This beneficial effect depended on a number of factors: an unusual environment, an inbred line, and perhaps most important of all, the production of such a large number of offspring that most could be discarded while still maintaining the population.

This indicates that exposure of humans to ionizing radiation will have far more harmful effects than beneficial ones. The frustrated lives caused by most unsuccessful mutations; our social mores which provide an existence for the idiot and the physically incapable; our protection of the rights of diabetics to have children; and our slow rate of reproduction—all would work against us if more mutations were produced. Moreover, the extra survival value of mental, physical, or moral abilities is minimized in our culture. Barring a dramatic departure from present civilization, an increased mutation rate would work strongly against humans, not for them. Moreover, such effects are insidious ones, often not appearing for many generations.

With this in mind, one may compare the observed natural mutation rate with the background radioactivity in which the organism lives. In the case of the fruit fly, the dose from background radioactivity is only sufficient to account for about 10–15 per cent of the natural mutation rate. Higher animals are more sensitive to ionizing radiation. In the mouse, the background radiation can account for about 30 per cent of the natural mutation rate. There is evidence to suggest that in humans the total body dose of approximately 10 rep over 30 years may account for more than 30 per cent of the observed mutations.

Because the background radiation has an effect on humans, and because it is desirable to decrease rather than increase the mutation rate in them, it is important to limit the radiation dose on people at least until they are past the reproductive age. One principal source of overdosage in the past has been the indiscriminant use of X rays for medical and dental tests. These often exceed the total body dose due to background radiation. It is desirable to avoid X-ray exposures of pregnant women under almost all circumstances; even dental use of X rays contributes a significant dose to the developing embryo.

Background radioactivity is due in part to cosmic rays, which are still beyond human control, and, in part, to radioactive elements in the air, soil, water, food, and our bodies. Since 1950, the total background radiation has risen detectably as a result of testing nuclear weapons. These tests release radioactive fission products into the upper atmosphere. Then radioactive atoms fall out over the surface of the earth, both near the original test site and farther away. The fall-out in 1961 had not reached such proportions that it greatly increased the background radiation, but any increase, no matter how small, can be expected to increase the mutation rate. It is not proposed to debate here whether the supposed benefits of testing atomic and nuclear weapons outweigh the best estimates of the genetic cost. It is important to emphasize that genetic damage to survivors would be a major long-term result of any war involving nuclear weapons.

The greatest immediate biological danger from fall-out appears to be the production of radioactive isotopes which are incorporated into the organism, particularly C^{14} and Sr^{90}. These had reached limits in 1961 in some parts of the world where the rate of carcinogenesis (production of new cancers) might be detectably increased by these isotopes. This type of damage would also be multiplied manyfold for the survivors of a nuclear war.

7. Summary

Many types of ionizing radiation produce similar effects in all living cells. The different types of radiation, their measurement in terms of dosage and target theory, and their action are discussed in this chapter. The cellular effects may be divided into two types: visible and genetic. The former consist primarily of changes in the pattern of cell division called mitosis, although other effects, particularly the death of lymphocytes, are also observed. Direct microbeam experiments show that some mitotic effects involve the direct action of the ionizing radiation on or near the chromosomes, whereas other effects result from irradiation anywhere within the cell. These studies have confirmed the role of the chromosomes in carrying genetic information and have emphasized the physical action of the centromere during mitosis.

Genetic effects produced by ionizing radiations and ultraviolet light include increasing the frequency of crossover and the production of mutations. The former is the predominant effect with ultraviolet irradiation, and the latter occurs with all the types of irradiation discussed in this chapter. The mutations consist primarily of lethal recessives; increased mutation rates are highly undesirable for mankind. In contrast, the controlled use of ionizing radiations has greatly enhanced genetic knowledge as well as made possible the production of better plant species.

Indiscriminate use of clinical X rays and increased fall-out from atomic testing both can produce increased mutation rates.   The present fall-out levels are just at the limit where the generation of new cancers and induction of the genetic effects might be detectable.   Both of these deleterious results would be manyfold worse among any population surviving a nuclear war.

REFERENCES

1. Miner, R. W., ed., "Ionizing Radiation and the Cell," (Monograph) *Ann. New York Acad. Sc.* **59**: 467–664 (1955).

    a. Bloom, William, R. E. Zirkle, and R. B. Uretz, "Irradiation of Parts of Individual Cells.   III.   Effects of Chromosal and Extrachromosal Irradiation on Chromosome Movements," pp. 503–513.

    b. Patt, H. M., "Factors in the Radiosensitivity of Mammalian Cells," pp. 649–664.

2. Hollaender, Alexander, ed., *Radiation Biology*: Volume I.   *High Energy Radiation* (New York: McGraw-Hill Book Company, Inc., 1954).

    a. Muller, H. J., "The Nature of the Genetic Effects Produced by Radiation," pp. 351–473.

    b. Muller, H. J., "The Manner of Production of Mutations by Radiation," pp. 475–626.

    c. Bloom, William, and Margaret A. Bloom, "Histological Changes After Irradiation," pp. 1091–1143.

3. Bovey, F. A., *Effects of Ionizing Radiation on Natural and Synthetic High Polymers* (New York: Interscience Publishers, 1958).

4. Bacqu, Z. M., and Peter Alexander, *Fundamentals of Radiobiology* (London, England: Butterworth & Co., Ltd., 1955).

5. Tatum, E. L., "The Status of Gene-Enzyme Relationship," part II, O. H. Gaebler, ed., *Enzymes: Units of Biological Structure and Function* (New York: Academic Press, Inc., 1956) pp. 107–176.

6. Zirkle, R. E., "Partial-Cell Irradiation," *Advances in Biological and Medical Physics*, J. H. Lawrence, and C. A. Tobias, eds. (New York: Academic Press, Inc., 1957) Vol. 5, pp. 103–146.

7. Benzer, Seymour, "The Elementary Units of Heredity," *A Symposium on the Chemical Basis of Heredity*, W. D. McElroy, and Bentley Glass, eds. (Baltimore: Johns Hopkins University Press, 1957) pp. 70–93.

8. U.S. National Committee on Radiation Protection, "Maximum Permissible Amounts of Radioisotopes in the Human Body and Maximum Permissible Concentrations in Air and Water," *National Bureau of Standards Handbook* 52 (Washington, D.C.: Government Printing Office, 1953).

9. U.S. National Committee on Radiation Protection and Measurements, "Permissible Dose From External Sources of Ionizing Radiations," *National Bureau of Standards Handbook* 59 (Washington, D.C.: Government Printing Office, 1954).

    a. Addendum to Handbook 59 (1958).

Several articles on fall-out and its effect on man can be found in *Science*.

II

The Absorption of Electro-magnetic and Ultrasonic Energy

I. Role of Nonionizing Radiation

Both electromagnetic and ultrasonic energy may be absorbed by tissues and cells without any specific damage at the cellular or molecular level. The energy absorbed is converted to heat. If the power absorbed becomes sufficiently large, the cells and their protein constituents heat up to such a high temperature that they are irreversibly altered. The result is identical to the changes produced by the direct application of heat.

Many types of irradiation do produce specific types of cellular damage. In the previous chapter, the action of ionizing radiation was considered. These ionizing radiations include electromagnetic radiation, provided the photon energy is sufficiently high. Photons of X-ray and γ-ray wavelengths produce ionizations or break bonds within biological cells. Photons of ultraviolet wavelengths excite reactive states in proteins and nucleic acids. In the present chapter, only electromagnetic energy of much longer wavelengths will be considered; this includes a broad band from the microwave region to d-c electrical currents.

Other types of radiation can damage cells without producing ionization. For example, under certain conditions single cells suspended in a liquid are fractured when irradiated with acoustic energy. This is always accompanied by a process called *cavitation*, in which small bubbles or holes form in the liquid. These and other destructive actions of ultrasonics are discussed in Chapter 11. If the acoustic power is not too high, or if cavitation is suppressed, exposed biological cells absorb some of the ultrasonic energy. This nondestructive absorption of ultrasound is also discussed in the present chapter.

When any type of energy is absorbed, it is eventually converted to heat. The phenomena considered in this chapter are grouped together because the conversion of incident energy to heat is the direct, immediate effect. The different tissues of the human body, and different single cells, all have differing absorptions, both for electromagnetic energy and for ultrasonic energy. Thus, it is possible to selectively heat certain tissues and certain portions of the human body. This heating action is known as *diathermy*. Local heating of tissues promotes recovery from many disorders. Diathermy is the direct medical application of the phenomena discussed in this chapter.

The absorption of electromagnetic and ultrasonic energy has, however, a more fundamental significance. It is an important tool for building a complete picture of the physical nature of biological cells and tissues. As such, it supplements knowledge gained by looking through a microscope and also supplements studies of molecular biology.

2. Electrical Impedances

The absorption of electromagnetic energy in tissues can be described only in the language of electricity and magnetism. Several important definitions are summarized in Table I of Appendix C. Any reader not well versed in electrical terminology and definitions is asked to study that appendix before proceeding with the current chapter. Magnetic terms were completely omitted from Table I, but magnetic fields exist whenever a current flows. Thus, if one passes an alternating current through tissues (or other conductors), a magnetic field $\vec{H}$ will be generated. Likewise, if a tissue (or other conductor) is subjected to a changing magnetic induction $\vec{B}$, an emf will be induced in it. The proportionality constant between $\vec{B}$ and $\vec{H}$ is called the magnetic permeability, μ. These added terms, along with a few others, are summarized in the following table.

Supplement to TABLE I, Appendix C

Quantity	Symbol	Defining Equation	Units
Magnetic induction	$\vec{B}$	$d\vec{F} = I(\vec{dl} \times \vec{B})$	webers/m²
Magnetic field	$\vec{H}$	$\vec{\nabla} \times \vec{H} = 4\pi \vec{J}$	ampere/m
Electric displacement	$\vec{D}$	$\vec{\nabla} \cdot \vec{D} = 4\pi\rho$	coulomb/m²
Dielectric constant	ϵ	$\vec{D} = \epsilon\vec{E}$	—
Magnetic permeability	μ	$\vec{B} = \mu\vec{H}$	—
Conductivity	σ	$\vec{J} = \sigma\vec{E}$	$(\text{ohm} \cdot \text{m})^{-1}$

In a vacuum, $\vec{B}$ is the same as $\vec{H}$, and $\vec{E}$ is the same as $\vec{D}$. The quantities $\vec{H}$ and $\vec{D}$ are generated by currents and fixed charges, respectively; accordingly, they do not include the specific medium such as tissue or cell. On the other hand, $\vec{B}$ and $\vec{E}$ represent the force on a unit current or charge, respectively; they do include the effects of the medium.

The properties of the medium itself, then, are included in the proportionality factors μ and ϵ. Likewise, the conductivity σ represents an additional proportionality factor depending only on the medium, not on the size of $\vec{E}$, $\vec{H}$, and so on.[1] Thus, one way of characterizing the electromagnetic behavior of a medium is to give values for μ, ϵ, and σ. For all biological cells and solutions of most compounds of biological interest, μ is less than 0.01 per cent different from μ_o, the permeability of free space. Studies utilizing these small differences are described in Chapter 28. For the material in the current chapter the approximation

$$\mu \doteq \mu_o$$

is well within experimental limits of error for all biological cells.

The basic equations describing electricity and magnetism are known as Maxwell's equations. These allow anyone adept at mathematics to predict the existence of propagated electromagnetic waves with wave velocity in free space

$$c_o = \frac{1}{\sqrt{\mu_o \epsilon_o}}$$

and velocity in a medium

$$c = \frac{1}{\sqrt{\mu\epsilon}}$$

Because ϵ for all cells, suspensions of cells. and tissues is much larger than ϵ_o, c is smaller than c_o.

---

[1] The conductivity σ for the axon and muscle-fiber membranes varies dramatically with the potential difference across the membrane. (See Chapter 4.)

When an electromagnetic wave falls upon a cell or group of cells (or any conductor, for that matter) a current will flow and energy will be dissipated. It is usually not possible to restrict the effects of a wave to an area smaller than a wavelength in diameter. Even with electromagnetic wavelengths of 5 cm in air the wavelength in the tissues will be about 1 cm. Thus, it is hard to confine electromagnetic waves to a small volume within tissues or cells.

The names given to the various parts of the electromagnetic spectrum are listed in a table in Chapter 21 on Spectrophotometry. That chapter also discusses atomic and molecular absorption of electromagnetic waves which are more important for higher frequencies. In the present chapter, radiofrequency and microwave absorptions and dielectric constants will be emphasized. These show neither sharp spectral bands nor rapid variation with wavelength. The frequencies included in this chapter range from 10 cps to 10^{10} cps.

In these spectral regions the tissues and cells may be characterized by an impedance (or an impedance of a unit crosssection). In Appendix C, it was noted that the impedance Z was defined by

$$Z = \frac{V}{I}$$

The impedance per unit length of a unit crosssection is

$$Z' = \frac{V}{J}$$

It has the units of ohm·cm. In Appendix C, it was also noted that the definition for Z was meaningful only if one used sinusoidal currents or if one used the Fourier transform of the current. Thus it is convenient to separate Z into two parts, R and X. In the complex notation,

$$Z = R + jX$$

The resistance R gives the ratio of the part of the potential in phase with the current to the current. The reactance X gives the ratio of the potential 90° out of phase to the current. The real part of Z' is the resistivity ρ. For d-c,

$$\rho = \frac{1}{\sigma}$$

The resistance R and reactance X can be used instead of the conductivity σ and dielectric constant ϵ to characterize the cells and tissues. Either pair will completely describe the electromagnetic properties of the biological system (with the unwritten addition that

$$\mu = \mu_o)$$

In general, all of the terms R, X, σ, and ϵ vary with frequency.   Studies of their variation should be interpretable in terms of the molecular structure of cells and cell membranes.   Such interpretations could either support or refute a given molecular model.   The electrical constants are obtained, in general, by measuring the electrical impedance of suspensions of cells and of aggregates of cells organized into tissues.   The success and limitations of this approach are discussed in the next section.

3. Biological Impedance

The membranes of most cells act as insulators at low frequencies. Thus, if one suspends cells in a saline solution, most of the current will flow around the cells.   The electrical current must then follow a longer path than in the absence of the cells.   In terms of electrical impedance, the resistance (or resistivity) will be higher for the suspension than for the pure suspending medium.   The difference in these two resistivities can be used to find the volume of the cell.

For tissues, likewise, the low frequency impedance is a measure of the free space between the cells.   It is interesting that this impedance is about the same for skeletal muscle, liver, and cardiac muscle.   The resistivity ρ is about 900 ohm·cm, dropping slowly as the frequency increases from 10 cps to 1,000 cps.   Blood, with fewer formed elements, has a much higher conductivity (that is, lower resistivity), whereas fatty tissues and bones have lower conductivities in this low frequency region.

Between 1 kc and 100 kc, the impedance of a suspension of single cells drops quite sharply to a lower value.   For a suspension of single cells of simple geometry in a saline solution, one can solve exactly the equations describing the flow of current.   A first approximation is to assume the cell is a spherical homogeneous conductor surrounded by a nonconducting (lipid) layer as shown in Figure 1.   This fits the impedance data in a qualitative fashion.   The lipid layer acts as a capacitor in series with the cell interior.   At low frequencies, the impedance of the capacitor (that is, the lipid shell)

$$Z_c = \frac{j}{\omega C}$$

is very high because the frequency ω appears in the denominator. Hence, little current can enter the cells, which then appear to be insulators.   At higher frequencies, Z_c becomes negligible and current can readily pass into the cell interior.   At such frequencies, the impedance of the suspension will be less than it is at lower frequencies.

A better quantitative fitting of the theory to the experiment can be realized by allowing the cell wall to be a leaky capacitor; that is, to be equivalent to a high resistance in parallel with a capacitor. Using the actual cell shape instead of spheres also improves the application of the theory to the experiment. This last is very hard except for simple symmetric shapes.

The properties of the cell wall are expressed as an areal capacity in microfarads per square centimeter, and an areal resistance in ohm·cm². The impedance of the cytoplasm can be represented as a resistivity, expressed in ohm·cm. At one time, it was believed that these cell constants could be interpreted to find the effective thickness of the cell

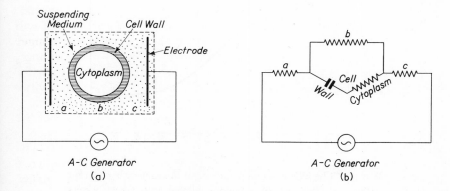

Figure I. (a) Diagrammatic representation of single cell in an electric field. The resistance of the suspending medium is lower in regions *a* and *c* than *b* because the cross section occupied by the suspending medium is greater at *a* and *c* than at *b*. (b) Equivalent lumped electrical parameters for the preceding diagram. The cell wall is represented as a capacitor. A better approximation would include a leakage resistance in parallel with the capacitor. Resistors *a*, *b*, and *c* represent the suspending medium in regions *a*, *b*, and *c* respectively.

membrane, but this hope has been unrealized as yet.   Perhaps the most impressive aspect of these data is their similarity from one cell type to another.   Plant cells, animal cells, nerve axons, and egg cells all overlap in their electrical constants.

The following are the orders of magnitude obtained for most cells. The internal or protoplasmic resistivity varies from 10 to 30,000 ohm·cm, with 300 being common for most mammalian cells.   For cat nerve, a value of 720 ohm·cm was measured.   However, for other nerves, values as low as 10 ohm·cm have been found.   The areal capacitance varies from 0.1 to 3 μfd/cm². Few values lie outside of the range 0.8 to 1.1. One low measurement of 0.01 μfd/cm² has been obtained for a frog nerve, but other nerve measurements are in the 0.6 to 1.2 μfd/cm² range. Values for the leakage areal resistance of the cell membrane vary from 25 to 10,000 ohm·cm² or higher. Nerve and muscle measurements have yielded both extremes.

Similar considerations apply to the electrical characteristics of whole tissues. Their impedance is hard to separate in terms of cellular

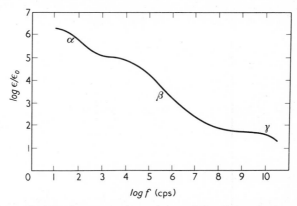

Figure 2. The frequency dependence of the dielectric constant of muscle. Note the three regions labeled with Greek letters indicating three types of relaxation. After H. P. Schwan and C. F. Kay, "Conductivity of Living Tissues," *Annals of the New York Academy of Sciences* **65**: 1007 (1957).

parameters but may be represented as a lumped resistivity and capacity. The ratio of the capacity to that of a vacuum is the dielectric constant. A plot of effective dielectric constants against frequency has the shape shown in Figure 2. It should be borne in mind that a variety of effects contribute to this general shape.

The region labeled β is the one related to the change from conductance around the cells to conductance through the cells. The complex shape of the curve indicates a variety of cell sizes and shapes. The region labeled γ is due to molecular relaxations discussed below. The low frequency changes labeled α indicate some other type of phenomena which is not clearly understood. Similar low frequency changes in resistivity can be seen in Figure 3. Although neither can be explained clearly, it appears likely that both are due to some common mechanism. Moreover, the low frequencies at which these occur indicate that comparatively large pieces of material are involved.

All molecules tend to become polarized in an electric field. In an alternating field, the molecule must reverse its polarization each half cycle.[2]   Above the *relaxation frequency* the electric field changes so fast that the molecular polarization no longer follows it.   The larger the molecule, the lower the relaxation frequency.   The dielectric constant and resistivity of the molecules drop fairly abruptly from higher values below the relaxation frequency to lower values above the relaxation frequency.   Proteins have relaxation frequencies in the range of megacycles apparently without effect on the lumped parameters of tissues.

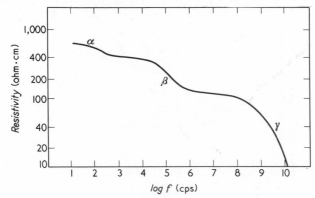

Figure 3. Resistivity of muscle as a function of frequency. Note the similarity of the relaxation regions for Figures 2 and 3. After H. P. Schwan and C. F. Kay, "Conductivity of Living Tissues," *Annals of the New York Academy of Sciences* **65**: 1007 (1957).

Small molecules such as those of water exhibit similar relaxations in the region of 10^{10} cps, giving rise to region γ in Figures 3 and 4.   The low frequency relaxation, in region α, must represent the behavior of some part of the cell that is large compared to a protein molecule.

The frequency dependence of the resistivity and dielectric constants of many different types of tissues are all similar.   These are also similar to that of blood.   The resistivity of blood, particularly at low frequencies, is lower than that of most other tissues, owing to its high water content. The values for muscle, liver, spleen, pancreas, lung, and kidney are all very similar, except that below 10^5 cps they are higher than that for blood.   Exceptions to the preceding general pattern are brain tissue, fat tissue, and bone.   The last, with its high content of calcium phosphate crystals, is very different from soft tissues.   Its impedance is

[2] For small molecules with a permanent dipole moment, this implies an actual physical rotation. For small molecules without a permanent dipole moment, and for all large molecules, this change involves a rearrangement of the electron orbitals and of the atomic spacings within the molecule.

much higher than that of the softer tissues, particularly at low frequencies.

Fatty tissue is very different because fat is an excellent electrical insulator. Tissues of this nature show a much higher resistivity and a much lower dielectric constant than do those with more water. The general shape of the resistivity and dielectric curves is similar to that for

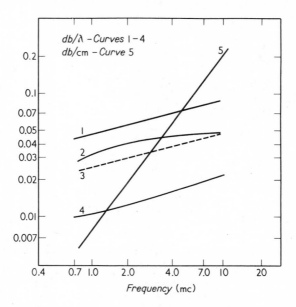

Figure 4. Ultrasonic absorption by blood. Curve 1 shows absorption per wavelength for packed red blood cells. Curve 2 illustrates similar absorption per wavelength for whole blood. Curve 3 is a plot of the absorption per wavelength for whole blood computed from the absorption of plasma proteins and hemoglobin. Curves 4 and 5 diagram the ultrasonic absorption of plasma in db per wavelength and db per cm, respectively. After E. L. Carstensen and H. P. Schwan, *J. Acous. Soc. America* **31**: 185 (1959).

muscle. Brain tissue has more fat-like material (lipids) than does muscle. At lower frequencies, its resistivity is close to that of fatty tissues. However, this resistivity falls rapidly as the frequency is raised from one to 10 megacycles (10^6 to 10^7 cps). Its value above this frequency range is close to that of the nonfatty tissues. Its dielectric constant is within the range of the watery tissues at all frequencies.

In concluding this section, it should be noted that the electrical impedance of biological cells supports the picture of a cell consisting of an electrically conducting cytoplasm surrounded by a poorly conducting, lipid membrane with a high dielectric constant. These electrical data are interesting as physical properties of the cells but have not yet been related in detail to the differences between cells.

4. Ultrasonics

Mechanical vibratory energy has the same end effect on cells and tissues as does the electromagnetic energy discussed in the previous section of this chapter, namely it heats them. The rate of heating is comparatively small for low frequency mechanical vibrations. The frequency range used for most heating studies is above the audible; it is referred to as ultrasonic. The absorption of ultrasonic energy is not inherently different from that of energy at audible frequencies. Some authors refer to nonauditory uses of acoustics as "sonics," but in this text the more common name "ultrasonic" is used.

Ultrasonic vibrations, then, are the sound waves whose frequency is above the audible range. The properties and mathematical descriptions of audible sound waves in air are discussed in Appendix A. There, it is emphasized that in air, sound waves are compressional waves characterized by a sound pressure (also called acoustic pressure) p and a local particle velocity v. The acoustic pressure p and particle velocity v are propagated throughout the medium with a characteristic wave velocity c. During the propagation, the wave may also be attenuated. The properties of the medium can be summarized in a quantity analogous to the electrical impedance, called the characteristic impedance Z. It is defined for plane waves as the ratio

$$Z = \frac{p}{v}$$

The real part of this impedance R represents the propagation of unattenuated sound waves. The value of R is given by the product ρc, where ρ is the density medium and c the velocity of sound. The imaginary part of Z represents attenuation, that is, the absorption per unit length. For many purposes, it is convenient to describe a medium in terms of the real part of the impedance ρc and the attenuation factor. This pair of numbers is completely equivalent to Z. The attenuation factor is the ratio by which the pressure amplitude is decreased in traveling one unit distance. Often, the log of this ratio is given, expressed, for example, as decibels/cm. (For a definition of decibels, see Chapter 1.)

Absorption of ultrasonic energy by biological cells and tissues is more complicated than similar absorption in a gas. In a solid or liquid, some of the longitudinal (that is, compressional) wave is converted into a transverse (or shear) wave. This wave is attenuated very rapidly in viscous media such as protoplasm. In addition, ultrasonic waves are scattered and absorbed at all cell interfaces. This is greatly accentuated when there is a large change in ρc, such as at a bone–soft tissue interface, but is an important factor even if the change in ρc is small.

The wavelength of ultrasonic energy is much smaller than that of electromagnetic energy of the same frequency. This means the passage of ultrasonic energy through tissues can be confined to a much smaller volume than can electromagnetic energy. For example, the ultrasonic wavelength is about 1.5 mm at 1 mc, whereas the electromagnetic wavelength is about 300 meters. An ultrasonic beam 0.25 mm in diameter is feasible at 1 mc; an electromagnetic beam would be at least 50 meters in diameter at the same frequency.

A result of this short ultrasonic wavelength is that ultrasonic absorption or reflection can be used, just as X rays, to determine the structures within living organisms. Various systems have been devised for this. All of them are superior to X rays, in that ultrasonograms (as they are called) have no known harmful effects. In contrast, more information is usually obtained from an X-ray photograph than from most of the ultrasonograms developed to date.

If the intensity and duration of the ultrasonic energy is raised sufficiently, destructive effects can be produced. These are discussed in greater detail in Chapter 12. In the present chapter, only non-destructive absorption will be discussed further.

5. Nondestructive Effects of Ultrasound

The absorption of ultrasonic energy at frequencies above about 250 kc has been studied for many different types of tissues obtained from various mammals. The real part of the acoustic impedance (that is, ρc) is essentially the same for all tissues. The exception is bone, which has a much higher ρc than any other tissue. In contrast, the absorption of ultrasonic energy varies markedly from one soft tissue to another. Perhaps the easiest data to interpret are those obtained for blood. It is possible to measure separately the contributions to the absorption due to the proteins dissolved in the plasma, the hemoglobin within the red blood cells, and the cellular structure itself. These measurements show that the absorption per wavelength increases monotonically as the frequency is raised from 0.5 to 20 mc. This gradual increase, however, is slower than would be expected for a simple viscoelastic medium.

The studies of blood showed that the ultrasonic absorption due to hemoglobin is similar to that due to the plasma proteins. Absorption by proteins represents the major part of the ultrasonic absorption in blood. A much smaller effect can be observed in dilute suspensions of blood cells, which may be attributed to the motion of the liquid relative to the cells. The absorption coefficient for whole blood is about 0.2 db/cm at 1 mc, or in other units about 0.03 db per wavelength. The second figure is correct within a factor of two throughout the frequency range 0.7 to 10 mc; that is to say, the absorption per wavelength increases only very slowly with increasing frequency. The graphs in Figure 4 show this variation. Figure 5 shows the variation of the absorption per wavelength over a greater frequency range.

This slow increase is extremely difficult to understand. All simple theories indicate that the absorption per wavelength should be proportional to the frequency. The failure of the simple theories is

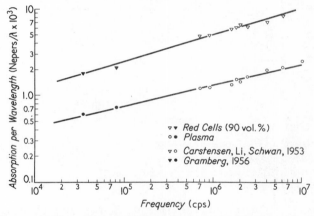

Figure 5. Ultrasonic absorption of red blood cells and plasma from 30 kc to 10 mc. Note that the absorption per wavelength changes only fivefold when the frequency changes three hundredfold. (To convert nepers to db, multiply by 8.7.) After E. L. Carstensen, with permission.

"explained" by saying that relaxations occur and that, as a result, the protein molecules no longer move as a whole at higher frequencies, or else somehow parts of the molecules become free to slip back and forth past other parts. Even on this model, the absorption per wavelength should be approximately independent of frequency only in a very narrow frequency region. Instead, the absorption depends only slightly on the frequency over the entire range from 0.3 to 20 mc (that is, almost a 100:1 ratio or about six octaves). It is still possible to explain away this discrepancy by stating that there are a large number of different relaxations which occur with a fairly uniform distribution of relaxation frequencies.   At best, this explanation is highly artificial because the origin of these relaxations is unknown.   It is possible that a more complete model of protein structure might increase the understanding of this process.   Conversely, these apparent relaxations are one type of data that can be used to test any theory of protein structure.   (The structure

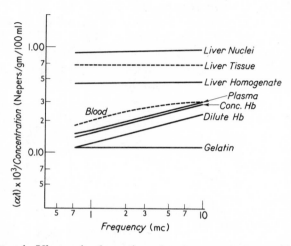

Figure 6. Ultrasonic absorption of various suspensions and of liver tissue. (To convert nepers to db, multiply by 8.7.) After E. L. Carstensen, with permission.

of proteins is discussed on the basis of X ray and chemical data in Chapter 17.)

Measurements on the values of ρc and the absorption coefficients for a wide variety of soft tissues are summarized in the reference by Goldman and Heuter.   These authors show that many measurements in various laboratories all support the similarity of ρc for tissue and water.   Similarly, all of these measurements indicate the relatively small dependence of the absorption per wavelength on frequency in the range 0.25 to 25 mc. The values for this absorption for many tissues are higher than that for blood.   Whether this is due to differences in the proteins or to scattering at the cell walls is not known.   Typical values for ultrasonic absorptions are shown in Figure 6.

A comparatively small number of isolated measurements at frequencies below 100 kc indicate that the absorption per wavelength is proportional to the frequency in this range.   If this is proved to be the case, it would further support the existence of mechanical relaxations although it would not give any clue as to the origin of them. However, the data in Figure 5, for example, indicate that if relaxation processes occur, there must be several for each protein molecule.

Much greater absorptions of ultrasonic energy occur at boundaries between media of very different density and hardness. For example, when an ultrasonic wave passes through soft tissue and is incident on bone, it encounters a region of much greater ρc. At this interface, a large part of the ultrasonic energy is converted into heat. This gross phenomenon, although easy to observe experimentally, is difficult to analyze in detail. Ultrasonic heating at bone surfaces forms the physical basis for many of the applications of ultrasonic diathermy.

6. Diathermy

Both ultrasonic and electromagnetic radiation are used clinically to heat selective portions of patients. This process is known as *diathermy*. It is more effective than the application of external heat because the heat is generated throughout the tissues. A variety of disorders are alleviated and recovery is speeded in others through the use of diathermy. The physical action is one of heating, although stirring the contents and surroundings of the cells may also be important in ultrasonic diathermy.

At very low frequencies, the absorption of both electromagnetic and ultrasonic radiations is so weak that neither is effective for diathermy. Absorption increases as does the frequency up to about 1 mc; as the frequency is raised above this the impedances (both electrical and ultrasonic) remain constant until much higher frequencies are reached. The depth of penetration measured in wavelengths also remains constant. Because the wavelength is inversely proportional to the frequency, the shorter wavelengths have a lower penetration. The extreme high frequency limit of electromagnetic diathermy is the use of an infrared or heat lamp whose radiations barely penetrate the skin.

In spite of their similarities, there are certain gross differences between ultrasonic and electromagnetic diathermy. Electromagnetic energy is only poorly absorbed in fatty tissues and hardly at all in bone. As a result, most of the heating occurs in the muscles. In contrast, ultrasonic energy is equally absorbed in fat and muscle and is markedly absorbed at the bone-tissue interfaces. It is used widely in the treatment of various bone diseases.

Another difference concerns the wavelength. At any given frequency, the wavelength of ultrasound is much shorter than that of an electromagnetic wave. Accordingly, ultrasonic diathermy treatment can be administered to a joint such as the elbow, or even part of a joint. Electromagnetic diathermy treatment would affect all the muscles of the arm at conventional frequencies (20 mc).

7. Summary

Ultrasonic and electromagnetic energy are absorbed by all tissues and cells.   These absorptions have been studied over a wide range of frequencies.   Such investigations have contributed to an understanding of the physical nature of biological cells and tissues.   Certain gaps in present knowledge are emphasized by these studies.

The electromagnetic absorptions are explained by the model of a cell consisting of an insulating dielectric wall surrounding an interior protoplasm which is a fair conductor of electricity.   The electrical impedance from 10 kc to 10 mc, both of suspensions of single cells and also of whole tissues, fits this model very well.   Above 10 mc, certain relaxation phenomena associated with the water itself·are important. These phenomena are predicted by conventional electromagnetic theory. Below 10 kc, other electrical relaxations occur in the tissues.   The origin or significance of the low frequency relaxations is not known.

Absorption of ultrasonic energy in cells fails to fit any simple viscoelastic model above 300 kc.   This failure emphasizes the incompleteness of current knowledge of protein structure.   The motion of single cells in blood contributes a small but measurable amount to the total ultrasonic absorption.   However, the major effect in blood-cell suspensions and tissues is due to the proteins.   Many different tissues with widely varying protein types have similar ultrasonic absorptions.   Thus, some common, but not understood, molecular property of proteins is measured by these experiments.

Both electromagnetic and ultrasonic irradiation of tissues are used clinically.   The success of this application has been the inspiration for many of the more basic studies of the cellular and molecular origin of these absorptions.

REFERENCES

1. Cole, K. S., and H. J. Curtis, "Bioelectricity: Electric Physiology," Otto Glasser, ed., *Medical Physics* (Chicago, Illinois: Year Book Publishers, Inc., 1950) Vol. 2, pp. 82–90.
2. Schwan, H. P., "Electrical Properties of Tissue and Cell Suspensions," *Advances in Biological and Medical Physics*, J. H. Lawrence, and C. A. Tobias, eds. (New York: Academic Press, Inc., 1957) Vol. 5, pp. 147–209.

3. Goldman, D. E., and T. F. Hueter, "Tabular Data of the Velocity and Absorption of High-Frequency Sound in Mammalian Tissues," *J. Acous. Soc. Am.* **28**: 35–37 (Jan. 1956).
4. Articles in *J. Acous. Soc. Am.* by Carstensen, E. L., Kam Li, and H. P. Schwan:
   a. "Determination of the Acoustic Properties of Blood and Its Components," **25**, pp. 286–289 (1953).
   b. "Absorption of Sound Arising From the Presence of Intact Cells in Blood," **31**, pp. 185–189 (1959).
   c. "Acoustic Properties of Hemoglobin Solutions," **31**, pp. 305–311 (1959).
5. Lehmann, J. F., "The Biophysical Mode of Action of Biologic and Therapeutic Ultrasonic Reactions," *J. Acous. Soc. Am.* **25**: 17–25 (Jan. 1953).

12

Destructive Effects of High Intensity Ultrasound

1. High Intensity Ultrasound

Acoustic energy of sufficiently great intensity can damage living cells in several ways. First, there is the nonspecific effect of heating. This type of destruction results from the absorption of high intensity ultrasonic waves in the manner described in the previous chapter. There are, however, two more specific types of effects which may occur. These are the rupture of single cells in watery suspensions when the medium is subjected to sufficiently intense sound fields, and the damage to nervous tissues which is highly specific as to which cells are destroyed.

These types of acoustic destruction are independent of hearing and can probably be demonstrated at almost any frequency. Some authors have suggested calling the entire spectrum from subaudible to superaudible by the name *sonic* when hearing is not involved. However, most of these destructive effects have been studied and used at frequencies above the limits of human hearing. Accordingly, they are referred to as *ultrasonic* in this text.

Ultrasonic destruction of single cells in suspension occurs in the presence of a phenomenon known as *cavitation*. Cavitation refers to the rupturing of the suspending medium, forming small bubbles or cavities whose density is negligible compared to the density of water. In general, these cavities are filled with air or other dissolved gases. If a gas-free liquid is used, the liquid vapor fills the cavities. During each period of the ultrasonic wave, these bubbles expand rapidly as the pressure decreases and then collapse to a much smaller volume as it increases.

The rupture of single cells can be applied for various purposes. One is to extract protein catalysts known as *enzymes* from whole cells. Enzyme extractions are important in order to study these catalysts in as pure a form as possible. However, the entire procedure is misleading unless the final, purified enzyme molecules are very similar to the original ones within the cell. In general, if several methods of extraction give purified enzyme molecules with the same chemical and physical properties, one tends to believe that the purified enzyme molecules are similar to those in the whole cell. Ultrasonic rupture of cells can often be used to confirm the validity of other methods of enzyme extraction. In a few known examples, enzyme extraction by ultrasonic techniques gives a higher yield than other methods. For instance, this is a very efficient method of preparing verdoperoxidase from white blood cells.

Similarly, subcellular particles can be extracted which have unique properties. In certain bacteria, it has been possible to obtain particulate fractions which will still synthesize proteins from amino acids. Gale has found the highest yield of such subcellular particles from cells fractured with ultrasonically generated cavitation. Other small particles made from ultrasonically ruptured, intracellular organelles called *mitochondria* have been used to study the mitochondrial structure.

A more basic approach to ultrasonic rupture of single cells in suspension is to investigate the physical parameters of the cell which control its sensitivity in a cavitating ultrasonic field. Measurements of the relative rates of destruction of different cell types indicate their relative fragility. It should be possible to relate these to other physical parameters of the cell structure. Approaches to this problem are considered both in this chapter and in the following one, Chapter 13.

A different type of ultrasonic destruction occurs when a portion of the central nervous system of a vertebrate is exposed to a high intensity ultrasonic beam. In this case, specific use is made of the very small wavelength to bring the ultrasonic field to focus in a small region of the brain. The evidence concerning the mode of action is not clear-cut, but the results are, nonetheless, very useful both for neurosurgery and for physiological studies of the actions of specific regions of the nervous system.

2. Cavitation

As was mentioned in the previous section, when cavitation occurs in an intense ultrasonic field, biological cells can be fractured.   If cavitation is suppressed, no cells are broken (unless the suspending medium is allowed to heat to a lethal temperature).   Accordingly, it is appropriate to examine the action of cavitation in more detail.   The following discussion presupposes a minimum knowledge of acoustics.   It is suggested that the student feeling unsure in this field first reread Section 2 of Chapter 1 and Section 4 of Chapter 11.

Associated with every sound wave, audible or not, is a variation in both the local pressure P and the local particle velocity v.   The acoustic pressure p has been defined as

$$p = P - P_o$$

where P_o is the average or atmospheric pressure.   The absolute pressure P in a gas cannot be negative.   Therefore, the acoustic pressure amplitude must always be less than the atmospheric pressure.

In contrast, liquids have a definite volume and can sustain negative pressures or tensions.   Pressure amplitudes of hundreds of atmospheres can be generated in water.   However, when the pressure becomes low enough (that is, the tension becomes great enough), the liquid will fracture.   The liquid breaks by forming small, more or less spherical holes, called *cavities*.

Various physical theories have attempted to predict the negative pressure at which pure water will fracture.   The most straightforward of these predicts about $-15,000$ atm.   This theory essentially calculates the work to pull two planes apart.   A somewhat more sophisticated theory employs both the spherical nature of the holes and another general semi-empirical theory called "absolute rate theory."   This combination, named nucleation theory, predicts cavitation thresholds of about $-1,500$ atm.

No one has ever reached this value.   The lowest threshold reported for cavitation (that is, liquid rupture) in water is -350 atm.   Apparently, dirt on the sides of the vessel, or suspended in the medium, even in triply distilled water, always limits the tension the liquid can withstand before rupturing.   For dirty liquids, saturated with gas and tiny gas nuclei, cavitation may occur at positive pressures.   Indeed, cellular disruption is sometimes found with pressure amplitudes of only 0.1 atm, that is, at positive pressures of 0.9 atm.

Cavitation can be observed by various techniques.   Intense cavitation is readily visible to the naked eye.   A hissing sound is often heard.   A probe microphone out of the main sound field will pick up noise radiated by the cavities. If the acoustic pressure is measured as a function of the energy applied to the transducer used to generate the ultrasonic field, a curve such as that sketched for p in Figure 1 is obtained. As the point of cavitation is reached, the curve bends over because the liquid tears rather than sustaining higher pressures. As the liquid fills with cavities, its density decreases; this permits the particle velocity to increase linearly with the square root of the applied energy to values well above the threshold for cavitation.

Cellular fracture and harmonic distortion of the pressure wave are observed at acoustic pressures lower than those shown by the break in

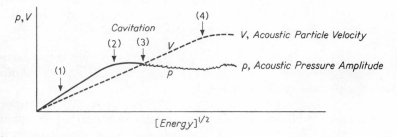

Figure I. Variation of acoustic pressure p and particle velocity V with energy supplied to transducer. The arrows indicate points at which cavitation occurs based on (1) cellular disruption; (2) break in the pressure curve; (3) generation of noise; and (4) break in the particle velocity curve.

the curve in Figure 1, labeled "cavitation." However, both cellular fracture and harmonic distortion can be suppressed by increasing the atmospheric pressure, a change which would interfere only with effects due to cavitation. These indicate that cavitation is occurring, at least to a limited degree, before the break in the curve. Thus, different tests for cavitation lead to different thresholds for cavitation.

Of course, care must be taken to distinguish cavitation from heating. When an intense ultrasonic field is generated in a small body of liquid, acoustic energy must be dissipated as heat. If no method is provided to remove this excess heat energy, the temperature will rise. Then all biological effects of ultrasound are masked by heating. Any practical exposure technique must involve either very short periods of time or some form of cooling.

All types of transducers can be built to include a cooling system. At the lowest frequencies practical, 0–10 kc, vibrating plates or diaphragms have been used to generate cavitating sound fields. From 6–60 kc, magnetostriction transducers are used.   Frequencies from 0.1–10 mc have several advantages.   It is comparatively easy to generate and control the necessary electrical power.   Quartz transducers make it possible to operate at sharply defined frequencies, whereas barium titanate elements permit focusing the sound field so that the region of maximum acoustic pressure appears away from the transducer face.

One problem which never has been completely solved is monitoring the ultrasonic intensity.   Hydrophones usually are sensitive to pressure variations and fail just where the interesting region of cavitation starts. Various ingenious devices have been used, although the most common method is simply to measure the power input to the transducer (or current through it).   This is easiest, but fails to take into account the dependence of transducer efficiency on load or cavitation.   (The latter may vary with the dirt or biological cells suspended in the liquid.)

3. Biological Cells and Cavitation

The destruction of biological cells in suspension occurs when cavitation is taking place.   For many years, it was suspected that some other parameter of the acoustic field or perhaps heating associated with cavitation could be responsible for the cellular destruction.   A large number of experiments with many types of cells including blood cells, protozoans, bacteria, and algae have all confirmed that the cells are broken by mechanical rupture as a result of cavitation.

At one time, it was believed that the large acoustic pressures, or perhaps the local particle velocities and accelerations, were in some way responsible for the observed cellular rupture.   All of these properties are, if anything, enhanced when cavitation is suppressed, either by increasing the applied pressure or by vacuum degassing.   In contrast, cellular destruction disappears or is greatly diminished when cavitation is suppressed.

In some ultrasonic phenomena, such as the detonation of explosives under water in the presence of cavitation, it has been shown that the local heating was the important parameter.   To prove that this heating is not the active agent when cavitation occurs near biological cells demanded additional experiments.   If local heating were important, the rate of cellular disruption should be strongly temperature dependent. Experiments with bacteria, red blood cells, and protozoa have shown that quite the reverse is true, that the rate of cell breakage is almost independent of the temperature from 0° to 30°C.   Another indication is to compare red blood cells heated to boiling with those agitated by a cavitating ultrasonic field. The heat-destroyed cells break into small spherical pieces, each containing some methemoglobin.[1] However, the red blood cells which are "ultrasonerated" form hemoglobin free ghosts and cellular debris; the hemoglobin itself is slowly converted to the met form.

Another action of cavitation is to break molecular bonds. For instance, H_2O molecules are fractured into H, OH, and HO_2 radicals and H_2O_2 is produced. Similarly, when a solution of NaCl is exposed to a cavitating ultrasonic field, Cl is produced. The Cl is apparently formed directly, for much more is present than could be formed by the H_2O_2 produced by the cavitation. Either free Cl atoms or H_2O_2 molecules could destroy biological cells. Quantitative studies, however, indicate that the concentrations of H_2O_2 and Cl are several orders of magnitude too small to account for the cellular disruption.

Electron-microscope studies of cells exposed to ultrasonic fields show that they are torn mechanically. Some typical electron micrographs are shown in Figure 2. This tearing could occur in any of several closely related fashions. In the presence of an expanding and collapsing bubble (that is, cavity), there will be very violent motions close to the bubble and relatively weak ones several diameters away. Thus, a part of the cell wall near the bubble will execute large motions relative to the rest of the cell wall. The resulting shearing strains could easily rip the cell wall. A model of this action is shown in Figure 3. Near the collapsing cavities, there is also an extremely vigorous stirring type of turbulence. The cell walls might be broken by the shearing stresses set up by this turbulence.

Similar mechanical rupture of cell walls of many types such as those of amoebae, yeast, and white blood cells can be produced by rapid local shearing stresses. For instance, a micromanipulator needle can be slowly inserted into and then removed from these cells without damaging them. However, a rapid jab will permanently destroy the cell wall. By analogy, one might suspect that not only the shearing stresses produced by cavitation but also the rapidity of their application are important.

Thus, cavitation may tear cellular structures by a combined effect of local shearing stress, local turbulence, and rapidly applied shearing action. When, and only when, cavitation occurs, are these effects observed.

---

[1] Methemoglobin is an altered form of hemoglobin with an optical absorption spectrum differing from that of the hemoglobin occurring normally in red blood cells.

4. Cellular Fragilities and Resonances

Biological cells such as protozoans, bacteria, algae, yeast, white blood cells, and red blood cells are destroyed in cavitating acoustic fields.

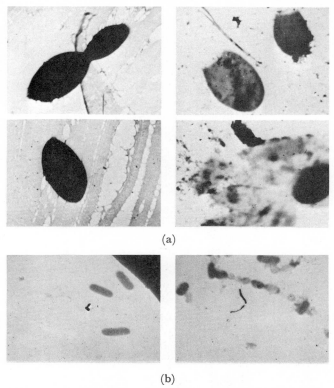

(a)

(b)

Figure 2. (a) Electron photomicrographs of *Saccharomyces cerevisiae*, unexposed cells illustrated on left. Cells exposed to 9 kc magnetostriction oscillator, illustrated on the right, show fragmented cells, some in which end has been broken, and some intact cells exhibiting marked irregularity in density. (b) Electron photomicrographs of *Escherichia coli*, strain B. Unexposed cells illustrated on left. Cells exposed to sound field, illustrated on the right, show increased debris and fragmented cells. After H. Kinsloe, E. Ackerman, and J. J. Reid, "Exposure of Microorganisms to Measured Sound Fields," *J. Bacteriology* **68**: 373 (1954).

The rate of destruction can be altered by a number of physical factors. Anything tending to decrease or suppress cavitation tends to protect the

cells. Increases in the viscosity and in the wetting ability of the suspending medium have been found to raise the ultrasonic pressure
necessary for cavitation. Thus, red blood cells in isotonic saline are
ruptured at lower ultrasonic pressures than are necessary in whole blood.

The threshold for cavitation always depends on the part of the field
where the greatest ultrasonic pressures
occur because stirring invariably
accompanies cavitation. For non-
focused sound fields, these maxima
occur at or near the transducer surface.
Experiments have shown that over a
wide frequency range, from perhaps
250 cps to 10 mc, the threshold is unchanged. By contrast, in focused
sound fields where cavitation occurs
away from the surface of the transducer, the ultrasonic pressure necessary to produce cavitation increases
rapidly as the frequency is raised.

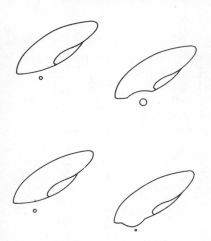

Figure 3. The distortions of a cell wall
which might be caused by an oscillating bubble near the cell. After
Eugene Ackerman, "Pressure Thresholds for Biologically Active Cavitation," *J. Appl. Physics* **24**: 1371 (1953).

The threshold for cavitation in the
body of the liquid is controlled, at a
given frequency, by the existence of
submicroscopic pockets of gas or vapor
called *nuclei*. If the amplitude of the
pressure changes during the ultrasonic
cycle is sufficiently great, the nucleus
grows, while the pressure is decreasing,
to such a large volume that it col-
lapses violently when the pressure starts to increase. The product of the
pressure amplitude times the period of ultrasonic wave determines the
pressure amplitudes necessary for violent collapse of the cavities. At about
10 kc, one atmosphere of pressure amplitude is sufficient, whereas at 1
mc the threshold for cavitation in air-saturated water is about 30 atm.

Over very wide frequency ranges, the *relative* rates at which different
types of biological cells are destroyed remain unaltered. These relative
rates can be used to indicate the relative fragility of different cell types.
To make this quantitative, one must study the time rate of cell destruction in a constant sound field. Studies of these rates show that as long
as at least 1 per cent of the population remains undamaged, one may
write

$$\frac{dN}{dt} = -RN \tag{1}$$

where N is the cell concentration, t is time, and R is the rate constant determining the probability of rupture per unit time.   At lower fractions of the original population remaining undamaged, this equation is not always obeyed.   The validity of Equation 1 is illustrated in Figure 4.

In integrated form, the preceding equation becomes

$$\ln\,(N/N_0)\,=\,Rt$$

Thus, a plot of N against time permits calculating a value for R.   The value of R is a fragility in arbitrary units, provided both the ultrasonic field and the suspending medium remain constant.

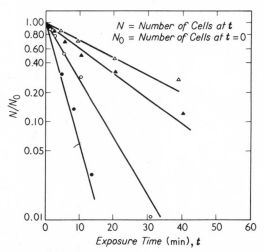

Figure 4. Log N/N_0 vs t. These four curves illustrate the linear dependence of log N/N_0 on the exposure time t. The four curves were obtained with different cells exposed to a constant cavitating sonic field.

The table on page 229 gives some typical values for relative fragilities, normalized so that human red blood cells (rbc) are unity.   Note the wide range which represents the different properties of the surfaces of different cells.   The larger ones tend to be more fragile as measured by this method, but there is no simple relationship between size and fragility.

Ultrasonic measurements of fragilities give results similar to other types of measurements.   For example, the fragility of red blood cells can easily be measured by another method.   This consists in suspending the cells in NaCl solutions of various concentrations.   As the concentration is lowered, the red blood cells swell and eventually burst (lyse).

TABLE I

Ultrasonic Fragilities of Various Cells

Cell Type	Relative Fragility	Average Diameter
Paramecium aurelia G's	16	80 microns
Paramecium caudatum	4	150
Amphibma tridactyla rbc	3	50
Trichomonas foetus	2	12
Human rbc	1	6
Rabbit sperm*	0.7	5
Amoeba proteus	0.4	200
T-2 bacteriophage	0.2	0.01
Escherichia coli U.W.	0.15	1
Escherichia coli B	0.01	1

* Destruction interpreted to mean removal of tail from sperm cell.

The lowest NaCl concentration at which lysis does not occur is an osmotic measure of fragility. Both osmotic and ultrasonic methods show that the fragility of human red blood cells increases as the cells age. The ultrasonic measurements show this increase sooner than do the osmotic ones. Thus, the two do not measure exactly the same properties of the cell.

The role of the cell surface in determining fragility can be illustrated dramatically by the protozoan, *Blepharisma*. These are pink ciliates somewhat similar to paramecia in shape. When a culture of *blepharisma* is exposed to suitable narcotics (for example, morphine sulfate) the animals shed their pink pellicles while retaining their shape, cilia, and so on. They look even more like paramecia without their pellicles than with them. The relative fragility of the animals is doubled after they shed their pellicles. This indicates that although the pellicle does not control the shape of the animals, it does contribute to their ability to withstand mechanical disturbances.

Although at most frequencies the relative breakdown rates are the same, at certain frequencies, experiments with paramecia, blepharisma, and red blood cells indicate greatly increased sensitivity to ultrasonically induced cavitation. It seems natural to interpret these frequencies as cellular resonances induced by cavitation. From a knowledge of these resonances, it should be possible to determine the elastic properties of the cell walls. This subject is sufficiently specialized for the entire next chapter to be devoted to it.

Thus, the rupture of single biological cells in a cavitating ultrasonic field has been useful not only for the preparation of enzyme and particulate extracts, but also to study the fragility and elastic properties of the outer surfaces of living cells.

5. Neurosurgery with Ultrasound

Ultrasonic agitation can be used for surgery within the central nervous system.　This application is very different from the effects of cavitation on single cells in suspension; further, it appears not to involve the general tissue heating discussed in Chapter 11.　Essentially, neurosurgery with ultrasound depends on the fact that neurons can be destroyed by short ultrasonic pulses at high acoustic pressure levels.　The pulses can be made sufficiently short so that negligible heating occurs.

The neuron damage can be restricted to a small volume by the use of sharply focused ultrasonic beams.　The wavelength of sound at 1 mc in water or tissue is

$$\lambda = \frac{c}{\nu} \doteq \frac{1.5 \times 10^5 \text{ cm/sec}}{10^6/\text{sec}} = 0.15 \text{ cm}$$

Thus, it should be possible by the use of suitable focusing devices to restrict the damage to a volume of about 1 mm^3, that is, about 10^{-3} ml. Very complex apparatus has been used to approach this extreme of focusing.

Neurosurgery with ultrasound has several advantages over more conventional surgery.　First, and perhaps most important, the pulse duration and intensity can be adjusted so that the blood vessels and supporting (glia) cells are undamaged.　Second, it is possible to destroy neurons within the brain without damaging the surface of the brain. As in other types of brain surgery, a part of the skull must be removed before the application of the ultrasound.

The action of destroying the neurons but leaving the surrounding cells undamaged is not clearly understood.　However, a number of possible explanations can easily be eliminated.　For example, the action on the neurons is not due to heating.　Experiments at different temperatures showed the same results.　Moreover, intermittent exposures produced the same destruction as continuous exposures of the same total exposure time.　Likewise, the neurosurgical effects do not depend critically upon the frequency of the applied signal.　Thus, they are not a resonant type of phenomenon.　Static pressures of a magnitude comparable to those occurring during the positive pressure of the acoustic cycle do not produce any damage.

The absence of other effects suggests cavitation as a possible cause of neuron destruction.　Traditionally, the most reliable test for cavitation has been to apply an excess static pressure.　If the effects observed are due to cavitation, these should be decreased when an excess pressure is applied.　This is, indeed, the case for the damage to neurons; at any ultrasonic pressure levels, the destruction is much less when a static excess pressure of about 13 atm is applied. However, as is illustrated in Figure 5, neuronal destruction is still observed when the acoustic pressure amplitude is 6 atm, whereas the static or average pressure is 13 atm. While making cavitation less likely as a cause for neuronal destruction, these observations do not rule it out completely because cavitation is observed in particulate suspensions at positive pressures.

Another criterion for cavitation is the existence of a sharp pressure threshold below which no effects would be observed. A sharp threshold

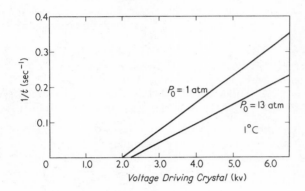

Figure 5. Minimum time for paralysis. The lines on the graph represent measurements, at two hydrostatic pressures, of the relationship of the driving voltage on the crystal to the reciprocal of the "minimum time for paralysis" for frogs cooled to 1 C. After W. J. Fry, "Action of Ultrasound on Nerve Tissue—a Review," *J. Acous. Soc. Am.* **25**: 1 (1953).

of this nature does exist for the ultrasonic destruction of neurons. Moreover, this threshold depends on the applied external pressure, although the rate of change is relatively small.

Thus, the application of extremely high intensity bursts of ultrasonic energy in destroying neurons is not fully understood. It appears possible that this might be a different sort of cavitation effect. Cellular injury due to effects other than cavitation was demonstrated by Goldman and Lepeschkin using algae and rotifers. This injury was similar to the neuron damage in that the cells were not disrupted. However, the injuries to algae and rotifers could be observed immediately after exposure to ultrasound, whereas the damage to neurons could not be detected histologically for the first ten minutes after exposure. Whatever its origin, the ultrasonic destruction of neurons is of clinical importance to the surgeon.

REFERENCES

1. Bergmann, Ludwig, *Der Ultraschall und seine Anwendung in Wissenschaft und Technik* (Zürich: S. Hirzel Verlag, 1954).
   a. Plus literature summary to 1957, a supplement to book.
   b. Read especially: "Biologische und Medizinische Wirkung des Ultraschalls," pp. 909–960.
2. Hueter, T. F., and R. H. Bolt, *Sonics: Techniques for the Use of Sound and Ultrasound in Engineering and Science* (New York: John Wiley & Sons, Inc., (1955). Read particularly pp. 215–244 on cavitation.
3. Gregg, E. C., Jr., "Ultrasonics: Biologic Effects," *Medical Physics*, Otto Glasser, ed. (Chicago, Illinois: Year Book Publishers, Inc., 1950) Vol. 2, pp. 1132–1138.
4. Grabar, Pierre, "Biological Actions of Ultrasonic Waves," *Advances in Biological and Medical Physics*, J. H. Lawrence, and C. A. Tobias, eds. (New York: Academic Press, Inc., 1953) Vol. 3, pp. 191–246.
5. Fry, W. J., in C. A. Tobias and J. H. Lawrence, eds., *Advances in Biological and Medical Physics* Vol. 8 (New York: Academic Press, Inc., 1958).

The destructive effects of high intensity ultrasound are discussed in a wide variety of articles in numerous journals, ranging from *J. Acous. Soc. Am.* and *J. Appl. Physiol.* to *J. Cell. & Comp. Physiol.* and *J.A.M.A.*

13

Mechanical Resonances of Biological Cells

I. Experimental Basis

In Chapter 12, it was shown that single biological cells in suspension are ruptured if the ultrasonic field is strong enough to produce cavitation. There seems little doubt that the destructive effects are produced by the shearing forces in the immediate neighborhood of these cavities, even though the exact details of how this occurs remain uncertain. Qualitatively, the same results are obtained at 1 kc/sec and 1 mc/sec. Most studies of ultrasonic rupture of single cells have employed only one frequency or, at best, an isolated set of frequencies. However, certain studies by the author and others have shown that frequency effects do occur; that is, at certain characteristic frequencies the cells of a particular type are ruptured much more readily than at neighboring frequencies. These optima are customarily referred to as resonances; they depend on the cell type and size.

Most mechanical structures have resonances. These in turn form a basis for studying the mechanical system. Mechanical resonances are used to investigate crystal structure, properties of liquids, and internal

233

friction in metals and polymers. It appears reasonable that if similar resonances occurred for biological cells, these resonances could be an indication of the physical properties of the cells.

The previous chapter referred to the existence of certain characteristic frequencies at which cells are more easily destroyed than at other frequencies. At a characteristic frequency, the relative rate at which a given type of cell is destroyed is greatly increased. Optical studies have also shown distortions in the shape of cells exposed to ultrasonic vibrations; these distortions occur to a greater extent at a lower ultrasonic pressure at certain frequencies characteristic of the geometry of the cell. The accompanying table shows the sizes and the characteristic frequencies of various strains of paramecia. Other studies have shown similar effects for red blood cells and for single cell types of algae. It is easiest to interpret these as due to mechanical resonances involving the cell surfaces. Similar surface resonances have been demonstrated and studied for air bubbles suspended in water and for rain drops.

TABLE I

Optimum Frequency versus Size

Cell Type	Maximum Diameter	Minimum Diameter	Optimum Frequency
P. caudatum	$223\,\mu$	$63\,\mu$	1.2 kc
P. bursaria	118	51	1.7
P. aurelia G's	124	29	3.3
P. trichium	80	38	4.1
RBC-*Amphiuma*	45	10	16.5

In this chapter, the mathematical theory for surface resonances of biological cells is discussed. It forms a link between cell models and the experiments demonstrating characteristic frequencies. In this chapter, the typical approach of the mathematical physicist is followed. First, very simple models are analyzed, then the conclusions are modified to fit more complex models which come closer to the physical form of the particular type of biological cells involved.

It was noted in the introduction that an attempt had been made to limit the level of mathematics necessary to understand this text but that a few chapters demonstrated that biophysics does use more advanced mathematical techniques where needed. The reader with an aversion to mathematical treatments is advised to omit the rest of the chapter. Those whose mathematics does not extend beyond calculus will find it necessary to accept several statements and conclusions on faith but should find most of the chapter understandable.

One might wonder why surface modes of resonance were referred to above as the basis for the characteristic frequencies for cellular disruption. Far more work has been done with pulsating bubbles in which the surface remains spherical than with bubble surface modes of vibration. However, all calculations show that any pulsating modes for biological cells (or any resonance dependent on the wavelength of sound in the suspending medium) should occur at much higher frequencies than those observed with cavitating sound fields. Accordingly, the characteristic

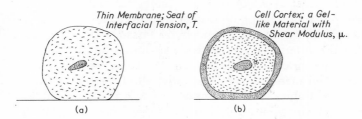

Thin Membrane; Seat of Interfacial Tension, T.

Cell Cortex; a Gel-like Material with Shear Modulus, μ.

(a)   (b)

Figure 1. The interfacial-tension model (a) and rigid-shell model (b). These two models of the surface of a biological cell are essentially different in that (a) presupposes that the cell wall lacks any rigidity or shear modulus whereas, by contrast (b) includes the rigidity of the outer cell layers but ignores any interfacial tension which may be present. Both disregard the contributions of the intracellular structure to the forces determining the cell shape.

frequencies seem to represent some other resonance of the biological cell such as surface vibrations.

Sections 2 and 3 deal with the mathematical development of two simple models of biological cells, both of which make resonances reasonable in the observed frequency ranges. These are illustrated in Figure 1. The first model treats the cell as if it were a sphere surrounded by a membrane possessing an interfacial tension but no rigidity. The internal viscosity of the cell is ignored in this first approximation. This model has been used to describe the results of centrifuge studies on cells, shape-distortion studies, and so forth. Because the model has proved useful for static studies, it seemed a promising one for dynamic studies such as observations of surface modes of resonances.

The second model also treats the cell as a fluid-filled sphere with negligible internal viscosity. However, it assigns a rigidity to the cell cortex, or outer layers. In both models, the cells are considered, then, to be spheres filled with one ideal, incompressible liquid and surrounded by another. Clearly, no biological cell fits this description. Thus, the

developments of Sections 2 and 3 can be regarded only as first approximations.   In Section 4, more exact solutions are outlined which include the
effects of viscosity, of compressibility, and of departures from spherical
shape.

2. Interfacial-Tension Model

This first model approximates the biological cell by a spherical shell
lacking any rigidity but possessing an interfacial tension.   The cell is
filled with liquid and surrounded by liquid.   It makes no difference
whether this interfacial tension is a true liquid-liquid interfacial tension,
a liquid-membrane interfacial tension, or a surface-tension residual
in a stretched membrane.   Physically, all of these may exist at the cell
boundary.   Values of this interfacial tension T computed from static
experiments ranged from 0.01 to 3.0 dynes/cm.   The theory discussed
here gives values of T from 0.03 to 15 dynes/cm for vertebrate red blood
cells and ciliate protozoans.

The surface motions of this model are very similar to the resonant
modes of a rain drop or of an air bubble in water.   The rain drop and the
bubble are different from cells in having liquid on only one side of the
boundary and also in possessing a much higher surface tension, around
75 dynes/cm.   Nonetheless, the general forms of the motions are similar.
Some typical modes for this geometry are illustrated in Figure 2.   These
types have been photographed for oscillating bubbles and for liquid
droplets.

In order to describe the resonant modes of this model quantitatively, it
is necessary to use a little mathematics.   Because the liquid is assumed
incompressible and its flow irrotational, the motion may be described in
terms of a velocity potential φ.   This velocity potential is defined so
that the negative of its gradient is the vector velocity $\vec{v}$; that is,

$$\vec{v} = -\vec{\nabla}\varphi \tag{1}$$

For noncompressible fluids, the divergence of $\vec{v}$ is zero; in terms of φ,

$$\nabla^2\varphi = 0 \tag{2}$$

Next, the equation of motion may be expressed in terms of this same
velocity potential.   Newton's second law for an incompressible fluid, in
the absence of any external-force field, is approximately given by

$$-\vec{\nabla}p \doteq \rho\,\frac{\partial \vec{v}}{\partial t} \tag{3}$$

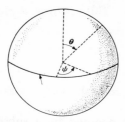

(a) Sphere. Illustrates definition of θ and ψ.

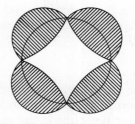

(b) Equatorial cross section ($\theta = \pi/2$). Shows distortion as a function of ψ in any mode P^2_{2n}.

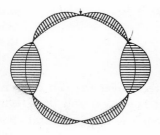

(c) Polar cross section ($\psi = \pi/4$ and $5\pi/4$). Shows distortion as a function of θ in P^2_4 mode.

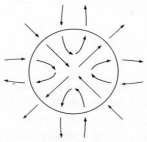

(d) Fluid motion. Shown for equatorial cross section ($\theta = \pi/2$) for a P^2_{2n} mode. Motion shown for $\frac{1}{2}$ cycle only.

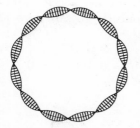

(e) Equatorial plane for mode characterized by $m = 6$.

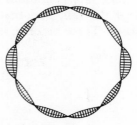

(f) Polar plane for mode characterized by $n - m = 4$. A three-dimensional combination of E and F illustrates P^6_{10}.

Figure 2. Various modes of oscillation for interfacial-tension model. Liquid flow lines assume irrotational flow. The symbols are explained in the text. Similar modes characterized by P^m_n for bubbles are easily observed for n greater than 8. The number of nodal diameters in the equatorial plane ($\theta = \pi/2$) is characterized by m. The number of "θ" nodal circles is given by $n - m$.

where ρ is the density, and p is the pressure. Substituting Equation 1 into Equation 3 and integrating leads to

$$p = \rho \frac{\partial \varphi}{\partial t} \tag{4}$$

This is an integrated equation of motion; it must be valid both within and outside the cell membrane.

Quantities outside the membrane will be denoted by a subscript o, whereas those within will be denoted by a subscript i. Using these, one may rewrite Equations 2 and 4 as

$$\nabla^2 \varphi_o = 0 \qquad \nabla^2 \varphi_i = 0 \tag{2'}$$

and

$$p_o = \rho_o \frac{\partial \varphi_o}{\partial t} \qquad p_i = \rho_i \frac{\partial \varphi_i}{\partial t} \tag{4'}$$

In the model, the two liquids may slip freely over the cell surface but still not lose contact with it. This latter condition will be satisfied if the component of $\vec{v}$ in the radial r direction is continuous at the cell surface, $r = a$. Analytically, this is

$$\frac{\partial \varphi_i}{\partial r} = \frac{\partial \varphi_o}{\partial r} \qquad \text{at} \qquad r = a \tag{5}$$

Other boundary conditions are that there is no net acceleration of the center of the cell, and that the velocity outside goes to zero at long distances. These become, in terms of φ,

$$\frac{\partial \varphi_i}{\partial r} = 0 \quad \text{and} \quad \frac{1}{r} \frac{\partial \varphi_i}{\partial \theta} = \frac{1}{r \sin \theta} \frac{\partial \varphi_i}{\partial \psi} = 0 \quad \text{at} \quad r = 0 \tag{6}$$

and

$$\frac{\partial \varphi_o}{\partial r} \to 0 \qquad \text{as} \qquad r \to \infty \tag{7}$$

where θ is the azimuthal angle and ψ the latitude.

The final boundary condition involves the cell membrane. This possesses an interfacial tension and in general will support a pressure difference Δp across it. Denoting by $R(\theta, \psi)$ the displacement of the membrane in the radial direction, one readily shows that at $r = a$

$$\Delta p = p_i - p_o = \frac{T}{a^2 \sin \theta} \frac{\partial}{\partial \theta} \left(\sin \theta \frac{\partial R}{\partial \theta} \right)$$

$$+ \frac{T}{a^2 \sin^2 \theta} \frac{\partial^2 R}{\partial \psi^2} - \frac{2T}{a^2} R + \frac{2T}{a} \tag{8}$$

where T is the interfacial tension. Differentiating Equation 8 with respect to time and recognizing that

$$\frac{\partial R}{\partial t} = -\frac{\partial \varphi}{\partial r} \quad \text{at} \quad r = a$$

one finds

$$\frac{\partial p_o}{\partial t} - \frac{\partial p_i}{\partial t} = \frac{T}{a^2 \sin \theta} \frac{\partial}{\partial \theta} \left(\sin \theta \frac{\partial^2 \varphi_i}{\partial r \partial \theta} \right)$$

$$+ \frac{T}{a^2 \sin^2 \theta} \frac{\partial^3 \varphi_i}{\partial r \partial \psi^2} - \frac{2T}{a^2} \frac{\partial \varphi_i}{\partial r} \quad \text{at} \quad r = a \quad (9)$$

The problem, then, is to find a solution to the Equation of continuity (2′) and the Equations of motion (4′) obeying the boundary conditions (5), (6), (7), and (9).

Because the problem has been set up in spherical coordinates, the most general solutions to Equation 2′ are

$$\varphi_i = \sum_{n=0}^{\infty} A_n r^n e^{-j\omega_n t} S_n(\theta, \psi)$$

$$\varphi_o = \sum_{n=0}^{\infty} B_n r^{-n+1} e^{-j\omega_n t} S_n(\theta, \psi)$$
(10)

where A, B, and ω are constants, j the square root of -1, and

$$S_n(\theta, \psi) = \sum_{m=0}^{n} a_m P_n^m (\cos \theta) e^{im\psi}$$

In this, the a's are constants and P_n^m is the mth associated Legendre polynomial of order n. It may be readily shown that

$$\frac{1}{\sin \theta} \frac{\partial}{\partial \theta} \left(\sin \theta \frac{\partial S_n}{\partial \theta} \right) + \frac{1}{a^2 \sin^2 \theta} \frac{\partial^2}{\partial \psi^2} S_n = \frac{n(n+1)}{2} S_n$$

It is possible to satisfy the boundary conditions only if the frequency has certain discrete values given by

$$\omega_n^2 = \frac{T}{\rho_i a^3} \frac{n(n-1)(n+2)}{\left[1 + \left(\dfrac{n}{n+1} \right) \dfrac{\rho_o}{\rho_i} \right]}$$
(11)

For the lowest possible mode, $n = 2$, this becomes for $\rho_i \doteq \rho_o \doteq 1$,

$$\omega_2^2 = 4.8 T a^{-3}$$
(12)

This formula has been used to estimate some of the interfacial tensions referred to earlier. When a higher harmonic is used, the values obtained for T are lower than those computed from Equation 12.

3. Gelatinous-Shell Model

The static experiments used to measure interfacial tensions of nonmobile or slowly moving cells could be interpreted in other ways. Some involving ultracentrifugation may measure the tensile strength of the cell membrane. Others, depending on the gravitational distortion of cell shape, may actually be measuring the rigidity of an elastic outer layer (or cortex) of the individual cell. In a like fashion, the optimum frequencies, or resonances, observed in the ultrasonic destruction of single cells in a ·cavitating suspension can also be interpreted as due to resonant vibrations of a rigid spherical cell immersed in, and filled with, an incompressible fluid.

This rigid-shell model is very different from the interfacial-tension model, in terms of both its mechanical structure and its biochemical make-up. However, its predictions for distortions and resonances of biological cells are very similar to those of the interfacial-tension model. Indeed, there is no simple way to distinguish one from the other.

The rigidity of the cell cortex is negligible compared to steel, glass, or even wood. Rigidities are described by elastic moduli called *coefficients of rigidity* or *shear moduli*, which are about 10^8–10^{10} dynes/cm^2 for solid objects. All protein gels have much smaller, but nonetheless measurable, shear moduli in the range of 10^3–10^5 dynes/cm^2. Assuming gelatinous properties for the outer layers of the single cell leads to predicted resonant frequencies in the ranges observed for protozoans and erythrocytes.

The rigid-shell model is considerably more complex than the interfacial-tension model. The analysis of the resonances of the rigid-shell model is similar to that of closed rigid shells in air. The restriction of a closed shell is important because most analyses of the vibrations of shells and plates assume no extension of the midsurface of the shell, a condition which cannot be met for closed shells.

For vibrations of rigid shells with extension of the midsurface in air, both the kinetic and potential energies are proportional to the shell thickness h. Most of the modes occur at frequencies independent of h. For the cell cortex, the liquid on both sides may move, as well as the cell cortex. Accordingly, some of the resonant frequencies depend on the effective thickness of the cortex h or, at any rate, on its ratio to the effective cell radius a. This is shown by a detailed derivation.

Rather than attempting to present the entire derivation, only the results will be described. Two general types of motion of the shell are considered, those which include radial motion as well as tangential motion, and those involving tangential motion only. The latter are simpler and will be described first.

The tangential-type modes are not affected by the intra- and extracellular liquids, to the extent that these liquids may be considered as having negligible viscosity. This tangential-motion-only mode may be described by a displacement in the ψ direction only, which will be denoted by Ψ. Because the liquids slip freely over the surface, these modes and frequencies are independent of h. They are described by

$$\Psi = A_n \frac{d}{d(\cos \theta)} \left[P_n \left(\cos \theta \right) \right] e^{-i\omega_n t}$$

$$\omega_n^2 = \frac{\mu}{\rho_s a} (n - 1)(n + 2)$$

(13)

where A_n is a constant, μ is the shear modulus and ρ_s is the shell density. Values of μ in the range of 10^3 dynes/cm^2 lead to the resonant frequencies in the ranges observed for the optima for cellular destruction in cavitating acoustic fields.

In modes with both radial and tangential motion, there are both a radial displacement $R(r, \theta)$ and a tangential displacement $\Theta(r, \theta)$. (This argument could be made more general by including a displacement Ψ, and allowing R, Θ, and Ψ to depend on ψ as well as r and θ. However, very little is gained at the expense of making the notation much more complex.) The problem with both R and Θ cannot be solved in a simple closed form analogous to Equations 10 and 13. However, the differential equation can be satisfied by

$$R_n = A_n P_n(\cos \theta) e^{-i\omega_n t}$$

and

(14)

$$\Theta_n = \Lambda_n \frac{\partial R_n}{\partial \theta}$$

where A_n is a constant and Λ_n a function of a, h, μ, and Poisson's ratio.

For given values of these parameters one can also find three values for ω_n. Two of these lead to absurd numerical contradictions. The third value of ω_n is in the range observed for optimum cellular destruction, if the shear modulus μ is around 10^3 dynes/cm^2, and h/a is in the range of 0.1–0.2.

Thus, this model predicts two different types of modes in the observed frequency range for cells having outer layers of protoplasm similar to a protein gel. If detailed observations on the cell shape during such resonance were possible, one could distinguish these two types of modes from each other and from interfacial-tension modes. In the absence of such observations, it is impossible to choose between these alternatives. For example, a photograph of a red blood cell in a cavitating ultrasonic field is shown in Figure 3. It strongly supports the existence of surface modes of resonance, but it is impossible to determine the number of nodal diameters, much less examine the details of the shape necessary to distinguish various modes.

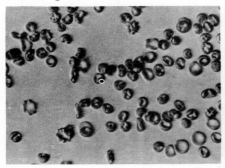 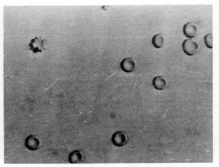

Figure 3. Photographs of rat red blood cells in ultrasonic fields. Note that there are some undistorted cells and some showing various modes of distortion. After L. Binstock and E. Ackerman.

4. More Exact Treatments

In deriving the expressions for the resonant frequencies in Sections 2 and 3, a number of assumptions were made. The validity of these is considered in more detail in this section. To a physicist, probably the most noticeable assumption was the absence of viscosity in the fluids. Readers with more biological training would emphasize the nonspherical shape of all real cells. Other factors, explicitly or implicitly neglected, include the effects of the compressibility of the liquids, the relationship of breakdown rate to resonance, and the actual modes present.

The major effect of viscosity is to damp any free vibration. With the geometries chosen in this chapter and typical viscosities measured for protoplasm, that is, coefficients of viscosity from 2 to 10 centipoise, this damping is very pronounced. The net result is to broaden the resonance curve as shown in Figure 4; the curve including viscosity has a mechanical Q of the order of 2.[1] Nonetheless, the resonant frequencies are only

[1] The quality factor Q of a resonance may be defined in several equivalent forms. For the purpose of this chapter, it may be considered to be defined by the relationship

$$Q = f_0/\Delta f$$

where Δf is the width of the band between the two frequencies at which the square of the amplitude of the response of a vibrator is decreased by a factor of two from its value at the resonant frequency f_0 provided the vibrator is driven by a force of constant amplitude. The greater the damping, the broader will be the resonance and the lower the Q.

slightly shifted.   The inclusion of viscosity complicates the analysis but has no effect on the orders of magnitude computed for the interfacial tension T in Section 2, or the shear modulus μ in Section 3.   It does, however, show that all modes must depend on ψ, the lowest possible varying as $P_2^2(\cos \theta)\, e^{2j\psi}$.

The effects of quite large departures from a strictly spherical shape are much less than those due to viscosity.   The exact shape is not critical because neither the kinetic energy nor the potential energy depends sharply on the shape.   This independence of exact shape is

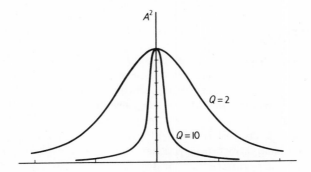

Figure 4. Effect of the quality factor Q on the shape of the resonance curve.

common to many types of resonances in all phases of physics, not only in elasticity.   The exact shape of cells is important for such effects as fluid flow past the cell and diffusion.   However, the resonant frequencies are very insensitive to changes in cell shapes.

The effects of the compressibility of the medium are also very small. This implies that surface modes are very hard to excite with plane acoustic waves.   In contrast, an extremely nonplanar waveform near small centers of cavitation could easily excite surface resonances of biological cells.   Likewise, streaming near a solid-liquid interface could excite surface resonances.

The cell disruption versus frequency curves at acoustic pressure levels near the threshold for cellular destruction can be characterized by an apparent Q that may be as large as 6.   This sharpness indicates that close to the threshold for cellular rupture, the rate of destruction increases much more rapidly than the amplitude of resonant vibration.   In contrast, at higher acoustic pressure levels, the apparent Q drops to values predicted for the vibration amplitude versus frequency curves.

Finally, it should be noted that the order of magnitude calculations in

Sections 2 and 3 were all based on the lowest possible mode being excited. However, similar studies with air bubbles showed that the higher modes were easier to excite than the lower ones. Similarly, photographs such as those in Figure 3 suggest that this is also true for biological cells; using a higher mode decreases the values of T calculated in Section 2 and of μ in Section 3. Because μ was barely high enough to be comparable with protein gels, whereas T was higher than estimated by static methods, the interpretation of the optimum frequencies as higher resonant modes slightly favors the interfacial-tension model.

5. Summary

A mathematical theory has been presented in this chapter in terms of which it is possible to explain observed maxima in the rates of destruction of ciliate protozoans and vertebrate erythrocytes in cavitating acoustic fields. Two different types of models were considered: one a cell surrounded by a membrane which is the seat of an interfacial tension, and the other a cell surrounded by a gel-like cortex. Both models, with reasonable physical constants, predict the observed resonances. The analyses were first performed on highly simplified models, and then the effects of the simplifications were discussed. It is impossible to choose between the various models in the light of the current experimental data. All agree with the available evidence.

REFERENCES

The following articles by the author and his co-workers discuss in more detail the material presented in this chapter.

1. Ackerman, Eugene, "Resonances of Biological Cells at Audible Frequencies," *Bull. Math. Biophys.* **13**: 93–106 (1951).
2. Ackerman, Eugene, "An Extension of the Theory of Resonances of Biological Cells, I. Effects of Viscosity and Compressibility," *Bull. Math. Biophys.* **16**: 141–150 (1954).
     a. "II. Cross-Section in a Plane Wave," *Bull. Math. Biophys.* **17**: 35–40 (1955).
     b. "III. Relationship of Breakdown Curves and Mechanical Q," *Bull. Math. Biophys.* **19**: 1–7 (1957).
3. Lombard, D. B., "Ultrasonic Rupture of Erythrocytes," Thesis, Pennsylvania State University (1955).
4. Binstock, L., "Photographic Studies of Erythrocytes in Ultrasonic Fields," Thesis, Pennsylvania State University (1960).

In addition, resonances of erythrocytes are discussed in:

5. Angerer, O. A., G. Barth, and W. Güttner, "Über den Wirkungmechanis-
mus biologischer Ultraschallreaktionen," *Strahlentherapie*. **84**: 601–610
(1951).

14

Structure of Viruses

I. Introduction

In the border zone between living cells and separate molecules, there is a class of particles having some characteristics of living cells and some characteristics of separate molecules. These are called *viruses*. For historical reasons, viruses infecting bacteria are given the separate name *bacteriophages*, or just *phages* for short. All viruses—plant, animal, and bacteriophages—have many common properties. These include extremely small size, 10–400 mμ; chemical simplicity (few types of molecules); lack of metabolism or reproduction outside of living cells; ability to attack only very specific cell types; absence of typical cellular structures such as membrane, nucleus, and granules; and ability to reproduce inside of the cell attacked, eventually destroying the host cell.

Virus studies have appealed to persons wishing to apply physics and chemistry to biology for a number of different reasons. First and foremost, no doubt, is the fact that viruses are simpler and exhibit a greater regularity than any single-celled plant or animal. At the same time, virus particles do reproduce and mutate in a fashion quite analogous to the more complex living organisms of a cellular nature. Another major reason biophysicists have been interested in virus research is that complex physical tools are necessary to study viruses; techniques used include electron microscopy, ultracentrifugation, spectrophotometry, and ionizing radiation. Although one can certainly use any of these without a knowledge of physics, it is also true that people with an inclination toward physics tend to feel more comfortable using these study tools. A third reason, albeit less important, is that many phases of virus research have involved mathematical manipulations of the data of a complex nature that appeals to certain physicists.

The existence of viruses, as well as many of their basic characteristics, however, were discovered by "pure" biologists. After it was established that bacteria and other microorganisms caused human (and animal) diseases, occasional cases were found in which no organisms of a microscopically visible size were associated with a disease. Eventually, it was discovered that diseases of this type even killed bacteria. The latter could be studied conveniently by conventional bacteriological techniques; the destructive agents were called bacteriophages.

The size, shape, and weight of viruses remained unknown until the development of modern physical equipment. In Table I are listed some

TABLE I
Some Physical Properties of Virus Particles

Type	Name	Shape	Dimensions
Plant	Tobacco Mosaic Virus (TMV)	Hexagonal rods	300 × 15 mμ
Plant	Bushy Stunt Tomato Virus (BSV)	Spheres	30 mμ in diameter
Animal	Influenza Virus	Flattened spheres	100–125 mμ in diameter; not all same
Animal	Poliomyelitis Virus	Spheres	30 mμ in diameter
Phage	E. coliphage T1	Hexagonal heads, long tails	Head 50 mμ wide Tail 150 × 10 mμ
Phage	E. coliphages T2, T4, and T6	Polyhedral heads	Head max. diameter 65 mμ; min. diameter 45 mμ Tail 100 × 25 mμ
Phage	E. coliphages T3 and T7	Hexagonal heads, short, stumpy tails	Head 47 mμ wide Tail 15 × 10 mμ
Phage	E. coliphage T5	Hexagonal heads, long tails	Head 65 mμ wide Tail 170 × 10 mμ

properties of a few viruses and bacteriophages. Those of the so-called "T series," which act on the bacterial species *Escherichia coli*, are all listed since these have been used in many studies. The T phages have the advantage that work in one laboratory can be compared with that in another; these T phages have been the "standard" for virus research for many years. Present knowledge indicates that they may be atypical viruses (and, hence, poor standards). Nonetheless, they have been studied so widely that most of the material in this chapter is based on experiments with T phages of *E. coli*. Figure 1 shows a T phage attached to a bacterial surface.

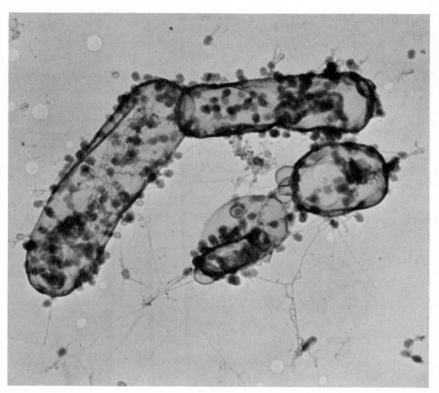

Figure I. Electron micrograph of T2 phage particles attached to ghosts of *E. coli B*. Note that many of the phage particles are attached to the bacterial ghosts by their tails. After T. F. Anderson, *American Naturalist* **86**: 91 (1952).

2. Phage Studies Using Bacteriological Methods

The routine method for analyzing bacteriophages involves bacterial plating techniques. To aid in understanding these techniques, the standard assay for determining bacterial concentration is first described. In this method, a large number of Petri dishes are made up with a sterile gelatinous medium on which the bacteria can grow. Each dish is carefully sterilized. One ml of the suspension of bacteria is poured into the dish and spread in a thin uniform film over the surface of the gel. (This is called a plate.) The plate is then covered, and the bacteria are allowed to grow for one or more days. If their initial concentration was of the order of 100 per ml, each will land on a separate spot on the plate and give rise to a small colony (also called a *clone*) which spreads out around the original bacterium. The clone has a size, shape, and color characteristic of the given type of bacteria. The clones can be counted visually after they have developed. Thus, the original number of bacteria in one ml can be determined.

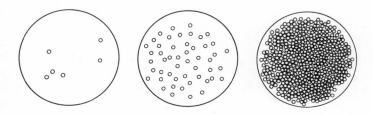

Figure 2. Bacterial plates for three different dilutions. The left hand plate represents a $10^7:1$ dilution which shows too few clones for meaningful counting, whereas the right hand one, a $10^5:1$ dilution, has far too many. However, the middle one, diluted $10^6:1$, shows about 50 clones. By counting duplicate plates at this dilution, one can find the original concentration of bacteria at the time of plating.

It is unlikely that the initial bacterial concentration will be in a range suitable for plating. Accordingly, a series of dilutions are made, each differing by a factor of 10. A few members of such a series are shown in Figure 2. On plates where the dilution is too great, too few clones develop to make counting statistically meaningful. On plates made up with too high a concentration of bacteria, many spots originate from two or more of the bacteria placed on the plate, and many clones overlap. In the extreme case, the entire plate will be covered with bacteria. Figure 2 illustrates typical plates after they have been incubated for two days.

When phages are studied by a plating method, bacteria are used at a concentration which would completely cover the plate in the absence of phage particles. If phages are present, clear areas develop on the surface of the plate. These result because each phage particle multiplies inside a bacterium until the cell wall is eventually ruptured. For every bacterium infected, as many as 300 new phage particles are sometimes produced. The new phage particles then enter other bacteria surrounding the original one, thereby producing a pattern which is characteristic of the particular phage. These clear spaces are called *plaques*. Figure 3 shows typical plaques for two strains of T2 bacteriophages infecting *E. coli*. Note that in Figure 2 the clones are bacteria on a clear background, whereas in Figure 3 the plaques are clear spots in a uniform layer of bacteria.

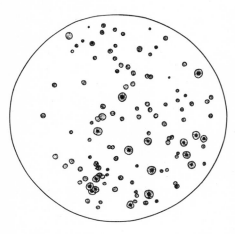

Figure 3. Phage plaques. This figure shows T2 plaques formed on *E. coli B*. The smaller plaques are wild type, whereas the larger ones are r-mutants.

This type of experiment and others using isotopic tracers have developed the following picture of bacteriophage activity. Outside the cell, the bacteriophage is initially attached reversibly to the bacterial cell wall. Once in contact, it opens a small hole through the cell wall and dumps the central part of the phage particle into the bacterium. Inside, the phage apparently breaks into smaller pieces. This can be shown by rupturing the bacteria sonically, after the phage has just entered. No active particles are found on plating.

Immediately upon entering the cell, the pieces of bacteriophage take over control of the cellular metabolism, directing it toward the production of many new phage particles. This period is called the *induction period* or the *eclipse*. Eventually (that is, after about 10 minutes at 37°C), the new phage particles start forming. When about a hundred of these are completed, the bacterium bursts, releasing the new phage particles into its surroundings. (This bursting is called *lysis*.) The new particles produced are replicas of the original one. If other bacteria are present, the cycle repeats; otherwise, the phage particles remain in suspension, not metabolizing or behaving in any fashion as living matter.

Because the phage particles are very small compared to the bacteria, more than one may enter a bacterium. If different types of phages are mixed, certain ones are able to "cross breed"; that is, some of the new phage particles have characteristics in between those of the two original strains. If two damaged phage suspensions are mixed, in some cases active phage can be produced by this cross-breeding process. In other words, *genetic recombination* has occurred.

It is also possible for a phage particle occasionally to change its characteristics, apparently spontaneously. (The characteristics include the size and shape of the plaque, the strains of bacteria it will infect, induction time, pH sensitivity, heat sensitivity, and shape and size as determined by the methods of Section 3.) This spontaneous change is called a *mutation*. Once a mutation has occurred, descendants of the mutant phage will reproduce the new characteristics faithfully.

Thus, bacteriophages are similar to living organisms in that they reproduce, exhibit genetic recombination, and also undergo mutations. They differ from living cells in not metabolizing outside of bacterial cells, in failing to show irritability outside of cells, and in the simplicity and uniformity of the complete bacteriophage. Other viruses behave similarly to bacteriophage in most respects. The largest ones such as influenza virus particles show neither the simplicity nor the uniformity of bacteriophages. However, the general pattern of initial attraction, cellular entry, induction period, production of many replicas of the original virus particle, and eventual cellular destruction is common to all viruses.

3. Virus Studies Using Physical Methods

A number of different types of physical techniques have been used to study the nature and activity of virus particles. Several of these methods are discussed briefly in this section: specifically, electron microscopy, ultracentrifugation, electrophoresis, and bombardment with ionizing radiation.

Electron microscopes are needed because virus particles are so very small. A few of the largest viruses have maximum diameters of about 400 mμ. The smallest separation resolvable with a light microscope is about one-half of this (see Chapter 23 for proof of resolution of the light microscope). Therefore, the largest viruses are barely visible in the light microscope. The phages and most viruses are much smaller, as is indicated in Table I. They cannot be seen with light microscopes.

Electron microscopes can resolve separations of 1 mμ (10 Å) or slightly less. Accordingly, suitable electron micrographs not only show the existence of the viruses and phages as separate particles, but also allow one to observe the shape and size of these particles. Rough particle counts show that the particles seen with the electron microscope are the same as those counted by plating techniques. The major disadvantage of electron microscopy is that the samples must be dried. As the air-water interface moves across the small particles, it may exert tremendous forces tending to distort them.

A novel way of avoiding this interface effect is to replace the water with ethyl alcohol and then liquid CO_2. This is then taken continuously

from the liquid to the gas by going around the critical point.   No interphase forces distort the specimen.   Phage particles attached by their tails
to *E. coli*, as shown in Figure 1, were prepared by this method.   The most
common method of avoiding surface-tension effects is by freeze-drying.

Another difficulty in using the electron microscope arises from the fact
that structures such as bacteria are so dense that it is not possible to
observe the phage developing within the bacteria.   This problem has

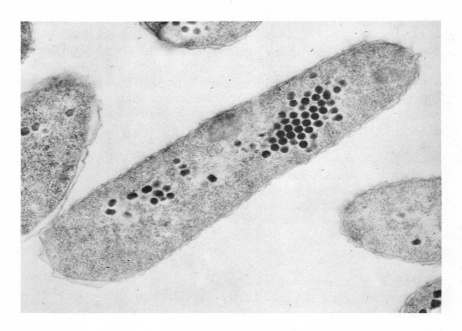

Figure 4. Electron micrograph of an *E. coli* bacterium infected
with T2 bacteriophages.   After E. R. Kellenberger, Labora-
toire de Biophysique, Université de Genève, Switzerland.

been solved by imbedding the bacteria in a suitable plastic and then
cutting sufficiently thin sections.   These show the phage particles
developing during the latter parts of the induction period.   A stained
section through an *E. coli* bacterium is shown in Figure 4.

As can be observed in Figure 1, the phage particles are all very
uniform.   This is characteristic of many different types of viruses.   The
extreme uniformity makes them similar to large molecules.   Molecules
can be crystallized, and so can many types of viruses.   The historical
example is a plant virus, tobacco mosaic virus, which infects tobacco
leaves.   Its crystallization led to an appreciation of the similarity of

large molecules and virus particles. Virus crystals have been studied by the technique of X-ray diffraction. These studies have led to models of the molecular arrangements within certain viruses.

The density and uniformity of virus particle size can be determined with an instrument known as the *ultracentrifuge*, in which the suspension containing the particles is subjected to accelerations 10^4 or more times gravity, by rapidly rotating it about an axis. The tube containing the suspension is at an angle to the axis of rotation. Particles heavier than the suspending medium will tend to migrate "down" the tube. The analytical ultracentrifuge is equipped with optical systems to make it possible to observe the migration of particles in the high gravity field during rotation.

By a series of calculations which will not be developed here, it is possible to use ultracentrifuge data to determine the molecular weight of small particles, as well as to determine the uniformity of particle size and shape. In addition to viruses, large, biologically important molecules can be measured in this fashion. At one time, it was believed that crystallization proved uniformity of particle size. Experiments with the ultracentrifuge have shown more than one component in certain crystalline viruses. Only one of the ultracentrifuge components was active as a virus.

Another physical property of large molecules is the rate of migration in an electrical field. This is called the electrophoretic mobility; it depends on the pH of the solution. Viruses, just as living cells, have a net negative charge at neutral pH and migrate to the anode. Electrophoretic studies have been used to demonstrate the uniformity of the virus particles, as well as changes in their charge as a function of pH. These studies, combined with ultracentrifuge and crystallization studies, have led to the picture of most viruses being uniform in particle weight, size, shape, and net charge.

A very different approach to virus studies consists in bombarding a dried layer of virus particles with ionizing radiation. It is then possible to apply target theory (see Chapter 16) to the virus and determine a critical volume throughout which energy transfer may occur. Such measurements show that on the average about 12 hits are necessary to destroy the infective properties of some viruses, whereas others are inactivated by single hit kinetics discussed in Chapter 16. These hits occur in a critical volume almost as big as the entire volume of the smaller viruses. For the larger viruses, the critical volume is much smaller than the particle size. In every case, this critical volume is about equal to the volume within the phage occupied by a class of substances called *nucleic acids*. Their properties are discussed further in the following section.

4. Physical Biochemistry of Viruses

Chemical analyses of the T series of coliphage show that those of this type consist of two classes of compounds: proteins and nucleic acids. Both are condensation type polymers; their chemical structure and form are discussed further in the next chapter. For the present, it is sufficient to note that proteins form part of the cell membranes and also part of all enzymes (that is, substances controlling the rate of biological reactions). The other class of compounds in T phages, the nucleic acids, is concerned with the transmission of genetic information and the synthesis of proteins. Two types of nucleic acids are known: DNA and RNA (Deoxyribose Nucleic Acids and Ribose Nucleic Acids). DNA is associated with genetic information in plants, animals, and bacteria, whereas both types appear to be associated with protein synthesis.

The bacteriophages all contain a large amount of DNA. This exists as a core inside a protein layer. The structure of some plant viruses is similar except that they contain RNA in place of DNA. The structure of some animal viruses is more complex, but all contain nucleic acid. The action of the bacteriophages has received more detailed study and will be discussed in the remainder of the section. The life cycle of a T phage is represented in Figure 5.

The T phages all attach to the bacterial surface by their tails. This attachment is at first reversible, but then certain enzymes, presumably proteins on the tip of the tail, make it irreversible. Certain receptor sites appear necessary for phage attachment. If the nucleic acid is removed from the phage (which can be done in the case of the even numbered T phages by osmotic shock) the phage particles attach to the bacterial surface exactly as if they were whole, but fail to reproduce. If an excess number of phage particles attack one bacterium, the cell undergoes "snap lysis"; that is, it breaks without reproducing phages. This also occurs when bacteriophages without nucleic acid are used.

After the complete bacteriophage attaches to the cell wall, it empties its nucleic acid content but none (or almost none) of its protein into the cell. The protein phage ghosts can be removed mechanically from outside the bacteria without interfering with phage reproduction. In contrast, if phages are mixed with broken pieces of bacterial cell walls, they attach to these pieces, emptying their nucleic acid content out through the other side of the cell wall.

Once the phage nucleic acid is inside the bacterium, it alters the metabolic processes of the bacterial cell. In some cases, the cell may divide for several generations carrying the phage with it in a latent form called a *prophage*. The cell is said to be in a *lysogenic* state. Eventually, the prophage is induced to enter the active phase called *vegetative*. The

T phages, in general, do not go through the lysogen stage but enter the vegetative stage directly.   In this stage, the bacterial cell starts manufacturing new proteins and nucleic acids typical of the phage.   At the end of a period of development, the nucleic acids are assembled.   The proteins are formed into doughnut-like forms about the nucleic acids.

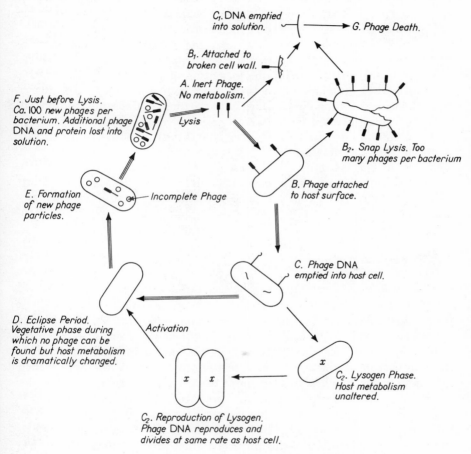

Figure 5. Life cycle of the bacteriophage.

These forms are then combined with other proteins to form whole phage particles.   Eventually, the bacterium bursts.   (This is called "lysis from within," in contrast to "snap lysis" which is lysis from without.)

The general character of many bacteria may be altered from without by two different processes, each of which bears some resemblance to the phage activity.   The first way is by mating or conjugation.   In this, two bacteria join together, some of the DNA from one passing into the other.   The one receiving the DNA takes on new characteristics typical of the donor.   These may include resistance to antibiotics, clone shape and size, form of cellular wall, and metabolic nutrients required. Essentially, the same results can be obtained by exposing the bacteria to high concentrations of DNA extracted from a strain having slightly different characteristics.   The DNA molecules apparently pass through the cell membrane and alter the genetic properties of the cell.

Infection by bacteriophage is an extreme example of adding foreign DNA (the result of which is the acquirement of new properties which are fatal to the cell).   During the formation of new phage particles, the nucleic acid threads appear to break and then recombine, not always with the same partners, but always with partners of the same length.   If a single cell is infected with several strains of the same type of phage, this recombination can lead to new phages having some properties of each of the parent strains.   This makes it possible to study phage genetics.   (The experimental evidence for recombination does not necessarily imply that the nucleic acid thread actually breaks.   Many other models of DNA replication also include the possibility of recombination.)

5. Phage Genetics

The techniques of recombination between phage strains have been used to study the genetic fine structure of the *E. coli* phage T4.   As was mentioned in Section 2, different genetic characteristics of phage strains have been described by such factors as plaque shape, strains of bacteria infected, rate of lysis, formation of lysogens, and details of the shape of the mature phage particles.   The relative frequency of the appearance of a new property when two strains of bacteriophage are mixed with the host bacteria is interpreted as the probability of recombination.   If both strains completely lack one property, such as the ability to form plaques on a given strain of bacteria, then it is comparatively easy to measure the occurrence of this property when the two phage strains are mixed.   The probabilities of recombination between two such strains to form phage particles when the property is lacking in both parent strains is a measure of the distance between the locations of the two mutations along the DNA chain of the bacteriophage.   In terms of these recombination probabilities, three types of units have been defined for mapping the genetic properties of the DNA of the bacteriophage.   These three units, the cistron, the recon, and the muton, were introduced in Chapter 10; they are redefined in this section in terms of the properties of the T4

E. coli bacteriophage.   The genetic fine structure of the T4 phage has been determined in more detail than has been possible for any other system.

The T4 bacteriophage has been used for these studies because it undergoes a particular type of mutation, labeled rII, which is easy to analyze for recombinations.   The r-type mutations were originally characterized by their rapid lysis of *E. coli* strain *B*.   Their genetic character is also shown by the types of plaques formed when plated with various strains of *E. coli*.   The r-type plaque, as shown in Figure 3, is larger than the usual *wild-type* plaque and has sharper edges.   Three different types of r-mutants can be distinguished in terms of the plaques formed with different strains of *E. coli*, as is described in Table II.   One may regard rII as a lethal mutation when the phage is grown on *E. coli K*.

TABLE II

Plaque Forms when Phage Strains are Plated on Various Host Strains

| Phage | *E. coli* Strain | | |
Strain	*B*	*S*	*K*
wild type	wild	wild	wild
rI	r	r	r
rII	r	wild	(m)*
rIII	r	wild	wild

* The (m) means minute, turbid plaques; these are only occasionally formed when rII is plated with *E. coli K*.

The three types of r-mutants can be considered to have one genetic character difference.   In terminology applied to higher organisms, each type of r-mutant of the T4 phage could be considered to have one gene altered.   In this terminology, three different genes, I, II, and III, each lead to the same expression of genetic character, rapid lysis and r-plaques, when the phage is grown on *E. coli B*.   The rII-strain is the most useful for studying (mapping) the fine structure of the gene (or genetic character) because these mutations are lethal on *E. coli K* but can be grown readily on *E. coli B*.   If two rII-mutant strains of T4 phage are mixed and grown on *E. coli B* and then plated on *E. coli K*, any genetic recombination can be readily observed by the appearance of wild-type plaques.   Thus, in a comparatively small number of experiments the frequency of recombination between the two mutants can be determined even if it is as low as one in 10^7.

In fruit flies and other higher organisms, the gene may be divided into units called *cistrons*.   As was discussed in Chapter 10, the cis and trans configurations are used to determine whether two mutations are in the same cistron. In the trans configuration, the two mutations are on different members of a pair of homologous chromosomes. If they lead to no normal (wild-type) offspring, the mutations are called *noncomplementary*. Two noncomplementary mutations are said to be in the same cistron provided that one normal chromosome can lead to normal offspring. This is checked in the cis configuration, with both mutations on the same chromosome.

In bacteriophage genetics, each phage particle is considered to be homologous to a chromosome. The wild-type phage is the homolog of the normal chromosome. The cis configuration of mixed rII-mutants and wild-type phage always leads to (normal) wild-type plaques (offspring). Thus, the trans configuration, a mixture of two rII-mutants, plated on *E. coli K*, can be used to determine whether the two mutants are in the same cistron. Studies with more than 200 different rII-mutants of T4 phages have shown that the "rII-gene" consists of two cistrons. When phage strains with mutations in different cistrons are mixed, grown on *E. coli B*, and plated on *E. coli K*, many wild-type plaques are found. By way of contrast, wild-type plaques are rarely found when mutants in the same cistron are mixed. Thus, the study of T4 genetics of the rII-mutants shows the existence of two cistrons which, together, may be considered to make up the rII-gene.

Just as the gene is divided into cistrons by a study of recombination probabilities, it is likewise possible to subdivide the cistron into smaller units called *recons* on the basis of similar recombination data. Although the probabilities for recombinations within the same cistron are small, they are not zero. A large number of experiments have indicated that the linear separation of two mutations is directly proportional to the probability of recombination. The advantage of the rII-mutants of T4 phage is that hundreds of mutants per cistron can be found, and that these mutations, although lethal on *E. coli K*, can be propagated on *E. coli B*. In this fashion, it is possible to show that the closest pairs of mutants, which will recombine to give wild-type plaques, are separated by a distance corresponding to a probability of 0.01 per cent. The ones farthest apart within a cistron are separated by a distance corresponding to 4 per cent. Thus, one may say the basic unit, the recon, is 0.01–0.02 per cent long whereas the cistron is 4 per cent long. Maps, such as the one in Figure 6, have been made showing the separation in recons of the various mutations. The recon length may be expressed in terms of physical lengths along the DNA chain if a few assumptions are made. These have led to an estimated length for the recon of about 10 Å, a length comparable to the separation of the monomers (nucleotide pairs) along the DNA chain (3.4 Å).

Another small unit of length used in locating mutations is the *muton*. This is defined as the smallest unit of length in which a mutation can occur. Again, because of the large number of mutations, lethal on *E. coli K* but viable on *E. coli B*, it is possible to obtain better estimates of the muton from studies of the genetics of T4 phage particles than from any other system. The determination of the length of a mutation is

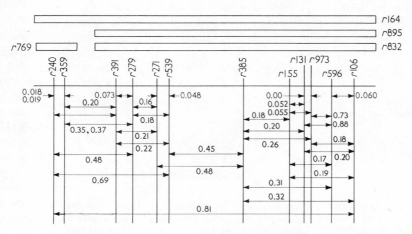

Figure 6. A map of the r164 region of the *A* cistron for rII-mutations of T4 *E. coliphages*. The numbers along the horizontal lines give the recombination probabilities. The code r131, for example, means the 131st rII-mutant isolated for T4. After S. Benzer, in *The Chemical Basis of Heredity*, W. D. McElroy and B. Glass, eds. (Baltimore, Md.: The Johns Hopkins Press, 1957).

based on recombination probabilities, just as the recon and the cistron are. If one considers three mutations arranged along the DNA chain as shown in Figure 7, it is clear that

$$M = L_{13} - L_{12} - L_{23}$$

Because the various lengths are proportional to recombination probabilities, one can determine the length M of mutation 2 in terms of probabilities. In this fashion, it has been shown that a mutation may correspond to different lengths from the single muton which corresponds to a probability of less than 0.05 per cent to almost the entire length of the cistron. In absolute length units, the muton is about 20 Å. Because mutations can have various lengths, it is possible for them to overlap, that is, cover the same region of the DNA chain. In this case, no recombinations which lead to wild-type plaques on *E. coli K* can occur. The use of a few longer mutations greatly speeded the mapping of more than 200 rII-mutants of T4, because recombination does not occur if the unlocated mutation includes a region covered by the located mutation.

The mapping of a large number of rII-mutants in two cistrons in the T4 phage has altered the interpretation of the genetics of higher organisms.   In particular, it has made untenable the idea that only a few mutations are possible per gene or even per cistron.   Further, this mapping of the rII cistrons of T4 phage particles has supported the fundamental role of DNA in inheritance, including the possibility of recombination between almost every DNA monomer (nucleotide pair) along the chain, and the possibility of a mutation involving only a few

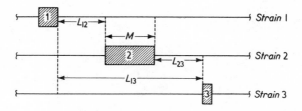

Figure 7. Diagrammatic representation of part of the *A* cistron for rII for T4 phage.   The locations of three mutations are shown on homologous pieces of the DNA chain.   After S. Benzer, in *The Chemical Basis of Heredity*, W. C. McElroy, and B. Glass, eds. (Baltimore, Md.: The Johns Hopkins Press, 1957).

such nucleotide pairs.   The interpretation in Chapter 10, that the critical volume for chromosome damage is greater than the muton, is based on the determination of the length of the muton through the mapping of rII-mutants of the T4 *E. coli* bacteriophage.   (The reader may recall from Chapter 10 that there is a critical volume in which ionizations must occur in order to produce a mutation.   This volume has a diameter of about 70 Å.   Because the diameter of the critical volume is larger than the muton, one may conclude that ionizations must occur near the DNA chain, but not necessarily in it, to produce mutations.)

6. Summary

Viruses and bacteriophages lie between living and nonliving materials in terms of their size, structure, and behavior.   Characteristic viruses infect all known living cells, causing the eventual death of the cell.

Virus particles are too small to view with the light microscope. They are studied by conventional bacteriological techniques and by many complex physical techniques including electron microscopy, ultra-centrifugation, tracer analysis, and electrophoresis. A clearer under-standing of the mode of action of viruses in general, and especially bacteriophages, has expanded knowledge of the cell surface, of the relationship of nucleic acids to metabolism, and most dramatically, of genetics.

REFERENCES

Viruses are responsible for serious diseases of man, plants, and animals. They have received much attention and are discussed in great detail in many books. Especially recommended for further reading are:

1. Smith, K. M., and M. A. Lauffer, ed., *Advances in Virus Research* (New York: Academic Press, Inc.). This appears annually; the first volume is dated 1953. Each volume contains at least one chapter which should be of interest to most biophysics students.
2. Pollard, E. C., *The Physics of Viruses* (New York: Academic Press, Inc., 1953).
3. Wolstenholme, G. E. W., and Elaine C. P. Millar, eds., *CIBA Foundation Symposium of the Nature of Viruses* (Boston, Massachusetts: Little, Brown & Company, 1957).

References 4 and 5 discuss Benzer's work on the genetic fine structure of the T4 *E. coliphage* which was reviewed in Section 5 of this chapter.

4. Benzer, Seymour, "The Elementary Units of Heredity," *A Symposium on the Chemical Basis of Heredity*, McElroy, W. D., and Bentley Glass, eds. (Baltimore, Maryland: Johns Hopkins University Press, 1957) pp. 70–93.
5. Lennox, E. S., "Genetic Fine-Structure Analysis," *Rev. Mod. Phys.* **31**: 242–248 (Jan. 1959).

DISCUSSION QUESTIONS—PART C

1. A table on page 188 in Chapter 10 gives a list of the relative biological effectiveness (RBE) of various types of ionizing radiations. How was each of these determined? Illustrate your answer with pertinent data.

2. What are the gross somatic (body) effects of high doses of ionizing radiations in mammals? Relate these insofar as possible to the material of Chapter 10.

3. Review the evidence for and against the one-gene, one-enzyme hypothesis. Indicate how ionizing radiations have been used as a study tool in testing this hypothesis.

4. Describe the construction of an ultraviolet microbeam apparatus for the irradiation of small parts of living cells. Explain its use by describing two experiments made possible by this apparatus.

5. Derive the equations for the lines of flow of electric current through (and around) a spherical biological cell model which is suspended in a conducting medium, subjected to an electric field having plane symmetry at long distances from the cell. Sketch the lines of current flow in the various frequency regions of interest.

6. Attempts have been made to calibrate electromagnetic diathermy apparatus with nonliving analogs. Describe one of these in detail. How well did the analog mimic the *in situ* heating?

7. Describe ultrasonic equipment suitable for the irradiation of humans. Give some measure of the intensities used. What specific disorders are treated in this fashion? Present data to indicate the success of the treatment.

8. Ultrasonic techniques have been used to determine the structures, both hard and soft, within a living human. Basically, this depends on a sonar type of measurement. Describe the equipment used and the results obtained. Compare these with X-ray data.

9. E. F. Gale has used ultrasonic cavitation to rupture *Staphylococcus aureus* in order to study the role of nucleic acids in enzymatic synthesis in cell-free systems. Review his findings about the synthesis of enzymes.

10. W. Nyborg and his associates have emphasized the role of microstreaming near cavitating nuclei. Describe their theory and experimental results, and the possible significance of this phenomenon in the disruption of single cells in cavitating ultrasonic fields.

11. Lamb developed the theory for the vibration of solid closed shells in air. Outline his analysis and apply it to biological cells.

12. Describe the essentially static experiments for measuring the interfacial tension of large biological cells, such as amoeba and marine eggs, using techniques of ultracentrifugation, shape distortion in a gravitational field, and stress-strain relationships.

13. Many investigators have been interested in the formation of DNA in the reproduction of new bacteriophage particles. Review the present evidence concerning the molecular mechanisms involved.

14. Tobacco mosaic virus (TMV) consists of RNA and protein. It is generally accepted that the RNA is essential for infection, but that the protein is not infectious. Most investigators believe that the protein protects the RNA, stabilizes it, and in some fashion helps it to enter the cell. Present an outline of the evidence for this role of protein and RNA in TMV.

15. Discuss the techniques of tissue culture. How have these been used to study the effects of ionizing radiations on single human cells? On the basis of these studies, compare the sensitivities of human cells and bacteria to ionizing radiations.

16. What are the distinguishing features of Poliomyelitis, Coxsackie, and ECHO viruses? Describe the occurrence, classification, chemical properties, physical dimensions, and infectivity of these enteric viruses. Indicate the significance of tissue culture techniques in studies of these viruses.

D

Molecular Biology

Introduction to Part D

In theory, all of biology could be explained in terms of
molecular phenomena. Such descriptions appeal to the
biophysicists as being in some way more fundamental;
they involve the properties of far simpler systems than
whole organisms. In this text, the earlier sections dealt
with properties of cells and groups of cells. In Part D,
the molecular mechanisms are discussed.

Chapter 15 describes the molecular form of two important classes of biological molecules, the proteins and the
nucleic acids. In Chapter 16, the interaction of these
molecules and ionizing radiations are considered. The
basic similarities between synthetic high polymers and
proteins and nucleic acids are emphasized.

One very important function of proteins is to control
the rate of biological reactions. Proteins which are
responsible for such catalytic action are called *enzymes*.
Chapters 17 and 18 present mathematical analyses of the
kinetics of enzyme catalyzed reactions.

Certain molecules owe their biological significance to
their reactions with light. The roles of these photosensitive molecules in vision and in photosynthesis are
described in the last two chapters of Part D.

15

X-ray Analyses of Proteins and Nucleic Acids

I. Protoplasm

Living matter is often referred to as *protoplasm*. This is a loose definition; it would be more exact to speak of the living cell and its contents, but the word protoplasm is shorter and easier. Protoplasm contains many types of structures and a wide variety of types of molecules. In this chapter, two types or families of molecules, both found in protoplasm, are characterized in terms of their physical shape and spatial arrangement. One of these families, the proteins, occurs abundantly in all living matter and forms an important part of all animal diets. The other, the nucleic acids, is found only in relatively small quantities but is very important for all life. Both families of compounds are high polymers, that is, molecules composed of many small units called *monomers*. Proteins and nucleic acids are large molecules with molecular weights as high as 10^7. These two families of molecules differ chemically in that they are polymerized from different types of monomers.

Some idea of the protoplasmic roles of proteins and nucleic acids may be obtained by considering a typical cell. A composite cell is shown in

Figure 1, illustrating the features of many different types of cells.   The structures shown in Figure 1 are based on the results obtained with a variety of techniques.   In the figure, there are two major subdivisions: the nucleus and its contents, often called *nucleoplasm*; and the remainder of the cell, sometimes called *cytoplasm*.   Both the nucleus and the cytoplasm are surrounded by membranes, as are also the smaller formed

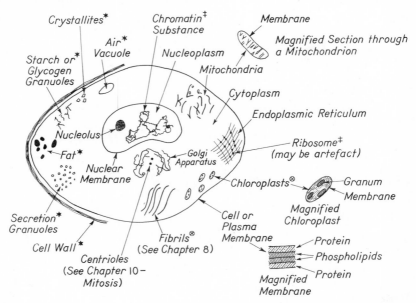

* = *Non-living, not present in all cells, does not contain protein*
⊗ = *Not present in all cells*
‡ = *Contain nucleic acids*

Figure 1. Composite cell.   Plasma membrane, nuclear membrane, chloroplast membrane, and mitochondrial membrane all probably have the form shown for the membrane on the right.   All elements except those marked with * contain proteins, whereas nucleic acids are found only in elements marked ‡.   The endothelial reticulum is believed to extend throughout the cytoplasm, possibly dividing it into vesicles or compartments.   After A. W. Ham, *Histology* (Philadelphia: J. B. Lippincott Company, 1957).

elements such as the *mitochondria* and the *Golgi bodies*.   These membranes consist partly of proteins and partly of other compounds called *lipids* (for example, fatlike compounds).   The membranes not only give physical form to the structures they surround, but also can use energy to transport molecules actively against electrochemical gradients. (Active transport is discussed in Chapter 23.)

Proteins are found in abundance within the formed elements, the contractile elements, the nucleus, and the endothelial reticulum shown in Figure 1. Some of these proteins serve structural purposes and others act as catalysts for the numerous biological reactions which must occur at controlled rates if the cell is to live. Other proteins are found in the liquid parts of the cytoplasm and nucleoplasm; these are probably mostly enzymes, although some may be concerned with the osmotic balance of the cell. The number and variety of different proteins seem almost limitless.

The nucleic acids are also found both in the cytoplasm and in the nucleoplasm. Those in the cytoplasm are all of a type called *Ribo-Nucleic Acids* (RNA); they probably exist primarily as small collections of RNA along the endothelial reticulum. Within the nucleus, there are two types of nucleic acids. One type is RNA, similar to that found in the cytoplasm; the other type, the *Deoxyribose Nucleic Acids* (DNA), occurs only in the nucleoplasm. Evidence was presented in the preceding chapter to show that DNA is associated with the transmission of genetic information. During cell division (see Chapter 10), the DNA in the nucleus of most plant and animal cells is organized into long threads, called *chromosomes*. The chromosomes contain both protein and DNA; they are referred to as nucleoproteins.

The RNA, in contrast with the DNA, is not restricted to the chromosomes or the cell nucleus. It is believed that DNA controls the synthesis of RNA which in turn controls the synthesis of proteins. Thus, both DNA and RNA act as biological catalysts, controlling ultimately the synthesis of protein-enzymes. These, in turn, control the rates of most other chemical reactions within the cell. The role of DNA is discussed further in Chapter 25. (As stated in Chapter 14, in the case of many plant viruses and some animal viruses, the genetic information necessary to build new virus particles is carried by RNA rather than DNA.)

There are many other types of molecules within the cell besides proteins and nucleic acids. In the typical living cell, there are more molecules of water than of any other compound. Water makes up as much as 80 per cent of the cell weight in some cases. The fatlike molecules, that is, lipids, have already been mentioned in connection with membranes but are by no means restricted to the membranes. Rather, lipids are found in varying roles throughout the cell. Those in fat globules are used to store energy, and a few lipids are hormones. However, the role of most lipids is unknown. Structures of a few lipids are shown in Figure 2. The typical lipid has a molecular weight between

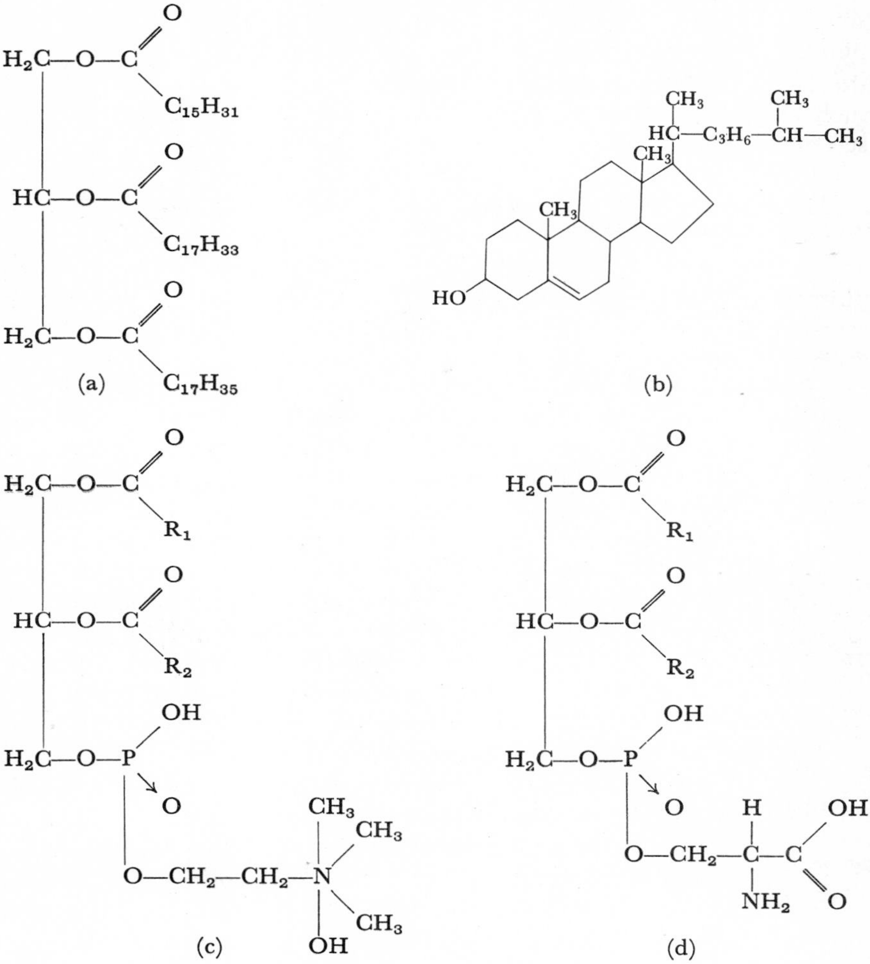

Figure 2. A few lipids. Lipids are one general class of molecules found in all cells. The phospholipids are a part of many cell structures. (a) Typical fat molecule; (b) cholesterol (a steroid); (c) α-lecithin (a phospholipid); and (d) phosphatidyl serine (another phospholipid). Many steroids act as hormones. The fats serve as storage depots for chemical energy which is not rapidly available to the cells.

100 and 1,000, which is small compared to those of proteins and nucleic acids.

Other molecules, found in all living cells, are called *carbohydrates*. These consist of carbon, hydrogen, and oxygen atoms, the latter two always occurring in the same ratio as in water. The carbohydrates sometimes are found as small ring or chain structures called *monoses*, or simple sugars having three to seven carbon atoms.   The most common number is six carbons, as exemplified by the common sugars glucose and fructose.   Carbohydrates are also found as compound sugars (or dimers) such as sucrose, and as long polymerized chains of monoses such as starches and celluloses.   Several carbohydrates are indicated in Figure 3.

Of the various compounds found in the cell, the proteins and nucleic acids have been singled out for attention in this chapter and in the three following ones for a number of reasons.   First, their structure and their action have been studied by means of the methods of physics and physical chemistry.   Second, their importance both for cell life and reproduction is understood.   In addition, they present a complexity and diversity which challenges man's abilities to investigate them, as well as a simplicity and uniformity in over-all plan which cannot but fill one with awe.

2. Proteins

To recapitulate briefly, proteins are one of the major classes of compounds found in all living matter.   Enzymes are protein catalysts controlling the rates of many biological reactions.   Muscular contraction depends on proteins, and active transport across cell membranes appears to be a lipoprotein function.   Many physical means have been used to study protein structure; currently accepted ideas lean heavily on the results obtained from studies of X-ray diffraction.   Before examining the X-ray data, the chemical composition of proteins will be briefly considered.

Proteins are natural high polymers built from small blocks, called *amino acids*.   These are molecules with an average molecular weight of about 120, each of which has an organic acid group,

$$-C \underset{\displaystyle OH}{\overset{\displaystyle O}{\big\langle}}$$

and a basic amino group, $-NH_2$. The acid and basic groups are attached to the same carbon leading to the form,

$$R-\underset{\displaystyle H}{\overset{\displaystyle NH_2}{C}}-C\underset{\displaystyle OH}{\overset{\displaystyle O}{\big\langle}}$$

where R is either H or any of a number of different organic radicals. This form is called an α-amino acid.

If one makes a three-dimensional model of such an α-amino acid, there are two steric arrangements of the α carbon which cannot be

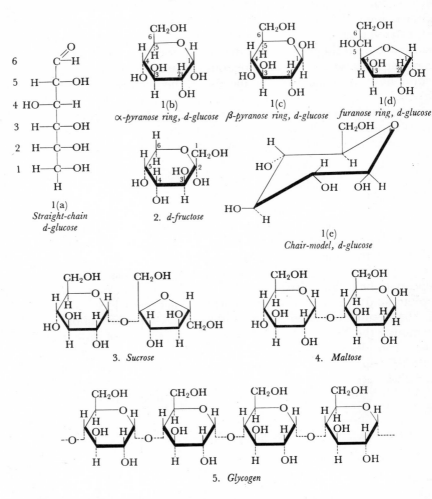

Figure 3. Some typical carbohydrates found in living cells. All hexoses can exist in solution in at least five forms: a straight chain, two six-membered (pyranose) rings and two five-membered (furnose) rings.   For glucose, most of the molecules are in the pyranose forms.   The chair model is closer to the actual molecular arrangement but is harder to draw.   The di- and polysaccharides exist in only one form.

rotated into one another (except when R is a proton). A carbon atom, which is sterically asymmetric in this fashion, is called optically active because in solution it rotates polarized light. The two stereoisomers are labeled *D* and *L* for dextro-rotary and levulo-rotary, respectively. Most test tube syntheses give equal amounts of the *D* and *L* isomers, but most living cells produce only one variety or the other. With very few exceptions, the amino acids polymerized into proteins in the living cell are all *L-α*-amino acids.

Two amino acid molecules may react to eliminate a molecule of water, thereby forming a peptide bond. Schematically, this can be represented as

The peptide bond so formed is very stable and the molecule is called a *dimer* or *dipeptide*. It is then possible to attach this molecule to other amino acid molecules, forming chains, or polypeptides. When these chains include 50 or more amino acids, they are called *proteins*. In some cases, the chains may be branched or cross linked; many proteins contain, in addition, a few small molecules other than amino acids. Molecular weights of proteins vary from several thousand into the millions.

The number of different amino acids conceivable has no known limit. A very large number have been synthesized in test tubes. Of these, approximately 20 *L-α*-amino acids make up almost all of the proteins of all living cells. Other amino acids occur in nature, especially in bacteria, but they are the exceptions rather than the rule. The 20 amino acids tabulated in the table on pages 275-277 are the building units which are polymerized to form complex polypeptide chains called proteins. The physical form and arrangement of these polypeptide chains is discussed further in Section 5 of this chapter.

The various proteins differ from one another in the number and order of the various amino acids in the polypeptide chains and in the configuration of these chains. Although the detailed order is known for only a few small proteins, pieces of many others have been studied to determine the order of the amino acids. Figure 4 gives the amino acid sequence for the protein, insulin.

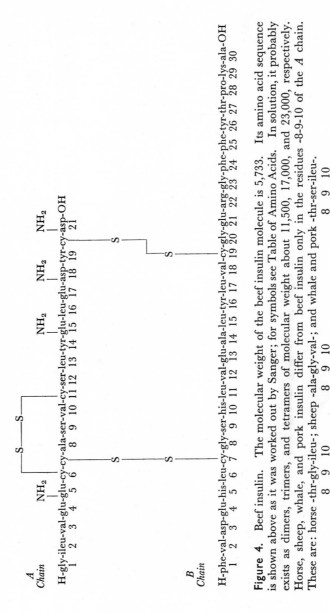

Figure 4. Beef insulin. The molecular weight of the beef insulin molecule is 5,733. Its amino acid sequence is shown above as it was worked out by Sanger; for symbols see Table of Amino Acids. In solution, it probably exists as dimers, trimers, and tetramers of molecular weight about 11,500, 17,000, and 23,000, respectively. Horse, sheep, whale, and pork insulin differ from beef insulin only in the residues -8-9-10 of the A chain. These are: horse -thr-gly-ileu-; sheep -ala-gly-val-; and whale and pork -thr-ser-ileu-.

TABLE I

Amino Acids

Amino Acid	Structure	Molecular weight	Abbreviation for residue in proteins
1. Glycine		75	—gly—
2. Alanine		89	—ala—
3. Valine		117	—val—
4. Leucine		131	—leu—
5. Isoleucine		131	—ileu—
6. Serine		105	—ser—
7. Threonine		119	—thr—
8. Phenylalanine		165	—phe—
9. Tyrosine		181	—tyr—

Amino Acid	Structure	Molecular weight	Abbreviation for residue in proteins
10. Tryptophan		204	—try—
11. Cysteine		121	SH | —cy—
11a. Cystine		240	—cy— | S | S | —cy—
12. Methionine		135 149	—met—
13. Aspartic Acid		133	—asp—
14. Glutamic Acid		163 147	—glu—
15. Lysine		146	—lys—
16. Arginine		174	—arg—

Structures:

10. Tryptophan:
H_2C—$\overset{H}{C}$—$C\overset{O}{\underset{OH}{}}$, NH_2 ; indole ring with H's and N—H

11. Cysteine:
CH_2—$\overset{H}{C}$—$C\overset{O}{\underset{OH}{}}$, HS , NH_2

11a. Cystine:
$\overset{HO}{\underset{O}{}}C$—$\overset{H}{\underset{NH_2}{C}}$—$CH_2$—$S$—$S$—$CH_2$—$\overset{H}{\underset{NH_2}{C}}$—$C\overset{O}{\underset{OH}{}}$

12. Methionine:
CH_2—CH_2—$\overset{H}{\underset{NH_2}{C}}$—$C\overset{O}{\underset{OH}{}}$, CH_3—S

13. Aspartic Acid:
$\overset{HO}{\underset{O}{}}C$—$CH_2$—$\overset{H}{\underset{NH_2}{C}}$—$C\overset{O}{\underset{OH}{}}$

14. Glutamic Acid:
$\overset{HO}{\underset{O}{}}C$—$CH_2$—$CH_2$—$\overset{H}{\underset{NH_2}{C}}$—$C\overset{O}{\underset{OH}{}}$

15. Lysine:
CH_2—CH_2—CH_2—CH_2—$\overset{H}{\underset{NH_2}{C}}$—$C\overset{O}{\underset{OH}{}}$, NH_2

16. Arginine:
CH_2—CH_2—CH_2—$\overset{H}{\underset{NH_2}{C}}$—$C\overset{O}{\underset{OH}{}}$, H_2N—C—NH , NH

Amino Acid	Structure	Molecular weight	Abbreviation for residue in proteins
17. Citrulline	$CH_2-CH_2-CH_2-$ ...	175	—cit—
18. Histidine		155	—his—
19. Proline		115	—pro—
20. Hydroxyproline		131	—hypro—

3. Nucleic Acids

As recently as 1950, many scientists regarded proteins as the fundamental "stuff" of life, controlling reactions, contracting, transmitting
genetic information, and reproducing themselves. This view has given
way to one which assigns proteins to a more restricted role but emphasizes
the importance of the nucleic acids in protein synthesis and genetic
transmission of information. The nucleic acids are high polymers, just
as are proteins, but are given a separate name because the monomers
from which nucleic acids are built are not amino acids. Consisting of
different structural units, the nucleic acids differ significantly from
proteins in their physicochemical properties, as well as in their biological
action.

The monomers from which nucleic acids are polymerized are called
nucleotides. Each nucleotide consists of a *nucleoside* condensed by the

elimination of a water molecule, with a phosphate group. A nucleoside in turn is the condensation product of a five-carbon *sugar* (pentose) plus an organic *base* derived from a purine or pyrimidine ring. Symbolically, this may be represented as

$$\text{Base} + \text{Sugar} \xrightarrow{\text{H}_2\text{O}} \text{Nucleoside}$$

$$\text{Nucleoside} + \text{H}_2\text{PO}_4^- \xrightarrow{-\text{OH}^-} \text{Nucleotide}$$

$$n\text{-Nucleotide} \xrightarrow{-(n-1)\text{H}_2\text{O}} \text{Nucleic Acid}$$

The number n is very large because the molecular weight of nucleic acid molecules usually runs in the millions.

There are two types of sugar molecules included in nucleic acids. Throughout any one nucleic acid molecule, all the sugar residues are the same. One sugar found in nucleic acids is called *D-ribose*, in which case the polymer is ribose nucleic acid (RNA); the other sugar possible is *D-2-deoxyribose*, in which case the polymer is deoxyribose nucleic acid (DNA). The structures of ribose and deoxyribose are shown below, in a ring form. The ring with carbon atoms at four of the corners is supposed, in this illustration, to appear to lie in one plane with the hydrogen and hydroxyl groups on bonds at right angles to the plane. Although this type of structure is often drawn, it is believed that the ring is not restricted to one plane but rather pleated, up and down, about the plane, as illustrated in the chair model in Figure 3.

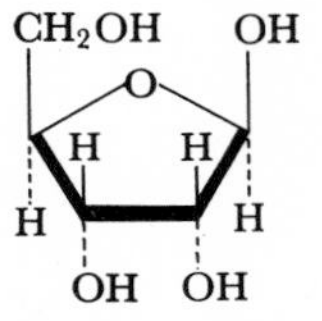

D-ribose 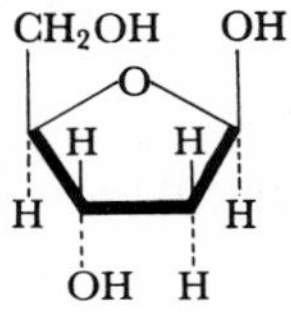   *D-2-deoxyribose*

The organic bases referred to above are derived from purine and pyrimidine rings. These rings have structures which can be shown as

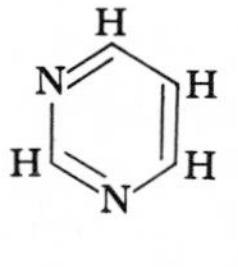

pyrimidine 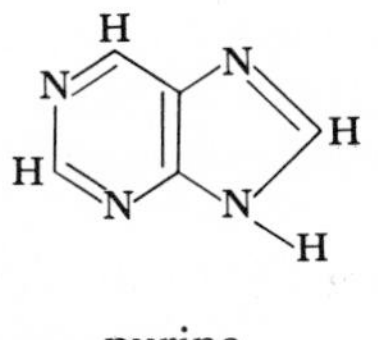   purine (where the corners without letters in the ring are to be interpreted as carbon atoms). The two pyrimidines found in DNA are *cytosine* (C)[1] and *thymine* (T), represented structurally by

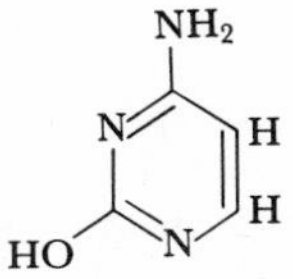

and

cytosine

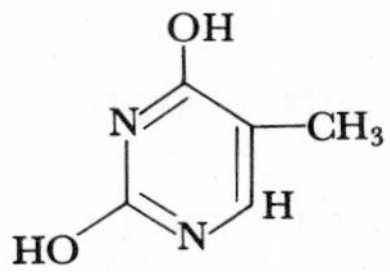

thymine

In RNA, two pyrimidines are also found. These are *cytosine* and *uracil*. The latter has the structure

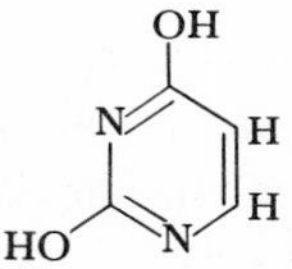

uracil

In both RNA and DNA, the same two purine-derived bases occur. These are called *adenine* (A) and *guanine* (G).[2] The structual formulas of adenine and guanine are

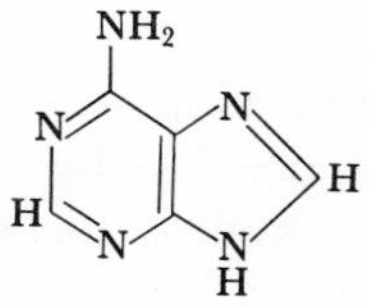

adenine

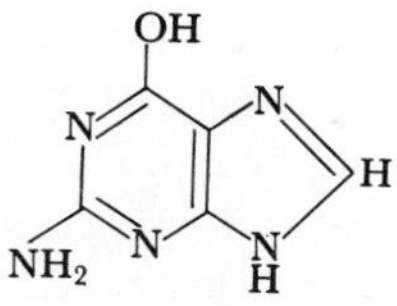

guanine

As mentioned above, most genetic information in plant and animal

---

[1] In certain bacteriophages, such as the coliform phages T2 and T4, the cytosine in the DNA is replaced by 5-hydroxy-methyl cytosine.

[2] Adenine-ribose-phosphate is the nucleotide AMP which was introduced in Chapter 8. It can be condensed with additional phosphate groups to form the energy-transport compounds, ADP and ATP.

cells is believed to be coded in DNA. This has only four monomers; these are nucleotides containing respectively A, T, C, and G. If it seems surprising that this alphabet is sufficient, it should be remembered that any English sentence can be written in Morse code which has three basic letters, a dot, a dash, and a pause.

4. X-ray Diffraction

The physical behavior of molecules found in biological structures can be investigated from different points of view. One of the most fruitful of these has been an analysis of the atomic architecture as determined by X-ray diffraction patterns. The term "X ray" is used to refer to a beam of photons (electromagnetic radiation) formed by bombarding a metal target with electrons. These X rays are shorter in wavelength than other electromagnetic radiation referred to as visible and ultra-violet light. (For a more complete discussion of the electromagnetic spectrum, refer to Chapter 26.)

The method of X-ray diffraction is a relatively new one in physical chemistry. X rays were discovered by Roentgen just before the start of this century. Quite a bit of simple X-ray crystallography was done between 1912 and 1920. However, accurate measurements of X-ray wavelengths and the corresponding studies of crystal structure have been possible only since about 1920. These studies profoundly affected scientists' ideas of the physical world at many different levels. The form of the periodic table, the exact values of the electronic charge e and of Avogadro's number N, and the arrangement of atoms in crystals and electrons within atoms, all have been based on X-ray measurements.

Although the diffraction of X rays by simple crystals, as NaCl, had been well studied for many years, the present interpretations of X-ray diffraction patterns of biologically interesting molecules were formulated since World War II. These were made possible by the same factor which is basic to so much of biophysics, namely the development of suitable electronic techniques. The detailed interpretation of X-ray diffraction data from complex molecules is possible only with the use of electronic analog computers and of high speed, digital electronic computers.

These studies of the diffraction of X-ray beams by biologically interesting molecules have influenced current ideas of the structure and action of almost all forms of biological compounds. The arrangement of the atoms within small molecules such as amino acids, purines, and sugars have been (or are being) determined. The chemical structural formula of certain antihistamines and the various isomers of vitamin A can best be investigated by their X-ray diffraction patterns. The helical structures of crystalline and fibrous proteins and of the genetic material, DNA, have been established from their diffraction of X rays.

The resolving power of an X-ray diffraction apparatus is much greater than that of a light microscope. In the light microscope, the limit of resolution is set by the wavelength of incident light employed. With X-ray diffraction patterns, no such restrictions exist. Using monochromatic X rays such as the Cu-K_{α_2} radiation, the wavelength λ is 1.54 Å but interatomic distances can readily be measured with an error of less than 0.01 Å. This can be compared with a theoretical limit of resolution of 2×10^3 Å for blue light.

One may ask why a crystal has to be used rather than a single molecule, if the resolving power is indeed of the order of 0.01 Å whereas the covalent bond lengths average about 1.5 Å. Perhaps the most obvious answer is that it is impossible to hold one molecule in place. In addition, some of the X-ray photons will break molecular bonds. Because many molecules are present, breaking a few bonds does not have an appreciable effect on the average diffraction pattern. Perhaps the most important advantage of a crystal is that it restricts the scattered rays to a finite number of maxima, giving sharp, intense reflections.

One of the difficulties of X-ray diffraction studies is that one ends up with a photograph or graph with a number of spots of varying intensity, such as that shown in Figure 5. The problem of reconstructing the crystal and the spatial arrangements of the molecules from these spots has a simple solution only for crystals of very simple molecules, such as NaCl or H_2O. For more complex molecules, a series of trial-and-error solutions is necessary. The analysis which follows is presented in the hope that those readers unfamiliar with this technique will acquire some idea of the problems involved.

Bragg showed that in treating X-ray diffraction by single crystals, one may regard the atoms as making up reflecting planes. A beam of X rays is shown incident on a single pair of such planes in Figure 6 (although there will in general be many planes for any given crystal). From Figure 6, one may see that there will be a maximum in the diffraction pattern if, and only if

$$n\lambda = 2d \sin \theta \qquad (1)$$

where n is an integer. With monochromatic X rays, one set of planes, at most, will give a maximum for a given θ, and for any arbitrary θ there will probably be no maximum in the diffraction pattern. This could be solved in Figure 6 by rotating the X-ray beam around the crystal or by rocking the crystal about an axis perpendicular to the plane of the paper. The latter alternative is more practical and is often employed.

Another type of diffraction pattern, called a *Laue pattern*, avoids this problem by using heterochromatic X rays of many wavelengths incident

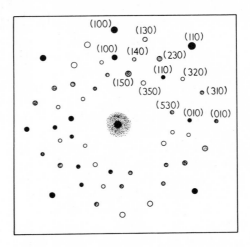

Figure 5. Laue pattern of NaCl. This has been redrawn from a photograph to emphasize the diffraction spots. The Miller indices of the corresponding planes have been labeled for some of the diffraction spots.

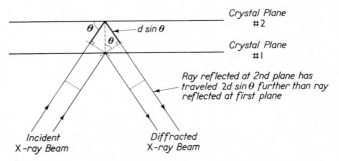

Figure 6. X-ray diffraction. The dotted lines show perpendiculars to the wavefront. For re-enforcement, the rays reflected at planes 1 and 2 must travel distances which differ by a whole number of wavelengths. This will be fulfilled if

$$n\lambda = 2d \sin \theta$$

where *n* is an integer.

in a fixed direction. However, because λ will not be known, one cannot find the distance between reflecting planes from a Laue pattern.

Figure 7 shows several planes in a cubic crystal, each with a number of atoms per plane. These planes are numbered by Miller indices (*hkl*) which are described in Figure 8. In Figure 7, one may notice that the planes are spaced at varying distances. By and large, as the Miller

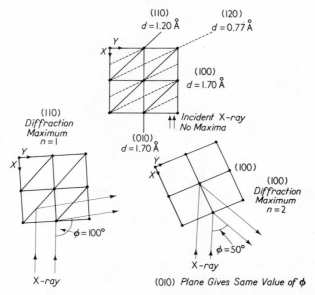

Figure 7. Diffraction of an X-ray beam. In working out angles, it is assumed that the X-ray wavelength λ is 1.52 Å and that the crystal had cubic symmetry with a lattice constant of 1.70 Å.

indices go up, the spacing *d* between adjacent planes decreases, and the number of maxima likewise decreases. For the example shown, there are two angles corresponding to $n = 1$ and $n = 2$ for the (010) and (100) planes. The (110) and (120) planes each have only one diffraction maximum corresponding to $n = 1$. The maximum for the (120) plane essentially reflects the incident beam back on itself and could not be observed. None of the higher planes will exhibit diffraction maxima. However, planes not perpendicular to the *xy* plane, such as (101) and (011), will give maxima whose diffracted beams will not lie in the plane of the paper. Thus, the maxima will form a two-dimensional pattern such as that shown in Figure 5. To show all the planes with monochromatic X rays, a number of different schemes have been developed which lead to an easier interpretation of the Miller indices of the planes giving rise to a given reflection. For complex molecules, such as proteins and nucleic acids, it is necessary to use one of these schemes. The reader is referred to Reference 4 for details of these techniques.

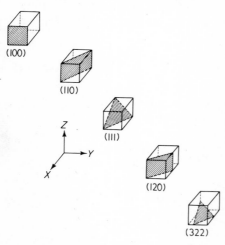

(100)

(110)

z

(111)

y

x

(120)

(322)

Figure 8. Miller indices (*hkl*) for some crystal planes illustrated for cubic crystals. The Miller indices are inversely proportional to the distance from the origin to the intersections with the crystal axes when these distances are expressed in terms of the lengths of the unit cell. The proportionality constant is so chosen that the Miller indices are the smallest possible whole numbers.

Instead of rocking the crystal, a powder of small crystallites can be used. Then the two-dimensional picture consists of a series of concentric circles. The powder pattern is harder to interpret but easier to obtain. It has been widely used in metallurgy and mineral sciences but has had few biological applications.

A sensitive test of an assumed atomic structure is to compare the relative intensities of the X-ray diffraction maxima observed with those computed from the model. The relative intensities are found by adding together the contributions of each atom, taking into account the phase differences due to the difference in pathlength to each atom. This is usually expressed by a crystal structure factor, F_{hkl}, for the beam perpendicular to the (*hkl*) planes. It can be found from

$$F_{hkl} = \sum_{n=1}^{N} f_n \, e^{2\pi i (hu_n + kv_n + lw_n)} \quad (2)$$

where

N = number of atoms in a unit cell of the crystal
n = a particular atom
f_n = atomic structure factor defined below
(u_n, v_n, w_n) = coordinates of the *n*th atom expressed as fractions of the unit crystal lattice lengths

The atomic structure factor *f* is defined by

$$f = \frac{\text{amplitude of the wave scattered by an atom}}{\text{amplitude of the wave scattered by an electron}}$$

In general, *f* depends both on the particular element (for example, Zn) and on the angle between the incident and the scattered beam; tables of *f* for various elements are available.

The relative intensity will be proportional to $|F_{hkl}|^2$. In a typical experiment, these are measured and the types of atoms present (and hence, the values of f_n) are known. Thus, the assumed values of u_n, v_n, w_n can be used to compute $|F_{hkl}|^2$. It remains to adjust u_n, v_n, w_n for each atom until the final structure agrees both with chemical data and also with the X-ray diffraction pattern.

Complex crystals or even simple crystals of complex molecules give rise to complex diffraction patterns. The number of points necessary increases both as the number of atoms per molecule and also as the size of the unit cell of the crystal increase. In order to obtain useful information from these complicated diffraction patterns, it is necessary to know the relative intensities of the various maxima as well as their direction.

In interpreting diffraction by complex molecules, it is more convenient to deal with electron densities than with atomic positions. After the electron density has been mapped, the atoms may be located at the center of the density maxima. From the preceding paragraphs, it may be seen that the crystal structure factor F_{hkl} can be defined by an absolute value $|F_{hkl}|$, and a phase angle a_{hkl}, as

$$|F_{hkl}| = \frac{\text{amplitude of the wave scattered by all atoms in the unit cell}}{\text{amplitude of the wave scattered by an electron}}$$

a_{hkl} = phase difference between the wave scattered by the unit cell and the wave scattered by an electron at the origin

Adding the contribution of each electron as before

$$F_{hkl} = \iiint \rho(u, v, w) \, e^{2\pi i(hu + kv + lw)} \, du \, dv \, dw \qquad (3)$$

where

$$\rho = \text{electron density at } u, v, w$$

Readers familiar with Fourier series will recognize that Equation 3 has the form of the coefficients of a Fourier series. Accordingly, one may rewrite it as

$$\rho(u, v, w) = \sum_h \sum_k \sum_l |F_{hkl}| \cos\{2\pi(hu + kv + lw) + a_{hkl}\} \qquad (4)$$

Thus, if one can guess the values of a_{hkl} and can measure a sufficient number of intensities $|F_{hkl}|^2$, then one can map the electron density ρ and hence, locate all the atoms. This is called a *Fourier synthesis*.

The problem of correctly guessing the phases either in Equation 2 or in Equations 3 and 4 has intrigued mathematically minded crystallographers. The general procedure is to guess phase values and then keep adjusting these to give sharper and sharper electron-density contours. If one gets on the right track, these contours define atoms of the types known to be present and at reasonable distances from other atoms to which they can be bonded.   (The bonds can often be found by the methods of classical organic chemistry.)   In the final analysis, phase guessing is very similar to working a crossword puzzle or solving a murder mystery story, and as in these, one finds, if successful, an answer which is no longer a guess.

Various schemes have been developed for the initial-phase guessing. One of the most successful involves placing a heavy atom such as I or Br within the molecule.[3]   The heavy atom diffracts more strongly than the others, so it may be located first.   To do this, Equation 2 is used, setting f_i to zero for all but the heavy atom.   Once it is located, approximate values for many of the phases can be determined at once.   With these as a starting point, one adjusts these phases and the others to give more and more sharply defined electron-density contours.   The final solution is an accurate determination just as in the crossword puzzle.

For certain crystals, the unit cell is symmetric about the center and, therefore, it can be shown that all the a_{hkl}'s have the value 0 or π. These are only two choices, but if 100 points are used there are 2^{100} or about 10^{30} possible sets of guesses.   By the use of heavy-atom substitution, this hopelessly large number may be reduced to a mere few billion. Protein and nucleic acid crystals are not even symmetric about the center of the unit cell, so that the problem is more difficult when using these molecules.

The entire adjustment of phase values and recomputing the F's and ρ is a lengthy, tedious process.   With an electrical desk calculator and a protein crystal, this would take many human lifetimes.   With electronic computers, it has been possible to find the details of the structural arrangements of the atoms within many smaller biological molecules (molecular weight $\leqslant$ 2,000).   The remainder of this chapter discusses the contributions of the method of X-ray diffraction to the determination of the structure of proteins and nucleic acids.

5. Protein Structure

In Chapter 8, it was mentioned that one class of proteins, the globulins, could exist in either a fiberlike or a globular state.   Most proteins do not have these two alternatives but, rather, are only fibrous or only globular.   X-ray diffraction studies have been applied to both types of protein structure with varying degrees of success.

---

[3] This technique is useful if the heavy atom does not alter the crystal structure; it is called isomorphic replacement.

The problem of determining the structure of fibrous proteins is quite different from that of crystalline proteins. If a fiber were made up of little crystalline regions all lined up, then one should obtain spots similar to those from a single crystal. If these were slightly disoriented, the spots would become arcs. If the crystallites were completely randomly disordered, the spots would become circles similar to those of a powder pattern. Early investigators took many pictures of X-ray diffraction patterns of fibrous materials but no one understood the results.

Around 1930, Astbury studied many protein and nucleic acid fibers. He showed that the proteins gave rise to two types of X-ray diffraction patterns called α and β. He recognized the α-configuration as a folded or more dense structure, and the β pattern as due to a stretched structure. To these, he assigned the forms

Astbury's α form   Astbury's β form

The double-bonded oxygen is slightly negative, whereas the hydrogen on the nitrogen is somewhat positive. Alternate rows of polypeptide chains were postulated to be held in place by the attraction between these two, called *hydrogen bonding*.

Astbury showed that wool and hair changed from an α to a β form on stretching. He postulated that in muscular contraction, the proteins changed from a β to an α form and this was generally accepted until about 1945. His models represented tremendous strides in understanding the structure of proteins but left many questions unanswered. His attempts to fit DNA and RNA patterns to his models were unsuccessful. Many spots in the diffraction pattern and the absence of other spots could not be explained in terms of his models. Thus, they represented a good first guess.

The current interpretations of X-ray diffraction patterns of fibers date back to about 1947. At that time, angles and configurations of many of the amino acids were investigated. Pauling and Corey, in 1951, showed that if they drew a polypeptide chain with the known bond angles on a piece of paper and twisted it into a helix, the various turns could hydrogen bond to one another. Astbury and others had tried helical models but always with an even number of amino acids per turn;

Pauling realized that this was a mistake. Pauling and Corey demonstrated that a helix with 3.7 amino acid residues per turn, a diameter of 6.8 Å and turns spaced 5.4 Å apart would be permitted by the observed bond angles. This is shown in Figure 9 for a right-handed helix. Left-handed α-helices are also possible. However, the diffraction pattern for X rays due to such a helical structure was more complex than that for any of the simpler models.

Cochran, Crick, and Vand carried out a theoretical study of the predicted X-ray pattern for helical structures. They showed that it was necessary to orient the X-ray beam at an oblique angle to the fibers. In general, the helical structures lead to patterns similar to that diagrammed in Figure 10. Whereas the simpler molecules and crystals involved such terms as cos $2\pi(hx + ky + lz + \alpha)$, the helical structures involved Bessel functions of the distance from the center of the helix.

The α-helical structure of Pauling and Corey fits very well to the diffraction patterns observed for synthetic polypeptides. It is generally accepted that many natural fibrous proteins occur as helices because their X-ray diffraction patterns are of the α-type which is similar to that of Figure 10. However, many unexplained spots are present. The data for the fibrous protein collagen can

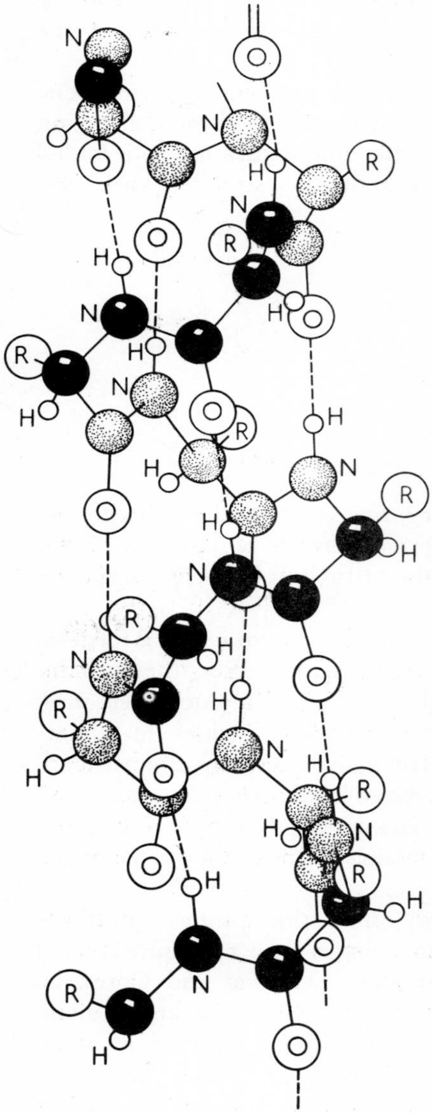

Figure 9. The α-helix of Pauling and Corey redrawn to emphasize helical polypeptide chain. Dotted lines indicate hydrogen bonding between =O of one turn with the H—N of the turn below. This is a close-packed structure. The polypeptide helix has a radius of 3.4 Å and an interturn distance of 5.4 Å. There are 3.7 residues per turn. The R groups are much larger than shown; they extend as far as 10 Å.

be fitted by a model involving a fiber made of three α-helices twisted around each other in a helical fashion.   By far, the most direct demonstration of the α-helix is in the globular protein myoglobin, discussed subsequently.

In addition to their α-helix, Pauling and Corey made pleated sheet models of proteins similar to the β model of Astbury but did not restrict the peptide bonds to one plane.   Both this and the α-helix have retained the ideas of the α structure being compressed and the β stretched out, and also of hydrogen bonds being responsible for holding the shape of the protein fibers.   They are superior to Astbury's earlier models in fitting known bond angles and in their agreement with the experimental results of X-ray diffraction studies.

Many attempts have been made to apply the general methods described in the previous section to crystals of globular proteins.   Perhaps the most studied crystal has been that of the blood protein, hemoglobin. However, the structure of the similar but simpler protein, myoglobin, was worked out to a resolution of about 6 Å before much progress was made with hemoglobin.   Myoglobin is a red pigment similar to hemoglobin but occurring in muscle rather than blood.   It is believed to function by buffering the oxygen concentration within the muscle.   Myoglobin has a molecular weight of about 16,000, very low for a typical protein.   This

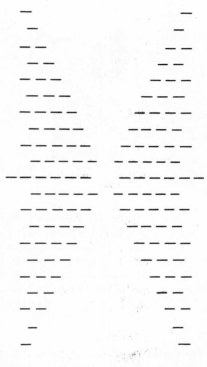

Figure 10. Diffraction pattern of a helix. Notice the clear area in the center of the pattern.

corresponds to 153 amino acid residues, that is, about 1,200 atoms other than hydrogen in each myoglobin molecule.   It means that to locate all of these atoms in the molecule, one would need to measure the intensity and to guess the phases of perhaps 20,000 diffraction spots.

The results of analyzing and adjusting the phase for about 400 diffraction spots for myoglobin crystals, substituted with heavy atoms, showed there were two myoglobin molecules per unit cell of the crystal and located the polypeptide chains and the iron-containing heme group within the myoglobin molecule. This procedure was then repeated to include 9,600 diffraction spots which showed the electron density of the myoglobin molecule with a resolution of about 2 Å. This is not quite sufficient to indicate the separate atoms. This resolution is sufficient to confirm that the major part of the myoglobin molecule consists of right-handed α-helices. To fit the single polypeptide chain of myoglobin

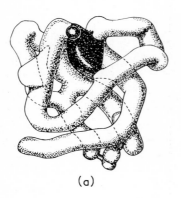
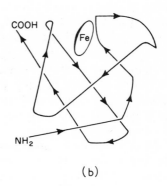

(a)   (b)

Figure 11. Kendrew's model of myoglobin. (a) General shape of the polypeptide chain. The gray area is the heme group. The round dark atom represents a heavy atom attached for isomorphous replacements. The tilt of the heme group is incorrect. (b) Course of the polypeptide chain as determined by a three-dimensional fourier synthesis with 2 Å resolution. After J. C. Kendrew, *et al.*, "Structure of Myoglobin," *Nature* 185: 422 (1960).

into one globular molecule, it must be bent and twisted at various corners. Where this occurs, the α-helical form is lost usually for 3 or 4 amino acid residues. There is also one group of about 13–18 amino acid residues not in the form of an α-helix.

Figure 11a shows a photograph of Kendrew's model of myoglobin, built to represent the structure which would give the 400 diffraction spots used. In addition, electron spin resonance measurements were used to locate the iron atoms in the heme group (see Chapter 28). However, the latter data were misinterpreted so that the heme group was tilted at the wrong angle. Figure 11b, for comparison, shows the form of the polypeptide chain revealed by the 9,600 diffraction spot study. Although not illustrated in the figure, all of the chains are shown by the latter study to be hollow, cylindrical tubes of the form

(c)

(d)

Figure 11 (*cont.*). Perutz's model of hemoglobin. The white units are an identical pair as are the two black units. Each unit is very similar to myoglobin in the shape of the peptide chain. (c) Hemoglobin model. The heme groups are indicated by grey disks. (d) Chain configuration in the two sub-units facing the observer. The other two chains are produced by the operation of the dyad axis. After M. F. Perutz, *et al.*, "Structure of Hemoglobin," *Nature* 185: 416 (1960).

expected for helices. As noted above, the straight chain portions are right-handed α-helices. In order to obtain Figures 11a and b, it was necessary to use four different substitutions of heavy atoms to check the results and obtain suitable starting points for phase guessing. The model in Figures 11a and b shows one continuous polypeptide chain as demanded by chemical evidence.

Similar studies of hemoglobin (molecular weight about 65,000) have shown that it consists of four subunits, each with a heme group. These studies at a resolution of 5.5 Å showed that each subunit of hemoglobin is a continuous polypeptide chain folded around itself in a form very similar to that of the myoglobin molecule. There are two identical pairs of subunits in each molecule. These are shown in black and white in the model illustrated in Figure 11c, which summarizes the X-ray diffraction studies of Perutz and his co-workers.

The myoglobin and hemoglobin studies involved three new ideas not used in the 1920's in X-ray determination of inorganic crystalline structure. The first was the technique of the substitution of heavy atoms into the unit cell (or isomorphous replacement, as it is called). The second involved the use of high-speed computers to adjust the phases until the electron density postulated and the diffraction spots observed were consistent with one another. The third novel technique was the use of electron spin resonance to locate the iron atoms. Everything indicates that with the development of higher-speed computers, with better programming for electronic computers, and with the preparation of increasing numbers of crystalline proteins, more and more protein structures will be studied by these methods.

6. Nucleic Acid Structure

Although it was known that DNA was included in the chromosomes, it was formerly believed that the nucleic acid was only significant for structural reasons. The current views completely interchange the protein and DNA role in the chromosome, regarding the protein as a protective agent for the DNA. A major factor in increasing the significance assigned to DNA was the determination of a satisfactory steric model by Crick and Watson. Their interpretation made use of the theory referred to in the last section for X-ray diffraction by helical structures.

Crick and Watson showed from the X-ray diffraction patterns that DNA consists of two antiparallel helices. The spiral is very large, having a diameter of 18 Å and a spacing between turns of 34 Å. Thus, it is a wide chain with lots of room for other molecules to fit in, if they are of the proper shape.   On the basis of chemical data and size considerations, Crick and Watson showed that the chains were made up of −sugar→phosphate–sugar→phosphate– and so forth, units.   Between the two chains, as rungs along a helical step ladder, were strung pairs of

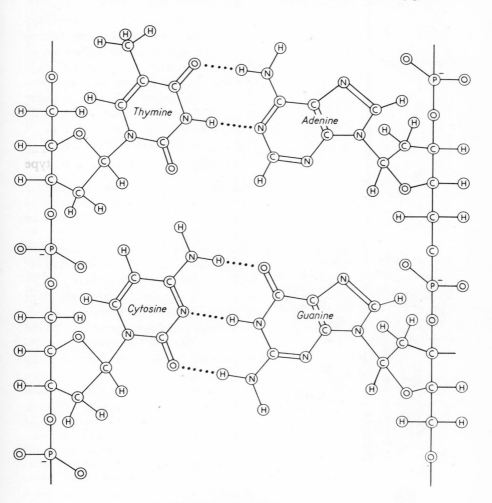

Figure 12. Double chain of DNA.

hydrogen-bonded bases of the form purine–H–pyrimidine.   These rungs are about 11 Å long.   A piece of a pair of chains is shown in Figure 12.
    This type of unit is repeated into a long double chain.   The entire double chain is then twisted to form the double helix shown in Figure 13,

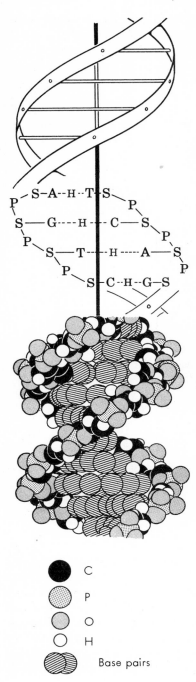

C

P

O

H

Base pairs

with about 10 rungs per turn. The pairs of bases fit across the chain as rungs being supported in the middle by hydrogen bonds. It is necessary that each pair of bases fit very exactly. Measurements based on X-ray diffraction patterns of crystals of the purine and pyrimidine bases have shown that these do indeed fit, provided that adenine (A) is paired with thymine (T), and guanine (G) with cytosine (C). If this is the case, one should have the relative concentrations of organic bases in DNA related as

$$[A]/[T] = [G]/[C] = 1.0$$

This relationship had been verified for all DNA and was one of the pieces of evidence used by Crick and Watson to construct their model.

Gamow tried to explain protein formation in terms of the location of residues along the DNA chain. The diagram in Figure 14 shows the type of blocks Gamow considered to determine amino acid arrangement. In the outlined cross, G, T, and C are independent, but the A is determined by

Figure 13. The helix of DNA, with three different ways of representing the molecular arrangement. Top, general picture of the double helix, with the phosphate-sugar combinations making up the outside spirals and the base pairs the cross-bars; middle, a somewhat more detailed representations: phosphate (P), sugar (S), adenine (A), thymine (T), guanine (G), cytosine (C), and hydrogen (H); bottom, detailed structure showing how the space is filled with atoms: carbon (C), oxygen (O), hydrogen (H), phosphorus (P) and the base pairs. After C. P. Swanson, *The Cell*, (Englewood Cliffs, N. J.: Prentice-Hall, Inc., 1960).

the T. Crosses of the nature outlined could determine amino acid order. However, several difficulties were present. A model of this nature made in three dimensions with actual bond angles, and so on, failed to show any good place to fit the amino acids. The model used each purine or pyridine in two crosses so that there would be an appreciable influence of one amino acid on the next; this has not been found in natural proteins. Finally, other biological data favor control of the synthesis of RNA by DNA. In turn, RNA is involved in protein synthesis. In spite of its obvious limitations, Gamow's model indicated information could be coded in DNA.

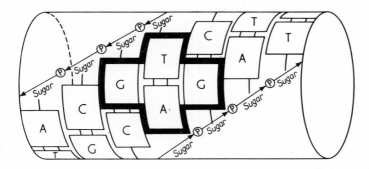

Figure 14. Gamow's model of DNA. After G. Gamow, "Information Transfer in the Living Cell," *Scientific American* 193: 70 (1955).

X-ray diffraction patterns have been studied for RNA as well as DNA. The structure of RNA is more complicated than that of DNA. The ratio of purine to pyrimidine is not one in RNA. The RNA chains may be branched. Its X-ray diffraction pattern suggests a single-chain helical symmetry. The detailed interpretation of this pattern still has not been accomplished.

In spite of this failure to determine the details of the structure of the RNA molecule, X-ray diffraction and electron scattering have been used to locate the nucleic acid within the RNA-type virus particles. This may be done for any of a considerable number of viruses which have been crystallized. The very existence of crystals implies detailed ordering at the atomic level, and accordingly a definite X-ray diffraction pattern. Figure 15 shows a model of tobacco mosaic virus (TMV) constructed to fit X-ray diffraction data. More recent models of TMV reveal that the RNA is held in a large vacuous helix similar to the DNA helix but with quite different physical dimensions. Instead of being supported by hydrogen bridges, the RNA helix in TMV is held in place and stabilized by the surrounding protein molecules which actually intermesh with the RNA (this is not illustrated in Figure 15).

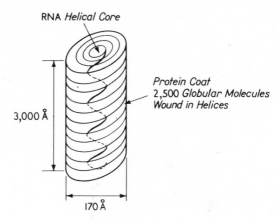

Figure 15. The structure of tobacco mosaic virus. The figure pictorially represents results of X-ray diffraction data.

Another plant virus whose gross structure has been determined is bushy stunt tomato virus (BSV). The particles of BSV are spherical, but, just as TMV, consist of a nucleic acid core plus a surrounding envelope of protein. These structures for TMV and BSV are in accord with the view of virus activity presented in the previous chapter.

7. Summary

The X-ray study of the structure of living matter is a fascinating and growing field. It has made possible discoveries of the steric form of complex high polymers such as proteins and nucleic acids, both of which are responsible for many of the properties of all living systems. These studies, based on X-ray diffraction, have revealed both a complexity that was previously beyond imagination, and a simplicity and an ordering of atoms on a much larger scale than had been previously suspected. Analyses at the molecular level have contributed many of the major steps taken in recent years to the understanding of living matter. The advances discussed in this chapter are not the result of X-ray diffraction studies alone; rather, a great many divergent approaches including those of chemistry, physics, crystallography, biochemistry, genetics, and virology have all been synthesized to elucidate the structure of proteins and nucleic acids. The task is far from complete and one may anticipate continued development of these techniques.

REFERENCES

Biochemistry

A number of good general biochemistry texts describe the properties of proteins and nucleic acids. The author suggests:

1. Kleiner, I. S., and J. M. Orten, *Human Biochemistry*, 5th ed. (St. Louis, Missouri: C. V. Mosby Company, 1958).

   The standard text on nucleic acid is:

2. Chargaff, Edwin, and J. N. Davidson, *The Nucleic Acids: Chemistry and Biology* (New York: Academic Press, Inc., 1955) 2 vols.

X-ray Diffraction

As a general introductory text, the author prefers:

3. Semat, Henry, *Introduction to Atomic and Nuclear Physics*, 3rd ed. (New York: Holt, Rinehart & Winston, Inc., 1954).

   A more advanced discussion can be found in:

4. McLachlan, Dan, *X-ray Crystal Structure* (New York: McGraw-Hill Book Company, Inc., 1957).

Journal Articles

The reader is strongly encouraged to read as many of the following journal articles as possible:

5. Watson, J. D., and F. H. C. Crick, "A Structure for Deoxyribose Nucleic Acid," *Nature* **171**: 737–738 (Apr. 25, 1953).
   a. "Genetical Implications of the Structure of Deoxyribonucleic Acid," **171**: 964–967 (May 30, 1953).
6. Pauling, Linus, and R. B. Corey, "Configuration of Polypeptide Chains," *Nature* **168**: 550–551 (Sept. 29, 1951).
7. Cochran, W., F. H. C. Crick, and V. Vand, "The Structure of Synthetic Polypeptides. I. The Transforms of Atoms on a Helix," *Acta Cryst.* **5**: 581–586 (1952).
8. Gamow, George, "Information Transfer in the Living Cell," *Scientific Am.* **193**: 70–84 (Oct. 1955).
9. Franklin, Rosalind E., "Structure of Tobacco Mosaic Virus," *Nature* **175**: 379–381 (Feb. 26, 1955).

10. ———, and Barry Commoner, "X-ray Diffraction by an Abnormal Protein (B8) Associated With Tobacco Mosaic Virus," *Nature* **175**: 1076–1077 (June 18, 1955).

11. Belozersky, A. N., and A. S. Spirin, "A Correlation Between the Compositions of Deoxyribonucleic and Ribonucleic Acids," *Nature* **182**: 111–112 (July 12, 1958).

12. Kendrew, J. C., "Three-Dimensional Structure of Globular Proteins," *Rev. Mod. Phys.* **31**: 94–99 (Jan. 1959).

The following two articles describe the Fourier syntheses to determine the structure of hemoglobin and myoglobin.   Both are in *Nature*, Vol. **185** (1960).

13. Perutz, M. F., M. G. Rossmann, Ann F. Cullis, Hilary Muirhead, Georg Will, and A. C. T. North, "Structure of Haemoglobin: A Three-Dimensional Fourier Synthesis at 5.5-Å Resolution Obtained by X-ray Analysis," pp. 416–422.

14. Kendrew, J. C., R. E. Dickerson, B. E. Strandberg, R. G. Hant, D. R. Davies, D. C. Phillips, and V. C. Shore, "Structure of Myoglobin: A Three-Dimensional Fourier Synthesis at 2 Å Resolution," pp. 422–427.

Several other articles in Volume 31 of *Reviews of Modern Physics* discuss protein and nucleic acid structures.

Replication of nucleic acids and their role in living cells are discussed in Chapter 25.

Radiation damage to nucleic acids and proteins is discussed in Chapter 16.

16

Molecular Action of Ionizing Radiations

I. Introduction

The effects of ionizing radiation on living matter can be considered at many different levels. The most complex is that of the entire animal or plant. Exposure of entire organisms to ionizing radiation may result, depending on the dose, in induction of cancers and mutations, radiation sickness, and even death. Although health physicists must learn what these complex responses are and at what dosages they are likely to occur, the complexity prohibits complete understanding at this time. Eventually, it is believed that the responses of higher animals and plants to ionizing radiation will be explained in terms of effects occurring at the cellular level. The latter have been discussed in Chapter 10. Particular stress was given to changes induced in the chromosomes. The cellular effects of ionizing radiations can be explained in part in terms of molecular changes. The current chapter emphasizes the effects on the molecular level, and in particular on the natural high polymers. Further logical extensions of this process of abstraction would be to consider the interactions of ionizing radiations with small molecules, atoms, and electrons. Although these levels are introduced briefly in Chapter 10 and are expanded upon in this chapter, a detailed treatment of atomic interactions with radiations is beyond the scope of this text.

Biologically important effects of ionizing radiations in living matter often involve two molecular species, proteins and nucleic acids. This is particularly true of the chromosomal changes, for chromosomes are composed of proteins plus nucleic acids. Both types of compounds are complex high polymers, occurring naturally. The effects of ionizing radiation on simpler high polymers are easier to interpret; these are discussed first. This information is then applied to the changes induced in proteins and nucleic acids by ionizing radiation.

Several different types of radiation produce ionization in all high polymers, both natural and synthetic. These same types of radiation produce ionizing effects in biological cells. Some of the physical characteristics of such radiations, which include α, β, and γ rays, proton, neutron, and deuteron beams, and X-ray photons, have been reviewed in Chapter 10. The action of all of these radiations is associated with ionization and the breaking of bonds. In certain cases, such as dried protein films, the local ionization in the polymer is the only active process. However, when proteins and nucleic acids are in solution, the ionization of the solvent plays an important role.

Ionizing radiations have clinical and pathological results. In addition, they are a tool to study the physical and chemical properties of proteins and nucleic acids, which is the basis for including this chapter in this text. Sections 5 and 6 are concerned with the properties of proteins and nucleic acids which can be discovered by bombardment of dried films with ionizing radiations.

2. Polymers, Proteins, and DNA

Chemically, both proteins and nucleic acids belong to a general class of compounds called polymers (or high polymers). As discussed in the previous chapter, a polymer is made up of a repeating type unit (the monomer), which is duplicated again and again; the repeating units making up proteins are called *amino acids*. Similarly, there are repeating units making up nucleic acids; their monomers are called *nucleotides*. The chemical structures of both proteins and nucleic acids are presented in Chapter 15.

The amino acids are joined together by peptide bonds to form proteins. Because a molecule of water is eliminated for each peptide bond formed, it is customary to state that the amino acids condense to form the proteins. Nucleic acids, too, are condensation-type polymers, a molecule of water being eliminated for each nucleotide joined to the chain. Both proteins and nucleic acids are complicated high polymers in that the long chains consist of a mixture of different types of residues or monomers arranged in a definite but complex pattern. It is easier to interpret the effects of ionizing radiations on simpler synthetic polymers, made up of one or at most two types of monomers, than on the more complex proteins and nucleic acids. A study of the radiation damage to these simpler polymers provides orientation toward the types of effects to be expected when proteins and nucleic acids are exposed to ionizing radiations.

Studies have been made of the effects of ionizing radiations on many different types of synthetic high polymers. Two used as examples in the next section are polyethylene and polyisobutylene. They have the structural forms shown in Figure 1.

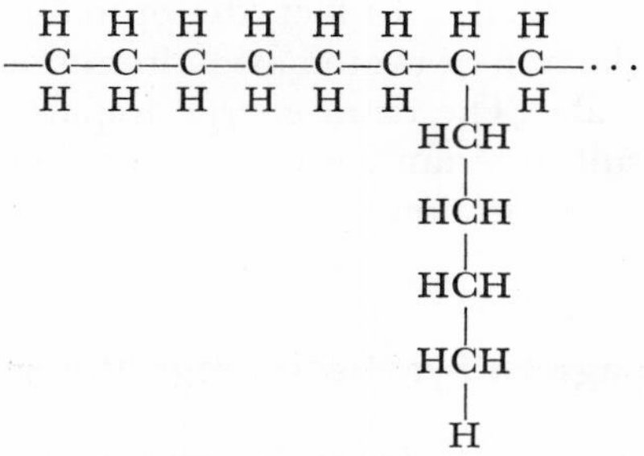

$$
\begin{array}{cccccccc}
H & H & H & H & H & H & H & H \\
-C-C-C-C-C-C-C-C- & \cdots \\
H & H & H & H & H & H & | & H \\
 & & & & & & HCH \\
 & & & & & & | \\
 & & & & & & HCH \\
 & & & & & & | \\
 & & & & & & HCH \\
 & & & & & & | \\
 & & & & & & HCH \\
 & & & & & & | \\
 & & & & & & H
\end{array}
$$

Polyethylene has branched sidechains. It is an "addition" polymer of ethylene, $CH_2{=}CH_2$.

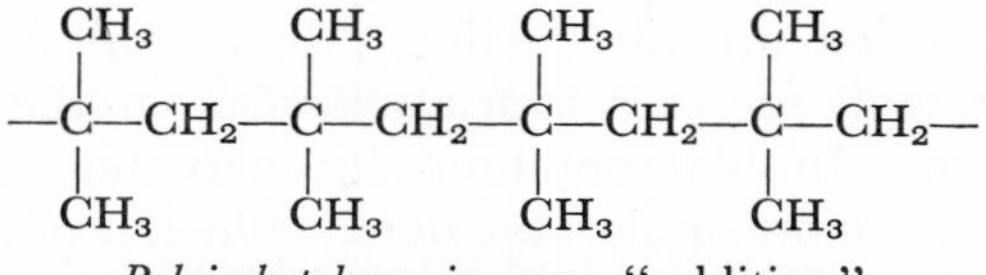

$$
\begin{array}{cccc}
CH_3 & CH_3 & CH_3 & CH_3 \\
| & | & | & | \\
-C-CH_2-C-CH_2-C-CH_2-C-CH_2- \\
| & | & | & | \\
CH_3 & CH_3 & CH_3 & CH_3
\end{array}
$$

Polyisobutylene is an "addition" polymer formed from isobutylene.

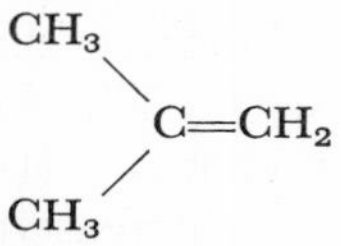

$$
\begin{array}{l}
CH_3 \\
\quad\diagdown \\
\qquad C{=}CH_2 \\
\quad\diagup \\
CH_3
\end{array}
$$

Figure I. Structure of polyethylene and polyisobutylene.

When the monomers (ethylene) molecules are added together to form polyethylene, it is possible to have carbon atoms surrounded by only seven electrons, as shown in Figure 2. Those atoms with unpaired

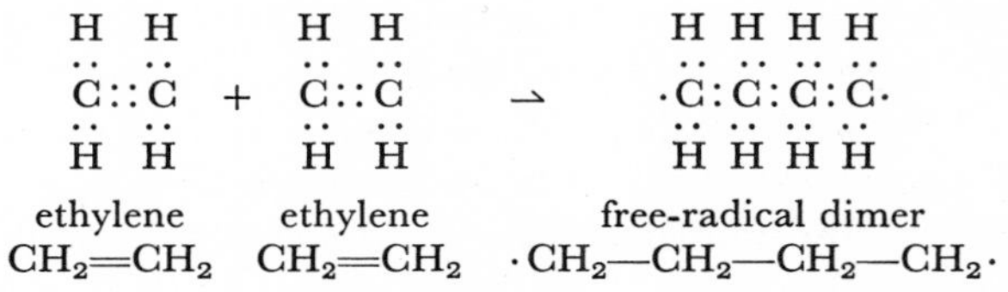

$$
\begin{array}{ccccc}
\text{H} \;\; \text{H} & & \text{H} \;\; \text{H} & & \text{H} \;\; \text{H} \;\; \text{H} \;\; \text{H} \\
\text{C} :: \text{C} & + & \text{C} :: \text{C} & \to & \cdot\text{C} : \text{C} : \text{C} : \text{C}\cdot \\
\text{H} \;\; \text{H} & & \text{H} \;\; \text{H} & & \text{H} \;\; \text{H} \;\; \text{H} \;\; \text{H}
\end{array}
$$

ethylene	ethylene	free-radical dimer
$CH_2{=}CH_2$	$CH_2{=}CH_2$	$\cdot CH_2{-}CH_2{-}CH_2{-}CH_2\cdot$

Figure 2. Free-radical formation during polymerization.

electrons are called free radicals. Many free radicals are extremely reactive; they are believed to be responsible for continuing a chain-type reaction once polymerization is started.

Free radicals are also responsible for some of the effects of ionizing radiations on high polymers. In fact, the primary action of the ionization is to knock an electron or proton away from the polymer leaving the latter as a free radical. The extra energy imparted to the polymer in this fashion may result in a number of different changes, a few of which are discussed in the next section.

3. Radiation Damage to Synthetic High Polymers

When high polymers are irradiated in solution, two different types of damage may occur. The first is that the polymer molecule itself may be irreversibly altered owing to the direct action of the radiation in producing ionizations within the polymer molecule. The second type of damage possible is due to indirect effects; these result from the reactions of the polymer with the free radicals formed in the solvent by the ionizing radiation. In dilute solutions, it is very likely that the indirect effects may be the more important ones. On the other hand, in the solid state, the direct actions of the radiation on the polymers are the only important type.

As a result of both direct and indirect damage, two major changes are found in synthetic high polymers. The first is called *crosslinking*, which means forming bonds between chains. It results in increased molecular weight, increased elastic moduli, increased transparency, and decreased solubility. The other type of effect, called *scission*, consists of breaking bonds along chains. It is characterized by the exact opposite of the effects described for crosslinking. The effects of crosslinking and scission are illustrated in Figures 3 and 4, respectively.

With both crosslinking and scission, a small molecule such as H_2 or

NH_3 is often eliminated. This third effect of small molecule elimination causes negligible changes in the molecular weight or physical properties of the polymers as compared to the changes due to scission and cross-linking. However, such small changes can completely alter the physiological actions of a protein.

Probably all high polymers undergo both scission and crosslinking when irradiated. However, in some, such as polyethylene, illustrated in Figure 3, the crosslinking is the predominant effect. Its physical

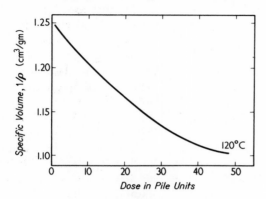

Figure 3. Crosslinking in polyethylene. Crosslinking results in many changes in physical properties. One of the more pronounced changes is the increased density; this change is most pronounced above the melting point at 105°C. After A. Charlesby and M. Ross, "Effect of Crosslinking on the Density and Melting of Polythene," *Proc. Roy. Soc.* **A217**: 122 (1953).

characteristics are changed in a fashion that indicates only the cross-linking. By contrast, polyisobutylene, illustrated in Figure 4, shows only the effects associated with scission when it is exposed to ionizing radiation.

The effects of ionizing radiations on all polymers are usually enhanced if oxygen is present. For example, if polyethylene is bombarded in the absence of oxygen, crosslinking occurs. If oxygen is present during the bombardment, considerably more crosslinking takes place. Likewise, the scission in polyisobutylene is greater if it is exposed to radiation damage in the presence of oxygen rather than in the absence of oxygen. The enhancement of the effects of bombardment is manyfold larger than expected from the ionization of the oxygen molecule by the radiation. The increased effects must result from the reactions of oxygen with the free radicals and other less stable forms produced by the ionizations.

In a molecule such as polymethylene, which is the same as poly-ethylene except that it has no side chains, there is no reason to suppose one carbon bond to be weaker than another. In other molecules, such as polyisobutylene, the carbon atoms attached to four other carbon atoms seem to be the weak links in the chain. In more complex poly-mers, there is usually one weakest bond. It appears that the extra energy imparted by the ionizing radiation is often carried to this spot. Thus, iso-octane breaks preferentially at one particular bond.

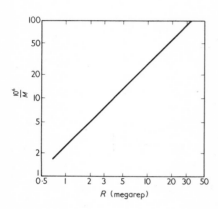

Figure 4. Scission in polyisobutylene. Decrease in molecular weight of polyisobutylene as a result of irradia-tion. The average molecular weight M was determined by viscosity measurements. After P. M. Alex-ander, R. M. Black, and A. Charlesby, "Radiation Induced Changes in the Structure of Polyisobutylene," *Proc. Roy. Soc.* **A232**: 31 (1955).

Another example of the transport of the ionization energy can be found in solutions. Some molecules which fluoresce because of the formation of free radicals will do so when the solution is irradiated, even if the ionization occurs in the solvent at a distance of 50 Å or more away. Similarly, most aromatic-ring comp-ounds tend to stabilize free radicals and can protect polymers. This occurs either if the aromatic com-pounds are placed in solution with the polymer or if they are incorporated into the polymer, as in polystyrene. The extra energy imparted by ioni-zation may be transferred within molecules or between molecules. In some cases, this involves charge transfer, but in others it does not. Exactly how the latter happens is not always understood.

There are situations in which the extra energy imparted by the ionizing radiation is not transferred. For instance, color changes and electrical-resistance changes in polyethylene, both of which are due to the presence of free radicals, may remain for weeks or even months after irradiation, provided oxygen is excluded. In this case, there is no doubt that the extra energy is not transferred through the polymer. No general rule exists to predict why the energy is transferred in some cases and not in others.

In the more complex natural polymers, all of the effects discussed above occur. The phenomena which should be considered in natural polymers are: direct and indirect action; crosslinking and scission; the elimination of small molecules; the role of oxygen; energy transfer; and damage protection. Dried protein films are simpler than protein solutions or biological cells, in that only direct effects are possible. From the variation of molecular destruction in dried films with dose rate, it is possible to compute a sensitive volume for the molecular species being studied.

4. Target Theory

Target theory can be used to compute a sensitive volume or target whenever doses of ionizing radiation are used to induce changes in whole animals, in cells, or in dried protein films. The interpretation of the target volume is least ambiguous in the case of dried protein films but use has been made of this concept in Chapters 10 and 14 in discussing the sensitive volume for genetic mutation. It was stated that this volume was computed to be equivalent to a sphere of around 70 Å diameter. In living cells, it is sometimes hard to distinguish single-hit targets from those requiring multiple hits to produce any result because the sensitivity may vary from one cell to the next. In a like fashion, even after one has found a sensitive volume, it is not self-evident whether this is associated with a particular molecule or with ionizations produced elsewhere in the cell, the excess energy being transferred to the critical molecules. In this section, the theory necessary to compute the target volume is discussed.

Suppose a beam of D ionizing particles per unit area strikes a given cell (or dried film). Further, assume that the only effects occur in one particular type of constituent, of which there are n in the cell (or film). For simplicity of discussion, it will be assumed that the particles of this constituent are individual molecules, although the theory is in no way altered if this is not true. If the probability of any one molecule of this species being damaged is equal to that of any other, then the probability that an incident particle will cause one change is proportional to the number of molecules n remaining unchanged. As the cell (or film) is bombarded by incident particles, n will decrease. This may be expressed symbolically by

$$\Delta n = -nS\Delta D \tag{1}$$

where the incremental dose ΔD is a small number of incident particles per unit area, which causes a decrease in n of an amount Δn, and S is a proportionality constant. The probability of reaction is included in the constant S which has the dimensions of an area; S is called a cross section.

Integration of Equation 1 leads to the equation

$$\frac{n}{n_o} = e^{-SD} \tag{2}$$

where n_o is the number of molecules before receiving total dose D, and n is the number left unaltered afterward.

If the number of ionizations along the track of the bombarding particle is sufficiently low, each may produce the destruction of one molecule. Then one may write

$$S = Vi \tag{3}$$

where V is the critical volume of the molecule and i is the number of ionizations per unit path length. (If there are too many ionizations per unit path length, Equation 3 must be modified. Moreover, if several hits are necessary for molecular destruction, Equation 3 must be changed in a different fashion.) To further simplify Equation 3, one may define a total ionization density I such that

$$I = Di \tag{4}$$

that is, I is the number of ionizations per unit volume. Using Equation 3, including its implicit assumptions, and Equation 4, Equation 2 may be rewritten as

$$\frac{n}{n_o} = e^{-NI} \tag{5}$$

Equation 5 is in a form that can be readily tested. Graphs of lines expected from this equation are shown in Figure 5. A wide variety of experiments ranging from genetic effects in whole animals and plants to the destruction of molecules in dried film all can be described by this equation if the ionization per unit path length is sufficiently small. It was used to compute the sensitive volume referred to in the discussion of genetic effects in Chapter 10, and its implications were considered in Chapter 14.

If instead of sparse ionizations, one considers the limiting case of a very large number of ionizations per unit path length, then Equation 2 can also be rewritten in a simpler form. In this case, there is certain to be at least one ionization within each molecule for each incident particle. Then S becomes a constant S_o, the cross section for destruction of the molecule if ionization occurs within it. Under these conditions, Equation 2 becomes

$$\frac{n}{n_o} = e^{-S_o D} \tag{6}$$

The calculations of the critical volume V and of the limiting cross section S_o are shown in Figure 5. The applications of these techniques are discussed in the following two sections.

5. Inactivation of Dried Protein Films

When dried protein films are subjected to ionizing radiation, the molecules are irreversibly altered. Because no solvent is present, the changes observed are of necessity direct ones in the protein itself. In most of the experiments described in this section, no attempt was made to exclude oxygen or determine its role, if any, in the final molecular alterations. Protein films are usually tested for molecular changes after redissolving them in suitable media (usually buffered water). Tests of the physical

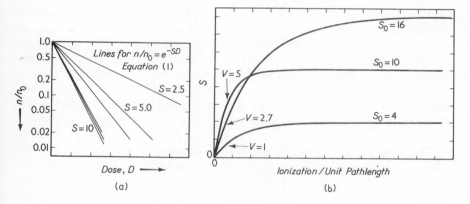

Figure 5. Curves illustrating the inactivation theory. (a) Curves show the predicted relationship for the number of particles remaining at different ionizations per unit path length. These were used to plot S below for the curve $S_0 = 10$. The ratio n/n_0 is the fraction of the molecules remaining unaltered after exposure to dose D. (b) Predicted curves for finding the critical volume V and limiting the cross section S_0. To determine these curves experimentally necessitates a series of experiments such as those illustrated in (a). The straight lines near the origin are predicted by Equation (5), whereas those parallel to the axis at the right edge of the graph are predicted by Equation (6).

and chemical properties of proteins are far more sensitive to any small change whatsoever than are those used on synthetic polymers. However, in most cases, even though a change can be detected, it is not possible to determine whether crosslinking or scission has occurred within the protein molecule. The polypeptide chains making up the protein appear to be so crosslinked that either scission or additional crosslinking can occur without altering the molecular weight. In other words, protein changes may be detected with a high sensitivity, but the tests yield no knowledge whatsoever of the intramolecular alterations.

An exception to this inability to distinguish scission from crosslinking is the molecule, hemocyanin, an iron-containing, oxygen-transport pigment found in snails and other invertebrates. When hemocyanin, molecular weight 7,000,000, is exposed to certain chemical agents such as urea, it undergoes scission, being split reversibly into eight pieces of equal molecular weight. Ionizing radiations also split hemocyanin; however, they split the molecule irreversibly in half.

One very sensitive criterion for physical changes in a protein is its solubility. Another is its isoelectric point (that is, the pH of the medium at which the protein molecule will not migrate in an electrical field). If the protein is an enzyme, the enzymatic activity is a very sensitive indication of its physical and chemical condition (see Chapters 17 and 18). Finally, other proteins react with specific antibodies; in this case, the protein is called an *antigen*. Its antigenicity may be altered after irradiation. Studies on a large number of dried protein films have shown all of the preceding changes. No dried protein films are completely unaltered by ionizing radiation.

The elimination of small molecules observed with synthetic high polymers can be readily demonstrated for proteins. When either the monomers (amino acids) or their high polymers (proteins) are exposed to ionizing radiation, a number of small molecules are eliminated. These include NH_3, CO_2, and CO. In the case of single amino acid molecules, the elimination of a smaller molecule represents a scission or a breaking of bonds. An amino acid which does not eliminate NH_3, CO_2, or CO during irradiation is cysteine, which contains a sulfhydryl group, —S—H. In the presence of O_2 or other oxidizing agents, two cysteines may be oxidized and then may unite to form one cystine. In proteins, there are some indications that such a high fraction of the free —S—H groups are oxidized that energy appears to be transferred preferentially to these sulfhydryl groups from other parts of the molecule. (In pure cysteine, in the absence of any oxidizing agent, H_2O_2 and H_2S are formed under the action of ionizing radiations. Proteins apparently stabilize the free radicals in the cysteine residues so that little or no H_2S is released.)

In spite of the indeterminancy of the nature of the changes in most dried proteins, it is possible to investigate energy transfer directly. Such studies are based on the single-hit target theory discussed in Section 4. If one assumes target theory and determines a damage or inactivation versus dosage curve, one can compute a critical volume according to Equation 5. If energy transfer may occur throughout the protein molecule, this critical volume should be the entire molecule. It is likewise conceivable that energy transfer could occur in only part of the molecule or, at the other extreme, energy transfer may take place between adjacent molecules. These conditions could lead to critical volumes which would be small or large, respectively, as compared to one protein molecule.

All three possibilities—critical volume equal to, smaller than, and larger than one molecule—have been observed by using dried films of different proteins. The case of the critical volume equal to the molecular volume has been observed for DNA-ase, invertase, and many other

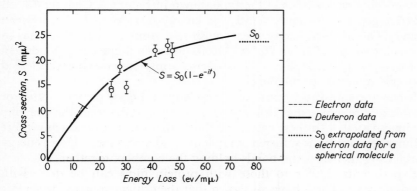

Figure 6. The critical volume and limiting cross section for DNA-ase. Points are shown for deuteron data only. After R. Setlow, "Radiation of Proteins and Enzymes," *Annals of the New York Academy of Sciences* **59**: 471 (1955).

proteins, as well as for one smaller molecule, penicillin, molecular weight 600. A plot of typical experimental data is shown in Figure 6. Although energy transfer throughout the molecule is a sufficient condition for the equality of the molecular and critical volumes, it is not a necessary condition. It is possible that any of a variety of small changes in various parts of the molecule would all lead to the same conclusion of protein damage. Thus, finding a critical volume which equals a molecular volume suggests that energy transfer may take place throughout the entire molecule but does not prove it.

In contrast, a critical volume smaller than the molecular volume proves that energy transfer cannot occur throughout the entire molecule. This is the case for catalase which has a critical volume, as determined by tests using enzymatic activity, corresponding to one-half its molecular weight. (If urea is added to the test medium, it is found that the critical volume corresponds to the entire molecular weight.) Bovine serum albumin is a more extreme example. When a monolayer is irradiated, the critical volume determined by antigenic tests corresponds to one-tenth its molecular weight. This implies that severe damage to nine-tenths of the molecule can leave the antigenic activity unaltered. Thus, both catalase and bovine serum albumin may be partially damaged without inactivating the remainder of the molecule.

Finally, some protein films are able to transfer excitation energy from one molecule to the next. Insulin films show a critical volume corresponding to a molecular weight of 23,000, whereas the usual value for the molecular weight is 12,000. This indicates that insulin in these films consists of *four* units of the type shown in Figure 4, Chapter 15, all linked together sufficiently tightly for energy transfer to occur between them. The digestive enzyme, trypsin, is similar in that it has a molecular weight of about 20,000, but its critical volume corresponds to a molecular weight of 34,000. Thus, energy apparently may be transferred from one molecule to the next.

If enzyme-substrate complexes (see Chapter 17) or enzyme-inhibitor complexes are exposed as dried films to ionizing radiations, the enzymes are inactivated. In these cases, it is found that one ionization anywhere within the complex is sufficient to inactivate the enzyme. Here, energy transfer occurs across the bonds holding the complex together.

Experiments similar to those with protein films can be done with dried viruses. These have all shown that the critical volume for genetic changes is comparable to the volume indicated by the nucleic acid content. Moreover, they have shown the complexity of the virus, that any gross criterion such as virus multiplication cannot be conveniently described in terms of Equation 5. Rather, to use Equation 5, one has the alternatives of measuring the rate of any genetic change whatsoever, or else comparing the rate of production of the same mutation as indicated by the methods presented in Chapter 14.

In summary of this section, it should be noted that the inactivations of dried protein and virus films by bombardment with ionizing radiations have indicated several features of the physical properties of proteins and viruses. The similarities between proteins and synthetic high polymers are emphasized by the similarity in the types of radiation damage, whereas the greater complexity of the proteins is emphasized by the greater sensitivity of tests for changes in the proteins. Differences between proteins are demonstrated by the various ranges of energy transfer; in some, the excess energy may be transferred throughout the entire molecule, in others it is restricted to part of the molecule, and in a third group energy transfer could occur between loosely bound pairs of molecules. Finally, the accepted role of the nucleic acids in virus multiplication is in accord with the results obtained through the irradiation of virus particles.

6. Indirect Effects on Proteins and Nucleic Acids

When solutions of proteins and nucleic acids are exposed to ionizing radiations, the changes observed are very similar to those found for dried protein films. However, if the concentrations are low enough, there can be little doubt that many of the effects are indirect, arising from ionizations occurring in the solvent. This is always true for proteins at physiological concentrations. In the case of nucleic acid solutions, and particularly of DNA solutions, the question of direct or indirect effects is not so clear cut. A great deal of evidence supports the direct target theory for DNA in chromosomes and bacteriophages. It shows that ionizations, leading to changes within a critical volume corresponding to about four nucleotides, are sufficient to alter genetic character. It is possible to believe therefore that energy is not transferred very far along the DNA polymer chain. However, the primary effect in living cells could be due to the formation of free radicals in the cellular water in a small volume close to the DNA molecule.

Because water plays an important role in damage to proteins in solution and may also be significant for DNA changes, effects of ionizing radiations on water have been carefully investigated. The primary process may be represented by

$$H_2O \rightarrow HO\cdot + H\cdot$$

where the dots signify free radicals. Alternative forms are also possible, for example,

$$H_2O \rightarrow \begin{cases} H_2O^+ \\ + e^- \end{cases} \begin{array}{l} \nearrow HO^+ + H\cdot \\ \searrow H^+ + HO\cdot \end{array}$$

$$e^- + H_2O \rightarrow H_2O^- \begin{array}{l} \nearrow OH^- + H\cdot \\ \searrow OH\cdot + H{:}^- \end{array}$$

These may then recombine in various forms to produce reactive molecules such as H_2O_2 and H_3O. All these reactive forms are known to alter proteins and DNA. The probability of producing H_2O_2 in water is greatly increased in the presence of dissolved oxygen.

Many experiments have confirmed that damage to both proteins and DNA in solution is much smaller either in the absence of oxygen or in the presence of a protective agent, which is more likely to react with the

H_2O_2 and free radicals than are the proteins and nucleic acids. Protective agents of this type can also reduce damage due to direct effects of the ionizing radiations because the extra energy may be transferred to the protective agent from the protein or nucleic acid. Among the most effective compounds of this nature are a group containing both —S—H or —S—S—groups and amino groups —NH_2, such as cysteamine and cystamine. These compounds protect not only proteins and nucleic acids, but also synthetic condensation-type polymers such as polymethacrylic acid. Other protective agents with very different structures have also been used, such as β-aminoethyl-isothiuronium-bromide-hydrobromide.

In terms of critical volumes, the net effect of the protective agent will be to reduce the critical volume far below the molecular volume. Various theories have been developed to explain the action of the protective agents on proteins as due to stabilizing terminal —S—H and —S—S— groups. However, because the same agents also protect synthetic polymers which do not contain sulfur, it appears unjustified to focus too much attention on one particular type of bond.

Studies have been conducted on the relative sensitivities of many amino acids, proteins, and nucleic acids to ionizing radiations. These have led to quite lengthy tables, but no one has succeeded in relating this information to protein structure. The relative sensitivities of different proteins can be indicated by a G value; this is the number of molecules altered per 100 ev (of a fixed type of irradiation). Some typical values are shown in the accompanying table which indicates the widespread range of G values.

The values in the table show that as the complexity of the molecule increases, there is some tendency for the molecule to become less sensitive to ionizing radiations. Thus, adenine is more sensitive by itself than when combined with ribose to form the nucleoside, adenosine. It in turn is more sensitive than the nucleotide, adenosine monophosphate (adenylic acid). Complete nucleic acids are another order of magnitude less sensitive. However, the variation of sensitivity with size is not always observed. Some proteins are almost as sensitive as a typical small molecule, whereas others are far less sensitive, so that no general rule can be maintained.

TABLE I

G Values for Biologically Active Molecules*

Protein enzymes	G
Yeast alcohol dehydrogenase	3.4
Carboxy peptidase	0.55
Hexokinase	0.033

TABLE I (*continued*)

Catalase	0.009
Nucleic Acids	
DNA	0.0039
RNA	0.0072
Nucleotides	
Adenylic acid (AMP)	0.161
Nucleosides	
Adenosine	0.196
Purine	
Adenine	0.676
Other Small Molecules	
DPNH	1.7
Ethyl alcohol	5.9
Coenzyme A	9.2
Glutathione	10.7

* *G* value is the number of molecules reacting per 100 ev. All for *x* irradiation in aerated solutions.

After E. S. G. Barron, "Effect of Ionizing Radiation on Systems of Biological Importance," *Annals of the New York Academy of Sciences* **59**: 575 (1955).

7. Summary

Exposures of proteins and nucleic acids to ionizing radiations have shown that all of these molecules may be altered with sufficient dosages. The similarity between the damages observed in proteins and nucleic acids, and those in synthetic high polymers, has been emphasized. These damages include: direct and indirect effects; crosslinking and scission; elimination of small molecules; and energy transfer. All play an important role in the irradiation of living matter by ionizing particles.

The data on the irradiation of dried protein films have also contributed to our knowledge of the physical properties of these proteins. However, the net return of knowledge has been very small, being limited to an indication of energy transfer and the relative sensitivity of the proteins to ionizing radiations. In this respect, the methods of X-ray analysis discussed in the previous chapter have been much more rewarding. Similarly, the approaches presented in the following two chapters, while dealing with a quite different aspect of proteins, namely enzymatic activity, have shown far more about the physiological role of proteins than has been discovered in experiments using radiation damage.

REFERENCES

The literature on the fields covered in this chapter is voluminous. This has resulted in part because the financial support for work in these areas has made it possible to print many books of essentially transient value. The author feels that of these the interested student will profit most by reading further in the following books. However, similar material can be found in other books and journal articles.

1. Bacq, Z. M., and Peter Alexander, *Fundamentals of Radiobiology* (New York: Academic Press, Inc., 1955).
2. Hollaender, Alexander, ed. *Radiation Biology* Volume I, Parts 1 and 2. *High Energy Radiation* (New York: McGraw-Hill Book Company, Inc., 1954).
3. Bovey, F. A., *Effects of Ionizing Radiations on Natural and Synthetic High Polymers* (New York: Interscience Publishers, Inc., 1958).
4. Miner, R. W., ed. "Ionizing Radiation and the Cell," (Monograph) *Ann. New York Acad. Sc.* **59**: 467–664 (1955).
   Particularly chapters by:
   a. Setlow, Richard, "Radiation Studies of Proteins and Enzymes," pp. 471–483.
   b. Barron, E. S. G., "The Effect of Ionizing Radiations on Systems of Biological Importance," pp. 574–594.

17

Enzyme Kinetics of
Hydrolytic Reactions

I. Introduction

Modern physics has emphasized the description of the properties of matter and energy in terms of the behavior of elementary particles. In a similar vein, molecular biology describes living systems in terms of their elementary particles, the molecules. This chapter is a discussion of an application of analytical methods to the dynamic behavior (kinetics) of a class of molecules called *enzymes*. Enzymes are biological catalysts of a primarily protein nature.[1] A catalyst is a chemical substance which alters a rate of reaction, although the catalyst itself is in the same state after the reaction as it was before the reaction. The catalyst may be altered during the reaction but returns to its original state after the completion of the reaction.

Many uncatalyzed systems exist in nonequilibrium conditions because the reaction rates to reach equilibrium are so slow. A catalyst speeds up the rate of attaining equilibrium but does not in itself alter the

---

[1] The chemical composition and structure of proteins are discussed in Chapter 15.

equilibrium. For example, glucose can remain in solution in the presence of oxygen for years without being significantly altered. In the presence of certain catalysts, however, the glucose and oxygen react rapidly to form carbon dioxide and water while releasing energy. One may regard the reaction as an equilibrium represented stoichiometrically by the equation

$$C_6H_{12}O_6 + 6O_2 \rightleftharpoons 6CO_2 + 6H_2O$$

This equilibrium so strongly favors the carbon dioxide and water that no detectable amounts of glucose are formed when carbon dioxide and water are mixed. The oxidation of glucose is catalyzed by a series of enzymes found in almost all living cells. These enzymes not only promote equilibrium but also convert part of the energy released to other forms of chemical energy used by the living cells. In the absence of catalysts, however, glucose and oxygen remain in solution in the nonequilibrium condition indefinitely.

Many biological reactions involve much more complex molecules than glucose. Others involving smaller, simpler molecules are easier to discuss. One such reaction, discussed in greater detail in the next chapter, is the dissociation of hydrogen peroxide, according to the scheme

$$2H_2O_2 \rightleftharpoons 2H_2O + O_2$$

Here, equilibrium also strongly favors the right-hand side of the equation. Nonetheless, hydrogen peroxide can be stored for years in a dark bottle in the absence of metallic ions. Many metal ions act as catalysts accelerating this reaction to the right. None of these is as effective as the protein catalyst *catalase*.

There are also examples of enzyme-catalyzed reactions whose equilibrium does not favor one side of the equation so strongly. A biologically important reaction of this type is the formation and destruction of carbonic acid according to the scheme

$$H_2CO_3 \underset{k_2}{\overset{k_1}{\rightleftharpoons}} H_2O + CO_2$$

In the absence of a catalyst, this reaction reaches equilibrium in a matter of minutes. However, this is too slow to remove the CO_2 from the blood stream during its time in the vertebrate gill or lung. The rate of attainment of equilibrium is increased fourfold by an enzyme present in all red blood cells called *carbonic anhydrase*.

In the foregoing equation, the symbols k_1 and k_2 have been introduced. These are *rate constants*. The first represents the fraction of carbonic acid molecules dissociating per unit of time. The second is a proportionality factor between the product of the carbon dioxide and water concentrations, and the new carbonic acid formed per unit of time. Analytically, this may be expressed by the differential equation

$$\frac{d[H_2CO_3]}{dt} = -k_1[H_2CO_3] + k_2[H_2O]\cdot[CO_2]$$

where the square brackets represent concentrations. One may also write a similar equation for the carbon dioxide

$$\frac{d[CO_2]}{dt} = +k_1[H_2CO_3] - k_2[H_2O]\cdot[CO_2]$$

Notice that k_1 and k_2 have different units; those of k_1 are sec^{-1}, whereas the units of k_2 are $concentration^{-1}\ sec^{-1}$.

In the foregoing paragraph, it was stated that k_1 and k_2 are rate constants. They certainly are rates but it is by no means obvious that they are constants, even if temperature and pH are maintained constant. The quantities k_1 and k_2 will be constants for many reactions, provided a number of conditions are met. The first is that the reaction scheme is complete and does not involve other steps. The addition of an enzyme which alters the reaction means that new rate constants must be defined in the presence of the enzyme. The second is that the reactants are sufficiently free to move about so that the probability of their colliding is proportional to their concentrations. (This is sometimes referred to as the law of mass action.) The final condition is that one really considers only the average behavior of large numbers of molecules, so that one may identify the rate of reaction with the concentration times the probability of a molecular reaction.

The foregoing examples illustrate the types of reactions analyzed in studies of enzyme kinetics; this type of reasoning has proved attractive to biophysicists and physical chemists. Enzyme studies have become part of biophysics for several additional reasons. For instance, many reactions are observed by the use of complex physical instruments such as recording spectrophotometers and paramagnetic resonance equipment. These have demanded a certain degree of training in physics (as well as skill in electronics) for their construction, maintenance, and the interpretation of their data. A quite different reason for including enzyme studies in biophysics is that enzyme kinetics are necessary for a study of enzyme thermodynamics. Physics, to the extent it has any unifying factor, has emphasized the point of view that energy is the most fundamental, most significant quantity. This approach, expressed through thermodynamics as applied to enzyme systems, is presented in Chapter 22.

2. Enzymes

Although many biophysicists have studied enzyme kinetics, most enzyme studies have not been the work of biophysicists. In this section, a minimal outline will be presented of the many types of enzymes known, primarily from a result of biochemical and physiological studies. It is hoped that this section will be of use to those readers with comparatively little biochemical background.

A complete classification of types of enzymes, in terms of the reactions they catalyze, can be found in many biochemistry texts. The first reference at the end of the next chapter has appealed particularly to the author and his students; the following four paragraphs contain a brief summary of the functional classification of enzymes found in that text. Six major classes are described. Most of the classes are named by attaching the suffix -*ase* to a word describing the reaction catalyzed. This same naming procedure is used for many individual types of enzymes.

The first such class consists of the *hydrolases*, which split molecules, adding H to one part and OH to the other. The kinetics of the hydro- lases are discussed in this chapter. One example of hydrolases are the phosphatases which catalyze the addition of water to an organic phos- phate to form the corresponding alcohol and phosphoric acid; sym- bolically, this may be represented as

$$R\!-\!O\!-\!PO_3H_2 + H_2O \rightleftharpoons ROH + H_3PO_4$$

In a like manner, *proteolytic enzymes* catalyze the splitting of peptide bonds adding H and OH to the two split parts. Other hydrolases are: *glycosidases* which catalyze the splitting of complex sugars to simpler sugars with the addition of water; and *lipases* and *esterases*, both of which catalyze the equilibrium between an ester and its hydrolyzed com- ponents. Acetyl cholinesterase, introduced in Chapter 4, is an example of this last group.

A second class of enzymes are the *transferases*, which catalyze the transfer of a piece of one molecule to another. For instance, *trans- phosphorylases* catalyze reactions in which phosphate groups are changed from one molecule to another. (If either the acceptor or donor of the phosphate is water [or phosphoric acid], the enzyme is a phosphatase rather than a transphosphorylase.) Other transferases may be defined in a similar manner; they include *transglycosidases*, *transpeptidases*, *trans- aminases*, *transmethylation systems*, and *transacylases*. The reaction cata- lyzed by each of these is contained in the name.

A third major group of enzymes are the *addition* enzymes, which catalyze the addition of two molecules, to form a single molecule. A fourth class, the *isomerases*, changes the isomeric form. Opsin, discussed in Chapter 19, belongs in this class because it acts as a *photoisomerase*. The fifth class of enzymes remove CO_2; they are called *carboxylases*.

Finally, as the sixth class, one may list the *respiratory enzymes*. The kinetics of some of their reactions are discussed in the following chapter. Respiratory enzymes include those which enter into oxidative reactions. Either O_2 or H_2O_2 may be the eventual source of oxygen, depending on the system of enzymes. These respiratory enzymes have been studied extensively by spectroscopic methods because many of them undergo changes in their absorption (and fluorescence) spectra during reaction. Many respiratory enzymes also have altered magnetic susceptibility during reactions.

Under each of the six major classifications just given, there are sub-classes and within each of these there are large numbers of enzymes. A major activity of biochemistry since about 1930 has been the discovery of more and still more enzymes. The number of known enzymes seems astronomical and is still growing. Almost every reaction which occurs in a living organism, or just outside it, is catalyzed by a specific enzyme. Complex reactions such as the oxidation of glucose, referred to earlier, involve many enzymes. Specifically, in the oxidation of glucose, more than 50 different enzymes participate, to form a complex pathway.

It is interesting that the same types of respiratory enzymes occur in almost every living cell from yeast to mammals. (A partial exception to this are the anaerobic bacteria.) On a molecular basis, the description of life must include a description of enzymes and enzyme kinetics. On a kinetic basis the similarities between the respiratory enzymes of various types of cells are much more impressive than their differences.

It has been facetiously remarked that the living cell is a bag full of enzymes. This is a gross oversimplification. Some of the enzymes are associated with particulate matter; others, such as digestive enzymes, act outside the cell altogether. The cell also contains many compounds not normally considered as enzymes. One class of compounds whose members act as catalysts, but are not considered enzymes, is the nucleic acids. These are discussed in Chapter 15. Nucleic acids are not considered enzymes because they are not proteins. Enzymes are usually distinguished from transport proteins such as hemoglobin, although here the basis of distinction is very weak.

At the start of this chapter, an enzyme was defined as a biological catalyst of a primarily protein nature. The word "primarily" was inserted because many enzymes consist not only of a protein molecule but also of a smaller molecule. In this case, the large protein portion of the enzyme is referred to as the *apoenzyme*. The smaller part is called the *cofactor, coenzyme,* or *prosthetic group.* No sharp dividing line separates these three types of smaller groups. By and large, the word "cofactor" is used for a loosely bound, small inorganic ion. Coenzyme usually implies a larger group which separates easily from the enzyme, such as diphosphopyridine nucleotide (DPN) illustrated in Chapter 18. Coenzymes probably separate and recombine with the various apoenzymes during normal physiological conditions. There may be many different types of apoenzymes for any given coenzyme. Although apoenzymes, like most other proteins, are irreversibly destroyed by prolonged boiling, the coenzymes in general are not so destroyed.

Prosthetic groups are small, nonprotein parts of enzymes which are attached so firmly that they cannot be easily removed without irreversibly altering the enzyme. Among the more frequently studied prosthetic groups are the hemes. A molecule consisting of a heme group and a protein is referred to as a *hemoprotein.* Examples include the carrier protein, hemoglobin, and the respiratory enzymes myoglobin, catalase, peroxidase, and about 20 different cytochromes. The chemical structure of the heme group is presented in Section 1 of the next chapter.

Hemoproteins are convenient to study because their optical absorption spectra change during their reactions. Their magnetic susceptibility also changes, which helps to elucidate their chemical structure. The occurrence of these heme compounds in relatively large amounts in most types of cells has also contributed to the ease of studying them. These studies have formed the basis of many of the accepted ideas of how specific enzymes catalyze reactions. The material in Sections 1 and 2 of the next chapter is concerned with the reactions of two heme enzymes, catalase and peroxidase.

3. Michaelis-Menten Kinetics of Hydrolases

The hydrolases were listed as the first group of enzymes because from many points of view they are the simplest. Most extracellular enzymes, such as those of the digestive tract, are hydrolases. By and large, it is relatively easy to obtain large quantities of these enzymes in an active form. Furthermore, most of them attack specific bonds rather than forming part of a complex chain or pathway.

Symbolically, one may represent these reactions by

$$S + H_2O \rightarrow \text{Products}$$

where S represents the substance hydrolyzed. It is called the *substrate.* For instance, the substrate might be sucrose, in which case the enzyme is called *sucrase* and the products *glucose* and *fructose*. (Sucrase is a glycosidase; it is often also called *invertase* because it inverts the optical rotation due to sucrose.) The reverse arrow is omitted because at equilibrium only the products of hydrolysis can usually be detected.

Most hydrolase reactions have a negligible velocity in the absence of any enzyme. If enzyme is added, the substrate is hydrolyzed at a measurable rate. As time progresses, this rate decreases because the substrate present decreases. One might be tempted to write the rate equation

$$\frac{d[S]}{dt} = -k[S] \tag{1}$$

The concentration of the water has been omitted because it is constant in dilute solutions and may be included in k.

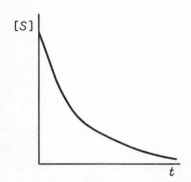

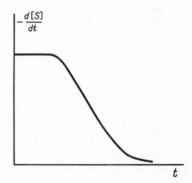

Figure 1. The concentration of the substrate S of a hydrolytic reaction as a function of time. This is actually observed.

Figure 2. The rate of disappearance of S as computed from the curve at left.

However, a graph of the rate of the enzyme catalyzed reaction plotted against $[S]$ shows that at higher concentrations the term k in Equation 1 is not constant. Similar studies show that this k is proportional to the enzyme concentration at low concentrations but not at high enzyme concentrations. This situation is illustrated in Figures 1, 2, 3, and 4.

Michaelis and Menten pointed out that this failure to obey the prediction of Equation 1 could easily be explained if the reaction mechanism were oversimplified. A simple scheme which they proposed is to assume that the enzyme and substrate formed an *intermediate complex* $E \cdot S$.   The complex $E \cdot S$ was assumed to be in quasi-equilibrium with E and S, but also to break down to form the products.   The reaction then would follow the scheme

$$\overset{e-p}{E} + \overset{x}{S} \underset{k_2}{\overset{k_1}{\rightleftharpoons}} \overset{p}{E \cdot S}$$

$$\overset{p}{E \cdot S} + H_2O \overset{k_3}{\longrightarrow} E + \text{Products}$$

where the letters above the reactants will be used to denote concentrations, thereby avoiding need for the square brackets.   Note that e is

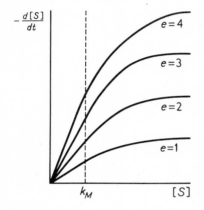

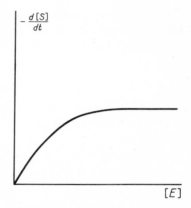

Figure 3. The rate at which a substrate S is hydrolyzed as a function of substrate concentration.   Curves are plotted for three concentrations of the enzyme E. Note that all three curves reach half maximum velocity at $[S] = K_M$.

Figure 4. The rate at which a substrate S is hydrolyzed as a function of the concentration of the enzyme E.   In general, curves of this type are more difficult to obtain than those as in Figure 3.

the total enzyme concentration added at time $t = 0$.   This situation is illustrated diagrammatically in Figure 5.   Although the shapes have no significance, the diagram illustrates the essentially cyclic nature of the enzyme process and also implies our belief that enzyme activity is dependent on the shapes of the reacting molecules.   Sometimes enzymes have been compared to a key fitting into a lock.   This is an oversimplification unless shapes are discussed in terms of the atomic configurations and of the electron orbitals in the substrate, intermediate complex, and products.

The foregoing stoichiometric equations can be rewritten as differential rate equations. These are

$$\frac{dp}{dt} = k_1(e-p)x - k_2 p - k_3 p \tag{2}$$

$$\frac{dx}{dt} = -k_1(e-p)x + k_2 p \tag{3}$$

The reaction rate V at which substrate is consumed is defined by

$$V = -\frac{dx}{dt} = k_1(e-p)x - k_2 p \tag{4}$$

These three equations can agree qualitatively with the empirical observations presented in Figures 1–4, provided suitable values are

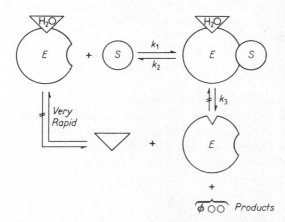

Figure 5. Diagrammatic representation of a hydrolytic reaction according to the Michaelis-Menten scheme. The shapes chosen here are purely for illustrative purposes and have no physical significance.

chosen for the rate constants k_1, k_2, and k_3. Because, in general, only one measured quantity, namely V, must be fitted by these data, it is perhaps not too surprising that suitable values can be found. If p could be observed directly, this would permit a separation of the constants and add considerable strength to the theory. For the more complex cases of catalase and peroxidase discussed in the next chapter, the intermediates can be observed, but for the hydrolytic reactions the intermediates never have been observed directly. Nonetheless, the success of this theory with the added approximations presented below has led to its general acceptance.   In the absence of additional data, it is the simplest explanation of the observed rates of reactions catalyzed by hydrolases.

The simultaneous differential Equations 2–4 are nonlinear.   In general, an analytical solution does not exist in closed form, subject to arbitrary initial conditions.   The equations can be solved by numerical computation, by analog computation, or by making suitable approximations.   The last method is so successful for these equations that it is the only one presented here.

In order to understand the approximations, consider the behavior of p and x for various values of the initial substrate concentration x_0 while holding e constant.   In all cases, p must be zero at the beginning of the reaction $(t = 0)$ and will return to zero at the end of the reaction. At the beginning of the reaction dp/dt, the rate of change of p given by Equation 2, must be positive; at the end it will be negative.   Some place in between, there will be a maximum value of p, designated by p_1, at which time dp/dt will vanish.   At this time, one may rewrite Equation 2 as

$$\left. \frac{dp}{dt} \right|_{p=p_1} = 0 = k_1(e - p_1)x - (k_2 + k_3)p_1 \tag{5}$$

It seems reasonable that as x_0 is made increasingly large, the maximum value p_1 will be reached increasingly rapidly, and also that p_1 will approach the total enzyme concentration e.   At very large values of x_0, it likewise would seem that the value of p_1 will remain close to that of e for a comparatively long time.   When this is true, the velocity V will have a maximum value V_1 given by

$$V_1 \doteq - \left. \frac{dx}{dt} \right|_{p=p_1} \doteq k_3 p_1 \doteq k_3 e \tag{6}$$

To show this, one may combine Equations 1 and 2 to give

$$-\frac{dx}{dt} = \frac{dp}{dt} + k_3 p$$

and use the relationships

$$\left. \frac{dp}{dt} \right|_{p=p_1} = 0 \quad \text{and} \quad p_1 \rightarrow e \quad \text{for large } x_0$$

If one solves Equation 5 for p_1 in the case where x_0 is not as large as considered above, one finds

$$p_1 = \frac{ex}{x + K_M} \tag{7}$$

and accordingly, one may write

$$V_1 = \frac{k_3 e x}{x + K_M} \tag{8}$$

where

$$K_M = \frac{k_2 + k_3}{k_1} \tag{9}$$

In this case, the intermediate p may only have the value p_1 for a very short time. Nevertheless, it is possible that the rate of change of the concentration of the intermediate complex dp/dt may be small compared to $k_3 p$, once p has reached its maximum value p_1. Should this occur, then Equations 5 through 9 may be retained for most of the reaction, keeping the subscript 1 on p and V, but with restriction that they apply only after p has reached its maximum. This is called the *quasi-static* approximation.

It is an empirical fact that this last approximation is valid for the reactions catalyzed by hydrolases. It is also found that k_1, k_2, and k_3 have such values that the time to reach p_1 can be ignored if x_0 is several times e. Accordingly, one may replace Equations 2 through 4, which cannot be solved exactly, by the approximations

$$\frac{dp}{dt} \doteq 0 \tag{10}$$

$$p \doteq \frac{e}{1 + K_M/x} \tag{11}$$

$$V \doteq \frac{k_3 e}{1 + K_M/x} \tag{12}$$

$$\therefore \quad k_3 e t \doteq (x_0 - x) + K_M \ln (x_0/x) \tag{13}$$

Figure 6 shows the comparison of the values for x, p, and V as computed numerically from Equations 2 through 4 and as plotted from Equations 11 through 13. Note the excellent agreement.

Equation 12 shows that for x large compared to K_M, V will have the maximum value V_{max} given by Equation 6. For x equal to K_M, V will be one-half of V_{max}. This is sometimes used to find K_M. In any case, one may rewrite Equation 12 as

$$V \doteq V_{max}/(1 + K_M/x) \tag{12a}$$

This form is particularly useful if the value of e is not known in absolute concentration units.

Equation 12a is not in a suitable form to determine graphically whether the reaction obeys these kinetics. As any physics student

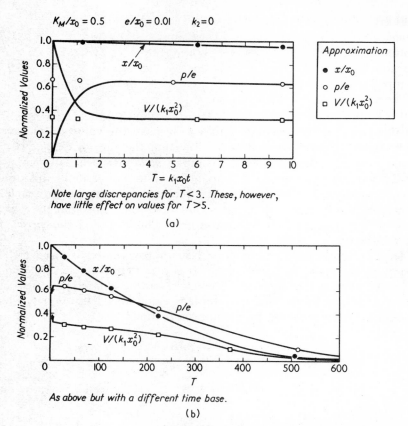

$K_M/x_0 = 0.5$ $e/x_0 = 0.01$ $k_2 = 0$

Note large discrepancies for $T < 3$. These, however,
have little effect on values for $T > 5$.

(a)

As above but with a different time base.

(b)

Figure 6. Exact and approximate solutions of Michaelis–
Menten equations for hydrolase kinetics. Lines show exact
values computed with electronic digital computer. Points
labeled show values predicted by the approximation.

knows, it is always best to plot a straight line graph. By taking recipro-
cals in Equation 12a, one obtains

$$\frac{1}{V} = \frac{1}{V_{max}} \left[1 + \frac{K_M}{x} \right] \tag{12b}$$

A graph of $1/V$ against $1/x$ is a straight line; it is known as a *Lineweaver–
Burk plot.* Figure 7a illustrates in this fashion that sucrase does obey
Michaelis–Menten kinetics. A better form is obtained by multiplying
both sides of Equation 12b by x, giving

$$\frac{x}{V} = \frac{1}{V_{max}} \left[x + K_M \right] \tag{12c}$$

This equation also predicts a straight line; its graph is also called a Lineweaver–Burk plot. It is illustrated in Figure 7b, where x/V is plotted against x. It is seen that the best points, obtained at large x, are now spread out over a major part of the graph instead of being cramped near the axis.

The strongest point of the foregoing Michaelis–Menten formulation is that it is the simplest theory which can be fitted to the reactions of most hydrolases. It also fits the reactions of several other types of enzymes. Its weakest point is that the intermediate complex has not been directly

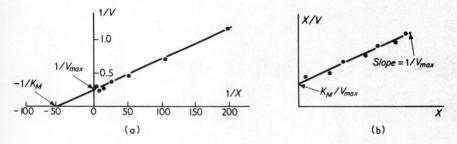

(a)   (b)

Figure 7. (a) Lineweaver-Burk plot of the hydrolysis of sucrose by sucrase. (b) Modified Lineweaver-Burk plot. After F. M. Huennekens, "Biological Reactions: Measurement and General Theory," *Technique of Organic Chemistry*, Vol. 8, *Investigations of Rates and Mechanisms of Reactions*, S. L. Friess and A. Weissberger, eds. (New York: Interscience Publishers, Inc., 1953).

observed for most reactions; it could easily be an oversimplification. In spite of these uncertainties, this type of kinetics is the basis for many studies. Almost all enzyme kinetics are described in the language of intermediate complexes and Michaelis constants.

4. Action of Inhibitors

Many enzyme reactions have been studied in part through the use of inhibitors. Specific inhibitors are useful for determining the role of particular enzymes. Other inhibitors (such as para-chloro-mercuri-benzoate, PCMB) are useful in determining the activity of certain groups (for example, sulfhydryl groups) in the enzyme activity. In this section, the action of inhibitors for systems obeying Michaelis–Menten kinetics will be analyzed.

Many inhibitors react with the enzyme in such a manner that the intermediate complex $E \cdot S$ cannot be formed. An inhibitor of this type is called a *competitive inhibitor*. Often, their structure is similar to that of the normal substrate. For example, the enzyme succinic dehydrogenase catalyzes the removal of hydrogen from succinic acid. The enzyme is competitively inhibited by malonic acid. The structural formulas in Figure 8a show the similarities of the normal substrate and its inhibitor.

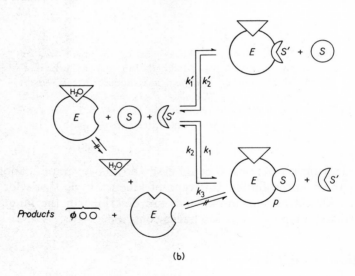

Figure 8. (a) Similarity between structures of enzyme substrate and competitive inhibitor. (b) Competitive inhibition of the hydrolysis of normal substrate *S* by inhibitor *S'*. The shapes chosen have no physical significance.

The general scheme is presented in a very symbolic form in Figure 8b.

A second group of inhibitors does not interfere with the formation of the intermediate complex but blocks its hydrolysis or further reaction.

The action of heavy metallic ions on many enzyme systems is an example of noncompetitive inhibition. This reaction scheme is presented diagrammatically in Figure 9. It is pictorially clear that noncompetitive inhibitions are more complex than competitive ones.

Accordingly, only the competitive inhibitors will be analyzed here. Either the normal substrate S or the inhibitor S' may react with the enzyme E, but not both of them. If x, the concentration of S, is much

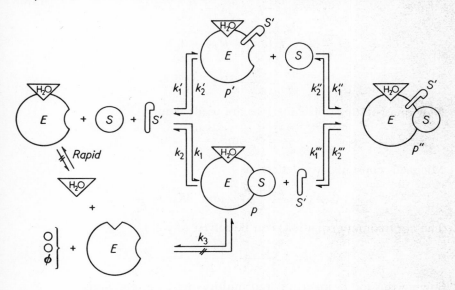

Figure 9. Noncompetitive inhibition of the hydrolysis of the normal substrate S by the inhibitor S'. The shapes chosen have no physical significance.

greater than x', the concentration of S', the reaction must proceed as if S' were not there. Thus, no matter how large the value of x', by choosing a sufficiently large value of x it is possible to obtain the uninhibited maximum velocity.

Stoichiometrically, a competitively inhibited Michaelis–Menten reaction can be represented by

$$\overset{e-p-p'}{E} + \overset{x'}{S'} \overset{k_1'}{\rightleftharpoons} \overset{p'}{E \cdot S'}$$

$$\overset{e-p-p'}{E} + \overset{x}{S} \overset{k_1}{\rightleftharpoons} \overset{p}{E \cdot S}$$

$$\overset{p}{E \cdot S} \overset{k_3}{\leftarrow} E + \text{Products}$$

As differential equations, these may be rewritten

$$\frac{dp'}{dt} = k_1'(e-p-p')x' - k_2'p'$$

$$\frac{dx'}{dt} = -k_1(e-p-p') + k_2p'$$

$$\frac{dp}{dt} = k_1(e-p-p')x - (k_2 + k_3)p$$

$$\frac{dx}{dt} = -k_1(e-p-p')x + k_2p$$

$$v = \frac{dx}{dt} = \frac{dp}{dt} + k_3p$$

Now quasi-static approximations are used; namely

$$\frac{dp}{dt} \doteq 0 \quad \text{and} \quad \frac{dp'}{dt} \doteq 0$$

Michaelis constants are defined as

$$K_M = \frac{k_2 + k_3}{k_1} \quad \text{and} \quad K_M' = \frac{k_2'}{k_1'}$$

The approximate equations can be solved to yield

$$p_1 \doteq \frac{K_M'ex}{x + (K_M) \cdot (x' + K_M')}$$

Solving this for V, inverting and multiplying by x, one finds

$$\frac{x}{V} = \frac{1}{V_{max}} \left[x + K_M \left(1 + \frac{x'}{K_M'} \right) \right] \tag{14}$$

The Lineweaver–Burk plot of Figure 7b would then represent a series of lines of constant slope, intersecting the x/V axis at points depending on x'/K_M'. This is illustrated in Figure 10a.

The case of the noncompetitive inhibitor is algebraically so complex that it is left to the interested reader to solve for himself. It is clear from Figure 9, however, that no matter what the relative concentrations of S and S', any trace of the inhibitor S' will slow down the rate of hydrolysis of S. Provided one is willing to assume that

$$\frac{k_2''}{k_1''} = \frac{k_2 + k_3}{k_1} = K_M \quad \text{and also that} \quad \frac{k_2'}{k_1'} = K_M' = \frac{k_2'''}{k_1'''}$$

then one can show that

$$\frac{x}{V} = \frac{1}{V_{max}} (x + K_M)\left(1 + \frac{x'}{K_M'} \right) \tag{15}$$

This equation indicates that the maximum velocity obtainable will be less than V_{max} even if only a trace of the inhibitor x' is present; it is illustrated in Figure 10b.   Other types of inhibitors have been found and studied.   For instance, some may react with $E \cdot S$ but not with E.

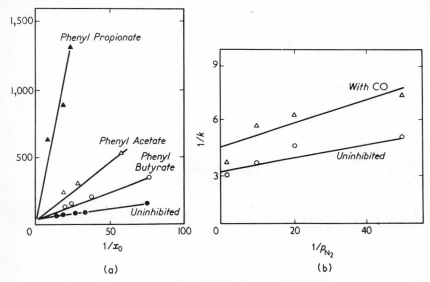

(a)   (b)

Figure 10. (a) Competitive inhibition of the hydrolysis of carboxybenzoxyglycyl-DL-phenylalanine by carboxypeptidase. The inhibitor concentrations were all $2 \times 10^{-3} M$.   (b) Non-competitive inhibition by CO of N_2 fixation in Azotabacter. The data could also be interpreted as indicating this reaction does not obey simple Michaelis–Menten kinetics.   After F. M. Huennekens, "Biological Reactions: Measurement and General Theory," *Technique of Organic Chemistry*, Vol. 8, *Investigations of Rates and Mechanisms of Reactions*, S. L. Friess and A. Weissberger, eds. (New York: Interscience Publishers Inc., 1953).

Many other variations are possible, but it does not seem fruitful to pursue their discussion here.

Inhibitors have been, and are, used widely to study enzymes and investigate enzymatic pathways.   In several cases, as in helping unravel the pathways of the utilization of glucose, inhibitors have proved helpful in blocking the process at desired points.   In other cases, the inhibitors have been misleading because they have had more than one action.   In a few cases, it has been possible to find certain details of the active surface of the enzyme by observing inhibitor action.

References on Enzymes are included at the end of Chapter 18.

18

Enzymes: Kinetics of Oxidations

1. Catalase

The respiratory enzymes catalyze the oxidation of many different substrates. Some are directly oxidized in one or two steps, whereas others follow a long pathway with many steps. The respiratory enzymes discussed in this chapter have been selected because of the reversible changes of their absorption spectra which occur during a catalyzed reaction. The changes in the absorption spectra of these enzymes can be related to the concentrations of intermediate compounds similar to $E \cdot S$, postulated in the last chapter. Quantitative time studies of the absorption spectra during reactions have led to an understanding of the mechanism of action of these enzymes. In this chapter, the mechanism is emphasized, deferring most of the details of absorption spectrophotometry to Chapter 26. The physical basis of molecular absorption spectra is discussed in Chapter 27 because these spectra are important in many other phases of biophysics, as well as in measuring the kinetics of enzyme-catalyzed oxidations.

The physiological role of the first respiratory enzyme discussed here, namely catalase, is not known.   In its purified form, it catalyzes two types of reactions.   The first of these, the so-called "catalatic reaction," is the destruction of hydrogen peroxide

$$2H_2O_2 \rightarrow 2H_2O + O_2$$

This is the oldest known biologically catalyzed reaction; its discovery was responsible for the name "catalase."   Another type of reaction catalyzed by catalase, the peroxidatic reaction, is an oxidation of any of a variety of reduced substrates.   The over-all reaction can be represented by

$$H_2O_2 + AH_2 \rightarrow H_2O + A + H_2O$$

where AH_2 is the reduced substrate (hydrogen donor) and A is its oxidized form.   This type of oxidation is catalyzed by both catalases and peroxidases.   Both are often grouped under the more general name "hydroperoxidase."   The kinetics of the peroxidases are, however, different from those of the catalases.

Catalase occurs in many mammalian cells, including red blood cells and liver cells; it is also found in large amounts in certain bacteria.   One role of catalase is to protect other proteins from destruction by hydrogen peroxide.   For example, a mutant human was discovered whose red blood cells lacked catalase; the hemoglobin in these cells was rapidly destroyed by hydrogen peroxide at concentrations often used for antiseptic purposes.   The hemoglobin of a normal person is unaltered under these conditions.   Thus, erythrocyte catalase protects hemoglobin from hydrogen peroxide.

Under normal physiological conditions, a limited amount of hydrogen peroxide is produced within living cells by reactions catalyzed by certain respiratory enzymes, such as xanthine oxidase.   Just how much peroxide is formed is not known, nor is its fate certain.   Accordingly, it is hard to guess at the physiological role of catalase, or to understand the reason for the very high catalase content of some species of bacteria.   In the extreme case, 1 per cent of the dry weight of the bacterial species, *Micrococcus lysodeikticus*, is catalase.

Catalases obtained from different types of cells, or from the same types of cells in different species, are different.   These differences lie in the protein (apoenzyme) portion of the molecule.   They alter the molecular weight, the molecular shape, and the reaction rates of the enzyme.   All catalases contain the same type of prosthetic group, called a *heme*.   The O_2-transport protein, hemoglobin, as well as the enzymes, myoglobin, peroxidase, and cytochromes, all contain heme groups.   A heme is a chelated Fe compound containing the tetrapyrrole (porphyrin) ring structure shown in Figure 1a.   The porphyrin ring also occurs in chlorophyll.

The alternating single and double bonds give rise to a so-called "resonance phenomenon," in which several different structures have the same energy levels.   For instance, in Figure 1b, if one exchanges all the single and the double bonds, and the dotted and solid chelating bonds, one has an equally possible molecule.   Modern quantum mechanics,

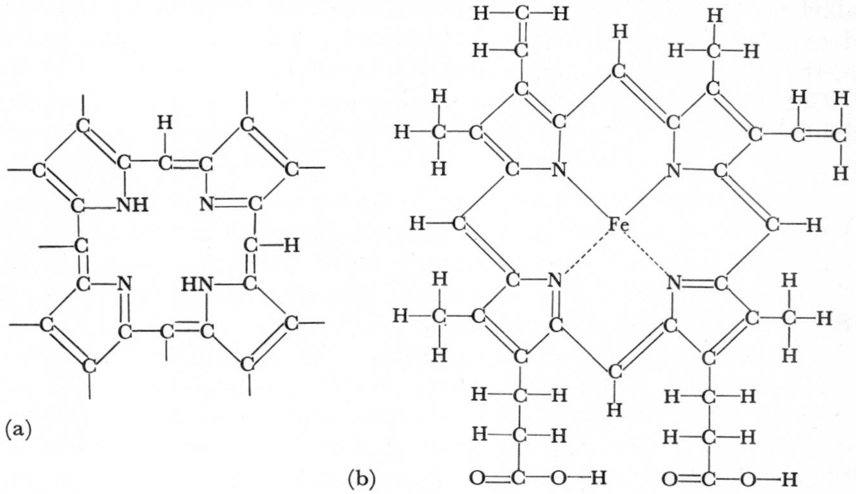

(a)

(b)

Figure 1. (a) Basic porphyrin structure is common to the prosthetic groups of hemoglobin, myoglobin, catalase, peroxidase, and cytochromes.   It is also found in chlorophyll.   Various groups are attached to the eight "dangling" bonds. (b) Ferroprotoporphyrin IX is the basic group of many of the heme proteins. Hemoglobin, myoglobin, and catalase contain this group. The other heme proteins contain either this porphyrin or ones derived from it by simple substitutions. The iron atom is in the ferrous state in both reduced and oxyhemoglobin and reduced and oxymyoglobin.   In peroxidase, it is in the ferric state.   Other heme proteins have their iron alternately reduced and oxidized during reactions.

discussed in Chapter 27, demands that one think of the molecule as existing not in either one or a second state, but as partly in one and partly in the other.   The orbitals of the bonding electrons, so-called "π electrons" (see Chapter 27) must be considered to include the entire structure. These lead to absorption bands in the visible and the near ultraviolet regions of the spectrum.   All of the heme proteins have one or two absorption bands in the yellow-green region of the spectrum and a very strong absorption band in the blue-violet region.   The last region is referred to as the Soret band or γ-band.   Typical spectra are shown in Figure 2.

When catalase catalyzes either the peroxidatic or catalatic reactions, the absorption in the Soret region decreases during the reaction, indicating the formation of an enzyme complex with peroxide.   The enzyme-peroxide complex appears as green.   On prolonged standing in the presence of an excess of hydrogen peroxide, an entirely different absorption spectrum is developed. In contrast to the first complex, the second one appears red. It is enzymatically inactive. Both types of complexes are easier to study with either methyl hydrogen peroxide, CH_3OOH, or ethyl hydrogen peroxide, C_2H_5OOH. Catalase reacts with these two alkyl peroxides to form both the green and the red complexes, but it does not decompose the alkyl peroxides. Spectra for the complexes with methyl hydrogen peroxide are shown in Figure 3.

Catalase reactions are convenient to study spectrophotometrically for another reason. Besides the possibility for rapid observations afforded

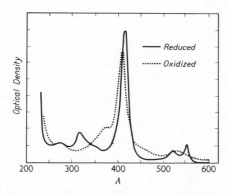

Figure 2. Spectra of the oxidized and reduced forms of an algal cytochrome, *Porphyra tenera*, cytochrome 553. Spectra from solutions of crystalized enzyme. After S. Katoh, "Crystallization of an Algal Cytochrome," *Nature* **186**: 138 (1960).

by the spectral absorption changes of the enzyme, the peroxide concentrations can also be observed by measuring the absorption in the ultraviolet region. The spectra of peroxides do not show sharp bands, but rather a curve which rises steadily as the wavelength is decreased from 300 mμ to less than 200 mμ. Because many proteins have a minimum in their absorption around 250–230 mμ, this wavelength band has been used to measure the peroxide concentration. Finally, in the peroxidatic reactions, it is often possible to observe the oxidation of AH_2 to A in terms of spectrophotometric changes.

Such studies have shown that the peroxidatic reaction can be represented by the stoichiometric equations

$$\overset{e-p}{E} + \overset{x}{S} \underset{k_2}{\overset{k_1}{\rightleftharpoons}} \overset{p}{E \cdot S}$$

$$\overset{p}{E \cdot S} + \overset{a}{AH_2} \overset{k_3}{\rightarrow} E + A + \text{Products}$$

where E is catalase, S is peroxide, and AH_2 is the substance being oxidized. As was done in the case of the hydrolase reactions discussed in the last chapter, one may rewrite these as the differential equations

$$\frac{dp}{dt} = k_1(e-p)x - k_2p - k_3ap$$

$$\frac{dx}{dt} = k_1(e-p)x + k_2p \tag{1}$$

$$\frac{da}{dt} = -k_3ap$$

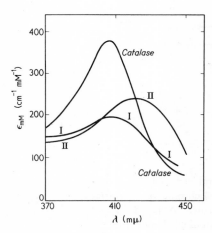

Figure 3. The spectra of catalase and its two complexes with methyl-hydrogen peroxide. After B. Chance, "Catalase Peroxides Spectra," *J. Biol. Chem.* **179**: 1331 (1949).

The algebra has become slightly more complex because two substances are used up in the reaction, instead of just one.

The set of equations in (1) are non-linear differential equations; they do not have an exact solution in closed form. Various approximations can be used just as in the case of the hydrolases. First, it should be noted that

$$da = dp + dx$$

If a quasi-steady state occurs, then p will have an approximately constant value p_1 and one may write the equations

$$\frac{dp}{dt} \doteq 0 \quad \text{and} \quad \frac{dx}{dt} \doteq \frac{da}{dt}$$

Under these circumstances, one may talk of a reaction velocity V defined as

$$V = -\frac{dx}{dt} = -\frac{da}{dt} = k_3ap_1 \tag{2}$$

The first equation of (1) can be solved to yield, under quasi-static conditions

$$p_1 = \frac{ex}{x + \dfrac{k_2 + k_3a}{k_1}} \tag{3}$$

and hence

$$V \doteq \frac{(k_3a)ex}{x + \dfrac{k_2 + k_3a}{k_1}} \tag{4}$$

The ratio $(k_2 + k_3a)/k_1$ is similar to a Michaelis constant K_M, except that instead of being constant it depends on the value of a.

The over-all rate V is the only rate measured for reactions of the hydrolases. For catalase, it is possible to find other relationships between k_1 and k_3 which can be measured experimentally. For example, one may measure p directly and find its absolute maximum value p_m. [Note: p_1 is quasi-steady state value; p_m is maximum of p_1.] If a_0 and x_0 are sufficiently large, they will not have changed appreciably from their maximum values when p reaches p_m. Moreover, k_2 will be appreciably less than k_3a_0. Accordingly, one may approximate Equation 3 as

$$p_m \doteq \frac{e}{1 + \dfrac{k_3a_0}{k_1x_0}} \tag{5}$$

or as

$$\frac{e - p_m}{p_m} \doteq \frac{k_3a_0}{k_1x_0} \tag{6}$$

Either form allows one to compute k_3/k_1.

The constant k_3 can be found from V by approximating Equation 4 at high values of x_0/a_0 to give

$$V \doteq k_3ae \tag{7}$$

Accordingly, one can compute k_1 and k_3 from measuring V and p_m. Moreover, one can find k_2 from the apparent Michaelis constant $(k_2 + k_3a)/k_1$, once k_1 and k_3 have been measured. Thus, this system allows one to find all three rate constants.

These same constants can be found from other measurements. For example, at the start of the reaction k_2p may be neglected because p will be very small. Moreover, the changes in a_0 and x_0 can also be neglected. Then the equation for dp/dt in (1) may be rewritten as follows

$$\frac{dp}{dt} \doteq k_1(e - p)x_0 - k_3pa_0$$

This equation may be integrated directly to give, for the first part of the reaction curve

$$p \doteq p_{\max} (1 - \epsilon^{-(k_1 x_0 + k_3 a_0)t}) \tag{8}$$

It is easy to confirm that the reaction follows a curve of this nature because the half-time is constant, being given by the expression

$$t_{p/2} = \frac{\ln 2}{k_1x_0 + k_3a_0} \tag{9}$$

[The half-time $t_{p/2}$ is the time for p to increase from any value p_a to a second value p_b such that

$$(p_{max} - p_a) = 2(p_{max} - p_b)$$

See Figure 4.]

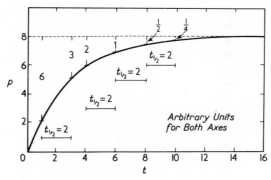

Figure 4. This illustrates Equations (8) and (9) given in the text.   The numbers above the curve give the value of $p_m - p$. It is seen that for a curve of this nature the half-time $t_{1/2}$ does not depend on the region of the curve used to measure it.

With either ethyl or methyl peroxide, it is possible to set a_0 to zero. Then equilibrium would result in all the measured enzyme being in $E \cdot S$, that is

$$p_{max} \doteq e \qquad \text{for} \qquad a_0 = 0$$

Equation 9 can be rewritten for this case as

$$t_{p/2} = \frac{\ln 2}{k_1 x_0} \tag{10}$$

Thus, one can measure k_1 directly for the alkyl peroxides.

Numerical studies have shown that k_3 can be approximated by a similar type of expression.   If one starts with large enough a_0 and x_0 so that a steady-state region exists, and measures p, a curve such as that in Figure 5 is obtained.   The maximum p_m of the intermediate complex $E \cdot S$, and the off-time $t_{1/2\downarrow}$, until p decreases to $\frac{1}{2}p_m$, are related approximately by the expression

$$k_3 \doteq \frac{1}{p_m t_{1/2\downarrow}} \frac{x_0}{a_0} \tag{11}$$

Equations 11 and 6 can be combined to yield

$$k_1 \doteq \frac{1}{(e - p_m) t_{1/2\downarrow}} \tag{12}$$

The technical difficulties of measuring $t_{1/2\downarrow}$ and p_m are less than those of measuring $t_{p/2}$. Accordingly, Equations 11 and 12 are convenient for precise measurement of k_1 and k_3. These values agree with those found by using Equations 5 and 7 and those found by using Equations 9 and 10.

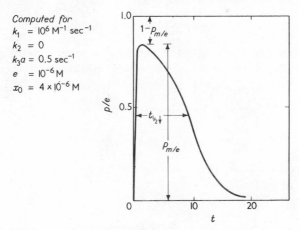

Computed for
$k_1 = 10^6 \ M^{-1} \ sec^{-1}$
$k_2 = 0$
$k_3 a = 0.5 \ sec^{-1}$
$e = 10^{-6} M$
$x_0 = 4 \times 10^{-6} M$

Figure 5. The intermediate complex for the peroxidatic reaction of catalase. The quantities shown above are used to compute k_1 and k_3. The curve illustrated is based on an analog-computer study. Similar curves can be found experimentally both for the enzyme-substrate complex of catalase and for complex II of peroxidase. After B. Chance, "Velocity Constants in Enzyme Reactions," *Arch. Biochem. Biophys.* **71**: 130 (1957).

The rate constant k_2 is more difficult to determine precisely. An upper limit for k_2 can be found by making suitable approximations from the data at the end of the reaction. Also, as noted previously, knowing k_1 and k_3 independently, one can obtain an estimate of k_2 from the apparent Michaelis constant. Some typical values for the different constants for bacterial catalase are

$X =$	H_2O_2	CH_3OOH	C_2H_5OOH	
$k_1 =$	2×10^7	0.9×10^6	1.0×10^4	$M^{-1} \ sec^{-1}$

$S =$	$HCOONa$	CH_3OH	C_2H_5OH	
$k_3 =$	175	91	13	$M^{-1} \ sec^{-1}$

An upper limit on the constant k_2 can be estimated as $k_2 \leqslant 0.0002 \ sec^{-1}$.

The other type of reaction discussed for catalase is the destruction of hydrogen peroxide. This reaction is similar to the peroxidatic reactions, except that hydrogen peroxide acts as both S and AH_2. The reaction may be represented stoichiometrically by the equations

$$\overset{e-p}{E} + \overset{x}{S} \overset{k_1}{\underset{k_2}{\rightleftharpoons}} \overset{p}{E \cdot S}$$

$$\overset{p}{E \cdot S} + \overset{x}{S} \overset{k_3}{\longrightarrow} E + \text{Products}$$

These equations, being somewhat different from the peroxidatic ones, lead to a slightly different set of differential equations, namely

$$\frac{dp}{dt} = k_1(e-p)x - k_2 p - k_3 px$$

$$\frac{dx}{dt} = -k_1(e-p)x - k_3 px + k_2 p$$

$$(13)$$

The quasi-static approximation applied to the first equation of (13) leads to the relationship

$$p_1 \doteq \frac{e}{1 + \dfrac{k_3}{k_1}} \tag{14}$$

if k_2 is negligible compared to $(k_1 + k_3)x$. This expression for p_1 is interesting because it does not depend on x. At the start of the reaction, p increases exponentially for large ratios of x_0/e. In this increasing range, the first equation in (13) predicts that

$$t_{p/2} \doteq \frac{\ln 2}{(k_1 + k_3)x_0} \tag{15}$$

It has been shown that the approximation Equation 15 can be improved by replacing x_0 with $(0.9)x_0$ to take account of the decrease of x as p is increasing.

In a similar fashion, the quasi-static approximation applied to the second equation of (13) leads to the differential equation

$$\frac{dx}{dt} = -2k_3 p_1 x \tag{16}$$

Integrating leads to an exponential curve

$$x = x_0 \epsilon^{-2k_3 p_1 t} \tag{17}$$

whose half-life is given by

$$t_{x/2} = \frac{\ln 2}{2k_3 p_1} \tag{18}$$

The three Equations, 14, 15, and 18, allow one to determine the two constants k_1 and k_3. Only two of these equations are necessary, the third providing an internal check on the validity of the equations in (13). The foregoing analysis shows that the differential equations chosen do agree with the data over wide ranges of concentration, ionic strength, temperature, and so forth. At very high concentrations of hydrogen peroxide, the equations in (13) apparently break down.

For any given catalase, the values of k_1 and k_2 will be the same for H_2O_2 entering either the peroxidatic or catalatic reactions. The constant k_3 is, in contrast, dependent on the hydrogen donor in the peroxidatic reaction. For the bacterial catalase, the value of k_3 for the catalatic reaction is about $1.7 \times 10^7 \, M^{-1} \, sec^{-1}$. In the catalatic reaction, there is no spectrophotometric evidence for the existence of a compound $E \cdot S \cdot S$. It seems almost inconceivable that a compound of this type does not have at least a transitory existence. It is likewise surprising that no complex of the form $E \cdot S \cdot AH_2$ has ever been detected. These will be commented upon further in Chapter 22.

The reactions of catalase have been discussed in comparative detail in this section, and those of peroxidase are presented in the next section. They have been emphasized because these reactions, although not obeying Michaelis–Menten kinetics, are strong supporting evidence for the existence of intermediate complexes during enzyme reactions. Because it is possible to observe the concentrations of all the intermediates and reactants, and to vary these concentrations, it is possible to check that the reaction does obey the equations chosen. There is no evidence that the hydrolase reaction does not also follow the equations for the peroxidatic reactions of catalase.

The spectra of catalase and peroxidase cannot be directly interpreted at the present time, other than giving the quantitative amounts of the various substances present. For additional information such as the electronic state of the iron, or the existence of other types of intermediates, one must turn to different lines of investigation. Some of these are discussed in Chapter 22 and still others in the chapter on magnetic measurements, 28.

2. Peroxidase

Peroxidases, like catalases, are heme compounds. They catalyze the peroxidatic but not the catalatic reactions. Peroxidases are widely distributed, being more abundant in plant cells than in animal cells. Almost any ferriheme protein (that is, one in which the iron is in the oxidized or ferric state) will act as a peroxidase. Even the ferric form of hemoglobin (called methemoglobin), although unsuitable for oxygen transport,[1] will act as a peroxidase. However, the enzymes named peroxidases have much more rapid reaction rates.

All peroxidases can use the respiratory enzyme, cytochrome c, as a hydrogen donor. Cytochrome c is part of the cytochrome chain which couples many oxidation chains to molecular oxygen (see Section 4). Thus, it seems possible that the peroxidases might function in normal respiration to use the enzymatically produced peroxides as oxidants. In spite of the relatively large concentrations of peroxidases in mammalian white blood cells, yeast, and the cells of several higher plants, no definite information is available concerning the physiological role of the peroxidases. They are presented here as a further, slightly more complicated, system to which the type of reasoning developed by Michaelis and Menten can be directly applied and the deductions tested spectrophotometrically.

Peroxidases are more complicated than catalases in that there are more complexes formed between the substrate and the enzyme. Whereas only one complex is enzymatically active in the case of catalase, two are active in peroxidase reactions. Symbolically, one may represent the reactions as in the case of a single hydrogen donor such as reduced cytochrome c by the following

$$\overset{e-p-p'}{E} + \overset{x}{S} \underset{k_2}{\overset{k_1}{\rightleftharpoons}} \overset{p}{E \cdot S_\mathrm{I}}$$

$$\overset{p}{E \cdot S_\mathrm{I}} + \overset{a}{A\mathrm{H}} \underset{k_4}{\overset{k_3}{\rightleftharpoons}} \overset{p'}{E \cdot S_\mathrm{II}} + A$$

$$\overset{p'}{E \cdot S_\mathrm{II}} + \overset{a}{A\mathrm{H}} \underset{k_6.}{\overset{k_5}{\rightleftharpoons}} E + \mathrm{Products} + A$$

In the case of a dual hydrogen donor such as ascorbic acid, the equations may be written

$$E + S \rightleftharpoons E \cdot S$$

$$E \cdot S + A\mathrm{H}_2 \rightleftharpoons E \cdot S_\mathrm{II} + (A\mathrm{H})^*$$

$$E \cdot S_\mathrm{II} + A\mathrm{H}_2 \rightharpoonup E + (A\mathrm{H})^* + \mathrm{Products}$$

$$2 (A\mathrm{H})^* \rightharpoonup A\mathrm{H}_2 + A$$

Evidence for this reaction scheme is based on electron spin resonance data. This method is discussed in Chapter 28.

The discussion here is restricted to the case of single hydrogen donors present in excess in the external medium. Furthermore, k_6 is assumed

---

[1] Both oxyhemoglobin and reduced hemoglobin are ferrous forms.

to always be unobservable. Under these conditions, the reaction may be presented by the following nonlinear differential equations

$$\frac{dp}{dt} = k_1(e-p-p')x - k_3pa + k_4p' - k_2p$$

$$\frac{dp'}{dt} = k_3pa - k_5p'a - k_4p'$$

$$\frac{dx}{dt} = -k_1(e-p-p')x + k_2p \tag{19}$$

$$\frac{da}{dt} = -k_3pa - k_5p'a + k_4a$$

Except for the very end of the reaction, the "back rates," k_2 and k_4, contribute very little to the kinetics. Considerable simplification can be obtained by ignoring them; they are cross-hatched in Equation 19. Even with these approximations, no exact solution in closed form exists for these equations.

Under many experimental conditions, a steady-state region is observed. At this time, one may make quasi-static approximations. As has been shown in the last chapter, these may be approximately valid a considerable time after a true steady state has ceased to exist. Symbolically, the quasi-static approximation is represented by

$$\frac{dp}{dt} \doteq \frac{dp'}{dt} \doteq 0$$

Subscript one will be used as previously to indicate the values of the intermediates computed by using these approximations. Solving the appropriate equations in (19), it is readily apparent that

$$p_1' = \frac{k_3}{k_5} p_1 \tag{20}$$

$$p_1 = \frac{ex}{x + \left\{ \dfrac{k_3 x}{k_5} + \dfrac{k_3 a}{k_1} \right\}} \tag{21}$$

and

$$V = \frac{dx}{dt} = -\tfrac{1}{2}\frac{da}{dt} \doteq k_3 a p_1 \tag{22}$$

For part of the reaction, the kinetics will resemble those of the hydrolases discussed earlier. However, the apparent Michaelis constant, K_M, will be given by the expression

$$K_M = \frac{k_3 x}{k_5} + \frac{k_3 a}{k_1} \tag{23}$$

This shows that K_M depends on both x and a.

As with catalase, the conditions as x or a approaches complete utilization are necessary to determine k_2 and k_4. These are difficult in that the auto-oxidation of the first complex becomes more important as the hydrogen-donor concentration decreases. Also similar to the catalase reaction is the approximation

$$k_5 \doteq \frac{1}{p_m t_{1/2\downarrow}} \frac{x_0}{a_0} \tag{24}$$

The value for the kinetic rate constant k_1 depends on whether S is hydrogen peroxide, methyl hydrogen peroxide, or ethyl hydrogen peroxide. The constants k_3 and k_5 are different for different hydrogen donors. All three vary for peroxidases from different sources. A typical set of values is

$$\left. \begin{array}{l} k_1 = 0.9 \times 10^7 \text{ M}^{-1} \text{ sec}^{-1} \\ k_3 = 2 \times 10^7 \text{ M}^{-1} \text{ sec}^{-1} \\ k_5 = 2.4 \times 10^5 \text{ M}^{-1} \text{ sec}^{-1} \end{array} \right\} \text{ for } \left\{ \begin{array}{l} E = \text{horse-radish peroxidase} \\ S = \text{H}_2\text{O}_2 \\ AH = \text{HNO}_2 \end{array} \right.$$

The values for k_3 are comparably large even when AH is the protein cytochrome c; this is particularly impressive when one considers the size of the molecules involved.

Studies of the kinetics of peroxidases agree with the reaction mechanism presented. This supports the reality of intermediate complexes of the type discussed in Michaelis–Menten kinetics. It also shows that the reactions may be far more complex than those postulated in the previous chapter.

3. Biological Oxidations

The previous two sections dealt with the enzymatically catalyzed oxidation of reduced compounds, using a peroxide such as HOOH as the oxygen donor. These reactions are convenient to study; they help to verify the physical existence of transient, enzyme-substrate complexes. However, both peroxidase and catalase are believed to be unusual respiratory enzymes in that the most frequent intracellular oxygen donor is the molecule O_2. The pathway from the reduced compound to the molecular oxygen is often a long one involving many catalyzed steps. (See, for example, the biological oxidation of glucose diagrammed in Chapter 8, Figure 8.) Only the last step actually involves molecular oxygen, but many steps along the way are spoken of as oxidations.

The oxidations within biological systems may be divided in many fashions into different types. One depends on whether the oxidizing substance (which itself becomes reduced) is O_2, H_2O_2, or some other compound. A second type of division separates those oxidations incorporating oxygen into the molecule from those involving the removal of hydrogen. These may be illustrated by the following two reactions of ethyl alcohol

$$(1) \quad CH_3CH_2OH + O_2 \rightarrow CH_3\overset{\displaystyle O}{\underset{\displaystyle OH}{C}} + H_2O$$

$$(2) \quad CH_3CH_2OH + O \rightarrow CH_3CHO + H_2O$$

$$(2') \quad CH_3CH_2OH + 2A \rightarrow CH_3CHO + 2AH$$

As far as the alcohol molecule is concerned, it cannot distinguish reactions (2) and (2′). Thus, any removal of atomic hydrogen is called a *biological oxidation.*

Biological oxidations occur within a watery suspending medium having an appreciable content of free protons (H^+). These can attach to the oxidized compound if it leads to a stable form. In contrast, if one removes an electron from a biological compound, an H^+ may dissociate, leaving the compound oxidized. Thus, removal of an electron is completely equivalent to the removal of a hydrogen atom. All biological oxidations may be considered to be the removal of electrons. For example, reaction (1) may be rewritten

$$CH_3CH_2OH + O_2 \rightarrow CH_3C^+_+H_2OH + O^{--} + O$$

$$CH_3C^+_+H_2OH \rightarrow CH_3C\overset{}{\underset{\displaystyle OH}{-}} + 2H^+ \qquad 2H^+ + O^{--} \rightarrow H_2O$$

$$CH_3C\overset{}{\underset{\displaystyle OH}{-}} + O \rightarrow CH_3\overset{\displaystyle O}{\underset{\displaystyle OH}{C}}$$

In a long chain of successive oxidations, one may consider each oxidation to be the removal of an electron. Thus, in the oxidation of glucose, electrons are transported from the glucose molecule to the oxygen molecules through a series of steps. This *electron transport* is usually implied by the term "biological oxidation."

Another type of division of biological oxidations is in terms of the type of molecule oxidized. For example, there are glucose oxidation pathways, carbohydrate oxidations, fatty acid oxidations, amino acid oxidations, and purine and pyrimidine oxidations. Most of these eventually convert the molecule being oxidized to CO_2, H_2O, and some nitrogen compound. In humans, the nitrogen of amino acids is converted to urea, whereas purine metabolism stops with the formation of uric acid which is then eliminated.

All of the oxidations within the living cell serve two purposes. The first is to convert the chemical energy of the molecules being oxidized into a form useful to drive intracellular syntheses, muscular contractions, and active transport. The second is to produce heat to maintain the cellular temperature in an optimum range. Because all the energy-conversion processes are less than 100 per cent efficient, some heat is always a by-product. The warm-blooded animals have internal systems to regulate the efficiency of energy conversion so as to maintain a more or less constant internal temperature. Some cold-blooded animals also tend to regulate their internal temperature but must vary their muscular activity to do so.

4. Oxidative Phosphorylation

In most animal cells, a major part of the energy released by oxidations is used to drive the reaction

$$\text{ADP} + \text{P} \rightarrow \text{ATP}$$

which may be written in structural form as

The ATP is formed primarily by the cytochrome chain which is located in intracellular organelles called mitochondria; these are shown in Figure 1, Chapter 15. The mitochondria also contain a set of enzymes which catalyze a cyclic process called *Krebs' cycle*. Two and three carbon fragments of glucose, fatty acids, and amino acids are coupled into Krebs' cycle. It, in turn, drives the cytochrome chain, thereby causing the conversion of the energy of oxidation to ATP. The molecule ATP can diffuse throughout the cell and couple with many enzyme systems. The reverse action

$$\text{ATP} \rightarrow \text{ADP} + \text{P}$$

can provide the energy to drive chemical syntheses, to cause active transport against a diffusion gradient, and to make muscular contraction possible.

The enzymes of the cytochrome chain consist of three known types. These are the pyridine nucleotides (PN) which contain the coenzyme DPN or TPN, the flavin-adenine-dinucleotides which contain the prosthetic group FAD, and the cytochromes (cyt), all of which contain a heme group. The structure of a heme group is shown in Figure 1 and that of DPN and FAD in Figure 6. In intact mitochondria, from vertebrates or yeast, these enzymes react as follows

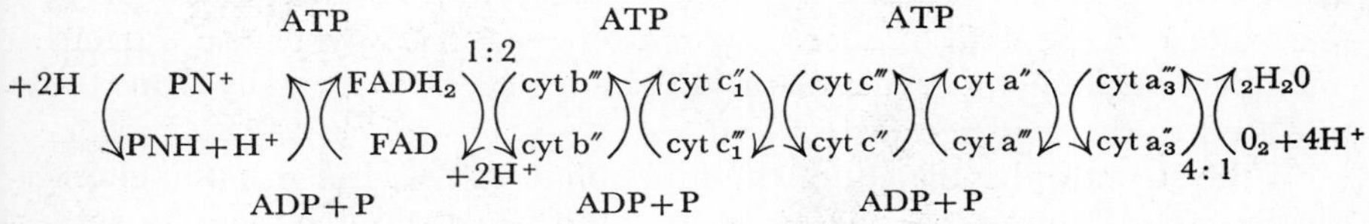

$$+2H \left(\begin{array}{c} PN^+ \\ PNH+H^+ \end{array} \right) \left(\begin{array}{c} FADH_2 \\ FAD \end{array} \right) \left(\begin{array}{c} cyt\ b'' \\ cyt\ b'' \end{array} \right) \left(\begin{array}{c} cyt\ c_1'' \\ cyt\ c_1'' \end{array} \right) \left(\begin{array}{c} cyt\ c'' \\ cyt\ c'' \end{array} \right) \left(\begin{array}{c} cyt\ a'' \\ cyt\ a''' \end{array} \right) \left(\begin{array}{c} cyt\ a_3''' \\ cyt\ a_3'' \end{array} \right) \left(\begin{array}{c} 2H_2O \\ O_2+4H^+ \end{array} \right)$$

with *ATP, ADP+P* at three positions, ratios *1:2*, *+2H⁺*, *4:1* as indicated.

The number of primes after each cytochrome indicates the valence

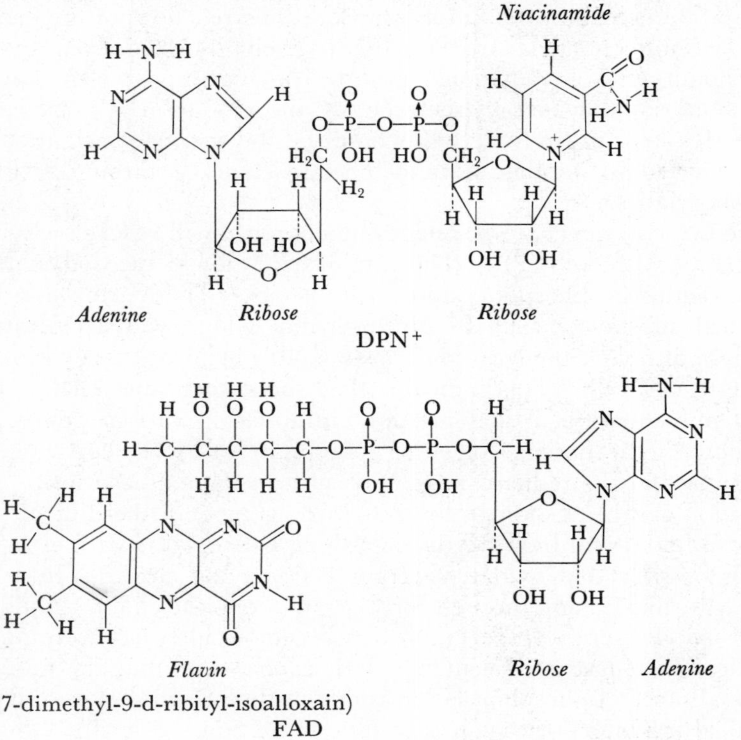

Niacinamide

DPN⁺

Flavin
(6,7-dimethyl-9-d-ribityl-isoalloxain)
FAD

Figure 6. Structure of DPN and FAD.

state of the iron; they do not show the charge on the molecule.   The pN and FAD reactions are two electron changes, whereas the cytochromes undergo one electron change.   Thus, two cytochrome b$'''$ molecules must be reduced for every $FADH_2$ oxidized.   Likewise, 4 cyt a$_3^{''}$ are oxidized by one O_2 molecule.

In the reactions of the cytochrome chain in intact mitochondria, no spectroscopically observable intermediate complexes have been found in the sense that a complex is formed between the hydroperoxidases and hydrogen peroxide.   This is similar to the absence of a spectrophotometrically detectable complex between the intermediate complex of peroxidase $E \cdot S_{II}$ and reduced cytochrome c.   However, the various members of the cytochrome chain do change spectroscopically from the reduced to the oxidized form.

If the structural integrity of the functional unit within the mitochondrion is not maintained, the reaction chain is altered.   Kinetic experiments show that the types and the order of the enzymes involved in oxidation, as well as the active ones, are a function of their relatively fixed positions within the mitochondria.   The reactions of the enzymes in intact mitochondria are also qualitatively different from those in mitochondria whose functional groups are disarranged.   In damaged mitochondria, the energy liberated by the oxidation is converted to heat.   By contrast, in intact mitochondria, the energy of oxidation may be converted to another form of chemical energy through oxidative phosphorylation.

The cytochrome chain in intact mitochondria will react slowly in the absence of ADP and Ⓟ .   The rate of oxidation is speeded manyfold when oxidative phosphorylation can occur.   There are also other chemical substances such as dinitrophenol which will accelerate the reaction, although these do not conserve the chemical energy in a form useful to the cell.   This indicates that the cytochrome chain, in the intact mitochondria, is in some sense inhibited at various points.   For instance, in the absence of either phosphate or ADP, cyt c tends to accumulate in the reduced form and cyt a in the oxidized form.   This inhibition can be accounted for with various models, the difficult thing being to find a real basis for distinguishing between the various models.

It is possible that oxidation represents carrying electrons in a semiconductor-like fashion through the proteins along the chain.   Oxidation might equally represent reactions between molecules, free to rotate and vibrate, about restricted centers.   It is conceivable that the inhibition in the absence of phosphorylation is due to the presence of an unknown chemical inhibitor, or that it is a steric inhibition.   A major limitation of testing the various hypotheses is the inability to vary the relative concentrations of most of the members of the chain without destroying the ability to phosphorylate ADP.   Under these circumstances, it is not surprising that data obtained by spectrophotometric studies have as yet failed to help select one among the various possibilities. Other techniques such as tracer studies and electron magnetic resonance methods may provide more information.

The mathematical analysis of the reaction equations for the cytochrome chain is very complex, no matter which model one chooses. The concentration of each member of the reaction depends on the kinetics and concentrations of all the other members. An electronic computer of some type is almost essential to even discover the concentrations predicted by a given model. Because these computations have so far failed to make it possible to select a particular model, they will not be pursued further here.

5. Summary of Enzyme Kinetics

Enzyme-kinetic studies apply to molecular biology the methods of mathematical analysis common to physics and physical chemistry. These strongly reinforce the view that many enzymes catalyze by entering the reaction forming intermediate complexes. In some cases, as with catalase and peroxidase, the intermediates have distinctive spectra which make it possible to follow the details of their formation and destruction. In other cases, as with the hydrolases, the intermediate complexes have been detected by inference from kinetic data. The actions of enzyme inhibitors have also been analyzed mathematically. Inhibitors give some indication of the order of reaction of various enzymes in a chain and also of the type of action involved.

Enzymes control the rate of most intracellular processes such as biological oxidations. In biological oxidations, there are, in general, many steps between the original substance being metabolized, for example glucose, and the final waste products such as CO_2 and H_2O. The oxidative steps include those which incorporate an atom of oxygen into the molecule, those which remove a hydrogen atom, and those which remove an electron. All are called biological oxidations.

Biological oxidations result in the formation of energy-carrier compounds, such as ATP, which can move throughout the cell and supply energy to the various life processes such as syntheses and muscular contraction. Much of the ATP in vertebrate cells and in yeast is formed by the cytochrome chain in the mitochondria. The characteristic spectra of some of the members of the chain have allowed their order of reaction to be determined. However, some of the steps in the synthesis of ATP from ADP and Ⓟ are still unknown.

From the point of view of biophysics, a major contribution of enzyme kinetics is that it forms a basis for the application of thermodynamics to molecular biology. Chapter 22 is concerned with this aspect of enzyme-catalyzed reactions.

REFERENCES

For more detailed information regarding enzyme chemistry, the reader is referred to the following:

1. Neilands, J. B., and P. K. Stumpf, *Outlines of Enzyme Chemistry* (New York: John Wiley & Sons, Inc., 1958).

For a picture of enzymes in the larger context of biochemistry and physiology, the following books are recommended:

2. Kleiner, I. S., *Human Biochemistry* 4th ed. (St. Louis, Missouri: The C. V. Mosby Company, 1954).
3. Heilbrunn, L. V., *An Outline of General Physiology* 3rd ed. (Philadelphia: W. B. Saunders Company, 1952). Chapters 4, 17, 21, and 22.

The following texts on enzyme kinetics are among those which were used as references in Chapters 17 and 18.

4. Friess, S. L., and A. Weissberger, eds., *Technique of Organic Chemistry*. Vol. 8. *Investigation of Rates and Mechanisms of Reactions* (New York: Interscience Publishers, Inc., 1953) [new ed. in prep.]

The following chapters are particularly pertinent:

   a. Huennekens, F. M., "Part I. Measurement and General Theory," pp. 535–627.
   b. Chance, Britton, "Part II. Reaction Kinetics of Enzyme-Substrate Compounds," pp. 627–643.
   c. Roughton, F. J. W., and Britton Chance, "Rapid Reactions," pp. 669–738.
5. Barron, E. S. G., ed., *Modern Trends in Physiology and Biochemistry* (New York: Academic Press, Inc., 1952).
   a. Chance, B., "Identification of Enzyme-Substrate Compounds," pp. 25–46.
6. Green, D. E., ed., *Currents in Biochemical Research* (New York: Interscience Publishers, Inc., 1956).

Especially the three chapters:

   a. Theorell, H., "Relations Between Prosthetic Groups, Coenzymes and Enzymes," pp. 275–307.
   b. Chance, B., "Enzyme-Substrate Compounds and Electron Transfer," pp. 308–337.
   c. Alberty, R. A., "Enzyme Kinetics," pp. 560–584.

A discussion of the cytochrome system, replete with references, is:

7. Lehninger, A. L., "Respiratory-Energy Transformation," *Rev. Mod. Phys.* **31**: 136–146 (Jan. 1959).

19

Molecular Basis of Vision

1. Color Vision and Photopigments

The phenomena of vision form the basis for Chapters 2 and 7. In these chapters, the eye was considered as an optical system which focuses images onto the retina. The retina was shown to act as a transducer converting the light to neural impulses. These, in turn, appear to be sorted and analyzed both within the retina and within the brain to give rise finally to the sensation of vision.

Part of the visual sensation consists in recognizing different colors. The color sensed is a function of the wavelength of the incident light; the complexity of this function is emphasized by the experiments described in Chapter 7. Nevertheless, any discrimination of different hues is due to the presence of receptors which selectively absorb light energy in certain wavelength regions. The photosensitive pigments are altered by the photons absorbed. These changes take place on a molecular level and are far too small to be revealed by any histological method. This particular aspect of vision is, therefore, in the realm of molecular biology.

All physiological or psychophysical experiments indicate that there must be at least three pigments within the retina of mammals. Whereas some experiments indicate that there may be many more than this, none indicate less than three.   In spite of this, only two photosensitive pigments have been isolated from human retinas.   One of these, rhodopsin, is found in the rods.   It has been studied in detail; its structure and action form the basis for the next section (and indeed most of this chapter).   Other mammalian pigments active in vision are introduced in Section 3 of this chapter.

The molecular basis for mammalian vision is far from being completely understood; this contrasts sharply with the knowledge of the geometrical optics of the eye.   Invertebrate vision has been even less well studied on a molecular level.   Although it is evident that many insects possess highly developed color senses which extend far into the ultraviolet, few of the photopigments responsible for insect vision have been isolated.

As stated earlier, molecular biophysics is regarded by some biophysicists as the most fundamental part of biophysics.   From this point of view, the most significant aspects of the biophysics of vision are the least well understood.

2. Rhodopsin

It had been known for many years that pigments which might be associated with vision existed in the retina.   In 1876, Boll named a pigment "Sehrot" which he saw in frog retinas.   It was described as a brilliant red pigment.   In 1878, Kuhne observed the bleaching of a pigment, rhodopsin, which he extracted with bile salts.   Rhodopsin has also been called visual purple because of its characteristic color.   It is by far the most studied of the photosensitive pigments.

Today, rhodopsin has been purified and studied in many laboratories. In order to extract it, fresh, dark-adapted retinas are mashed in a dim red light.   The mashed retinas are then subjected to differential centrifugation until a fairly pure suspension of rods is obtained.   The rods are hardened with alum, which makes most proteins insoluble.   Then the hardened rods are extracted exhaustively with buffers to remove all water-soluble material, after which they are dried.   The rods are next extracted exhaustively with petroleum ether to remove all fat-soluble substances.   This leaves insoluble particles which can be suspended only with suitable detergents.   The particles containing the pigment rhodopsin are suspended in a 2 per cent solution of digitonin, or in bile salts.   The entire purification must be carried out in a deep red light in order to have an appreciable yield of rhodopsin.

Is the rhodopsin one ends up with anything like the original?   Tests show that it has almost the same absorption spectrum, although at physiological pH the peak is shifted several $m\mu$. This similarity is taken as evidence that the purified rhodopsin is essentially the same as the initial rhodopsin. If the extraction is performed in a bright light, no rhodopsin is present in the final suspension; only the protein, opsin, remains.

Rhodopsin is a protein complex with a molecular weight of approximately 40,000. It is a conjugated complex of a particular protein, *opsin*, with a much smaller hydrocarbon group, called *neoretinene b* or *retinene*. Retinene$_1$ is the aldehyde[1] of vitamin A_1. Vitamin A_1 has the structure shown in Figure 1. The carbon atoms in the ring and along the chain are numbered for convenient reference. Compounds with a ring structure of this type, plus a chain of about nine additional carbon atoms, are referred to as carotenoids because many of them are found in carrots. Vitamin A_1 is one of these carotenoids.

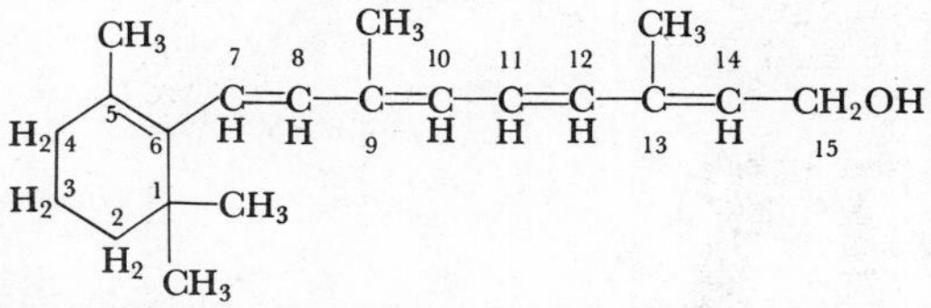

Figure I. Structural formula of vitamin A_1.

For every double bond along the vitamin A_1 chain, there are two spatial isomers. If one of the atoms on each carbon is hydrogen, one can represent the *cis* isomer as

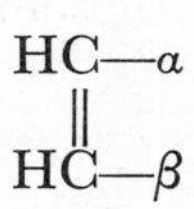

$$\begin{array}{c} HC\!-\!\alpha \\ \| \\ HC\!-\!\beta \end{array}$$

and similarly the *trans* isomer as

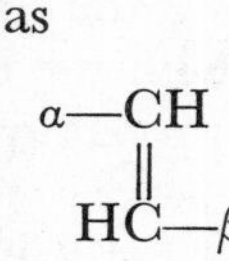

$$\begin{array}{c} \alpha\!-\!CH \\ \| \\ HC\!-\!\beta \end{array}$$

In many cases, it is possible to distinguish between the cis and trans compounds either by chemical or by X-ray techniques. In more complex cases, this distinction is difficult to demonstrate. In the case

[1] An aldehyde is a compound containing the structure $-\overset{\overset{\textstyle H}{|}}{C}\!=\!O$. Neoretinene (and all other retinenes) have this structure on the fifteenth (terminal) carbon atom. Vitamin A_1 has an alcohol structure on this atom, as is shown in Figure 1. The aldehyde form is an oxidized form, whereas the alcohol is a reduced form.

of vitamin A_1 (or retinene), there are 2^4 or 16 different isomers which can be drawn with pencil and paper. Only one of these isomers is physiologically active.

Essentially, one may regard the visual process as the splitting of retinene from opsin and then the resynthesis of rhodopsin, as shown in Figure 2. Unfortunately, this is a gross oversimplification. For if the usual form of vitamin A is converted to retinene, it does not react with opsin at all. This is because the common vitamin A is the all-trans isomer. If retinene is split from rhodopsin, it is also the all-trans isomer and will not recombine. Chemical methods can show that the active retinene is a mono-cis compound but cannot distinguish between the four possible isomers having the cis configuration at the 7–8, 9–10, 11–12, and 13–14 positions, respectively. On the basis of a study of the

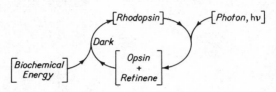

Figure 2. Simplified version of the visual cycle of rhodopsin.

actual dimensional configurations, Pauling predicted that the only four stable isomers should be the all-trans, 9-cis, 13-cis, and 9–13 di-cis. Of these, only the 9-cis isomer reacts with opsin, and, although forming a photosensitive pigment, does not form rhodopsin. Thus, retinene cannot be one of the more probable forms.

The other mono-cis isomers, 7–8 and 11–12, are hindered forms. The interaction between different parts of the molecule twists the long side chain and the ring, distorting the normal planar form. Of these two hindered forms, the isomer with the cis bond at the 11–12 position is less hindered and so is more probable for the active form, which is called *neoretinene b* or *retinene₁*.

The plane projection of the 11–12 cis compound is illustrated in Figure 3. This compound possesses a large steric hindrance between 13-CH_3 and the 10-H. The 7–8 cis compound possesses a still stronger hindrance between the 9-CH_3 and the 1- and 5-CH_3 groups. The conversion from the all-trans form of vitamin A aldehyde to neoretinene b occurs in the presence of iodine and light. It is believed to occur also within the retina where the conversion is enzymatically catalyzed.

There is another type of enzyme within the retina (and almost all other body tissues for that matter) which is known as alcohol dehydrogenase (abbreviated ADH). This enzyme interacts with the visual cycle because it acts as a catalyst maintaining an equilibrium ratio between the aldehyde retinene and the corresponding alcohol, vitamin A. This equilibrium is in the direction of much greater concentration of the alcohol. If, however, the aldehyde concentration is sufficiently low, the enzyme catalyzes the aldehyde production from the alcohol. To function, alcohol dehydrogenase needs a coenzyme, diphosphopyridine nucleotide (DPN^+) to accept the hydrogen atoms removed from the aldehyde (see Chapter 18). In the living retina, as in all other tissues, there is an abundant supply of DPN^+ and DPNH.

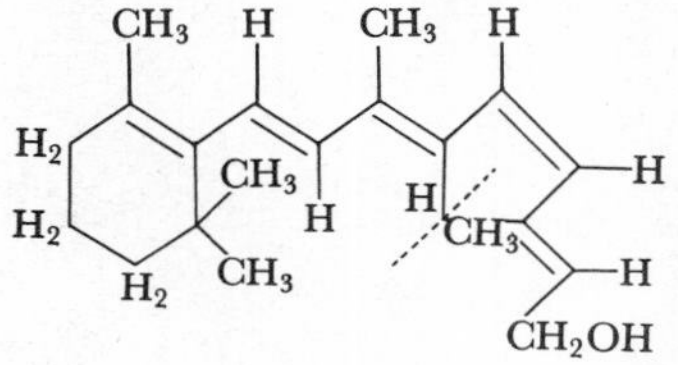

Figure 3. The 11-12 mono-cis isomer of vitamin A_1. The plane projection is distorted so that it does not show the steric hindrance. This is indicated by the broken line between the methyl group at 13 and the hydrogen attached to position 10.

The vitamin A produced by the action of alcohol dehydrogenase and DPNH can pass through the rod membrane and into the blood stream. The vitamin A in the retina is in equilibrium with that in the blood under steady-state light conditions. The vitamin A in the blood stream is, in turn, maintained at a more or less constant concentration by the liver, which stores any excess of vitamin A.

The over-all process is then a complex cycle, which is shown in diagrammatic form in Figure 4. In the dark, the cycle is stopped by all the opsin being bound in the form of rhodopsin. In the light, an equilibrium must be established with a steady-state concentration of rhodopsin. The concentration may be very close to zero, but a small part of the opsin should always exist in the form of rhodopsin.

From the point of view of the alcohol dehydrogenase, one may regard the opsin as a trapping reagent which effectively shifts the equilibrium so that the alcohol (vitamin A_1) is converted to the aldehyde (retinene$_1$). The reaction of retinene$_1$ with opsin is exothermic and goes spontaneously. From the point of view of the retinene, the opsin acts as an enzyme, converting the retinene with the help of the photon $h\nu$ from the less probable cis form to the more probable all-trans form. One may describe the protein opsin as a photo-isomerase.

An additional feature of this reaction is that it tends to stabilize the reactants. Opsin and retinene$_1$ are both relatively unstable. For instance, by changing the pH of an opsin solution from a neutral 7.0 to either 5.0 or 8.0, opsin is 50 per cent irreversibly altered (denatured) in an hour.   The cis retinene is relatively easy to "isomerize" to the all-trans form and is primarily converted to the alcohol (vitamin) form. In contrast to opsin and retinene, the compound rhodopsin presents remarkable stability as indicated by the extraction procedure.   It is stable over the pH range 3.9 to 9.6.   It is easy to imagine that in vitamin

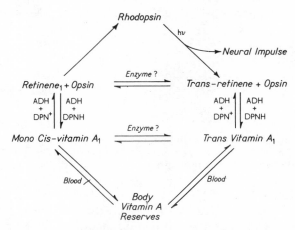

Figure 4. The visual cycle of rhodopsin in the retina.

A deficiency, the opsin might quickly degenerate.   (Indeed, the rods do show very rapid degeneration.)   On addition of vitamin A to the diet, the opsin formed would be stabilized as rhodopsin.   Hence, the rods (and cones?) could rebuild.   This suggests that opsin is a type of adaptive enzyme.   This mutual stabilizing may be typical of other adaptive enzymes.

Under certain conditions, the step from rhodopsin to trans retinene and opsin may be stopped at two intermediate points.   If a dried film of rhodopsin is exposed at $-70°C$, a new compound, lumirhodopsin, is formed.   On heating to 20°C, this spontaneously changes to meta-rhodopsin.   This compound is stable when formed from squid rhodopsin.   Metarhodopsin from vertebrate rhodopsin changes spontaneously in the presence of water to trans retinene and opsin.

No evidence exists concerning the possible appearance of lumi-rhodopsin and metarhodopsin in the normal visual process.   It is possible that one of these is stable in the cones, giving rise to the δ cone postulated in Chapter 7.   Perhaps partially bleached rhodopsin is converted to one of these intermediates under the conditions of color vision and gives rise to an absorption curve different than the scotopic relative luminosity curve.

The nature of the bond between the carotenoid retinene and opsin has been investigated. Certain proteins are known to possess free —S—H groups called *sulfhydryl* groups. These are very reactive with a variety of compounds but are inhibited by the compound para chloromercuribenzoate (PCMB). The reaction of opsin and retinene is also inhibited by PCMB; quantitative studies indicate that the reaction may involve two sulfhydryl groups per retinene$_1$ molecule. This is pictorially represented in Figure 5. This, however, may be an oversimplification. During the reac-

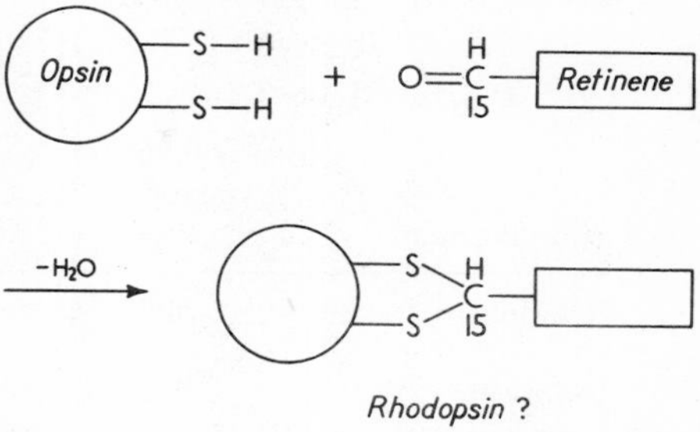

Figure 5. Pictorial representation of the reaction of retinene with the postulated sulfhydryl groups of opsin.

tion, the pH changes in a manner which corresponds to blocking or tying up a base such as histidine. The detailed reaction of opsin and retinene is not known.

3. Other Photopigments

The cones of the human eye have yielded another pigment similar to rhodopsin but having a different absorption maximum. This pigment, called *iodopsin*, is of uncertain physiological action because its spectrum does not correspond to any observed physiologically. In the scheme diagrammed in Chapter 7, Talbot avoided this issue by adding a contribution labeled "dz" from the rods and the hypothetical δ cones. Because the latter are only postulated, one certainly can account for any physiological spectrum, but this theory lacks a conviction similar to that presented by the similarity of the scotopic luminosity curve and the rhodopsin absorption curve.

An examination of iodopsin (from cones) shows that it is very similar to rhodopsin. Iodopsin is a conjugated compound consisting of retinene$_1$ and another protein, cone opsin or photopsin. (The rod protein is referred to in various places as rod opsin and scotopsin.) The rod opsin and the cone opsin extracted from a wide variety of animals, including all the vertebrates, are essentially similar.

Some animals have a different aldehyde called *retinene$_2$* instead of retinene$_1$. Retinene$_2$ is the aldehyde of vitamin A$_2$, which differs from A$_1$ in having an extra double bond in the ring between 3-C and 4-C.

Retinene$_2$ is also a mono-cis compound, but the location of the cis bond has not been determined.

A list of some of the known pigments of this general type is given in the accompanying table.

TABLE I

Pigment	Absorption maximum mμ	Carotenoid	Protein	Source
Rhodopsin	500	retinene$_1$	rod opsin	Land vertebrates, marine fishes
Iodopsin	562	retinene$_1$	cone opsin	Birds, turtles, mammals
Porphyropsin	522	retinene$_2$	rod opsin	Fresh water fish
Cyanopsin	620	retinene$_2$	cone opsin	Turtles, tench
Isorhodopsin	487	9-cis retinene$_1$	rod opsin	In vitro only
Isoiodopsin	510	9-cis retinene$_1$	cone opsin	In vitro only
Isoporphyropsin	507	cis-isomer retinene$_2$	rod opsin	In vitro only
Isocyanopsin	575	cis-isomer retinene$_2$	cone opsin	In vitro only

Birds and reptiles have mostly cones in their retinas and probably lack rods. These cones contain bright colored oil globules between the inner and outer cone segments. These oils are all carotenoids. Wald extracted 1,600 bird eyes to isolate the following oils

Carotenoid	Absorption maximum, mμ	Color
Astacin	497	purplish red
Xanthophyll	463	golden yellow
Galloxanthine	450	greenish yellow

Color vision is clearly possible with just these filters and iodopsin.

4. The Origin of the Neural Spike

Many experiments indicate that one photon dissociates one retinene$_1$ group from one rod opsin molecule. It is completely unknown how one or two such dissociations can give rise to a neural spike. This is one of the most fundamental questions which may be asked about the molecular changes in vision. One suggestion is that somehow the retinene alters the permeability of the rod when it is dissociated from the opsin. The rhodopsin in a fixed rod has been shown by electron microscopy to be arranged in a regular array of disks which essentially fill the rod. The arrangement of rhodopsin molecules within the disks is not known. The disks are about 250 mμ diameter and 50 mμ thick. It is possible that this array of disks acts somehow as a semiconductor (or even transistor) whose conduction depends on the number of impurity centers (dissociated retinene molecules). But this cannot be proved. In common with hearing, olfaction, and taste, it is impossible to describe the method by which the neural impulse is started.

REFERENCES

1. Wolken, J. J., ed., "Photoreception" (Monograph) *Ann. New York Acad. Sc.* **74**: 161–406 (1958).
2. Wald, George, "The Biochemistry of Visual Excitation," O. H. Gaebler, *Enzymes: Units of Biological Structure and Function* (New York: Academic Press, Inc., 1956) pp. 355–367.

20

Photosynthesis

I. Introduction

The surface of the earth continually receives radiant energy from the sun. This may be dissipated as heat or used to drive the syntheses of new molecules. These new molecules, in turn, can serve as sources of energy for later reactions and syntheses. The primary synthesis of new compounds driven by radiant energy is called *photosynthesis*. It is catalyzed by colored pigments found in many plants. Photosynthesis occurs in all green plants, including all of the higher plants and some of the algae. In addition, many other unicellular forms carry out photosynthesis. The blue-green algae and bacteria of a variety of colors all photosynthesize. There is also a genus of one-celled animals, called *euglena*, which contain a green-pigmented organelle capable of catalyzing photosynthesis. (In fact, some taxonomists prefer to call euglena a plant.)

All living processes, other than photosynthesis, involve the degradation of chemical energy to heat energy. Eventually, all sources of chemical energy would be consumed and life on earth would stop if photosynthesis did not occur. This process of building up of the chemical energy available to living organisms is continuously driven by the sun.   It can best be described in terms of entropy or information, an approach followed in more detail in Chapters 21 and 25.

Photosynthesis is necessary for life on earth for another quite different reason.   The entire chemistry of the surface of the earth has a net reducing property which, in the absence of photosynthesis, would bind all oxygen in the form of oxides.   If this happened, protoplasm as we know it, which depends on oxidations to use chemical energy, would not be possible.   However, photosynthesis produces sufficient molecular oxygen that it actually "controls" the oxygen in our atmosphere, raising it to an equilibrium value of about 20 per cent.   Thus, photosynthesis is necessary for living organisms, as they exist on the surface of the earth, both in supplying the necessary energy-rich organic compounds and also in producing the oxygen necessary to use the energy in these compounds.

The over-all reaction occuring in photosynthesis is the fixation of CO_2 and water to form a sugar and molecular oxygen.   This may be written symbolically as

$$6CO_2 + 6H_2O + nh\nu \rightarrow C_6H_{12}O_6 + 6O_2 \qquad (1)$$

In this formula, $h\nu$ represents a photon of visible light, n the number of photons necessary, and $C_6H_{12}O_6$ a hexose sugar.   At one time, it was believed that the number of photons per CO_2 molecule should be constant and various models were built on the size of this constant.   The number n may be regarded as a measure of the efficiency of the photosynthetic process; as shown in Section 6, this is by no means a constant but varies with many different parameters.

The foregoing stoichiometric equation is deceptive in its simplicity. Actually, many steps and subprocesses occur at the molecular level in the photosynthetic reactions summarized by this equation. The principal aim of this chapter is to describe the current knowledge of these molecular steps.   Research in photosynthesis has moved rapidly forward since about 1940 and there is no indication that the process has stopped.   Increasingly, it has involved the tools and the ideas of the biophysicist.

2. A Little Plant Histology

All green plants and euglena contain organelles called *chloroplasts*. The chloroplasts can be removed from the cells by suitable fractionation procedures and, when resuspended in media containing the necessary additives, will catalyze photosynthesis at rates comparable to those in the intact plants.   The chloroplasts contain the pigments primarily responsible for the green color.   A wide variety of experiments indicate that photosynthesis in green plants and euglena occurs only in the chloroplasts.

The size and shape of the chloroplasts vary quite widely.   The most studied organisms are two genuses of one-celled green algae called *Chlorella* and *Scenedesmus*.   A diagram of a cross section through a chlorella cell is shown in Figure 1a.   Chlorella has only one cup-shaped chloroplast per cell.   It differs in this respect from many other algae

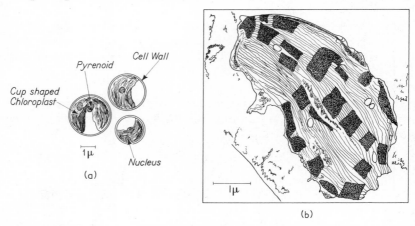

Figure 1. (a) Three *Chlorella* cells.   This diagram emphasizes that the single cup-shaped chloroplast occupies most of the cell. The pyrenoid is associated with starch and/or protein synthesis and/or storage.   (b) A corn chloroplast.   Sketch of an electron micrograph of a chloroplast from *Zea mais*.   The dark regions are the grana.   They are cylinders about 4,000 to 6,000 Å in diameter and 5,000 to 8,000 Å in height.   After E. I. Rabinowitch, *Photosynthesis*, II, 2 (New York: Interscience Publishers, Inc., 1956), from Vatter, unpublished, modified.

and most higher plants, all of which have many chloroplasts per cell. The chloroplasts of higher plants are shaped like a saucer with a diameter of 4 to 6 μ and a thickness of 0.5 to 1.0 μ.   In nongreen plants, the pigmented organelles responsible for photosynthesis are called by other names such as chromoplasts.   A more general term used for both chloroplasts and chromoplasts is *plastid*.

The algal cells have one to 50 plastids per cell.   When these plastids first form they are homogeneous, but as they develop, structure appears. They are filled with smaller dark bodies called *grana*, which contain all the photosynthetic pigment.   A simplified cross section of a corn plastid is shown in Figure 1b.   In euglena, the entire chloroplast is one granum. In most other organisms, there are 10 to 100 grana per plastid.   All of the chlorophyll, and presumably all of the light absorbing pigments of the plastid, are contained in the grana.

The grana can be isolated by breaking the plastids and then centrifuging.   They contain large amounts of lipid material.   Each granum is a highly oriented system of anisotropically arranged molecules.

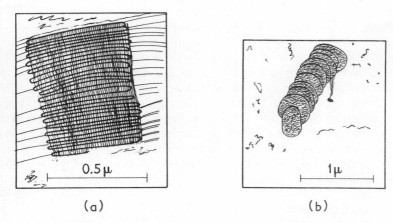

(a)   (b)

Figure 2. Green grana of corn leaves.   (a) A sketch of an electron micrograph of a section of granum within an intact chloroplast of *Zea mais*.   There are about 50 such grana per chloroplast.   Each granum has about 15 parallel lamellae which are about 400 Å thick and about 4,000 Å in diameter. (b) A sketch of an electron micrograph of a granum which is believed to be dissociated into separate disks.   After E. I. Rabinowitch, *Photosynthesis*, II, 2 (New York: Interscience Publishers, Inc., 1956), from Vatter, unpublished, modified.

Figure 2 shows the lamellar structure found within grana by electron microscopy.   The granum appears to be made up of piles or stacks of plates.   The individual plates are about 100 Å (10 mμ) thick; there are about 40 plates per stack.   The structure is very similar to that of the rods of the vertebrate retinas.   As shown in Figure 1b, the grana are regions where the density of lamellae is greater than elsewhere.   Many of the lamellae are continuous with those outside the granum.

Although apparently endless variations exist on the structures outlined in the preceding paragraphs, the general characteristics are common to all photosynthetic organisms, except bacteria; namely, the absorbing pigments are oriented on a molecular level in small plates.

Probably each plate is surrounded by a very thin membrane. The plates are assembled or stacked up in larger ordered structures called grana, each surrounded by its own membrane. The grana in turn are located in an oriented fashion within the chloroplasts, each within its own membrane. The chloroplasts tend to be arranged in a random fashion in the cytoplasm of the cell, although chloroplasts of many cells are oriented in the light.

3. Basic Chemistry of Photosynthesis

The over-all reaction of photosynthesis consists of the conversion of CO_2 to carbohydrate at the expense of the energy contained in photons of visible light. The over-all process in green plants may be divided into three parts, each of which can, under suitable conditions, be independently observed. These are (a) the conversion of the carbon dioxide to sugar, (b) the light reaction resulting in the splitting of water, and (c) photosynthetic phosphorylation. Each part has involved studies which fill many books. In this text, only some of the established processes will be mentioned.

A. CO_2 Conversion

The fixation of CO_2 and its reduction to sugars is, in one sense, the central, net result of photosynthesis. The simple sugars formed have the general formula $C_nH_{2n}O_n$ where n is in the range of three to seven. These sugars may exist in either a straight chain or in one of several ring forms, as discussed in Chapter 15. The six-carbon sugars and their polymers are the ones produced in largest amounts. The various hexoses are all stereo-isomers differing only in the relative locations of the —H and —OH groups. They can be converted from one form to another by suitable catalysts with very little expenditure of energy. Thus, if the cell forms or obtains one hexose, it can, with suitable enzymes, readily convert it to other hexoses.

Forming the hexose from CO_2 and water requires energy. Specifically, it requires Gibbs' free energy. (This is discussed in the following chapter more fully.) In describing energy changes, it is customary to divide Equation 1 by six, giving

$$CO_2 + H_2O \rightarrow \tfrac{1}{6}(CH_2O)_6 + O_2 \qquad (2)$$

The value of the extra Gibbs' free energy per mole, ΔG_0, necessary to drive this reaction to the right, has been measured to be

$$\Delta G_0 = 116 \text{ kcal/mole} \qquad (3)$$

This value may be compared with the energy of photons of red (680 mμ) and violet (400 mμ) light. These are

$$\Delta G_0 = 41 \text{ kcal/mole} \quad \text{(red photons)}$$
$$\Delta G_0 = 65 \text{ kcal/mole} \quad \text{(blue photons)} \tag{4}$$

(Often purists object to speaking of a mole of photons and use the unit of 1 einstein which is really the same thing.) If the process were 100 per cent efficient, about 3 moles (einsteins) of red photons would be needed for each mole of CO_2 converted to hexose.

There is no reason why the energy for this process need come from photons. Indeed, under suitable conditions all living cells fix CO_2 and reduce the product to hexose. In other words, CO_2 conversion to hexose is not a unique property of photosynthetic cells. In most cells and tissues, this conversion takes place at the expense of metabolic energy. Photosynthetic tissues are distinguished by fixing CO_2 and converting the product to hexose, using the energy obtained by the absorption of photons of visible light to drive the reactions.

B. Photodissociation of Water

In the over-all process of photosynthesis in green plants, CO_2 is used up and O_2 appears. In any experiment with whole cells lasting more than a minute or two, the moles of O_2 produced are almost equal to the moles of CO_2 fixed. It is therefore natural to guess that the oxygen might come from splitting CO_2. However, in nonphotosynthetic tissues, CO_2 is fixed without O_2 production or the need for water. Thus, if CO_2 fixation is similar in photosynthetic and nonphotosynthetic cells, the oxygen released in photosynthesis might come from the splitting of water rather than CO_2.

Experiments using tracer techniques have shown that the photosynthetic oxygen does ultimately come from splitting water in photosynthesis. If water of the form $H_2O^{18} + H_2O^{16}$ is used, the oxygen formed contains $O^{16}O^{18}$. In contrast, if H_2O^{16} and $CO^{16}O^{18}$ are used, the photosynthetically produced oxygen is all O^{16}. Thus, CO_2 fixation in photosynthetic and nonphotosynthetic cells is basically similar, in that the CO_2 molecule is not split. As discussed in Section 4 of this chapter, the pathway followed by the carbon is, however, different.

There is no evidence that water is simply split in photosynthesis to molecular oxygen and hydrogen. Rather, a variety of experiments indicate that the mechanism includes the reduction of oxidized pyridine nucleotide, as

$$PN^+ + H_2O \xrightarrow{h\nu} PNH + H^+ + \tfrac{1}{2}O_2 \tag{5}$$

The pyridine nucleotide may be either diphosphopyridine nucleotide,

DPN, or triphosphopyridine nucleotide, TPN. The structure of DPN is shown in Chapter 18.

If chloroplasts are separated from other cellular debris and washed with water, they lose the ability to fix CO_2 but can still split water according to the scheme

$$nh\nu + A + H_2O \xrightarrow{\text{chloroplasts}} AH_2 + \tfrac{1}{2}O_2 \qquad (6)$$

where A may be any of a wide variety of substances which can be oxidized. This is known as the Hill reaction. Because it is easy to demonstrate, it was used for many years to study the activity of chloroplast preparations. At one time, it was believed that the Hill reaction was just a fluke or an indication of an improperly functioning chloroplast. When A is oxidized pyridine nucleotide, the Hill reaction is currently regarded as an essential part of photosynthesis.

C. Photosynthetic Phosphorylation

Besides the energy used to split H_2O, additional energy is necessary to convert CO_2 into hexose. This energy is supplied by the splitting of the coenzyme ATP (adenosine triphosphate) to ADP and (P), (adenosine diphosphate and inorganic phosphate). As mentioned in Chapter 18, many oxidations lead to the formation of ATP, the over-all process being called *oxidative phosphorylation*.

It would seem possible that under some circumstances the ATP necessary to form hexoses could come from respiratory oxidation. As will be discussed further, this appears to be the case. However, most of the ATP comes from the chloroplasts themselves. They catalyze phosphorylation (that is, the formation of ATP from ADP and (P)) in the presence of light, even if no molecular O_2 is present. By analogy with oxidative phosphorylation, this last process is called *photosynthetic phosphorylation*.

Photosynthetic phosphorylation differs from oxidative phosphorylation in that it does not involve molecular oxygen. However, there are a number of cytochromes as well as flavins and pyridine nucleotides within the chloroplast. Photosynthetic phosphorylation does involve a series of oxidations and reductions. The initial step may be regarded as the formation of two separate compounds which can serve as the oxidized [OH] and reduced [H] ends of the phosphorylating chain.

To recapitulate, the chloroplast not only catalyzes the splitting of water to form the reduced compounds necessary for CO_2 fixation but also effectively splits water to drive the photosynthetic phosphorylation chain. If the latter is limited by the ADP available, then the two uses of "split water" must keep in step. For if the CO_2 fixation goes faster, then the ADP available will increase, thereby speeding up the rate of phosphorylation. Likewise, if phosphorylation proceeds more rapidly for a time, then the ADP supply will be depleted and the rate of phosphorylation decreased. This is a simple example of the action of negative feedback on a chemical scale serving to keep the two processes in step.

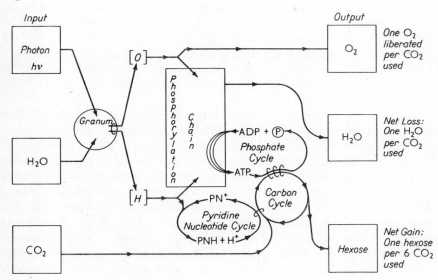

Figure 3. Block diagram of reactions within chloroplast. The brackets around the H and O indicate that these do not imply molecular or atomic hydrogen and oxygen, but rather reducing and oxidizing compounds. Considerable evidence indicates there is a flavin mononucleotide intermediate between (H) and pyridine nucleotide. The circle for the carbon pathways and the square for the phosphorylating chain are purely diagrammatic. The carbon pathway is discussed in more detail in Section 4. There is not an instantaneous balance between CO_2 fixed and O_2 released. A feedback mechanism, controlling the rate of phosphorylation, assures that over a period of time the number of moles of O_2 released is equal to the number of moles of CO_2 fixed.

One may then summarize the action of the chloroplast schematically as shown in Figure 3. This shows H_2O, CO_2, and photons being used up, and H_2O, O_2, and hexose being formed. It emphasizes the three types of reactions catalyzed by the chloroplasts, the splitting of water, the fixation of carbon dioxide, and photosynthetic phosphorylation.

4. The Path of Carbon in Photosynthesis

The pathways followed by the carbon of the CO_2 during its fixation and conversion to hexose have been studied with radioactive carbon as a tracer. To do this, $C^{14}O_2$ is introduced into a suspension of photosynthesizing cells or isolated chloroplasts. If the reaction is stopped after a brief time, one may determine from cellular extracts the compounds containing labeled carbon. Many similar experiments may be performed using different times of exposure to $C^{14}O_2$; from these data the relative amounts of the radioactivity in the various labeled compounds may be plotted as a function of time. Thus, it is possible to establish the order in which the compounds appear and hence, their relationship to one another.

In order to separate the various labeled compounds, a system called *paper radiochromatography* is used. (The word chromatography is very misleading because colors are not involved.) In paper chromatography, the cellular extract is placed near one corner of a large square of filter paper and dried. An edge is then immersed in a solvent (phenol water); the various components at the origin migrate in a line. The paper is dried, turned 90°, and the adjacent edge immersed in a new solvent. The partly separated compounds migrate at different rates in the two different solvents and so are arranged in a two-dimensional array. The filter paper is dried. To find the radioactive, labeled compounds, the filter paper is placed against a sheet of X-ray film. The location of labeled compounds identifies them; the intensity of the darkening of the film shows the extent of labeling.

Because the initial compounds form in a fraction of a minute, very short exposures are necessary. Several of the steps known to occur from these studies are summarized in Figure 4. Note that the final compound formed is the hexose sugar, fructose-6-phosphate. Enzymes exist within the chloroplast to change some of the fructose to glucose. Some of the glucose in turn is polymerized to starch, whereas the remainder is combined with fructose to form sucrose. This can be represented by straight-chain formulas as shown in Figure 5.

In order to confirm the scheme shown in Figures 4 and 5, it was necessary to introduce the labeled CO_2 very rapidly into the mixture. Then the entire process had to be stopped in a matter of seconds. It was possible that the compounds found labeled might have reflected the method used to stop the photosynthetic reaction. However, plunging into boiling water, strong acid, and strong alkali all showed 3-phospho-glyceric acid as the first compound and confirmed the general scheme shown.

The initial reaction of CO_2 with ribulose-1,5-diphosphate is interesting in that it is exothermic, liberating energy and apparently going even in the absence of any specific enzyme. Reduced pyridine nucleotide is used to convert 3-phospho-glyceric acid to 3-phosphoglyceraldehyde.

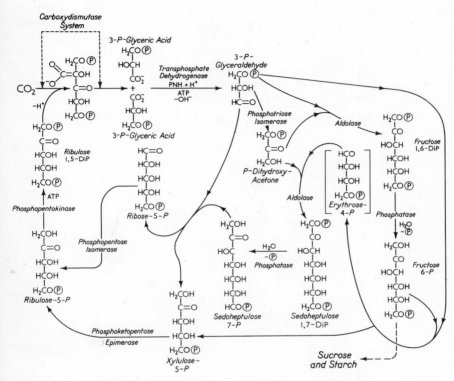

Figure 4. Some of the steps in photosynthesis. ⓟ stands for phosphate in the diagram and P for phosphate in the names. Note that all compounds with five or more carbons are sugars and probably exist primarily in a ring isomer; straight-chain formulas are for convenience only. After J. A. Bassham and M. Calvin, *The Path of Carbon in Photosynthesis* (Englewood Cliffs, N.J.: Prentice-Hall, Inc., 1957).

ATP is used at this step and in the formation of the ribulose-1,5-diphosphate.

Although the scheme shown in Figures 4 and 5 may seem extremely complex, all evidence indicates that it is an oversimplification. Nonetheless, the general cyclic character and the need for reduced pyridine nucleotide (PNH) and ATP seem established beyond question. The steps at which ATP and PNH are used are the ones utilizing free energy, ultimately derived from the absorption of visible light. Each PN$^+$ reduction requires about 8 kcal/mole. The cycle of Figure 4 uses two

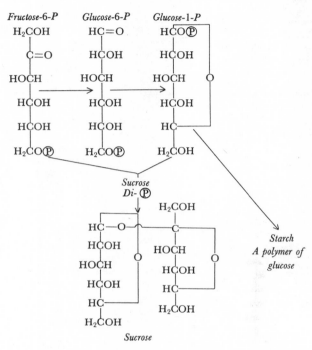

Figure 5.   The conversion of fructose-6-phosphate to sucrose and starch.

reduced pyridine nucleotides and three ATP's per molecule of CO_2. Thus, the total free energy required for this scheme is about 135 kcal/mole of CO_2, just a little higher than the 116 kcal/mole necessary to form hexose. The pigments responsible for this conversion are described in the next section; their operation and efficiency are discussed in Section 6.

5. The Photosynthetic Pigments

The grana within the chloroplasts contain the pigments responsible for the absorption of light and its conversion into the forms useful for photosynthesis. These pigments may be grouped in three classes: the chlorophylls, the carotenoids, and the phycobilins. All photosynthetic cells contain chlorophyll. Carotenoids are likewise found in grana from all photosynthetic cells.   The phycobilins are pigments found in some algae and bacteria.   In some fashion, all of these pigments act together so that light photons absorbed by any of them are equally effective for photosynthesis.   (Some carotenoid pigments occur outside of chloroplasts and are completely ineffective for photosynthesis.)

All chlorophylls contain a porphyrin structure, similar to that of the heme groups discussed in Chapter 18.   An atom of magnesium rather than iron is found in chlorophyll.   Attached to the hydrophilic porphyrin ring is a long hydrocarbon side chain which is soluble in lipids. (Thus, chlorophyll should be a detergent!)   All green plants have a type of chlorophyll called chlorophyll *a* and most also have another, namely, chlorophyll *b*.   The two can be converted from one to the other in extracts, but no such change has ever been demonstrated in whole

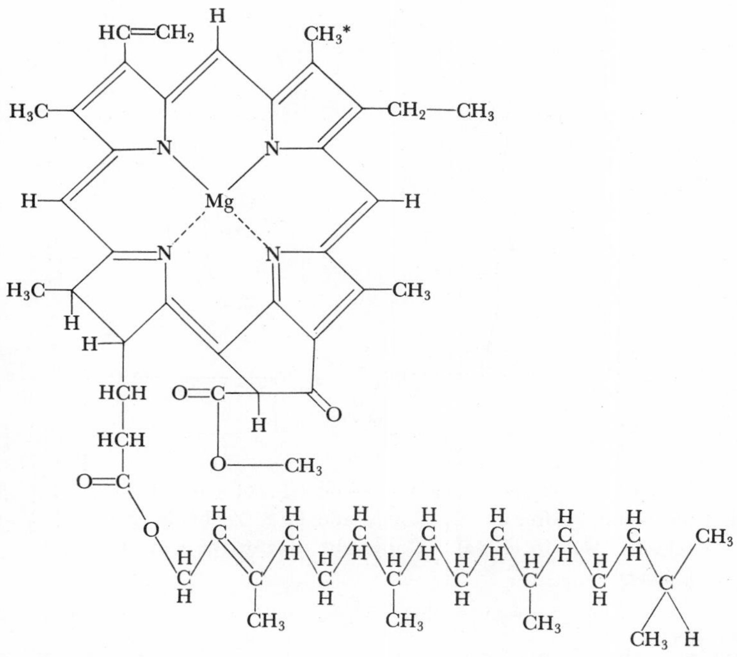

Figure 6.   Structure of chlorophyll *a*.   Chlorophyll *b* differs in having a carboxyl group —C(=O)OH in place of the starred —CH_3.

chloroplasts.   The structure of chlorophyll *a* and its absorption spectrum are shown in Figures 6 and 7.   The absorption spectrum shifts to the red on extraction from the whole cell.

Similar chlorophylls are found in blue-green algae.   The chlorophylls in bacteria, however, have different absorption maxima and slightly different structures.   Some form of chlorophyll is found in all photosynthetic organisms.   Those in euglena are chlorophylls *a* and *b*.

Carotenoid pigments are involved in photobiology, not only in photosynthesis but also in vision.   As described in the preceding chapter, many vertebrate visual pigments involve a carotenoid derivative called retinene.   In addition, the eyes of snakes and birds have carotenoid

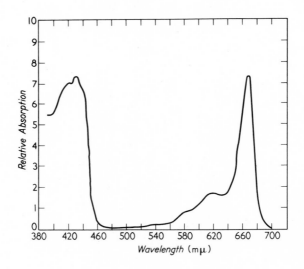

Figure 7. Relative extinction coefficient of chlorophyl *a* in methanol.   After D. G. Harris and F. P. Zscheille, *Botanical Gazette* 104: 515 (1943).   Copyright 1943 by the University of Chicago.

oil droplets which appear to act as filters.   A variety of carotenoid pigments are also found in chloroplasts.   The general structure of carotenoids is shown in Figure 8, while two absorption spectra are illustrated in Figure 9.   The carotenoids apparently act to absorb the photons which the chlorophylls miss and somehow pass the energy on to the chlorophyll.

The action spectrum, that is, the relative yield of hexose, at constant light intensity is shown in Figure 10.   The most striking feature of this

light photons absorbed by pigments other than chlorophyll are effective in photosynthesis.

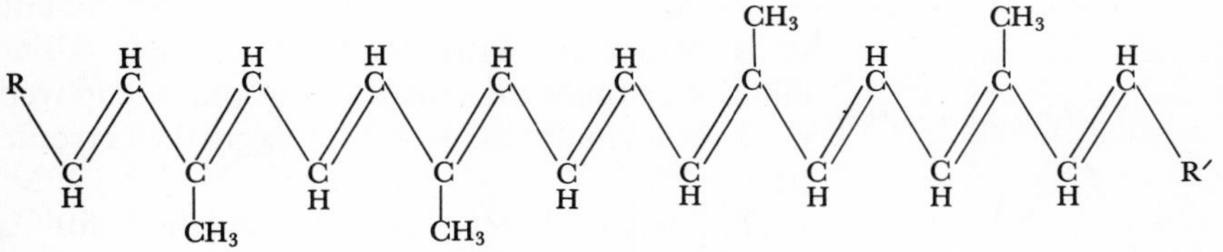

(a). *Carotenoid structure*

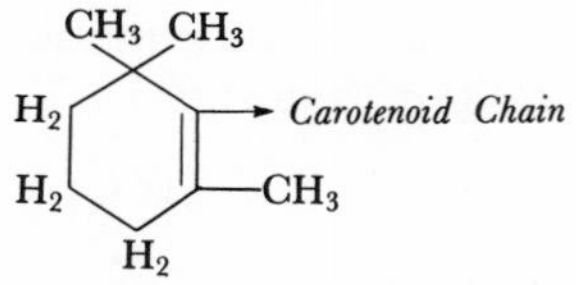

(b). *R and R' for β-carotene*

Figure 8. Carotenoid structure. Different carotenoids have different R and R' groups and exist as various cis and trans isomers. The all-trans isomer is illustrated. For β-carotene, both R and R' have form shown in (b).

Chlorophylls, when extracted, fluoresce very strongly, and each type exhibits a characteristic fluorescence spectrum. Whole green cells also fluoresce, always exhibiting the chlorophyll *a* fluorescence spectrum. This is true no matter what wavelength is used to illuminate the cells. Thus, all light energy absorbed which can be used in photosynthesis is in some fashion coupled to the chlorophyll *a* molecules. How this occurs is uncertain; the details of the light reaction are discussed in the next section.

(Chlorophyll *a* fluoresces much less in the bound state in the chloroplast than it does in extracts. In this sense, it is similar to flavin groups which also lose most of their fluorescence upon binding to protein. Pyridine nucleotides, however, do not fluoresce appreciably when free but do so when bound to protein. No general interpretation for these changes in fluorescence exists.)

6. The Light Reaction

Of the three parts of photosynthesis—photodissociation of water, conversion of carbon dioxide to hexose, and photosynthetic phosphorylation—the first is unique. Just how it occurs is not fully understood. Clearly, photons are absorbed or, in terms of electronic structure, an electron is raised from its lowest energy state to an excited one. Thereafter, this energy is used to drive the phosphorylation chain and to reduce pyridine nucleotide. Considerable evidence supports the existence of intermediate states associated with the light reaction. The lifetime of these intermediates is long compared to that normally expected for excited electronic states.

One very direct line of evidence for a comparatively stable intermediate comes from a study of the Hill reaction. In the presence of an excess of electron acceptors, the reaction follows the rate equation, relating O_2 production to light intensity I

$$\frac{d[O_2]}{dt} = \frac{K_d I}{K_d + I} \qquad (7)$$

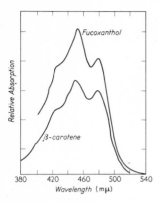

Figure 9. Absorption spectra of two carotenoids. These were both dissolved in hexane. The solvent alters the location of the maxima as well as the height of the curve. Different carotenoids in the same medium have different peaks. The two curves shown are not plotted on the same scale along the absorption axis. The β-carotene is after F. P. Zscheille, J. W. White, B. W. Beadle, and J. R. Roach, *Plant Physiol.* 17: 331 (1942). The fucoxanthol is after E. I. Rabinowitch, *Photosynthesis*, II, 1 (New York: Interscience Publishers, Inc., 1951), from Wald, unpublished, modified.

which is similar to that for Michaelis–Menten kinetics. As in the latter case, the simplest interpretation of Equation 7 is that a stable intermediate must exist within the chloroplast. In a similar fashion, one may measure the relationship of the rate of photosynthesis in intact cells to light intensity. The resulting curves flatten out as the light intensity increases. This phenomenon also supports the concept of light-induced stable intermediates.

Another quite different indication of intermediates comes from observing the effects of flashing lights. From the previous analysis of photosynthesis into three parts, it seems almost trivial that a part of the reaction could proceed with the light off, but historically this was not always understood. At high light intensities, the photosynthetic yield of carbohydrates (or oxygen) per incident photon is greater with a flashing light than with a constant light. Essentially, the light may be thought of as inducing stable intermediates up to saturation during the "on" period, which continue to drive the phosphorylation chain and carbon cycle during the "off" (or dark) period.

If the flashes are shortened to 0.5 msec, it is found that one flash does not result in the liberation of oxygen from whole cells. A flash of the

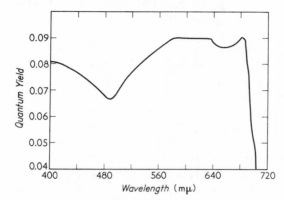

Figure 10. Action spectrum of chlorella. Note the extremely flat curve as compared with those of Figures 7 and 9. After R. Emerson and C. Lewis, "Dependence of the Quantum Yield of Photosynthesis on Wave Length of Light," *American J. Botany* **30**: 165 (1943).

same total number of photons but spread over a 25 msec interval does result in the liberation of oxygen. (In the Hill reaction, even the short flash results in the liberation of oxygen.) Two consecutive flashes lead to a greater evolution of oxygen than twice that produced by one flash. Thus, each flash leads to the production of stable intermediates. It is not clear in the flashing-light experiments whether this is merely converting all the ADP to ATP the first flash, or whether it is the same intermediate indicated by the light-saturation experiments.

The most direct evidence for the existence of an intermediate compound in an excited state comes from studies of electron spin resonance. This technique is discussed in Chapter 31, "Magnetic Measurements." Essentially, it is based on the inherent magnetic moment (spin) possessed by all electrons. In most organic compounds encountered in biological materials, the electrons exist as pairs with their magnetic moments opposing one another and thereby cancelling. There also exist certain excited forms of compounds normally expected to have paired electrons only, in which one electron is missing, or an extra electron is present. In either case, the compound has a net magnetic moment and is called a *free radical*. Magnetic studies with chloroplast materials indicate that such free radicals form when light falls on the chloroplast. The very nature of the magnetic studies makes it impossible to tell just what compound contains the unpaired electron. In contrast to most free radicals, this is one of the minority class called *stable free radicals*, which can be maintained for a comparatively long time. (Most free radicals, for example OH, are highly reactive and therefore cannot be kept as such except for very short periods.)

By repeating the magnetic measurements at 25°C and −150°C, it is possible to show that the free radical builds up in a fraction of a second at both temperatures. This suggests that the free-radical production does not involve a separate chemical reaction. The unpaired electrons disappear much more rapidly at the higher temperature. This indicates that their disappearance is associated with a chemical reaction.

The available evidence on the nature of the light reaction, then, may be summarized as follows. Photons may be absorbed by any of a number of pigment molecules, raising these to an excited level. All the different types of pigments are somehow coupled together so that energy absorbed by any one of them may be transferred to any other one. (This is indicated by the appearance of the chlorophyll *a* fluorescence spectrum in intact chloroplasts. The quantum mechanical basis for this process is under study.) In some fashion, the energy is converted into a charge separation, and the charges so separated form comparatively stable free radicals. (Calvin describes this by saying that the free electrons fall into "traps.") These free radicals then react to form chemical free radicals which are able to move about and lead to the ultimate reactions necessary for photosynthesis. Various models of the grana of chloroplasts have been built and are constantly being revised in order to try to make this picture of the light reaction seem reasonable in terms of molecular form and arrangement. It appears that the lamellar structure of the granum may be intimately associated with the over-all process of energy conversion.

One of the reasons for supposing that the energy of excitation appears directly as a charge separation is that the over-all efficiency is very high. Another reason is that the resonant structure of single and double bonds in both the chlorophyll and also the carotenoid pigments may make both suitable for short semiconductors. (Alternate double and single bonds are discussed in Chapter 27.) To justify the statement about the efficiency of photosynthesis, one needs to measure this efficiency. These measurements give variable results depending on how they are carried out; at one time, these efficiencies were the source of an active controversy between research workers in the field of photosynthesis.

The efficiency of photosynthesis has been of interest for a number of reasons. Before photophosphorylation and the carbon cycle were understood, attempts were made to find the minimum number of steps in photosynthesis. It was assumed (albeit incorrectly) that each photon necessary catalyzed a different step and schemes were built for photosynthesis involving as many as eight hypothetical steps. Although completely valueless today, these models emphasized the complexity of photosynthesis and inspired the experiments which led to the unraveling of the carbon cycle. Another interest in photosynthetic efficiency has been to predict the maximum yield obtainable and hence the maximum number of living organisms (humans) that can be sustained on earth. Perhaps most important of all, describing photosynthesis in terms of its over-all energy efficiency is using the language which appeals to the physicist and the chemist.

In a previous section, it was noted that to convert 1 mole of CO_2 to hexose, 117 kcal of free energy were needed. With the scheme shown in Figure 4, 135 kcal of free energy were necessary. The last number would represent 3 red photons per CO_2 molecule or 2 blue ones. The various numbers of photons per CO_2 molecule, observed experimentally, have varied from 1 to 13. Most recent values for prolonged photosynthesis range from 4 to 8 photons per CO_2; that is, 30–60 per cent efficiency.

These measurements have been plagued by a variety of errors. Many of the earlier determinations were based on manometry and short experiments, although the manometers could not respond sufficiently rapidly to make this meaningful. Also, it was necessary to know the respiration in the light, which was determined eventually by means of tracer techniques. The tracer techniques used the stable isotopes $O^{18}O^{16}$ in the gas phase and H_2O^{16} in the liquid. By following the uptake of O^{18}, it was shown that the rate of respiration was the same in the light as it had been in the dark. However, after rapid photosynthesis, the respiratory rate increased in the dark owing presumably to the ease of oxidizability of some of the photosynthetic intermediates shown in Figure 4.

Taking account of respiration, measuring CO_2 in terms of its infra-red absorption and O_2 in terms of its magnetic moment (with a Pauling oxygen meter), and measuring light intensity with a bolometer gave values for photosynthetic efficiency which bridged the gap between the various other investigators whose results appear to conflict. Data obtained in this fashion for very short flashes gave apparent efficiencies of 200–300 per cent. (This can be interpreted to indicate that ATP and PNH produced outside the chloroplasts can be used for short periods to assist photosynthesis.) At low light intensities, a sustained rate of about 4 photons per CO_2 molecule (that is, about 60 per cent efficiency) was observed. At very high light intensity, a rate of 7.4 photons per CO_2 molecule (that is, about 30 per cent efficiency) was indicated.

This last variation with intensity is in accord with the model of the excitation energy of the pigment molecules being transferred to charge separation and the charges being trapped (or held as stable free radicals) at certain sites. At low intensities, the probability of the sites being available is high and hence, more of the absorbed energy should be available for photosynthesis. In contrast, at higher intensities fewer trapping sites would be available and more of the absorbed energy would be converted to heat.

The models presented in this chapter, particularly those in Figures 3 and 4, suggest that one should be able to do many kinetic experiments and determine many different types of rates. This is indeed the case. Each experiment must, if these models are valid, involve the interplay of several rate constants and concentrations. The results are somewhat frustrating in that no one has really succeeded in disentangling the various constants. Such steps in building a better model of photosynthesis still lie in the future.

7. Summary

Photosynthesis is the trapping of the free energy of the photons of visible light, converting the energy into stable chemical forms. The process of photosynthesis makes life as it exists on earth possible, both by producing carbohydrates, the ultimate source of food energy for almost all organisms, and also by liberating molecular oxygen into the atmosphere. Photosynthesis is catalyzed by all green plants, by the green protozoan, euglena, by the blue-green algae, and by a variety of pigmented bacteria.

In all of the higher forms, photosynthesis is catalyzed by intracellular organelles called *chloroplasts*. Within the chloroplasts there are smaller organelles called *grana* which contain the pigments necessary for photosynthesis. The reactions can be divided for convenience into three parts: (a) a light reaction or quantum conversion which occurs in the grana and leads to the dissociation of H_2O; (b) the phosphorylation of ADP to ATP; and (c) CO_2 conversion to carbohydrate. Of these, only the last is understood in detail. CO_2 fixation and conversion to hexose can occur in all types of tissues, although it follows somewhat different pathways. Similarly, phosphorylation is a concomitant of oxidation in known living cells. The light reaction, however, is unique to photosynthesis.

In the light reaction, the incoming photon is first absorbed by any of a variety of pigments in the grana, including chlorophyll *a*, chlorophyll *b*, carotenoid pigments, and phycobilins. By a mechanism not clearly understood, the electronic excitation can be passed from one molecule to another. This occurs with very high efficiency and accordingly must be very rapid. In some fashion, the electronic excitation produces a charge separation, the resulting unpaired electrons being trapped or stored at certain sites where they may be regarded as stable free radicals. These then react to drive the phosphorylation chain of enzymes and the carbon cycle. The entire reaction has a very high efficiency; 30 to 60 per cent of the photon energy absorbed is used to produce carbohydrate and oxygen.

The study of photosynthesis is in a state of transition. In the not too distant past, standard histological techniques and simple chemical procedures were used to reveal many of the basic characteristics of photosynthesis. More recently, highly specialized chemical and physical tools have become an essential part of photosynthetic studies. It appears that the outstanding advances of the future will involve the application of physical techniques such as the X-ray determination of molecular structure and arrangement.

REFERENCES

The number of books and articles on photosynthesis is very large. Owing, however, to the rapid advances in this field, many of these become outdated very rapidly. This applies especially to the interpretation, on the molecular level, of the mechanism of photosynthesis. The following selections should be helpful to readers interested in more detailed discussions of photosynthesis than it was possible to include within the limits of this text.

1. Calvin, Melvin, "Energy Reception and Transfer in Photosynthesis," *Rev. Mod. Phys.* **31**: 147–156 (Jan. 1959).
   a. "Free Radicals in Photosynthetic Systems," pp. 157–161.
2. Kasha, Michael, "Relation Between Exciton Bands and Conduction Bands in Molecular Lamellar Systems," *Rev. Mod. Phys.* **31**: 162–169 (Jan. 1959).
   To understand the previous article it is helpful to read:
   a. Livingston, Robert, "Intermolecular Transfer of Electronic Excitation," *J. Phys. Chem.* **61**: 860–864 (July 1957).
   b. Rabinowitch, E., "Photosynthesis and Energy Transfer," *J. Phys. Chem.* **61**: 870–878 (July 1957).
3. Gaffron, Hans, et al., ed., *Research in Photosynthesis* (New York: Interscience Publishers, Inc., 1957). An advanced text of transient interest.
4. Arnon, D. I., "Localization of Photosynthesis in Chloroplasts," *The Enzymes: Units of Biological Structure and Function*, Gaebler, O. H., ed. (New York: Academic Press, Inc., 1956).
5. Bassham, J. A., and Melvin Calvin, *Path of Carbon in Photosynthesis* (Englewood Cliffs, N.J.: Prentice-Hall, Inc., 1957).
   Extremely complete compendia replete with references:
6. Rabinowitch, E. I., *Photosynthesis and Related Processes*. Vol. I. *Chemistry of Photosynthesis, Chemosynthesis and Related Processes In Vitro and In Vivo* (New York: Interscience Publishers, Inc., 1945).
   a. *Spectroscopy and Fluorescence of Photosynthetic Pigments: Kinetics of Photosynthesis.* Vol. II, Part I (New York: Interscience Publishers, Inc., 1951) pp. 603–1208.
   b. *Kinetics of Photosynthesis* (cont.). Vol. II, Part II. Addenda to Vol. I and Vol. II, Part I (New York: Interscience Publishers, Inc., 1956) pp. 1211–2088.

DISCUSSION QUESTIONS—PART D

1. One of the smaller proteins whose structure is being intensively studied is the enzyme ribonuclease. Describe its extraction and purification as well as its enzymatic actions. What is known at present about its molecular structure?

2. A fibrous protein which has been widely studied is the silk molecule. What is known about large angle and small angle X-ray scattering by silk? What is the present state of knowledge of the structure of silk?

3. Although many different lines of evidence have all been shown to be in accord with the Crick-Watson double helix of DNA, no one, at the time of writing this text, has been able to produce a satisfactory structure for RNA. Describe the best current model of the RNA molecule.

4. Electron spin resonance, discussed in Chapter 28, was used to locate the Fe atoms in the myoglobin unit cell. Describe in detail how this was accomplished.

5. The enzyme fumarase catalyzes the hydration of fumarate to L-malate. This reaction has been repeatedly studied by Alberty and his co-workers, as well as several other scientists. Write suitable stoichiometric equations and describe the corresponding kinetics for fumarase.

6. The enzyme fumarase referred to in question 5 can be inhibited by various compounds. What are some of these inhibitors? Describe their action. What is learned about the action of fumarase by using these inhibitors?

7. Mitochondria are small subcellular organelles found in almost all cells (except bacteria and red blood cells). These organelles contain many important enzyme systems. Describe the techniques and necessary precautions for isolating functional mitochondria.

8. One action of the mitochondria is to phosphorylate ADP to ATP. How is the P/O ratio defined? Discuss techniques for measuring the P/O ratio with various substrates.

9. The enzyme chains in intact mitochondria have been most clearly demonstrated through the use of selective inhibitors. Describe how this can be accomplished, giving specific examples of useful inhibitors.

10. A large segment of the literature about enzyme action deals with the role of —S—H groups which can be readily oxidized and reduced. In which enzymes are —S—H groups important? How is this demonstrated? What role do —S—H groups play in hemoglobin?

11. The enzyme invertase catalyzes the hydrolysis of sucrose, thereby inverting the optical rotation of the solution. Describe the kinetics of this reaction in the symbolism of calculus.

12. Describe the enzymes active in the oxidation of fatty acids.   Include a discussion of the methods of observing changes in these enzymes and also of the energy changes which occur.

13. Describe the changes in the mechanical properties of several high polymers following exposure to ionizing radiations.   Correlate these changes with other changes in the polymer properties.

14. Catalase activity is altered in various fashions by ionizing radiations, depending on the temperature at which dry catalase films are irradiated. Discuss the form of the temperature curve and its significance.

15. Review the evidence indicating that all forms of ionizing radiations have effects on single films of proteins which can be described by the equations for target theory.   Cite specific examples.

16. Describe the difficulties of assigning a specific inactivation cross section to virus particles.

17. Describe the metabolic and morphological changes which occur in euglena when they are transferred from a well-lighted environment to a dark one.

18. Review the history of the development of our knowledge of chloroplast structure and function.

19. Describe the evidence for the existence of free radicals during photosynthesis.   What role do these free radicals play in the photosynthetic process?

20. Review in detail the experiments which have led to the present ideas about the path of carbon in photosynthesis.

21. How was the photosynthetic phosphorylation shown to be one of the major parts of the photosynthetic processes occurring in the chloroplast?

22. Review the interpretation of the evolution of fishes and higher vertebrates necessary to explain the distribution of retinal pigments.   What other lines of evidence also support this interpretation?

23. Describe the current theories concerning the role of the carotenoid oil-droplets in the vision of snakes and birds.   What is the evidence supporting these theories?

24. How and where is retinene synthesized in the human body?   How is this demonstrated?

25. What is the evidence that the red eye-spot in euglena actually functions as a visual receptor?

E

Thermodynamics and Transport Systems

Introduction to Part E

Thermodynamics and statistical mechanics are major branches of physics and physical chemistry. They emphasize the application of the concept of energy and its conservation law; these have proved extremely fruitful in modern physics as well as in classical physics and physical chemistry. Therefore, it is quite appropriate that the application of thermodynamics should be a basic part of biophysics.

The concepts of chemical thermodynamics which are important for biophysics are introduced in the first chapter in this section. These ideas are applied in two succeeding chapters to enzyme reactions and to the diffusion of molecules through fluids and their transport through membranes. The preceding ideas are used in the next chapter to develop molecular models to explain the nature of the action potentials in nerves. In the last chapter in this section, information theory is introduced; its relationship to thermodynamics and kinetic theory is emphasized.

Thermodynamics is a part of physics and is described best in the language of physics, namely mathematics. All the chapters in this section could be called mathematical biophysics (as could also parts of several other chapters). It is important that the mathematical developments be related to experiments or else they become nonsense. In Part E, the experimental applications are outlined, but the mathematical analyses are granted a greater allocation of space. It is the author's belief that the approach taken in these chapters will increasingly become typical of all of biophysical research.

21

Thermodynamics and Biology

I. The Role of Thermodynamics in Biology

Thermodynamics is one of the major fields of classical physics. The concepts of energy and of its changes of form are central to thermodynamics. Many physicists and chemists have come to regard this approach as the most basic and most important. Accordingly, they consider the application of thermodynamics to biological systems as the central core of biophysics.

Thermodynamics can be applied to various aspects of living systems. The chapters in this part of the text illustrate some of these applications. They include the behavior of enzyme systems, the transport of molecules against chemical and electrical gradients, and the molecular basis of nerve conduction. There is virtually no field of biological science to which the concepts of thermodynamics cannot be applied.

Thermodynamics has long been recognized to be of prime importance to biophysics. One of the most distinguished of the early biophysicists of the current century, A. V. Hill, is best known for his heat measurements on muscles. Other biophysicists have followed this path toward an understanding of life.

Unfortunately, to apply thermodynamics to biological systems one must know something about thermodynamics. It is inherently a physical discipline whose theory is expressed most readily in mathematical terms. Because of this, and because the theory and applications of thermodynamics are often found in separate courses, many students receive a B.S. degree in physics or chemistry with little or no knowledge of thermodynamics.

Accordingly, the development of thermodynamics is included in this chapter. No attempt has been made either to include rigorous proofs or to eliminate the fundamentally mathematical symbolism involved. Those terms and parts of thermodynamics of greatest application to biology are emphasized, particularly the concepts of energy, entropy, and Gibbs' free energy. The last-mentioned concept is applied in the concluding sections of this chapter to a discussion of chemical equilibria. This application has received the greatest attention by biologists; it is one of the more important uses of thermodynamics in describing biological systems.

2. The Laws of Thermodynamics

Thermodynamics is a study of the exchange of heat between bodies and of the conversion of heat to and from other forms of energy. Energy is not something which we see or feel; it is a concept constructed by humans to describe the external world. Energy is defined as the ability to do mechanical work W. This in turn is defined as the product of a force F exerted times the distance s moved in the direction of the force. (In the language of integral calculus, this last statement becomes

$$W = \int_1^2 \vec{F} \cdot \vec{ds}$$

where W is the work done by $\vec{F}$ in moving from position 1 to 2 and the arrows indicate vectors.)

Mechanical energy may exist in two general forms, potential and kinetic. Potential energy includes elastic energy and gravitational energy. Sound or acoustic energy is a mixture of potential and kinetic energy. In a frictionless system, mechanical energy would always be conserved. Because friction occurs in all real systems, mechanical energy is lost. Moreover, mechanical energy sources are also known, for example, human beings, so that in a real system mechanical energy may be both generated and dissipated.

To physicists, the idea of conservation is a pleasing one. It was proposed to retain the concept of conservation of mechanical energy even in the presence of friction and heat driven machines, by including heat as a form of energy. Joule proved experimentally that for every unit of mechanical energy dissipated, a fixed number of heat energy units were generated. Moreover, if heat energy were used to operate a machine, the same ratio of energies was valid. By extending the concept of energy to include electric and magnetic energy, chemical energy, and finally mass energy, it has been possible to retain the conservation of energy as a fundamental law.

Another name for this fundamental law is the *first law of thermodynamics*. Symbolically, it may be written

$$dE = \delta Q - \delta W \tag{1}$$

In this expression, E is the internal energy, Q the heat put into the system, and W the work done by the system. The symbol δ is used instead of d for differences, because neither δQ nor δW is an exact differential. A differential is the difference in a thermodynamic quantity when the system is changed from one equilibrium state to a neighboring equilibrium state. (The states are defined in thermodynamics by the pressure p, volume V, temperature T, and concentrations c_i.) In the above expression, dE is an exact differential because it depends only on the initial and final states, whereas δQ and δW will vary with the path between these two states. In fact, if one considers a heat engine going around a cycle, dE, dT, dp, dV, and dc will all be zero for a complete cycle or any integral number of cycles. In contrast, δW and δQ will increase with each complete cycle.

It is always preferable to work with exact differentials, if this is possible. Those who have studied differential equations will know that it is often possible to multiply by a suitable function, known as an integrating factor, to make a differential exact. This can be done for both δQ and δW. It is then possible to rewrite the first law using exact differentials only.

The differential of added heat δQ may be made exact by dividing by the absolute temperature. The resultant differential dS, where

$$dS = \frac{\delta Q}{T} \tag{2}$$

is called the differential of *entropy*. (For reasons not germane to our present discussion, dS can be calculated only for reversible changes between equilibrium states.) The entropy S is interpreted in statistical mechanics as a measure of the disorder of the components of the system. In information theory, the entropy is a measure of the information to be gained by determining the locations, and so on, of all the parts of the system. From the point of view of thermodynamics, the importance of entropy is that it returns to its original value after a complete cycle; that is, dS is an exact differential.

The differential of work done δW may be represented as a sum of inexact differentials, each of which can then be made exact by suitable integrating factors. If the system is a gas, then δW is particularly simple; dividing it by the pressure p gives the differential of volume dV. In other words,

$$\delta W = pdV$$

For more complex systems, it is convenient to discuss the difference $\delta W'$, defined by

$$\delta W' = \delta W - pdV \tag{3}$$

This work, other than expansion, may be: elastic or mechanical, $\delta W'_M$; electromagnetic, $\delta W'_E$; or chemical, $\delta W'_c$. In each case, it is possible to find an expression similar to pdV.

For any elastic or mechanical type of work, one may always write

$$\delta W'_M = Fd\xi$$

where F is a suitably defined force and $d\xi$ the displacement in the direction of the force. If many forces are present, $\delta W'_M$ is the sum of terms such as the preceding equation, that is,

$$\delta W'_M = \sum_{i=1}^{N} F_i d\xi_i \tag{4}$$

Likewise, the differential of the electromagnetic work, represented as the sum of products of potentials ϵ, times differentials of charge q, is given by

$$\delta W'_E = \sum_{i=1}^{M} \epsilon_i dq_i \tag{5}$$

For biomolecular studies, the most important term of this type is often the differential of the chemical work $\delta W'_c$. It may be represented as

$$\delta W'_c = \sum_{i=1}^{N} n_i \Pi_i d(1/c_i)$$

where n_i is the number of moles of the ith substance, Π_i its osmotic pressure, and $1/c_i$ the volume per mole of this substance. (Note that Π_i is analogous to P and $n_i d(1/c_i)$ to dV.) In the case of ideal solutions, it is possible to further simplify the preceding equation. Just as for one mole of an ideal gas

$$pV = RT$$

so for ideal solutions

$$\Pi(1/c) = RT \qquad \text{that is,} \qquad \Pi = cRT$$

Substituting for Π_i, one finds

$$\delta W'_c = - \sum_{i=1}^{N} n_i RT d(\ln c_i) \tag{6}$$

(For nonideal solutions, it is possible to define a dimensionless quantity called the fugacity f such that

$$\delta W'_c = \sum_{i=1}^{N} n_i RTd(\ln f_i)$$

is correct. However, it will not be necessary to use f_i in the specific topics considered in this text.)

The first law of thermodynamics may be rewritten by combining Equations 1 through 6 into the form

$$dE = TdS - pdV + \sum n_i RTd(\ln c_i) - \sum F_i d\xi_i - \sum \epsilon_i dq_i \qquad (7)$$

The last sum is biologically important at membranes, whereas the next to last sum is significant in problems involving muscular contraction or the elastic properties of tissues. In discussions of enzyme activity, both of the last two sums may be set to zero.

There are two other laws of thermodynamics, both of which may be expressed in terms of the entropy. The *second law of thermodynamics* is concerned with the direction of time. In all of mechanics and in electricity and magnetism, there is nothing to distinguish the positive and negative directions of time. The second law of thermodynamics states essentially that the positive direction of time is that in which heat flows from a hot body to a cold body in an isolated system. When a given amount of heat δQ leaves a body at T_1 and flows to a colder body at T_2, the net change of entropy

$$dS = \frac{\delta Q}{T_2} - \frac{\delta Q}{T_1}$$

is greater than zero. The second law of thermodynamics states that in an isolated system the entropy will be a maximum at equilibrium. The conditions for equilibrium of an isolated system then are

$$dS = 0$$
$$dE = 0$$
$$d^2S < 0, \text{ that is, } S \text{ is a maximum}$$

Although it is mathematically useful to discuss isolated systems, they are as unreal as frictionless systems; no system is known which is completely thermodynamically isolated. In a real system, the entropy may decrease with time.

The *third law of thermodynamics* is a more recent invention than the first and second laws. The third law is concerned with what happens to the entropy as the absolute temperature approaches zero. Equation 2 shows that the definition of dS has a factor of $1/T$. If the specific heat of a substance remained greater than zero as the absolute temperature approached zero, then the entropy change would approach minus infinity when a body was cooled toward absolute zero. The third law states that this is not true; that the entropy change remains finite. In other words, the third law states that the specific heat of all substances goes to zero at least as fast as the temperature in the neighborhood of absolute zero.

A somewhat stronger form of the third law states that the entropy of all single crystals is the same at absolute zero and may be conveniently chosen as zero. This means, for example, that if one measures the entropy changes for two moles of hydrogen and one of oxygen from zero absolute to room temperature and adds the entropy due to the formation of liquid water, then the final sum should be identical to the entropy change from ice at 0°K to water at room temperature. This stronger version of the third law has been verified for many substances and never refuted for any substance tested.

3. Other Thermodynamic Functions

Three thermodynamic functions, other than the entropy, are more satisfactory for discussing equilibrium conditions in nonisolated systems. One of these is the enthalpy H defined by

$$H = E + pV \tag{8}$$

In an isobaric system[1], doing only pdV work

$$dH = dE + pdV + Vdp = \delta Q \quad \text{because} \quad dp = 0$$

For this reason, the enthalpy is sometimes called the *heat* or *heat function*. It should be clear that these names are misleading.

The other two functions are both called *free energy*; one or the other is designated by F in many texts. A less ambiguous approach is to use A for the Helmholtz free energy defined by

$$A = E - TS \tag{9}$$

and G for the Gibbs' free energy defined by

$$G = H - TS \tag{10}$$

A little manipulation shows that

$$dA = -SdT - \delta W \tag{11}$$

and

$$dG = -SdT + Vdp - \delta W' \tag{12}$$

[1] Constant pressure.

If the system, instead of being isolated, is maintained at constant temperature, then

$$dA = -\delta W \qquad \text{because} \qquad dT = 0$$

At equilibrium, in this isothermal system

$$dA = 0 \quad (A \text{ is a minimum})$$

If this system starts out other than at equilibrium, the Helmholtz free energy in excess of the equilibrium minimum value is the maximum work obtainable from the system.

Most biological changes occur with external restraints which maintain not only the temperature but also the pressure approximately constant. Under these conditions, Equation 12 shows that

$$dG = -\delta W' \tag{13}$$

and equilibrium corresponds to a minimum of G

$$dG = 0 \tag{14}$$

If one starts with reactants in a nonequilibrium condition, the excess of the Gibbs' free energy above this minimum is the work (other than pdV) available from the system.

In a system which is restricted by its surroundings to isobaric, isothermal conditions, and in which $\delta W''$ consists only of chemical work, one may write

$$dG = \sum n_i RT d(\ln c_i) \tag{15}$$

In this case, it is possible to integrate dG, providing all the n_i are held constant. A useful quantity, for chemical thermodynamics, is the partial molal Gibbs' free energy, $\tilde{G}_i$. This is the Gibbs' free energy per mole of i, which the system possesses because of the presence of substance i. From Equation 15, one finds readily that

$$d\tilde{G}_i = RT d(\ln c_i) \tag{16}$$

This is simple to integrate from a standard concentration $c_i^{(0)}$ to the actual concentration, since the factor T is constant because the system is isothermal. Integrating and rearranging terms, one may write

$$\tilde{G}_i = \tilde{G}_i^0 + RT \ln (c_i/c_i^{(0)}) \tag{17}$$

The term $\tilde{G}_i^0$ is the value of $\tilde{G}_i$ when the concentration is $c_i^{(0)}$. We may choose the latter as unit concentration and rewrite Equation 17 as

$$\tilde{G}_i = \tilde{G}_i^0 + RT \ln c_i \tag{17'}$$

It is important in (17') to realize that c_i represents, not the concentration, but really a dimensionless concentration ratio, because one cannot take logarithms of numbers with dimensions. This problem may be avoided by using activities or fugacities in place of c, but these are also meaningless unless one specifies the standard concentration.

The term $\tilde{G}_i^0$ will depend on T, p, and the standard concentration of substance i. It may also depend on the concentrations of the other molecular species. To uniquely define $\tilde{G}_i^0$, it is necessary to state all of these standard (or unit) concentrations. This group of standard concentrations is called the *standard state*. To recapitulate, the quantity $\tilde{G}_i^0$ is the Gibbs' free energy per mole of substance i, due to the presence of substance i, when the system is in its standard state at absolute temperature T and pressure p.

The standard state need not be a real state. For instance, one might use 1 mole per liter for the concentration of catalase in the standard state. A concentration of 1 millimole per liter is a large one for catalase, and 1 mole/liter is physically unrealizable. In this case, $\tilde{G}_i^0$ means the value of the partial molal free energy obtained by extrapolating from infinite dilution to the standard state under the hypothesis that the solution acted as an ideal one. Even though this hypothesis is obviously absurd, the term $\tilde{G}_i^0$ is a useful one for thermodynamic calculations.

From Equation 10, one sees that it is possible to write

$$\tilde{G}_i^0 = \tilde{H}_i^0 - T\tilde{S}_i^0 \tag{10'}$$

Changing the standard state by decreasing $c_i^{(0)}$ by a factor of 10^3 will decrease $\tilde{G}_i^0$ by an amount $RT \ln 10^3$. Because the partial molal enthalpy, in the standard state $\tilde{H}_i^0$, is not dependent on $c_i^{(0)}$, this change in $\tilde{G}_i^0$ must be an increase in $\tilde{S}_i^0$ of $R \ln 10^3$. Statistical mechanics interprets this increase as the equivalent of saying a mole of substance i can be distributed 10^3 times more ways at 10^{-3} of the original concentration.

In order to assign meaning to $\tilde{S}_i^0$, it is necessary to have a zero for entropy. This is provided by the second statement of the third law of thermodynamics as the entropy of a simple single crystal of a single substance at $0°K$. By varying the standard state concentration, it is possible to change even the sign of $\tilde{S}_i^0$. Thus, no significance *per se* can be attached to either the magnitude or sign of $\tilde{S}_i^0$; it is a useful mathematical construction only.

4. Equilibrium Constants

The concepts of thermodynamics, and particularly the Gibbs' free energy, may be applied directly to the enzyme kinetic rates discussed in previous chapters. In cases where all (or most) of the kinetic constants are known, equilibrium constants can be found directly, as well as from the rate constants, and also from thermodynamic arguments. All three types of values are found to be in good agreement. The equilibrium constant K for the reaction

$$B_1 + B_2 \underset{k_2}{\overset{k_1}{\rightleftharpoons}} C_1 + C_2 \tag{18}$$

is defined by the equilibrium value of the ratio

$$K = \frac{[C_1][C_2]}{[B_1][B_2]} \tag{19}$$

where the square brackets indicate concentrations. The constant K is independent of the concentrations of the reactants but may depend on temperature, dielectric constant of the suspending media, pH, ionic strength, and so forth.

The equilibrium constant K is directly related to the rate constants k_1 and k_2. By definition of the latter, the rate of formation of $[C_1]$ is given by

$$\frac{d[C_1]}{dt} = k_1[B_1][B_2] - k_2[C_1][C_2]$$

At equilibrium, this expression must vanish. Rearranging the resultant equation, one finds that

$$K = k_1/k_2 \tag{20}$$

In the case of reactions involving equal numbers of molecules on both sides of the equation, the equilibrium constant K is dimensionless if the same units are used on both sides of the equation. Even if this is not convenient, it is still possible to regard K as dimensionless, provided one regards the square brackets as ratios of the concentrations to those in the standard state.

In general, the number of molecules on the two sides of the equation are unequal; one must either specify a standard state or treat K as a number with dimensions. Although, for most purposes, the second of these is a satisfactory procedure, it is necessary to use some artificial construct as the standard state to relate K to the Gibbs' free energy G.

In the last section, it was noted that under isobaric, isothermal conditions equilibrium occurred at a minimum for the Gibbs' free energy G; that is, dG must vanish at equilibrium. To relate Gibbs' free energy to K, it is necessary to obtain an expression for dG for a small disturbance of the equilibrium in Equation 18. Symbolically, one may represent G for the reactants in Equation 18 by

$$G = V([B_1]\tilde{G}_{B_1} + [B_2]\tilde{G}_{B_2} + [C_1]\tilde{G}_{C_1} + [C_2]\tilde{G}_{C_2}) \tag{21}$$

where V is the volume and where the partial molal free energy has been defined by Equation 17' as

$$\tilde{G}_{B_i} = \tilde{G}^0_{B_i} + RT \ln [B_i]$$

Differentiating Equation 21, using the definition of $\tilde{G}$ in Equation 17', leads to the relationship

$$dG = \left(\frac{G}{V}\right)dV + V(\tilde{G}_{B_1}d[B_1] + \tilde{G}_{B_2}d[B_2] + \tilde{G}_{C_1}d[C_1] + \tilde{G}_{C_2}d[C_2])$$

$$+ RT(d[B_1] + d[B_2] + d[C_1] + d[C_2])\, V \qquad (22)$$

The various differentials are restricted by Equation 18 so that, if the volume remains constant

$$d[B_1] = d[B_2] = -d[C_1]. = -d[C_2] = dx \qquad (23)$$

in which x is an arbitrary parameter expressing the amount the reaction in Equation 18 has progressed to the right. Substituting Equations 23 into 22 and setting $dV = 0$, one arrives finally at the desired equation

$$dG = V[\tilde{G}_{B_1} + \tilde{G}_{B_2} - \tilde{G}_{C_1} - \tilde{G}_{C_2}]dx \qquad (24)$$

for the change of Gibbs' free energy for a small displacement of Equation 18 from equilibrium.

For equilibrium, this last expression must vanish. Replacing the $\tilde{G}$'s by their expressions in Equation 17' and rearranging terms, leads to

$$\tilde{G}^0_{B_1} + \tilde{G}^0_{B_2} - \tilde{G}^0_{C_1} - \tilde{G}^0_{C_2} =$$
$$RT (\ln [C_1] + \ln [C_2] - \ln [B_1] - \ln [B_2]) \qquad (25)$$

The left-hand side of this equation is the difference in the partial molal free energies of Equation 18 when all substances are in their standard state. This is usually denoted by $-\Delta G^0$, defined by

$$\Delta G^0 = \tilde{G}^0_{C_1} + \tilde{G}^0_{C_2} - \tilde{G}^0_{B_1} - \tilde{G}^0_{B_2} \qquad (26)$$

The right-hand side of Equation 25 may be recognized as $RT \ln K$, thereby allowing one to write

$$\Delta G^0 = -RT \ln K$$

or

$$K = e^{-\Delta G^0/RT} \qquad (27)$$

The preceding was carried through for two reactants on each side of the equation. If one assumes the osmotic pressure is constant, then the volume will be constant also.

(The more general case is somewhat more complex. The most general reaction may be represented by

$$\nu_1 B_1 + \nu_2 B_2 + \nu_n B_n \underset{k_2}{\overset{k_1}{\rightleftharpoons}} \mu_1 C_1 + \mu_2 C_2 + \mu_n C_n \qquad (18')$$

where the ν's and μ's are positive integers and the B_i's are distinct molecular species reacting reversibly to form the molecular species C_i. In this case, the equilibrium constant becomes

$$K = \frac{C_1^{\mu_1} C_2^{\mu_2} \cdots C_m^{\mu_m}}{B_1^{\nu_1} B_2^{\nu_2} \cdots B_n^{\nu_n}} \qquad (19')$$

Equation 20 is unaltered; that is

$$K = \frac{k_1}{k_2} \qquad (20')$$

The expression for the Gibbs' free energy may be written as

$$G = V\left[\sum_i^n [B_i]\tilde{G}_i + \sum_i^m [C_j]\tilde{G}_j \right] \qquad (21')$$

As in the earlier case, one can show that, if

$$dV = 0$$

$$dG = \left[\sum_i^n \tilde{G}_i - \sum_i^m \tilde{G}_j \right] dx + RT \left[\sum_i^n \nu_i - \sum_i^m \mu_j \right] dx \qquad (24')$$

For equilibrium, one must demand that dG vanish, which leads to

$$K = e^{\sum \nu_i - \sum \mu_j} e^{-\Delta G^0/RT} \qquad (27')$$

where

$$\Delta G^0 = \sum_j^n \mu_j \tilde{G}_j^0 - \sum_i^m \nu_i \tilde{G}_i^0 \qquad (26')$$

If, instead of constant volume, the reaction were restricted to constant osmotic pressure, Equation 27' would be replaced by

$$K = e^{-\Delta G^0/RT} \qquad (27'')$$

Although the latter is simpler, Equation 27' appears to be a more realistic one for biologically significant reactions.)

Equations 27 and 27' are general relationships for reactions in a liquid. Neither these equations nor the equilibrium constants indicate how rapidly a solution of reactants will reach equilibrium. Nonetheless, Equation 27' is used in the discussion of absolute rate theory in the next chapter. A simple example of the application of Equation 27' is considered in the following section.

In words, Equation 27 says that equilibrium will favor the side of a chemical equation which has the lowest total partial molal Gibbs' free energy in the standard state; that is, the bigger the difference in the free energies of the standard states, the greater will be the tendency of the equilibrium to favor one side of the reaction equation. In cases where the value of ΔG^0 is not known, it can be determined by a graph of $\ln K$ plotted against $1/(RT)$. Equation 27, as well as Equation 27', states that this graph should be a straight line. A graph of this nature is called an *Arrhenius plot*. It is discussed in more detail in the following chapter.

5. Reactions of Catalase

In this section, the equilibrium theory embodied in Equation 27' is used to amplify the discussion of the catalatic reaction of catalase presented in Chapter 18. Equation 27' specifically is used to find the amount of H_2O_2 in equilibrium with air-saturated water in the absence of and in the presence of the enzyme catalase. It is also used to find the "back" rate for the production of intermediate complex and H_2O_2 from catalase, oxygen, and water.

The over-all reaction being considered obeys the equation

$$2H_2O_2 \overset{k_1}{\underset{k_2}{\rightleftharpoons}} 2H_2O + O_2 \tag{28}$$

As standard states, one may choose 1 mole per liter for both hydrogen peroxide and oxygen, and 55 moles per liter for water. The free energies of these compounds, relative to gaseous molecular hydrogen and oxygen at normal temperature and pressure, may be found in the International Critical Tables. For this reaction

$$\Delta G^0 = 2\tilde{G}^0_{H_2O} + \tilde{G}^0_{O_2} - 2\tilde{G}^0_{H_2O_2}$$

Therefore, the following sum is needed

$$
\begin{aligned}
2\tilde{G}^0_{H_2O} &= 2(-56,560) &= -113,120 \text{ kcal/mole} \\
\tilde{G}_{O_2} & &= + \quad 3,904 \\
-2\tilde{G}^0_{H_2O_2} &= -2(-31,470) &= + \quad 62,940 \\
\hline
& \Delta G^0 &\doteq - \quad 46,300
\end{aligned}
$$

All these numbers are for 15°C. Because there is one more molecule on the right than on the left in the preceding Equation 28, Equation 27' becomes

$$K = e^{(\Sigma \nu_i - \Sigma \mu_j)} e^{-\Delta G^0/RT} \doteq e^{-1} e^{+46,300/600} \doteq 10^{+33}$$

This extremely large equilibrium constant implies that at equilibrium it will be very difficult to detect any hydrogen peroxide. In fact, if one chooses practical values for the ratios of the oxygen and water concentrations to the standard state concentrations, one may compute the equilibrium hydrogen peroxide concentration as follows

$$\therefore \quad [H_2O_2]^2 = [H_2O]^2[O_2]/K$$
$$[H_2O] = 1$$
$$[O_2] = 0.24 \times 10^{-3} \text{ (in equilibrium with atmosphere)}$$

$$\therefore \quad [H_2O_2]^2 \doteq 2.4 \times 10^{-37}$$
$$\text{or} \quad [H_2O_2] \doteq 5 \times 10^{-19}$$

This value is so low that it represents, on the average, less than 10 molecules of hydrogen peroxide per milliliter. This very low concentration must be interpreted as the probability that there will be a molecule of hydrogen peroxide in a milliliter of H_2O.

Anyone can go to a neighboring drug store and buy a bottle of hydrogen peroxide solution. This is a nonequilibrium solution. It will remain in this nonequilibrium condition in a dark bottle for many years providing there are no catalysts present to speed the attainment of equilibrium. Many substances will accomplish this catalysis, including ferric, ferrous, and cupric ions. Per iron atom, the most effective catalyst is the enzyme catalase. None of these catalysts alter either the value of ΔG^0 or K, but they do alter the rate at which equilibrium is attained.

It was shown in Chapter 18 that the reaction catalyzed by catalase could be represented as two successive reactions

$$\overset{e-p}{E} + \overset{x}{S} \underset{k_2}{\overset{k_1}{\rightleftharpoons}} \overset{p}{E \cdot S}$$

$$\overset{p}{E \cdot S} + \overset{x}{S} \underset{k_4}{\overset{k_3}{\rightleftharpoons}} E + 2H_2O + O_2$$

where E represents catalase, S represents hydrogen peroxide, and $E \cdot S$ is the intermediate complex. For each of these two reactions, there is an equilibrium constant defined as

$$K_1 = \frac{p}{(e-p)x} \quad \text{and} \quad K_2 = \frac{(e-p)[H_2O]^2[O_2]}{p \cdot x}$$

Both K's can be represented as quotients of rate constants

$$K_1 = k_1/k_2 \quad \text{and} \quad K_2 = k_3/k_4$$

or as exponentials involving changes in free energy

$$K_1 = e e^{-\Delta G_1^0/RT} \quad \text{and} \quad K_2 = e^{-2} e^{-\Delta G_2^0/RT}$$

Because catalase acts as a catalyst, these equilibrium constants and ΔG^0's are related to those for the spontaneous decomposition of hydrogen peroxide as

$$K = K_1 K_2 \quad \text{and} \quad \Delta G^0 = \Delta G_1^0 + \Delta G_2^0$$

If it were possible to measure all four rate constants directly, it would be possible to confirm these last relationships. No one has been able to measure k_4 for this reaction. However, the free energy change ΔG_2^0 can be used to compute k_4. This allows a qualitative check on the reaction mechanism, as it shows that k_4 is so small that it should not be detected experimentally.

To show this, one must substitute numbers into the formulas above. Referring to Chapter 18, one may use

$$k_1 = 2 \times 10^7 \text{ sec}^{-1}$$
$$k_2 = 2 \times 10^{-4} \text{ sec}^{-1}$$
$$k_3 = 2 \times 10^7 \text{ sec}^{-1}$$

all relative to the standard state

$$[O_2]^{(0)} = [H_2O_2]^{(0)} = [E]^{(0)} = [E{\cdot}S]^{(0)} = 1 \text{ mole/liter}$$

and

$$[H_2O]^{(0)} = 55 \text{ moles/liter}$$

Solving for k_4 gives

$$k_4 = \frac{k_3 k_1}{k_2 K} \doteq 2 \times 10^{-15} \text{ sec}^{-1}, \text{ relative to the above standard state}$$

Similarly, it can be shown that

$$K_2 = 10^{22}$$
$$K_1 = 10^{11}$$

both relative to the preceding standard state.

The foregoing value of K_2 can be used to find the equilibrium concentration of hydrogen peroxide in an air-saturated catalase solution. Appropriate concentration ratios relative to the standard state are

$$[O_2] = 0.24 \times 10^{-3}$$
$$[E] = 5 \times 10^{-6}$$
$$[H_2O] = 1$$

Because only a negligible fraction of the total enzyme exists in complex form, we may write

$$[E{\cdot}S] \doteq [H_2O_2] = x$$

Under these conditions, the value of the peroxide concentration x is about

$$x^2 = \frac{[O_2][E][H_2O]^2}{K_2} \doteq 10^{-32}$$

or

$$x \doteq 10^{-16} \text{ moles/liter}$$

Likewise, p would be of the order of 10^{-16} moles/liter.

Although this number is much larger than the hydrogen peroxide concentration computed for a solution of oxygen in water, it is still far less than can be detected at the present time. Conceivably, one might find a compound AH_2 which would react with the intermediate $E \cdot S$

$$AH_2 + E \cdot S \rightarrow A + E + 2H_2O$$

so that equilibrium would favor the right-hand side more strongly than in the reaction

$$E \cdot S + S \rightleftharpoons E + O_2 + 2H_2O$$

In this case, catalase could serve to oxidize AH_2. At present, no such compound is actually known.

Even though it is not possible to carry out any direct experiments to verify the value of k_4, it is always assumed to actually exist. Many other enzyme systems are simpler than catalase in that they can be observed to catalyze reactions in either direction, depending on the initial concentrations of the reacting molecular species. Catalase has been discussed in detail because it illustrates an example of a reaction to which the reasoning of thermodynamics can be applied to determine an additional rate constant from equilibrium data.

The interpretation of equilibrium data in terms of Gibbs' free energy is a very important area in which thermodynamics can be used to describe biologically significant events. Other related areas are found in the following chapters.

REFERENCES

1. Glasstone, Samuel, *Textbook of Physical Chemistry* 2nd ed. (New York: D. Van Nostrand Company, Inc., 1946).
2. Glasstone, Samuel, K. J. Laidler, and Henry Eyring, *Theory of Rate Processes: The Kinetics of Chemical Reactions, Viscosity, Diffusion and Electrochemical Phenomena* (New York: McGraw-Hill Book Company, Inc., 1941).

3. Johnson, F. H., Henry Eyring, and M. J. Polissar, *The Kinetic Basis of Molecular Biology* (New York: John Wiley & Sons, Inc., 1954).

4. Höber, Rudolf, D. I. Hitchcock, J. B. Bateman, D. R. Goddard, and W. O. Fenn, *Physical Chemistry of Cells and Tissues* (Philadelphia: The Blakiston Company, 1945).

22

Thermodynamics of Enzyme Reactions

I. Collision Theory of Reactions

Thermodynamics deals with the gross, macroscopic properties of a system. It can also be related to events on a molecular scale by kinetic theory. This chapter is concerned with the latter aspects of thermodynamics as applied to enzyme reactions. As discussed in Chapters 17 and 18, most biological reactions are enzymatically controlled. The current chapter may be considered as an application of thermodynamics to molecular biology. Using thermodynamics and kinetic theory, it is possible to relate the energy changes during enzyme reactions to the changes of the reaction rate constants[1] with temperature. Thus, the temperature dependence of the rate constants can be used to find energy changes other than those discussed in the last two sections of the last chapter. Before applying the theory to enzyme reactions, the theory of reactions in general will be developed. Because gas phase reactions are easiest to discuss, they are introduced first.

The idea of energy changes during a chemical reaction may appear

[1] For a discussion of reaction rate constants, see Chapters 17 and 18.

to be a trivial one.   Suppose two molecular species, say hydrogen and oxygen, are mixed together.   Under suitable conditions, the reaction goes off with a bang, producing water and heat.   By controlling the reaction, one can carry it out at several temperatures and measure ΔG^0 as mentioned in the last chapter.   The simplest assumption would be that each time two hydrogen molecules and an oxygen molecule approached each other, they reacted, giving up energy.

The obvious oversimplification of this picture can be emphasized by considering what happens at room temperature.   One can introduce a considerable concentration of hydrogen into air.   Although many oxygen-hydrogen collisions occur, no reactions are noticed unless some local region is heated by a spark or match.   This illustrates that the reaction rate rises sharply as the temperature rises.   Many studies on reacting gases have confirmed that reaction rates vary much more rapidly with temperature than do collision rates.

A reasonable explanation of this variation, which was essentially originated by Arrhenius, is as follows: Suppose two molecular types, A and B, are mixed and can react to form a third molecular type C. When far apart, A has an internal energy E_A and B has an internal energy E_B.   The total internal energy of the two molecules is then

$$E_A + E_B = E_T$$

As they approach each other, there are repulsive forces which tend to keep A and B apart.   While they were far apart, their internal energy was all in the form of kinetic energy.   As they approach each other, this is converted into potential energy.   Figure 1 shows the case where E_T is less than the height of the energy barrier E_a, and the molecules cannot even approach close enough to react.   Let us assume that A and B are approaching each other at r_3; they will continue toward each other until they are separated by the distance r_1.   By the time they reach r_2, their relative motion has been slowed.   At r_1, they stop moving because E_T is completely potential energy.   Because there are repulsive forces which are responsible for the energy barrier to the right of r_0, the molecules will not remain at r_1 but will move apart again, maintaining the same total internal energy E_T.

Next, consider a case in which a reaction does occur.   This is shown in Figure 2, where E_T is greater than E_a at r_3.   The molecules again move toward each other, this time having a minimum velocity at r_0.   At r_{-1}, A and B give up internal energy, dropping down to E'.   Now they have become the molecule C within the potential well.   The total energy given up $E_T + E'$ must appear eventually as heat.   If the average temperature is maintained constant, E^0 will be the average heat developed. The height of the peak E_a is usually called the activation energy.

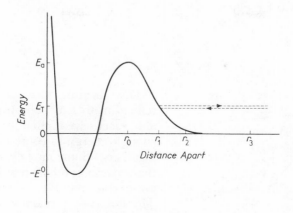

Figure 1. Molecular collision. The solid curve represents the potential energy of a molecule of A and a molecule of B when separated by a distance r. It is seen that their thermal energy E_T is less than the activation energy E_a. As a consequence they cannot come close enough together to react. The broken line represents their motion relative to one another.

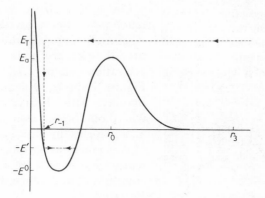

Figure 2. Molecular reaction. In contrast to the two molecules depicted in Figure 1, the two here have a sufficient thermal energy E_T to come closer together than r_0. They react at r_{-1}, releasing the energy $E_T + E'$.

To complete this picture, one then needs the fraction of the collisions between molecules having a total internal energy greater than E_a.

Kinetic theory shows that this fraction is $e^{-E_a/RT}$. If Z is the collision rate, in the standard state, then the collision theory outlined above predicts that the reaction rate k for

$$A + B \xrightarrow{k} C$$

should be

$$k = Ze^{-E_a/RT} \tag{1}$$

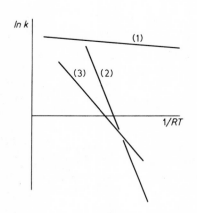

Figure 3. Arrhenius plots. Curves expected for different reactions when the log of the rate constant is plotted against $1/RT$. On the basis of this plot, one determines a slope μ called the Arrhenius constant. As discussed later, low values of μ for reactions in liquids (that is, curve Number 1 above) suggest the reaction may be diffusion controlled. However, high values of μ (curves Number 2 and Number 3 above) probably reflect the intrinsic properties of the reacting molecules.

This formula can be somewhat refined in that all colliding pairs may not react even though they have enough energy to come close enough together. Some may fly apart rather than reacting; others may be oriented unsuitably relative to one another. The absence of reaction in some of the collisions for which E_T is greater than E_a may be included in Equation 1 by introducing a probability factor a (less than one). Thus, one has

$$k = aZe^{-E_a/RT} \tag{2}$$

One test of this collision theory of reactions is to plot log k against $1/RT$. A straight line should result if the preceding theory is correct, and if the activation energy E_a is constant. Figure 3 shows typical lines of this nature. This theory, even in cases where one cannot estimate either a or Z, still forms the basis for our concepts of how reactions occur on a molecular scale. For gases, it is possible to compute Z, and hence, to find a from Equation 2.

The problem of applying Equation 2 to liquids poses many difficulties. There are even a number of questions which one may raise about its application to gaseous reactions. Most fundamental of these is why the activation energy E_a should remain constant with temperature.[2] Per-

---

[2] A constant value of E_a implies, for example, that the intramolecular bonds of the reacting molecules do not change size with temperature changes, and that the shape of the active sites on enzymes is temperature independent.

haps the enthalpy, or some other similar function, really should remain constant. If one of the latter were true, the interpretation of a would be more complex, but one would still find a straight line by plotting $\log k$ against $1/RT$. To avoid this question, some people call the slope of the lines in Figure 3 the *Arrhenius constant* μ. (The graph itself is often called an *Arrhenius plot*.)

Another moot point involves the concepts of entropy and Gibbs' free energy. From the point of view of kinetic theory, entropy is a measure of the randomness of the system. If A and B are initially separate molecules and become pairs during the reaction, the total entropy has decreased. Where on the potential curve should one first consider A and B as one molecule C? The answer is not obvious. If one starts at point r_1, say in Figures 1 and 2, then it is really the Gibbs' free energy which must exceed some minimum value $\Delta G^{\ddagger}$. By definition, one may write

$$\Delta G^{\ddagger} = \Delta H^{\ddagger} - T\Delta S^{\ddagger}$$

for an isothermal change. In this case, Equation 2 should have been

$$k = aZe^{-\Delta H^{\ddagger}/RT}e^{+\Delta S^{\ddagger}/R} \tag{3}$$

If $\Delta H^{\ddagger}$ and $\Delta S^{\ddagger}$ are independent of temperature, then $\Delta H^{\ddagger}$ will be the slope of the Arrhenius plot. If one also may write

$$\Delta H^{\ddagger} = \Delta E^{\ddagger} + P\Delta V$$

for an isobaric reaction, and if ΔV is proportional to the absolute temperature, then $\Delta E^{\ddagger}$ will be the slope of the Arrhenius plot. (It is easiest to read the "$\ddagger$" as activation.) In almost all cases, the constant a cannot be obtained by any other means than from the Arrhenius plot. Accordingly, the exact interpretation of μ, the slope of the Arrhenius plot, cannot be definitely determined.

All of the foregoing schemes predict qualitatively that the reaction rate should vary exponentially with the temperature. The temperature dependence of the collision frequency Z is so small as compared to the exponential variation that it cannot be detected in most cases. The preceding theory also indicates that there should be no obvious connection between the net energy obtained from the reaction E^0 (or ΔG^0), and the activation energy $\Delta G^{\ddagger}$ which determines the stability of the reacting molecules.

The height of the potential energy barrier $\Delta G^{\ddagger}$ determines the ease with which a reaction can occur. The action of a catalyst, such as an enzyme, may be thought of as distorting the shape of one or both reactants so that the effective value of $\Delta G^{\ddagger}$ is lowered without changing in any way the value of ΔG^0.

2. Collision Theory Applied to Enzyme Reactions

Qualitatively, one may picture an enzyme as acting by lowering the potential energy barrier $\Delta G^{\ddagger}$. However, the detailed application of collision theory to enzyme reactions is difficult for two reasons. The first is that it is possible to make measurements only over a narrow temperature range. A more fundamental limitation is our inability to compute either the probability factor a or the collision rate Z for reactions in the liquid phase. To understand this phase, let us consider briefly some ideas contained in the kinetic theory of liquids.

In a liquid, as in a solid, there are equilibrium distances from one molecule to the next molecule. In a solid, these are maintained in a regular pattern for astronomically large numbers of molecules. In a liquid, by contrast, the order is only local, falling off rapidly a few molecular diameters away. Diffusion in a liquid occurs as a result of the diffusing molecule jumping from one quasi-equilibrium lattice position to the next. As the molecule is in the quasi-stable position, it vibrates and rotates, colliding many times with its neighbors before moving on to its next position. The period of time during which two reacting molecules are in neighboring sites is called an *encounter*. The rate of encounter Z_e can be readily computed. In contrast, the kinetic theory of liquids is far too poorly developed to compute the collision rate Z.

Two extreme types of reactions can be distinguished. In the first, called *diffusion limited*, each encounter leads to a reaction. Anything lowering the diffusion rate will decrease the encounter rate and hence, decrease the reaction rate. For a diffusion-limited reaction, the reaction rate and encounter rate are the same, that is

$$k = Z_e \qquad (4)$$

The encounter rate will be proportional to the diffusion constant. In this case, the slope of the Arrhenius plot represents the temperature dependence of the diffusion constant and yields no information relative to the reacting molecules. For water the slope of the log of the diffusion rate plotted against $1/RT$ is around 3 kcal/mole for many solutes. This suggests that reactions with a μ of 6 kcal/mole or more are not diffusion controlled, whereas those with a μ of around 3 kcal/mole may be. (However, this is not a good criterion for diffusion control. For if the molecular shape is temperature dependent, it is possible to imagine diffusion-controlled reactions with much larger values of μ than 3 kcal/mole. In this case, it would indicate the temperature dependence of the change of shape of the reacting molecules. Likewise, even though $\mu \doteq 3$ kcal/mole, the reaction need not be diffusion controlled.)

The other extreme type of reaction is one in which most encounters end by the molecules jumping apart. Then, decreasing the diffusion rate decreases the number of encounters per unit time but increases the length of each encounter. Accordingly, the collision rate Z will not be greatly altered, and the reaction rate should be independent of the coefficient of diffusion. Such a reaction is called a diffusion-independent reaction. The slope of μ of the Arrhenius plot for such a reaction is an intrinsic property of the reacting molecules. Its interpretation, however, is exceedingly difficult unless one uses absolute rate theory, presented in the next section. (By making the incorrect assumption that the collision rate is the same in gases and liquids, one can arrive at values of a. Although, by definition, a is less than one, this misleading calculation produces values of a much larger than one for some enzyme reactions!)

In spite of its limitations, μ is a characteristic of a given enzyme reaction and can be used to compare different enzyme preparations and different types of enzymes, as well as to express in one number the temperature dependence of the reaction. Actually, an equivalent quantity called Q_{10} is used more frequently. By definition, it is the ratio of the reaction rates measured at two temperatures 10°C apart. That is, symbolically defined

$$Q_{10} = \frac{k_{t+10}}{k_t} \tag{5}$$

where the subscripts on the k's indicate the temperatures. By manipulating Equations 5 and 2, one can show that

$$Q_{10} \doteq e^{-\frac{10\mu}{RT^2}}$$

or

$$\mu \doteq \frac{RT^2}{10} \ln Q_{10} \tag{6}$$

For biological reactions, Q_{10} is generally in the range of 1.2 to 4, with the majority of reactions having Q_{10}'s very close to 2.0. Expressed in terms of μ, these values are 3.4 kcal/mole to 25 kcal/mole with a maximum number of reactions having $\mu \doteq 12.5$ kcal/mole. The quantity Q_{10} is easier to compute and is used more widely than μ. Since most biological reactions can be observed only over a narrow range of temperatures, the representation of the data in terms of Q_{10} is completely equivalent to describing them in terms of the slope μ of the Arrhenius plot.

3. Absolute Rate Theory

The proportionality constant a in Equation 2 of the collision theory is a sort of "correction factor" to make theory and experiment agree. In the case of gaseous reactions, a is often very small, having values in some reactions as low as 10^{-10}. A somewhat different thermodynamic analysis called *absolute rate theory* has been outstandingly successful in predicting these small values of a for gaseous reactions. Its application to reactions in liquids is considerably more tenuous, although the theory is widely accepted.

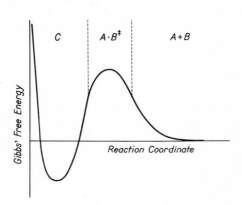

In order to describe absolute rate theory, it is convenient to again use the potential energy diagram of the form found in Figures 1 and 2. Now, three separate regions must be distinguished as shown in Figure 4. The abscissa does not have to be regarded as simply a distance apart. It is called the *reaction coordinate* and will, in general, have the dimension of length. When the reactants are far out on the reaction coordinate, they are considered as separate molecules A and B. Above the highest part of the potential barrier, they are considered as an activated complex $A \cdot B.^{\ddagger}$ Finally, in the region of the potential well there is a single molecular species C. This method of analysis is an approximation method because the region in which the activated complex exists is arbitrary.

Figure 4. The absolute rate theory. The absolute rate theory postulates an activated complex $A \cdot B^{\ddagger}$, which must be in equilibrium with $A + B$ in order to apply this theory to k. The rate of crossing the barrier from $A \cdot B^{\ddagger}$ to C is an absolute quantity if certain general assumptions are valid.

The reasoning employed is very similar to that used to develop Michaelis–Menten kinetics in Chapter 17. The complexes introduced in that chapter and here both control reaction rates. However, the intermediate complex of enzyme kinetics stays in existence for a much longer time, and its rate of breakdown cannot be determined on *a priori* grounds. The rate of breakdown of the activated complex $A \cdot B^{\ddagger}$, on the contrary, is always

$$\frac{1}{[A \cdot B^{\ddagger}]} \frac{d[A \cdot B^{\ddagger}]}{dt} = \frac{RT}{Nh} e^{+\Delta S_i/R}$$

where R is the gas constant per mole; T is the absolute temperature; N is Avogadro's number; and h is Planck's constant. The term ΔS_i represents the contribution to the entropy of $A \cdot B^{\ddagger}$ due to motion along the reaction coordinate. (Note: ΔS_i is a part of the partial molal entropy of the activated complex $A \cdot B^{\ddagger}$.) The reasoning necessary to obtain the absolute rate of breakdown of the activated complex has been presented in several equivalent forms by Eyring and his co-workers. All these developments involve more quantum mechanics than can be included in this text.

If the reaction is not diffusion controlled, $A \cdot B^{\ddagger}$ may be thought of as being in quasi-equilibrium with the reactants A and B. As demonstrated in the last chapter, this allows one to write

$$K = \frac{[A \cdot B^{\ddagger}]}{[A][B]} = e^{-\Delta G^0 / RT} \tag{7}$$

where ΔG^0 is the difference in the standard state between the free energy of $A \cdot B^{\ddagger}$ and $A + B$. Because the factor $-\Delta S_i/R$ appears shortly, it is convenient to divide ΔG^0 as

$$\Delta G^0 = \Delta G^{\ddagger} + T \Delta S_i$$

where the activation free energy $\Delta G^{\ddagger}$ is computed, omitting the contribution to the entropy from the reaction coordinate. Equation 7 may be rewritten

$$[A \cdot B^{\ddagger}] = [A][B] e^{-G^{\ddagger}/RT} e^{-\Delta S_i/R}$$

The absolute rate of transformation of $A \cdot B^{\ddagger}$ to C leads one to the expression

$$\frac{d[C]}{dt} = \frac{RT}{Nh} e^{\Delta S_i/R} [A \cdot B^{\ddagger}] = [A][B] \frac{RT}{Nh} e^{-\Delta G^{\ddagger}/RT}$$

From this equation, one finds that

$$k = \frac{1}{[A][B]} \cdot \frac{d[C]}{dt} = \frac{RT}{Nh} e^{-\Delta G^{\ddagger}/RT} \tag{8}$$

The term $\Delta G^{\ddagger}$ may be replaced as before giving

$$k = \frac{RT}{Nh} e^{-\Delta H^{\ddagger}/RT} e^{\Delta S^{\ddagger}/R} \tag{9}$$

Equation 9 contains the prediction that the slope of the Arrhenius plot should be $\Delta H^{\ddagger}$ (or $\Delta E^{\ddagger}$ as noted earlier). All the terms in Equation 9 may be found experimentally except $\Delta S^{\ddagger}$. Accordingly, it might be possible to test absolute rate theory by determining $\Delta S^{\ddagger}$ by some other means. If this is not possible, it is hard to see any real advantage to an arbitrary correction factor $\Delta S^{\ddagger}$ as opposed to the arbitrary product aZ of the Arrhenius collision theory.

For those familiar with quantum mechanics, a rigorous derivation of reaction rate theory can be found in the text by Kimball and Eyring. They show that under certain conditions the rate constant can be approximated by an expression of the type found in Equation 9. But even collision theory can be interpreted to give an expression of this type, as was previously noted. The really outstanding positive implication of absolute rate theory is that the complex $E \cdot S^{\ddagger}$ does have a physical existence, and that $\Delta S^{\ddagger}$ does have a real significance as an entropy change. These implications are extremely difficult to check in most enzyme reactions.

Equation 9 applies equally well to monomolecular reactions, bimolecular reactions, and polymolecular reactions, provided that one uses dimensionless concentration ratios in defining k. For any reaction except a monomolecular one, both k and $\Delta S^{\ddagger}$ have meaning only if they are specified relative to some standard state.

The term $\Delta S^{\ddagger}$ could in theory reveal a great deal about what is happening at the molecular level during the reaction. Various factors may contribute to $\Delta S^{\ddagger}$. For monomolecular reactions, $\Delta S^{\ddagger}$ represents a change in bond structure; a positive value means denaturation or loosening of bonds and a negative value the opposite. In polymolecular reactions, $\Delta S^{\ddagger}$ includes changes in bond structure as well as changes associated with decreasing the number of free particles in forming the activated complex. The values of $\Delta S^{\ddagger}$ are per mole so that the bond structure changes are independent of the standard state. However, the value of $\Delta S^{\ddagger}$ due to the change in the number of particles will depend on the standard state. (If charged molecules react, dielectric effects will also contribute to $\Delta S^{\ddagger}$.) In some reactions, such as that between hemoglobin and oxygen, it is possible by changing the standard states used to alter the sign of $\Delta S^{\ddagger}$. It is meaningless then, concerning a polymolecular reaction, to consider just the sign of $\Delta S^{\ddagger}$; it is necessary to consider how this value compares with that obtained by assuming that no changes occur in the bond structure, except along the reaction coordinate.

The activated complex $A \cdot B^{\ddagger}$ of absolute rate theory should not be confused with the intermediate complexes of Chapters 17 and 18; the two types of complexes are very different. The distinction can be illustrated as shown in Figure 5 for the reaction of hydrogen peroxide with catalase.   As discussed in Chapter 18, there is one intermediate complex formed; it is fairly stable and has a unique optical absorption spectrum.   The sketch in Figure 5 shows that there should be two activated complexes for this reaction although neither has been observed directly by any method.

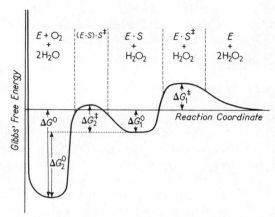

Figure 5. Absolute rate theory diagram for catalase.   This diagram distinguishes the activation energies and the free energy changes due to the reaction.   It also emphasizes the difference between the intermediate complex $E \cdot S$ and the activated complexes $E \cdot S^{\ddagger}$ and $(E \cdot S) \cdot S^{\ddagger}$.

There are several difficulties in the application of absolute rate theory to enzyme reactions.   First, it is difficult to do experiments over a wide enough temperature range to have significant values for $\Delta H^{\ddagger}$ and $\Delta S^{\ddagger}$. Second, it has never been determined whether or not most enzyme reactions are diffusion limited.   Unless this is known, the application of absolute rate theory is certainly questionable.   As noted previously, it is often quite difficult to arrive at an independent measure or even estimate of $\Delta S^{\ddagger}$.   Finally, no one has ever demonstrated any physical change associated with the formation of the activated complex.

Optical-spectrum absorption changes and magnetic moment changes have been observed for several intermediate complexes in the reactions of the heme proteins.   These increase our faith in the existence of intermediate complexes even for those enzymes for which no such change has ever been demonstrated.   However, the intermediate complexes were postulated long before any were ever observed.   It may be that new techniques will some day make possible the direct verification (or refutation) of the activated-complex hypothesis.

In addition to the foregoing, in the derivation of the absolute rate of transformation of the activated complex to its products, there are a number of approximations which could easily not apply to enzyme reactions. Unless one is able to observe the activated complex by physical measurements or can verify the entropy of activation by an independent set of measurements, one cannot rule out the possibility that absolute rate theory does not apply to some (or even all) enzyme reactions. In spite of these uncertainties, absolute rate theory forms the basis in terms of which reaction-rate data are often presented.

4. Denaturation Studies

Absolute rate theory applies in liquids only to reactions which are not diffusion limited.[3] All reactions which involve changes in one molecule only are by definition not limited by diffusion. This section deals with a particular type of monomolecular reaction characteristic of proteins. The changes produced by these reactions are called *denaturations*; they result from submitting the protein molecules to various physical changes such as heat, cold, vibration, and so on. If denaturation does not proceed too far, it may be reversible; under more extreme conditions, denaturation becomes irreversible.

Enzymes are particularly suitable for denaturation studies because small changes in their internal structure may produce dramatic changes in their rates of reactivity. Almost all enzymes rapidly lose their activity irreversibly at temperatures around the boiling point of water. By and large, the rate of denaturation depends exponentially on the reciprocal of the absolute temperature. The Arrhenius coefficients (or activation energies) vary widely but are all larger than 15 kcal/mole.

A typical denaturation study involves the rate at which trypsin digests a given protein. To observe reversible denaturation, one measures the rate of reaction at various temperatures. In the low temperature range, the slope of the Arrhenius plot is about 10 kcal/mole and the reaction can be described by the typical equations

$$E + S \rightleftharpoons E \cdot S$$

$$E \cdot S \rightarrow E + \text{Products}$$

where E is trypsin, S is the protein, and the products are the hydrolyzed (that is, split) protein.

---

[3] If the reaction is diffusion limited, absolute rate theory may be applied to the diffusion, but not to the reaction itself.

Above about 45°C, it is observed that the reaction rate increases less rapidly and then decreases as the temperature is raised.   If the trypsin is cooled, it regains its old activity.   This behavior may be represented as a competitive reaction

$$E \rightleftharpoons E^{\ddagger} \rightleftharpoons E'$$

where $E^{\ddagger}$ is an activated form and E' a reversibly denatured form of the enzyme.

At still higher temperatures, above 70°C, the reaction rate decreases further.   On cooling, the enzyme does not regain its original activity. Under these conditions, the trypsin is said to be irreversibly denatured. In the symbolism of absolute rate theory, this situation can be represented by

$$E' \rightleftharpoons E'^{\ddagger} \rightarrow E''$$

where E'' is the irreversibly denatured form.

It was noted previously that a monomolecular reaction such as a denaturation is not diffusion limited.   This in no way implies that the reaction does not depend on collisions.   Quite the opposite is the case. In the kinetic theory, heat energy is represented as random motion of the constituent particles.   In a fluid, the random vibrations of the protein molecule are thought of as continually bringing about collisions between one part of the protein and another, and between the parts of the protein molecule and the vibrating fluid molecules.   Denaturation will occur when an excess of energy is delivered by a series of collisions to a particular bond or group of bonds.

Absolute rate theory can be used successfully to describe denaturation, but collision theory has little to offer.   The difficulties of applying collision theory to a denaturation-type reaction are worse than for a bimolecular reaction.   Not only is one unable to quantify collision frequencies and probabilities, but one does not even know the location or the type of the critical colliding groups.   Thus, except for implying (correctly) that an Arrhenius coefficient should exist, collision theory per se can yield little insight into the nature of denaturation.   It offers no explanation for the spread of values of the energy of activation for denaturation, although it does imply correctly that these should be high in order that the enzymes be stable at room temperature.

The proponents of absolute rate theory have emphasized its application to denaturation studies.   On purely theoretical grounds, there is less reason in hesitating to apply it to these reactions than to any others. The reactions are essentially monomolecular, hence, there is no problem of diffusion.   The equilibrium between the activated form and the normal enzyme appears quite plausible. Finally, the assumptions necessary to derive the rate of decay of the activated form seem reasonable for denaturation-type reactions.

Stearn has collected data for a large number of denaturation-type reactions. These are summarized in the table on page 415. For irreversible reactions, data are given on the values of $\Delta H^{\ddagger}$ and $\Delta S^{\ddagger}$ to form the activated complex. For one reversible reaction, these and also values of ΔH^0 and ΔS^0 for the over-all equilibrium are listed. The lists are impressive but do not in themselves support absolute rate theory. Other evidence can be shown to make these numbers reasonable, and thereby justify the application of absolute rate theory to these reactions.

In order to compare these experimental results with theoretical predictions, an additional assumption is needed. This is that the activated form is similar to the final form of the molecule. For denaturation, this implies that chemical bonds are broken or at least weakened during the formation of the activated complex. Thus, one would expect that $\Delta S^{\ddagger}$ should be positive for all denaturations. (Because the standard state does not alter the value of $\Delta S^{\ddagger}$ for monomolecular reactions, it is possible to assign meaning to the sign of $\Delta S^{\ddagger}$ independent of the standard state.) It will be noted in the table that $\Delta S^{\ddagger}$ is indeed positive for all denaturations, as is ΔS^0, also.

By various means, different authors have estimated values for ΔH and ΔS associated with breaking the types of bonds found in proteins. The estimates for ΔH/bond vary from 4 to 8.5 kcal/mole, and for ΔS/bond from 10 to 15 kcal/(mole°K). Taking the average of ΔH/bond, one may express the probable number of broken bonds represented by the experimental values of $\Delta H^{\ddagger}$ and ΔH^0. Similarly, the experimental values of $\Delta S^{\ddagger}$ and ΔS^0 can be used to find a probable number of bonds broken. These estimates are shown in the following table. The differences are small in comparison to the range of theoretically calculated values for ΔH/bond. Thus, this evidence strongly supports absolute rate theory.

Although the values of $\Delta H^{\ddagger}$ vary by a very large amount from one enzyme to the next, the calculated values of $\Delta G^{\ddagger}$ are much more nearly constant. This has been interpreted as supporting absolute rate theory. However, the statement that $\Delta G^{\ddagger}$ is almost constant is equivalent to the statement that the denaturation rates are all within the same order of magnitude. Perhaps those enzymes with a more rapid denaturation rate cannot be studied, whereas those that are much less rapidly denatured are not attractive for denaturation studies.

In any case, it is clear that absolute rate theory is more useful than collision theory in a discussion of denaturation of enzymes. One may expect that this would be true of any monomolecular reaction in solution.

TABLE I

Thermodynamic Denaturation Constants for Various Proteins*

Substance	$\Delta H^{\ddagger}$	$\Delta S^{\ddagger}$ (meas.) (1)	Bonds broken, no.[†]	$\Delta S^{\ddagger}$ (calc.) (2)	Ratio (1)/(2)
Enterokinase	42,200	52.8	8	96	0.55
Trypsin kinase	44,300	57.6	9	108	0.53
Proteinase, pancreatic	37,900	40.6	7	84	0.48
Lipase, pancreatic	45,400	68.2	9	108	0.63
Amylase, malt	41,600	52.3	8	96	0.55
Emulsin	44,900	65.3	9	108	0.60
Average					0.56
Pepsin	55,600	113.3	11	132	0.86
Leucosin	84,300	185.0	17	204	0.91
Egg albumin	132,000	315.7	26	312	1.01
Hemoglobin	75,600	152.7	15	180	0.85
Hemolysin, goat	198,000	537.0	40	480	1.12
Vibriolysin	128,000	326.0	26	312	1.04
Tetanolysin	172,600	459.0	36	432	1.06
Peroxidase, milk	185,300	466.0	37	444	1.05
Rennin	89,300	208.0	18	216	0.96
Average					0.99
Trypsin	40,200	44.7	8	96	0.47
Trypsin	67,600[§]	213.0[‖]	14	168	1.27
Egg albumin					
pH 7.7	134,300	317.1	27	324	0.98
pH 3.4	96,800	223.7	19	228	0.98
Yeast invertase					
pH 5.7	52,400	84.7	10	120	0.71
pH 5.2	86,400	185.0	17	204	0.91
pH 4.0	110,400	262.5	22	264	0.995
pH 3.0	74,400	152.4	15	180	0.85
Egg albumin					
pH 1.35	35,200	36.3	—	—	—

* $\Delta H^{\ddagger}$ in cal per mole; $\Delta S^{\ddagger}$ in cal per mole per degree.
† Computed from number of broken bonds = $\Delta H^{\ddagger}/5,000$; $\Delta S^{\ddagger}$ calc. = (Number of broken bonds) · 12.
§ ΔH^{0} for denaturation.
‖ ΔS^{0} for denaturation.

After A. E. Stearn, "Kinetics of Biological Reactions with Special Reference to Enzymic Processes," pp. 25–74, in *Advances in Enzymology*, **9**. (New York: Interscience Publishers, Inc., 1949.)

5. Diffusion Studies

To properly apply absolute rate theory to enzyme reactions, other than denaturation, it is necessary to know whether the reactions are diffusion controlled.   Surprisingly little information is available in the literature on this subject.   The reactions of the transport protein, hemoglobin, with oxygen and carbon monoxide have been shown to be independent of the diffusion rate at room temperature.   However, for the catalatic reaction of the heme-type enzyme, catalase, with hydrogen peroxide, it has been shown that the reaction rate constants, k_1 and k_3, both become diffusion controlled at viscosities several times that of water.[4]   The reaction of the heme protein, myoglobin, with oxygen is similar in its diffusion dependence to that of catalase with hydrogen peroxide.   The intermediates of horse-radish peroxidase react with reduced cytochrome c at rates which are altered both by the viscosity of the medium and also by the dielectric constant.

The results for catalase can be used in the diffusion-controlled region to compute a radius r for the active site at which the hydrogen peroxide reacts.   It can be shown that the encounter rate is

$$Z_e = DrNf\Omega \cdot 10^{-3} \tag{10}$$

where

D = diffusion constant in cm^2/sec
r = radius in cm
N = Avogadro's number
f = factor which includes electrostatic effects
Ω = solid angle through which the molecules may approach one another to react.

When catalase reacts with hydrogen peroxide, the rates of reaction are independent of dielectric constant, ionic strength, and pH.   Therefore, the factor f in Equation 10 will be one.   In the diffusion-controlled region, k_1 and k_3 for catalase will be approximately equal to Z_e.   A graph of k_1 or k_3 plotted as a function of D allows one to evaluate $r\Omega$. If it is assumed that the hydrogen peroxide can diffuse at any angle within a hemisphere, it is found that for both k_1 and k_3

$$r \doteq 1 \text{ Å}$$

The small value indicates strongly that the reaction occurs at the iron atom in the heme group on the catalase, and that the protein does not act as a semiconductor for the purposes of this reaction.

Similar experiments for cytochrome c and horse-radish peroxidase indicate that electrostatic effects are important, the two reactants behaving as dipoles oriented to oppose the reaction.   Using dipole moments of one electron-Å, it is found that the closest approach is

---

[4] See Chapter 18 for definition of k_1 and k_3 for this reaction.

about 1.5 Å. In other words, it is necessary for the iron atoms in the two heme groups to come directly into contact with one another.

In the diffusion-independent region, absolute rate theory may be applied to both the catalase and the peroxidase reaction. The accompanying table summarizes the data. It can be seen that low values for $\Delta H^{\ddagger}$ do not imply diffusion control.

TABLE II

Absolute Rate Theory Parameters for Catalase and Peroxidase

Enzyme	Rate Constant	$\Delta H^{\ddagger}$	$\Delta S^{\ddagger}$ re 1 M
Catalase*	k_1	0 kcal/mole	-25 entropy units/mole
Catalase*	k_3	5	-7
Peroxidase*	k_5	8	-5

* Cf. Chapter 18 for definition of rate constants.

The values of $\Delta S^{\ddagger}$ were computed relative to a standard state of 1 mole per liter concentration of all reactants in water-like solutions. If no changes occurred in bond structure in forming the activated complex, one would predict that 7 entropy units would be lost owing to fewer particles present. Thus, the second and third reactions in the table are, within experimental error, in agreement with this number. The values for $\Delta S^{\ddagger}$ suggest that the activated complex does not alter or restrict the freedom of the reactants, except to the extent that they may be regarded as one instead of two molecules.[5]

The value of $-\Delta S^{\ddagger}$ for k_1 is much higher. An attempt to estimate a maximum for $-\Delta S^{\ddagger}$ indicates that if all the freedom of the peroxide were lost, $\Delta S^{\ddagger}$ should be -28 entropy units/mole. Thus, the intermediate value observed is in accord with the concept that most of the entropy of the peroxide is lost.

6. Summary

In this chapter, thermodynamics and kinetic theory have been applied to a discussion of enzyme rate constants. Two types of theories were discussed, collision theory and absolute rate theory. The first is always valid but is difficult to apply to enzyme reactions because it introduces the product of two factors, neither of which can be measured or computed directly. However, collision theory does predict correctly that

---

[5] An alternative interpretation is that bound water must be released during the formation of the activated complex. As this would increase the entropy, there would then have to be a loss of freedom on the part of the reactants.

most rate constants should have an exponential dependence on temperature. A graph of the natural logarithm of the rate constant plotted against $1/RT$ is called an *Arrhenius plot*. The negative of the slope of the resulting straight line is called an *activation energy* or *Arrhenius constant*.

Reactions in a liquid may be diffusion controlled or diffusion independent. The last may be treated by the second type of thermodynamic theory called *absolute rate theory*. It is based on quantum mechanics. It considers any reaction to consist first of the formation of an activated complex and then its dissociation to products. Absolute rate theory interprets the Arrhenius constant as the energy (or enthalpy) necessary to form the activated complex. It allows one to compute an entropy of activation. This leads to consistent values for denaturation reactions, but its meaning is ambiguous in the case of reactions of some heme proteins.

REFERENCES

1. Glasstone, Samuel, *Textbook of Physical Chemistry* 2nd ed. (New York: D. Van Nostrand Company, Inc., 1946).
2. Eyring, Henry, J. E. Walter, and G. E. Kimball, *Quantum Chemistry* (New York: John Wiley & Sons, Inc., 1944).
3. Glasstone, Samuel, K. J. Laidler, and Henry Eyring, *Theory of Rate Processes: The Kinetics of Chemical Reactions, Viscosity, Diffusion, and Electrochemical Phenomena* (New York: McGraw-Hill Book Company, Inc., 1941).
4. Friess, S. L., and A. Weissberger, *Technique of Organic Chemistry.* Vol. 8. *Investigation of Rates and Mechanisms of Reactions* (New York: Interscience Publishers, Inc., 1953).
   a. Livingston, Robert, "General Theory of Rate Processes," pp. 1–68.
   b. Livingston, Robert, "Evaluation and Interpretation of Rate Data," pp. 169–230.
   c. Chap. 6: "Reactions in the Liquid Phase," pp. 303–420.
      (1) Leffler, J. E., and Ernest Grunwald: Part 1. "General Methods of Study," pp. 303–335.
      (2) Morse, B. Kathleen, and S. L. Friess: Part 2. "Specific Experimental Techniques," pp. 335–420.
5. Stearn, A. E., "Kinetics of Biological Reactions With Special Reference to Enzymic Processes," Nord, F. F., ed., *Advances in Enzymology and Related Subjects of Biochemistry* (New York: Interscience Publishers, Inc., 1949) Vol. 9, pp. 25–74.
6. Ackerman, Eugene, R. L. Berger, and G. K. Strother, "Effects of Temperature on Formation of Intermediate Compound of Catalase With H_2O_2," Johnson, F. H., ed., *Influence of Temperature on Biological Systems* (Washington, D.C.: American Physiological Society, 1957) pp. 25–35.
7. Johnson, F. H., Henry Eyring, and M. J. Polissar, *The Kinetic Basis of Molecular Biology* (New York: John Wiley & Sons, Inc., 1954).

23

Diffusion, Permeability, and Active Transport

I. Introduction

In the preceding chapter, the theory and terminology of thermodynamics were used to discuss the rate constants of enzymatically catalyzed reactions. In the current chapter and in the following one, the motions of molecules in diffusing through living systems and in permeating cell walls are presented. The treatment of diffusion and permeability is similar to the discussion of enzyme kinetics in that both are strongly based on the ideas of energy and of thermodynamic equilibrium.

Diffusion is a very rapid process when it occurs within a single biological cell. However, on a macroscopic scale it may be very slow if unaided by stirring and convection. For example, if one puts several spoonfuls of sugar into a cup of coffee, the sugar will sink to the bottom. Soon, there will be a thin layer of coffee which is saturated with sugar. In the absence of stirring, the sugar molecules will slowly spread, that is, diffuse, throughout the coffee. On the gross scale of the coffee cup, it may take days to approach equilibrium. (Usually we stir the sugar into the coffee rather than waiting for diffusion.) On the microscopic scale of biological cells, and on the still smaller scale of reacting molecules, diffusion becomes very rapid. To diffuse throughout a cell requires only milliseconds.

From the point of view of molecules, the diffusing solute may be thought of as jumping from one quasi-equilibrium site to the next, perhaps an Ångström unit away. There will be greater probability of a molecule jumping from a region of higher concentration than vice versa. Thus, diffusion will lead toward an equalizing of concentration. When the concentration is equal throughout the container, the partial molal free energy $\tilde{G}$ will also be equal throughout. Diffusion leads toward the equilibrium condition:

$$d\tilde{G} = 0$$

At boundaries separated by membranes (for example, cell membranes), the rate of diffusion may be markedly slowed. Although not really a different type of phenomenon, the rate of diffusion through a limiting membrane is called the *permeability*. Most membranes are permeable only to certain substances. If the concentrations of substances to which the membrane is impermeable are different on the two sides of the membrane, the solvent will tend to move toward the greater concentration. This is described by assigning an osmotic pressure to the solution.

When some of the molecules which cannot pass the boundary are charged, an electrical potential may be developed across the membrane. This is called a *Donnan potential*. In this case, the equilibrium concentrations of the ionic species may be different on the two sides of the membrane.

In Chapter 4, on the conduction of nerve impulses, it was pointed out that the ion concentrations inside nerve axons are different from those outside. These differences cannot be explained by passive diffusion through a membrane subject only to osmotic and electrical forces. Rather, certain ions are actively transported at the ultimate expense of metabolic energy. Active transport is not restricted to membranes of axons. Forced diffusion in a direction different than indicated by electrical and concentration gradients probably is a common occurrence in all cells.

Many experiments have been carried out to measure diffusion rates and permeabilities, as well as to demonstrate the role of active transport against electrochemical gradients. Behind each of these experiments, indeed as an essential part of each, is the mathematical theory of diffusion and permeability. Without it, the experiments would be meaningless. In this chapter, the basic mathematical development is presented. It is hoped that the reader will not be misled into feeling that the experiments are less important than the theory, for this is surely not the case.

The mathematical theory can never be completely divorced from experiment any more than the opposite is possible.

The development both of the individual sections and of the over-all chapter illustrates the approach of the mathematical physicist as well as of the biophysicist. One feature of this approach is to start with simple idealized situations which can be described exactly by mathematical formulae. These are then gradually expanded, improved, made to correspond more exactly to nature. In the process, the theories may become mathematically cumbersome, but throughout the entire development, the intuitive picture is colored and influenced by the simple, idealized approximation which can be exactly solved.

2. Diffusion Equations

The example of diffusion which is easiest to describe in mathematical terms is that in which diffusion occurs in one dimension (direction) only. This mathematical development is presented in this section, the more

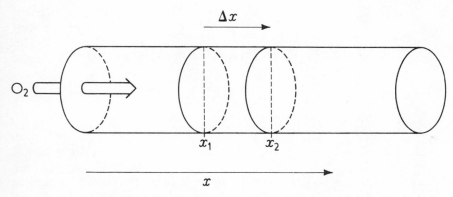

Figure I. One-dimensional diffusion. In this figure, oxygen is considered to be diffusing down a long pipe, such that the concentration is constant all over the plane at x_1. The concentration value at a second plane at x_2 however may be different from that at the plane at x_1.

general case of three dimensions being left to the reader. The unidimensional situation can be visualized as some substance, for example O_2, diffusing through a liquid which fills a long pipe of constant cross-sectional area A. This is illustrated in Figure 1. With suitable precautions, the concentration c of the O_2 will be constant throughout any given cross section. In contrast, c will vary from one cross section to the next.   At any given cross section, c will also vary in time.   These variations can be described by a single partial differential equation.   This equation will now be developed.

Consider two planes at x_1 and x_2, spaced as shown in Figure 1.   In a homogeneous liquid, the probability of a molecule jumping either in the $+x$ or $-x$ direction is equal.   The mass per unit time of molecules jumping from plane x_1 to plane x_2 will be proportional to the concentration c_1 at x_1.   Likewise, the mass per unit time going from x_2 to x_1 will be proportional to c_2.   These masses will also be proportional to the cross-sectional area A.   Analytically, one may express this as

$$\frac{\Delta m}{\Delta t} = \beta A(c_1 - c_2) = -\beta A \Delta c \qquad (1)$$

where Δm is the net mass transfer in the $+x$ direction across the surface at x_2, and β is a probability parameter.

It seems clear that if the two planes x_1 and x_2 are far enough apart, the probability constant β must be very low, whereas if they are close, β should be large.   The exact dependence of β on the separation can be approximated by

$$\beta = \frac{D}{x_2 - x_1} = \frac{D}{\Delta x} \qquad (2)$$

where D is a constant.   Then Equation 1 may be rewritten

$$\frac{\Delta m}{\Delta t} = -DA \frac{\Delta c}{\Delta x}$$

Taking the limits as Δt and Δx go to zero reduces this to

$$\frac{\partial m}{\partial t} = -DA \frac{\partial c}{\partial x} \qquad (3)$$

Equation 3 can be derived starting from thermodynamics as well as from other points of view.   Although several of these add refinements, they all contain the basic assumption made in writing Equation 2.   This assumption can be justified empirically because experiments with a wide variety of gases and solutes in different solvents confirm Equation 3. For most purposes, it is correct; however, it is meaningless to apply Equation 3 to distances of the order of a few angstrom units or times comparable to the period that a molecule remains in a quasi-equilibrium state (10^{-14} sec).   The cases discussed in the remainder of this chapter have been restricted to those to which Equation 3 can be applied.

Equation 3 is all that is necessary to mathematically analyze the diffusion problems encountered in this text.   The constant D is called the diffusion constant or sometimes the *Fick diffusion constant*.   Equation 3 is often called the *Fick diffusion equation* or *Fick's law*. It can be expressed in an alternate form which is easier to handle, although conceptually identical. To derive this alternative form, consider again the pipe of constant cross section A, and so on, redrawn in Figure 2. The mass

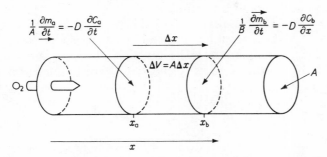

Figure 2. One-dimensional diffusion and continuity. This figure is used to illustrate the relationship of the change of concentration within ΔV to the O_2 diffusing in at x_a and out at x_b.

change per unit time in the volume ΔV between planes x_a and x_b is the difference between that entering at x_a and that leaving at x_b. That is

$$\frac{1}{A} \Delta \left(\frac{\partial m}{\partial t} \right) = D \left[\frac{\partial c_b}{\partial x} - \frac{\partial c_a}{\partial x} \right]$$

or dividing both sides by Δx and taking the limit as Δx goes to zero,

$$\frac{\partial c}{\partial t} = D \frac{\partial^2 c}{\partial x^2} \tag{4}$$

This is an alternative form of Equation 3, valid for the case in which no oxygen is generated or destroyed.

Equation 4 can be readily generalized to the three-dimensional diffusion equation as

$$\frac{\partial c}{\partial t} = D \left[\frac{\partial^2 c}{\partial x^2} + \frac{\partial^2 c}{\partial y^2} + \frac{\partial^2 c}{\partial z^2} \right] \tag{5}$$

Both Equations 3 and 5 may be written in the vector notation. By defining the mass current $\vec{J}$ as

$$\vec{J} = \left(\frac{1}{A} \frac{\partial m}{\partial t} \right) \vec{n} \tag{6}$$

where $\vec{n}$ is a unit vector normal to A, Equation 3 may be rewritten as

$$\vec{J} = D \vec{\nabla} c \tag{7}$$

In vector notation, Equation 5 becomes

$$\frac{\partial c}{\partial t} = D\nabla^2 c \tag{8}$$

Equations 8 and 5 as well as Equation 3 are often called *Fick's diffusion equation* or *Fick's law*. Equation 8 is also referred to by physicists and chemists as "the heat equation" because its form is identical to that for the variation of temperature as a function of space and time in the absence of any sources or sinks[1] of heat. Although the substance considered in Equations 3 and 5 was called oxygen for convenience, there is nothing that restricts the use of these equations to oxygen. They are restricted, however, to the case in which the substance is not being either generated or used up chemically.

Actually, oxygen is almost always either being used or being liberated within a living cell. In most cells it is being used, and in others that are photosynthesizing, it is being produced. If the rate of production per unit volume is called q, Equation 8 must be replaced by

$$\frac{\partial c}{\partial t} = D\nabla^2 c + q \tag{9}$$

A negative value of q implies use of oxygen (or, at any rate, of the substance to which the equation applies). In general, the production rate q may vary with x, y, z, and t in any arbitrary manner. Equation 9 is known as the *inhomogeneous* diffusion equation.

Equation 9 is the final form of the diffusion equation which is developed here. It can be used to analyze many different types of situations of biological significance, some of which will be considered in subsequent sections of this chapter. However, Equation 9 is not in a form which is useful at cell membranes. The remainder of the current section is devoted to deriving suitable expressions, describing mathematically the permeability of cell membranes. These, when combined with Equation 3, 5, or 9 as appropriate, are used in the problems considered in the remainder of this chapter.

Across the membrane there may be a very large change in concentration. In theory, the membrane and surrounding fluids could be treated as three regions, as indicated in Figure 3. In each region there will be a different diffusion constant. By and large, the membranes are so thin that no empirical meaning can be assigned to the concentration c_2 within the membrane. Instead, the membrane is usually characterized

---

[1] A heat sink is a place where heat energy is removed (of course being converted into some other type of energy).

by a permeability k such that the mass per unit time passing through the membrane is given by

$$\frac{1}{A}\frac{\partial m}{\partial t} = k(c_1 - c_3)|_{membrane} \tag{10}$$

This in turn must equal the mass flux entering and leaving the membrane. The equations describing this are

$$D_1 \frac{\partial c_1}{\partial x}\bigg|_0 = -k\left(c_1\bigg|_0 - c_3\bigg|_h\right) = D_3 \frac{\partial c_3}{\partial x}\bigg|_h \tag{11}$$

Equations 9 and 11, with the proper values for the diffusion coefficient D, the permeability k, and the rate of generation of the substance q, completely define all biological diffusion problems, from a mathematical point of view.[2] Although in principle they can always be solved, in practice this is not always easy. In the remainder of the chapter, certain examples are worked out. However, there are two restrictions to Equations 9 and 10 which should be noted.

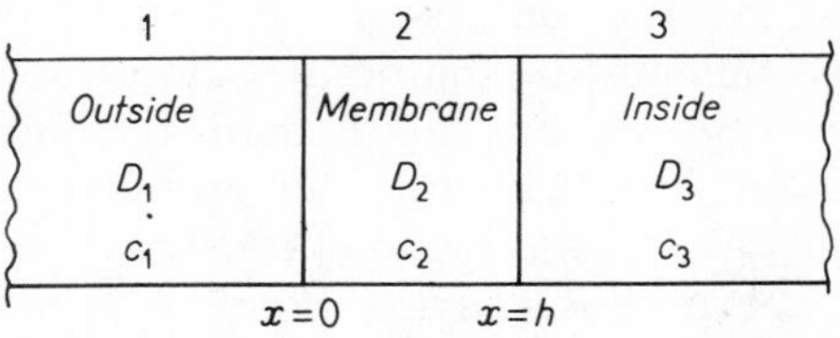

1	2	3
Outside	Membrane	Inside
D_1	D_2	D_3
c_1	c_2	c_3

$x=0 \qquad x=h$

Figure 3. Idealized membrane. This is used in permeability discussions. The membranes around many cells and subcellular structures are actually three layers thick. The outer two layers are believed to be protein monolayers, whereas the central layer is phospholipid about two molecules thick.

First, it has been assumed that stirring did not occur. If random or turbulent stirring is present, one may include it by using appropriately larger values for D. It also has been implicitly assumed in the foregoing derivation that no electrical potential gradients are present. Most protoplasm conducts electrical charge so well that potential gradients can exist only across the membranes. If these are present, Equation 11 must be modified, replacing the middle expression by

$$-k\left(c_1\bigg|_0 e^{-zFV/RT} - c_3\bigg|_h\right)$$

where z is the charge on the ion, F the Faraday, R the gas constant per mole, T the absolute temperature, and V the electrical potential difference across the membrane. This extra factor occurs because the partial molal free energies inside and outside differ by zFV when the concentrations are equal.

[2] Throughout this chapter, the purist will insist that it would be better to use activities than concentrations. Although this is true, there appears to be little advantage in this distinction in the examples discussed in this chapter.

3. The Diffusion of Oxygen into Cells

There are many applications of the equations developed in the last section. In this chapter, three applications will be discussed. These are the diffusion of oxygen in single cells, the permeability of red blood cells, and the evidence for active transport across cell membranes.

In the absence of active transport, the problem of oxygen diffusion is one of finding a suitable solution to Equations 9 and 11, subject to the concentration of oxygen far from the cell being held constant. In mathematical terms, this is a boundary-value problem. Equation 9 is studied in heat problems and in quantum mechanics. No matter what significance one assigns to the symbols, Equation 9 always has the same mathematical solutions. Only in certain very special geometrical symmetries are mathematical solutions in a closed form[3] possible. That is, in general, the problem can be solved only numerically by means of lengthy computational procedures.

From this starting point, one may take several approaches to the oxygen-diffusion problem (besides the trivial one of giving up altogether). The first is to restrict the discussion to cases in which permeability plays the dominant role. This is pursued in Section 4.

If effects other than permeability are considered, there still remain several avenues of approach. The most exact is to set up the problem for a numerical solution by a high-speed electronic computer. This has the disadvantage of yielding only very specialized solutions and little or no insight into the general nature of diffusion problems; it will not be pursued further here. Another course is to approximate all values by average ones. This is discussed briefly below. The other approach considered in this section is to approximate the cell by a geometry (namely spherical) in which Equation 9 can be solved.

The Average-Value Approach

In this approach, any arbitrary-shaped cell is approximated by either a rod or a pillbox. The ends are treated as circles and the curved sides are further approximated as planes. Finally, it is assumed that the average concentration $\bar{c}$ exists throughout the inner part of the cell. This allows one to approximate the concentration gradient at the inside of the cell wall by

$$\left.\frac{\partial c}{\partial r}\right|_{r_1} \doteq \frac{2(c_1 - \bar{c})}{r_1}$$

where c_1 is the concentration at r_1 (see Figure 4).

---

[3] That is to say, a solution exists in terms of known or tabulated functions.

It is further necessary to assume that in a short distance δ the concentration c' outside the cell reaches the value c_0' it has at long distances. Then the concentration gradient outside the cell wall may be approximated as

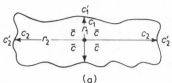

$$\left.\frac{\partial c'}{\partial r}\right|_{r'} = \frac{c_0' - c_1}{\delta}$$

where r' is the average cell radius.

With some juggling, it is possible to rewrite Equations 9 and 11 as

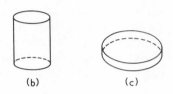

(a)

$$\frac{d\bar{c}}{dt} \doteq -3D\left(\frac{\bar{c} - c_1}{r_1^2}\right) - 3D\left(\frac{\bar{c} - c_2}{r_2^2}\right) + \bar{q}$$

$$2D\frac{(\bar{c} - c_1)}{r_1} = k(c_1 - c_1') = D'\frac{c_1 - c_0'}{\delta}$$

(b)   (c)

$$2D\frac{(\bar{c} - c_2)}{r_2} = k(c_2 - c_2') = D'\frac{c_2' - c_0'}{\delta}$$

where D' is the diffusion constant outside the cell.

These terms may be further approximated to show that for the case

$$\bar{q} = \text{constant}$$

one may write

$$\bar{c} = c_0 + \lambda\bar{q} + A\lambda e^{-t/\lambda}$$

$$\bar{c} \xrightarrow[t\to 0]{} c_0 + \lambda\bar{q} + A\lambda \qquad \bar{c} \xrightarrow[t\to\infty]{} c_0 + \lambda\bar{q} \quad (12)$$

In this expression, c_0 and λ are complicated constants involving the parameters k, D, D', r_1, and r_2. This entire approach is developed in detail in the reference by Rashevsky; it is hoped that more mathematically inclined readers will refer to this text.

Figure 4. The average value approach. An arbitrary cell is shown in Figure (a) with average radii r_1 and r_2. It is assumed that the concentration in the central part of the cell is constant reaching the value of the average concentration $\bar{c}$ at $r_1/2$ and $r_2/2$ from the center. It is further assumed that the cell can be replaced by a rod or pillbox as shown in Figures (b) and (c). The general patterns of diffusion which do not depend on exact cell geometry are then investigated. After N. Rashevsky, *Mathematical Biophysics* (Chicago: University of Chicago Press, 1948).

The approximate expression, Equation 12, emphasizes that after a sufficient length of time a steady state will be set up if $\bar{q}$ is time independent. The preceding solution also shows the form of result to expect from any approximation. Comparing Equation 12 with exact expressions for spheres allows one to demonstrate that the exact cell shape is not important.

Spherical-Cell Approximations

A mathematically less cumbersome technique than that of the average-value method is to replace the cell by a model of simple geometry and solve the problem exactly. As indicated above, there will, in general, exist a steady-state solution. This is usually the only one which can be measured.

In this subsection, the diffusion of oxygen into a living cell is approximated by a steady-state spherical model. The rate of use of oxygen per unit volume q is assumed constant if the concentration c of oxygen inside the cell is greater than zero. Depending upon the cell radius r_0, the diffusion constants inside and outside the cell D and D', and the permeability k, there may exist a region in the center of the cell in which the oxygen concentration is zero. The symbol r_α will be used to designate the radius of this last region.

For this case, Equations 9 and 10 may be written as

$$\text{Outside} \quad r > r_0 \qquad \frac{D'}{r^2}\frac{d^2(r^2 c')}{dr^2} = 0$$

$$\text{Inside} \quad r_0 > r > r_\alpha \qquad \frac{D}{r^2}\frac{d^2(r^2 c)}{dr^2} = -q \tag{9'}$$

$$r_\alpha < r \qquad\qquad c = 0$$

$$\text{Membrane } r = r_0 \;\; D'\frac{dc'}{dr} = k(c - c') = D\frac{dc}{dr} \tag{10'}$$

In addition, one may require

$$\text{Far outside } r = \infty \qquad\qquad c' = c_0'$$

This set of equations appears complex but, actually, it is one of the simplest cases. The mathematically trained can easily show that a solution is

$$c' = c_0' + \frac{q}{3}\frac{r_0^3 - r_a^3}{D}\frac{1}{r} \qquad\qquad r > r_0 \tag{13}$$

$$c = c_0' + \frac{q'_0}{3k} + \frac{q}{6D}(r_0^2 - r^2) + \frac{qr_0^2}{3D'} - \frac{qr_\alpha^3}{3}\left(\frac{1}{D'r_0} - \frac{1}{Dr_0} + \frac{1}{kr_0^2} + \frac{1}{3Dr}\right)$$

$$r_0 > r > r_\alpha \tag{14}$$

$$c = 0 \qquad\qquad r_\alpha > r$$

If no oxygen-free region exists, slightly different equations and solutions can be written. However, their general character is not altered.

Equations 13 and 14 can be tested experimentally. There can be little doubt that the experimental values for oxygen uptake by single cells plotted as a function of oxygen pressure fail to fit these theoretical predictions. The steady-state, spherical model can be brought closer to the experimental data by including several steps in the utilization of O_2; these alter the values for q. Mathematically, if one is willing to include enough arbitrary constants, one can fit any experimental curve. The model in Figure 5 is supported by some biochemical evidence and can fit any measured curve merely by juggling parameters.

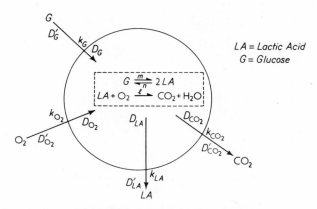

Figure 5. Spherical-cell model. This model with its numerous constants can account for O_2 diffusion into living cells. The model is also supported by metabolic studies of other types.

The spherical-cell model shows that a simple assumption such as the constancy of the rate of oxygen utilization cannot be maintained. More complex chemical reactions and equilibria must be included to fit the O_2-uptake data. Although diffusion and permeability play an important role, they are not the only rate-limiting steps in the intracellular use of O_2.

4. Permeability of Red Blood Cells

The mathematical problems of analyzing diffusion into biological cells can be greatly simplified if the rate at which a substance penetrates the cell membrane is slow compared to its rate of diffusion on either side of this membrane. Mammalian red blood cells have proved very useful for studies of this nature. They are especially convenient because the cells act as "osmometers," swelling or shrinking accordingly as their internal osmotic pressure varies. In spite of very large variations in the volume, the surface area of the erythrocytes remains almost constant.

In this fashion, the volume can be used to indicate the internal concentrations, and because the surface area remains constant, one may compute the permeability constant k. In actual practice, the area is constant and not measured; rather the permeability P is used. It is defined by

$$P = kA_r \tag{15}$$

where A_r is the surface area of the erythrocyte.

Equation 10 is particularly suited to this case. If S is the mass of substance s inside the cell, then Equation 10 becomes

$$\frac{\partial S}{\partial t} = kA_r(c_i - c_S) \tag{16}$$

where c_i and c_S are the concentrations of s inside and outside the cell, respectively. Because diffusion occurs rapidly as compared to penetration of the cell membrane, c_i may be replaced using

$$c_i = \frac{S}{V}$$

where V is the cell volume[4]. Equation 16 can then be rewritten

$$\frac{\partial S}{\partial t} = P\left(\frac{S}{V} - c_S\right) \tag{17}$$

As the concentration of substance s within the cell rises, there will be a flow of water into the cell. This will result, in turn, in a change of the cell volume V. The flow of water must also obey Equation 10 for the mass flow through the cell wall. It takes a few algebraic manipulations to rewrite this equation for water flow as

$$\frac{dV}{dt} = P_W\left(\frac{c_0V_0 + S}{V} - c_S - c_M\right) \tag{18}$$

where c_0 is the initial concentration of nonpenetrating solutes within the cell, V_0 the initial cell volume, and c_M the concentration of nonpenetrating solutes in the external medium. If more than one penetrating solute is present, S and c_S must be regarded as the sum of all the various values.

If the volume changes are observed, Equations 17 and 18 may be used to compute values for P and P_W. In the most general case, only numerical solutions are possible. There exist, however, a number of simplified conditions under which P and P_W may be found.

First, if there are no nonpenetrating solutes in the external medium,

[4] The symbol V is used for volume in this section. The same symbol is used for electrical potential in Sections 2 and 5 of this chapter.

c_M may be set equal to zero. If, in addition, there are no penetrating solutes, S and c_S will also be zero. Equation 15 can also be simplified for solutes penetrating far more rapidly than water. Such solutes can be described by $c_S = S/V$ because a rapidly penetrating solute will equilibrate before a change in water occurs. In either case, that is, no penetrating solutes or very rapidly penetrating ones, Equation 18 may be approximated by

$$\frac{dV}{dt} = P_W\left(\frac{c_0 V_0}{V}\right)$$

which can be integrated directly to give

$$V^2 = V_0^2 + 2P_W c_0 V_0 t \tag{19}$$

Equation 19 may be used to find the value of P_W for erythrocytes. The value per unit surface area is 10 to 30 times greater than for most other biological cells. This high value will be commented on further in the next section.

Because the value of P_W is so high for red blood cells, it follows that most solutes will penetrate more slowly than water. Then, one may solve Equation 17 for the penetration of the solute, assuming that the water equilibrium is attained instantaneously. This is equivalent to the assumption that the external concentration c_S is always iso-osmotic with c_0, the original concentration within the cell (provided that c_M is zero). Accordingly, one may write

$$S \doteq c_S(V - V_0) \qquad \text{or} \qquad dS \doteq c_S dV$$

This last differential may be substituted into Equation 17, describing the flow of s into the cell. The variable S disappears, giving

$$\frac{dV}{dt} = -P\frac{c_S V_0}{V}$$

On integrating, this becomes

$$V^2 = V_0^2 - Pc_S V_0 t \tag{20}$$

Using this relationship, the permeability P may be found for all solutes which penetrate less rapidly than water.

Equations 19 and 20 allow one to compute the time for 90 per cent saturation of the cell, assuming that diffusion within the cell is sufficiently rapid that the concentration within the cell is constant. Similarly, Equation 5 could be used, assuming that P was infinite. Such calculations have been carried out for a number of different solutes. It was found that the times for intracellular diffusion are negligible compared to the time for permeating the cell membrane.

The values for P and D vary in very different fashions from one solute to the next. For large molecules, for example, the diffusion constant D varies roughly as the square root of the reciprocal of the molecular weight. On the other hand, the permeability for urea is

$$k = \frac{P}{A} = 7{,}000 \text{ cm/hr}$$

whereas for glycerol it is 54 cm/hr and for sucrose 0 cm/hr. Moreover, the times for 90 per cent saturation for these three solutes would all be less than 10^{-3} sec, if the limitation of the cell membrane could be ignored, but range from 0.5 sec to ∞, including the limitations at the membranes.

Certain general rules can be found for the relative values of P measured for erythrocytes. First, the more soluble the solute is in lipids, the greater is the value for P. For example, glycerol has a much lower value for P than does its larger, lipid soluble ester, monacetin. Therefore part, at least, of the red blood cell membranes appears to be of a lipid nature. (This is also supported by other lines of evidence; however, it appears unlikely that the lipid forms a simple film or monolayer around the cell.)

The second general rule for the variations of P is that, given the same lipid solubility, the smaller molecule goes through faster. For instance, the rates for ethylene glycol, diethylene glycol, and triethylene glycol decrease in the order of increasing molecular weights. This supports a molecular-sieve picture of the cell membrane in which bigger molecules, even though lipid soluble, have a hard time going through the pores.

In spite of these general rules, there exist other molecules such as water, urea, and sodium ions, which appear to go through the cell membrane at inordinately high rates. No simple picture of the cell membrane can explain these very high rates. One must think of the cell membrane as in some sense actively transporting certain molecular species.

5. Active Transport

The extremely high permeability constants of erythrocyte membranes for certain molecules suggest that in some fashion the cell membrane actively moves these molecules rather than merely permitting them to passively diffuse through the membrane, as described in Section 2 of this chapter. Similar evidence for active transport comes from a variety of other sources. It appears probable that all membranes actively transport certain substances.   In Chapters 4 and 8, it was stated that the concentration of potassium ions within nerve axons and muscle fibers is higher than in the surrounding solution, whereas the concentration of sodium ions was lower.   Because these membranes are charged, it is not sufficient to merely measure concentration differences; the concentrations must be compared with those predicted for the electrical potential differences measured across the membrane.   This reasoning shows that the Na^+ ions, although demonstrated by tracer techniques to pass from the outside medium into the cell, must be continually pumped out against an electrochemical gradient to maintain equilibrium.

Whenever molecules and ions are pumped against an electrochemical gradient, the phenomenon may be called *active transport*.   This has been demonstrated to occur in the kidney tubules, in the epithelium of the stomach mucosa (H^+ transport), in the epithelium of the intestines (transport of ions, water, simple sugars, fatty acids, amino acids, and so on), and in frog skin.   Active transport may involve this pumping against an electrochemical gradient, or it may involve pumping to increase the net flow in the direction of an electrochemical gradient, as perhaps the entrance of urea into the red blood cell.   In either case, the cell expends metabolic work and alters the relative rates of flux of a molecular species in passing through the membrane in the two directions. The detailed molecular mechanisms are not known in any case so far studied, although ATP (adenosine triphosphate) appears to be an energy source for some of them.

A mathematical theory has been developed by Ussing to determine whether active transport occurs.   This theory seems particularly important because the detailed mechanisms are not known on a molecular basis.   The mathematical theory involves the relative rates of transport of tracer-labeled molecules across the membrane in the two directions.   These are compared with actually measured values.

At equilibrium the rate of transport of molecules across the membrane in the two directions must be equal, or else the concentrations would not be at their equilibrium values.   If the membrane is uncharged, the concentrations on both sides must be equal at equilibrium.   If the flux from the right to the left is called J_{RL} and in the opposite direction J_{LR}, then probability considerations dictate that, in the absence of active transport or of membrane potentials

$$\frac{J_{RL}}{J_{LR}} = \frac{c_R}{c_L} \tag{21}$$

where c_R is the concentration on the right side of the membrane and c_L that on the left.   This same conclusion can be reached from considerations of Gibbs' free energy, or of chemical potentials.

Likewise, if the membrane is charged, one may start from any of these bases and arrive at the formula

$$\frac{J_{RL}}{J_{LR}} = \frac{c_R}{c_L} e^{zFV/RT} \qquad (22)$$

In this, F is the Faraday, z the charge on the molecule, and V the potential difference between the right and left sides; RT has its usual meaning. As mentioned earlier, the exponential factor appears because the partial molal free energies on the two sides of the membrane differ by zFV when the concentrations are equal. When the two fluxes are equal, equilibrium is established although the concentrations need not be equal. By using two different labeled isotopes on the two sides of the membrane, one may measure the ratio of the fluxes.

Equations 21 and 22 are sometimes referred to as *Ussing's equations*. Their theoretical basis is sound except for the point that chemical activities rather than concentrations should be used. Although this difference is highly significant in many concentrated solutions, there is little evidence that it is important in most biological systems.

Equations 21 and 22 have been used to design experiments to test for active transport across many membranes. If the flux ratio is different than predicted, it implies that the assumption of passive transport necessary to derive Equation 22 must be wrong. Somehow, the membrane must be pumping or forcing the molecules in a preferred direction. One of the easiest examples to discuss is the isolated frog skin. The experimental arrangement is diagrammed in Figure 6. Perhaps this is a rather poor example, for the membrane (or membranes) responsible for the pumping action are not known. However, the frog skin can be used to demonstrate active transport because it can separate two media whose concentrations can be controlled.

If an isolated live frog skin is used to separate two containers of Ringers' solution, it develops a 60 millivolt potential difference between the two solutions, the outside of the skin being negative relative to the inside. For equal Ringers' solutions, and a 60 mv potential across the membrane, a direct substitution of numbers into Equation 22 shows that actually the efflux may be as low as one tenth of the influx, a factor of 100 difference between theory and experiment, if active transport is omitted. Accordingly, it is concluded that Na^+ is actively transported inwardly. It is known that frogs can take up sodium ions from their surroundings even if the external concentration is as low as 10^{-5} M. Similar tests show that Cl^- and HCO_3^- are not actively transported by frog skins, whereas if Li^+ is present, it is actively transported.

Because the frog skin actively transports Na^+ and develops an electrical potential, it may be used as a battery to drive a current through an external circuit. This demands energy, which in turn must be related to some metabolic process. Inhibitors which block the active transport of Na$^+$ do not uniformly block O_2 consumption. In fact, one of the most effective, dinitrophenol (DNP), stimulates O_2 respiration while

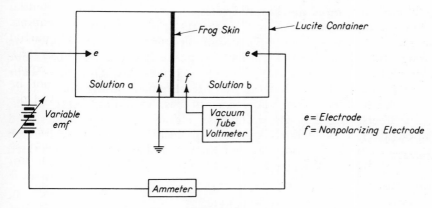

Figure 6. Diagram of apparatus for determining currents through and potential across frog skin. Air is bubbled into both solutions. The variable emf is adjustable over both positive and negative values. For an open circuit potential, the variable emf is adjusted to cause the ammeter to read zero, whereas for short-circuit current determinations, the variable emf is set to zero.

decreasing the production of ATP. This latter suggests that ATP may be the ultimate energy source for active transport in frog skin. As noted earlier, the detailed molecular mechanism is not known for this or any other of the numerous cases of active transport.

6. Summary

Mathematical theories describing the diffusion of molecules in solutions and their penetration through membranes have been presented in this chapter. These theories can be used to describe the uptake of oxygen by cells of various shapes. This last description emphasizes the important role of the rate-limiting, enzymatically catalyzed steps. Attempts to oversimplify lead to theoretical predictions that disagree with experiments. However, the oversimplified theory is easier to carry through and gives one a qualitative feeling for the types of phenomena which occur.

Red blood cells can be used to measure diffusion through the cell membrane. The permeability of the membrane has been studied for a wide variety of molecules. These emphasize the lipoid nature of the membrane, the pore-size properties of the membrane, and the existence of a few molecules which, in spite of size or solubility, pass through the membrane at comparatively rapid rates.

The last phenomena may well be the result of active transport which uses metabolic energy to pump certain molecules in a preferred direction through the membrane. Diffusion and permeability theory allows one to predict the relative rates of flux of molecules through a membrane if active transport does not occur. Measurements using tracer techniques have shown that many membranes, including nerve axons, muscle fibers, frog skin, gastric mucosa, kidney-tubule epithelium, and red blood cells, do actively transport molecules and ions. Although the molecular mechanisms are not known, it has been demonstrated that active transport depends eventually on metabolic energy.

REFERENCES

1. Rashevsky, Nicolas, *Mathematical Biophysics* (Chicago, Illinois: University of Chicago Press, 1948).
2. Jacobs, M. H., "The Measurement of Cell Permeability With Particular Reference to the Erythrocyte," Barron, E. S. G., ed., *Modern Trends in Physiology and Biochemistry* (New York: Academic Press, Inc., 1952) pp. 149–172.
3. Ussing, H., "Active Transport of Inorganic Ions," Brown, R., and J. F. Danielli, eds., *Active Transport and Secretion* [Symposia No. 8, Society for Experimental Biology] (New York: Academic Press, Inc., 1954) pp. 407–422.

Although there are numerous articles and references on the topics discussed in this chapter, the author feels that the above-mentioned three are especially worth the detailed study of anyone wishing to pursue further the topics discussed here.

24

The Molecular Basis of Nerve Conduction

I. Donnan Membrane Potentials

In Chapter 4, the basic phenomena of nerve conduction were described in detail. Their molecular interpretation was deferred to this chapter since it leans heavily on the ideas of active transport, diffusion, permeability, and thermodynamics. As a first approach, the expression for the Donnan potential across a membrane will be derived. The remainder of the chapter is concerned with three simplified systems for studying nerve conduction.

Historically, physics has substituted simplified systems for more complex ones; after studying the simplified system, the original becomes more understandable. For instance, in mechanics, real machines with friction are described in terms of the behavior of an ideal frictionless machine. In this chapter, three types of simplified systems are discussed; all of them attempt to study effects which might lead to a more complete understanding of the molecular phenomena involved in the conduction of impulses by nerves. The first system discussed attempts to mimic the rapid spike potential by a subthreshold direct current.

The second is based on biochemical experiments dealing with extracts of nervous tissue. The third type of simplified system makes use of electronic potential clamps to study the variations of current with time at a fixed membrane potential or after a predetermined potential change.

Classically, the oldest type of simplified system used to attempt to account for nerve potentials was the Donnan membrane potential.

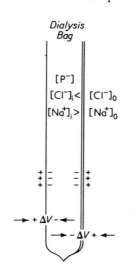

Because Donnan potentials are used in the ideas presented in this chapter, they will be developed here in detail. The Donnan membrane potential arises when a semipermeable membrane separates two solutions, one of which contains three ions, two of which can permeate the membrane and one of which cannot.

This is pictured in Figure 1. Initially, one may conceive of filling a dialysis bag with a solution of sodium chloride and sodium proteinate. The dialysis bag is placed in distilled water, resulting in the configuration shown in Figure 1, where some of the Na^+ and Cl^- ions have left the dialysis bag to enter into the surrounding fluid. It seems intuitively clear that because there are more Na^+ ions than Cl^- ions, a few more of the Na^+ ions might permeate the membrane, charging the outside positive relative to the inside. As soon as the potential difference became appreciable, it would discriminate against Na^+ ions coming out, so that the net external concentration of Na^+ and Cl^- would be almost exactly equal and no appreciable error would be made in neglecting the difference in these two concentrations.

Figure I. Donnan membrane potential. The potential developed across a semipermeable membrane is used as part of the explanation of nerve membrane potentials in Section 4 of this chapter.

Thermodynamics can be used to find the magnitude of the potential developed across the membrane. According to the formulas developed in Chapter 21, equilibrium will represent a minimum in the Gibbs' free energy for the system; that is

$$dG = 0$$

In order that this be true, there must be no change in G when a few Na^+ ions are moved from one side of the membrane to the other. This implies that $\tilde{G}_{Na^+}$, the partial molal free energy of sodium ions, must be the same on both sides of the membrane, and $\tilde{G}_{Cl^-}$ must be also.   Using the subscript i for inside and o for outside, one may write this as

$$\tilde{G}_{Na^+,i} = \tilde{G}_{Na^+,o}$$
$$\tilde{G}_{Cl^-,i} = \tilde{G}_{Cl^-,o} \tag{1}$$

Referring again to Chapter 21, one can show that in the presence of an electrical potential V, the partial molal Gibbs' free energy of an ionic species is given by

$$\tilde{G} = \tilde{G}^0 + RT \ln c + zFV \tag{2}$$

where z is the valence of the ion and F is the Faraday.[1]   In this expression, $\tilde{G}^0$ is the value of $\tilde{G}$ in the standard state with $V = 0$.   For Na^+, z is $+1$ and for Cl^-, z is -1.   Substituting Equation 2 into Equation 1 and rearranging, one obtains

$$RT \ln \frac{[Na^+]_i}{[Na^+]_o} = zF\Delta V$$
$$RT \ln \frac{[Cl^-]_i}{[Cl^-]_o} = -zF\Delta V \tag{3}$$

where ΔV is the potential difference across the membrane, the outside being positive for $\Delta V > 0$.

Adding together the equations in (3) and rearranging shows that

$$[Na^+]_i[Cl^-]_i = [Na^+]_o[Cl^-]_o \tag{4}$$

Because both sides of the membrane have approximately no net charge, it is clear that

$$[Na^+]_o = [Cl^-]_o$$
$$[Na^+]_i = [Cl^-]_i + [P^-] \tag{5}$$

where $[P^-]$ is the proteinate concentration.   Because

$$[Na^+]_i > [Cl^-]_i \quad \text{whereas} \quad [Na^+]_o \doteq [Cl^-]_o$$

Equation 4 allows one to conclude that

$$[Na^+]_i > [Na^+]_o \quad \text{and} \quad [Cl^-]_i < [Cl^-]_o$$

Accordingly, Equation 3 indicates that ΔV is positive; that is, the outside of the membrane is positively charged.

This is the direction of the potential difference observed with fibers such as nerve and muscle.   As predicted, the K^+ ions are at a higher concentration inside than outside the membrane.   But the Na^+ ions

---

[1] In this chapter, V is used for electrical potential.   The same symbol was used for volume in Chapter 21, in discussions of Gibbs' free energy.

are distributed in the opposite fashion.   On the other hand, equilibrium thermodynamics demands that the values of $\tilde{G}$ be equal on the two sides of the membrane for all ionic species present.   In other words, the ratio of the Na^+ concentration inside and outside muscle fibers is in complete disagreement with the belief that Na^+ ions were free to permeate the fiber membrane which acted as a passive semipermeable membrane.

However, tracer experiments show that Na^+ ions do pass through the membrane in both directions.   Thus, there can be little doubt that the Na^+ concentrations are maintained at nonequilibrium ratios by active transport out of the fiber at the expense of metabolic energy.

If the membrane were suddenly to become much more permeable to Na^+, one would expect the membrane pump to be completely shunted by the membrane permeability.   If this occurred, the membrane potential should reverse in sign, approaching that predicted by Equation 3 for Na^+.   Such an effect is observed at the peak of the spike potential. Various types of studies attempting to unravel the molecular details of how this occurs are discussed in the following sections.

2. Quasi-Static Analogs

The first type of study discussed in this section attempts to mimic the action potential by direct currents which are too weak to elicit a transmitted spike potential.   This model has been pursued most fully by Tobias and is discussed in Reference 1b.   Tobias points out that when a spike potential travels down an axon, local currents will flow, having the form shown in Figure 2.   Similar electrical currents are produced by a subthreshold direct current, as is shown in Figure 3.   The figures indicate that a subthreshold direct current does mimic the currents accompanying the conduction of a spike potential.   The current in the anodal region is directed from the outside region into the axon just as are the currents in the recovering part of the axon after the spike has passed.   Similarly, the currents near the cathode in Figure 3, and near the part about to be excited, Figure 2, both flow from within the axon into the external medium.

In other words, the direct currents accompanying subthreshold stimulation are similar in direction to those accompanying the spike potential.   Although the changes per unit time may be small, the subthreshold current can be maintained indefinitely.   By observing the results of prolonged subthreshold currents, it is hoped to emphasize physical and chemical changes accompanying spike conduction.   The situation represented in Figure 3 is then the analog of the spike potential diagrammed in Figure 2.   The analog integrates these changes over a long period of time; some may be more readily observed in the analog than in the conducting axon.

Other experiments support this analog.   Spike potentials usually

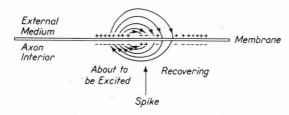

Figure 2. Current patterns near a spike conducted along an axon. After J. M. Tobias, "Nerve Ultrastructure and Functions," in *Modern Trends in Physiology and Biochemistry*, E. S. G. Barron, ed. (New York: Academic Press, Inc, 1952).

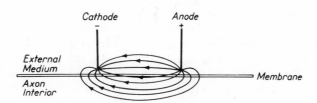

Figure 3. Current patterns for subthreshold d-c stimulus applied to an axon.   Note similarity of current patterns *inside* axon in Figures 2 and 3.   After J. M. Tobias, "Nerve Ultrastructure and Functions," in *Modern Trends in Physiology and Biochemistry*, E. S. G. Barron, ed. (New York: Academic Press, Inc., 1952).

start near a region of cathodal polarization.   Conduction rate is faster near an external cathode, slower near an anode.   Anodal polarization relieves blocks caused by chemical agents producing depolarization. These all can be predicted from the analog.   That it is only an analog, however, is emphasized by the observations that anodal polarization also relieves chemical blocks not associated with depolarization, contrary to the predictions of this analog.

In an axon polarized by a subthreshold direct current, various changes are seen.   By and large, opposite changes occur near the cathode and anode.   These changes are represented in tabular form on page 442 and then discussed briefly.

TABLE I

Cathode	Anode
Swelling	Shrinkage
Decreased opacity	Increased opacity
Decreased light scattering	Increased light scattering
"Looser" structure	Tighter structure
Lower threshold for spike formation	Higher threshold for spike formation
Decrease of $[Ca^{++}]/K^+$	Increase of $[Ca^{++}]/K^+$

The swelling at the cathode and the opposite effect at the anode may be due to electro-endosmotic movement of water. (When a current flows in a limited region, water as well as ions may be transported because of potentials generated along the boundaries.) Likewise, the decrease of the ratio $[Ca^{++}]/[K^+]$ could also cause the swelling. Various investigators have hypothesized peristalsis-like waves which might travel along the axon, giving rise in themselves to the action potential. All the mathematical schemes indicate such waves would have to be continually supplied with additional energy. Nonetheless, this peristalsis-like motion might contribute to the spike potential or its rate of conduction.

The "loosening" of the protoplasmic structure and the decreased scattering of light could be interpreted as a breaking up of the protein structure of the axon membrane in the region, mimicking "about to be excited." The Ca^{++} and K^+ changes also tend to support this view. The clotting of both mammalian blood and sea urchin eggs depends on the presence of Ca^{++}, and is decreased by K^+. Thus, one may think of the area near the cathode as being in some sense "solvated" and that near the anode as "clotted."

The ions Ca^{++} and K^+ have "antagonistic" effects not only on protein action but also on nerve conduction in general. An excess of K^+ (or an absence of Ca^{++}) in the external medium tends to lower the threshold for the production of a spike potential. If the excess K^+ is carried to an extreme, the axon fires repeatedly without any stimulus; it thus produces tetany and eventually blocks conduction. An excess of Ca^{++} (or the absence of K^+) tends to raise the threshold for excitation, and in the extreme it blocks conduction of spike potentials. Thus, the ion changes shown by the model appear highly significant.

Several valid criticisms can be raised regarding the simplified system discussed here. First, none of the chemical or mechanical effects presented lead to an all-or-none type of spike potential. Further, they are inherently incapable of revealing a threshold and are not connected in an obvious way to any energy-supplying mechanism. The observations made with this model tell us nothing about the behavior of the

Na^+ ions or about acetylcholine, both of which clearly play an important role in conduction of the spike potentials.   In short, this model cannot in itself lead to an explanation, on a molecular basis, of the excitation of and conduction along axons.   It is possible that these chemical and mechanical changes, noticed from the analog, are all secondary effects. Most of them are observations of the axoplasm as a whole, but squid axons continue to conduct spikes even if more than half of their axoplasm is replaced by an iron rod.

The model has been included here for several reasons.   First, it emphasizes the approach of the physicist in trying simplified systems. Second, unlike the next two systems discussed, it indicates the essential role of Ca^{++} ions.   And finally, it shows that structural rearrangements of the protein membrane may really occur during conduction of the spike potential.

3. Biochemical Extractions

An approach oriented more towards biochemistry is to first study extracts of nerve axons, and then to investigate the effects of added amounts of the characteristic compounds or their inhibitors.   The compounds which have been studied most are the ester, *acetylcholine*, and the enzyme which hydrolyzes it, called *cholinesterase*.   This work is reviewed by Nachmansohn in Reference 4.

As discussed in Chapter 4, acetylcholine is an ester formed by removing one molecule of water from acetic acid and the lipid molecule choline. In terms of chemical symbolism, this is

Acetic Acid   *Choline*

Acetylcholine

These are long formulas; it is easier to write AH for acetic acid, Ch for choline, and ACh for acetylcholine.

Most esters require free energy for their formation.   At equilibrium at room temperature, almost all of the ester should be hydrolyzed to the component acid and alcohol.   Enzymes which promote this equilibrium are called *esterases*.   In all nerve tissues, there are certain specific enzymes called *cholinesterases* which split acetylcholine at a much faster rate than do the other esterases.   If acetylcholine is released, or injected, its action is limited to a short period of time because the enzyme, cholinesterase, hydrolyzes the ACh in 1 or 2 msec.

As discussed in Chapter 4, acetylcholine was discovered as a secretion from the ends of the vagus nerve in the heart.   Stimulation of the vagus nerve slows the heart rate; this was shown to be mediated by acetylcholine.   Numerous experiments have shown that acetylcholine may be active in transmitting nerve impulses across synapses.   This has been most strongly supported by studies of neuromuscular junctions.   In these external cases, acetylcholine is able to produce the secondary effect without the primary nerve impulses.

Some of the evidence for the action of acetylcholine comes from a study of electric eels.   These animals have electric organs which are effectively a series of potential generators.   For a few milliseconds, they can discharge as much as 6 KW with potential differences as high as 250 volts.   The electric organs are modified motor end plates; in the normal muscle, the motor end plate is stimulated by a nerve ending. Indirect evidence from many lines indicates that at the active nerve ending, acetylcholine is secreted which then produces the response in the motor end plate.   The size of the eel's electric organ makes it very suitable to study this response directly, using chemical extraction procedures.   Nachmansohn has shown that the amount of cholinesterase is proportional to the emf developed.   This suggests strongly that acetylcholine plays an essential role in the potential discharge of the electric organ.   Likewise, Nachmansohn and his co-workers have shown that the formation and hydrolysis of acetylcholine in extracts can be coupled to the energy-storing mechanisms of the cell, phosphocreatine and adenosine-triphosphate (ATP).

In explaining the action of acetylcholine in the conduction of spike potentials along axons, it was hypothesized that ACh was released by the approaching spike.   The permeability of the membrane to Na^+ and K^+ ions was increased by the combination of ACh with the membrane.   As the spike passed, the permeability was reduced because of the hydrolysis of ACh by cholinesterase.   Then, the ACh was resynthesized using energy from cellular metabolism.   The ACh was postulated to be synthesized in a bound form in order that it not act on the membrane again.   The resynthesis, after the spike had passed, is based on very sensitive heat determinations, which revealed that heat was generated after, not during, the spike. The interrelated biochemical processes are shown in Figure 4.

There are a number of weaknesses of the ACh hypothesis. Most

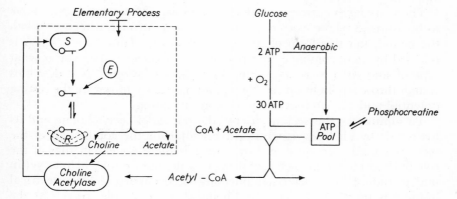

Figure 4. Sequence of energy transformations associated with conduction and integration of the acetylcholine system into the metabolic pathways of the nerve cell. The elementary process of conduction may be tentatively pictured as follows:

(1) In resting condition acetylcholine (O—➤) is bound, presumably to a storage protein (S). The membrane is polarized.

(2) ACh is released by current flow (possibly hydrogen ion movements) or any other excitatory agent. The free ester combines with the receptor (R), presumably a protein.

(3) The receptor changes its configuration (dotted line). This process increases the Na ion permeability and permits its rapid influx. This is the trigger action by which the potential primary source of emf, the ionic concentration gradient, becomes effective and by which the action current is generated.

(4) The ester-receptor complex is in dynamic equilibrium with the free ester and the receptor; the free ester is open to attack by acetylcholinesterase (E).

(5) The hydrolysis of the ester permits the receptor to return to its original shape. The permeability decreases, and the membrane is again in its original polarized condition. After D. Nachmansohn and I. B. Wilson, in *Currents in Biochemical Research—1956*, D. E. Green, ed. (New York: Interscience Publishers, Inc., 1956).

glaring is its failure to provide a possibility for all the rate constants shown necessary in the next subsection. In addition, if a compound blocking cholinesterase is applied to a nerve, the action potential is blocked but the resting potential remains unaltered. If the ACh hypothesis presented a complete picture of axon potentials, it would be hard to understand why ACh would not accumulate slowly, completely abolishing the resting potential.

There are large gaps in the ACh hypothesis. Many compounds have to be assumed whose existence cannot be demonstrated directly. Even the bound, inactive form of ACh is not known. How or why ACh is released by an oncoming action potential is unknown. How or at what type of sites ACh increases permeability is not known. Nor does this system throw any light on the Na$^+$ pump necessary to restore the resting potential and the equilibrium ionic concentrations.

To summarize this section briefly, the release of acetylcholine and its hydrolysis by cholinesterase appear essential for the conduction of the spike potential. In spite of this, neither is there a clear picture of the role of these compounds on a molecular scale, nor do they help as yet in understanding the electrical phenomena occurring. The electrical impulse is the central fact. No chemical, no molecule, travels at the rate of the spike potential—only an electrical disturbance is transmitted.

4. Clamped Nerve Experiments

The third simplified system discussed here was used originally by Hodgkin and Huxley on the giant axons of squids and cuttlefish. They used five electrodes, two within the axon and three outside; in this manner, the current to the axon could be electronically controlled to hold the membrane clamped at a potential difference determined by the experimenter. The current passed between electrodes not used for the potential measurements so that polarization effects did not interfere with the action of the electronic clamp. By a suitable electrode arrangement, it was also possible to measure the current through a predetermined length of axon, across which the potential was essentially constant. Figure 5a is a pictorial sketch of the electrode arrangement, whereas Figure 5b is a schematic cross section.

The current applied to the membrane is supplied to electrodes a and e. The potential drop across the membrane is measured from b to c, whereas the current through the membrane section studied is measured in terms of the potential drop from c to d. This arrangement results in a relatively long axon membrane all of which will have the same potential drop across it at any given time. The long electrodes and plastic separators also result in all currents in the central compartment (containing electrodes b, c, and d) flowing in the radial direction only. Because the current supplied goes from electrode a to electrode e, these may become polarized.   However, no current flows from b, c, and d to the external circuit.   Hence, these electrodes will not be polarized and can be used for potential measurements.

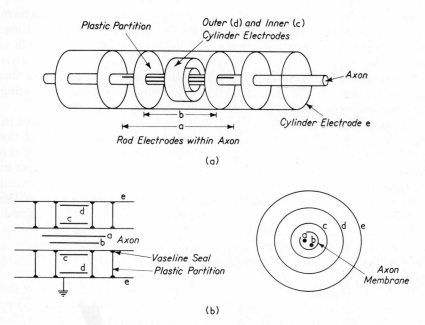

(a)

(b)

Figure 5. (a) Pictorial sketch of electrodes used in voltage clamp experiments.   The hollow cylinder electrode e is filled with saline or other solution.   Electrodes a and b are actually wires wrapped around a glass cylinder; the wires are insulated except in the region shown as electrodes in the sketch.   (b) Schematic arrangement of electrodes used in voltage clamp experiments. The electrodes a, b, c, d, and e are all metallic.   The axon is sealed to the plastic insulators with vaseline.   Current flows from electrode a to electrode e; potential and current measurements are made only between the two central insulators to eliminate end effects.   The electrode and insulator sizes are not to scale.   After A. L. Hodgkin, A. F. Huxley, and B. Katz, "Current-Voltage Relation in Nerve," *J. Physiol.* **116**: 424 (1952).

This experimental arrangement is useful for voltage clamp studies. It also can be used to follow both the current and the potential changes, if a pulse stimulus is applied.   The simplest experiment of this type was to apply a pulse of current between electrodes a and e and record the potential changes of the membrane with time.   The results of a series of experiments showed that when a negative current was applied, that is, the membrane potential was increased in the direction of the resting potential, the membrane potential changed rapidly, and then fell slowly to its equilibrium value.   If this were a passive element, it should have returned to zero at the end of the 8 μsec surge to charge the capacity; instead, it was still appreciably different at the end of 1 msec, or 1,000 μsec!

The results were very different when pulses were used to depolarize the membrane.   If the depolarization was sufficiently weak, the curve shape was similar to that obtained with increased polarization.   At a sharp threshold around 18 mμ coulombs/cm^2, a dramatically different type of response occurred resembling a spike potential.   In this case, the membrane potential changed to a different equilibrium value determined by the membrane, the change occurring more rapidly the greater the stimulus.

These experiments showed the membrane was not passive.   The experiments also revealed that comparatively long sections of the membrane could be excited to produce a potential whose time course resembled a transmitted spike potential.   The current-voltage curves were difficult to interpret unless some physical parameter was held constant.

In order to hold the potential across the membrane constant, an electronic feedback circuit was used.   A simplified form is presented in Figure 6.   The membrane potential is measured essentially between electrodes b and c.   This is applied to a high-input impedance amplifier, so that no current will flow and the electrodes will not become polarized. A predetermined voltage V_0 is then subtracted from V.   The difference is amplified and fed to the current generator in such a fashion that $V - V_0$ is reduced to zero.   The current flowing through the membrane is measured in terms of the potential difference between electrodes c and d, plus a knowledge of the resistance of the external medium used. These electrodes are also applied to a high-input impedance amplifier to avoid polarization.   The amplified current is indicated on the graphic recorder.   This circuit supplies the necessary current so that the membrane potential will remain clamped at $V = V_0$, no matter how the membrane impedance may change with time.   The clamped voltage can be easily and rapidly changed by the experimenter.   Records obtained are presented in Figures 7 and 8.

One phenomenon illustrated by these curves is the smallness of currents obtained for increased polarization, compared to those obtained for decreased polarization.   Another is that of both effects having a marked time dependence.   Most remarkable is that above a certain threshold, the initial current on depolarization is in the opposite direction from that expected for a passive membrane. This current reverses itself after a period of time. Finally, as the depolarization is reduced

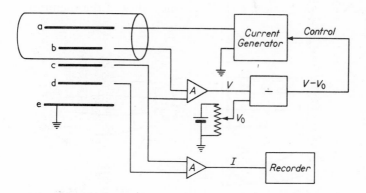

Figure 6. Simplified diagram of clamped nerve circuit. In actual practice, V was read between electrodes b and e, then compensated for the drop from c to e. For a pictorial sketch of electrodes, see Figure 5. After A. L. Hodgkin, A. F. Huxley, and B. Katz, "Current-Voltage Relation in Nerve," *J. Physiol.* 116: 424 (1952).

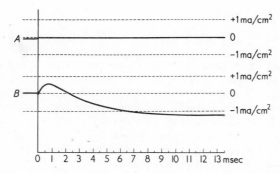

Figure 7. Records of membrane current under a voltage clamp. At zero time, the membrane potential was increased by 65 mV (record A) or decreased by 65 mV (record B); this level was then maintained constant throughout the record. The inward current is shown as an upward deflection. Temperature 3.8°C. In a passive system, the current in record B should always have been outward (downward deflection). After A. L. Hodgkin, A. F. Huxley, and B. Katz, "Current-Voltage Relation in Nerve," *J. Physiol.* 116: 424 (1952).

to -117 mv the initial hump disappears and by -130 mv a hump in the opposite direction has appeared.

By removing the Na^+ from the external medium and replacing it with choline$^+$, Hodgkin and Huxley showed that the initial hump was due to Na^+ conduction.   If the permeability of the membrane to Na^+

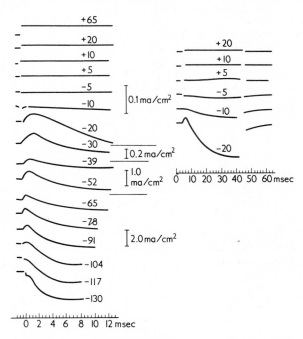

Figure 8. Further records of membrane current under a voltage clamp.   The displacement of membrane potential (V) is given in millivolts by the number attached to each record. Inward current is shown as an upward deflection.   Six records at a lower time base speed are given in the right-hand column. Experimental details as in Figure 6.   After A. L. Hodgkin, A. F. Huxley, and B. Katz, "Current-Voltage Relation in Nerve," *J. Physiol.* **116**: 424 (1952).

suddenly increased, one would expect a hump proportional to the difference between the sodium potential and the resting membrane potential.   The emf associated with these Na^+ ions is in the reverse direction from the resting potential and is about 117 mv below the resting potential.   If due to Na^+, the hump should disappear at a depolarization of 117 mv, and then reverse at greater polarizations.

The results indicate that the sodium current can be expressed as the difference between the membrane potential V and the Donnan potential V_{Na}, computed using Equation 3 for Na^+ ions only. In symbolic form, this is written

$$V - V_{Na} = R_{Na}J_{Na}$$

where R_{Na} is the membrane areal resistance for a sodium-ion current density, J_{Na}. The resistance was shown to be a function of V only and to be independent of V_{Na} by varying the external Na^+ concentration. Actually, Hodgkin and Huxley computed and used the areal conductance,

$$g_{Na} = 1/R_{Na}$$

The conductance is slightly easier to discuss because it varies directly as the permeability of the axon membrane. The conductance g_{Na} is a function both of the membrane potential V and of time; hence, the permeability to sodium must depend on these variables also.

Having found the part of the current associated with the Na conductance, one may subtract to find the K conductance. Qualitatively, it is clear that the K conductance increases with decreasing polarization, but the change occurs very slowly at first as compared with the Na conductance.

These experiments may be made more complex by changing the polarization first to one value V_1, and then after a few milliseconds t to a second value V_2. By observing the effects of different values of V_1, V_2, and t, it was possible to confirm that the potassium-ion currents obeyed the relationship

$$J_K = g_K(V - V_K)$$

where V_K was at about 10 mv above the resting potential. In addition, a small leakage current also existed given by

$$J_L = g_L(V - V_L)$$

The terms g_L and V_L were treated as constant, whereas V_K depended (in theory) on the external potassium concentration, and g_K on both V and time.

Thus, the electronic arrangement diagrammed in Figure 6 proved useful in studying the magnitude and time dependence of the currents associated with Na^+ and K^+ in a nerve membrane held clamped at a fixed potential. Qualitatively, these may be summarized by three events which follow a decrease in the membrane polarization. First, the membrane permeability to Na^+ increases markedly, although after a finite time delay. Second, the membrane permeability to K^+ increases. And finally, the membrane permeability to Na^+ decreases, although not to the original value. When the membrane polarization is increased, both the permeability to Na^+ and the permeability to K^+ drop rapidly. The time dependence of the changes as well as the size of the changes are uniquely determined by the original and final values of V. All of these permeabilities and rates are temperature dependent.

Hodgkin and Huxley accumulated a vast array of data; however, they went further in that they summarized these data in terms of a minimum number of formulas. Although this minimum presented on page 454 may seem large, it is nevertheless small compared to the original data.

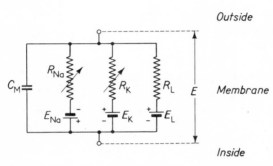

Figure 9 shows the equivalent circuit of an axon. This circuit was used to describe the permeability changes in electrical terminology. Note that the sodium emf is directed opposite to the potassium and leakage emf's. According to this picture, at the resting potential currents would flow within the membrane. This is equivalent to saying that the membrane, at its resting potential, must use energy to keep its "pumps" going, thereby maintaining E_{Na}. Note that R_K

Figure 9. Equivalent membrane circuit. The symbol E is used for the absolute value of the potentials; whereas V is used for the differences from the resting potential. The symbol R is an areal resistance in ohm·cm^2 and C_M is an areal capacitance in fd/cm^2. After A. L. Hodgkin and A. F. Huxley, "A Quantitative Description of Membrane Current and its Application to Conduction and Excitation in Nerve," *J. Physiol.* 117: 500 (1952).

and R_{Na} are variable to include the fact that they must depend on E and on the time t.

Through the use of mathematical symbols, it is possible to develop differential equations which summarize all the books of data on one or two pages, and which permit a simple comparison with data of other investigators. Moreover, this summary, with one additional assumption, allows one to predict the form of the transmitted spike potential in the normal axon.

The development of these equations is quite straightforward. It is reviewed here because it illustrates the power of mathematical tools when applied to quantitative biological data. Nonetheless, some readers may feel that their mathematical interests are too limited to justify following even this simplified presentation. If they skip to page 457, they will find the conclusion of the mathematical analysis listed without having to struggle through the intervening details and symbols.

In order to analyze the behavior of the equivalent circuit of the membrane shown in Figure 9, it is convenient to use some additional symbols. Let the areal conductances be given by g_K, g_{Na}, and g_L respectively, for the potassium, the sodium, and the leakage conductances. The units of g are mhos/cm^2. Because all potentials are measured relative to the resting potential E_r, all of the equations are written referring to the potential change V; that is

$$V = E - E_r$$

Similarly, one may define relative potentials for sodium, potassium, and leakage; that is

$$V_{Na} = E_{Na} - E_r$$
$$V_K = E_K - E_r$$

and
$$V_L = E_L - E_r$$

Let J represent the current density flowing through the membrane. This current density will consist of a part which charges the membrane capacitance and of an ionic-current density J_i; that is

$$J = C_M \frac{dE}{dt} + J_i$$

In turn, J_i may be represented as

$$J_i = J_{Na} + J_K + J_L$$

where the different ionic currents are given as noted previously by

$$J_{Na} = g_{Na}(V - V_{Na})$$
$$J_K = g_K(V - V_K)$$
$$J_L = g_L(V - V_L)$$

From the preceding definitions, curves for the variation of g_{Na} and g_K with V and time can be calculated. This still leaves a massive catalog of data. To compress this catalog, Hodgkin and Huxley developed differential equatins wohich would fit all the data. If such differential equations are to be useful, it should be possible to show that the equations also predict other properties of the system. Hodgkin and Huxley were successful in predicting the behavior of the conducting axon from their differential equations based on voltage clamp experiments.

They found that the following five equations could predict all their results. These are labeled H1–H5.

$$g_K = \bar{g}_K n^4 \qquad\qquad 0 < n < 1 \qquad\qquad \text{(H1)}$$

$$\frac{dn}{dt} = a_n - (a_n + \beta_n)n \qquad\qquad\qquad \text{(H2)}$$

$$g_{Na} = \bar{g}_{Na} m^3 h \qquad\qquad 0 < m < 1 \qquad\qquad \text{(H3)}$$

$$\frac{dm}{dt} = a_m - (a_n + \beta_m)m \qquad\qquad\qquad \text{(H4)}$$

$$\frac{dh}{dt} = a_h - (a_h + \beta_h)h \qquad\qquad\qquad \text{(H5)}$$

These equations summarize all their data in terms of six constants. Functional forms for these constants are summarized in Table II.

TABLE II

A. Functional form of constants in Hodgkin and Huxley's differential equations

$$\alpha_n = (0.01)(V + 10)/(e^{(V + 10)/10} - 1)$$
$$\beta_n = 0.125 e^{V/80}$$

$$\alpha_m = (0.1)(V + 25)/(e^{(V + 25)/10} - 1) \qquad \alpha_h = 0.07 e^{V/20}$$
$$\beta_m = 4 e^{V/18} \qquad\qquad\qquad\qquad \beta_h = (e^{(V + 30)/10} + 1)^{-1}$$

B. These values are all at 6°C. The constants all increase about threefold for a 10° rise in temperature ($Q_{10} = 3$).

C. It is doubtful if the functional forms of α and β have any theoretical significance.

D. Alternative forms: If the membrane potential is changed from V_0 to V at $t = 0$, the equations H2, H4, and H5 have as solutions

$$n = n_\infty - (n_\infty - n_0)e^{-t/\tau_n}$$
$$m = m_\infty - (m_\infty - m_0)e^{-t/\tau_m}$$
$$h = h_\infty - (h_\infty - h_0)e^{-t/\tau_h}$$

In these, the constants are given by

$$n_\infty = \alpha_n/(\alpha_n + \beta_n) \qquad m_\infty = \alpha_m/(\alpha_m + \beta_m) \qquad h_\infty = \alpha_h/(\alpha_h + \beta_h)$$
$$\tau_n = (\alpha_n + \beta_n)^{-1} \qquad \tau_m = (\alpha_m + \beta_m)^{-1} \qquad \tau_h = (\alpha_h + \beta_h)^{-1}$$

The foregoing differential equations describe adequately the form of the voltage clamp currents over a wide range of V and $[Na^+]$, as well as for various axons and temperatures. They indicate the need for six rate constants, all of which are functions of both V and temperature. Any model failing to supply these constants is incomplete. Even though the exact form chosen for the equations may be wrong, it does not appear that the data can be fitted with fewer rate constants. This discovery in itself makes the analytical effort worthwhile (although it would not justify including its outline in this text).

As already mentioned, these same equations can be used to predict the behavior of the conducting axon. To demonstrate this, consider the following: As the spike potential travels down the axon a potential gradient exists along the axon. To distinguish quantities outside and within the axon, the subscripts 1 and 2 respectively are used as shown in Figure 10. If r represents the resistance per unit length, then Ohm's law states that

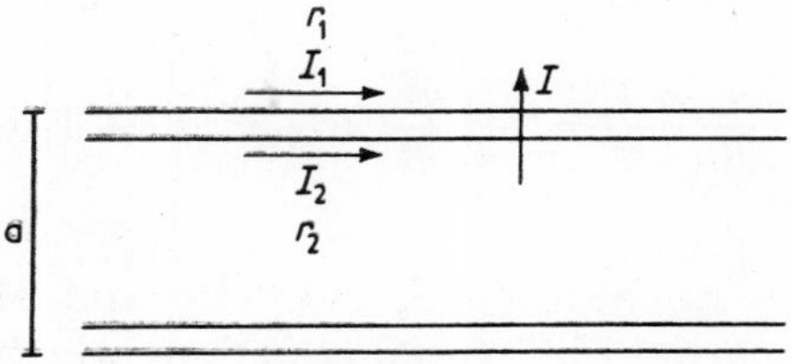

Figure 10. Current flow along an axon. Some of the symbols used in the text to develop Equation (H6) are illustrated.

$$r_1 I_1 = \frac{\partial V_1}{\partial x}$$

and

$$r_2 I_2 = \frac{\partial V_2}{\partial x}$$

The internal and external currents can be altered only by the current I flowing through the axon membrane (or else large charges would accumulate). Analytically, this is expressed by

$$I = \frac{\partial I_1}{\partial x} - \frac{\partial I_2}{\partial x}$$

Likewise, the membrane potential V is given by

$$V = V_1 - V_2$$

Combining the four preceding relationships leads to

$$I = \frac{1}{r_1 + r_2} \cdot \frac{\partial^2 V}{\partial x^2}$$

In the squid axon experiments

$$r_1 \ll r_2$$

so r_1 may be discarded from the last equation. It is convenient to discuss the current per unit area of membrane J and to replace r_2 by the resistivity R_2'. The last equation can then be rewritten

$$J = \frac{a}{2R_2'} \frac{\partial^2 V}{\partial x^2}$$

where a is the axon diameter. Combining this with the earlier definitions, and with Equations H1 and H3, leads to the differential propagation
equation

$$\frac{a}{2R_2'}\frac{\partial^2 V}{\partial x^2} = C_M\frac{\partial V}{\partial t} + \bar{g}_K n^4(V - V_K) + \bar{g}_{Na}m^3 h(V - V_{Na}) + g_L(V - V_L)$$

$$\text{(H6)}$$

Equations H2, H4, H5, and H6 then form a set of simultaneous
partial differential equations which are to be solved for V as a function
of x and t. Although these equations do not appear excessively involved,
it is not possible to solve them even by numerical methods without an
additional assumption. Since it is known that the spikes maintain
their shape as they propagate along the axon, it is assumed that there
exists a constant θ, such that

$$\frac{\partial^2 V}{\partial x^2} = \frac{1}{\theta^2}\frac{\partial^2 V}{\partial t^2}$$

$$\text{(H7)}$$

This is to say V obeys a wave equation with propagation velocity θ.

Assuming this is true, one may eliminate the space derivatives,
arriving at

$$\frac{a}{2R_2\theta^2}\frac{d^2 V}{dt^2} = C_M\frac{dV}{dt} + \bar{g}_K n^4(V - V_K) + \bar{g}_{Na}m^3 h(V - V_{Na}) + \bar{g}_L(V - V_L)$$

$$\text{(H8)}$$

Now the system has been reduced to ordinary differential equations
which can be integrated numerically. One may conclude that if the
answers are reasonable, the assumption of the wave equation was correct.

Computations show that if θ is chosen too large, V goes to $+\infty$ for a
small initial stimulus, and if θ is chosen too small, V goes to $-\infty$. There
exists a narrow range for θ, within which finite solutions are obtained for
V. These values of θ agree with the experimental values within 15
per cent.

The theoretical solutions for the original experiment described, of
stimulating a length of membrane with a current pulse, agree well with
the empirical data. Likewise, the computed form and amplitude of
the propagated spike potential are in accord with the experimental
measurements. The theory and experiment agree on a number of
other aspects of axon behavior. The only outstanding disagreement
with theory is that the calculated exchange of K^+ ions is higher than
that found in cuttlefish axons.

Figure 11 shows the agreement between theory and experiment for
the form of the transmitted spike potential. The successes of the
differential equations derived for data from voltage clamped axons are

presented in more detail in the references at the end of the chapter. The results emphasize both the importance of the clamped nerve

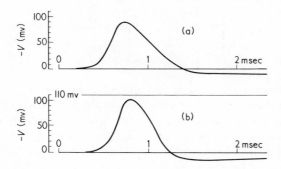

Figure 11. Predicted and observed action potential. (a) shows the curve predicted by equations developed in this section, whereas (b) is a tracing of an actual action potential observed on an axon. After A. L. Hodgkin and A. F. Huxley, "A Quantitative Description of Membrane Current and its Application to Conduction and Excitation in Nerve," *J. Physiol.* 117: 500 (1952).

experiments and the significance of the minimum of six rate constants found.

5. Summary

The equations and experiments of Hodgkin and Huxley have been checked by other investigators and found essentially correct. These equations rule out all previous molecular models and they rule out passive diffusion of Na^+ ions. However, the equations cannot supply any model related to known molecules.

One could fit the acetylcholine activity into these equations by permitting ACh to react with a variety of molecules in the membrane having a variety of effects. To do this, one has to produce a mysterious (that is, unknown) mechanism for releasing an amount of ACh which is a complex function of the membrane potential. Although Nachmansohn's conclusions, that is, ACh and cholinesterase are necessary for the conduction of spike potentials in axons, appear quite justified, the work of Hodgkin and Huxley makes it clear that these can be but two of a number of molecules necessary to explain the action of the neuron membrane.

The effects of ACh as well as the mechanical and chemical effects uncovered by the subthreshold analog may all be relatively unimportant secondary manifestations of the primary process of the conduction of spike potentials. The analog experiments emphasize the important role of Ca^{++} not used explicitly in the equations based on the voltage clamped nerves. (The Ca^{++} action must be there implicitly because $\bar{g}_K$, $\bar{g}_{Na}$, g_L, and V_L, as well as all the α's and β's, probably depend on the concentration of calcium ions.)

The data from voltage clamped nerves make the axon appear far more complex than it did to investigators in the 1930's who were successfully applying electronic techniques to biological phenomena. The molecular basis for the resting potential as well as the spike potential is a challenging, unsolved problem. These are two facets of the more general problem of how membranes actively transport small ions against a concentration gradient.

REFERENCES

The following references were used in preparing this chapter:

1. Barron, E. S. G., ed., *Modern Trends in Physiology and Biochemistry* (New York: Academic Press, Inc., 1952).

    a. Grundfest, H., "Mechanisms and Properties of Biological Potentials," pp. 193–229.
    b. Tobias, J. M., "Ultrastructure and Function in Nerve," pp. 291–322.
    c. Nachmansohn, D., "Chemical Mechanisms of Nervous Activity," pp. 230–276.

2. Grundfest, Harry, C. Y. Kao, and Mario Altamirano, "Bioelectric Effects of Ions Microinjected Into the Giant Axon of Loligo," *J. Gen. Physiol.* **38**: 245–282 (Nov. 20, 1954).

3. Clamped Nerve Experiments:

    a. Hodgkin, A. L., A. F. Huxley, and B. Katz, "Measurement of Current-Voltage Relations in Membrane of Giant Axon of Loligo," *J. Physiol.* **116**: 424–448 (Apr. 28, 1952).
    b. Hodgkin, A. L., and A. F. Huxley, "Currents Carried by Sodium and Potassium Ions Through Membrane of Giant Axon of Loligo," *J. Physiol.* **116**: 449–472 (Apr. 28, 1952).
    c. Hodgkin, A. L., and A. F. Huxley, "Components of Membrane Conductance in Giant Axon of Loligo," *J. Physiol.* **116**: 473–496 (Apr. 28, 1952).
    d. Hodgkin, A. L., and A. F. Huxley, "Dual Effect of Membrane Potential on Sodium Conductance in Giant Axon of Loligo," *J. Physiol.* **116**: 497–506 (Apr. 28, 1952).

    e. Hodgkin, A. L., and A. F. Huxley, "A Quantitative Description of Membrane Current and Its Application to Conduction and Excitation in Nerve," *J. Physiol.* **117**: 500–544 (Aug. 1952).

4. Nachmansohn, D. A., and I. B. Wilson, "Trends in the Biochemistry of Nerve Activity," Green, D. E., ed., *Currents in Biochemical Research—1956* (New York: Interscience Publishers, Inc., 1956) pp. 628–652.
5. Nachmansohn, D. A., Consulting Ed., "Second Conference on Physico-chemical Mechanism of Nerve Activity and Second Conference on Muscular Contraction," (Monograph) *Ann. New York Acad. Sc.* **81**: 215–510 (1959). Most of the articles in this monograph are pertinent to the material in this chapter.

25

Information Theory and Biology

I. Languages

It is often said that mathematics is the language of physics. Perhaps, more strictly speaking, one should assign this role to calculus. Isaac Newton was a leader in the development of this branch of mathematics; calculus enabled Newton and those who followed him to more conveniently describe the physical world. Ever since Newton's time, calculus and its ramifications have developed side by side with physics. Some purely mathematical theorems have been later applied in physics; and some physicists have developed mathematical tools which could not be justified or made rigorous for years to follow.

In this chapter, information theory is presented as a branch of applied mathematics which has become a convenient language in many varied fields. It is included in this section of the text because information theory is so closely related to the ideas of thermodynamics, particularly the concept of entropy. In biophysics, research workers describe experiments in terms of information theory when discussing sensory biophysics, molecular biology, genetics, and the operation of special equipment. It is extremely easy to mistake the role played by a language. In literature, it is well understood that a book can be translated into many different languages and still express approximately the same ideas. Absolutely everything in physics which is discussed in mathematical terms—every proof and every theorem—could be presented without any mathematical symbols or terms whatsoever. However, the length of time and the number of words involved would be so great that most of the concepts of physics could not be developed within a lifetime.

The mathematical language tells us nothing new about the physical universe. A knowledge of advanced calculus is in no way synonymous with an understanding of intermediate physics. Nonetheless, it is almost inconceivable that anyone would discuss the details of quantum mechanics without considerable training in advanced mathematics. In contrast, in Newton's day, all physical theorems could be expressed and discussed in words rather than in mathematical symbols.

Information theory consists of mathematical methods for assigning quantitative values to information. It is a language and as such cannot reveal anything new or unsuspected about the universe. It can help to express ideas and theorems and to realize similarities and analogies between widely diverse fields. Information theory is a successful language in that it can achieve an economy in thought processes and words. However, it is a far less successful language than calculus; its applications are not as forceful and its economies are not nearly as great. It is important in studying information theory neither to be misled into assigning it too important a role nor to be blinded into ignoring it altogether.

2. Information Theory—General Discussion

Information theory consists of mathematical methods for quantifying information. In order to do this, one must understand what is meant by information. In the technical, restricted sense, information may be regarded as removing uncertainty or doubt. From this point of view, the ordering of randomly arranged objects is removing doubt concerning their location, and hence, increasing their informational content.

A few examples may help clarify this idea of information as the removal of doubt. Suppose a teacher asks one of his students if he has answered correctly at least three-quarters of the questions on a class test. If the teacher has little previous knowledge of the student or his work, either a "yes" or a "no" answer is equally probable. After receiving the student's answer, the teacher's uncertainty will be less, but it will not be removed completely. In the language of information theory, the answer is masked by the "noise" caused by the student's inability to assess his own work. If, instead of asking the student, the teacher had "asked" his test paper (that is, corrected it), all uncertainty would have been removed.

Again, suppose the teacher asks a student if he likes ice cream. It is extremely likely that he does, so the teacher can receive only very little information if the student answers "yes." This time the answer will remove all uncertainties. (Unless, for instance, the student has such poor diction that the teacher cannot understand his speech.)

From these examples, one can note that the more uncertain the a priori choice, the more information there is that can be supplied by the answer. Further, the more certainty that exists after the answer, the greater the amount of information received. The quantitative form of information must reduce to zero if the initial probability of the answer p_i is one, and must be a maximum if the final (or output) probability p_0 is one. The ratio p_0/p_i varies as the information but does not go to zero when p_i (and therefore p_0) are unity. A function which does behave as information, and which is always positive, is log (p_0/p_i). For historical reasons, *information is defined in information theory as*

$$I = \log_2 (p_0/p_i) \tag{1}$$

The unit of I is called a *bit*, an abbreviation for *binary integer*. Because p_0 is greater than, or at worst equal to, p_i, information I as defined by Equation 1 will always be positive.

As an example of Equation 1, one may ask if a given neuron is conducting a spike potential at a given time. The two possible answers are yes and no, so that the a priori probability p_i is

$$p_i = 1/2$$

If the question is asked with suitable measuring equipment, the answer may be definitely yes; that is, the output probability p_0 is one. The information gained is

$$I = \log_2 \frac{p_0}{p_i} = \log_2 \frac{1}{\frac{1}{2}} = \log_2 2 = 1 \text{ bit}$$

Electrical engineers were the first to use information theory. Many electronic circuits exist in one of two stable positions. In digital electronic computers, all decimal numbers are reduced to binary numbers which involve making several yes-no choices. The base 2 logarithm appears to be the natural one, not only for the electronics engineer, but also for the physiologists and biophysicists who work with nerves which follow a yes-no pattern. (Historically, the physiologists have preferred the words "all-or-none.")

Table I compares decimal and binary integers. It also gives the decimal value of the base 2 logarithm of the number. Table II gives the arithmetic rules for the binary system and illustrates multiplication in both systems. The binary arithmetic rules are easier and involve fewer complex processes than decimal arithmetic. This simplicity is obtained at the cost of larger number of digits. Although the decimal system is more economical for writing and speaking, the binary system is more satisfactory for electronic computers; it is the only system known to be used along nerve fibers.

TABLE I

Decimal and Binary Numbers

Decimal	Binary	$\log_2$ in bits
0	0	$-\infty$
0.5	0.1	-1.00
1	1	0.00
2	10	1.00
3	11	1.59
4	100	2.00
5	101	2.33
6	110	2.53
7	111	
8	1,000	3.00
10	1,010	3.33
17	10,001	
100	1,100,010	
128	10,000,000	

TABLE II

Binary Arithmetic Rules

$$0 + 1 = 1 + 0 = 1 \qquad 0 \times 0 = 0$$
$$0 + 0 = 0 \qquad 0 \times 1 = 0 = 1 \times 0$$
$$1 + 1 = 10 \qquad 1 \times 1 = 1$$

Same Multiplication

Decimal	Binary
535	1,000,010,111
472	111,011,000
1,070	0,000,000,000
37,45	00,000,000,00
214,0	000,000,000,0
	1,000,010,111
252,520	10,000,101,11
	000,000,000,0
	1,000,010,111
	10,000,101,11
	100,001,011,1
	111,101,101,001,101,000

To recapitulate, information theory treats information as the removal of uncertainty. The theory measures information quantitatively in accord with Equation 1, the base 2 logarithm being used because all problems are reduced to equivalent yes-no type answers. In many cases, it is hard to know the values of p_0 and p_i; accordingly, Equation 1 is difficult to apply. In other cases, p_0 and p_i may be simply known.

For example, suppose that the number of impulses transmitted by a given nerve fiber are recorded for 1,000 seconds. Then one can make out a distribution table and compute the probabilities p_i as has been done in Table III. Suppose a few minutes later, one measures the

TABLE III

Transmitted Spikes

Impulses/sec	Number of occurrences	Probability = p_i
0	20	.02
1	50	.05
2	100	.10
3	100	.10
4	250	.25
5	250	.25
6	100	.10
7	50	.05
8	30	.03
9	20	.02
10	20	.02
11	10	.01
Total	1000	1.00

number of impulses for one second and finds four of them. Then one may write

$$p_0 = 1.0 \quad p_i = 0.25 \quad I = \log_2 \frac{p_0}{p_i} = 2 \text{ bits}$$

Because so many different possibilities exist, any definite number such as four gives information. However, four is a relatively probable value, so this is a minimum of information. If the measurement is repeated a few minutes later and 10 impulses are measured, more information is obtained because 10 is a priori less likely. In this case, the appropriate values are

$$p_0 = 1.0 \quad p_i = 0.02 \quad I = \log_2 \frac{p_0}{p_i} = \log_2 50 = 5.6 \text{ bits}$$

For the system as described, p_0 is always one. This is called a *noiseless system*. If, instead of counting impulses, one recorded a current, it might have read 9.6 impulses instead of 10. The answer is still probably 10 but the output probability p_0 is no longer one. A reasonable choice might be

$$p_0 = 0.6 \quad p_i = 0.02 \quad I = 4.9 \text{ bits}$$

The information has been reduced by the "noise" in the system.

The foregoing examples are admittedly oversimplified and not very practical. Nonetheless, they illustrate the meaning of the word "information" as used in information theory. A somewhat less simplified picture of any system can be represented schematically as shown in

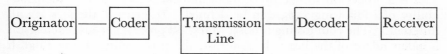

Figure I. Schematic diagram of an information system.

Figure 1. For a telegraph, the meaning of the boxes is obvious. For the process of hearing, the originator might be a piano player. The coder would be the piano. The transmission line represents the air. The decoder is the ear of the listener, and the receiver is his central nervous system. Similar analogies can be made for the synthesis of proteins, the genetic processes, vision, and so on.

In the example illustrated by Table III, vastly different amounts of information were received from one second to the next. Information theory calls the impulses received in a given period of time the *message*. In a noiseless system, the information in a given message is

$$I_i = -\log_2 p_i \tag{2}$$

The average information per message H is then

$$H = \sum_{i=1}^{M} p_i I_i \tag{3}$$

or, using Equation 2

$$H = -\sum_{i=1}^{M} p_i \log_2 p_i \tag{4}$$

The last equation is very similar to the statistical-mechanics definition of entropy, except for a minus sign. Accordingly, the average information in a message H is often called *negative entropy*.

There are a number of other terms used in the "jargon" of information theory, some of which are included here for completeness.

A. Stochastic Process

This is a process which "generates" symbols, for example, words or amino acids, in a random fashion, but in which the frequency of occurrence (that is, probability) approaches a limiting value as the number of symbols is increased. For example, a stochastic process is tossing a penny which generates the symbols "heads" and "tails." The frequency of occurrence of heads for a small number of tosses is random but approaches 1/2 as the number of tosses is increased.

B. Markhoff Process

This is a process in which intersymbol influences exist, so that the probability of i following j, p_{ij}, can be defined. In general, the p_{ij}'s are all different. The coin tossing is not a Markhoff process because each result is independent of the last. In contrast, the probability of one English letter following another is measurable. A process generating English letters in words, for example, writing, is a Markhoff process.

C. Ergodic Sequence

This is a sequence of symbols in which the intersymbol influence falls off exponentially or disappears after a finite number of symbols. In English, the probability of a given letter following the first one is not random. Nor is the probability of a second or third following letter determined at random. Definite intersymbol influences can be found out to eight letters. Thereafter, the probability is essentially random. Thus, English letters form ergodic sequences.

(The word "ergodic" comes from the Greek; literally, it means energy pathway. Its relationship to the foregoing is not trivially obvious. Students of statistical mechanics will recognize that the foregoing definition in terms of intersymbol influences is synonymous with the definition in terms of energy pathways as used in Gibbs' statistics. Information theory borrowed this word from statistical mechanics.)

D. Redundancy

If intersymbol influences exist, not all the symbols are necessary. A different coding could reduce the number of symbols. Redundancy is desirable in that it tends to increase the signal to noise ratio.

One example of redundancy is the written English language. The average information per letter H_1 has been computed, including various intersymbol influences. These are given in Table IV, which shows that a redundancy of about 1 bit, that is, twofold, exists.

TABLE IV
Average Information of English Letters

Letters	H_1
Random	4.7 bits
English frequency	4.15 bits
Intersymbol influences for 2 letters	3.57 bits
Intersymbol influences for 8 letters	3.25 bits

The twofold redundancy in English greatly reduces the error rate due to noise, such as blurred printing, bad spelling, poor lighting, and so on. The error rate is reduced because there are a large number of possible messages excluded. The number of 1,000 symbol messages M_r, if all random arrangements of letters were possible, would be

$$M_r \doteq 10^{1400} \text{ messages}$$

If one includes all influences up to eight symbols away, the number of messages M_8 is reduced to

$$M_8 \doteq 10^{700}$$

A 1,000 symbol message is about a typed page. The number M_8 is certainly astronomical in size, but it is microscopic compared to M_r.

Similar redundancies may exist in many biological processes. It seems likely that the endocrine systems of mammals have more interacting glands than are necessary. This redundancy makes possible the action of extreme feedback (homeostatic) mechanisms. It also appears to be a reasonable guess that the pigment myoglobin is not necessary. Its presence in the muscles is a redundancy tending to further smooth out oxygen variations.

The most striking example of redundancy occurs in the higher plants. Some are so-called "polyploids," in which, instead of having pairs of chromosomes, all the body cells have sets of four or even eight homologous chromosomes. Each member of each set controls the same characteristics. This redundancy should markedly reduce the error rate during cell multiplication. (At any rate, this possibility exists whether or not the plant uses it!)

3. Information and Sensory Perception

The senses provide the link between the central nervous system and the outside world. All information reaching the central nervous system comes through the senses. It seems appropriate therefore that the language of information theory can be used to describe what man perceives. Consider first the theory of hearing.

A. Hearing

All the examples in the previous section dealt with discrete phenomena. Sound is continuous both in amplitude and in time. (As mentioned in Chapter 1, the representation in time may be replaced by a corresponding one in frequency.) Any discussion of the information content of sound must include some method of handling continuous variables.

Such theories have been developed. They show that for amplitudes with no noise level, or messages of infinite length in either frequency or time, the average information per message is infinite. However, all sounds have a noise limit provided by molecular thermal motions, a finite time of duration, and a finite frequency span, the latter two being limited by the ear.

If speech is analyzed in terms of the physical noise level and the frequency response of the human ear, one may easily arrive at tremendous values for the information per second. Although these values represent the information which can be detected by a microphone or other physical detector, they have no meaning for human hearing. The information received is limited by the ear itself.

Frequencywise, humans hear about 10 octaves from 20 cps to 20 kc. Few people can distinguish more than 12 tones per octave. This says there are essentially 120 distinguishable pure tones. If each is equally probable, all the p_i's are the same. One may write

$$p_i = \frac{1}{120}$$

and the average information associated with a tone H_f is

$$H_f = -\sum_1^{120} p_i \log_2 p_i = \frac{120}{120} \log_2 120 = 7 \text{ bits/tone}$$

Similarly, from the threshold of hearing to the threshold of pain, man can distinguish about 250 steps. Again, one may assume all steps equally probable and find the average information associated with the sound pressure level

$$H_L = \log_2 250 = 8 \text{ bits/impulse}$$

For a pure tone, then, man's auditory apparatus can receive about 15 bits of information. For a complex tone, this must be increased to about 20. Human auditory systems can distinguish about 10 tones per second. Therefore, the rate H' of receipt of useful information by the ear is

$$H' \doteq 200 \text{ bits/second}$$

This represents the ability of the ear to code information as neural impulses. The limiting factor is most clearly the ear itself. Much more information can be coded from a microphone onto magnetic tape.

Although 200 bits/second may reach the brain, it in no way follows that these are recorded or used by the brain. When a person is asleep or daydreaming, most auditory information is lost. When we concentrate on reading, we deliberately discard most auditory information.

If we listen to a friend talking in a noisy room, most of the information reaching our ears is consciously or unconsciously blocked from our conscious mind; that is, we listen only to his speech and not to the background noise.

Even with the utmost concentration under ideal conditions, it is rarely possible to use all of the 200 bits/second reaching the brain. For short pure tones, most people can detect not more than one correct choice of six possibilities. Hence, we should write

$$H_f = 2.5 \text{ bits/tone}$$

of useful information. (Some people with perfect pitch can detect 8 bits per piano tone. They use information of more than one frequency and of the relative intensities of the different harmonics. They must hear the tone longer than 0.1 second.)

Again, for sound-pressure-level choices, people on the average can choose only one of six possibilities. As above, one may recompute H_L to give

$$H_L = 2.5 \text{ bits/impulse}$$

Adding another 2.5 bits for quality of a complex tone, we find that 7.5 bits can be detected each 0.1 second. The rate of receipt of useful information by the brain is

$$H'' = 75 \text{ bits/second}$$

Interpretation of the information received from words is more complicated. The best estimates give

$$H''_{\text{word}} = 50 \text{ bits/second}$$

of useful information at the brain.

In terms of the language of computers, the rate is limited by the ability to read information into the brain. The sound waves in the ear, and even the impulses in the eighth cranial nerve, carry far more information than can be read into the brain.

B. Vision

A similar analysis can be carried out for the visual system. Analogous to sound information, most light information is destroyed by the eye. Vision is very different from hearing in that information may be received and transmitted to the brain at a much greater rate.

In the eye, there are about 10^7 receptor units, each feeding into a separate ganglion cell. The receptor units are made up of individual receptors, that is, rods and cones. Except in the most sensitive region of the eye, the *fovea centralis*, several receptors combine to form one receptor unit. (There are about 7×10^6 cones and 10^8 rods in the human eye.)

Each receptor unit is believed able to respond in a characteristic fashion to about 100 just noticeable differences in intensity between the visual threshold and the pain threshold. The average information per receptor unit then is

$$H_1 = \log_2 10^2 \doteq 7 \text{ bits}$$

The eye sees a new picture about 10 times a second. Accordingly, the rate of receipt of useful information is

$$H_1' = 70 \text{ bits/sec/receptor unit}$$

or for the entire eye

$$H' = 7 \times 10^8 \text{ bits/second}$$

This can be compared with a television channel which carries about 10^7 bits/second.

The optic nerve which carries this information has about 10^6 fibers. Each carries a maximum of 300 spikes per second. Hence, in each 0.003 second, each fiber carries 1 bit of information. The optic nerve, then, has a capacity for transmitting information of

$$C = 3 \times 10^8 \text{ bits/sec}$$

a number identical, within experimental error, with the receipt of useful information by the eye.

In the central nervous system, one can make crude estimates of the information received that is associated with acuity and with color vision. These lead to

$$H_{\text{brain}}'' = 5 \times 10^8 \text{ bits/second}$$

The optic nerve is extremely well coded. Its channel capacity is not many orders of magnitude larger than the auditory nerve. However, the rate of information entering the conscious part of the brain is perhaps 10^7 times as large.

The coding of the optic nerve may be compared to a television channel. One of the limitations of television broadcasting is poor encoding of information. Many engineers have realized that a system which indicated changes of intensity only would be far more efficient in transmission of information. (In other words, much narrower channels could be used.) The high efficiency of the optic nerve as indicated by the foregoing estimates suggests that such a system is used. Evidence from electrophysiology and histology supports this view (see Chapter 7). The approach of information theory helps to understand the histology and the electrophysiological data.

Although the visual information reaching the brain is very great, the amount actually stored or analyzed is much smaller. This is similar to the read-out limitation in a high speed computer. To completely translate into the human memory, all the information received in a 0.1 sec flash takes more than 0.1 sec. By blinking the eyes open and shut, it is possible to notice many details such as height, width, length, brightness, hue, shade, tint, orientation, and shape. It takes many seconds to store all these in the brain memory.

4. Information Theory and Protein Structure

Information theory is a mathematical technique used to give a quantitative value to information. Its basic definitions, embodied in Equations 1 and 4, were used in the last section as a language to describe sensory information. Information theory is not restricted to this field alone but can also be used as a language to describe other types of information. Only a few of these can be included in this text. In this section, information theory is applied to protein structure.

To assemble a protein, it is necessary to choose the proper amino acids and arrange them in a given order with a suitable spatial configuration. There are many ways in which this ordering can be done with the same amino acids. It is too complex to illustrate this for a complicated protein with a hundred amino acid residues, but some intuitive feeling can be gained by considering a polypeptide with five residues. Suppose these are all different; for example, one glycine (g), one phenylalanine (p), one tryptophane (t), one valine (v), one methionine (m). These can be arranged in 5! fashions because the nature of the peptide bond is asymmetrical; that is, gp ≠ pg. These 5! forms include

gptvm	gtpvm	gvtpm	gmtvp
gptmv	gtpmv	gvtmp	gmtpv
gpvtm	gtvpm	gvptm	gmvtp
gpvmt	gtvmp	gvpmt	gmvpt
gpmtv	gtmpv	gvmtp	gmptv
gpmvt	gtmvp	gvmpt	gmpvt

There are four other equal sets making a total of 120, that is, 5!.

If two of the amino acids had been the same, the number of possibilities would have been reduced by a factor of two. And if three were the same the number of distinct possibilities would have been reduced by a factor of 3! or 6. If only two different amino acids are present, for example three glycines and two plenylalanines, the only possibilities are

$$
\begin{array}{ll}
\text{gggpp} & \text{gppgg} \\
\text{ggpgp} & \text{pgggp} \\
\text{ggppg} & \text{pggpg} \\
\text{gpggp} & \text{pgpgg} \\
\text{gpgpg} & \text{ppggg}
\end{array}
$$

that is, 10 or $\dfrac{5!}{3!\,2!}$

In general, there are N amino acid residues of m types in a protein, such that there are n_1 of the first, n_2 of the second, and so on. The number of types m is less than or equal to 21. The number of ways of arranging these in a straight chain is

$$
P = \frac{N!}{(n_1!)(n_2!)\cdots(n_m!)} \tag{5}
$$

If all are equally likely, the information necessary to build a particular protein is

$$
I = +\log_2 P = \log_2 N! - \sum_1^m \log_2 (n_i!)
$$

The average information per amino acid residue is

$$
H_R = \frac{I}{N} = \frac{1}{N}[\log_2 N! - \sum_1^m \log_2 (n_i!)] \tag{6}
$$

Because N is large compared to one, Sterling's formula can be used, namely that

$$
\therefore \quad \log_2 N! = (\log_2 e)\log_e N! \doteq 1.45\, N \log_2 N
$$

Therefore, the average information per residue, or negative entropy per residue, is

$$
H_R = 1.45 \log_2 N - \frac{1}{N}\sum_1^m \log_2 (n_i!) \tag{7}
$$

If, in addition, all the n_i are large, this expression becomes

$$
H_R = 1.45 \log_2 N - 1.45 \sum_1^m \frac{n_i}{N} \log_2 n_i = -1.45 \sum_1^m \frac{n_i}{N} \log_2 \frac{n_i}{N} \tag{8}
$$

In a long molecule, the ratio n_i/N is the relative probability of finding an amino acid of the ith variety, so that (except for a numerical constant) the foregoing formula is identical to the previous form for H. Unfortunately, the values of n_i are so small that Equation 7 must be used.

The values for I and for H_R can vary widely even though both the total number of residues N and the number of types of residues m are fixed. In the five-amino-acid residue, polypeptide, discussed earlier, if there are four glycines and one phenylalanine, then there are only five possible arrangements

ggggp   gggpg   ggpgg   gpggg   pgggg

The information has been reduced from

$$I = \log_2 10 = 3.33 \text{ bits}$$

for three (g)'s and two (p)'s to

$$I = \log_2 5 = 2.33 \text{ bits}$$

for four (g)'s and one (p).

For larger values of N and m, the variation is much greater. In general, one can compute an I_{max} and an I_{min} for fixed N and m. Because there are usually about 20 types of amino acids within the cell, one can also compute an $I_{max}^{(20)}$ for fixed N and 20 types of residues. It is instructive to consider the ratios

$$\frac{I}{I_{max}}, \quad \frac{I}{I_{min}}, \quad \text{and} \quad \frac{I_{max}}{I_{max}^{(20)}}$$

It has been found for all proteins tested that I/I_{max} is greater than 0.5. For all proteins within living cells, in fact, this ratio is greater than 0.7, and for most it is greater than 0.85. The information per residue is about

$$H_r = 3.6 \text{ bits/amino acid}$$

for a typical protein. No values are less than half this or greater than 5 bits. For instance, for a protein such as albumin with over 500 residues, this is a total information of 2,000 bits needed to build the molecule. Fibrinogen has 3,400 amino acid residues; a total information of 10,000 bits is necessary to distinguish it from all other proteins with the 3,400 amino acid residues and the same types of amino acids.

It is not just because there are no other possibilities that these values are so high. For albumin, the ratio of I/I_{min} is about 15. Nor does replacing I_{max} with $I_{max}^{(20)}$ alter the situation very much. The ratio of the last two is not very different from one.

Thus, information theory has emphasized a common feature of all natural proteins, namely that for a given number of residues N and a given number of types m of amino acids, the information contained in the protein molecule is close to a maximum. In terms of entropy, this states that the amino acids are ordered in such a fashion as to minimize the entropy. Information theory was not necessary to reach this conclusion, but it helped focus attention in this direction.

5. The Coding of Genetic Information

Information theory also is used in discussions of genetics and reproduction. Complex vertebrate organisms grow from a single cell during the reproductive process. Within that cell, in a microscopic or submicroscopic volume, is coded the information necessary for building a complete organism. The amount of information stored is extremely large, yet it takes up very little space.

Various attempts have been made to estimate the amount of genetic information necessary. Although these do not agree exactly, they indicate the general orders of magnitude expected. The following is an outline of such an estimate. In every type of nucleus, there are chromosomes characteristic of the particular animal or plant. Along these there are sites functionally connected with different properties of the organism and with the various enzymes within the cells. These sites are called *genes*. Each gene has several different possible forms called *alleles*. Estimates indicate there may be as many as 16 viable alleles per gene. Thus, the average information per viable gene is about

$$H_g = \log_2 16 = 4 \text{ bits}$$

Inclusion of nonviable alleles would raise H_g.

The number of genes in vertebrates has been estimated as low as 3×10^4 and as high as 10^6. Thus, the total information I necessary to be transmitted from generation to generation probably lies in the range

$$10^5 < I < 10^7 \text{ bits}$$

These are certainly only estimates. However, it would be very surprising if the estimate of the lower limit was a factor of 10 too high or of the upper limit a factor of 10 too low.

One test of the hypothesis that DNA carries the information of cellular reproduction is to ask if this amount of information can be coded in the DNA in one cell. As was shown in Chapter 15, DNA consists of a double helical chain with "rungs" between the two chains. These rungs are made of the pairs adenine-thymine, (AT), and guanine-cytosine, (GC). If there is a method of sensing the chain direction then there are four possible rungs, AT, TA, GC, CG. Discovering one of these rather than the others reduces the uncertainty, that is, increases information by

$$I = \log_2 4 = 2 \text{ bits}$$

Within the nucleus there are more than 10^9 such rungs. Because this number is larger than the maximum estimate of information needed for reproduction, DNA may be the storehouse of such information.

Other tests of this hypothesis have involved studies of the minimum distances apart at which one can break a chromosome or alter it to form various alleles.   Best estimates place this at about the length along the DNA helix of one rung.   Likewise, experiments with fractured bacterial DNA indicate that pieces as small as 4 rungs may still carry information. This would be just 2 bits more than is necessary to specify one amino acid.

The language of information theory makes it easier to understand the transmission of genetic information during reproduction.   It emphasizes the coding problem along the DNA, focusing attention in that particular direction.   Information theory is a language.   It cannot in itself find the coding system.

6. Summary

It has been shown that the language of information theory can be used in various fields of biology.   Information theory emphasizes the quantitative, mathematical approach appealing to the physicist.   Information theory is a successful language in that it increases the rate of transmission of information from one person to another and helps focus research thoughts in new directions.   It is a new language and as yet a far less successful language in biology than calculus is in physics.

REFERENCES

1. Goldman, Stanford, *Information Theory* (Englewood Cliffs, N.J.: Prentice-Hall, Inc., 1953).
2. Quastler, H., ed., *Essays on the Use of Information Theory in Biology* (Urbana, Illinois: University of Illinois Press, 1953).
3. Shannon, C. E., and Warren Weaver, *Mathematical Theory of Communications, and Recent Contributions to the Mathematical Theory of Communication* (Urbana, Illinois: University of Illinois Press, 1949).   This is the "classical" book in the field.
4. Yockey, H. P., R. L. Platzman, and H. Quastler, *Symposium on Information Theory in Biology* (New York: Pergamon Press, 1958).
5. Elsasser, W. M., *The Physical Foundation of Biology* (New York: Pergamon Press, 1959).

Many journal articles and recent publications deal with the applications of information theory to biology.   The following three are among the earlier ones on information theory and perception:

6. Jacobsen, Homer, "Information and the Human Ear," *J. Acous. Soc. Am.* **23**: 463–471 (July 1951).

7. Pollack, Irwin, "The Information of Elementary Auditory Displays," *J. Acous. Soc. Am.* **24**: 745–749 (Nov. 1952).
8. Halsey, R. M., and A. Chapanis, "On the Number of Absolutely Identifiable Spectral Hues" (Letter to the Editor) *J. Opt. Soc. Am.* **41**: 1057–1058 (1951).

DISCUSSION QUESTIONS—PART E

1. Discuss the heat changes observed in intact muscles from the point of view of thermodynamics.

2. Describe the energy changes occurring during the flight of insects. What is the effect of temperature on the rate of wing beat?

3. How is a body temperature regulated in humans? Include in your answer a discussion of the metabolic rate, the temperature receptors, the portions of the central nervous system active in temperature regulation, and the role of the endocrine system.

4. How does the equilibrium constant K vary with temperature for the reaction

$$Mb + O_2 \rightleftharpoons MbO_2$$

where Mb is myoglobin? Use this to find the Gibbs' free-energy difference between the two sides of the equation each referred to an appropriate standard state.

5. Compute the difference in Gibbs' free energy for $CO_2 + H_2O$ and H_2CO_3. In terms of this result, discuss the variations of this equilibrium with the temperature.

6. Outline the rigorous development of absolute rate theory based on the quantum mechanical approach of Kimball and Eyring.

7. The enzyme systems called *luciferase* are responsible for the bioluminescence of fireflies and various other organisms. These systems have been studied in detail as a function of temperature and pressure. Describe the results of such studies in the terminology of absolute rate theory.

8. Carry through in detail the average-value approach discussed in Chapter 23, pages 426-427, including an algebraic evaluation of the parameter λ in Equation 12, Chapter 23.

9. Discuss the hole theory of liquids, comparing it with other models of liquids.

10. Diffusion theory has been applied to fumerase to show that it is a diffusion-limited reaction. Discuss this proof.

11. Develop rigorously Equations 17 and 18 of Chapter 23.

12. Review the evidence for the concept that the secretion of HCl by the gastric mucosa is an example of active transport.

13. Describe in detail the experiments which indicate that active transport occurs across the mucosa of the small intestine, resulting in the selective absorption of certain metabolites and ions.

14. Which molecules and ions have been demonstrated to be actively transported across membranes surrounding various portions of the kidney tubules? Which ions are believed to be actively transported although the evidence is weak? How could you test to see whether active transport occurs?

15. Describe the anatomy of one of the electric eels, emphasizing the structure of the electric organs. Cite numerical values supporting the role of acetylcholine in triggering the discharge of these organs.

16. Review the theory for peristalsis-like surface type waves traveling along nerve axons.

17. What is the cable model of an axon? Describe how this is used to theoretically analyze the conduction of impulses between nodes along a large "myelinated" nerve fiber.

18. Grundfest and his co-workers injected various ionic solutions into the axoplasm of squid axons. What effect would you predict this to have on the resting potential and on the height of the action potential? Why? Were these predictions verified by the experiments?

19. Develop in detail the application of information theory to a study of enzyme specificity.

20. Design a set of experiments in which the language of information theory could be applied to the sense of taste.

F

Specialized Instrumentation

Introduction to Part F

It is important that a biophysicist include mathematical biophysics in his tool box without becoming lost in mathematics. It is likewise important that he be familiar with special physical equipment used in biological research without becoming a gadgeteer. To present this point of view, the last six chapters deal with selected examples of biophysical instruments. The theory of their function is emphasized rather than the engineering details of their construction.

Extra emphasis is given to absorption spectrophotometry; its discussion occupies the first two chapters of Part F. The important role of spectrophotometry in current biological research, coupled with the store of information potentially available from molecular spectra, make these two chapters very important. The remaining four chapters each present a different field of instrumentation, namely magnetic measurements, microscopy, tracer techniques, and electronic computers. The only justification for these choices rather than any of numerous other, equally important types of instrumentation is that they are ones with which the author is not only familiar but which he also feels are instructive to students in a variety of disciplines. It is hoped that this concluding section of the text will give a balanced view of biophysics, ranging from purely mathematical analyses to applied instrumentation, and from the characteristics of complete organisms to the form of the molecules which compose them.

26

Absorption Spectrophotometry

I. Role of Absorption Spectrophotometry in Biology

Absorption spectrophotometry plays an important role in many areas of biophysical research. The techniques and equipment used have been specialized and developed to be increasingly more precise and more versatile. This special physical equipment allows one to extract information from biological systems which would otherwise keep their secrets from the investigators. In contrast to the previous chapter, which dealt with the description of information in the language of information theory, the current chapter describes equipment used to obtain information.

Electromagnetic spectra have been important in many areas of natural science. For example, the characteristic emission spectra of light radiated from atoms formed one of the major parts of the supporting evidence that led to the development of the theory of quantum mechanics, an important field of modern physics. Characteristic absorption spectra have played an equally important role in modern physiology, biochemistry and biophysics. Spectroscopy can reveal far more than can most chemical tests; these show only the general class to which a compound belongs. In biological systems, there are many similar molecules, as for instance the heme proteins, which are difficult to separate by chemical techniques. However, each of the heme proteins has a characteristic absorption spectrum which makes possible not only its identification but also a measure of the amount of the compound present, both in the test tube and in the living cell.

Absorption spectroscopy has been important both for compounds with characteristic spectra and for many others which form characteristically colored compounds on reacting with another substance. In measuring blood sugar level, for example, a reaction is produced which leads to a colored product. The amount of this characteristic product is determined spectrophotometrically.

Nor is absorption spectroscopy limited to visibly colored pigments. Although the eye responds to electromagnetic energy only if its frequency is within a particular octave, there exist detectors which can measure electromagnetic energy from very low frequencies to very high frequencies. The different parts of the electromagnetic spectrum are presented in Table I. The various ranges are purely arbitrary; there are

TABLE I

Electromagnetic Radiation

Frequency ν, cps	Wavelength λ	Name
0–5.5×10^5	∞–5.50 m	Long wavelength, low frequency
5.5–15×10^5	550–200 m	Broadcast band (AM)
1.5–15×10^6	200–20 m	Short wave band
1.5–60×10^7	30–0.5 m	Ultra high frequency (TV, FM)
6–$3,000 \times 10^8$	50–0.1 cm	Radar (microwave)
1.5×10^{10}–1.5×10^{13}	20–0.02 mm	Heat, far infrared
1.5–40×10^{13}	20–0.75 μ	Near infrared, fingerprint region
4–8×10^{14}	750–350 mμ	Visible light
0.8–30×10^{15}	350–1 mμ	Ultraviolet
3–30×10^{16}	10–1.0 Å	Soft X rays
3–300×10^{18}	1.0–0.01 Å	Hard X rays
3×10^{19}–∞	0.1–0 Å	Gamma rays

no sharp dividing lines. Each range demands the use of a different type of emitter and detector. However, between any two adjacent regions, there is an overlap where both techniques may be employed. This fact emphasizes the essential continuity of the electromagnetic spectrum; all the types of radiation described propagate as disturbances in the electrical and magnetic fields. In a plane wave, these disturbances are at right angles to each other as well as to the direction of propagation.

Any absorption or emission of electromagnetic energy which varies in a characteristic fashion with wavelength can be used to study the nature of, or measure the amounts of, certain biochemical substances. By and large, one obtains different types of information from different regions of the spectrum. The specific absorption bands of many biologically important molecules lie in the visible and ultraviolet regions of the spectrum. Measurements in these regions will be emphasized in this chapter.

A number of different terms are used to describe the equipment employed to measure spectra in the visible, ultraviolet, and infrared regions. An instrument which presents the spectrum in such a fashion that it can be observed with the eye as a detector is called a *spectroscope*. Apparatus arranged to measure the wavelengths at which bright emission lines or dark absorption lines occur is referred to as a *spectrometer*. If a detector other than the eye is used, the spectrometer is not restricted to visible light. A *colorimeter* is made by placing spectrally selective filters in the path of a white light; the colored light beam so produced may be split in two and passed through two solutions. Any piece of apparatus which compares the absorption of two solutions or emission of two sources is called a *photometer*. A *monochromator* selects a narrow wavelength band from the incident light. A monochromator combined with a photometer is called a *spectrophotometer*. The latter is the most widely used form of analyzing equipment in current biochemical and biophysical research, although colorimeters are still used for some clinical measurements. Spectrophotometry was markedly improved by the development of electronic circuits. Although spectrophotometry was used before the impact of electronics was felt in biology, the widespread application of spectrophotometry has resulted from the availability of convenient electronic equipment. Today, every clinical hospital laboratory, every biochemical research laboratory, and most microbiology and physiology laboratories make use of absorption spectrophotometry.

A large number of basic physical concepts are necessary in order for one to understand the origin and the nature of characteristic spectra of biochemical molecules. Complex physical equipment is necessary to make optimum use of the information available from these spectra. Accordingly, absorption spectrophotometry is one of the important fields of instrumentation within the general framework of biophysics.

The present chapter is a description of some types of equipment used in spectrophotometry. No attempt has been made to be complete or to provide an instruction manual for the use of a specific spectrophotometer. Rather, it is hoped that the reader will find an indication of the types of measurements possible, as well as of certain modifications of standard spectrophotometers which increase their utility for biological research.

It is quite possible to use a spectrophotometer without any idea of the physical basis for the observed spectra.   However, spectrophotometry is so important in biological studies that it is hoped the reader will want to know more about the spectra in order to appreciate both the limitations and the unexplored possibilities of spectrophotometry.   The physical basis for the characteristic absorption spectra of biological molecules is described in the following chapter.

2. Units and Symbols of Absorption

Almost all biophysics, biochemistry, and physiology laboratories use some form of spectrophotometry.   The most frequently used types are absorption spectra of compounds in liquid suspension or within the

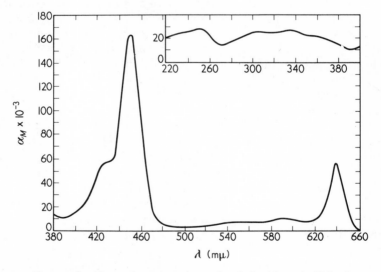

Figure I. Absorption spectrum of ethyl chlorophyllide *b*. This spectrum is essentially identical to that for chlorophyll *b*. See Chapter 20 for a discussion of chlorophylls.   After A. S. Holt and E. E. Jacobs, *Am. J. Botany* **4I**: 710 (1954).

living cell.   These absorption spectra are used both to identify compounds and also to quantify the amount of a given compound in solution (or in the cell).   Typical absorption spectra are shown in Figures 1 through 4.

Although absorption spectra are widely used, the units and symbols with which the data are reported are very varied. In the language of information theory, the spectrophotometrically obtained information is coded in different ways. It is necessary to know which code is being used. This section describes some of these codes and their basis in the physical theory of absorption of electromagnetic radiation.

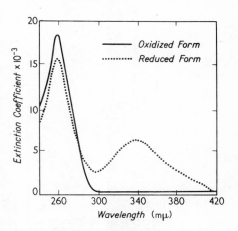

Figure 2. Absorption spectra of reduced and oxidized diphosphopyridine nucleotide. The role of DPN in oxidative phosphorylation is discussed in Chapter 18. After J. B. Nielands and P. K. Stumpf, *Outlines of Enzyme Chemistry* (New York: John Wiley and Sons, Inc., 1958).

Suppose a beam of monochromatic light is incident normally on a thin sheet of material of thickness Δx, as illustrated in Figure 5. The incident intensity is represented by I_1. In passing through the material, some of the light will be absorbed. The intensity I_2 leaving the thin sheet will be less than I_1. If the sheet is sufficiently thin, the change in intensity ΔI will be proportional to Δx. Experimentally, it is found also that ΔI is proportional to I_1 for monochromatic light. Expressing these ideas symbolically, one may write

$$\Delta I = I_2 - I_1 = -\mu I_1 \Delta x \qquad (1)$$

where μ is a proportionality constant depending on the material making up the thin sheet.

If now one allows the thickness Δx to become infinitesimal, Equation 1 may be rewritten as

$$\frac{dI}{dx} = -\mu I \qquad (2)$$

A sample of finite thickness x may be considered to be composed of many such thin sheets. If I_0 now is defined to mean the intensity entering the sample at $x = 0$, and I_x is the final intensity leaving the sample at x, Equation 2 may be integrated to yield

$$I_x = I_0 e^{-\mu x} \qquad (3)$$

This is known as *Lambert's law*[1] and μ is called the *absorption coefficient*.

---

[1] Also called *Bouger's law*, in some texts.

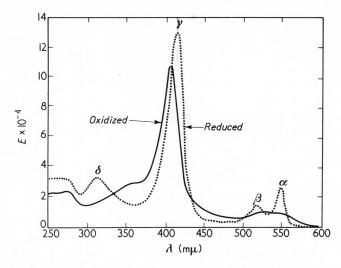

Figure 3. Spectra of reduced and oxidized cytochrome c. The role of cytochrome c is discussed in Chapter 18. After E. Margoliash, in D. Keilin and E. C. Slater, "Cytochrome," *British Med. Bulletin* **9**: 89 (1953).

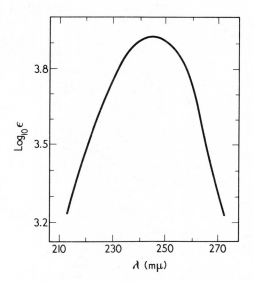

Figure 4. Absorption spectrum of ascorbic acid (vitamin C) in ethanol. After H. H. Wasserman and F. M. Precopio, "Studies on the Mucohalic Acids," *J. Am. Chem. Soc.* **74**: 326 (1952).

If scattering occurs as well as true absorption, one may rewrite the preceding by setting

$$\mu = \mu_a + \mu_s \qquad (4)$$

where the subscript a means absorption and s scattering. If μ_s is too large relative to μ_a, some energy will be scattered more than once, re-entering the original beam. Then Lambert's law will no longer be valid. However, in many cases this rescattering is not important and Lambert's law is useful. If the scattering is too great, it is possible sometimes to use not the light transmitted in the original direction as shown in Figure 5, but instead, all the transmitted light.

Equation 3 is a correct form of Lambert's law only if μ is constant over the wavelength band present. The value of μ will in general vary with the wavelength. In this case, one may represent the initial intensity I_0 as an integral over the range of wavelengths present. This is expressed by

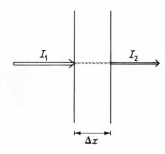

$$I_0 = \int I_{0\lambda}\, d\lambda \qquad (5)$$

where $I_{0\lambda}\, d\lambda$ is the incident intensity between $\lambda + d\lambda$. For each $I_{0\lambda}\, d\lambda$, μ will be constant, so that a more general form of Lambert's law is

Figure 5. Attenuation of light on passing through a sheet the thickness of which is Δx. The incident intensity is I_1, and the attenuated intensity leaving the sheet is I_2.

$$I = \int I_{0\lambda}\, e^{-\mu x}\, d\lambda \qquad (6)$$

Because μ depends in a complex fashion on λ, there is no way of simplifying the preceding integral. Equations 5 and 6 are very complicated to use. For precise work, narrow bands of wavelengths are used.

Since absorption is a probability phenomenon, one expects that the more absorbers there are in the light beam the greater will be the absorption. For solutions with low concentrations, when Lambert's law is valid

$$\mu = \beta c \qquad (7)$$

where c is the concentration of the absorbing molecule and β, the *extinction coefficient*, is a constant. This is called *Beer's law*. At high concentrations, Beer's law and Lambert's law fail. In any experiment, one must be sure that the concentration range is such that these laws are valid at the wavelengths used.

Provided that Beer's law is valid for all the molecular species involved, it is possible to determine the contribution to μ of any one type of compound by measuring μ for solutions with and without that compound. The difference in the two values of μ rather than the two absolute values is important. Most spectrophotometers are constructed so as to read this difference directly.

In actual practice, instead of using μ which is defined by

$$\mu = \frac{1}{x} \ln \frac{I_0}{I} \tag{8}$$

it is more customary to measure the optical density D where

$$D = \log_{10} \frac{I_0}{I} \tag{9}$$

The two are simply related; since

$$\log_{10}(I_0/I) = \frac{1}{2.3}\left[\ln\frac{I_0}{I}\right]$$

one may write

$$\mu = \frac{D}{2.3x} \tag{10}$$

The values of μ and β may be specified in a number of ways, depending on the units used for x and c; different symbols are often used for the same form. Table II on page 489 gives some of the more common terms and symbols. All of these and other coefficients are used at one place or another in the literature. Usually, $x = 1$ cm, and its dimensions are ignored. Probably the most widely used member of this group of coefficients is ϵ_{mM}.

A familiarity with the symbols and units indicated allows one to compare and correlate the work of different authors and the contents of different textbooks. In terms of these units, one may use measured optical densities to compute concentrations and to identify biologically significant molecular species.

3. Spectrophotometers

The remainder of this chapter is devoted to specific equipment useful in spectrophotometry. The large number of variations and combinations in existence illustrate the widespread use of spectrophotometry, in both research and routine clinical procedures. The purpose of this section is to review the general types of spectrophotometric equipment, their advantages and disadvantages. From the equipment standpoint, every

TABLE II
Symbols Used in Absorption Spectrophotometry

Term	Symbol	Alternative symbols	Defining equation	Units
1. Transmittance	τ	T	$\tau = 100(I/I_0)$	Per cent
2. Optical density	D	$o.d., E, D$	$D = \log_{10}(I/I_0)$	Pure number
3. Extinction coefficient	ϵ	K	$\epsilon = D/x$	x in cm, ϵ in cm^{-1}
4. Specific extinction coefficient	ϵ_{sp}	ϵ	$\epsilon_{sp} = \dfrac{D}{cx}$	c in gm/L, ϵ_{sp} in L/(gm cm)
5. Molar extinction coefficient	ϵ_{mol}	$\epsilon_M, \underset{E}{\epsilon}$	$\epsilon_{mol} = \dfrac{D}{cx}$	c in moles/L, ϵ_{mol} in L/(mole·cm)
6. Millimolar extinction coefficient	ϵ_{mM}	ϵ	$\epsilon_{mM} = \dfrac{D}{cx}$ $\epsilon_{mM} = \dfrac{\epsilon_{mole}}{1{,}000}$	c in millimoles/L ϵ_{mM} in L/(millimole·cm)
7. Absorption ratio	A	—	$A = \dfrac{cx}{D}$	c in gm/ml x in cm A in gm cm/ml
8. Absorption coefficient	μ	κ, a	$\mu = \dfrac{1}{x}\ln(I/I_0)$	μ in cm^{-1}
9. Molar absorption coefficient [extinction coefficient]	β	β_{mol}	$\beta = \dfrac{\mu}{c}$	L/(mole·cm)

spectrophotometer has several components. These include the light source, the monochromator, the sample holder, the detector, and the associated electronic amplifiers and recorders. These are discussed briefly on the following pages.

A. Light Sources

For spectrophotometers operated in the visible and ultraviolet regions, light sources are usually either gas discharge tubes or heated filaments. The discharge tubes give a line spectrum at long wavelengths and a continuous spectrum at the shorter ultraviolet wavelengths. The heated filaments emit continuous light from the "near" infrared region to the "near" ultraviolet region.

For most studies, a continuous spectrum is desired from the light source. This makes it possible to study absorption spectra as a continuous function of wavelength. For the excitation of fluorescence and for the calibration of monochromators, a line spectrum is more useful. Usually, it is not possible to have one source of light which is satisfactory over both the visible and the ultraviolet spectra. Most characteristic absorption spectra are measured between 200 and 1,000 mμ.

In the infrared regions of the spectrum, still other light sources are needed. Generally, some form of hot glowing object is used, the visible rays being filtered off from the infrared. Nernst glowers of rare earth oxides and Globars of carborundum are the most frequently used infrared sources.

In any wavelength region, the electrical power source operating the light must be carefully stabilized. Otherwise, fluctuations in light intensity due to the changes in the electrical power may be greater than the differences due to the absorption being measured. This is illustrated forcefully in the case of the incandescent filament. The power delivered to the filament is roughly proportional to the square of the applied electrical voltage. The temperature of the filament will vary almost proportionally to the power consumed. The light emitted, however, is proportional to the fourth power of the absolute temperature, and hence, to the eighth power of the voltage. Thus, if the voltage is represented by V and the light intensity emitted by I

$$I \propto (V)^8$$

If V changes from V_0 to $V_0 + \Delta V$, I changes from I_0 to $I_0 + \Delta I$. The apparent optical density change ΔD due to the change in I will be

$$\Delta D = \log \frac{I_0 + \Delta I}{I_0} \doteq \frac{1}{2.3} \frac{\Delta I}{I_0}$$

if $\Delta I/I_0$ is small.   From $I \propto (V)^8$, one may write

$$\frac{I_0 + \Delta I}{I_0} = \frac{(V_0 + V\Delta)^8}{V_0} \doteq \frac{V_0 + 8V}{V_0}$$

Combining the last two relationships leads to

$$\Delta D \doteq 3\frac{\Delta V}{V_0} \tag{11}$$

If only the intensity in a narrow wavelength band is measured, the numerical coefficient in Equation 11 might come out closer to 4.

If it is desired to measure optical densities or optical-density changes as small as 0.001, then the electrical power source must be so constant that the voltage changes are less than 3 parts in 10^4.   For sensitive spectrophotometry, necessary to observe small changes in enzyme concentrations, it is sometimes essential to have an optical-density noise level below 10^{-5}.   This means the maximum noise voltage must be no greater than 3 parts in 10^6.

B. Monochromators

In order to make spectrophotometric measurements, as contrasted to photometric measurements, it is necessary to have some method of distinguishing light of different wavelengths.   Our eyes do this in a complex fashion, presenting the information as the sensation of color. In a colorimeter, a series of colored glasses or filters is used for this purpose.   These separate rather broad wavelength bands of light.   For precision work, it is more convenient to produce narrow, sharp wavelength bands with monochromators than with filters.   Two general types of monochromators are widely employed; these are the prism type and the grating type.

The action of a prism of dispersing a white light into a spectrum of colored light was discovered by Isaac Newton (the "father of physics"). It is illustrated in Figures 6, 7, and 8.   The case shown in Figure 6 is simplest to analyze.   The angle φ between the incoming and outgoing rays is called the *deviation*.   It is a minimum when the light rays in the prism are parallel to the base.   The more general case shown in Figure 7 is harder to analyze.

For all transparent media, n varies with the wavelength.   Accordingly, the deviation φ will also vary with the wavelength.   Figure 8 is a simplified diagram of a prism monochromator.   The filament source emits light which passes through slits S_1.   These act as a point source for lens 1, which converts the light beam to parallel light.   On passing through the prism, the light is dispersed, light of each wavelength coming out at an angle dependent on the index of refraction n.   Lens 2 focuses the light so that the beams of any given angle reach a spot in the plane of slits S_2. The slits permit only one narrow wavelength band to pass, thus giving rise to monochromatic light. By rotating the prism about an axis perpendicular to the plane of Figure 8, light of different wavelengths can be brought to S_2. The monochromator can thus be adjusted to any desired wavelength.

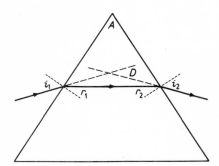

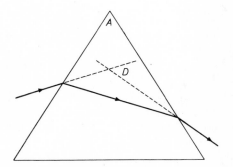

Figure 6. Minimum angle of deviation for light refracted by a prism. Most elementary physics texts show that if A is small

$$\Phi = (n - 1)A$$

$$i_2 = \gamma_1 = \frac{A}{2}$$

$$i_1 = \gamma_2 = \frac{(nA)}{2}$$

where n is the index of refraction.

Figure 7. Refraction by the prism illustrated in Figure 6. A different wavelength gives a greater deviation.

In general, there is not a simple relationship between the angle of deviation and the wavelength. The dial adjusting the prism (and hence, the wavelength selected) must be calibrated for the substance used to form the prism. The purity of the light is controlled by width of the slits S_1 and S_2. For most prisms the slit width W is related to the band width passed by a relationship approximately given by

$$\Delta\lambda/\lambda = kW$$

where k is a constant independent of wavelength or slit width. In other words, for fixed slit width, the fractional or logarithmic bandwidth is approximately constant.

A monochromator for which the wavelength calibration depends on geometry only, and for which there is a constant bandwidth, that is

$$\lambda = k'S$$

can be constructed by using a grating in place of the prism to provide spectral dispersion. There is little or no inherent advantage (or disadvantage) in a grating rather than a prism for a spectrophotometer used to measure the absorption of biologically interesting molecules.

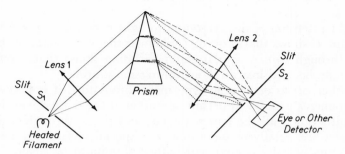

Figure 8. Simplified diagram of a prism monochromator.

Both can be calibrated far more precisely than has any meaning in biological studies, and both can be designed to pass comparable amounts of light at the same wavelength bandwidth.

A grating spectrophotometer is schematically illustrated in Figure 9 for a transmission type grating. Light generated by the heated filament passes through slit S_1 located in the focal plane of lens L_1. The parallel light so produced falls on the grating G. Each line of the grating acts as a source of light giving rise to diffracted rays which are focused by the lens L_2 onto the plane of the slits S_2. The path lengths

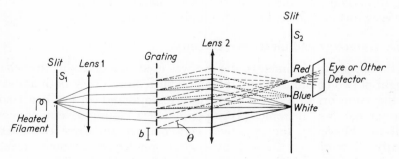

Figure 9. Simplified diagram of a grating monochromator.

from each successive slit to the lens differ by an amount depending only on the angle θ. For most wavelengths, the light from the different lines of the grating will cancel and for only one will they reinforce. In first physics courses, it is shown that the condition for reinforcement is given by

$$b \sin \theta = m\lambda$$

where b is the spacing between the lines of the grating and m is an integer.

A slight extension of this reasoning to light rays not perpendicular to the grating G shows that rotating G changes the wavelength of the light passing through S_2. A similar slight variation shows that a reflection grating may be used instead of a transmission grating.

For either prism or grating type monochromators, it is necessary to use components which will permit operation at the desired wavelengths. In the ultraviolet, all the lenses, prisms, and plates through which the light passes are usually made of quartz. Special surfaces are necessary for reflectors, usually coated with either aluminum or silver. In the visible region of the spectrum, glass of various types is used. For infrared spectrophotometers, prisms are made from rock salt. Lenses, transparent for infrared radiation, are difficult or impossible to construct, so focusing must be accomplished with suitably curved mirrors. In general, special parts are necessary for any desired wavelength region.

C. Sample Holders

For spectrophotometric measurements in the visible and ultraviolet, the samples are usually held in small glass (or quartz) containers called *cuvettes*. If a direct measure of the millimolar extinction coefficient is desired, the cuvette must have plane parallel faces, at right angles to the light beam and separated by a known distance, most often 1 cm. In spectrophotometers designed for curved cuvettes, it is necessary to calibrate against a standard of known optical density.

D. Detectors and Electronic Circuits

In the simplest colorimeters, the eye was used as a detector, the relative height of two columns of liquid being adjusted until they both appeared at the same brightness. A hand spectroscope and an eye can resolve sharper bands than some spectrophotometers costing several thousand dollars. However, the eye gives very poor quantitative estimates of relative intensities. In sensitive spectrophotometry, some form of detector is used which converts the light intensity into an electrical current or voltage. Various photocells, phototubes, and photomultipliers are used.

For measurements which do not change rapidly with time, the optical density can be determined by reading a meter or by balancing a bridge. To observe rapid reactions, some means of graphic or photographic recording is necessary.   This is not difficult with appropriate electronic circuits.

The essential role of electronics in all of the natural sciences cannot be overemphasized.   This has been especially true in biophysics, where almost all measurements are made with electronic equipment.   The material in every chapter in this text depends for its validity on measurements made with electronic tools.   Spectrophotometry is no exception to this rule.

4. Flow Systems

To study rapid reactions, it is necessary to mix the reactants and start observing the reaction before it has progressed too far.   Often this is not possible in cuvettes, where the time to mix the reactants is at least 1 sec.   To avoid this difficulty, flow systems are used in which the mixing occurs just before the solution enters the path of the light beam. For reactions which are not too rapid, the flow is stopped after mixing is completed.   Then the changes in optical density are recorded.   This is called the *stopped-flow method*.   It can be used for reactions whose half-times are greater than 30 msec.

Some reactions take place so rapidly that the stopped-flow method is too slow to be useful, so that it is necessary to observe the reaction during flow.   If the liquid flows at a constant velocity, a constant optical density will be detected.   This can be repeated at varying velocities to obtain the optical density at varying times after mixing. If, instead, the velocity is varied during flow, it is possible to observe the reactions at various times after mixing.   In principle, one could also vary the distance, d, from the mixer to the observation point but this is mechanically more cumbersome.

A suitable flow system is diagrammed in Figure 10.   The two reactants are stored in tanks T_1 and T_2 respectively.   When the stopcocks C_1 and C_2 are set in an appropriate fashion, liquid may be pulled from the storage tanks into the syringes by raising the connecting bar.   With the stopcocks turned as shown in the diagram, liquid may be pushed from the syringes, mixing at M, before flowing through the path of the light beam d centimeters downstream.   If the linear flow velocity is v, the time t, after mixing, is given by

$$t = \frac{d}{v}$$

When flow starts, the old reactants are in the observation tube and mixing chamber.   Some of the mixed reactants may also have diffused back up from M toward the stopcocks.   The initial changes then have little significance.   The curves in Figure 11 show the type of results to be expected from a stopped-flow and an accelerated-flow reaction, both of which are exponential in their time course.   More rapid reaction

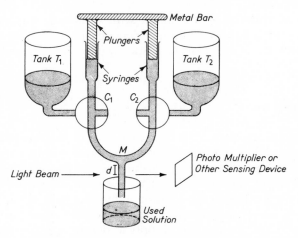

Figure 10. Rapid flow apparatus. C_1 and C_2 are three-way stopcocks allowing one to fill the syringes from the storage tanks and then discharge the syringes into the mixing chamber M.   The optical density changes are observed at d cm down the flow tube.

rates can be detected by flow-type measurements than by measurements in cuvettes.   However, there are larger experimental errors associated with the flow-type measurements.

5. Split-Beam and Dual-Beam Spectrophotometers

In absorption spectrophotometry, the light intensities transmitted by a standard and a test sample are compared.   Errors will be introduced into the optical densities so measured if the output of the light source changes.   Similarly, if one measures the transmitted intensity at several wavelengths first for the standard and then for the test sample, it is important to compare readings at exactly the same wavelength.   These operations can be simplified and the errors reduced by using slightly more complex equipment, namely a *split-beam spectrophotometer*.   In this, the beam from the monochromator is split so that it alternates rapidly, passing first through the standard and then the test sample.   Thereafter, the split beam is recombined to fall on a common detector.   The optical density of the test sample relative to the standard is found electronically or by mechanically controlling the intensity of the source so that the light passing through the standard gives rise to a constant voltage.

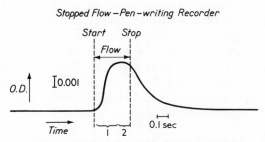

Stopped Flow –Pen–writing Recorder

Region 1. *Old reactants removed by flow down tube.*
Region 2. *New reactants do not react during time to flow down tube.*

(a)

Accelerated Flow — Oscilloscope Tracing

(b)

Figure II. Rapid flow records. (a) Stopped flow as made by a pen-writing recorder. (b) Accelerated flow as indicated by an oscilloscope tracing.

The split-beam method has another advantage, besides reducing the sensitivity to light-source fluctuations and increasing the ease of obtaining spectral measurements. For example, the absorption spectra of a suspension of cells in the presence and absence of oxygen can be compared by using one of these suspensions as a standard and the other as the test sample.   The spectrum obtained in this fashion is a difference spectrum.

In some cases, a suspension of cells or cell fragments will undergo specific changes in absorption during the reaction as well as more general changes due to such factors as settling and swelling.   This can be taken into account by measuring the optical density at two neighboring wavelengths, only one of which is altered specifically by the reaction being studied.   If the original light beam is passed alternately through two monochromators, and these two beams are then recombined to pass through a common sample, the nonspecific changes in optical density can be subtracted out by the associated electronic equipment.   The device used for this operation is called a *dual-beam spectrophotometer*.   It is less sensitive to light-level fluctuations than is a single, unsplit-beam spectrophotometer.

Both the split-beam and dual-beam spectrophotometers employ some form of light chopper.   All light choppers have an inherent noise which cannot be eliminated.   Accordingly, one can measure smaller changes in optical density by regulating the light source than one can through the use of split- or dual-beam spectrophotometers.   The extremes of light regulation necessary to do this with a single beam make split- and dual-beam spectrophotometers more convenient for most purposes.

Instead of presenting a detailed description of split- and dual-beam spectrophotometers, the action of one particular split-beam spectrophotometer is outlined below.   It is shown in block-diagram form in Figure 12.

Light proceeds through the monochromator and is then reflected alternately by the sector mirror R, so that it passes through sample holder C_1, and by the fixed mirror M, so that it passes through sample holder C_2.   Thereafter, the light is reflected by two fixed mirrors M' and M'' so that it converges on the photomultiplier cathode.   To detect low signal intensities, the load resistor must be large.   A d-c amplifier with feedback acts as a current amplifier, presenting sufficient current to operate the following circuits.   The potential from the d-c amplifier is proportional to the intensity, I_1, of light coming through C_1 for half a cycle and then to I_2 coming through C_2 for the next half cycle.   This potential is passed through the logarithmic attenuator; the signals produced are proportional to $\log I_1$ and to $\log I_2$ respectively, each for half a cycle.   The output of the logarithmic attenuator is fed into an a-c amplifier.

The a-c amplifier responds only to the differences from the average of the two signals.   Denoting its rms output by ϵ, one may write

$$\epsilon = A\,[\log I_1 - \log I_2] = A \log \frac{I_1}{I_2}$$

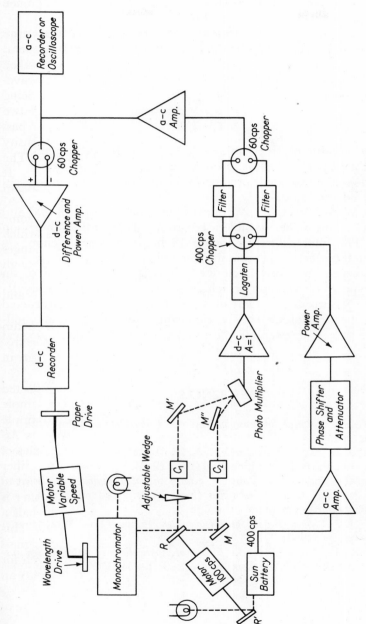

Figure 12. Split beam spectrophotometer. R and R' are rotating sector-mirrors. M, M', and M'' are fixed mirrors. The recorders plot the difference in optical density of the solutions in cuvettes C_1 and C_2. After W. L. Blair, Thesis, The Pennsylvania State University, 1958.

where A is a proportionality constant. Thus, the output of the a-c amplifier is proportional to the optical density.

If the signal is very small, the losses in the logarithmic attenuator are excessive. In this case, it may be omitted, since

$$\log \frac{I_1}{I_2} = \log \left(1 + \frac{I_1 - I_2}{I_2}\right) \doteq \left(\frac{I_1 - I_2}{I_2}\right)\Big/ 2.3$$

if

$$(I_1 - I_2) \ll I_2$$

Under these conditions, the optical density will be proportional to $I_1 - I_2$. If a 10 per cent error in optical density can be tolerated, the approximation may be used, provided that the total change of optical density does not exceed 0.05.

Motor Number 2 in Figure 12 controls both the wavelength dial and the recorder. This makes possible a recording of the entire absorption spectrum. The filter shown in Figure 12 helps to remove chopping noise and high-frequency photomultiplier noise.

This instrument has been described as a specific example of an absorption spectrophotometer which is more complex than a single-beam one. Numerous commercial as well as laboratory-constructed models of spectrophotometers—single-beam, split-beam, and dual-beam—have played an essential role in research in all of the biological sciences.

REFERENCES

1. Brode, W. R., *Chemical Spectroscopy* 2nd ed. (New York: John Wiley & Sons, Inc., 1943).
2. Harrison, G. R., R. C. Lord, and J. R. Loofbourow, *Practical Spectroscopy* (Englewood Cliffs, N.J.: Prentice-Hall, Inc., 1948).
3. Oster, Gerald, and A. W. Pollister, eds., *Physical Techniques in Biological Research.* Vol. I. *Optical Techniques* (New York: Academic Press, Inc., 1955). Particularly Chapters 1 through 7.
4. Blair, W. L., *A Split Beam Spectrophotometer* Thesis, The Pennsylvania State University (1958).
5. Bauman, R. P., Consulting ed., *Biological Applications of Infrared Spectroscopy* (Monograph) *Ann. New York Acad. Sc.* **69**: 1–254 (1957).

27

Quantum Mechanical Basis of Molecular Spectra

I. Introduction

In the last chapter, some of the types of spectrophotometers used in biological research were described. All of these depend on molecular absorption spectra. It is quite customary to use molecular spectra as a tool with little or no basis for understanding the physical origin of these spectra. By contrast, this chapter is intended to present an elementary, physical picture of the molecular basis for absorption spectrophotometry.

A good deal of space and many words are devoted to the various symbols and to the terminology common in spectrophotometry. Although these may seem far from biology, discussions of photobiology and of energy transformations in biology use the symbols and concepts of molecular spectroscopy. Thus, these symbols and ideas are important not only for their direct application toward understanding spectroscopy, but also for describing other biologically significant types of events.

In order to understand molecular-absorption spectra, it is necessary first to have some ideas about molecular-energy levels. These in turn can be adequately described only in the language of quantum mechanics. The ideas and theories of quantum mechanics have been supported by a wide variety of experiments, such as those dealing with characteristic spectra, specific heats, and the photo-electric effect. The original observations which most forcefully demanded the creation of quantum mechanics for their explanation were the regularities of the characteristic spectra of atoms. It seems quite fitting to present a discussion of quantum mechanics in a chapter on spectrophotometry.

2. An Elementary Approach to Quantum Mechanics

A rigorous presentation of the theory of quantum mechanics is far beyond the scope of this text. Rather, it is hoped that this discussion will serve to acquaint biologically oriented readers with the concepts of quantum mechanics, and to orient the physically inclined to thinking of quantum mechanics in terms of its application to spectra of biological materials.

One of the fundamental ideas of quantum mechanics is that many physical quantities such as energy, momentum, volume, and mass come in small finite chunks, called *quanta*. It is not permissible even to think of further subdividing these quanta. They are all so very small that in the macroscopic world one is not generally aware of their existence. However, on a submicroscopic scale, quantum mechanics is the only theory which correctly predicts the behavior of small molecules, atoms, electrons, and subatomic particles. The absorption spectra of interest in biophysics involve changes within molecules. Hence, one can hope to understand these spectra only in terms of quantum mechanics.

The idea that mass also comes in chunks is familiar to all readers. It is drilled into children in elementary school and high school so that no one any longer questions the realities of molecules and atoms. When one divides a molecule, it is no longer the same substance; and as soon as one divides an atom, it is no longer the same element. Likewise, subatomic particles have fixed masses.

However, the concepts that energy, angular momentum, space, and time come in minimum-size pieces are harder to appreciate. The typical high school science teacher has heard of it but probably can't explain it. Even many elementary physics courses at the college level pass over these ideas as quickly as possible. Yet these ideas are no more surprising or unusual than the existence of atoms and molecules.

Quantum mechanics arose because of an apparent duality of nature— both electrons and radiant energy seeming like waves in some experiments, and in others, like particles. For example, classical experiments of diffraction and interference emphasize that light is transmitted as a wave. (This does *not* mean that something is wiggling or waving back and forth. Rather, it means that the transmission of light obeys the same type of descriptive equations as do elastic waves which one can see and feel.) However, the radiation from black bodies and the photo-electric effect can only be explained by assuming that electromagnetic energy is emitted and absorbed in finite chunks called *photons*. Each photon has an energy E which is related to the frequency of the trans-mitted wave by

$$E = h\nu \qquad (1)$$

In this, h is Planck's constant and ν is the frequency. The numerical value of h is 6.6×10^{-27} erg·sec. In general, the wavelength λ rather than ν is measured in diffraction and interference experiments. Accord-ingly, Equation 1 is often rewritten

$$E = \frac{hc}{\lambda} \qquad (2)$$

Thus, light behaves in transmission as a wave, but in absorption and in emission as a particle.

Electrons also exhibit this apparent duality. In experiments such as those in which the charge e on an electron is measured, the electron acts as a particle. It can be accelerated; it can possess kinetic energy; and in many other ways it can act as a particle obeying Newton's laws of motion. There are other experiments however, which cannot be explained in terms of the particle-like properties of electrons. For example, electrons exhibit interference when reflected by a crystal, and their transmission through an electron microscope can be described accurately through the use of the phenomenon of diffraction. When treated as a wave, their wavelength is given by

$$\lambda = \frac{h}{p} \qquad (3)$$

and their frequency by

$$\nu = \frac{E}{h}$$

where p is the momentum and where E is the total relativistic energy mc^2. Thus, just as photons are, electrons also are transmitted as a wave but act in many places as particles.

These apparent dualities can be resolved by treating both matter and electromagnetic energy as made up of small particles, that is, both are *quantized*. These particles do not individually obey Newton's laws of motion, although a large aggregate of these small particles will appear, on the average, to behave as predicted by Newtonian mechanics. The individual particles move in such a manner that only the relative probability of their being at a certain place can be described. This relative probability is given by the square of the amplitude of a mathematical expression called a *wave function*. The general theory which predicts this behavior is called *quantum mechanics*.

Quantum mechanics has been verified by a wide variety of phenomena. These involve measurements of specific heats, entropies, behavior of gases in discharge tubes, magnetic experiments, and interactions of atomic particles, as well as the characteristic spectra associated with atoms and molecules. Modern quantum mechanics leads to the picture of an atom consisting of a small (about 10^{-12} cm diameter), heavy, positively charged nucleus surrounded by a smeared out cloud of electrons. Within the nucleus of the atom are the protons and neutrons. The electrons cannot be pinpointed at any spot or orbit, but they spend a greater amount of time in certain most probable regions called *orbitals*. (Similarly, it is impossible to specify their instantaneous momentums or energies.) There is a certain region within which there is close to 100 per cent probability of finding all the electrons associated with a given nucleus. This region constitutes the atom; it has a diameter of the order of 10^{-8} cm (1 Å).

The indeterminancy and peculiar effects of quantum mechanics apply only to very small particles. One of the fundamental principles which any quantum mechanical statement must obey is that when applied to large masses, high energies, and long times, quantum mechanics reduces to (or corresponds to) the laws of classical physics. This is known as the *correspondence principle*; it is important for an intuitive grasp of quantum mechanics as well as for a complete mathematical analysis.

Quantum mechanics, when formulated in the symbolism of mathematics, can be shown to lead directly to another general principle, the so-called (*Heisenberg*) *uncertainty principle*. It states that there exist various pairs of variables (called canonically *conjugate variables*) which cannot both be known precisely simultaneously. For example, if Δx indicates the uncertainty about the location of a particle, and Δp the uncertainty concerning its momentum, then the uncertainty principle states that the product of the absolute values obeys the inequality

$$|\Delta x|\,|\Delta p| > \frac{h}{2\pi} \tag{4}$$

In other words, no matter how one goes about measuring the location x of the particle, the measurement will alter the momentum p so that

Equation 4 will be valid. Another canonically conjugate pair of variables are energy E and time t. Again, one may write an inequality; for those variables it is

$$|\Delta E| \, |\Delta t| > \frac{h}{2\pi} \tag{4'}$$

This states that if one describes an atom or molecule in terms of its exact energy, it is impossible to tell when it had this energy.

Table I illustrates the application of the uncertainty principle to two large particles, a piece of chalk and a bacterium, *Escherichia coli*, and to two subatomic particles, a neutron and an electron. The location of the edge of the chalk and of the *E. coli* are uncertain to the order of one interatomic distance. The neutron's location is known only in that it may be restricted to a region within an atomic nucleus. A rather hypothetical calculation shows the results of attempting to restrict the electron to the atomic nucleus; the calculation shows this is absurd because the uncertainty in the electron's velocity would be greater than the velocity of light. This is one of several lines of evidence indicating that one cannot know the position of the electron this precisely.

TABLE I

Examples Illustrating the Uncertainty Principle

Item	Mass Mass in gm	Mass in amu*	$\lvert\Delta x\rvert$ in cm	$\lvert\Delta p\rvert = h/\lvert\Delta x\rvert$ in gm c/sec	$\Delta v = \Delta p/m$ in cm/sec	Uncertainty
Chalk	2	—	10^{-8}	10^{-19}	5×10^{-20}	Negligible
E. coli	1.6×10^{-13}	10^{11}	10^{-8}	10^{-19}	6×10^{-7}	Negligible
Neutron	1.7×10^{-24}	1.0	10^{-12}	10^{-15}	6×10^{8}	Important
Electron (in atoms)	5×10^{-4}		10^{-8}	10^{-19}	10^{8}	Important
Electron (in nucleus)	5×10^{-4}		10^{-12}	10^{-15}	10^{12}	Absurdly large

* amu = atomic mass units.

The uncertainties in the momenta of the chalk or even of the *E. coli* cannot be experimentally detected. By way of contrast, the uncertainties in the velocities of the electron within an atom or the neutron within a nucleus are of major importance. The uncertainty Δv for the neutron is one-fiftieth the velocity of light.

In addition to the correspondence and uncertainty principles, there are other general conclusions basic to quantum mechanics which can be derived by the mathematically adept. One of the more important of these is the existence of *characteristic* (or *eigen-*) *functions*. With the eigenfunctions, there are associated *eigenvalues* of the variables described by *quantum numbers.*   This result is a direct consequence of the wave type equations used to describe the transmission of particles.

Quantum mechanics associates wave-like functions with all particles. If one is sufficiently skilled in manipulating these mathematical wave functions, one can deduce all the measurable characteristics of the particle such as momentum and energy.   These wave functions in many ways resemble those describing the motion of vibrating strings. Such a string has certain resonant modes, each of which can be represented by a suitable characteristic function.   For each resonant mode,

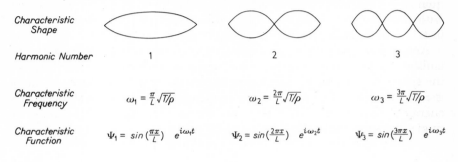

Characteristic Shape			
Harmonic Number	1	2	3
Characteristic Frequency	$\omega_1 = \frac{\pi}{L}\sqrt{T/\rho}$	$\omega_2 = \frac{2\pi}{L}\sqrt{T/\rho}$	$\omega_3 = \frac{3\pi}{L}\sqrt{T/\rho}$
Characteristic Function	$\Psi_1 = \sin\left(\frac{\pi x}{L}\right)\ e^{i\omega_1 t}$	$\Psi_2 = \sin\left(\frac{2\pi x}{L}\right)\ e^{i\omega_2 t}$	$\Psi_3 = \sin\left(\frac{3\pi x}{L}\right)\ e^{i\omega_3 t}$

$$\omega = 2\pi v$$

Figure I. Eigenvalues and eigenfunctions for a string.

there is a certain resonant or characteristic frequency.   Any arbitrary motion of the string can be described as sums of characteristic functions, each multiplied by appropriate amplitudes.   For example, a piano string of length L, linear density ρ, and tension T, vibrates in resonant modes which look something like those shown in Figure 1.   Any arbitrary motion of the string can be described by a wave function Ψ given by

$$\Psi = \sum_{n=1}^{\infty} A_n \Psi_n \qquad (5)$$

where the A_n's are the appropriate amplitudes which are independent of both x and t.

This same mathematical reasoning is valid in quantum mechanics, provided that minor changes are made in the terminology.   Quantum mechanicians usually use the words "quantum number" instead of "harmonic number," and the German word "eigen" instead of the English word "characteristic."   Thus, they talk of eigenfrequencies, eigenfunctions, and eigenvalues.

In the case of the vibrating string, a knowledge of the eigenfrequencies is insufficient to determine the energies associated with the different modes.   In a quantum mechanics problem, however, one obtains the energy from the eigenfrequency through the use of Equation 1, namely

$$E = h\nu \tag{1}$$

The string has one set of numbers which specify the particular harmonic.   The resonant modes of a vibrating plate have two characteristic numbers associated with them, whereas those of a resonant room have three numbers.   Electrons, in general, have five characteristic or quantum numbers associated with them, provided the electrons are within an atom.   The nature of these numbers will be discussed further in the next section.

Another of the central ideas of quantum mechanics deals with the emission of photons.   These have definite sizes which are determined by the spacing between the eigenvalues for the energy.   A photon of light is emitted when an atom (or molecule) changes from one eigenstate with energy E_1 to another eigenstate with lower energy E_2.   In this case, the single photon emitted has an energy E given by

$$E = E_1 - E_2 \tag{6}$$

The wavelength of the photon is then given by Equation 2 as

$$\lambda = \frac{hc}{E} \tag{2'}$$

Conversely, if a photon of just the proper energy E approaches the atom or molecule when it is in the lower eigenstate E_2, the photon may be absorbed, raising the atom (or molecule) to the eigenstate with energy E_1.

This process may sound self-contradictory.   The molecule is either in the state with energy E_1 or in that with energy E_2.   It never has energy values between these two.   Yet, in the emission of the photon, it jumps from one to the other and in so doing must surely pass through all in-between values.   The solution to this dilemma lies in the uncertainty principle.   Since

$$|\Delta E|\,|\Delta t| > \frac{h}{2\pi} \tag{4'}$$

the energies E_1 and E_2 are only average values of the energies.   During a very short time, the energy may be very different from either of the values E_1 and E_2.   It seems helpful to have some idea for how long a time the uncertainty ΔE may be comparable to $E_1 - E_2$.   For this purpose, let us try a numerical example, carrying out the computations only very approximately.

Suppose the photon is in the green region of the spectrum, with a wavelength of 5,500 Å. Then

$$\lambda \doteq 600 \text{ m}\mu = 6 \times 10^{-5} \text{ cm}$$

The energy of the photon is

$$E = \frac{hc}{\lambda} \doteq \frac{6 \times 10^{-27} \times 3 \times 10^{10}}{6 \times 10^{-5}} \doteq 3 \times 10^{-12} \text{ ergs}$$

The time Δt during which there is an uncertainty ΔE in the atomic energy comparable to E is

$$\Delta t \approx \frac{h}{(2\pi E)} = \frac{\lambda}{(2\pi c)} \doteq 3 \times 10^{-16} \text{ sec}$$

This indicates that the emission or absorption of such a photon must take place in 10^{-15} sec or less. During this period of time, it is possible for the energy to have any intermediate value between E_1 and E_2. (For shorter periods of time, the energy may vary still more. The law of conservation of energy is not valid for such short periods of time. This law describes only averages over periods of time long compared to 10^{-15} sec.)

The foregoing example indicates that the statement that E_1 and E_2 are average values means that the average is taken over periods of time which are long compared to 10^{-15} sec. It is extremely difficult to measure periods of time as small as this. The average energy is the one which would be measured by almost any method except the emission or absorption of a photon of energy E.

As stated previously, certain quantities such as time and energy cannot both be known precisely. Other quantities can be known at the same time. (These latter are called *commutable*, in the language of quantum mechanics.) One set of variables, all of which can be known at the same time for an electron, consists of its energy, its total angular momentum, the projection of its total angular momentum on any given axis, and its orbital angular momentum. Having read that electrons are not restricted to orbits, the reader may justifiably feel surprised to see the word "orbital" used here, and he also may feel puzzled at the difference between total angular momentum and orbital angular momentum. Perhaps the next paragraph may make these statements a little clearer.

Many small particles, such as electrons, have an intrinsic angular momentum called *spin*. It is convenient to think of the electron spinning like the earth about some internal axis. This leads to certain difficulties with the theory of relativity, so most physicists today simply mumble "intrinsic angular momentum" and let it go at that. In addition, the electron has an average angular momentum about an external axis due to its motion in the field of the atom.   For historical reasons, the latter is called an *orbital angular momentum*.   The vector sum of the intrinsic and orbital angular momenta is called the *total angular momentum*. Because these momenta are all averages, it is not surprising that the average projection of these momenta on any prechosen axis is also *quantized*, that is, it can have only a discrete set of eigenvalues.

In applying quantum mechanics, it is important to distinguish that which is small and hence described by quantum mechanics from that which is large and adequately interpreted by classical physics.   In general, angular momenta may be compared to Planck's constant, h; distances may be compared to the radius of a hydrogen atom; energies— to the lowest possible for the given system; and masses—to atomic masses.   From the point of view of quantum mechanics, a virus particle, too small to observe with the light microscope, is still a macroscopic object.   In fact, for some considerations of quantum mechanics, even a protein molecule is a macroscopic object.

Quantum mechanics of proteins and nucleic acids becomes significant only when one discusses the nature of the bonds between atoms and the absorption spectra characteristic of that particular species of molecules. In the following sections, it will be shown that modern quantum mechanics is useful for a qualitative understanding of molecular spectra.

3. Molecular Spectra—Rotational and Vibrational Bands

As described in the last section, a photon will be absorbed only if its energy is just sufficient to raise the molecule to another eigenstate. Molecules excited by thermal or other means may fall to a lower energy eigenstate by emitting a photon.   In addition to the necessary energy values, there are certain selection rules, correctly predicted by quantum mechanics, which give the energy-level changes most likely to produce absorption or emission spectra.   The energy changes can be related to wavelengths through the use of Equation 2.

Molecular spectra result from changes in energy levels within molecules.   Three types of molecular energy can be readily distinguished; rotational, vibrational, and electronic.   The spacings of rotational-energy levels are small compared to the average thermal energy kT at room temperature.   (For $T \approx 300°K$, $kT \doteq 4 \times 10^{-14}$ ergs.)   At equilibrium, at this temperature, a group of molecules will be distributed among various rotational levels.   In a collision between two molecules, either or both may jump from one energy level to another.   Spectral absorption of photons of the proper energy to raise the molecules to a higher level is also of interest. Rotational spectra are discussed in subsection A, to follow.

By contrast, differences in vibrational energy levels are large compared to kT. At room temperature, most of the molecules will be in the lowest vibrational state. When a photon is absorbed with energy sufficient to increase the vibrational-energy level, there may be a change in the rotational-energy level as well. Vibrational spectra are discussed in subsection B.

Spacings of electronic-energy levels are still larger. Thus, to increase the electronic-energy level, the photons must be in the visible or ultraviolet regions of the spectrum. At equilibrium, usually only the lowest electronic state is occupied. (Some molecules have electronic eigenstates whose energy levels are very close to the lowest one. *Resonance* between these low-energy states gives such molecules added stability.) Electronic spectra are described in the next section.

A. Rotational Spectra

The rotational changes involve the smallest energy differences of any of the types of spectra considered in this chapter. The photons absorbed and emitted by rotational changes correspond to comparatively long wavelengths ranging from the "microwave" region where the wavelength is of the order of 1 cm, to the "far infrared" where the wavelength is of the order of 10^{-2} cm. If the molecule could be thought of as a "classical" (Newtonian) rotor, with moment of inertia I, its angular momentum P_φ would be

$$P_\varphi = I\omega \tag{7}$$

where ω is 2π times the frequency of rotation. The kinetic energy E_K of the rotor is

$$E_K = \tfrac{1}{2} I\omega^2 = (P_\varphi^2)/(2I) \tag{8}$$

Quantum mechanics allows one to retain Equations 7 and 8, provided that P_φ and P_φ^2 are properly interpreted. Neither may be known precisely at any instant. However, their averages over long periods of time are given by

$$\overline{P_\varphi} = \frac{Jh}{2\pi}$$

and

$$\overline{P_\varphi^2} = J\frac{(J + 1)}{4\pi^2}$$

where J is a positive integer or zero. These average values will be correct provided that the time of measurement Δt is long compared to $h/(2\pi E_K)$. Algebraic manipulation reduces this restriction to

$$\Delta t \gg \frac{1}{\omega} \frac{2}{J + 1}$$

In other words, at low J values one must observe the angular momentum for periods of time long compared to the average period of rotation of the molecule (divided by 2π), whereas at higher values of J the necessary time becomes negligible compared to a molecular period. This is in accord with the correspondence principle.

A number of different lines of evidence confirm the relationship between $\overline{P_\varphi}$ and $\overline{P_\varphi^2}$. Spectroscopic evidence demanded it long before quantum mechanics had developed to the point of predicting it. Again, at the higher energy

$$\lim \; (\overline{P_\varphi^2}) \doteq (\overline{P_\varphi})^2$$

also as demanded by the correspondence principle.

Quantum mechanics predicts not only that P_φ is quantized, but also that its projection P_Z on any prechosen axis is quantized. In particular

$$P_Z = M_J h/2\pi$$

where

$$M_J = -J, \; -(J-1), \cdots -1, 0, +1, \cdots (J-1), J$$

A knowledge of M_J is necessary to predict the relative intensity of spectral lines and also to describe their changes in a magnetic field.

Molecules may radiate or absorb energy by changing their rotational energy level which is specified by J (and by M_J in an electrical or magnetic field). However, not all molecules will do so. Classically, electrical dipole changes were thought of as responsible for radiation. The correspondence principle indicates that dipole changes must occur in all cases. Thus, homopolar molecules such as O_2, N_2, H_2, and so on should not be expected to exhibit purely rotational spectra. However, asymmetric molecules such as HCl and H_2O have characteristic absorption spectra due to changes in their rotational levels.

For transitions involving the absorption or emission of a photon, not all changes in J are permissible. There is a so-called selection rule which states

$$\Delta J = \pm 1$$

(This rule applies only to "electrical dipole" changes. Absorption can also occur because of electrical quadrapole changes, magnetic dipole changes, and so on. These are less probable; usually they are called *forbidden lines.*)   Absorption corresponds to an increase of J from J_1 to $J_2 = J_1 + 1$.   In this case, the photon energy will be

$$E = E_2 - E_1 = \frac{h^2(J_1 + 1)(J_1 + 2)}{8\pi^2 I} - \frac{h^2 J_1(J_1 + 1)}{8\pi^2 I} = \frac{h^2(J_1 + 1)}{4\pi^2 I}$$

(Actually this is a slight oversimplification, because the effective value of I depends on the value of J.   Classically, this would be expected for a nonrigid rotor, that is, one which could vibrate as well as rotate.   As all molecules vibrate, a better approximation for the molecular energy E_K is

$$E_K = AJ(J + 1) - BJ^2(J + 1)^2$$

Values for both A and B can be found from spectroscopic measurements for molecules which are asymmetrical rotators.)

To the best of the author's knowledge, purely rotational spectra have never been used in biophysical research.   They have been introduced here because rotational-energy levels affect the vibrational and electronic spectra.   Rotational levels are closer in behavior to our ideas of classical macroscopic bodies than are the vibrational and electronic-energy levels.   Rotational levels are easier to visualize, and thus these form a good introduction to molecular spectra.

B. Vibrational Spectra

A somewhat more complicated mathematical problem arises when one considers the vibrational modes of motion.   A quantum mechanical treatment of a simple harmonic vibrator shows its energy is quantized so that

$$E = h(v + \tfrac{1}{2}) \qquad v = 0, 1, 2, 3, \cdots \tag{9}$$

If the vibrator may also rotate, one should write

$$E = h(v + \tfrac{1}{2}) + \frac{h^2 J(J + 1)}{8\pi^2 I} \tag{10}$$

Note that in the lowest energy state there is still the vibrational energy

$$E = \tfrac{1}{2}h$$

In other words, even at 0°K, the vibrator still possesses kinetic energy of vibration.

The vibrational-energy levels of diatomic molecules are more complex than those of a simple harmonic vibrator.   Polyatomic vibrations are still more complicated.   Thus, the expressions for the energy in Equations 9 and 10 are oversimplified, but at low values of v, they are good approximations.   The more exact expressions for E permit one to calculate dissociation energies from spectroscopic data.   These values agree well with chemical data; the spectroscopic data are often more precise.

If the change in the vibrational-energy level involves a change in the average electrical dipole, radiation can occur. The selection rules are

$$\Delta v = \pm 1$$
$$\Delta J = \pm 1, 0 \text{ except } 0 \rightarrow 0$$

(Read expression $0 \rightarrow 0$ as "zero to zero is forbidden.") For every change in v, there will be a band of changes in J. (In fact, there will be three bands, one for $\Delta J = +1$, one for $\Delta J = -1$, and one for $\Delta J = 0$. They are different because the energy and the moment of inertia I both depend on J and v.)

Qualitatively, the foregoing concept is valid for all molecular bonds. For the more complex molecules, however, the sharp lines within a band are smeared out by interactions with other groups within the molecules and with neighboring molecules. To some extent, these interactions can be reduced by taking the spectrophotometric measurements at very low temperatures, but the smearing out of the rotational bands associated with a vibrational transition cannot be completely removed.

A variety of covalent bonds have characteristic absorption peaks due to vibrational transitions. From the location and relative magnitude of these absorption peaks, it is sometimes possible to determine the bond types present and also the number of bonds of a given type. So many peaks occur in the spectral region of $3 \rightarrow 20\mu$ that this type of analysis is most successful for choosing one of several structures for a given molecule or determining the amounts of two or, at most, three different types of molecules after purification. Spectra in this region are complex but characteristic of the particular molecular species present. This band is often called the *fingerprint region* of the spectrum.

A characteristic spectrum is shown in Figure 2. Many more are shown in the book by Randal, *et al.* included in the references. When their book was published in 1949, the actual type of vibration was not known for all absorption bands. They do, however, identify a large number. Since then, additional studies have multiplied the known absorption spectra manyfold.

The problems of comparing different data from different laboratories have been complicated by lack of absolute calibrations and failure to appreciate the limitations of the equipment. Infrared measurements of vibrational bands are also difficult because of the extremely high absorption of water in this spectral region. Some experiments have compared spectra in H_2O and D_2O to eliminate the high background absorptions. Most experiments involved specimens prepared either in a hydrocarbon gel (as nujol) or as part of a pressed KBr disc.   The preparation by either method does alter the spectrum.   Some typical absorption bands are given in Table II.

TABLE II

Infrared Absorptions

Group	λ_{max} in μ	Group	λ_{max} in μ
$>C=N$	5.95 or longer	$>NH$	2.88–3.28
$>C=S$, $-N=O$ } $-N=N-$, $S=O$ }	6.28–6.8	$-SH$ $-OD$	3.72–3.9 3.6 –3.8
$>SO^4$	8 –8.5	$>ND$	3.85–4.15
$-OH$	2.66–2.98	$>CH$	3.05–3.7

The various types of covalent bonds each have several absorption maxima corresponding to different types of vibrations.   Randal and

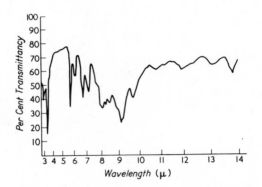

Figure 2. Infrared absorption spectrum of 1-α-dimyristoyl cephalin.   Absorption bands in the infrared are due to molecular vibrations and rotations.   After H. P. Schwarz *et al.*, "Infrared Studies of Tissue Lipids," *Annals of the New York Academy of Sciences* **69**: 116 (1957).

co-workers classify the vibrations responsible for the absorption spectra as: (1) stretching (along the bond); (2) bending (across the bond); (3) deformation—a bending which changes the bond angle; (4) wagging —an entire group moving perpendicular to the plane of symmetry; (5) rocking—similar to wagging but in the plane of symmetry; (6) twisting—an entire group rotates around a bond to the rest of the molecule; (7) breathing—completely symmetric stretching—usually in rings; and (8) others not yet identified.

Qualitatively, the description of the simple harmonic vibrator adequately describes the type of spectra observed and predicts that they should be located somewhere in the infrared. However, such details as the wavelength at which —C—H bonds absorb or the shape of the absorption bands cannot be predicted a priori. Rather, the absorption bands of known structures are measured, and these are used to interpret

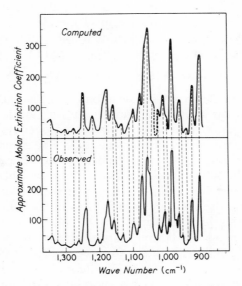

Figure 3. Infrared absorption spectra of 3-desoxytigogen. Computed and observed spectra are compared. The wave number, used here for the abscissa, is the reciprocal of the wavelength. After R. N. Jones *et al.,* "Infrared Intensity Measurements Applied to the Determination of Molecular Structure," *Annals of the New York Academy of Sciences* **69**: 38 (1957).

the bonds present in unknown compounds. Even here, there are only empirical rules to indicate how a particular compound will alter the absorption band due to a bond as $>C{=}O$. A successful application of these rules is illustrated in Figure 3.

To recapitulate, then, vibrational absorption bands show the bonds which are present. The spectral fingerprints of most biologically important compounds are so complicated in the spectral region from 2–20μ that purified solutions are necessary. These absorption spectra can be used to identify the bonds in a compound or determine the relative amounts of a few similar compounds (for example, steroids) present in a given fraction or sample.

4. Electronic Levels of Atoms and Molecules

Rotational and vibrational spectra involve the relative motion of atoms or groups of atoms. It is also possible to change the energy levels of an electron within a molecule without changing the location of the atoms. In the most general case, a transition of the electronic-energy level is accompanied by a change in vibrational and rotational levels. Symbolically, the energy change may be represented as

$$\Delta E = \Delta E_r + \Delta E_v + \Delta E_e \tag{11}$$

This predicts the existence of bands of bands of lines about any spectral line representing an electronic change. In the liquid and solid states, these bands of bands of lines are all smeared out into one continuous absorption band for each electronic change. The absence of sharp lines is due to interactions of the various parts of the same molecule and to collisions with the solvent molecules or with the neighboring molecules. These interactions and collisions may either add or subtract small amounts ΔE_i to the photon energy ΔE in Equation 11, resulting in a continuous absorption band.

The details of the qualitative nature of electronic-energy levels of molecular spectra are very similar to those of atomic spectra. Because the atomic spectra are somewhat less complicated they are described first. The same types of quantum numbers exist for the electronic-energy levels of both atoms and molecules. However, only the atomic wave functions can be computed exactly.

A. Electronic Spectra of Atoms

The electronic-energy levels of atoms can be found from a knowledge of the numbers of electrons and the charge on the nucleus. The wave functions for one-electron atoms such as H, D, T, He^+, Li^{++}, Be^{+++}, and so on, can be represented exactly in closed form. So can the electron wave functions for two-electron atoms such as He, Li^+, Be^{++}, B^{+++}, and so on. In all other cases, iterative approximation methods allow one to come as close as desired to the eigenfunctions, energy levels, and spectral lines.

Atomic wave functions for isolated atoms can be used to derive very exact expressions for the wavelengths of absorption and emission lines. Five quantum numbers are used to specify the energy state of each electron. These numbers are represented by certain letters. Also, some of their numerical values are specified by letters rather than numbers. A large number of letters is summarized in Table IV in the next subsection. Not only are many letters used but several have more than one meaning. These letters are the language of quantum mechanics and spectroscopy. If one wishes to discuss the nature of absorption bands, it is customary to describe them in terms of these letters.

Although the atomic electronic wave functions are simpler than the molecular ones, they are by no means as simple as those describing molecular rotations and vibrations. In order to designate an electron within an atom completely, there are two sets of five numbers, either set of which may be specified. Both include a total quantum number n, an orbital quantum number l, and a spin quantum number s. There are two possible choices for the other two numbers. One may specify the projection of l and s on a given axis by the quantum numbers m_l and m_s, or one may specify the total angular momentum by the quantum number j and its projection on a given axis by m_j.

These quantum numbers are restricted for an electron so that

$$s = \tfrac{1}{2}$$
$$n = 1, 2, \cdots$$
$$l = 0, 1, 2, \cdots n-1$$
$$m_l = -l, l+1, \cdots -1, 0, +1, \cdots l-1, l$$
$$m_s = \pm \tfrac{1}{2}$$
$$j = |l+s|, |l+s|-1, \cdots |l-s|$$
$$m_j = -j, -j+1, \cdots -\tfrac{1}{2}, +\tfrac{1}{2}, \cdots j-1, j$$

The total quantum number n appears in the energy and in the eigenfunction. The others are all related to angular momenta in the same fashion as J is to the rotational angular momentum of a molecule. For example, if p_s is the intrinsic momentum, then

$$\overline{p_s} = sh/2\pi$$

and

$$\overline{p_s^2} = s(s+1)h^2/4\pi^2$$

Again, for the projection of the total angular momentum on the z axis p_z, one may write

$$p_z = m_j h/2\pi \quad \text{and} \quad \overline{p_z^2} = m_j(m_j+1)h^2/4\pi^2$$

Just as in the case of rotational and vibrational spectra, there are selection rules for absorption and radiations involving electrical dipoles. For a single electron change, these selection rules are

$$\Delta l = \pm 1$$
$$\Delta s = 0$$
$$\Delta j = \pm 1, 0$$

In addition, in a weak magnetic field there is also the selection rule

$$\Delta m_j = \pm 1, 0$$

whereas in a strong magnetic field

$$\Delta m_l = \pm 1, 0$$
$$\Delta m_s = 0$$

For reasons which have far outlived their original meaning, the electrons are designated by different letters according to their value of the orbital quantum number l.   These are

$$l = 0 \ 1 \ 2 \ 3 \ 4 \ 5 \ 6 \text{ and so on}$$
$$\text{letter} = s \ p \ d \ f \ g \ h$$

Notice that the letter s has been used both for the spin quantum number and for an electron with no orbital angular momentum.   It is important not to confuse these two.   (In naming the electrons, originally s = sharp, p = principal, d = diffuse, and f = fundamental.   These words are devoid of anything but historical significance.   This inappropriate ordering of letters to represent different values of l is, however, employed by chemists and physicists alike.   This situation is reminiscent of some of their strongest criticisms of descriptive biology.)

The five quantum numbers for an electron can be extended to a complete atom.   In so doing, one introduces more letters.   The total quantum number n must be specified for each electron.   However, the angular momenta of the various electrons can add vectorially.   Both the values of the individual momenta and some of their sums are quantized.   Capital letters are used for whole atom values corresponding to the lower-case letters for single electrons.   For instance, for two electrons, in some cases

$$
\begin{aligned}
L &= (l_2 - l_1), (l_2 - l_1 + 1), \cdots (l_2 + l_1) \\
S &= s_1 \pm s_2 \\
M_L &= -L, (-L+1), \cdots (L-1), L \\
M_S &= -1, 0, +1 \\
J &= (L-S), (L-S+1), \cdots (L+S)
\end{aligned}
$$

In other cases, the orbital angular momentum and atomic spin are not quantized but, instead, the total angular momentum is quantized. Then one may write

$$
\begin{aligned}
J &= (j_2 - j_1), (j_2 - j_1 + 1), \cdots (j_2 + j_1) \qquad j_2 > j_1 \\
M_J &= -J, (-J+1), \cdots (J-1), J
\end{aligned}
$$

This last case is called *j–j coupling* and the former is called *L–S* or *Russel–*

Saunders coupling. The reader may readily extend these concepts to more than two electrons.

Selection rules for atomic spectra are very similar to those for single electrons, namely

$$\left.\begin{array}{l} \Delta L = \pm 1 \\ \Delta S = 0 \\ \Delta J = \pm 1, 0 \quad 0 \to 0 \end{array}\right\}$$

In a weak magnetic field

$$\Delta M_j = \pm 1, \quad 0 \to 0$$

and in strong magnetic fields

$$\left.\begin{array}{l} \Delta M_L = \pm 1 \\ \Delta M_S = 0 \end{array}\right\}$$

The letters used for different L values are the same as those for different l values except that capitals are used. For a given value of L and S, there are at most $2S+1$ values of J; this is sometimes called the *multiplicity*. The quantum state of an atom due to its electronic configuration is often represented by symbols such as $^3P_0$. The superscript 3 is the value of $2S+1$; in this example, it tells one that $S = 1$. The letter P is the value of L, namely 1. The subscript 0 is the value of J.

(So many letters having been introduced to describe the state of the electrons within an atom, a few more will be included for completeness. In X-ray studies, photons are emitted when a free electron falls into an atom. These photons are absorbed when an electron is raised from a lower energy level to a much higher level. The X-ray researchers have their own letter scheme for representing quantum numbers. They refer to the different values of n as shells, and of l as subshells. Each shell is designated by a letter starting with K, as shown in Table III.)

TABLE III

X-ray Terminology for Electron-Energy Levels

$n =$	1	2		3			4			
shell	K	L		M			N			
$l =$	0	0	1	0	1	2	0	1	2	3
subshell	K	L_1	L_2	M_1	M_2	M_3	N_1	N_2	N_3	N_4

(As another aside, attention should be drawn to the Pauli exclusion principle which states that no 2 electrons within the same atom may have the same 5 quantum numbers. Because s is always 1/2, it is sometimes not counted; then the exclusion principle states that the number of quantum numbers which may not be identical is 4. Using this exclusion principle, it is possible to predict the general form of the periodic table. By and large, the lowest values of n and l correspond to the lowest energy levels and these are filled in first. Thus, $n = 1$, $l = 0$, $m_j = 1/2$ corresponds to the lowest level for hydrogen. In helium, both electrons are in the state $n = 1$, $l = 0$ but one has $m_j = +1/2$, and the other $m_j = -1/2$. The full development is beyond the scope of this text. See, for example, the reference by White.)

The major energy-level changes are determined by the initial and final values of n and l. Most spectroscopic lines due to electron transitions within an atom have a fine structure determined by the quantum number j. Still higher resolution shows that, in many cases, each of these lines has a hyperfine structure. Some hyperfine structure is due to the presence of several isotopes, others to the existence of a net nuclear spin. The nuclear spin has a quantum number I which is coupled to the total electronic angular momentum specified by J to give a total atomic angular momentum specified by the quantum number K.

Atomic spectra are employed quite widely in biological research. Perhaps the most frequently used are in flame spectrophotometric studies to identify the amount of sodium, potassium, and calcium in blood, urine, tissues, and food. Atomic spectra due to X-ray absorption are used to locate Ca and other elements within tissues and even within parts of the cells. However, the details of fine and hyperfine structure of atomic spectra are rarely used in biological studies.

B. Electronic Spectra of Molecules

The energy states of electrons within a molecule are described by the same types of quantum numbers as those which apply to electrons within an atom. To distinguish the molecular levels from atomic ones, Greek letters are often used. Lower case Greek letters are used to describe the levels of individual electrons within a molecule and capital Greek letters to designate the sums of the electronic properties for the whole molecule. Thus, the total electron spin is represented by the quantum number Σ and the total orbital momentum by the quantum number Λ. As in atomic spectra, electronic states with a given value of Λ are designated by the corresponding Greek capital letters; that is

Λ	0	1	2	3	4 and so on
letter	Σ	Π	Δ	Φ	Γ

Note that no attention is paid to the order of either the Greek or the English alphabets; rather, the Greek letter closest to the corresponding English letter is used.

In some cases, the sum of Λ and Σ is also quantized, just as in atomic spectra.   Here, the letters start running out and often ones duplicating those of atomic spectra are used.   Symbols are also used to indicate whether the bond due to a pair of electrons is symmetric or antisymmetric about the origin, about a plane of symmetry, or about a line of symmetry.

The symbols used for atomic and molecular electronic levels are summarized in Table IV.

TABLE IV

Some Symbols Used in Spectroscopy for Electronic States

Quantum number	Individual electronic states		Electronic configuration	
	in atom	in molecule	in atom	in molecule
Total	n	—	—	—
Spin	$s = \frac{1}{2}$	$\sigma = \frac{1}{2}$	S	Σ
Orbital	l	λ	L	Λ
Orbital projection	m_l	m_λ	M_L	M
Total angular	j	J	J	J
Angular projection	m_j	m_J	M_J	M_J
Nuclear spin	—	—	I	—
Nuclear plus electronic	—	—	K	—
Multiplicity	$2s+1=2$	$2\sigma+1=2$	$2S + 1$	$2\Sigma + 1$
Orbital quantum number equals				
0	s	σ	S	Σ
1	p	π	P	Π
2	d	δ	D	Δ
3	f	φ	F	Φ
4	g	γ	G	Γ
5	h		H	
6	j		J	
7	k		K	

X-ray shells and subshells—see Table III (page 519)

Molecular levels

g—gleich $\left.\vphantom{\begin{matrix}a\\b\end{matrix}}\right\}$ parity
u—ungleich

$+\left.\vphantom{\begin{matrix}a\\b\end{matrix}}\right\}$ reflection
$-\int$ in a plane

$s\left.\vphantom{\begin{matrix}a\\b\end{matrix}}\right\}$ symmetry about
$a\int$ an axis

For molecular spectra resulting from dipole transitions, there are a set of selection rules which include

$$\Delta\Sigma = 0$$
$$\Delta\Lambda = \pm 1, 0$$

For two electrons comprising any bond, their total spin may be 1 or 0; that is, the multiplicity may be 3 or 1. The state of multiplicity 1, called the *singlet state*, has, in general, a lower energy than the states of multiplicity 3, called the *triplet states*. (A notable exception to this is the molecule O_2, whose lowest or ground state is a $^3\Sigma$ state; that is, $\Sigma = 1$, $\Lambda = 0$.) According to the selection rule, a molecule in the lowest triplet state is "forbidden" to radiate its energy to reach the still lower singlet state. Thus, energy may be "trapped" in the molecule. This type of trapping has been included in several schemes to explain the action of chlorophyll during photosynthesis.

In general, single, covalent bonds have relatively large spacings between successive electronic-energy levels. It is usually not feasible to measure absorption spectra due to single covalent bonds. On the contrary, the compounds whose spectra are of greatest biological interest usually have a system of alternate double and single bonds, called a *conjugated system*. Examples include vitamin A and rhodopsin, discussed in the chapter on vision, and heme groups and heme proteins, which are so markedly colored. As more and more bonds are added to a conjugated system, the energy difference between the lowest and the first excited states decreases; the absorption band is shifted progressively toward the red.

It is convenient to write a chain of alternate single and double bonds as

Although simple, this form is probably misleading. A more significant symbolism might be

where the number 3 indicates that three pairs of electrons have orbitals encompassing the dotted region. (Recall that orbital means the locus of the most probable locations and *not* that the electrons travel around fixed orbits.)

The pairs of electrons within the dotted region cannot have spherically symmetric orbits because the chain shown would be stretched out in the plane of the paper and would extend only slightly above and below. Because Σ state (that is, $\Lambda = 0$) implies spherical symmetry, this state is ruled out. The next lowest possibility energywise is a Π state. Accordingly, the electrons not bound to a particular atom must be in π states. These π electrons are believed to be responsible for the characteristic spectra of most biologically interesting molecules.

One approach to quantum mechanical models of more complex molecules is the so-called "method of *molecular orbitals*." In this method, one needs X-ray or other data describing where the atoms are located. The "innermost" electrons (for example, the K shell of C and N) are assumed to be undisturbed and are described by the same wave functions and charge distributions as in the free atoms. Next, one forms linear combinations of the wave functions representing the valence electrons in the free atoms. The form of the new functions is restricted by symmetry requirements and by other considerations. Finally, suitable approximations can be made and constants can be adjusted until the new computed orbitals predict the observed molecular properties. Many chemists and physicists have felt that this method has revealed important information about the molecule. Others feel the necessary approximations and the adjustment of the constants limit the validity of this method of molecular orbitals. In recent years, this method has been used to produce wave functions (that is, molecular orbitals) which correctly predict the spectra of tetrapyrrole ring structures and other dyes.

As far as basic information regarding the structure of molecules is concerned, the infrared studies have yielded much more information than those involving the absorption of light in the visible and ultraviolet regions. However, as a physical tool for research and analysis, the visible and ultraviolet spectra have been far more useful. These spectra have been determined purely empirically. The maxima of the characteristic absorption spectra are used for routine assays, kinetic studies, and analysis of new compounds in all phases of biochemistry and biophysics. By analogy, the use of the absorption peaks is similar to distinguishing that one person is speaking German, another French, and a third Chinese without understanding enough of their words to comprehend what they are saying. Most of the information inherent in the pattern of the absorption peaks is lost because no one can decode it in terms of the electronic configurations of the molecule.

REFERENCES

1. This book is recommended especially for physics students interested in the philosophical basis of quantum mechanics.

Lindsay, R. B., and Henry Margenau, *Foundations of Physics* (New York: John Wiley & Sons, Inc., 1936). Republished by Dover Publications, New York, 1958.

2. This book is recommended especially for students in the biological sciences wishing to read further on quantum mechanics and its relationship to spectrophotometry.
Semat, Henry, *Introduction to Atomic and Nuclear Physics* 3rd ed. (New York: Rinehart & Company, Inc., 1954).

3. Randall, H. M., R. G. Fowler, N. Fuson, and J. R. Dangl, *Infrared Determination of Organic Structures* (New York: D. Van Nostrand Company, (1949).

4. White, H. E., *Introduction to Atomic Spectra* (New York: McGraw-Hill Book Company, Inc., 1934).

5. Herzberg, Gerhard, *Atomic Spectra and Atomic Structure* 2nd ed. Translated by J. W. T. Spinks, with the cooperation of the author. Reprinted by Dover Publications, Inc., New York, 1944.

6. Oster, Gerald, and A. W. Pollister, eds., *Physical Techniques in Biological Research*. Vol. I. *Optical Techniques* (New York: Academic Press, Inc., 1955). Particularly Chaps. 1 through 7.

28

Magnetic Measurements

I. Magnetic Effects in Biology

Constant or slowly varying magnetic fields are not detected directly by any of the human senses. As such, magnetic fields are different from other physical changes, many of which act as external stimuli. Light, sound, heat, pressure, acceleration, gravitational forces, electrical potentials, and chemicals—all may be perceived directly by at least one of the human sensory organs. There is no theoretical reason for this insensitivity to magnetic fields. Perhaps there are other organisms in a different place in the cosmos which do sense magnetic fields. Some persons have believed that homing pigeons could sense the earth's magnetic field and could use it as a guide.

The belief continues to exist among a small minority of scientific investigators that magnetic fields can affect living organisms. Several papers have been presented at technical meetings describing subtle effects claimed in animals (usually rats) raised in high magnetic fields. No changes reported in the past due to magnetic fields have ever been confirmed.

There appears to be no sensory or metabolic response to magnetic fields. Nonetheless, magnetic effects can be used to study the properties of biochemical molecules, particularly a small group called *paramagnetic molecules*. These possess a net magnetic dipole moment which tends to align with the magnetic field, thereby reinforcing the field. This property of paramagnetism can be used to determine molecular electronic structure as well as reaction kinetics. The effects are all extremely small; to observe them, the paramagnetic substance usually must be highly concentrated compared to its naturally occurring state.

Paramagnetic changes have been studied particularly during enzyme-catalyzed reactions. The nature of enzyme reactions has been discussed in detail in Chapters 17, 18, and 22. For the present chapter, it is sufficient to know that enzymes are proteins which catalyze most of the reactions in living systems. Enzyme reactions are usually observed by the spectrophotometric methods discussed in Chapter 26. Sometimes thermal changes are studied, and sometimes direct chemical analyses are performed. For many of the enzyme-catalyzed reactions, chemical analysis is too slow to reveal much information about intermediates. Paramagnetic changes offer an alternate means of studying rapid enzyme reactions. It is possible to use paramagnetic rate constants to confirm spectrophotometric ones and also to detect new intermediates.

The paramagnetic measurements are directly related to the electronic-energy levels within the molecule, discussed in the last chapter. Most organic molecules are normally diamagnetic; that is, they possess no permanent magnetic dipole moment. Those containing metal atoms or free radicals, in contrast, often possess a net dipole moment. The magnetic susceptibility, which quantitatively measures the para- (or dia-) magnetism, can be used to determine the state of the metal atoms or the presence of free radicals.

2. Paramagnetism and Diamagnetism

If one holds a bar magnet near a piece of iron, the iron is strongly attracted to the ends of the bar magnet. These reactions are easy to observe. Materials such as iron which are strongly attracted by a magnet are called *ferromagnetic* or sometimes just *magnetic*. No living systems are known to contain ferromagnetic substances.

Although it is more difficult to demonstrate, some nonferromagnetic substances are attracted by the bar magnet and others are repelled by it. Those attracted are called *paramagnetic* and those repelled are called *diamagnetic*. The diamagnetic are the most common for biologically important molecules.

To put this on a quantitative basis, it is convenient to define a few terms used in describing magnetism. If a current flows through a loop of wire, it gives rise to a magnetic field $\vec{H}$. If a loop of wire carrying a current is brought into the magnetic field, it will be acted on by a force determined by the magnetic induction $\vec{B}$. In most materials, $\vec{B}$ and $\vec{H}$ are proportional to one another, that is

$$\vec{B} = \mu\vec{H}$$

where μ is a constant called the *permeability*. In ferromagnetic substances, the permeability μ, measured in electromagnetic units (emu), is very large compared to one. Moreover, for ferromagnetic substances, μ is not a true constant but depends on H. For low field strengths, μ is around 10^3 for some iron alloys.

Nonferromagnetic substances all have values of μ very close to one. If μ is greater than one, the substance is paramagnetic; if less than one, it is diamagnetic. In both cases, the values are very close to one. (In a vacuum, the permeability is unity.) For the diamagnetic substance, water, for example

$$\mu = 0.99999928 \text{ emu}$$

Writing all these nines is rather annoying; a more convenient quantity is the susceptibility κ defined by

$$\kappa = \mu - 1$$

For water, the susceptibility is

$$\kappa = -7.2 \times 10^{-7} \text{ emu}$$

Paramagnetic substances have a positive susceptibility. In such a substance, the individual molecules act like small bar magnets, tending to line up with the magnetic field and to reinforce it. This property is found only in molecules with net permanent dipole moments which are due to the electron orbital motion or the inherent spin of the electron. (Both of these are discussed in Chapter 27.) In filled shells or subshells of electrons, there is no net magnetic moment; pairs of electrons will always be present with their spins in opposite directions and with their orbital moments cancelling. If, however, there are unpaired electrons present, as in most iron compounds, cupric compounds, and so on, then there will be a net magnetic dipole moment. Certain substances, notably the molecule O_2, although possessing an even number of electrons, have two electrons whose spins are unpaired. These so-called "antibinding electrons" make molecules of oxygen paramagnetic.

Diamagnetic substances have pairs of electrons whose magnetic moments cancel. There are no net dipoles to align with the magnetic field and thus reinforce it. One may think of the pair of electrons as being analogous to two parallel current loops with the current flowing in opposite directions. The magnetic field will tend to alter both current loops. According to the principle of Le Chatelier,[1] the net change is in such a fashion as to oppose the magnetic field applied.

All atoms possess this basic diamagnetism. Paramagnetism, when it is present, tends to be a larger effect. In enzymes, one is interested in the excess of κ over the basic diamagnetism rather than in the actual value. In large molecules, the individual electrons cannot change the orientation of their orbital momentum to line up with the magnetic field. The quantity of interest is the paramagnetic contribution to κ, which is due to unpaired electronic spins.

A striking example is the reaction of reduced hemoglobin Hb and oxygen O_2 to form oxyhemoglobin HbO_2; that is

$$
\begin{array}{cccc}
\text{Hb} + \text{O}_2 \rightleftharpoons \text{HbO}_2 & & \textit{Reactants} \\
4 \quad\quad 2 \quad\quad\quad 0 & & \textit{Unpaired Electrons}
\end{array}
$$

where Hb represents a heme iron. The numbers below the reactants are the unpaired electrons. Thus, hemoglobin and oxygen, both paramagnetic, react to form diamagnetic $Hb \cdot O_2$. Because both Hb and $Hb \cdot O_2$ have an even number of unpaired electrons, it is concluded that the iron has lost an even number of electrons; that is, it is in the ferrous state in both Hb and $Hb \cdot O_2$.

The susceptibility changes of enzymes are measured in the presence of an excess of water. For 10 μM ferric iron, the maximum susceptibility difference from pure water is, at room temperature

$$\Delta\kappa = 1.4 \times 10^{-10} \text{ emu}$$

If this is to be measured with 5 per cent accuracy, one must be able to detect

$$\Delta\kappa = 7 \times 10^{-12} \text{ emu} = -10^{-5} \times \kappa_{H_2O}$$

Thus, the total susceptibility must be measured with an accuracy of one part in 10^5. (If one tried to work with the permeability μ, one would need an accuracy of one part in 10^{12}!) This iron concentration, 10 μM, is high for enzyme studies.

3. Static Measurement Techniques

Several different techniques have been used to measure magnetic susceptibility in biological materials; three methods are discussed in this chapter. The Gouy balance is a static susceptibility measuring device. At one time, it was the most widely used type of apparatus for measuring

---

[1] This principle is usually referred to as *Lenz's law* when describing magnetically induced currents.

susceptibility of biologically active molecules. A novel detector with a more rapid response time is a modification of the Rankine balance at the Johnson Research Foundation at the University of Pennsylvania. A third, completely different, method utilizes the phenomenon of electron-spin resonance. It is described in the following section.

The Gouy balance consists essentially of an ordinary analytical chemistry balance and a strong magnet. It is shown diagrammatically

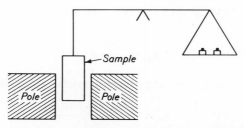

Figure 1. The principle of the Gouy magnetic susceptibility balance. After P. W. Selwood, *Magnetochemistry* (New York: Interscience Publishers, Inc., 1956).

in Figure 1. The sample extends from the region of maximum magnetic-field strength to a region of minimum magnetic-field strength. Under these conditions, it is shown in texts on electricity and magnetism that there exists a force per unit volume df/dv on the sample given by

$$\frac{df}{dv} = \kappa H \frac{\partial H}{\partial x}$$

where x is the direction in which f is measured. If the sample is immersed in a medium of susceptibility κ_0, the foregoing expression becomes

$$\frac{df}{dv} = (\kappa - \kappa_0) H \frac{\partial H}{\partial x} \tag{1}$$

For a sample extending from maximum field H_m to zero field, Equation 1 can be integrated to

$$\frac{f}{v} = \tfrac{1}{2} (\kappa - \kappa_0) H_m^2 A \tag{2}$$

where A is the sample cross section and v is the sample volume.

By comparing the weight of the sample in the Gouy balance with its normal weight, one finds the excess force designated by f in Equation 2. Then κ can be computed. Equation 2 may be rewritten

$$f = F(\kappa - \kappa_0) \tag{3}$$

where F is the proportionality constant

$$F = \tfrac{1}{2} H_m^2 A v \tag{4}$$

In practice, F is determined from Equation 3 by finding f for a sample of known susceptibility κ in the instrument.

Having found the susceptibility κ in emu, it is possible to compute the number of free electrons per molecule. If the molar concentration is c (the moles per milliliter is $10^{-3} c$), one may define a molar susceptibility χ_m by

$$\chi_m = \frac{10^3}{c} \kappa$$

It can be shown that χ_m for many paramagnetic atoms is given by

$$\chi_m = \frac{N^2 g \beta^2 J(J + 1)}{3kT}$$

where N is Avogadro's number, g the Landé factor,[2] β the Bohr magneton, J the total momentum quantum number, k the Boltzmann gas constant, and T the absolute temperature. For a paramagnetic molecule (instead of a single atom), J is replaced by S, the spin quantum number, and g by the spin-only value, g_s. For a single electron, $g_s \doteq 2$.

The theoretical basis of the Rankine balance is the same as that of the Gouy balance. However, instead of having a stationary magnet and observing the force on the sample, it uses a fixed sample holder and measures the force on a suspended magnet. A diagram illustrating this principle is shown in Figure 2. The quartz suspending fibers tend to minimize the effects of the earth's magnetic field, and the symmetry of the suspension reduces the effects of vibrations. The mirror is part of an optical lever system for measuring the rotational displacements of the suspension accompanying changes in force upon the magnet.

In the Johnson Foundation instrument, two samples are used, one on each side of the magnet. These are in the form of half cylinders. The difference in susceptibility between the solutions in the two half cylinders

---

[2] The Landé g factor is the ratio

$$g = \frac{p}{\mu} \cdot \frac{2mc}{e}$$

where p is the total angular moment, μ the magnetic moment, c the velocity in a vacuum, and e the charge on an electron. The Landé g factor is always between one and two. In terms of quantum numbers

$$g = 1 + \frac{J(J + 1) + S(S + 1) - L(L + 1)}{2J(J + 1)}$$

is then determined. The entire apparatus is very small. The magnet is about 2 cm long and each half cylinder holds about 0.5 ml. Instead of allowing the magnet to move, a servo system is employed to hold the

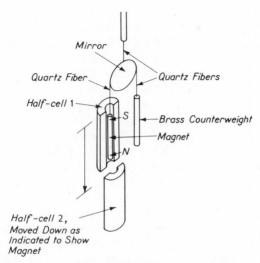

Figure 2. The principle of the Rankine magnetic susceptibility balance. After A. S. Brill, H. den Hartog, and V. Legallais, "Fast and Sensitive Magnetic Susceptometer for the Study of Rapid Biochemical Reactions," *Rev. Sci. Instr.* **29**: 383 (1958).

magnet in place; the servo current is recorded. This instrument is not an absolute one; it must be calibrated using solutions of known susceptibility. This problem is discussed in considerable detail in the reference by Brill and co-workers. The use of a flow system and a rapid mixing chamber makes it possible to resolve short times after the start of the reaction, as discussed in Chapter 26.

4. Resonance Measurements

Both of the balances described in the previous section measure the static magnetic susceptibility of a sample. This includes the effects of all the paramagnetic and diamagnetic molecules in the sample. There is no simple way of separating the various contributions. Resonance methods, in contrast, allow one to separate the effects of different paramagnetic species. Resonance methods are based on the quantum mechanical effect that magnetic dipoles are restricted so that their projection on the direction of a magnetic field can have only certain discrete values. Each discrete value possesses a different energy of interaction with the magnetic field, but the differences are so small that at room temperature all possibilities are present. Photons will be absorbed if they possess just the right energy to flip the dipole from one characteristic angle with the magnetic field to another. Because the photon energy is determined by its frequency, this is called a *resonance phenomenon*.

Resonance methods may be applied to the study of paramagnetism due either to electron spins or to nuclear spins. In the second case, this method is called *nuclear magnetic resonance* (NMR) and in the former case, *electron paramagnetic resonance* (EPR) or *electron spin resonance* (ESR). The theory for both of these is essentially the same, although the frequencies at which the resonances occur are very different. It is possible to measure the resonant frequency ν (if H is constant) or, as is usually more convenient, one may measure the magnetic field H that makes a fixed frequency ν be the resonant one. It is also possible to measure the sharpness of the absorption peaks which then indicates the strength of the interactions with neighboring groups of atoms.

From this discussion, it might seem that all hydrogen nuclei would have the same resonant frequency. However, different types of bonding appreciably alter the location of the resonant frequency. For example, in ethyl alcohol, three frequencies are found using NMR. All three correspond to hydrogen nuclei; one of the absorptions is due to the three methyl-hydrogens, another to the two methylene-hydrogens, and a third to the hydroxyl-hydrogen. NMR is a powerful tool for studying atomic species whose nuclei possess a net spin I different from zero. Unfortunately, most nuclei have a spin $I = 0$.

Electron-spin resonance can be used to study molecules, such as free radicals, which have unpaired electrons. For a single electron, the spin must be either parallel or antiparallel to the magnetic field. The energy difference ΔE between these two is

$$\Delta E = gS\beta H \tag{5}$$

where all the symbols are as defined previously in this chapter. If now a photon of exactly this energy ΔE is applied, it will be absorbed, flipping an electron spin from antiparallel to parallel; that is, there is a resonance at the frequency

$$\nu = \frac{gS\beta H}{h} \tag{6}$$

where h is Planck's constant. For a free electron, g is 2, and S is one-half. For unpaired electrons in a molecule, g may have slightly different values.

In the terminology of electron-spin resonance, it is customary to call the spin magnetic moment of one electron (that is, $1/2\beta$) μ, and to replace the product $2g_sS$ by the spectroscopic splitting factor g. Rewriting Equation 6, it then becomes, in ESR notation

$$\nu = \frac{g\mu H}{h} \tag{7}$$

By varying either ν or H, one can find a value for g. Technically, it is easier to vary H. The form of the apparatus is shown in Figure 3.

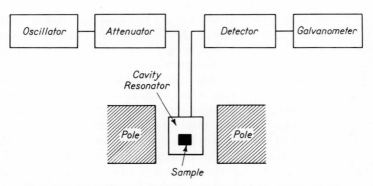

Figure 3. The principle of magnetic resonance absorption measurements. To tune the apparatus, H is usually varied rather than the oscillator frequency. For a free electron

$$\nu = 2.8H,$$

whereas for a proton

$$\nu = 2 \times 10^{-3}H.$$

In these formulae, ν is the oscillator frequency in mc and H the field strength in gauss. For $H = 5 \times 10^3$ gauss, $\nu_{el} = 14$ kmc and $\nu_{pr} = 20$ mc. After P. Selwood, *Magnetochemistry* (New York: Interscience Publishers, Inc., 1956).

For crystalline materials, electron-spin resonance methods give a much higher resolution and more information than does any other method available. However, water, a necessary part of all enzyme reactions, absorbs electromagnetic waves. This problem can be reduced by placing the sample in a capillary tube at an electric node of a waveguide, but the water still remains the limiting factor. In spite of this limitation, ESR is more sensitive than other magnetic methods for the detection of free radicals.

5. Limitations and Applications of Magnetic Measurements

For enzyme studies, two important limitations of magnetic susceptibility measurements are the concentrations needed and the total amount of enzyme needed. The concentration is important for two reasons. First, it is hard to get high concentrations in protein solutions. Secondly, at very high concentrations the proteins may react in a different fashion than at low concentrations. The total enzyme needed is an important limitation because it is difficult to extract large amounts of purified enzymes.

The resolving time or response time of the apparatus is also important in many enzyme experiments. The higher the concentrations, the faster the reactions become. Many enzyme reactions are over in the time required to make the first measurement with the Gouy balance. At maximum sensitivity, the Rankine balance has a slow response time (about one second), but compensates for this by having a long period of flow at constant velocity. By using moderate velocities, it is possible to have the fluid arrive at the cell only 50 milliseconds after mixing.

The properties of the three types of apparatus discussed in the last sections are compared in the accompanying table. The large volume needed for the Rankine balance is used to maintain temperature equilibrium. The poor temperature control is a very undesirable feature of the apparatus described in Reference 3 but is in no theoretical way inherent in the equipment. It seems reasonable to suppose that the

TABLE I

Properties of Susceptibility Measuring Apparatuses

Type	Gouy balance	Rankine balance	ESR	
			Static	Flow system
Quantity measured	Force in μgrams	Force in μdynes	Absorption in per cent	
Minimum concentration needed (about)	300 μM	10 μM	500 μM*	500 μM*
Active volume	0.3 ml	5 ml	0.1 ml	0.1 ml
Volume used	0.3 ml	300 ml	0.1 ml	0.1 ml
Enzyme needed	0.1 μmoles	3 μmoles	0.1 μmoles*	1.0 μmoles*
Minimum time after mixing	1 min	0.05 sec	0.5 sec	0.005 sec
Ability to resolve different paramagnetic molecules	No	No	Yes	Yes

* Values depend critically on the line width.

volume used could be reduced to the active volume. Likewise, the high minimum-concentration limit on the electron spin resonance apparatus can be reduced by compensating for the water absorption.

The Gouy balance has been used to investigate heme proteins including hemoglobin, catalase, peroxidase, and cytochrome c. In several cases, more than one stable form can be prepared. It has also been used to observe the cuprous-cupric change in the enzyme laccase.

The Rankine balance at the Johnson Foundation has been used to observe the reactions of metmyoglobin, catalase, and peroxidase. It has also been used to observe free radicals in the conversion of xanthine to uric acid catalyzed by xanthine oxidase. These free radicals were not detected by spectrophotometric methods.

Electron-spin resonance apparatus has been used to study metmyoglobin and methemoglobin reactions in the frozen state. It has also been used to demonstrate free radicals in dried chlorophyll and in protein pastes. ESR data have been interpreted to indicate that certain flavoprotein-enzyme intermediates are free radicals. Some of these experiments are discussed in papers cited in References 5 through 9. The use of electron-spin resonance in locating the iron atoms in heme-protein crystals is referred to in Chapter 15.

A striking example of the use of electron-spin resonance techniques occurred in studies of the peroxidation of ascorbic acid. Absorption spectrophotometry showed that the enzyme, peroxidase, reacted with hydrogen peroxide to form a first intermediate complex. This then reacted with ascorbic acid to form a second intermediate complex and then the free enzyme. However, the enzyme complexes change in steps involving one electron, whereas the oxidation of ascorbic acid and reduction of hydrogen peroxide involve two electron changes. Measurements of electron-spin resonance showed the existence of a free radical. It was postulated that the following scheme could account for all the observations

$$E + H_2O_2 \rightarrow E \cdot S_I$$
$$E \cdot S_I + AH_2 \rightarrow E \cdot S_{II} + AH \cdot$$
$$E \cdot S_{II} + AH_2 \rightarrow E + AH \cdot + 2H_2O$$
$$2AH \cdot \rightarrow A + AH_2$$

where

$$E = \text{peroxidase}$$
$$AH_2 = \text{ascorbic acid}$$
$$AH \cdot = \text{ascorbic acid free radical}$$
$$E \cdot S = \text{enzyme-substrate intermediate complex}$$
$$A = \text{dehydroascorbic acid}$$

This reaction scheme was analyzed as in Chapter 17 by the assumption of a quasi-steady state. The conclusion of this analysis was that the concentration of free radicals $[AH \cdot]$ should be proportional to the square root of the enzyme concentration. This relationship was confirmed experimentally by measurements of electron-spin resonance at varying enzyme concentrations. In order to carry out the experiments, it was necessary to use a flow system to reduce the minimum time necessary after mixing until observations were possible.

REFERENCES

1. Selwood, P. W., *Magnetochemistry* (New York: Interscience Publishers, Inc., 1956).
2. Blois, S., "Magnetic Measurements," Chap. 8, pp. 393–440, Oster, G., and A. W. Pollister, eds., *Physical Techniques in Biological Research*. Vol. 2, *Physical Chemical Techniques* (New York: Academic Press, Inc., 1956).
3. Sogo, P. B., and B. M. Tolbert, "Nuclear and Electron Paramagnetic Resonance and its Application to Biology," pp. 1–36, Lawrence, J. H., and C. A. Tobias, eds., *Advances in Biological and Medical Physics*, Vol. 5 (New York: Academic Press, Inc., 1957).
4. St. Whitelock, O. V., ed., "Nuclear Magnetic Resonance," *Ann. New York Acad. Sc.* **70**: 763–930 (June 1958).
5. Brill, A. S., H. den Hartog, and V. Legallais, "Fast and Sensitive Magnetic Susceptometer for the Study of Rapid Biochemical Reactions," *Rev. Sc. Instr.* **29**: 383–391 (May 1958).
6. Gibson, J. F., and D. J. E. Ingram, "Location of Free Electrons in Porphin Ring Complexes," *Nature* **178**: 871–872 (October 1956).
7. Gibson, J. F., D. J. E. Ingram, and P. Nicholls, "Free Radical Produced in Reaction of Metmyoglobin with Hydrogen Peroxide," *Nature* **181**: 1398–1399 (May 1958).
8. Commoner, B., *et al.*, "Biological Activity of Free Radicals," *Science* **126**: 57–63 (July 1957).
9. Yamazaki, I., H. S. Mason, and L. Piette, "Identification, by Electron Paramagnetic Resonance Spectroscopy, of Free Radicals Generated from Substrates by Peroxidase," *J. Biol. Chem.* **235**: 2444–2449 (August 1960).

29

Microscopy

I. Types of Microscopes

The development of the microscope was one of the major advances in physical instrumentation which made modern biology possible. The bright-field light microscope is so familiar that it hardly seems necessary to comment on it in a biophysics text. However, since about 1935, a number of different forms of microscopes have appeared; these have made possible far more detailed studies of the ultrastructure of cells, as well as the nondestructive observation of the structures within living cells. These new forms of microscopes are all specialized physical instruments; they were developed by scientists who had both an interest in biology and a basic understanding of the physical principles of the bright-field light microscope.

In this chapter, the Abbé theory of the resolving power of the bright-field light microscope is presented in some detail. This is followed by brief descriptions of the dark-field microscope, the phase-contrast microscope, the interference-contrast microscope, the polarizing microscope, the ultraviolet and the X-ray microscopes, and the electron microscope. The theories for these are essentially similar to that of the bright-field light microscope. The differences and distinctive features, as well as the advantages and disadvantages of each of these

types of microscopes, are emphasized.   This is by no means an exhaustive
survey of the varieties of microscopes used in current biological research.
New and different variations are being introduced and used.   However,
the basic theory outlined in this chapter remains unaltered, as do the
goals of obtaining more and more contrasting images of almost identical
objects and at the same time decreasing the lower limit of resolution.

2. The Bright-Field Light Microscope

The essentials of the *bright-field light microscope* (ordinary light microscope)
are shown in Figure 1.   Light from a source strikes the mirror and
passes through the condenser and diaphragm.   The condenser can be
adjusted so that the light is focused on the specimen or so that the light
is a parallel beam at the specimen.   The diaphragm can be regulated
to control the light reaching the specimen.   The objective forms a
real image of the specimen about 20 cm above in the microscope tube.
This real image is finally magnified by the eyepiece which forms a
virtual image 25 cm from the eye.   The magnification of the objective
is the ratio of the image distance divided by the object distance.   The
image distance is fixed by the geometry of the microscope, but the
object distance can be varied.   The stronger the lens, the smaller this
distance and hence, the greater the magnification.

The useful magnification is limited by the resolving power; that is,
there is a certain minimum distance of separation below which the images
of two points cannot be separated, no matter how great the magnification may be.   This limit of resolution is determined both by the wavelength of light used and by the geometry of the objective.   The discussion which follows is an outline of the mathematical proof of the
equation for the limit of resolution.

To develop the expression for the limit of resolution of a microscope,
consider first the simpler problem of a grating placed in the path of a
parallel light beam, as shown in Figure 2.   If the diffracted light then
passes through a converging lens, all parallel rays incident on the lens
will be focused onto a line in the focal plane of the lens.   At some lines
in the focal plane, the various light rays originating from different lines
on the grating will cancel, whereas at others they will reinforce.   These
bright lines are called the *diffraction orders*.   From Figure 2, one can see
that bright lines will occur at angles θ, satisfying the relationship

$$n\lambda = b \sin \theta \qquad (1)$$

where n is an integer, λ the wavelength, and b the space between lines on the grating. The integer n is called the *order of the diffraction line*; $n = 0$ is the central, undiffracted beam.

The light reaching any one of the bright lines in the focal plane of the lens is in phase. Accordingly, if a screen is placed so that only the

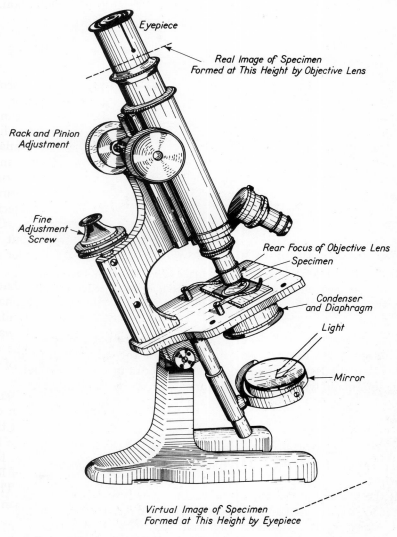

Figure 1. Essentials of the ordinary light microscope. This is referred to in the text as the bright-field light microscope to distinguish it from other types of microscopes.

light of one of these bright lines can pass, the transmitted light will spread out past the focal plane as if from a single line source.   If, however, light from two of the lines in the focal plane is allowed to pass the

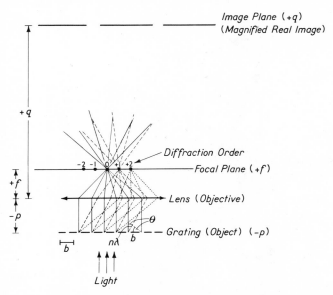

Figure 2. Grating and lens.   This figure is used in derivation of the limit of resolution of a lens such as the objective lens of a microscope.

screen, interference will occur.   The interference pattern will have just the proper form to give rise to an image of the original grating, provided that the latter was more than a focal distance from the lens.   In fact, the image will occur at a distance q given by the lens formula

$$\frac{1}{q} - \frac{1}{p} = \frac{1}{f} \qquad (2)$$

In this, $-p$ is the distance from the grating to the lens and f is the focal length of the lens.   The plane at q is called the *image plane of the objective*.

If the spacing of the grating is decreased, the number of bright lines in the focal plane will also decrease because $\sin \theta$ cannot exceed one.   As this happens, the distance between the various diffraction orders increases.   In the extreme cases, even the first-order diffraction line will disappear, leaving only the central line.   When this occurs, no image of the grating can be formed by the lens.

As is seen in Figure 3, the limiting case of just the first-order diffraction line and the central line occurs when b becomes so small that the angle θ_1 of the first-order diffraction line is given by

$$\tan \theta_1 = \frac{2a}{-p} \qquad (3)$$

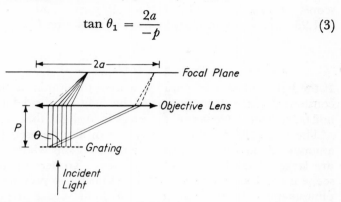

Figure 3. Limiting case of only one order of diffraction other than the central spot.

where a is the lens radius. For most microscope objectives, $-p$ is just slightly greater than f, and θ_1 is a small angle. Accordingly, the foregoing condition of a first-order diffraction (and hence, an image) just barely existing can be approximated by

$$\frac{2a}{f} \doteq \tan \theta_1 \doteq \sin \theta_1 = \frac{\lambda}{b}$$

or

$$b \doteq \frac{f}{2a} \doteq \frac{\lambda}{2 \sin \theta_1} \qquad (4)$$

Equation 4 gives the resolving power for a lens, provided the object is illuminated by parallel light. The wavelength λ is that of the medium between the object and the lens. If this medium is different from air, one may express λ in terms of the wavelength λ_0 in air by the expression

$$\lambda = \frac{\lambda_0}{n}$$

Further, the product $n \sin \theta_1$ is often called the *numerical aperture* NA. Thus, Equation 4 may be rewritten

$$b = \frac{\lambda_0}{2\text{NA}} \qquad (5)$$

The last equation was developed for a single lens. In the microscope, a compound lens, namely the objective, limits the resolving power. However, this introduces no major changes in the foregoing theory. Equation 5 can still be used to find the limit of resolution of a microscope. Using blue light λ, about 0.45 micra, and a numerical aperture of 1.25,[1] one can find that the limit of resolution b is

$$b = \frac{0.45}{2 \times 1.25} = 0.2 \text{ micra}$$

If the light, other than parallel, is used to illuminate the specimen, the constant 2 in the denominator of the right-hand side of Equation 5 will not be correct. However, the error is so slight that it may be ignored.

The bright-field light microscope can also be used to determine the amounts of various pigments present in regions whose linear dimensions are larger than the limit of resolution. To accomplish this, a microscope is combined with a spectrophotometer to produce a microspectrophotometer. In this variation, the light source is passed through a monochromator; the eyepiece is replaced by a lens which forms a real image at the surface of a light-sensing device such as a photomultiplier tube. By measuring the relative optical density of neighboring portions of a cell at various wavelengths, it is possible to locate many pigments such as cytochromes within a cell. In all microspectrophotometers, resolution is sacrificed to make quantitative absorption measurements possible.

The bright-field light microscope is a standard tool. In order that it be useful, the specimen must possess regions in which different amounts of light are absorbed and must have linear dimensions larger than 0.2 micra. The former restriction makes it necessary to fix and stain most specimens. The microscope in itself cannot help to distinguish artifacts due to fixing and staining from the inherent properties of the specimen. Further, the limit of resolution prohibits the observation of virus particles and makes it difficult to resolve the details of the structure of bacteria and mitochondria.

3. The Dark-Field Microscope

This section and the three following deal with methods of increasing the contrast of the images seen in a microscope without resort to staining and fixing techniques. By far, the oldest of these methods is *dark-field microscopy*, also called *ultramicroscopy*. In this method, the specimen is illuminated by a beam of light which has such a shape that no direct

[1] For air, the numerical aperture, NA, is always less than one. The value 1.25 is typical of a high quality of immersion lens.

light can enter the objective. Anything in the specimen which diffracts or scatters light sufficiently will appear bright against a dark background. A condenser arrangement to make this possible is shown in Figure 4.

The microscope used with a dark field is called an *ultramicroscope* not

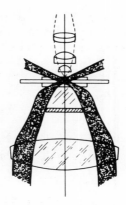

Figure 4. Dark-field illumination. Accomplished by substituting for the upper lens of an Abbé condenser a special dark-field element provided with a stop on the lower surface. After W. B. Rayton, in *Medical Physics*, Vol. 1, O. Glasser, ed. (Chicago, Ill.: Yearbook Publishers, Inc., 1944).

because it has a greater resolving power, but because it reveals unstained elements which are not visible with the bright-field microscope. For example, most living protoplasm appears homogeneous when viewed with bright-field illumination, but numerous small particles oscillating in Brownian motion become visible in dark-field illumination. Protozoans in a liquid are almost transparent in bright-field illumination but show up as bright images against a dark background in the dark-field microscope.

However, the dark-field microscope has a number of limitations. The numerical aperture cannot exceed one, which decreases the resolving power[2] of oil-immersion lenses. The image produced is often a diffraction pattern rather than a true image and may have little resemblance in shape to the original. The images seen are only of those objects which diffract light strongly enough so that it enters the objective.

The dark-field microscope can be looked upon as a special extreme

[2] It is often customary to call the reciprocal of the limit of resolution the *resolving power*. Thus, a lower limit of resolution means a higher resolving power.

case of the phase-contrast microscope, discussed in the next section, which is somewhat less limited in its application than the dark-field microscope.

4. Phase-Contrast Microscopy

The *phase-contrast microscope* is another optical variation of the basic bright-field microscope, its purpose being to increase the contrast of almost transparent specimens. In the phase-contrast microscope, the

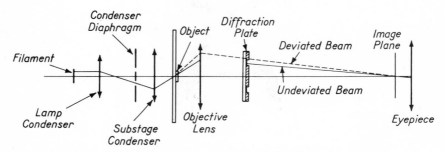

Figure 5. The phase-contrast microscope. Figures 5, 6, 7, and 8 are all after H. Osterberg, in *Physical Techniques in Biological Research*, Vol. 1, *Optical Techniques*, G. Oster and A. W. Pollister, eds. (New York: Academic Press, Inc., 1955).

light beam incident on the specimen is of such a shape that, in the absence of a specimen, it would pass through the objective and all be concentrated in a ring in the focal plane of the objective lens. This result is very similar to the diffraction pattern introduced in Section 2. If part of the specimen has an index of refraction slightly different from the surrounding medium, the light through it will pass through a different region in the focal plane of the objective. This is illustrated in Figure 5, where the light is called *undeviated* if it is transmitted as it would be in the absence of a specimen, or *deviated* if its direction is altered by the specimen.

Because the deviated and undeviated beams are separate in the focal plane of the objective, it is possible to alter one and not the other at this point. Perhaps the simplest alternative to consider is to absorb the undeviated beam partially and change the phase of the deviated beam. This is accomplished by the diffraction plate illustrated in Figure 6.

Just as the different diffraction orders of the grating were combined in Section 2 to form the final image, so in the phase-contrast microscope the deviated and undeviated beams combine at the image plane of the objective to give the image which finally is magnified by the eyepiece. If the diffraction plate introduces about a half-wavelength phase difference, then the deviated and undeviated beams will subtract from one another, giving a dark spot where they are equal. In this fashion, an almost transparent object, which refracts the light even slightly, will appear dark. This occurs because some of the light going through it will be in the deviated beam and some in the undeviated beam, and these two are combined to form the final image.

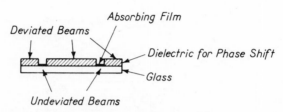

Figure 6. A diffraction plate.

In the phase-contrast microscope, an object or area scattering or refracting very little light will appear bright, as its image will be produced almost entirely by the undeviated beam. Moreover, an object strongly refracting the light passing through it will appear bright because its image will be produced by the deviated beam. By varying the amount of absorption in the undeviated beam, one can increase the contrast of various objects. By making the phase change slightly wavelength dependent, one can make colorless, almost-transparent objects appear colored. This process is called *colored phase-contrast microscopy*.

The extreme of absorbing the undeviated beam consists of removing it altogether. In this case, one has the dark-field microscope as a special example of the phase-contrast microscope.

Phase-contrast microscopy is very useful for counting living sperm cells, observing changes within living cells, and showing structures not readily apparent with staining. The resolving power, using phase-contrast microscopy, is, in general, higher than with dark-field microscopy but is lower than with bright-field light microscopy. In particular, many small objects are surrounded with an extra ring (halo) which cannot be removed by focusing or by altering the phases.

5. Interference-Contrast Microscopy

In the phase-contrast microscope, the final image is produced by the interference of beams coming through the same or neighboring regions of the specimen. At sharp changes of the refractive index, such as at the edge of the nucleus, light beams coming through the nucleus and through the surrounding cytoplasm interfere in the image to produce a halo. The *interference-contrast microscope* is a similar variation of the

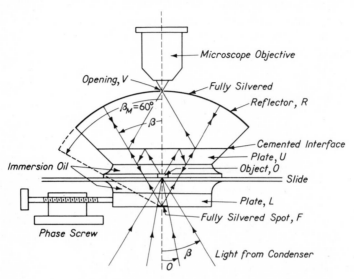

Figure 7. Dyson's interference contrast microscope. Both the object and the fully silvered spot F are focused with unit magnification on the opening V at the vertex of the spherical reflector R. Basically, the light is split into two beams at the upper surface of L which is half-silvered. The reference beam goes from the upper surface of L down to F and then back to V. The object beam goes from the upper surface of L through the object and thence to V. Both surfaces of plate V are half-silvered. The phase screw moves the slightly wedge-shaped plate L, thereby allowing the adjustment of the phase of the reference beam.

ordinary microscope in which the final image represents the interference of two (or more) beams of light. One beam is transmitted directly through the specimen. The interference-contrast microscope differs from the phase-contrast microscope in that the second beam comes through a very different part of the object. This avoids the halo formation at the edge of the nucleus and similar artifacts.

One form of the interference-contrast microscope is illustrated in Figure 7 and another in Figure 8. In the first form, one external beam is combined with the transmitted beam to give an interference pattern.

This pattern will, in general, consist of sharp contour lines representing equal differences of optical path length[3] between the object and its surroundings.   The interference-contrast microscope is most useful when the maximum difference in the optical path lengths in the region of interest is less than a quarter of a wavelength.   Usually, if a rapid change occurs in the optical path length as at the edge of a cell, the interference pattern will be very complicated.

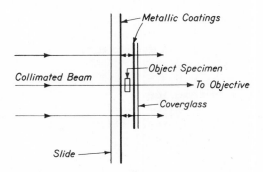

Figure 8. Multiple-beam interferometer adapted for biological specimens.   The final image is made up of beams of light which have passed through the specimen many times.   Small differences in optical pathlength are made more significant by multiple reflections.

The interference-contrast microscope, shown in Figure 8, essentially superimposes the specimen on one plate of an interferometer.   If the specimen is platelike in nature, distinct equal height contours will be produced.   The specimen height can then be measured to a small fraction of a wavelength.   In fact, with crystalline samples the limit of resolution is of the order of 0.1 mμ.   However, the width- and the length-resolving powers are somewhat less than for the bright-field light microscope.

The greatest single advantage of interference-contrast microscopy is that it enables the measuring of the heights of particles (or determining the optical path lengths) with a precision that cannot be equalled by any other method.   In the usual biological applications, one is more interested in determining the length and width; for these the interference-contrast microscopes of Figures 7 and 8 offer only slight advantages over the phase-contrast microscope.   Even the heights can be

[3] The optical path length is defined as the product of the path length times the index of refraction.   It enables one to find the length of the path in wavelengths.

accurately measured only if the area of the object is large compared to the square of the limit of resolution of the bright-field light microscope. Knowing both the height and area allows one to compute a volume and hence, a mass for subcellular structures.

The interference-contrast microscope can be combined with a phase-contrast microscope to give certain practical advantages in resolution and contrast. Both of these types of microscopes and their numerous variations have the end result of making visible unstained structures which are almost transparent and which differ only slightly from their surroundings. Another method of obtaining two interfering beams to accomplish this same result is discussed in the next section.

6. The Polarizing Microscope

The *polarizing microscope* shown in Figure 9 consists of a bright-field microscope with two (or three) added pieces. Below the specimen is the

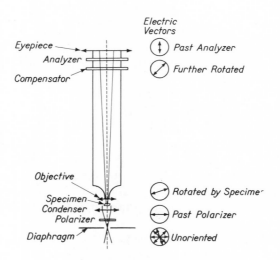

Figure 9. The polarizing microscope.

so-called "polarizer." It functions to pass light only if the electrical vector is in a particular direction, for example, parallel to the plane of the drawing. (The electrical vector will always be perpendicular to the direction of propagation of the light beam. The direction of the light beam and the direction of the electrical vector together define the plane of polarization.) Above the objective is placed an analyzer which rejects all light whose electrical vector (plane of polarization) is that determined by the polarizer. Under these conditions, the polarizer and analyzer are said to be crossed; the background will appear dark, as will any homogeneous isotropic object.

In contrast, most fibers, all helices, and all asymmetric carbon atoms are optically active; that is, they rotate the plane of polarization of light passing through them. Optically active crystals or fibers have one (or more) preferential direction(s) called the *optic axis* (*axes*). If the plane of polarization of the incident light is either parallel to or perpendicular to the optic axis, it will not be rotated. A maximum rotation of the plane of polarization occurs when the optic axis is perpendicular to the direction of propagation of the light and at 45° to the plane of polarization.

Materials so oriented that they rotate the plane of polarization will appear bright, or at any rate gray against a dark background. The action of the optically active materials may be considered as splitting the incident beam into two beams polarized at right angles to each other and traveling with different velocities through the sample. One of these beams, the ordinary beam, obeys the ordinary laws of refraction and has an index of refraction n_0. The other beam, the extraordinary beam, travels through the sample with a different velocity. In terms of its velocity, one may define an index of refraction n_e. Optically active materials are said to be birefringent, the degree of birefringence being given by

$$\Gamma = n_e - n_0$$

Because Γ is different from zero, there will be a phase difference between the ordinary and extraordinary beams when these are combined by the analyzer. Most biological samples are so thin that the phase difference is very small. It may be enhanced by a number of methods. One of these introduces an additional difference of phase through the use of a compensator plate located below the analyzer. This brightens and colors the background and also emphasizes the phase change introduced by the birefringent material in the specimen.

Almost all biological samples are birefringent. Accordingly, the polarizing microscope has been widely used since its commercial introduction about 1945. It made possible observations such as of the form of the chromosomes, the spindles, and the mitotic figures in living, dividing cells. Various additional methods have been introduced to increase its utility further through combining polarization and interference-contrast microscopes. However, the resolution of the polarizing microscope is never better than that of the bright-field light microscope.

Dark-field, phase-contrast, interference-contrast, and polarizing microscopes have all made it possible to observe living cells in the microscope without staining. These techniques have shown that the structures seen in stained preparations were almost all real and not artifacts. They also have shown that most structures of size greater than 0.2 μ had been seen with the stained preparations. However, the various modifications make more rapid, easier measurements possible, as well as allowing one to observe directly the course of physiological changes in single cells.

7. Ultraviolet and X-ray Microscopes

Referring to Equation 5, it can be seen that one way of increasing the resolving power (that is, decreasing b) is by decreasing λ_0. Wavelengths of electromagnetic radiation just shorter than visible are called *ultraviolet* and those quite a bit shorter are called *X rays*. If one is willing to use a photographic image in place of direct visual observation, it is perfectly feasible to build ultraviolet and X-ray microscopes. In theory, they should be able to resolve smaller distances b than can the visual bright-field microscope. In practice, the ultraviolet and X-ray microscopes are very useful for microspectrophotometry but have not led to better resolution than the visual light microscope.

The ultraviolet microscope is limited primarily by the problem of focusing. In order to gain an increase in the theoretical resolution of a factor of two, one must go to wavelengths around 200 mμ. The image must first be formed on a fluorescent screen in order to focus the microscope, and then a photograph must be taken. To get a reasonably good photograph, it is necessary to have the focus very close to perfect. Any small deviation from exactly proper focusing leads to a loss in resolution; a factor of two or more is almost always lost.[4]

In spite of this the ultraviolet microscope, when used as a microspectrophotometer, has played a very important role in the developing analytical picture of the living cell. Perhaps its greatest importance arises from the unique characteristic absorptions of the nucleic acids DNA and RNA. The ultraviolet microspectrophotometer has been used to show that all the DNA is in the chromosomes in dividing cells and that the RNA is distributed throughout the nucleus and the cytoplasm in living cells. The ultraviolet microscope can also be used to locate a wide variety of other important biological compounds whose characteristic absorption spectra are in the ultraviolet.

X-ray wavelengths are shorter than ultraviolet, shorter even than

---

[4] The use of reflection systems in place of lenses allows focusing with visible light and then use in the ultraviolet, thereby reducing the difficulties of focusing.

10 mμ. Accordingly, one might hope to obtain resolutions of the order of 10 mμ with X-ray microscopes. However, one cannot use ordinary lenses. Special curved mirrors "illuminated" at grazing incidence can be used to create an X-ray optical system with a theoretical limit of resolution of 7 mμ. Owing to imperfections in construction, alignment and focusing, no X-ray microscope of this type has resolved separations smaller than 500 mμ (as compared to 200 mμ with the bright-field light microscope!).

Another technique is to use an extremely tiny pin hole to give an X-ray source spreading out from a point. If the specimen is placed close to the pin hole and a photographic film is located many times this distance away, a magnified image (shadow) will be found in the photographic image. This may be further enlarged by ordinary photographic methods in forming the final image. In this fashion, images of quite good quality can be obtained in which separation of the order of 500 mμ can be resolved.

The principal application of the X-ray microscope has been in microspectrophotometric studies. These can be useful in locating atoms of heavier elements such as calcium, phosphorus, iodine, and sulfur within the tissues. For this application, a parallel beam of X rays falls on a sample and is photographed. Repeating this at several wavelengths and examining the photographs with a light microscope (or with a microdensitometer) allows one to locate these heavier elements.

8. The Electron Microscope

All of the special forms of microscopes discussed to this point had limits of resolution larger than, or at best equal to, that of the light microscope. The electron microscope is unique in having a far greater resolving power (that is, far smaller limit of resolution) than any light microscope. The impact of electron microscopy on biology has been particularly pronounced. The study of viruses discussed in Chapter 14 is very dependent on electron microscopy. In a similar fashion, the cytologists' pictures of cell membranes, of the bacterial surface, and of the subcellular structures are fashioned from electron micrographs. At one time, mitochondria were small bodies within cells exhibiting characteristic staining patterns. This view has been replaced by a structure with a double membrane, cristae, and so on, whose appearance in an electron micrograph has a characteristic form. Besides the fields of virology and cytology, numerous others including the form of the visual receptors (see Chapter 7), the chloroplasts (see Chapter 20), and the contractile elements of muscles (see Chapter 8) depend on electron microscopy for their basic structural pictures.

Electron microscopes focus electrons instead of light beams. The electrons may be considered as waves in the same sense as electromagnetic waves, or may be treated as rays of particles just as light may be. The significant difference is that electron microscopes can resolve separate images of points so close together that their images would fuse in the conventional optical microscopes. The theory of the operation of the electron microscope, and indeed its physical structure, are in every way analogous to those of a light microscope. However, the resolution of the electron microscope is far greater. The higher resolution is possible because the electron wavelength is much shorter than the wavelength of a visible photon.

As discussed in the last chapter, quantum mechanics represents an electron by a packet of waves of proper phases and slightly varying frequency. The wave velocity varies with the frequency. The component waves cancel except in a small region, and this region moves with a velocity called a *group velocity* which is different from the wave velocity. Modern quantum mechanics shows that ν, the average frequency of the electron wave, and λ, its average wavelength, can be represented by the expressions

$$E = h\nu = mc^2$$

$$p = mv = \frac{h}{\lambda}$$

where E is the total energy of the electron, p is its momentum, v is its velocity, h is Planck's constant, c is the velocity of light in a vacuum, and m is the (relativistic) mass of the electron moving with velocity v. (For computing λ and ν for electrons within an electron microscope, m is approximately the same as m_0, the rest mass. Hence, the frequency is constant, and the change in frequency is negligible.)

If an electron is accelerated by passing through a potential difference, V, it gains momentum

$$p = \sqrt{2mVe}$$

and hence, has a wavelength

$$\lambda = \frac{h}{\sqrt{2mVe}}$$

For a potential difference of 50 kilovolts (a typical value for an electron microscope), the electronic wavelength is

$$\lambda = 0.08 \text{ Å}$$

Even if the lenses are so poor that the resolution obtained is 100 times worse than the theoretical limit, one can still obtain separate images from two points whose distance apart b is

$$b = 10 \text{ Å}$$

This is about the actual limit of resolution in the better electron microscopes.

Electron lenses are necessary to focus the electron beam if one wishes to obtain magnification. As discussed in the previous paragraph, when the potential changes, the electron wavelength changes, but its frequency remains approximately constant. Accordingly, one may treat V as

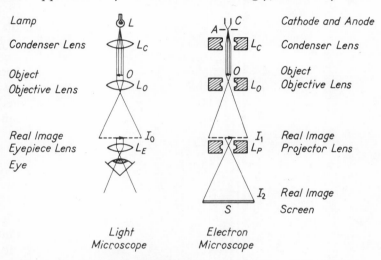

| Light
Microscope | Electron
Microscope |

Figure 10. A comparison of the light microscope and the electron microscope. After C. P. Swanson, *The Cell* (Englewood Cliffs, N.J.: Prentice-Hall, Inc., 1960).

analogous to n, the index of refraction for light waves. Properly shaped electrostatic fields act on electrons just as glass lenses of the same shape act on photons. This type of electron lens is called an *electrostatic lens*.

Another type of electron lens is the so-called "electromagnetic type." Electromagnetic theory shows that electrons moving in a magnetic field effectively experience an increase in potential. Electromagnetic coils around the beam can form lenses just as can the electrostatic ones. The detailed theory is somewhat more complex and will not be pursued here.

Whether electromagnetic or electrostatic lenses are used depends on practical engineering details. In either case, the parts of an electron microscope are analogous to those of a light microscope. This analogy is presented in Figure 10. The electrons are emitted from a heated filament and accelerated through a high potential, perhaps 50 kilovolts. This is equivalent to producing light photons from a heated filament (except that the electrons are monochromatic and the photons are not). The photon and electron beams are then collimated by lenses, pass through the object, and are magnified by an objective lens and finally

Figure II. A crystal of the rhombic type of tobacco necrosis virus in which the molecular order is unusually good, × 84,000. After L. W. Labaw and R. W. G. Wyckoff, "The Electron Microscopy of Tobacco Necrosis Virus Crystals," *J. Ultrastructure Research* **2**: 8 (1958).

by a projector (or eyepiece lens). The image so formed is suitably detected.

Electrons are more highly absorbed when going through a solid specimen than are photons of visible light. Even a glass cover slide would so absorb the electrons that no useful image could be obtained. For electron microscope studies of biological materials, a small round metallic screen is used to support the specimens. These screens are about ¼ inch in diameter and have approximately 400 wires per inch. The electron beam passes through the holes in the screen. The object can be moved around so that different parts are viewed just as in the conventional light microscope. When the beam strikes a wire of the screen, no electrons come through; the open areas between wires, however, are large compared to the field of observation of the electron microscope.

Figure 12. Bacterial flagella at 41,700 × (left) and 73,400 × having the external contour of a counterclockwise double helix. After L. W. Labaw and V. M. Mosley, "Periodic Structure in the Flagella and Cell Walls of a Bacterium," *Biochim. et Biophys. Acta* **15**: 325 (1954).

For particulate suspensions, such as bacteria, phages, or mitochondria, a thin plastic film is placed over the screen and then the suspension is dried on the film. It is necessary to dry all the material because the electron beam in the electron microscope operates only in vacuum. In some studies, the specimens are shadowed with metallic atoms; in others, replicas are made with carbon or other types of films. Whether the particles are directly studied, or shadowed, or reproduced, they must first be dried. (This necessitates that only nonliving specimens can be studied.) The drying may introduce many artifacts. To reduce these, several alternative schemes have been followed, including quick freezing before drying; fixing in osmic acid; and replacing the water with liquid CO_2, and then going around the critical point. Although some of these schemes have added to the detail observed, none of them have dramatically altered the final images obtained with electron microscopes. Because several different methods of specimen preparation all lead to the same final images, this indicates that the electron-microscope images do represent the original objects.

To prepare tissues for electron microscope studies, it is necessary to imbed the tissues in a suitable plastic and then section, before placing them on the wire screens. The sections must be no more than 0.1 micron thick. These sections are so thin that it is possible to section not only tissues, but also bacteria and red blood cells. The disadvantage of these very thin sections is the large number of serial sections which must be viewed in order to obtain a complete picture of a single cell, and the still larger number to obtain a perspective view of tissue structure. In spite of this limitation, electron microscopy is one of the most important physical tools used in research in cytology. Figures 11 and 12 show electron micrographs of biological specimens.

REFERENCES

1. Oster, Gerald, and A. W. Pollister, eds., *Physical Techniques in Biological Research.* Vol. 1. *Optical Techniques* (New York: Academic Press, Inc., 1955).

2. Mellors, R. C., *Analytical Cytology: Methods for Studying Cellular Form and Function* 2nd ed. (New York: Blakiston Company, 1959).

3. Palade, G. E., "Electron Microscopy of Mitochondria and Other Cytoplasmic Structures," Gaebler, O. H., ed., *Enzymes: Units of Biological Structure and Function* (New York: Academic Press, Inc., 1956) pp. 185–215.

4. Rayton, W. B., "Microscopes," Glasser, Otto, ed., *Medical Physics* (Chicago, Illinois: Year Book Publishers, Inc., 1944) Vol. 1, pp. 733–750.

30

Tracer Techniques

I. Introduction

Tracer methods have come into vogue since the later 1930's.   In theory, they are extremely elementary.   Essentially, they consist of putting an unusual isotope of an element into a biologically important metabolite (or foodstuff) and following the progressive reactions of this metabolite by determining the fate of the tracer isotope.   The use of tracers has been made possible by the development of methods to prepare and concentrate isotopes other than the commonly occurring ones.   The production and detection of these isotopes are possible only through the use of complex physical equipment.   Accordingly, tracer methods have been included in this text among the specialized physical tools used in biology.

Most chemical elements consist of more than one isotope.   All isotopes of the same element have the same chemical properties but different atomic weights.   The atomic weight of an isotope is approximately equal to the sum of the number of neutrons plus the number of protons in the nucleus.   In contrast, the chemical properties are determined only by the number of protons, that is, the atomic number.   (Owing to their different atomic weights, two isotopes of the same element may have different rates of reaction.)   Often, the isotope number is shown by a superscript. For example, C^{14} is a carbon isotope with six protons and eight neutrons. Other carbon isotopes such as C^{11}, C^{12} and C^{13} all have six protons per nucleus but have 5, 6, and 7 neutrons, respectively, in the nucleus. (Sometimes the atomic number is shown as a subscript $_6C^{12}$, but this subscript is redundant.)

Some naturally occurring isotopes are radioactive; these emit three different types of particles. All of them emit either an alpha particle (an He^4 nucleus) or a negative beta particle (a high-velocity electron). In addition, many emit the third type, gamma rays, which are high-energy electromagnetic photons. Few naturally occurring radioisotopes are useful as biological tracers. (Two naturally occurring radioisotopes, H^3 and C^{14}, are widely used for tracer studies.)

Most artificially produced radioactive isotopes emit beta particles; some emit positive ones and others negative ones. Often, gamma rays accompany the radioactive decay. In some cases, it is easier to detect the gamma rays (photons) than the beta rays (electrons). Artificial radioisotopes form the basis for most biological tracer studies. Rather than attempting to produce a catalog of all isotopes, three selected radioactive isotopes, C^{14}, I^{131}, and P^{32}, are presented. These were chosen because they are among the most common species used. Although they have been employed in many types of experiments, only a few examples are described. These are meant to be illustrative rather than complete.

Nonradioactive isotopes can also be used for tracers, provided the naturally occurring isotope ratios are varied. It is possible to measure these ratios by means of mass spectrometer-type techniques. These techniques are illustrated by the nonradioactive isotope N^{15}, which normally occurs at concentrations that are small compared to N^{14}. By concentrating the N^{15}, one may prepare samples of metabolites with an excess concentration of N^{15}.

In general, the tracer element is used in a form diluted with a carrier; that is, radioactive C^{14} is used only diluted in a large excess of nonradioactive C^{12}. These can then be studied in systems which are in over-all thermodynamic equilibrium, that is, with respect to carbon atoms, but are far from equilibrium for the tracer isotope. Tracer techniques make possible the study of equilibrium biological processes without altering the chemical equilibria.

2. Radioactive Tracers

Radioactive tracers continually disintegrate during an experiment. The probability of one atom disintegrating appears to be a purely random phenomenon; the number of disintegrations per second is proportional to the number of radioactive atoms present. Expressed analytically, this is

$$\frac{dN}{dt} = -\lambda N \tag{1}$$

where N is the number of atoms present, t is time, and λ is a constant characteristic of the particular isotope. Equation 1 can be integrated to

$$N = N_0 e^{-\lambda t} \tag{2}$$

where N_0 is the number present at zero time. Equation 2 may be solved for the time τ in which N decreases by a factor of two; namely

$$\tau = \frac{\ln 2}{\lambda} \tag{3}$$

The time τ is called the *half-life*. During each half-life, the number of atoms of the isotope decreases by a factor of two. The half-life τ, rather than λ, is customarily used to describe an isotope.

In order that an isotope be useful for tracer studies, τ must be in a reasonable range. If τ is too short, that is, of the order of seconds, the isotope decays before one can do most tracer experiments. However, if τ is too long, then the number of disintegrations per second becomes prohibitively low for the detection of usual tracer concentrations. The isotope C^{14} with a half-life of 5,700 years is close to the too-long limit.

The activity of a sample of radioactive material is usually described by the number of disintegrations per second. The number occurring in 1 gm of radium, 3.7×10^{10} per second, is called a *curie*. One thousandth of this, that is, a millicurie, is a more useful unit for biological tracer studies. The number of atoms per millicurie is related to the half-life. If there is 1 millicurie present

$$\frac{dN}{dt} = 3.7 \times 10^7 = -\frac{\ln 2}{\tau} N$$

Or, solving for N

$$N = -\frac{\tau}{\ln 2} \times 3.7 \times 10^7 \text{ atoms}$$

This number can readily be converted to gram atoms, or grams, using Avogadro's number and the atomic weight.

The radioactive isotopes are assayed by detecting their characteristic radiations. These, in the case of artificial radioactive isotopes, usually consist of a β ray and, in addition, sometimes a γ ray. In the case of orbital electron capture,[1] only a photon is emitted. The energy of the

---

[1] Orbital electron capture means that one of the electrons combines with the nucleus to decrease the atomic number by one.

γ particles (photons) and the maximum energy of the β particles are characteristic of the particular isotope. Usually, the energies of both types of particles are measured in terms of the energy an electron would acquire in being accelerated by a given potential difference. These units of energy include electron-volts (ev), or kiloelectron-volts (Kev). The size of the unit most convenient for description of radioactive tracers is the megaelectron-volt, Mev, that is, the energy an electron acquires in "falling through" 10^6 volts. The different energy ranges are compared in Figure 1.

The radioactively emitted particles produce a response in a detector. The responses may then be counted by some type of electronic circuit. In the past, the most widely used type of detector was the Geiger–Mueller (G-M) tube, also called *Geiger counter*. As shown in Figure 2, it consists of a wire in the center of a gas-filled cylindrical chamber. The central wire is insulated from the outer cylinder and maintained at a high potential relative to it. Ionizing particles entering the cylinder produce a chain of ionization ending in a pulse of current, provided the tube potential is sufficient. Figure 3 shows the dependence of the size of the current on the potential between wire and cylindrical wall. In region A, the height of the pulse is proportional to the energy of the incoming particle, whereas in region B, it is independent. Finally, at C the tube tends to conduct current continuously once one particle starts it.

Geiger counters are used in the plateau region B. The gas in the tube, the exact geometry, and the purity of the wall material all affect the operation of the tube. The pulses from the Geiger tube are counted by electronic circuits. Eventually, one reads a count on a bank of lights, or a dial, or a paper tape. Other electronic circuits permit a direct measure or recording of pulse rate.

Pulse counters can be designed to discriminate against all but pulses within a certain height range. In this fashion, a proportional counter similar to a Geiger tube, but designed to operate in region A of Figure 3, can be used to detect one type of radioactive isotope in a mixture. This is possible because each isotope emits particles of characteristic energy, which in turn give rise to pulses of characteristic heights from the proportional counter.

Another type of detector with numerous advantages is the scintillation counter. This uses the tiny bursts of light produced when ionizing radiations fall on many types of crystals and liquids. The light occurs at a wavelength characteristic of the scintillator. The size of the light burst (scintillation) is proportional to the energy lost by the particle. The scintillations are detected, in turn, with a photomultiplier, whose output is fed through a pulse-height selector to a counter. In this

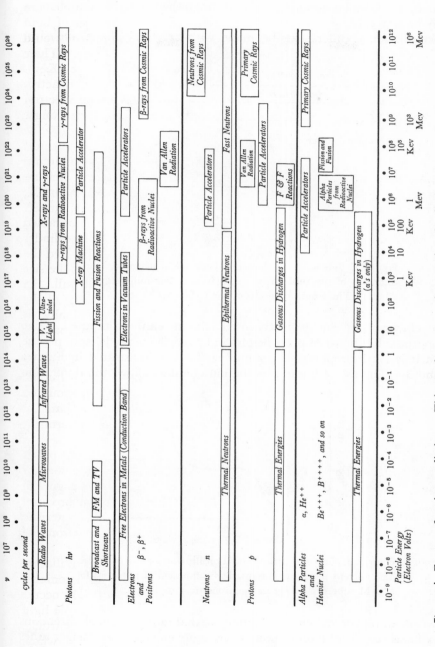

Figure 1. Energy of various radiations. This graph contrasts the energies of radiations from radioactive nuclei with the energies of other particulate radiations. The terms high and low energy as used in this chapter refer to subdivisions within the range of radiations from radioactive nuclei. Figure modified from *Vectors*, Hughes Aircraft Company, Culver City, California, **2**: (No. 42), pp. 12–13 (1960).

fashion, a particular isotope can be distinguished from a mixture or a noisy background.

Scintillation counters can be made with arbitrary shape and size.

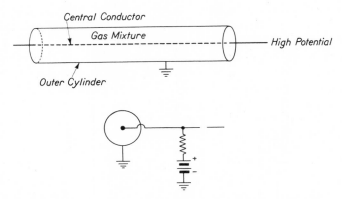

Figure 2. Side and end views of a Geiger-Mueller tube. The diameter of the tubes used varies from a few millimeters to 25 cm. The length varies from one to 50 cm.

The efficiency of the geometry used can be easily computed. The proportionality between pulse height and particle energy is more precise than it is for a proportional counter of the type illustrated in Figures 2 and 3. The use of liquid scintillation counters allows the immersion

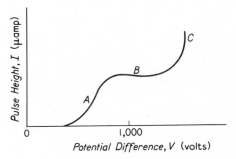

Figure 3. Current-voltage relationship for a G-M tube. The current per pulse is plotted as a function of potential for a G-M tube excited by monochromatic γ rays.

of weak samples or low-energy emitters, so that radiations in all directions may be used. Scintillation counters are more efficient than Geiger tubes for gamma ray detection. However, for certain applications G-M tubes used as proportional counters have a slightly better signal-to-noise ratio than most scintillation counters.

The methods described were concerned with precise measurements of the activity of the radioisotope present. This activity is determined by counting. However, for some problems it is not so important to know the exact rates of disintegration, but rather to distinguish in which portion of a cell the radioisotope is located. A similar problem occurs in paper chromatography in which various compounds are spread out over a large piece of filter paper. Then one wants to find the radioactive spots on the paper. To discover this, one may place a tissue section (or filter paper) against a piece of photographic paper. The latter will be exposed by the radiation and when developed shows the location of the radio-active isotopes. Such a film is called an *autoradiograph*.

Any of the three detection methods described (as well as others) can be used with any radioisotope available. Although there are radio-active isotopes known for all elements, only a limited number have been widely used in biological research. Among the most popular of these have been C^{14}, I^{131}, and P^{32}. Each will be discussed briefly in the following sections.

3. C^{14}

Naturally occurring carbon consists almost entirely of the stable isotope C^{12}. In addition, there is a small amount (about 1 per cent) of the stable isotope C^{13} and a trace of the radioactive element C^{14}. Using artificial means, it is possible to produce C^{14} and also the radioactive isotopes C^{10} and C^{11}. (The isotope C^{15} has been detected but is not useful for tracer studies.) The isotopes C^{10} and C^{11} have half-lives of 19 sec and 20.5 minutes respectively, both emitting positive beta particles and decaying to the corresponding Be isotopes. These half-lifes are so short that C^{14} is usually the only radioactive carbon isotope employed in biological tracer studies. Because carbon is an essential part of all biological compounds, C^{14} is a very widely used isotope.

The isotope C^{14} can be prepared by a number of reactions. If C^{13}-enriched carbon is bombarded by neutrons, some of it is converted to C^{14} according to the scheme

$$C^{13} + n' \to C^{14} + \gamma^0$$

Similarly, if the C^{13}-enriched carbon is bombarded by deuterons, C^{14} is formed, this time by the reaction

$$C^{13} + D^2 \to C^{14} + H'$$

Neither of these is desirable because a mass spectrometer must be used to concentrate first C^{13} and then C^{14}.

The most efficient reaction for forming C^{14} consists in bombarding N^{14} with neutrons.[2]   This reacts as

$$N^{14} + n' \rightarrow C^{14} + H'$$

The compounds NH_4NO_3 and $BeNO_2$ are often used as nitrogen sources. The C^{14} can then be removed by standard electrochemical techniques. A certain amount of C^{14} is formed in this fashion by cosmic rays acting on the N^{14} in the atmosphere.   This results in about 10 counts per minute per gram of carbon in equilibrium with the CO_2 in the atmosphere.

The half-life of C^{14} is about 5,760 years.   Thus, comparatively high concentrations are necessary to obtain a measurable counting rate.   In disintegrating, C^{14} emits only a negative beta particle and no gamma rays; it becomes N^{14}.   The maximum energy of the emitted beta particles (electrons) is about 0.154 Kev.   This is comparable to the energy of a clinical X-ray tube and is much lower than particles from many other radioactive isotopes.   It is difficult to detect these low-energy beta particles.   Sometimes the C^{14}-containing sample is made into a $BaCO_3$ disk and pressed against the end of a Geiger tube (or inside it).   Certain Geiger tubes are designed to admit the C^{14} in the form of CO_2 gas. Various liquid scintillators are also used.   In any case, the sample cannot be very thick because all the emitted beta particles are absorbed in passing through a few millimeters of solid or liquid sample.

In other words, C^{14} is not an ideal tracer element.   Its half-life is too long, and its emitted beta particle has too low an energy.   In spite of this, C^{14} has been very important in research.   Two specific examples, chosen from a multitude of applications, are protoporphyrin synthesis and carbon dating.

Protoporphyrin is part of the heme group, which is the prosthetic group of hemoglobin and several enzymes.   Its structural formula is shown in Chapter 18.   Several experiments indicated that the amino acid glycine is used in the formation of protoporphyrin.   Accordingly, two forms of glycine were prepared

$$
\begin{array}{cc}
\text{NH}_2 \quad \text{O} & \text{NH}_2 \quad \text{O} \\
\mid \quad \nearrow\!\!\!/ & \mid \quad \nearrow\!\!\!/ \\
\text{H}-\text{C*}-\text{C} & \text{H}-\text{C}-\text{C*} \\
\mid \quad\quad \searrow & \mid \quad\quad \searrow \\
\text{H} \quad\quad \text{OH} & \text{H} \quad\quad \text{OH}
\end{array}
$$

where the * indicates the tracer atom, in this case C^{14}.   It was found with the first of these that radioactivity was incorporated into the porphyrin

---

[2] The manufacture of radioactive isotopes by neutron bombardment often employs neutrons from a pile (atomic reactor).   Neutrons from such a source are plentiful and relatively inexpensive.

ring, whereas with the second it was not. These experiments indicate that glycine is used in the biosynthesis of protoporphyrin, but that the carboxyl [COOH] carbon is removed during the synthesis. Although this example may seem very simple, it has not been possible to determine this role of glycine by any other method than tracer techniques. N^{15} experiments have also shown that glycine is a precursor of protoporphyrin.

A rather different application of C^{14} is carbon dating. In this, the radioactivity of a sample of wood or other organic material is determined. If it is part of a recently living system, the carbon atoms are in dynamic equilibrium with the CO_2 of the atmosphere which produces about 10 counts/min/gm of carbon due to C^{14}. In material which has been nonliving for a long time, the C^{14} gradually disintegrates and is not replaced. Thus, a piece of ivory about 5,760 years old would be expected to have half as much C^{14} per gram of carbon as recent material. A piece of wood about 11,500 years old should have one-quarter as much (that is, 2.5 counts/min/gm of carbon). The radioactivity due to the C^{14} is small and weak. Nonetheless, with suitable precautions to eliminate counts due to cosmic rays, other disintegrations, background radioactivity in the room, and electronic noise, it is possible to measure the C^{14} content very accurately. When it has been possible to compare the date computed from C^{14} measurements with that known from other sources, these two have agreed within experimental error. For carbon-containing objects, between 2,000 and 50,000 years old, the C^{14} date can be computed more precisely than any other type of date. For many objects of significance to archeology, anthropology, and evolution, C^{14} dates are the only ones possible.

4. I^{131}

Stable, naturally occurring iodine consists primarily of isotope I^{127}. Many radioactive isotopes of iodine are known; among these are I^{128}, I^{129}, I^{130}, and I^{131}. The isotope I^{128} has a half-life of 25 minutes, and I^{130} a half-life of 12 hours. Both have been used for biological studies but are too short-lived for most experiments. The isotope I^{129} has a half-life of more than 10^7 years; this is too long-lived to be useful as a tracer. However, I^{131} has a half-life of 8.0 days which is a very convenient length. It implies a much higher disintegration rate per gram atom than C^{14}. In the matter of a few months, the I^{131} is almost completely disintegrated and it no longer represents a health hazard. Owing to its short half-life, the counts obtained must always be interpreted in terms of the fraction of the original sample not yet disintegrated.

In disintegration, I^{131} emits many particles; these include negative beta particles of 0.6 and 0.3 Mev maximum energy, as well as gamma rays of 0.08, 0.28, 0.37, and 0.64 Mev. The last two pass readily through tissue and through thin aluminum sheets; they can be detected very easily. By surrounding the detector with a metal shield, it is possible to reduce the background noise without excessive loss of sensitivity to the gamma rays.

The isotope I^{131} can be made by bombarding I^{130} with neutrons. A more satisfactory method is to bombard Te^{130} with neutrons. In this way, I^{131} is formed which can be separated in a highly purified form from all other elements. Most I^{131} production is by separation of fission products. For biological studies, I^{131} is usually converted to iodide.

Iodine is an important metabolite for vertebrates because it forms part of the thyroid hormones. The concentration of iodine in the thyroid is 10,000 times greater than in any other body organ. Only very small amounts of iodine are needed daily by humans, approximately 100 micrograms per day. If less is included in the diet, the person develops various thyroid difficulties.

The tracer isotope I^{131} has been used to follow the course of iodine from its ingestion through its concentration in the thyroid, distribution throughout the body in thyroid hormones, and its final excretion. A specific example is the uptake of intravenously injected iodide by the thyroid. Before the advent of tracers, it was impossible to demonstrate this process in normal individuals injected with physiological amounts of iodide.

Experiments have been conducted in which varying amounts of I^{131} were injected into guinea pigs, rats, dogs, humans, and so on. In every case, at low iodide injections, a large part or perhaps all of the injected iodide was concentrated within the thyroid within 24 hours. With high "pharmacological" doses of 5 mg of I^{131} per kilogram of body weight, the thyroid concentrated a small fraction of the injected iodide in 5 minutes and thereafter became saturated. Keeping subjects on an extra-high iodide diet also saturated the thyroid. Experiments with inhibitors showed that the thyroid concentrates iodide *per se*, even if it is inhibited from forming di-iodo-tyrosine and thyroxin. These experiments emphasize that the thyroid of a person receiving a normal human diet is not saturated with iodine but is in a position to absorb it against tremendous concentration gradients (at least 500:1 for blood/thyroid iodide ratio).

5. P³²

Phosphorus is an important constituent of all living matter. It is an essential part of the nucleic acids which transmit genetic information and form templates for protein synthesis. Phosphorus is used by living cells in the energy-storing compound ATP (adenosine triphosphate). It plays an important part in many syntheses and oxidations. Calcium phosphate is a major constituent of bone. Naturally occurring phosphorus is all P^{31}.

Phosphorus has one biologically important radioactive isotope, P^{32}. It is made from sulfur by the reaction

$$S^{32} + n' \rightarrow P^{32} + H'$$

For economic reasons, the reaction is carried out using neutrons from a nuclear pile. Phosphorus isotope P^{32} can be separated from the other reaction products by chemical methods.

The isotope P^{32} has a half-life of 14.3 days. Just as is true of I^{131}, it is convenient to use because its half-life is long enough to permit experiments but short enough to produce an easily detectable rate of disintegration. Both C^{14} and P^{32} emit only negative beta particles. Those from C^{14} are difficult to detect because their maximum energy is only about 0.15 Mev; particles from P^{32} are easy to detect because they have a maximum energy of 1.7 Mev, more than a factor of 10 greater than that of C^{14}.

The tracer isotope P^{32} has been used to study the rate of renewal of deoxyribose-nucleic acid (DNA) and ribose-nucleic acid (RNA).[3] In brain tissue, less than 1 per cent of the DNA is renewed per day. In liver tissue, it approaches 1 per cent, whereas in the mucosa of the small intestines it may be as high as 15 per cent. This illustrates that in cells that are not multiplying rapidly, there is comparatively little turnover of DNA. In embryonic tissue and cancer tissue, the rate of DNA removal (or new synthesis) is even greater than in the mucosa of the small intestines. This evidence is one of the lines indicating that DNA is associated with genetic information.

RNA is synthesized much more rapidly than DNA in all tissues except the most rapidly growing ones. Although the rate of synthesis of RNA is somewhat higher in the mucosa of the small intestines than in the liver, the difference is only a factor of two or three, as opposed to a factor of 15 between the DNA rates. This evidence is in accord with the idea that RNA is not directly responsible for the transmission of genetic information.

6. Stable Isotopes

In addition to radioactive isotopes, stable ones may also be used as tracers. However, there is no comparably simple way of detecting the

[3] See Chapter 15 for a discussion of nucleic acids.

presence or amount of stable isotopes.   Instead, it is necessary to use a mass spectrometer to measure the relative isotope abundance.   In this analysis, the material must first be converted to a gas.   It is then admitted under low pressure to a region in which it is bombarded with electrons; this occurs in the ionizing chamber, region (1) in Figure 4.

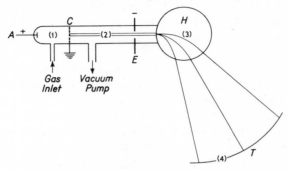

Figure 4. Essentials of a mass spectrometer.

(1) ionizing chamber   (3) velocity spectrometer
(2) accelerating region   (4) detector

A anode   *E* electrode at high nega-
C cathode with holes to   tive potential
     permit passage of "canal   *H* magnetic field
     rays"   *T* target

The bombarding electrons tend to knock a valence electron out of the atoms, which then become positive ions.   These positive ions, if the pressure is sufficiently low, are accelerated toward the cathode.   They pass through "canals," that is, holes in the cathode, and are accelerated by a high voltage between the cathode and electrode *A* shown in Figure 4. All the singly charged ions acquire the same kinetic energy *E*, namely

$$E = \tfrac{1}{2}mv^2 = eV$$

The velocities will be different for each isotope.   The ions are then separated according to velocity by bending in a magnetic field or other means and are finally detected.

Mass spectrometers can be used to separate measurable amounts of isotopes or to detect the ratio of various isotopes present.   A mass spectrometer is larger and more complex than a scintillation counter, but in theory it presents no additional problems.

7. N¹⁵

Many stable isotopes are used as tracers in biological problems.   The specific example discussed here utilizes nitrogen isotope N^{15}.   Nitrogen is common to all living organisms, being found in many building blocks including amino acids, purines, pyrimidines, porphyrins, and flavins. Amino acids are the units polymerized to form proteins; thus, all proteins contain nitrogen. Likewise, the nucleic acids, DNA and RNA, contain purines and pyrimidines and hence, nitrogen.

Naturally occurring nitrogen consists of the isotopes N^{14} (99.64 per

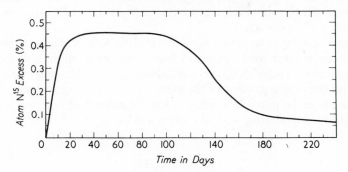

Figure 5. A tracer experiment. N^{15} excess in heme of human erythrocytes after feeding N^{15} labelled glycine for 3 days. After D. Shemin and D. Rittenberg, "Life Span of the Human Red Blood Cell," *J. Biol. Chemistry* **166**: 627 (1946).

cent) and N^{15} (0.36 per cent). Because the natural abundance of the N^{15} is so much lower, it forms an ideal isotope for stable-isotope studies. The longest-lived radioactive isotope, N^{13}, has a half-life of only 10 minutes. Accordingly, it can be used only in a limited number of experiments. The isotope N^{15} is the one used for most biological tracer studies involving nitrogen.

One example discussed of the use of C^{14} was the incorporation of the amino acid glycine into protoporphyrin and hence into heme and hemoglobin. Similar studies using N^{15}-labeled glycine gave similar results. The N^{15}-labeled hemoglobin has then been used to study the average lifetime of red blood cells.

For these studies, humans were fed for 3 days on N^{15}-labeled glycine. As shown in Figure 5, the N^{15}-excess built up rapidly in the heme in the red blood cells. This is interpreted to represent the rate of "birth" of new cells. For more than 60 days, few cells are destroyed. At sometime around 80 days, the amount of excess N^{15} decreases. Using the curve shown in Figure 5, it is possible to compute the average life span of human red blood cells as 127 days. These and similar experiments with labeled Fe and with C^{14} have confirmed this average life span and also that the heme group is not re-used.

8. Summary

Tracer techniques use unusual isotopes in many different ways. In this chapter, examples were cited of studies on a pathway of synthesis, on the fate of an ingested compound, on a turnover or resynthesis rate, and on a life span of a given cell type. In other chapters in this text, reference has been made to isotope tracer studies. These have been included in discussions of the role of viruses in Chapter 14 and of studies on active transport in Chapter 23.

The use of tracers depends upon several factors, namely, their availability from reactor and cyclotron bombardments, their half-lives, the energies of their radiations, the availability of suitable detecting equipment, and the concentration of the element in the living system. Tracer experiments make possible studies of kinetic rates and reaction mechanisms, without interfering with the chemical equilibria.

REFERENCES

A large number of books have been written on the use of tracer techniques. It is hard to open a journal dealing with physiology, or biochemistry, or biophysics, and avoid reading articles using tracer techniques. The following references are only meant to be typical, not complete.

1. Lawrence, J. H., and J. G. Hamilton, eds., *Advances in Biological and Medical Physics* (New York: Academic Press, Inc., 1948) Vol. 1; 1951, Vol. 2.
   a. Lawrence, J. H., and C. A. Tobias, eds., *Advances in Biological and Medical Physics* (New York: Academic Press, Inc., 1953) Vol. 3.
2. Arnoff, Samuel, *Techniques of Radiobiochemistry* (Ames, Iowa: Iowa State College Press, 1956).
3. Comar, C. L., *Radioisotopes in Biology and Agriculture: Principles and Practice* (New York: McGraw-Hill Book Company, 1955).
4. Kamen, M. D., *Radioactive Tracers in Biology* 2nd ed. (New York: Academic Press, Inc., 1951).

A complete table of isotopes and their products can be found in:

5. Strominger, D., J. D. Hollander, and G. T. Seaborg, "Table of Isotopes," *Rev. Mod. Phys.* **30**: 42, Part II, 585–904 (1958).

31

Electronic Computers

I. Need for High Speed Computation

In physics, it is customary to analyze simple (or simplified) situations so that the mathematical description can be written in a closed (or complete) form. For example, in mechanics, most calculations ignore the role of friction. Similarly, in the study of thermodynamics and of electricity and magnetism, the physical systems emphasized are those capable of description in terms of known mathematical functions. For the development of general physical theorems, and for an intuitive understanding of physical principles, this simplified approach has been very instructive. Ignoring many experimental details which failed to fit the simple theory (or explaining them away) has been an essential step in the development of classical physics.

However, applications of basic theory to increasingly complex problems have become an important part of science, in engineering, in modern physics, and in physiology. Biophysicists likewise often encounter complex problems which do not have a simple mathematical solution. The physical description of the motion of the cochlea in the inner ear, the equations describing enzyme reactions, the theory of the diffusion of oxygen into cells, and the mathematical description of the conduction of impulses by nerves are all problems which cannot be solved exactly in terms of known mathematical functions.

If basic differential equations can be developed (which is true in the foregoing examples), then in principle one can sit down with a pencil and paper and solve by numerical methods each specific problem.   In practice, this is not too easy because there are often certain parameters (such as kinetic rate constants) for which values must be chosen in order to make the theory fit the data.   If it takes two years to solve the problem for each choice of parameters, it might take several human half-lives to find the answer.   Some problems which are only a little too time-con-suming for pencil and paper solutions can be hastened by the use of mechanical aids such as slide rules, desk calculators, and tables of logarithms.   However, the mathematics of most problems amenable to solution with desk calculators has been worked out rather thoroughly. The most challenging problems remaining are too complex for these methods.   All of the problems referred to in the previous paragraph would require many human lifetimes, if attacked with a desk calculator.

Automatic computational devices, which are far more rapid than the desk calculator, have become important physical tools used in biological research.   There are two general types of automated computers.   One type, the analog computer, solves problems by analogies between the elements of the real physical system and other physical variables, such as the potential across certain resistors or the torques on various shafts. The other type, the digital computer, carries out the same types of operations as does a desk calculator (of course, very much more rapidly); in addition, the digital computer can make logical choices.

2. Analog and Digital Computers

Analog computers operate by setting up analogies to physical problems. Many such problems occurring within the realm of biophysics and physiology cannot be solved mathematically in an exact closed form. Many of the analog computers used in physiological research involve complex physical equipment combined in imaginative fashions; as such, they belong in the part of biophysics concerned with physical techniques used in biology.

The use of analogies in biology is by no means restricted to analog computers.   For example, temperatures are measured in terms of the length of a column of fluid.   And pressures are often measured in terms of the height of a column of mercury.   In analog computers, this process is carried slightly further; completely unrelated variables such as the concentration of hydrogen peroxide and the voltage across a given resistor are said to be analogs.   In this case, the circuit is so designed that the potential difference in volts is proportional to the concentration of the hydrogen peroxide in millimoles per liter.

Analog computers at best can do a limited number of types of operations. However, they are rapid, comparatively inexpensive, and have a precision comparable to most biophysical data (that is, at best ± 0.1 per cent, but more usually ± 10 per cent). When similar types of problems are solved repeatedly, analog computers may be the most economical method of obtaining numerical answers. Many analog computers, and all digital computers, use electronic techniques. In this chapter, two electronic analog computers are described to illustrate this general approach. Both use electrical potentials to represent different physical variables.

Digital computers are far more versatile than analog computers. Their versatility arises from their ability to make choices. The machine senses when it has finished one operation; then it automatically goes on to the next. A digital computer can compare numbers, and, depending on their relative sizes, can go to one of several alternative next steps. A high speed digital computer can complete in 1 second as many as 10^5 elementary operations, such as addition and multiplication of 10 digit numbers. Digital computers are very rapid, very sensitive, and very expensive. They can be programmed, that is, instructed, to do any of an almost infinite variety of different problems, provided the programmer is sufficiently ingenious. Digital computers are discussed in the last section of this chapter.

3. A Bone-Density Analog Computer

Analogs can be formed for many different types of problems. The one to be considered here uses several analogies. This computer was designed for the quantitative measurement of bone densities from X-ray films. It is impossible to determine the bone density or bone calcium directly from an X-ray photograph of a bone in a limb because one knows neither the conditions of exposure nor the sensitivity curve of the film as used and developed. To determine the last two, a wedge of an aluminum-zinc alloy is exposed with the bone. Suitably made wedges have the same shape of absorption and scattering curves when plotted as a function of wavelength as does the calcium phosphate in mammalian bones. For each point along the image of a bone it is possible to find a wedge thickness that gives the same film darkening. These equivalent thicknesses could be integrated numerically to find the equivalent wedge mass of a given slice of bone. If the volume were known from other data, one could then compute an average density for the bone slice. This process so far has used one analogy, that of the bone and wedge.

Calculation, or even measurement, of all the points as described in the last paragraph would make this so slow and laborious that it could be used in only a limited number of experiments. No simple analytical rules exist relating film darkening and wedge thickness. If broad-band X rays from a clinical-type X-ray tube are used, the absorption of the wedge will not increase exponentially with wedge thickness. The density of the film will be a complex combination of emulsion sensitivity, developer strength, and so on.

To shorten the computing time, various electrical analogs are used. The wedge is scanned with an optical densitometer, and the curve of optical density versus wedge thickness is recorded with a potentiometer-type recorder. The curve represents the functional relationship between optical density of the film and wedge thickness.

This function is then used to set up what is called a "function transformer." It operates so that, when a voltage is fed to it corresponding to a given optical density, another voltage is produced which is then proportional to the wedge thickness corresponding to that optical density. (The function transformers used in several bone-density computers are electromechanical function transformers which convert the electrical input into a mechanical displacement and then into a new voltage. However, this is purely fortuitous; completely electronic function transformers could equally well be employed.) The output of the function transformer represents equivalent wedge thickness. Thus, if the wedge were traced at a constant velocity, a straight line graph should be obtained for the output of the function transformer against time.

If, instead of retracing the wedge, the optical densitometer is set to trace the photograph along a line across the image of the bone, then the function transformer output against time is the analog of the equivalent wedge thickness plotted against distance across the bone. To obtain average values, this output is integrated electronically. A final output number is obtained whose units are unrelated to bone mass, but whose value is linearly proportional to the bone mass along the path traced. Again, if one knows the cross-sectional area, this mass may be described by an average bone density.

Figure 1 shows an X-ray photograph of a rat and a wedge. Curves of the optical density and of the equivalent wedge mass are shown in Figures 2 and 3. In this computation, wedge thickness and bone mass are considered to be analogs of one another, as also are optical density and voltage, and distance and time. In addition, another voltage has been made analogous to the mass of the calcium phosphate.

If the bone is surrounded by soft tissue, the problem is more difficult. The X-ray absorption coefficients of soft tissue and of bone have very different variations with wavelength. Thus, any wedge which is a

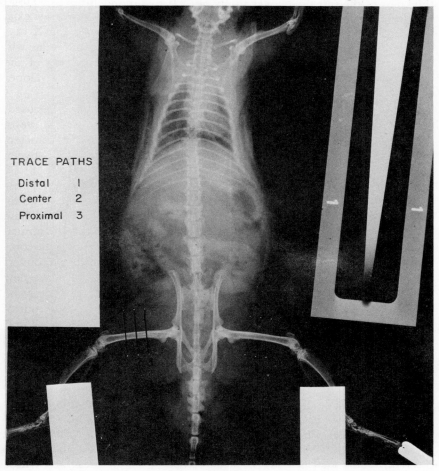

TRACE PATHS

Distal 1
Center 2
Proximal 3

Figure 1. Bones and wedge. X-ray photograph showing rat, the three trace paths used, and the aluminum-zinc alloy wedge used for calibration. After H. Schraer, The Pennsylvania State University; original figure.

good analog of bone is a poor analog of soft tissues. Although various approximations are made to try to use the apparent equivalent wedge mass of the soft tissue, these approximations introduce errors as large as ± 30 per cent into the computed equivalent wedge thickness of a bone surrounded by a large amount of soft tissue.

The soft-tissue problem may be simplified somewhat by using monochromatic X rays.   In this case, the equivalent wedge thickness of the
soft tissue has some meaning.   However, it is still necessary to guess the
thickness of the soft tissue over the bone.   If two monochromatic X-ray
photographs are taken at different wavelengths, each with the same bone

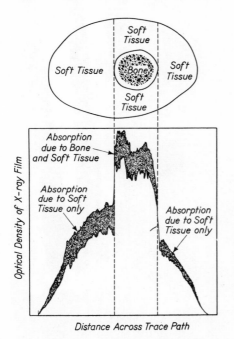

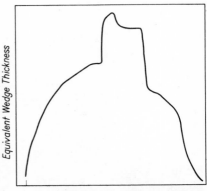

Figure 2. A cross section through the
humerus.   The upper figure shows the
bone and soft tissue distribution.   The
lower figure shows the optical density
of the X-ray film.   Based on original
data   of   H.   Schraer.   The
Pennsylvania State University.

Figure 3.   Equivalent wedge thickness.   This is for the same trace path
shown in Figure 2.   The abscissa
(distance axis) is the same in both
figures.   The ordinate scales have
been adjusted to make the peaks
coincide.

and wedge on the picture, then it is possible to determine independently
the mass of both the bone and the soft tissue lying around it.

A similar procedure has been employed using two wedges, one an
analog of the bone and the other an analog of the soft tissue.   These
are placed in the path of two monochromatic X-ray beams of different
wavelengths which pass through the wedges, soft tissue, and bone to
scintillation counters.   The limb is moved across the beam and the
wedges adjusted to give a constant intensity at both wavelengths at the

scintillation counters. The wedges are adjusted by a feedback servotype system. A record of wedge positions across the limb gives a measure of both soft tissue and bone mass. Inherently, such a null system is less convenient but far more accurate than any of the film techniques.

4. Curve Fitters

The analog computer described in the last section carried out an actual calculation; starting with the experimentally determined data (the X-ray photograph of bone and wedge), it computed the bone density. Another type of problem for which analog computers are widely used is to determine the parameters of an equation to give the best fit of the theoretically computed curves to the experimental data.

For example, it is known that the electron density ρ in a crystal must have the form in any plane perpendicular to the w axis[1]

$$\rho(u, v) = \sum_{h,k} |F_{hk}| [\cos \varphi_{hk} \cos (2\pi hu + 2\pi kv)$$

$$+ \sin \varphi_{hk} \sin (2\pi hu + 2\pi kv)] \quad (1)$$

where (u, v) are fractions of the unit cell length, $|F_{hk}|$ are amplitudes determined by X-ray diffraction, φ_{hk} are parameters depending on z only, and h, k are positive integers or zero. To determine the electron density, one must know the parameters φ_{hk}. In general, there is no experimental method to measure them. To find the electron density, one must guess the values of φ_{hk}, compute ρ, and then ascertain if it leads to a reasonable atomic arrangement. For a complex crystal, each such computation without the aid of electronic computers would take many human lifetimes. The analog computer X-RAC can compute $\rho(u, v)$ for all u, v and for 400 φ_{hk} parameters in 1 second. The result is displayed on an oscilloscope screen as equal-density contour lines; this result can then be compared with the investigator's notions of the particular atoms present and the probable bonds between them.

The initial choice of the values for the parameters φ_{hk} is a very difficult one. Once one is reasonably close, it is possible to adjust these values to bring the electrons into sharper and sharper contours about atomic locations. This is very much like focusing a microscope. The initial choice of the φ_{hk}'s for crystals of complex molecules is usually calculated with a digital computer.

[1] This can be derived from Equation 3 of Chapter 15.

Curve-fitting problems also arise in other fields associated with bio-physics. One of these is the problem of finding the suitable rate constants for enzyme-catalyzed reactions as discussed in Chapters 17 and 18. Here, the rate constants are the parameters which are to be adjusted to give curves which give the best fit to the experimental data. An analog computer which does this calculation electronically was constructed at the Johnson Research Foundation at the University of Pennsylvania. Its use will be described here as applied to the oxidation by H_2O_2 of a one-electron donor AH, when catalyzed by the enzyme peroxidase (E). (This example is chosen for convenience of description.)

The reaction scheme for this problem can be written

$$\overset{e-p-p'}{E} + \overset{x}{S} \underset{k_-}{\overset{k_+}{\rightleftharpoons}} \overset{p}{E \cdot S_I}$$

$$\overset{p}{E \cdot S_I} + \overset{a}{AH} \overset{l_+}{\rightarrow} \overset{p'}{E \cdot S_{II}} + A$$

$$\overset{p'}{E \cdot S_{II}} + \overset{a}{AH} \overset{m_+}{\rightarrow} E + A + H_2O$$

where E is peroxidase and S is H_2O_2. The concentrations are represented by letters above the reactants. The intermediates are spectrophotometrically distinct from the enzyme and from each other.

The reaction scheme can be represented mathematically by the differential equations

$$\frac{dx}{dt} = -k_+x(e-p-p') + k_-p$$

$$\frac{dp}{dt} = -l_+ap - k_-p + k_+x(e-p-p')$$

$$\frac{dp'}{dt} = l_+ap - m_+ap'$$

$$\frac{da}{dt} = -l_+ap - m_+ap'$$

and the initial conditions

$$x = x_0$$
$$a = a_0$$
$$p = 0 \quad \text{at } t = 0$$
$$p' = 0$$

These differential equations cannot be solved exactly in terms of known mathematical functions.

In order to handle these differential equations numerically, it is desirable to rewrite them as integral equations. This is to avoid numerical differentiation, in which one subtracts two numbers. If both numbers contain random errors, the percentage error in the difference will be larger than in either number. However, in integration one adds numbers, thereby decreasing the fractional error due to random errors. Rewritten, the four equations become

$$x - x_0 = \int_0^t (-k_+ x\{e-p-p'\} + k_- p)\,dt$$

$$p = \int_0^t (-l_+ ap - k_- p + k_+\{e-p-p'\})\,dt$$

$$p' = \int_0^t (l_+ ap - m_+ ap')\,dt$$

$$a - a_0 = -\int_0^t (l_+ ap + m_+ ap')\,dt$$

Experimental curves can be measured for the time dependence of x, p, p', and a. The mathematical problem is to choose the constants k_+, k_-, l_+, and m_+ in such a fashion as to obtain an optimum fit.

The integral equations can be solved in 1 second by an analog computer. Each concentration is represented by the electrical potential between a specified binding post and ground. Likewise, the reaction-time units are represented by other time units. If, then, the potential on any of these binding posts is connected to the vertical axis amplifier of an oscilloscope and the horizontal axis to a sweep generator, a curve will appear of potential V, against sweep time τ. This is now interpreted that V is analogous to some concentration x, the height of the deflection in centimeters being proportional to the concentration in millimoles per liter. The horizontal distance on the oscilloscope tube face measured in centimeters is the analog of the reaction time; however, this proportionality constant is different from the one relating this same distance to real (sweep) time units.

The problem can be solved because electronic units are available to integrate, multiply by a constant (that is, amplify), multiply two variables, add, and subtract. Such units are standard equipment and are diagrammed below, using this symbolic code

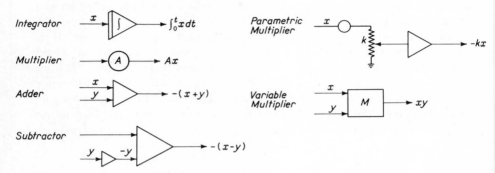

Using these types of elements, one can compute the behavior of the reactants for any chosen set of rate constants, k_+, k_-, l_+, and m_+. A block-diagram type of circuit is shown in Figure 4. Note that the feedback loops fix the size of x, p, p', and a so that they obey the differential equations. The clamps C hold the voltage at ground (zero) until time zero and then release it to take on the values dictated by the circuit.

5. Digital Computers

Digital computers are far more versatile than analog computers. When properly instructed, they can carry out very complex calculations. However, it is necessary to understand the language of the computer in order to instruct it properly. The set of instructions given the computer is called the *program*; the utility of a digital computer depends on the abilities of the programmer.

Basically, there are only a limited number of types of operations which a digital computer can do (about 100 for an IBM 704). These include: add, subtract, multiply, divide, round off, shift the decimal point, read numbers in, read numbers out, choose the larger of two numbers, choose the smaller of two numbers, and change the sign of a number. These are all essentially arithmetic operations. The computer also must have a memory unit where it can store numbers, a control unit which determines what it will do next, and a read-in and read-out unit.

The computer itself understands the steps which it should follow only in terms of sets of two to four (decimal) digit numbers. These are hard for the programmer to learn and remember, whereas sets of three letters are much easier to remember, particularly if they resemble English words. Various schemes have been developed to make it possible to use abbreviations resembling English and algebraic symbols with which to write these codes. For example, in one such code, CLA means clear and add, MPY means multiply, FSB means floating (point arithmetic) subtract, and LXD means load index from decrement. Another

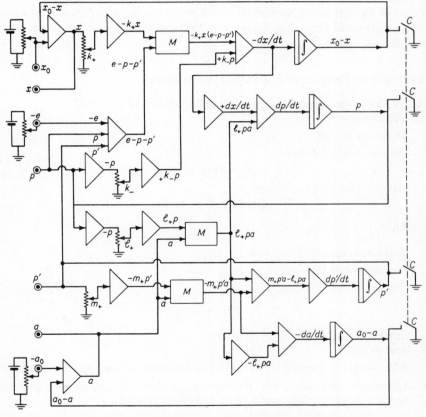

Figure 4. An analog computer to simulate peroxidase reactions. An oscilloscope may be connected to display voltage at terminals x, p, p', and a. Clamps C hold terminals at ground until time zero. Constants e, a_0, k_+, k_-, l_+, and m_+ may be varied by twiddling knobs. The entire pattern repeats about once a second. Note use of feedback loops to produce analogs of the differential equations.

coding system shown in the example that follows allows the programmer to write statements even more like algebra and English. These systems all demand additional computer time in order to translate the program to a code the computer can follow.[2] However, the saving in the time of the programmer and the ease of spotting errors often make these systems worth while.

The following example, the computation of a square root, has been included to illustrate the steps followed by the computer. This problem is in itself trivially short, and it would not be profitable to use a computer. However, a slight extension of the example, such as printing a table of square roots, would be quicker with a high-speed digital computer and would cost less than having a person compute the table using a desk calculator.

Example of Programming Digital Computers

A. The problem: Find the square root of y, when $0 < y < 1$.
B. Algebraic method.

   Guess an answer x_1

   Assume correct answer is $x = x_1 + \Delta x_1$

   $$\therefore\ y = x^2 = x_1^2 + 2x_1\Delta x_1 + (\Delta x_1)^2$$

   Assume $(\Delta x_1)^2$ is negligible,

   $$\therefore\ y - x_1^2 = 2x_1\Delta x_1$$

   Or $$\Delta x_1 \doteq \frac{y - x_1^2}{2x_1}$$

   2nd guess answer is $x_2 = x_1 + \Delta x_1$

   Assume correct answer is $x = x_2 + \Delta x_2$

   Assume $(\Delta x_2)^2$ is negligible,

   $$\therefore\ \Delta x_2 = \frac{y - x_2^2}{2x_2}$$

   3rd guess answer is $x_3 = x_2 + \Delta x_2$
   and so on.

   Process may be stopped when $|\Delta x|$ is less than some pre-assigned limit of error.

C. Computer program. For illustrative purposes, the program has been written with English words and algebraic symbols. For actual digital computer programs, one must write the various operations in the numerical code built into the computer, or else use a system as shown in Part D of this example. The program there must be translated by the machine into a program it can understand, and then this program must be fed back into the computer.

[2] For the IBM 704, CLA must be translated to the binary code 000 101 000 010 and MPY to 000 010 000 000.

Step	Operation	Result
1	Read in y	Computer learns value of y
2	Store at memory location y	Computer stores value of y at assigned location in its memory
3	Store 1.0 at x	Computer stores the first guess, namely 1.0, at location assigned to x
4	Clear and add x	Computer puts x into arithmetic unit
5	Multiply by x	Computes x^2
6	Multiply by -1	Computes $-x^2$
7	Add y	Computes $y - x^2$
8	Divide by 2.00	Computes $(y - x^2)/2$
9	Divide by x	Computes $(y - x^2)/(2x) = \Delta x$
10	Store result at z	Stores value of Δx at memory location assigned to z
11	Add x	Computes $z + x$
12	Store at x	Replaces contents of memory location x with the next guess for x
13	Clear and add $\lvert z \rvert$	Brings absolute value of z into arithmetic unit
14	Subtract 0.0001	Computes $\lvert z \rvert - 0.0001$ [0.0001 is limit of error assigned here to x]
15	If $\begin{bmatrix} (\lvert z \rvert - 0.0001) > 0 \text{ Go to } 4 \\ (\lvert z \rvert - 0.0001) < 0 \text{ Go to } 16 \end{bmatrix}$	Reiterates if Δx exceeds limits of error. Proceeds if final answer has been reached
16	Read out x	Records final answer
17	Stop	Computer awaits further manual instructions

D. FORTRAN program for IBM 650 or IBM 704:

Statement Number	Statement	
Comment	FIND SQ RT (Y)	Note: This procedure would actually be available as a special subroutine labeled SQRTF and does not have to be programmed each time. It is included here for illustrative purposes only.
1	READ 1, Y	
2	$X = 1.0$	
3	DELX $= (Y - (X^{**}2))/(2.^{*}X)$	
4	$X = X +$ DELX	
5	IF (ABSF(DELX) $-$ 0.0001) 6, 6, 3	
6	PUNCH 1, X	
7	END	

E. Actual calculations of computer for $y = 0.18000$. Step numbers refer to Part C.

Step	First Iteration	Second Iteration	Third Iteration	Fourth Iteration	Fifth Iteration
1	$Y = 0.18000$	—	—	—	—
2	$Y = 0.18000$	—	—	—	—
3	$X_1 = 1.00000$	—	—	—	—
4	$X_1 = 1.00000$	$X_2 = 0.59000$	$X_3 = 0.44671$	$X_4 = 0.42484$	$X_5 = 0.424265$
5	$X_1^2 = 1.00000$	—	—	—	—
6	$-X_1^2 = -1.00000$	$-X_2^2 = -0.34810$	$-X_3^2 = -0.199550$	$-X_4^2 = -0.180489$	$-X_5^2 = 0.1800007$
7	$Y - X_1^2 = -0.82000$	$Y - X_2^2 = -0.16810$	$Y - X_3^2 = -0.019550$	$Y - X_4^2 = -0.000489$	—
8	$Y_1 - X_1^2/2X_1 = -0.41000$				
9	$Z_1 = -0.41000$	$Z_2 = -0.14329$	$Z_3 = -0.02187$	$Z_4 = -0.000575$	$Z_5 = 0.0000008$
10	$Z_1 = -0.41000$	—	—	—	—
11	$X_1 + Z_1 = 0.59000$	—	—	—	—
12	$X_2 = 0.59000$	$X_3 = 0.44671$	$X_4 = 0.42484$	$X_5 = 0.424265$	$X_6 = 0.4242642$
13	—	—	—	—	—
14	$|Z_1| - 0.0001 = 0.40090$	0.14319	0.02177	0.000389	-0.0000992
15	Go to 4	Go to 4	Go to 4	Go to 4	Go to 16
16	—	—	—	—	$X = 0.4242642$
17	—	—	—	—	Stop

Note: $(0.4242642)^2 = 0.18000011$

Digital computers have made it possible to undertake statistical studies of a greater magnitude than formerly possible, at the same time relieving the investigators of tedious, time-consuming detailed calculations. Similarly, the discovery of the shape of the myoglobin molecule was possible only through the use of high-speed digital computers. The problem involved such lengthy numerical calculations that it was not feasible to do it by any other method.

Throughout the areas of biology which can be investigated by physical techniques and reasoning, new problems are continually appearing for which theories cannot be fully developed without resort to numerical techniques. The high-speed, electronic, digital computers are specialized physical instruments which make these investigations possible. The digital computers are large, expensive to operate, and very slow as compared to an analog computer. Accordingly, both types of electronic computers have an important role to play in the technology of biophysics.

REFERENCES

1. Barkeley, E. C., and L. Wainwright, *Computers, Their Operation and Applications* (New York: Reinhold Publishing Corporation, 1956).
2. Johnson, C. L., *Analog Computer Techniques* (New York: McGraw-Hill Book Company, Inc., 1956).
3. Pepinsky, R., *Computing Methods and the Phase Problem in X-ray Crystal Analysis* (Department of Physics, Pennsylvania State University, University Park, Pennsylvania, 1952).
4. Chance, Britton, D. S. Greenstein, Joseph Higgins, and C. C. Yang, "The Mechanism of Catalase Action. II. Electric Analog Computer Studies," *Arch. Biochem.* **37**: 322–339 (June 1952).
5. Brown, W. N., Jr., and W. B. Birtley, "A Densitometer Which Records Directly in Units of Emulsion Exposure," *Rev. Scientific Instr.* **22**: 67–72 (Feb. 1951).
6. Mackay, R. S., "X-ray Visualization and Analysis of Multicomponent Subjects" (Abstr.), *Science* **128**: 1622–1623 (Dec. 26, 1958).
7. Jacobson, Bertil, "Dichromography—A Method for In Vivo Quantitative Analysis of Certain Elements" (Abstr.), *Science* **128**: 1346 (Nov. 28, 1958).

DISCUSSION QUESTIONS—PART F

1. An alternative to rapid flow systems for observing spectrophotometric changes during reaction is to introduce a sudden pulse of heat, thereby raising the temperature, and to measure the spectrophotometric changes as the reaction mixture approaches a new equilibrium. This method is sometimes called a *relaxation method*. Describe suitable apparatus for such measurements on myoglobin.

2. The technique of neutron activation is used to locate spots on a chromatogram containing phosphorus. For this purpose, the chromatogram is placed in the neutron flux of a reactor. Afterward, the chromatogram is autoradiographed. Discuss the details, advantages, and disadvantages of this technique.

3. One of the advantages of phase microscopy is that one can measure quantitatively the thickness of parts of cells. Develop the necessary symbolic expressions to describe quantitatively how this is done.

4. The ultraviolet microscope can be made more useful by translating a given ultraviolet wavelength to a visible one on a television tube screen. RCA has developed a three-color scheme using three ultraviolet wavelengths. Describe the equipment briefly. What are its advantages? Its disadvantages?

5. Certain absorption bands of cytochromes can be intensified by reducing the temperature to that of liquid nitrogen. Describe briefly the necessary equipment and the type of results obtained. In so far as possible, explain these on a theoretical basis.

6. Electrophoresis refers to the motion of charged ions in an electrical field. It is used to separate different types of molecules, including very similar proteins. Develop the theory of electrophoretic separation.

7. Two frequently used types of electrophoresis are paper and Tiselius. Describe the necessary equipment for each and the advantages and disadvantages of each.

8. Some laboratories labeled "biophysics" owe their existence and unique character to measurements made with the analytical ultracentrifuge. Describe this apparatus and outline the theory necessary to interpret ultracentrifuge data. Cite specific examples of its use.

9. Some persons labeled "biophysicists" have worked with equipment measuring oxygen concentrations in terms of the current through a platinum electrode. Describe the necessary apparatus and indicate how it operates. What is the advantage of having the electrode rotating or vibrating? Why are the electrodes often covered with a plastic film?

10. One technique mentioned in the text for the preparation of electron microscope samples involved replacing the H_2O with CO_2 and then going around the critical point. What is the advantage of this? What types of results are obtained by this method? Cite specific examples.

11. Describe the replica method for the preparation of electron microscope samples. Give examples of its use.

12. The analog computer X-RAC was referred to in Chapter 31. Describe this computer briefly, including an indication of the theoretical basis and of analogies used.

13. Electron spin resonance was described in Chapter 28. Proton spin resonance is also used for biological studies. Describe one of these.

14. Describe the preparation and use of radioactive sodium isotopes. Give specific examples of their use in biological studies.

15. Describe the preparation and use of a radioactive isotope of sulfur. Give specific examples of its use in biological studies.

16. What are Raman spectra? How can they be observed? What applications do they have to biological problems?

17. What is meant by the term "fluorescence?" Describe the necessary apparatus for observing it quantitatively. Cite several examples where this type of observation has been used in biological studies.

18. What is the nature of the evidence for free radicals in laccase reactions?

19. Outline the mathematical theory necessary to find molecular orbitals for tetrapyrrole ring structures.

20. Describe the technique of column chromatography. What is its physical basis?

Appendix A

Auditory Acoustics

The purely physical part of hearing belongs within the field commonly referred to as auditory acoustics; it is discussed in this appendix in more detail than it is presented in Section 2 of Chapter 1. Acoustics is defined as a study of vibration and sound. Sound refers to the propagation of elastic disturbances in a continuous (3 dimensional) medium, whereas vibration often is restricted to elastic disturbances in simpler systems, such as springs or loudspeakers. In either case, what happens is that certain particles are displaced from their equilibrium positions, thereby developing potential energy. Later, these same particles are restored to their equilibrium positions releasing energy. These motions can be handled mathematically only if they are sufficiently small. Theories using the approximation of very small vibrations are called *infinitesimal amplitude acoustics*. They describe most of the properties of sound which are important in a study of hearing.

This appendix is a compilation of various physical terms used to characterize audible sound. They are summarized in Table I on page 590; each is described briefly in the text.

Any vibration or elastic disturbance may occur only once, or the phenomenon may be repeated. If it is repetitive, one can distinguish a certain frequency, that is the number of times per second that the particle has the same displacement and velocity. A very simple case arises if the motion of a given particle can be described by

$$\xi = A_1 \sin 2\pi \nu t + A_2 \cos 2\pi \nu t \qquad (1)$$

TABLE I

Terms Used in Physical Characteristics of Sound

Quantity	Symbol	Quantity	Symbol
Displacement	$\vec{\xi}$	†Sound pressure level	L
Time	t	Density	ρ
†Frequency	ν	†Absolute pressure	P
Particle velocity	$\vec{v}$	†Equilibrium pressure	P_0
Local acceleration	$\vec{a}$	Bulk modulus	B
Wave velocity	c	Specific heat ratio	γ
†Wavelength	λ	Electrical impedance	Z
†Sound pressure	p	Distance	x, y, z
†Intensity	Υ	Angle	φ
Specific acoustic			
impedance	z	Laplacian operator	∇^2
Characteristic impedance	ρc	$\sqrt{-1}$	j
		Amplitudes	A_1, A_2, C

Subjective Equivalents

†Pitch or tone ~ Frequency
†Loudness ~ Sound pressure level
†Quality or timbre ~ Harmonic content

† Discussed in Chapter 1, Section 2.

where ξ is the displacement, t is the time, ν is the frequency, and A_1 and A_2 are constants (either of which may be zero). This is referred to as a simple harmonic motion, or as a pure tone. The resolution of a complex motion into simple harmonic terms was illustrated in Figure 1 of Chapter 1. This type of analysis, known as Fourier analysis, can be applied to any complex time dependent phenomena. Because any speech pattern or any other sound can be represented as a sum (or integral) of simple harmonic terms, most of the following discussion will be restricted to single frequencies.

In discussing sound waves, it is easiest to start from the particle displacement $\vec{\xi}$ which represents the distance a particle is displaced from equilibrium. Because $\vec{\xi}$ is a function of time, its first and second derivatives, the particle velocity $\vec{v}$, and the local acceleration $\vec{a}$, will, in general, be different from zero. For many acoustic analyses, $\vec{v}$ is slightly easier to manipulate than is $\vec{\xi}$.

Particularly, if $\vec{\xi}$ is simple harmonic, it is convenient to use the so-called "complex notation." In this procedure, $\vec{\xi}$ is represented by a complex number which is easier to manipulate than the real part. Only the latter represents the experimental value.   To illustrate this, one may write the following

$$\textit{Real part} \qquad\qquad\qquad \textit{Complex notation}$$

$$\xi = A_1 \cos 2\pi\nu t + A_2 \sin 2\pi\nu t \qquad \xi = Ce^{j2\pi\nu t} \qquad C = A - jB \qquad (2)$$

$$v = \frac{d\xi}{dt} = 2\pi\nu[-A_1 \sin 2\pi\nu t + A_2 \cos 2\pi\nu t]$$

$$v = \frac{d\xi}{dt} = 2\pi\nu j Ce^{j2\pi\nu t} = 2\pi\nu j \xi \qquad (3)$$

$$a = \frac{d^2\xi}{dt^2} = -(2\pi\nu)^2[A_1 \cos 2\pi\nu t + A_2 \sin 2\pi\nu t]$$

$$= -(2\pi\upsilon)^2\xi$$

$$a = \frac{d^2\xi}{dt^2} = -(2\pi\nu)^2 Ce^{j2\pi\nu t}$$

$$= -(2\pi\nu)^2\xi \qquad (4)$$

No matter what type of object is vibrating, be it a piano-wire, an organ pipe, or a part of the ear, these same relationships are valid.

In addition to a local particle velocity, the *wave velocity c* is often used in acoustics.   When a displacement is transmitted, the rate at which a wave front moves through the medium is called the *wave velocity*.   For media such as air, water, and most tissues, c is independent of frequency. For any non-viscous fluid

$$c = \sqrt{B/\rho_0} \qquad (5)$$

where B is the adiabatic bulk modulus and ρ_0 is the average (or equilibrium) density.   For gases, B is related to the average pressure p_0 by the equation

$$B = \gamma p_0 \qquad \text{and hence} \qquad c = \sqrt{\gamma p_0/\rho_0}$$

In this expression, γ is the ratio of the specific heat at constant pressure to the specific heat at constant volume.   For air under normal pressure and temperature $c \doteq 3.4 \times 10^4$ cm/sec.   For ideal gases, the ratio p_0/ρ_0 is proportional to the absolute temperature.   Hence, their wave velocity c will increase as the square root of the absolute temperature.

It is shown in physics and math texts that the equation

$$\frac{\partial^2 v}{\partial t^2} = c^2 \nabla^2 v \qquad (6)$$

will describe the motion of a nonviscous medium subject to infinitesimal displacements. The operator ∇^2 introduced in this expression in Cartesian coordinates means the following

$$\nabla^2 f = \frac{\partial^2 f}{\partial x^2} + \frac{\partial^2 f}{\partial y^2} + \frac{\partial^2 f}{\partial z^2}$$

Although Equation 6 can be used for many calculations useful in bio-acoustics, such as diffraction patterns, its use here is restricted to one observation. Any phenomenon described by an equation of the same type as Equation 6 is known as a *wave phenomenon*, and this type of equation is called a *wave equation*. For the mathematically initiated, this equation, with its few symbols, expresses the wide variety of physical properties such as interference and diffraction associated with wave motion. (For plane acoustic waves in a fluid, the vector particle velocity $\vec{v}$ is parallel to the direction of the propagation of the wave. Such waves are called *longitudinal* (or *compressional* or *irrotational*). These properties are not expressed by Equation 6.)

Most acoustic experiments measure not the wavelength or the particle velocity but the sound pressure p (or acoustic pressure) defined by the relationship

$$p = P - P_0$$

where P is the instantaneous total pressure and P_0 the average (or equilibrium) pressure. For a plane wave traveling in the positive x direction, one can show (although it is not shown here) that

$$p_+ = A e^{j 2\pi v(t - x/c)}$$

and

$$p_+ = \rho c v_+$$

The sensation of pitch, it has been noted, is associated with frequency and the sensation of loudness with the sound pressure amplitude. The quality of a musical note is recognized by the number and relative intensity of the harmonics present. Not only are the harmonics import-ant but in a few cases the relative *phases* are important. Qualitatively, one may think of the relative phase as the indication of the displacement and velocity at the time $t = 0$. Symbolically, p at a given place is represented by

$$p = A_0 e^{j\varphi} e^{j 2\pi v t} \qquad [\text{or } p = A_0 \cos{(2\pi v t + \varphi)}]$$

where A_0 is a real number and $2\pi v t + \varphi$ is called the *phase angle*. If the acoustic pressure wave is made up of two frequencies v_1 and v_2, then one may represent p at a specific place by the expression

$$p = A_{0_1} e^{j\varphi_1} e^{j 2\pi v_1 t} + A_{0_2} e^{j\varphi_2} e^{j 2\pi v_2 t}$$

The difference, $\varphi_2 - \varphi_1$, is called the *phase difference*. Under most conditions, the ear is insensitive to phase differences, but for clicks, drum beats, piano attacks, and so on, these phase differences between the various audible components are very important.

To those familiar with electrical theory, the analogies between acoustics and electricity are striking. There are many analogies possible; one is presented in Table II. These analogs help the person trained in

TABLE II

Electroacoustic Analogs

Acoustic	Electric
Pressure	Voltage
Particle velocity	Current
Intensity	Power dissipated
ρc	Resistance

physics or engineering to apply to acoustics the mathematical symbolism and proofs developed for electrical circuits and transmission lines.

To use this analogy, it is customary to define a specific acoustic impedance z, such that

$$z = \frac{p}{v}$$

It is analogous to the electrical impedance Z, where

$$Z = \text{voltage/current}$$

For plane waves going in the ^+x direction

$$z = \rho c$$

This value of z is called the characteristic impedance.

When an electrical transmission line is joined to another element having the same impedance, a maximum power transfer will occur. If the two have an impedance ratio much different from one, relatively little power transfer takes place. Likewise, if two acoustic media with very different characteristic impedances are in contact, a plane wave will be primarily reflected at the interface. For example, air has a characteristic impedance

$$\rho c_{\text{air}} = 42 \text{ cgs units}$$

whereas water and tissue have characteristic impedances

$$\rho c_{\text{H}_2\text{O}} \doteq \rho c_{\text{tissue}} \doteq 1.5 \times 10^5 \text{ cgs units}$$

Thus, sound energy is transmitted readily from water to tissue but very little is transmitted from air to tissue. This difference in characteristic impedance means that only a very small portion of the power incident on the ear can be used in hearing. However, the sound pressure amplitude remains approximately the same in the tissues of the ear as in the incident air.

It is generally assumed in acoustics that if a generator sends out waves of a given frequency, then only these will be transmitted by the medium and received by the ear. This is a consequence of Equation 6 which applies not only to velocity but also to pressure and to excess density. Actually, no real medium propagates sound in the fashion predicted by Equation 6, but the deviations from it are often so small as to be undetectable by human ears. At high amplitudes, and in certain special cases even at low amplitudes, the shape of a propagated wave may change in a fashion that cannot be predicted from Equation 6. An extreme example is the surface waves on the ocean. In this case, the wave velocity c depends on the frequency. As a consequence, waves rise up to a maximum at some places and then seem to disappear; others actually double back and form breakers. In the inner ear, incident waves likewise pile up to give a maximum amplitude at a location which depends on their frequency.

The waveform is distorted by the production of harmonics in the transmission of waves in air at sound pressure levels in excess of about 120 db in the audible range. These effects are referred to as nonlinear; they contradict the assumptions of infinitesimal amplitudes made in traditional acoustics. Similar production of harmonics can be observed in the ear. However, in most cases the harmonic distortion due to nonlinearities is not important in hearing. It is quite possible, however, that they produce some of the important effects when tissue is subjected to ultrasound.

There are many other acoustic terms used to describe auditory acoustics. It is the author's belief, however, that a familiarity with the words and symbols of Table I is sufficient to understand most journal articles and more advanced texts dealing with the physical aspects of hearing.

REFERENCES

1. Hunter, J. L., *Acoustics* (Englewood Cliffs, N.J: Prentice-Hall, Inc., 1957).
2. Morse, P. M., *Vibrations and Sound* 2nd ed. (New York: McGraw-Hill Book Company, Inc., 1948).
3. Hueter, T. F., and R. H. Bolt, *Sonics: Techniques for the Use of Sound and Ultrasound in Engineering and Science* (New York: John Wiley & Sons, Inc., 1955).

Appendix B

Geometrical Optics

The formulas of geometrical optics are used to describe the image-forming properties of the eye. These are not different from those of lenses in general. A thorough background in geometrical optics will help one to understand the image-forming function of the eye. The formulas describing image formation by thick lenses will be discussed in this appendix. As in Chapter 2, use is made of the index of refraction defined by

$$n = \frac{c}{v} \tag{1}$$

where c is the velocity of light in a vacuum and v is that in any given medium. The relative index of refraction n_{12} for any two media is defined by

$$n_{12} = \frac{v_2}{v_1} \tag{2}$$

Before the properties of lenses are discussed, the approach of geometrical optics is used to derive Snell's law. This proof is characteristic of the general methods used. Consider a medium of index of refraction n bounded by a plane surface, as shown in Figure 1. Here the line $\overline{AB}$ represents the boundary between this medium and a vacuum. The line $\overline{\alpha\beta}$ is the normal of this surface. Now consider a plane wavefront at $\overline{DE}$ at time $t = 0$.

A short time later, this wavefront will have moved to $\overline{D'OE'}$. The wavefront no longer is straight since the portion of the wave in the right hand medium moves more slowly than that still in the left hand medium. At a still later time, it will be entirely in the second medium at $\overline{D''E''}$.

The angle between the normal to the interface $\overline{\alpha\beta}$ and the normal to the incident wave $\overline{Oy}$ is called the angle of incidence θ. Likewise, the angle between $\overline{\alpha\beta}$ and the normal to the refracted wave $\overline{O\delta}$ is called

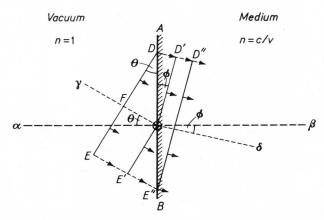

Figure 1. Refraction of a plane wave at a plane interface. (This diagram is used to derive Snell's Law.)

the angle of refraction φ. The properties of right triangles can be used to show that both angles labeled θ in the drawing are equal, as are both angles labeled φ, and that

$$\overline{FO} = \overline{DO} \sin \theta \quad \text{and} \quad \overline{DD'} = \overline{DO} \sin \varphi \qquad (3)$$

Because $\overline{FO}$ is the distance the light ray traversed in the vacuum while a similar ray was traveling $\overline{DD'}$ in the medium, one may equate the times of travel. Thus

$$\frac{\overline{FO}}{c} = \frac{\overline{DD'}}{v}$$

Using Equation 1, one may rewrite this last relationship as

$$\overline{FO} = n\overline{DD'} \qquad (4)$$

Combining Equations 3 and 4 and rearranging terms, one obtains Snell's law

$$n = \sin \theta / \sin \varphi \qquad (5)$$

Using this law, one has only to draw the lines representing the incident and refracted rays, $\overline{O\gamma}$ and $\overline{O\delta}$ in Figure 1; drawing lines for the wave-fronts is superfluous.

From the point of view of mathematical theory, Snell's law describes the simplest case of refraction possible. In analyzing lens systems, including the eye, it is necessary to treat curved interfaces between two media and curved wavefronts. The type of curved interface which is

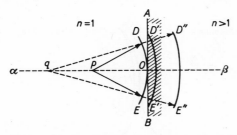

Figure 2. Refraction of a spherical wave at a plane interface. A virtual image is formed at q due to the object at p. Curvature of wavefront is changed because it does not all reach interface at the same time. Image is virtual because wavefront diverges as if it came from q; in other words, q is negative.

simplest to treat mathematically is a spherical interface. Even this is complex when used for an analysis of lens action; only small sections of spherical surfaces are simple to treat. Although insufficient for making optical lenses, an analysis of refraction by small sections of spheres is sufficiently complex to describe the action of the eye because the interfaces between the various media in the eye are very close to small sections of spheres.

A curved wavefront will, in general, undergo a change in curvature when it is refracted. This is illustrated in Figure 2 for a plane interface. The point p from which the incident wave diverges is called the *location of the object*, whereas the point q to which the refracted wave converges is called the *location of the image*. Objects are called *real* if they are on the side of the interface from which the light is coming; images are called *real* if they are on the side of the interface toward which the light is going. Objects and images which are not real are called *virtual*.

For camera or eye action, it is necessary to have real final images. In the following examples, only real initial objects, real final images, and positive (converging) surfaces are illustrated. The convention is adopted of treating distances as positive or negative, according to their location relative to the lens or to the surface of discontinuity of index refraction. Thus, a real object will be located at a negative distance p, whereas a real image will be located at a positive distance q.

Consider now the case shown in Figure 3 of a curved interface. A section of a sphere AOA' with center at r separates two media of indices of refraction n_1 and n_2. A section of a spherical wave BOB' with center at p reaches the spherical surface at time $t = 0$. A short time later, BB' has reached AA'. The waves in the second medium move more slowly. Consequently, the portion of the wavefront initially at O has

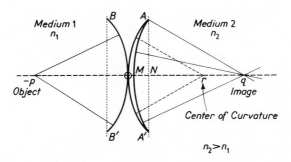

Figure 3. Refraction of a spherical wave at a spherical interface. Light is traveling from left to right. A real object is located in medium 1 at $-p$ and a real image in medium 2 at q.

only reached M during the time in which the wavefront in the first medium has moved from B to A. Thus, a real image will form at q due to the change in the curvature of the wavefront.

To find a relationship between p, q, r, n_1, and n_2, one proceeds just as in Snell's law to equate the time for light to travel from O to M and from B to A; symbolically

$$n_1 \overline{AB} = n_2 \overline{OM} \tag{6}$$

The entire problem (which is still far simpler than the refraction in the eye) can be simplified mathematically by assuming only small sections of spheres. This allows one to make the following approximations

$$\overline{AA'} \doteq \overline{BB'} \qquad \qquad \overline{AB} \doteq \overline{LN}$$

$$\overline{LO} \doteq \frac{\overline{AA'}^2}{2p} \qquad \overline{MN} \doteq \frac{\overline{AA'}^2}{2q} \qquad \overline{ON} \doteq \frac{\overline{AA'}^2}{2r} \tag{7}$$

The last three are based on the sagittal approximation illustrated in Figure 4. Noting in Figure 3 that

$$\overline{LN} = \overline{LO} + \overline{ON} \qquad \text{and} \qquad \overline{OM} = \overline{ON} - \overline{MN} \tag{8}$$

and turning the handle of the algebraic crank several times leads to the final relationship

$$\frac{n_2}{q} - \frac{n_1}{p} = \frac{n_2 - n_1}{r} \tag{9}$$

Several aspects of Equation 9 should be emphasized because they are characteristic of all lens systems. For simplicity, only the case in which $(n_2 - n_1)/r$ is greater than zero will be considered. It is possible then to construct Table I. The point $-f_1$ is called the *back focal length*, whereas f_2 is the *front focal length*. Objects more than $10 f_1$ behind the interface will produce real images within 10 per cent of f_2. This is the case for most objects focused by the eye.

The implications of Equation 9 for the refraction of spherical wavefronts at a spherical interface can be represented by a ray diagram, as shown in Figure 5. Just as in the illustration of Snell's law, the ray diagram makes detailed drawings of the wavefronts superfluous. In Figure 5, the optic axis passes through the center of curvature r of the interface and the central point of the interface o. Another line labeled (a) is drawn from the end of the object, located at $-p$, parallel to the optic axis until it reaches the interface. Because this ray is parallel to the axis, it is

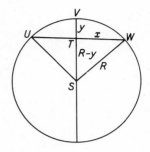

Figure 4. The sagittal approximation. The sagittal approximation for small spherical sections is derived as follows:

$$x^2 + (R - y)^2 = R^2$$
$$\therefore \quad x^2 - 2Ry + y^2 = 0$$
If $\qquad y \ll R$
$$\therefore \qquad y \doteq \frac{x^2}{2R}$$

TABLE I

Objects and Images for Equation 9

Object		Image	
Parallel light $\quad -p = \infty$		$q = r\dfrac{n_2}{n_2 - n_1} = f_2$	*Real*
Real $\quad p < 0$ $\quad -p > r\dfrac{n_1}{n_2 - n_1} = f_1$		$q > f_2$	*Real*
$-p = f_1$		$q = \pm\infty$	*Parallel light*
$-p < f_1$		$q < 0$	*Virtual*
Virtual $\quad p < 0$		$f_2 > q > 0$	*Real*

Values above valid if $f_1, f_2 > 0$.

bent to pass through the front focal point f_2.   Line (b) is constructed in a similar fashion.   Finally, (c) is a line joining the end of the object with the center of curvature r.   This line is undeviated as it is normal to the interface.   Any two of the three lines (a), (b), and (c) are sufficient to locate and to determine the size of the object.   The three points $-f_1$, f_2, and r are sufficient with the optic center o to permit all constructions. The point r is related to f_1 and f_2 by the equation

$$r = f_2 - f_1 \qquad (10)$$

In the eye, light passes through four approximately spherical surfaces, separating media of different indices of refraction.   Equation 9 could be

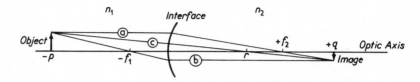

Figure 5. Ray diagram illustrating refraction by a curved interface between two media of indices of refraction n_1 and n_2. The interface is a small spherical section with center of curvature at r.   Any two of the three rays, a, b, and c, are sufficient to determine the location and size of the image.

used successively at each of these surfaces, noting that the image formed by one surface is the object of the next.   It is quite possible to have virtual objects under these conditions.

Although the preceding is all that is necessary to discuss the geometrical optics of the eye, a somewhat more generalized approach that lumps the effects of several surfaces is neater.   For example, by applying Equation 9 twice, one can solve the problem of a single lens.   To illustrate this, suppose a medium of index of refraction n_2 separates two others of indices of refraction n_1 and n_3, respectively.   The surfaces of separation are assumed to be small sections of spheres whose line of centers is referred to as the *optic axis*.   The radius of the surface separating the media of indices of refraction n_1 and n_2 will be designated by r_a, and the radius of the other surface by r_b.   If the object is located at a distance $-p$ along the optic axis from the first surface, one may find the location of the image q' by solving Equation 9 in the form

$$\frac{n_2}{q'} - \frac{n_1}{p} = \frac{n_2 - n_1}{r_a} \qquad (11)$$

This image q' is the object for the second surface.   If the distance between surfaces is denoted by t, the distance from the second surface to its object p' is

$$p' = q' - t$$

Hence, one can find the location of the final image q by applying Equation 9 again to yield

$$\frac{n_3}{q} - \frac{n_2}{q' - t} = \frac{n_3 - n_2}{r_b} \tag{12}$$

Tedious but straightforward algebraic manipulations of Equations 11 and 12 allow one to eliminate q', arriving at

$$\frac{n_3}{q - \beta} - \frac{n_1}{p - \alpha} = \frac{1}{\Phi} \tag{13}$$

where q is the image distance from surface b
$\quad -p$ is the object distance from surface a

$$\alpha = -\frac{n_1 f_a t}{\gamma} \tag{14}$$

$$\beta = -\frac{n_3 f_b t}{\gamma} \tag{15}$$

$$\Phi = -\frac{n_2 f_a f_b}{\gamma} \tag{16}$$

$$\gamma = n_2(f_b - f_a) - t \tag{17}$$

$$f_a = \frac{r_a}{n_1 - n_2} \tag{18}$$

$$f_b = \frac{r_b}{n_1 - n_2} \tag{19}$$

The form of Equation 13 can be simplified in various fashions. Three different cases will be considered.

A. *Thin lenses:* In this case, one may neglect t. Then α and β are both zero. If, in addition, n_1 and n_3 are equal and one denotes by n the ratio

$$n = \frac{n_2}{n_1}$$

then Equation 13 reduces to

$$\frac{1}{q} - \frac{1}{p} = \frac{1}{f} \tag{20}$$

whereas Equations 16 through 19 become simply

$$\frac{1}{f} = (n - 1)\left(\frac{1}{r_a} - \frac{1}{r_b}\right) \tag{21}$$

A ray diagram for the thin lens is illustrated in Figure 6.   Note that because the front and back focal lengths are equal, the center r as defined by Equation 10 is at 0.

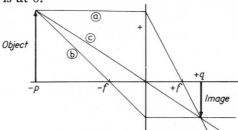

Figure 6. Ray diagram for a thin lens.   The lens is shown as a straight line because it is thin.   The plus sign indicates f is positive.

B.   Thick lens with same medium on both sides: In this case, it is no longer possible to neglect t.   However, if one defines P, Q, and F as

$$P = p - \alpha \tag{22}$$

$$Q = q - \beta \tag{23}$$

$$F = n_1 \Phi \tag{24}$$

then Equation 19 becomes

$$\frac{1}{Q} - \frac{1}{P} = \frac{1}{F} \tag{25}$$

This is completely analogous to Equation 20, except that now the object distance and back focal length are measured from a plane called the *first principal plane*, which is normal to the optic axis and intersects it at the point called the *first principal point*, which is at a distance α from the first surface.   The image and front focal length are measured from the second principal plane, located at a distance β from the second surface. The ray diagram describing the thick lens is illustrated in Figure 7. Note that if one imagined that the space between the two principal planes did not exist, the diagram would be essentially the same as Figure 6.

C.   Thick lens separating two different media: For this case, one can use Equations 22 and 23 to simplify Equation 19 slightly to yield

$$\frac{n_3}{Q} - \frac{n_1}{P} = \frac{1}{\Phi} \tag{26}$$

This is identical in form to Equation 9 for refraction at a single spherical surface, provided one interprets $(n_3 - n_1)\Phi$ as an equivalent radius.

All of the interpretations of Equation 9 apply also to Equation 26, provided one measures distances from the appropriate principal planes. For example, there will be a back focal length $-F_1$, given by

$$-F_1 = n_1\Phi$$

and a front focal length F_2, such that

$$F_2 = n_3\Phi$$

A ray diagram for this case is shown in Figure 1 of Chapter 2. By analogy with Figure 5, the ray from the object labeled (c) must intersect

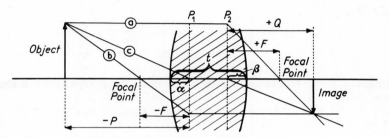

Figure 7. Thick lens ray diagram. Notice in this figure that F, P, and Q are all measured from the planes P_1 and P_2. These planes at which the rays a and b change direction are called *principal planes* and their intersections with the axis of symmetry are called *principal points*. Likewise, the points at which ray c proceeds toward and then away from are called *nodal points*. If the media on both sides of the lens are the same, the nodal and principal points coincide. The case of different media on the two sides of the lens is illustrated in Chapter 2, Figure 1.

the optic axis at a point called the *first nodal point*, which is at the distance $(n_3 - n_1)\Phi$ from the first principal point. This ray then runs along the optic axis to the second nodal point, located at the distance $(n_3 - n_1)\Phi$ from the second principal point. Thereafter, the line (c) must proceed to the image, running parallel to the first part of (c). Thus, the image subtends the same angle about the second nodal point as the object about the first.

The six points, namely, two foci, two principal points, and two nodal points, describe the refraction due to any pair of lens surfaces[1] to the extent that the approximation developed in Figure 3 is valid. These

---

[1] Actually, only four of the six points are necessary.

six points are called the *cardinal points*. This conclusion is not restricted to two surfaces. Because Equation 26 is identical in form to Equation 9, one can consider two surfaces separating media of different indices of refraction as equivalent to only one surface. This surface can be combined mathematically with a third surface, provided the latter can be approximated by a small section of a sphere whose center lies on the optic axis of the first two. This argument then may be generalized to any number N of surfaces separating media of different indices of refraction, provided the surfaces can all be approximated by small sections of spheres, all of which have a common line of centers. These six cardinal points are used in Chapter 2 to describe the refraction of light in the eye.

REFERENCES

1. Stuhlman, Otto, Jr., *An Introduction to Biophysics* (New York: John Wiley & Sons, Inc., 1943).

2. Ogle, K. N., *Optics: An Introduction for Ophthalmologists* (Springfield, Illinois: Charles C. Thomas, 1961).

3. Glasser, Otto, ed., *Medical Physics* (Chicago, Illinois: Year Book Publishers, Inc., 1944) Vol. 1.

    a. Luckiesh, Matthew, and F. K. Moss, "Light, Vision and Seeing," pp. 672–684.

    b. Sheard, Charles, "Optics: Ophthalmic, With Applications to Physiologic Optics," pp. 830–869.

For a more thorough discussion of optics at an intermediate physics level, see:

4. Robertson, J. K., *Introduction to Physical Optics* 2nd ed. (New York: D. Van Nostrand Company, Inc., 1935).

Appendix C

Electrical Terminology (Used in Chapters 4 through 7)

There are a number of electrical terms which are used in the discussion of nerve action. The more important ones are included in Table I on page 606. This appendix is devoted to a discussion of some of these quantities and their units.

The concept of electrical charge is hard to define. The unit of charge may be defined in terms of Coulomb's law giving the force of interaction between two charges separated by a distance r; that is

$$F = \frac{q_1 q_2}{Kr^2}$$

If K is given the appropriate value for mks units, namely $4\pi\epsilon_0$,[1] and F is in newtons and r in meters, the q's will be in coulombs. The force will be repulsive if the two charges have the same sign and attractive if the signs are opposite.

Because there exist forces between charges, it will in general require work to bring a new charge into any region of space. The work necessary to move a unit charge between two points is called the potential difference V. Symbolically, this is expressed as

$$\Delta V = \frac{dW}{dq}$$

If a potential difference exists between two points, there will be a

---

[1] The symbol ϵ_0 stands for the dielectric constant of free space.

TABLE I

Electrical Terms and Units

Term	Symbol	mks Unit*	Defining Equations
Charge	Q, q	coulomb	—
Electron charge	e	1.6×10^{-19} coulombs	—
Potential difference	V, E	volt	$\Delta V = \dfrac{dW}{dq}$
Field strength	E	volt meter	$\vec{E} = \dfrac{d\vec{F}}{dq} = -\vec{\nabla}V$
Current	I	ampere	$I = \dfrac{dq}{dt}$
Current density	J	ampere/square meter	$J = \dfrac{dI}{dA}$
Resistance	R	ohm	$R = V/I \qquad \left(R = \dfrac{dV}{dI}\right)$
Capacity	C	farad	$C = \dfrac{Q}{V}$
Inductance	L	henry	$E = -L\dfrac{dI}{dt}$
Impedance	Z	ohm	$Z = V/I$
Reactance	X	ohm	[for single frequency] $Z = R + jX$
Power	P	watt	$P = \dfrac{dW}{dt} \quad P = RI^2$
Dielectric constant	ϵ		$\epsilon = C/C_0$

Other Symbols Used Above and in Text

Term	Symbol	Unit	Equation
Force	F	newton	—
Work	W	joule	$W = \int \vec{F}\cdot\vec{dx}$
Distance	x, r	meter	—
Area	A	meter^2	—
Time	t	second	—
	j		$j = \sqrt{-1}$
Vector operator del	$\vec{\nabla}$	meter^{-1}	$\vec{\nabla}V = \vec{i}\dfrac{\partial V}{\partial x} + \vec{j}\dfrac{\partial V}{\partial y} + \vec{k}\dfrac{\partial V}{\partial z}$
Unit vectors	$\vec{i}, \vec{j}, \vec{k}$	none	
Free space	Subscript $_0$		
Complex amplitude	Subscript $_0$		

*The mks (meter-kilogram-second) units are used in most of this text for electrical quantities.

tendency for charge to flow. In many bioelectrical experiments, the physical quantity measured is a potential difference in volts.

In intermediate courses in electricity, the potential V is defined in terms of the electric field strength $\vec{E}$ by the equation

$$E = -\vec{\nabla}V$$

The electric field strength is the magnitude and direction of the force per unit charge at a given place in space. Symbolically, $\vec{E}$ is defined by

$$\vec{E} = \frac{d\vec{F}}{dq}$$

The value of $\vec{E}$ determines among other things the point at which an insulator will "break down" passing a spark to ground or the surrounding medium. This discharge is used in spark plugs to cause a spark when the field strength at its points becomes sufficiently great. In dry air, the critical field strength is about 3×10^6 v/m. If the spark plug is sufficiently worn away, the separation between the two points becomes too large and, accordingly, the field strength never attains this value.

If a direct (unidirectional) current flows between two points, then one may compute the ratio R called the *resistance*, defined by

$$R = \frac{V}{I}$$

Ohm's law states that R is independent of I. It is approximately true for many substances over large ranges of I. Substances for which R is low are called *conductors*, those for which R is high are *insulators*.

If other forms of energy are reversibly converted to electrical energy when a current flows, the generated potential difference is called an *electromotive force* (emf). It is often distinguished by the symbol E. Electrochemical cells, electromechanical transducers such as motors and microphones, and junctions between dissimilar metals all give rise to an emf. When the emf causes the current to flow, nonelectrical energy is converted to electrical energy. If the current is caused to flow in the opposite direction, electrical energy is removed by the emf. Some direct current circuits are illustrated in Figure 1 of Chapter 4.

A term used frequently in discussing biological tissues is capacity. If two conductors are separated by an insulating medium, then the ratio

$$C = \frac{Q}{V}$$

is called the *capacity*. A current cannot flow from one conductor to the other through the capacitor. However, while the capacitor is being charged, positive charges flow to one conductor and away from the other. In an alternating current, the capacitors are continually charged, discharged, and then charged in the reverse direction, thereby effectively transmitting an alternating current. Because the charge on the capacitor is proportional to the voltage across the capacitor, the current through the capacitor must precede the voltage changes across it. In an alternating circuit, the current through a capacitor leads the voltage across it by 90°.

An element in which the current lags the voltage by 90° is called an inductance L. If a coil is formed, it is found that an emf E is induced in it, as the current changes. This emf is so directed that it opposes the current change. The self-inductance L is defined by

$$E = -L\frac{dI}{dt}$$

An inductance does not alter a steady direct current but hinders the flow of an alternating current.

Many of the interesting bioelectric phenomena involve currents and potentials which change in time. As was mentioned in Chapter 1, any complicated function of time can be represented as a sum of terms at single frequencies, or at worst, an integral of a frequency distribution function. Thus, if one can describe the behavior of any circuit element as a function of frequency, one can compute its response to a transient. Accordingly, it is useful to be familiar with the terminology applied to sinusoidal alternating currents.

Such an alternating current, just as an alternating acoustic pressure, may be described by an expression such as

$$I = A \cos{(\omega t + \varphi)} \tag{1}$$

where A and φ are constants and ω is 2π times the frequency. It is often more convenient to treat the measured current as the real part of the complex current[2]

$$I = I_0 e^{j\omega t}$$

where the complex current amplitude is related to Equation 1 by

$$I_0 = A e^{j\varphi} \tag{1'}$$

Using a similar complex notation for the potential V, one may form the complex ratio

$$Z = \frac{V}{I} = \frac{V_0}{I_0} \tag{2}$$

---

[2] It is important not to confuse the electronic charge e with the base of the natural logarithm $e = 2.7182818\ldots.$ The latter occurs in Equation 1'.

which is called the impedance. Equation 2 has meaning only for sinusoidal currents and potentials or for Fourier transforms of currents and potentials. The ratio Z is called the *impedance*. It can be represented in the form

$$Z = R + jX$$

where both R and X are real numbers. If the impedance Z is real (that is, $X = 0$), the voltage and current are said to be in phase. In this case, at all times, the instantaneous ratio of V to I is the same constant. The real part of Z is called the *resistance R*. However, if R is zero, but the reactance X is different from zero, V and I will be 90° out of phase. An a-c circuit is illustrated in Figure 2 of Chapter 4.

Only the resistance R contributes to the power dissipated by an element in an alternating circuit. In a direct current circuit, one may write

$$P = VI$$

This same formula may be used for an alternating current circuit, providing one uses the real instantaneous values of V and I and averages over a period. For a sinusoidal current

$$P = \frac{|I_0|^2 R}{2} = \frac{|V_0|^2 R}{2|Z|^2}$$

where the vertical lines indicate the absolute values of the complex quantities. In the neuron, the power dissipated is so small compared to metabolic heat losses that it is in general unimportant.

Other electrical terms and symbols are discussed in Section 2 of Chapter 11. For references, see Chapters 4 and 11.

Appendix D

Ionizing Radiations

The biological effects of ionizing radiations were discussed in Chapters 10 and 16. Some of the physical properties of these radiations are outlined here.

Ionizing radiations may have a number of different origins. So-called "naturally radioactive materials" give off α, β, or γ rays. Artificially produced radioactive isotopes emit positive and negative β's and γ's. (Artificially produced isotopes include the products of nuclear fission.) In addition, neutrons may be obtained from a nuclear reactor. High energy protons, deuterons, alpha particles, and electrons can be produced with the appropriate types of accelerators. The different types of particles are listed in Table I on page 611, along with their properties.

All of these radiations, when striking an atom, impart energy to it by either exciting its electrons to a higher energy state or knocking one (or more) electrons from the atom. For each type of radiation, the energy loss per centimeter, the shape of the path, and the stopping distance, all have characteristic values.

Alpha particles have the greatest rest mass of the various types of radiation considered here. The alpha particles are helium nuclei. Each has an atomic weight of 4 and a positive charge equal to twice the magnitude of the charge of an electron. Alpha particles interact strongly with electrons, losing their excess kinetic energy in a matter of a tenth of a millimeter of tissue or less. They are only harmful to biological cells if the α-emitter is incorporated in the cell or in a neighboring one.

Other massive positively charged particles are the deuteron and the

TABLE I

Radiations

Name	Other Names	Sources	Rest Mass	Charge	Spin	Path Length
Alpha particle	He⁴ nucleus	Natural radioactivity	4 amu	+2	0	Heavily ionized straight paths
Deuteron	D⁺	Accelerator beam	2	+1	1	
Proton	H⁺, p	Accelerator beam	1	+1	$\frac{1}{2}$	Lightly ionized paths not straight
Neutron	n	Atomic fission Nuclear reactions	1	0	$\frac{1}{2}$	
Electron	β^-	Natural radioactivity Artificial radioactivity Accelerator	$1\,m_e$	−1	$\frac{1}{2}$	Ionized twisted paths
Positron	β^+, positive electron	Artificial radioactivity	$1\,m_e$	+1	$-\frac{1}{2}$	As electron above but ends with large burst of energy
Photons	*Ultraviolet *X ray *γ ray	Arc discharge Electron bombardment of metals Radioactivity—natural and artificial	0	0	1	Resonance absorption; { Long straight paths through matter with comparatively light ionization }
†K-mesons	Several labeled $\kappa, \theta, x, \kappa_\mu, \kappa_\pi$	Cosmic rays	$966\,m_e$	+1, −1, and 0	Integer	Radioactive; also create dense bursts of ionization when striking nucleus
†L-mesons	π^- π^+ π° μ^- μ^+	Cosmic rays and reactions after bombardment with accelerator beams of sufficient energy	273 273 264 207 207	−1 +1 0 −1 +1	0 0 0 $\frac{1}{2}$ $\frac{1}{2}$	π^- reacts strongly with all nuclei. All are unstable but may also collide with nuclei causing dense bursts of ionization
†Neutrino	‡Leptons	Accompany β^- emission	0	0	$+\frac{1}{2}$	Interact very weakly with matter. Travel diameter of earth with one or less ionizations
†Antineutrino		Accompany β^+ emission	0	0	$+\frac{1}{2}$	

* These are specific types of photons. See Chapter 21.

‡ This name also includes photons.

m_e = electron rest mass.

amu = atomic mass unit.

† Other radiations not included in text—included for completeness in table.

proton. These are both hydrogen nuclei having a positive electronic charge of 1 and the atomic weights of 2 and 1, respectively. Neither protons nor deuterons are emitted by any naturally occurring atomic nuclei. However, beams of both can be formed in high energy accelerators and used to bombard biological cells or layers of proteins. The cell layers must be very thin for, just as alpha particles, both protons and deuterons react very strongly with electrons. The ionization along their path through the cell is very intense.

Alpha particles, protons, and deuterons are all much heavier than electrons. Accordingly, these heavy, positively charged particles are only slightly deflected when reacting with electrons. The atomic nuclei deflect all these three types of radiation if the particles come close to them, but this happens infrequently. The paths of all three types are fairly straight; given equal starting energies, the pathlengths of each type are distributed quite close to the average value. This is illustrated in Figure 1 of Chapter 10.

Neutrons have about the same mass as protons but have zero charge. They do not react appreciably with electrons; their primary effect is in interactions with atomic nuclei. In material containing hydrogen, that is, water, proteins, nucleic acids, and protoplasm in general, one major result of neutron irradiation is the knocking out of hydrogen nuclei (protons) from the molecules by elastic collisions. As a result of these collisions, the path of the neutrons may be very twisted and intertwined. Neutrons can also react with various atomic nuclei. The destructive action of neutrons in living matter is much greater than indicated by their ionizing powers.

Neutrons with kinetic energies comparable to the molecules about them are called *thermal neutrons*. These have sufficient energy to enter only a few of the nuclei of the elements found in living tissues. Moreover, neutrons are radioactive, decaying to proton and beta particles with a half-life of about 13 minutes. That is, each 13 minutes the number of neutrons is decreased by a factor of two. Neutrons which are not thermal are called *high energy neutrons*.

Electrons have a mass about 1/2000 that of a proton. Rapidly moving electrons are called *beta rays*. The word electron is usually used for negative ones; anti-electrons with an equal mass and a charge of equal magnitude but opposite sign are called *positrons*, or *positive beta particles* or *positive electrons*. Both positive and negative electrons passing through matter interact both with electrons and with atomic nuclei. In addition, a positron can combine with an electron, resulting in their mutual annihilation and the formation of photons (γ rays). The paths of electrons in tissues are very twisted. Both those from radioactive atoms and those from accelerators do not penetrate very deeply into an organism on the average. However, a few will always penetrate much further into the tissues. On a cellular level, both positive and negative electrons have the same types of effects as alpha particles, deuterons, and protons.

Certain particles with no rest mass are called photons; these particles are also called electromagnetic radiation. The most energetic photons are X rays and γ rays. X-ray photons are made by bombarding a metallic surface with electrons, whereas γ rays are emitted by atomic nuclei during transitions. Both X-ray and γ-ray photons interact comparatively weakly with matter. Their paths through an entire human are quite straight. Both of these types of photons can impart energy to electrons, causing them to be excited or knocked out of their orbitals.

Slightly lower energy photons are called *ultraviolet*. Those with a wavelength of around 2,600 Å are strongly absorbed by certain compounds within the cell called *nucleic acids*. In this case, the entire photon is absorbed and an electron is raised to a higher energy level. There is a small, but observable, probability that the entire nucleic acid molecule will then be ruptured.

When a beam of ionizing radiation interacts with a biological cell, it is possible that the ionizations produced throughout the cell are equally effective or that only those in a certain critical volume are important. This critical volume is called the *target*; the theory necessary to find its size is referred to as *target theory* or *single hit theory*. The latter theory is discussed in Chapter 16.

Index

A

Absolute rate theory, 222, 408–412
    denaturation studies, 412–415
Absorption bands:
    infrared, 514
Absorption coefficient, 485, 487, 489
    molar, 489
Absorption ratio, 489
Absorption spectrophotometry, 481–500
    (see Spectrophotometry, absorption)
A-c, 73, 608–609
Accelerated-flow method, 496, 497
Accommodation, 36, 38
Acetylcholine, 85, 145, 180, 443
Acetylcholinesterase, 85, 145, 443
ACh, 85, 443–446
    cycle in nerve cell, 445
    synthesis, 444
Acid, organic, 271
Acoustic (sound) pressure, 5, 7, 8, 592
    amplitude, 5, 7, 8, 10, 13
Acoustic streaming, 243, 262
Acoustics, 4–10, 589–594
    finite amplitude, 594
    infinitesimal amplitude, 589
Actin, 148, 152
Action current, 72
Action potential, 70 (see also Spike
        potential)
    heart, 165–166
    muscle, 145–146
Activated complex, 408
Activation energy, 404
Active transport, 420, 432–436, 477–478
    frog's skin, 434–435
    Ussing's equations, 433–434

Adenine, 149, 279
Adenosine, 149
Adenosine diphosphate, 149–151 (see also
        ADP)
Adenosine monophosphate, 149
Adenosine triphosphate, 148–151 (see also
        ATP)
Adenylic acid, 149
ADP, 149–151, 346, 366–369
Alanine, 275
Albumin, 473
Alcohol dehydrogenase (ADH), 354–355
Aldehyde, 353
Algae:
    blue-green and photosynthesis, 360
    damage by ultrasound, 231
    and photosynthesis, 360
Allele, 474
All-or-none response, 80
Alpha ray (or particle), 185, 610
α-rhythm, 98
α-waves, 98
Amino acids, 148, 271–277
Amino group, 271
Amoeba:
    relative fragility, 229
AMP, 149
Ampere, 72
Amplitude distribution, 6
Analyzer, 548–549
Anaphase, 190
Angular momentum:
    orbital, 508–509
    spin, 508–509
    total, 508
Antigen, 308
Anti-node, 9

Aorta, 161
Aperture, 37
Apoenzyme, 319
Aqueous humor, 37, 50
Arginine, 276
Arrhenius constant, 405
Arrhenius plot, 396, 405
Arteriole, 158
Artery, 158
Ascorbic acid spectrum, 486
Aspartic acid, 276
Astacin, 358
Astigmatism, 39, 65
ATP, 148–151, 346, 366–369
Attenuation factor, 213
Audible frequency range, 5, 12
Audiometer, 15
    Bekesy, 15, 16
    pure tone, 16
    speech, 16
Auditory acoustics, 589–594
Auricle:
    of the ear, 19
    of the heart, 161–163
Auriculo-ventricular (a-v) node, 162, 165
Auriculo-ventricular (a-v) values, 163
Autocorrelator, 97, 180
A-v bundle (of His), 165
A-v node, 162, 165
Axon, 70, 74, 75
    cable theory, 478
    current patterns, 441
    "myelinated", 74
    "nonmyelinated", 83
    peristaltic-like wave, 442, 478

B

Bacteria:
    photosynthetic, 360
Bacteriological plate, 249
Bacteriophage, 246 (*see also* Phage)
Ballistocardiograph, 181
Basilar membrane, 24–25, 105–106
Bats, 53–58
Beer's law, 487
Bekesy audiometer, 15, 16
β-carotene, 372–373
Beta ray, 185, 610, 611
β-waves, 98
Binary integer, 462
Biomechanics, 137
Bird navigation, 61–63, 65
Birefringence, 549
Bit, 462
Blepharisma, 229
Blind spot, 35, 36
Blinking reflex, 40
Blood:
    density, 158
    pressure, 158–161
        diastolic, 159–160
        systolic, 159–160
    velocity, 158–161
Bohr magneton, 530

Bone conduction, 14
Bouger's law, 485
Bovine serum albumin, 309–310
Brain, 90
    electrical potentials of, 88–102
    ventricle, 90
Brain stem, 90
"Brain wave", 89

C

Canonically conjugate variables, 504
Capacitor, 73
Capacity, 73, 607
Capillary, 158
Carbohydrates, 270–272
Carbon dating, 565
C^{14}, 201, 563–565
Carbonic anhydrase, 316
Carboxylase, 319
Cardinal points, 30, 37, 603
Carotenoid, 353, 358, 370–372
Carotenoid oil droplets, 358, 381
Catalase, 309, 316, 332–341
    diffusion studies, 416–417
    thermodynamic interpretation, 396–399
Catalytic reaction, 333
Catalyst, 315–316
Cavitation, 205, 221–224
    rupture of biological cells, 224–225
    rupture of molecular bonds, 225
Cavitation threshold, 222
Cellulose, 271–272
Cellular fragility:
    determined by ultrasound, 226–229
Central nervous system, 75, 89–92
    auditory pathways, 114–115
    visual pathways, 134
Centromere, 189–190
Centrosome, 190
Cerebral cortex, 90
Cerebral hemisphere, 90
    occipal lobe, 134
    temporal lobe:
        auditory area, 114–115
Cerumen, 20
Characteristic frequency, 8 (*see also* Resonance)
Characteristic function, 9, 505
Chemical releasers, 65
Chlorella, 362
    action spectrum, 374'
Chlorophyll, 370
    a, 370–372
    b, 370–372
    bacterial, 370–371
    ethylchlorophyllide b, 484
Chloroplast, 361–362, 381
Cholesterol, 270
Choline, 443
Cholinesterase, 85, 145, 443
Choroid layer, 34
Chromatic aberration, 49
Chromaticity, 120
Chromatin material, 189–190

Chromosome, 189–191, 269
Ciliary muscle, 36
Circulatory system, 157–158
Cisisomer, 353
Cistron, 199, 256–258
Citrulline, 276
Clone, 249
Cochlea, 19, 24, 105–107, 180
  arm analogs, 111–113, 180
  hydrodynamic analog, 109–110
  hydrodynamic models, 109, 180
Cochlear duct, 24
Cochlear microphonics, 107–108, 110–111
Cochlear potentials, 107–111
Coefficient of rigidity, 240
Coenzyme, 320
Cofactor, 320
Collision rate, 404
Collision theory, 401–405
  enzyme reactions, 406–407
Color:
  complementary, 120
  white, 120–122
Colorimeter, 483
Color vision, 119 (*see also* Vision, color)
Coma, 36, 65
Commutable, 508
Composite cell, 268
Compressional wave, 214
Computer:
  analog, 572–580
    bone-density, 573–577
    for enzyme studies, 578–580
    X-RAC, 577–578
  digital, 572–573, 580–586
    memory, 581
    program, 580
    program example, 583–585
  electronic, 571–586
Complex notation, 591
Condenser (of microscope), 538
Conductivity, 173, 206
Conductor, 607
Cones, 35, 41–43, 45–50, 124–129
Conjugated system, 522
Conjugation, 255–256
Cornea, 34, 37, 40, 49
Correspondence principle, 504
Craniosacral division, 76
Creatine, 151
Creatine phosphate, 151
Crossing over, 191
Crosslinking, 302–303
Cross section, 306, 381
Crystalography, 280–286
Curie, 559
Current density, 173
Current source, 172
Cyanopsin, 358
Cysteine, 276
Cystine, 276
Cytochrome, 333, 335
Cytochrome a, 347–348
Cytochrome a_3, 347
Cytochrome b, 347

Cytochrome c, 347–348, 486
Cytochrome c_1, 347
Cytochrome system, 150, 347–349
Cytoplasm, 268
Cytosine, 279

D

Dark-adapted, 46–48
D-c, 73
Decibel, 10
δ-waves, 98, 101
Dendrites, 74
Deoxyribose, 278
Deoxyribose nucleic acid, 254 (*see* DNA)
Depth of focus, 36, 37
Deuteranopia, 122, 128
Deuteron, 185, 612
Diamagnetism, 526–528
Diaphragm (of microscope), 538
Diathermy, 205, 217–218, 262
Dielectric constant, 206
Diffraction, 7, 31, 32
  of X rays, 280–286
Diffraction orders, 538
Diffraction plate, 545
Diffuse, d, 518
Diffusion, 419–429
  constant, 422
  equations, 421–425
  Fick diffusion constant, 422
  Fick's law, 423–424
  inhomogeneous equation, 424
  into cells, 426–429
    average-value approach, 426–427, 477
    spherical approximation, 428–429, 477
Dimer, 273
Diopter, 30
Dipeptide, 273
Diphosphopyridine nucleotide, 347 (*see* DPN)
Dipoles, electrical, 171–175, 511
Displacement, 21, 589–590
DL, 17 (*see* Loudness)
DNA, 254, 269, 277–295, 300–302, 567
  helical form, 292–295
  information theory, 474
DNA-ase, 309
Dominant, 190, 197
Dominator, 130
Donnan membrane potential, 437–440
Dorsal cochlear nucleus, 115
Dosage, 187–189
DPN, 347, 355–356, 366, 485
Drosophila, 197

E

Ear, 1–4, 19–25, 104–111
  anatomy, 19–25
  inner, 19, 24–25, 104–111
  middle, 19, 21–24
  outer, 19–21
Ear canal, 19
Ear drum, 19

Echo-location, 53–59
  bats, 53–58, 65
    jamming, 55
    physical characteristics of pulse, 55–58
  oilbird, 58
  porpoise, 59
  radar, 54, 57
  sonar, 54, 57
  swiftlet, 59
Eclipse, 250
Eeg, 88
Eeg equipment, 97
Eeg patterns:
  and age, 99
  and anesthesia or sleep, 99
  spike, 101
  spike and wave, 101
Eeg potentials:
  origin, 99–100
Eigenfrequency, 8, 506
Eigenfunction, 9, 505
  string, 506
Eigenvalue, 505
  string, 506
Eighth (cranial) nerve, 19, 24, 114
Einstein, 46
Einthoven's law, 170, 171
Ekg, 163, 168–171
  abnormal, 182
  lead, 169
  orthogonal system of leads, 177
  P wave, 169–170
  QRS complex, 169–170
  T wave, 169–170
  U wave, 166, 169
Electrical charge, 605
Electrical current, 72
Electrical displacement, 206
Electrical field strength, 78, 607
Electrical fish (electrical eels),
    59, 180, 444, 478
Electrical impedance, 205–208, 609
Electrical potential, 72, 605
Electrical terminology, 605–609
Electricity, 72–74, 605–609
  table of terms and units, 606
Electric organ, 444
Electroacoustic analogs, 593
Electrocardiograph, 163 (*see also* Ekg)
Electrocardiography, 168–171 (*see also* Ekg)
  vector, 175–177
Electroencephalogram, 89
Electroencephalograph, 89
Electroencephalographic patterns,
    96–100, 180
  abnormal, 100–102
Electroencephalographic potentials, 88–89
Electroencephalography, 88–89
Electromagnetic energy:
  absorption, 204–213, 217–218 (*see also*
    Spectrophotometry)
Electromagnetic radiation table, 482
Electromotive force, 74 (*see also* Emf)
Electron:
  negative, 185, 612

Electron (*Cont.*)
  positive, 612
Electron density, 285
Electronic computer, 571–586
Electron microscope, 551–556
  muscle, 151–154
  virus, 251–252
Electron paramagnetic resonance (EPR),
    532
Electron spin resonance (ESR), 532
Electron transport, 345
Electron volt, 560
Electrophoresis, 587
Electroretinograms, 181
Emf, 74, 607
Encounter, 406
Encounter rate, 406
Endocrine system, 70–71
Endolymph, 24
End plate, 84–87, 144–145
Energy, 386
  various radiations, 561
  relativistic, 503
Energy level:
  electronic, 516
  molecular:
    table of symbols, 521
  rotational, 510
  vibrational, 512
  X-ray terminology, 519
Energy transfer, 304
Enthalpy, 390
Entropy, 387
  negative, 465
Enzyme, 197, 315–350
  adaptive, 356
  addition, 318–319
  classification, 318–320
  denaturation, 412–415
  diffusion effects, 415–417
  digestive, 319
  extraction by ultrasound, 221, 229
  fatty-acid oxidation, 381
  hydrolase:
    inhibitors, 327–331
    Michaelis-Menten kinetics, 320–327
  kinetics of hydrolytic reactions, 315–331
  kinetics of oxidations, 332–350
  proteolytic, 318
  respiratory, 319
Epilepsy, 100–102
Equal loudness curves, 17, 18
Equilibrium constant, 393
  related to Gibbs' free energy, 394
  related to rate constants, 393
  thermodynamic interpretation, 392–396
Ergodic sequence, 466
E. coli:
  damage by ultrasound, 226
  relative fragility, 229
Esterase, 318, 444
Euglena, 65, 360
  eye-spot, 381
Eustachian tube, 21, 23

Evolution:
  and eye pigments, 358, 381
  influenced by ionizing radiation, 200
Exact differential, 387
Exponential curve, 338
External auditory meatus, 9, 19–20
Extinction coefficient, 487, 489
  millimolar, 489
  molar, 489
  specific, 489
Eye, 34–43
  anatomy, 39–43
    geometrical optics of, 37–39
    gross, 34–37
    histology, 39–43
  pigments, 50, 358
Eyeball, 34
Eyepiece, 538

F

FAD, 347
Fall-out, 201–202
Far-sighted, 39
Fat molecule, 270
Feedback, 22, 71, 92–96, 180
  negative, 71, 92–96
  and the nervous system, 92–96, 180
  positive, 94
Ferromagnetism, 526
Ferroprotoporphyrin IX, 334
Fibrinogen, 473
Fick diffusion equation, 423–424
Field curvature, 36, 65
Filaments of muscle:
  thick, 151–154
  thin, 151–154
Finger-print region, 513
Focal points, 30
Forbidden lines, 512
Fourier series, 6
Fourier synthesis, 285
Fourier transform, 6, 180
Fovea (centralis), 35, 48–50, 127
Free energy, 147 (*see also* Gibbs' free energy)
Free radical, 302, 311–312, 375, 380,
  533–536
Frequency, 5
  difference limen, 18
  just noticeable differences, 17
Fructose, 271–272, 368–369
Fructose-6-phosphate, 368–369
Fucoxanthol, 373
Fumerase, 380, 477
Function transformer, 574
Fundamental, f, 518
Fundamental frequency, 8
Funnelling, 112

G

GABA (gamma-amino-butyric acid), 180
Galloxanthine, 358
Gamma ray, 185, 613
  wavelengths, 482

Ganglion, 75
Geiger counter, 560
Gene, 197
  enzyme relationship, 197
Genetic recombination, 191, 250
Genetics:
  phage, 256–260
Gibbs' free energy, 147, 364, 370, 390
  definition, 390
  and equilibrium, 391
  partial molal, 391–392
Globar, 490
Globulins, 148
Glucose, 150, 271–272, 368–369
Glutamic acid, 276
Glycine, 275, 564
Glycolytic enzymes, 150
Glycosidase, 318
Golgi body, 268
Gouy balance, 528–530
Grana, 362–363
Guanine, 279
G value, 312–313

H

Hair cells, 25, 111
Half-life, 559
Harmonic, 8
Hearing, 1–5, 10–25, 65, 104–118, 467–469
  arm analog, 111–113
  cochlear mechanism of neural excitation,
    108–111
  cortical representation, 113–116
  hydrodynamic theory, 108–113
  information theory, 467–469
  limits, 12–18
  neural mechanisms, 104–118
  place theory, 104–108
    lesions, evidence from, 107–108
  quantum effect in, 18
  resonator theory, 105–108
  special uses of, 52–64
  telephone theory, 104–108
  tests, 10–19
  threshold of, 10–19
Hearing loss, 16
  pure tone, 16
  speech, 16
Heart, 157–179
  energy relationships, 166
  fish and amphibian, 161–162
  mammalian, 161–163
  rate, 165, 181
  reptilian, 161–162
  sequence of events, 163–168
    electrical events, 164–166
    over-all sequence, 163–164
  vector, 171–177
Heat equation, 424
Helicotrema, 24
Helmholtz free energy, 390
  and equilibrium, 391
Heme, 333–334
Hemocyanin, 308

Hemoglobin, 289–292, 333–334, 528
Hemoprotein, 320
Hill reaction, 373
Histidine, 277
Hodgkin-Huxley equations, 453–456
  functional form of parameters, 454
Hormone, 70–71
Hue, 120
Hydrogen bonding, 287, 293–294
Hydrolase, 318
Hydroxyproline, 277
Hyperopic, 39

I

Image distortion, 65
Impedance:
  electrical, 73, 207, 608–609
    of biological cells, 208–210
    of biological tissues, 210–213
    definition, 207
  ultrasonic:
    characteristic, 213
Index of refraction, 29, 595
Inductance, 74, 608
Induction period, 250
Inferior colliculus, 115
Information, 462
Information theory, 460–476
  average information per amino acid, 472
  average information per message, 465
  general discussion, 461
  genetic code, 474–475
  hearing, 467–469
  noise, 464, 468
  protein structure, 471–473
  redundancy in English, 466–467
  redundancy and polyploidy, 467
  role of languages, 460–461
  sensory perception, 467–471
  vision, 469–471
Infrared:
  wavelengths, 482
Inhibitor:
  competitive, 328–330
  non-competitive, 329–331
Instrumentation, 479–588
  Insulator, 607
  Insulin, 274, 310
  Intensity, 8, 10, 33
Interfacial tension, 236
Interference, 31
Intermediate complex, 321–322
Interneuron, 90
Interphase, 189–190
Invertase, 309, 321, 380
I^{131}, 565–566
Iodopsin, 124, 357–358
Ionizing radiation, 185–203, 299–314,
    610–613
  background radioactivity, 200–201
  as a biological tool, 185–187
  cellular events produced by, 185–203
  critical volume (also called sensitive
    volume), 195, 199, 306

Ionizing radiation (*Cont.*)
  dried protein film bombardment,
    307–310
  elimination of small molecules, 303
  enhancement of effects by oxygen, 195,
    303
  free radical formation, 196
  genetic effects, 196–201
  G value, 312–313
  indirect effects, 304, 311–313
  molecular action, 299–314
  protective agents, 196
  visible cellular effects, 190–196
  water, radicals formed by, 311
Iris, 36, 95, 180
Isocyanopsin, 358
Isoiodopsin, 358
Isoleucine, 275
Isomerase, 319
Isometric, 141
Isomorphic replacement, 286
Isoporphyropsin, 358
Isorhodopsin, 358
Isotonic, 141
Isotope, 557

J

j-j coupling, 518–519
Junction:
  neuromuscular, 84–87

K

Kinetic energy, 159
King crab, 45, 129
K$_M$, 325
Krebs' cycle, 150, 346

L

Lactic acid, 150–151
Lambert's law, 485, 487
Lande g factor, 530
Laplacian equation, 173
Lateral lemniscus, 115
Lateral line organs, 180
Laue pattern, 282
Legendre polynomial, 239
Lens, 29–30, 600–604
  crystalline, 36–38, 41, 49–50
  electromagnetic, 553
  electrostatic, 553
  strength of, 30
  thick, 30, 602–604
  thin, 601–602
Lenz's law, 528
Leucine, 275
Light:
  electromagnetic wave aspect, 31–33
  and the eye, 27–51
  photons as, 33–34
  quantum aspect, 33–34
Light-adapted, 46–48
Light chopper, 498
Limulus, 45, 129, 131, 181
  plexus, 131

Lineweaver-Burk plot, 326
Lipase, 318
Lipid, 268–270
Local response, 81, 85
Loudness, 7–10, 17–19
    difference limen, 17
    just noticeable differences, 17
Loudness level, 10
L-S coupling, 518–519
Luciferase, 477
Luminosity, 120
Lumirhodopsin, 356
Lysine, 276
Lysis, 250
    snap, 255
    from within, 255
Lysogenic state, 254

M

Macula lutea, 35
Magnetic effects in biology, 525–526
Magnetic field, 205–206, 526
    sensory system for, 52, 65, 525
Magnetic induction, 205–206, 527
Magnetic measurements, 525–536
    resonance type, 531–533
    static, 528–531
    table of comparison, 534
Magnetic permeability, 205–206, 527
Magnetic susceptibility, 527
    molar, 530
Malleus, 21–22
Malonic acid, 328
Markhoff process, 465
Mass action law, 317
Mass current, 423
Mass spectrometer, 568
Medial geniculate body, 115
Meiosis, 190–191, 192
Membrane:
    idealized for permeability studies, 425
Meninges, 90
Message, 465
Metaphase, 189–190
Metarhodopsin, 356
Methionine, 276
Michaelis constant, 325 (see K_M)
Michaelis-Menten kinetics, 321
Micrococcus lysodeikticus, 333
Microelectrode, 145
Microscope:
    bright-field light, 538–542
    dark-field, 542–544
    electron, 551–556
    interference-contrast, 545–548
        Dyson's, 546
        multiple-beam interferometer, 547
    phase-contrast, 544
        colored, 545
    polarizing, 548–550
    types, 537
    X-ray, 550–551
    ultraviolet, 550

Microscopy, 537–556
Microspectrophotometer, 542
Microwave wavelengths, 482
Miller indices, 283–284
Millicurie, 559
Mirror points, 177
Mitochondria, 140, 268, 380
    rupture by ultrasound, 221
Mitosis, 189–191
Mitral valve, 162, 164
Modulator, 130
Molecular biology, 265–382
Molecular orbital, 523
Molecular spectra, 501–524
    electronic, 520–523
    and quantum mechanics, 501
    rotational bands, 509–512
    vibrational, 509–510, 512–516
Molecular vibrations, types of, 514
Monochromatic, 120
Monochromator, 483, 491–494
    grating, 492–494
    infrared, 494
    prism, 491–493
    ultraviolet, 494
Monomer, 267
Monose, 271
Motor end plate, 84 (see End plate)
Multiplicity, 519, 522
Muscle, 67, 137–182
    A band, 139–141, 151–154
    anatomy, 138–141, 151–154
        electron microscopy, 151–154
    cardiac, 140
    chemistry, 147–151
    end plate, 84 (see End plate)
    fiber, 139, 181
    heat production, 146–147
    H zone, 139–141, 151–154
    I band, 139–141, 151–154
    involuntary, 141
    J disc, 139
    Q disc, 139–141, 151–154
    smooth, 139–141
    striated, 139–141
        skeletal, 140
        special, 140
    voluntary, 141
        control of, 95–96
    Z disc, 139–141, 151–154
Muscular contraction, 141–154
    initiated by nervous system, 144–146
    sliding model, 153
    tension and length, changes of, 141–143
Mutation, 197, 251
    lethal, 197
Muton, 199, 256, 259
Myelin sheath, 74, 77
Myofibril, 139–141, 151–154
Myoglobin, 141, 148, 289–292, 333–334, 477
Myoneural junction (*also* neuromuscular junction), 84–87, 144–145
Myopic, 39
Myosin, 148, 152

N

Near-sighted, 39
Negative after-potential, 80, 81
Negative feedback, 71, 92–96
Neoretinene b, 353–354
Nernst glower, 490
Nerve, 67–136, 180–182, 437–459 (*see also* Axon and Neuron)
  afferent pathway, 75, 89
  auditory fibers of moths, 180
  clamped, 446–457
    prediction of spike potential, 455–456
  efferent pathway, 76, 90
  impulse conduction, 69–87
  membrane:
    ionic conductances, 451
  membrane potential, 70, 78–83
    and ACh, 443–446
    and Donnan potential, 439
    ionic currents, 449–452
  molecular basis of conduction, 437–459
  peripheral, 75
  specific, 75
Nervous system, 69–71
Neural sharpening, 111–113
Neuromuscular junction, 84–87
  ACh packets, 86
Neuron, 69, 74
  anatomy and histology, 74–78
  bipolar (in retina), 125–126
    amacrine, 125–126
  cell body, 74, 77
  conduction rate, 80–83
  ganglion cells (in retina), 126
Neurospera, 197
Neutron, 185, 612
  high energy, 612
  thermal, 612
Neutron activation, 587
Newtonian fluid, 182
Nissl substance, 74, 77
Nitella, 81, 180, 181
N^{15}, 568–569
Nodal points, 30, 603
Node, 9
Node of Ranvier, 74, 77
Noise:
  physiological, 14
Nonionizing radiations, 204–205
Nonlinearity, 20, 22, 594
Nuclear magnetic resonance (NMR), 532
Nucleic acid, 253, 269, 277–296
  structure, 277–296
Nucleoli, 189
Nucleoplasm, 268
Nucleoside, 277–278
Nucleotide, 277–278
Nucleus:
  in central nervous system, 75, 90
Numerical aperture, 541
Nvt, 188

O

Objective, 538
Olfaction, 52, 65
Ommatidia, 45, 129, 131–132
Opsin, 353
Optical activity, 273, 549
Optical density, 488–489
Optic axis, 600
Optic disk, 35
Optic nerve (second cranial nerve), 119
  coding of information, 470
Optics (geometrical), 29–34, 37–39, 595–604
  focal length, 599
  image, 597
  object, 597
  real, 597
  virtual, 597
Orbital, 504
Orbital electron capture, 559
Organ of Corti, 24–25, 105
Oscillation:
  modes of, 237
Osmotic pressure, 388
Ossicles, 21–24, 65
  anvil, 21
  hammer, 21
  incus, 21
  malleus, 21
  stapes, 21
  stirrup, 21
Oval window, 22
Overtone, 8, 9
Oxidation:
  biological, 344-346
Oxidative phosphorylation, 346–349

P

Pacemaker, 161, 165
Pacian corpuscle, 146
Pain, 52
Paper radiochromatography, 368
Para-chloro-mercuribenzoate, 327
Paramagnetism, 525–528
Paramecium:
  optimum frequency *vs* size, 234
  relative fragility, 229
Parasympathetic system, 76
Partial molal thermodynamic quantities, 391–392
PCMB, 327
Penicillin, 309
Peptide bond, 273
Perilymph, 24
Permeability, 420, 425, 429–432
  altered by ACh, 444
  constant, 425
  P, 430
  red blood cells, 429–432
    various solutes, 432
    to water, 430–431

Peroxidase, 333, 341–344, 535
   diffusion studies, 416–417
   reaction with ascorbic acid, 342, 535
   reaction with cytochrome c, 342, 578–580
Peroxidatic reaction, 333
Phage, 246
   genetics, 256–260
   life cycle, 255
   r-type plaque, 257
   studied by bacteriological methods,
      248–251
   studied by electron microscope, 251–252
   T series of E. coliphages, 247
   vegetative stage, 254
   wild-type plaque, 257
Phase, 592
Phase angle, 592
Phenylalanine, 275
Phon, 10
Phonons, 18
Phospholipid, 270
P^{32}, 566–567
Photoisomerase, 319, 355
Photometer, 483
Photon:
   emission or absorption, 507
Photopic vision, 46–48
Photopigment, 351–352
Photosynthesis, 360–379
   basic chemistry, 364–367
   CO$_2$ conversion, 364–365
   charge separation, 375
   efficiency, 376
   free radicals in, 375–376, 381
   light reaction, 373–377
   path of carbon, 368–370, 381
   photodissociation of water, 365–366
   pigments, 370–372
   reactions within the chloroplast, 367
Photosynthetic phosphorylation, 366–367,
      381
Phycobilin, 370–372
Physical microbiology, 183–263
π-electron, 334, 520–523
Pile unit, 188
Pinna, 19
Pitch, 5
Planck's constant, 18, 503
Plane wave, 592
Plaque, 250
Plastid, 362–363
Pneumoencephalograph, 100
PN$^+$, PNH, 347, 366 (see DPN and TPN)
Poisson probability distribution, 44
Polarized light:
   role in vision, 65
Polarizer, 548
Polyethylene, 301, 303
Polyisobutylene, 301, 304
Polymer, 267, 300–302
   synthetic:
      radiation damage, 302–305, 381
Polymethylene, 304
Polypeptide, 273
Porphyrin, 333–334

Porphyropsin, 358
Positive after-potential, 80, 81
Positron, 612
Potential energy, 159
Pressure:
   absolute, 158
   acoustic, 5 (see Acoustic pressure)
Pressure amplification, 20, 23
Pressure, gauge, 158
Principal, p, 518
Principal plane, 602
Principal points, 30, 602
Proline, 277
Prophage, 254
Prophase, 189–190
Proportional counter, 560
Proprioception, 52, 96, 146
Prosthetic group, 320
Protanopia, 122, 128
Protein, 268–269, 271–277, 286–292,
      300–302
   structure, 286
      α-form, 152, 287
      α-helix, 288–292
      β-form, 152, 287
      fibrous proteins, 287–289
      information theory, 471–473
Protein gels, 240
Proton, 185, 612
Protoplasm, 267
Protoporphyrin, 334, 564, 569
Pulse, 182
Purine, 278
Purkinje fibers, 170
Pyridine nucleotide, 347, 366 (see also
      DPN, TPN)
Pyrimidine, 278

                  Q

Q$_{10}$, 407
Quality of sound, 5
Quanta, 33, 502
Quantum mechanics, 33–34, 501–524
   elementary approach, 502–509
Quantum number, 506
   atomic, 517–520
   atomic one-electron:
      m$_l$, m$_s$, and m$_j$, 517
      orbital, l, 517
      spin, s, 517
      total angular momentum, j, 517
      total, n, 517
   molecular:
      electronic, various, 520–521
      rotational, 510–511
      table of symbols, 521
      vibrational, 512–513
      X-ray terminology, 519
Quantization, 503, 509
Quasi-static approximation, 325

                  R

Rad, 187
Radiations (table), 611

Rankine balance, 529–531
Rate constants, 316–317
Rayleigh criterion, 32, 48
Rbe, 188
Reactance, 73, 207, 609
Reaction coordinate, 408
Reaction rate, 316–317
   diffusion-independent, 406–407
   diffusion-limited, 406
Reb, 187
Recessive, 190, 197
Recon, 199, 256–258
Red blood cells, 569
   permeability, 429–432
   relative fragility, 229
Redundancy, 466
Reisner's membrane, 24
Relative luminosity, 46
Relaxation:
   frequency, 211, 215–218
   mechanical, 215
   method, 587
Rem, 187
Rep, 187
Resistance, 73, 207, 607
   ultrasonic:
      characteristic, 213
Resolution, limit of, 538
Resolving power, 32, 538, 543
   bright-field light microscope, 541
Resonance, 8
   of biological cells, 229, 233–244
      more exact treatments, 242–244
      experimental basis, 233–236
      interfacial-tension model, 235–239
      rigid-shell model (*also* gelatinous-shell
         model), 235, 240–242
      mixed mode, 241
      tangential mode, 241
   magnetic, 532
   of molecular bonds, 334
   pulsating mode, 235
   Q factor, 242–243
   surface, 234–236
Resonant frequency, 9
Resonator:
   Helmholtz, 65, 105
Resting potential, 78, 145–146
   muscle, 145–146
   nerve, 78
Retina, 35, 41–43, 48–50, 119, 124–127
   model, 124–127
Retinene, 353, 381
Retinene₁, 353–354
Retinene₂, 357
Rhodopsin, 124, 127, 352–357
   daylight, 124
Ribonuclease, 380
Ribose, 278
Ribose nucleic acid, 254 (*see* RNA)
Ribulose-1, 5-diphosphate, 368–369
RNA (ribose nucleic acid), 254, 269,
   295–296, 567
Rods, 35, 41–43, 45–48, 124–129
Roentgen (r), 187

Rotifers:
   damage by ultrasound, 231
Round window, 21, 22
rII-mutant, 257
Russel-Saunders coupling, 518–519

S

S-a node, 161, 162, 164–165
Sarcolemma, 140
Sarcomere, 140
Satellite cell, 77
Saturation, 120
Scala media, 24
Scala tympani, 22, 24
Scala vestibuli, 22, 24
Scenedesmus, 362
Schematic eye, 37, 38
Schwann cell, 74, 77
Scintillation counter, 560
Scission, 302, 304
Sclera, 34, 40
Scotopic vision, 46–48
Selection rules, 511, 513, 517–518, 521–522
Semilunar valve, 162, 164
Sense of direction, 59–61
   ants, 59–60, 65
   bees, 60–61, 65
Sensory systems, 52–53
   special, 1–65
Serine, 275
Servomechanism, 94, 180
Sharp, s, 518
Shear modulus, 240
Shear wave, 214
Silk, 380
Singlet state, 522
Sink, 424
Sino-auricular node, 161 (*see also* S-a node)
Sinus venosus, 161, 162
Snell's law, 595–597
Sone, 10
Sonic, 220
Soret band, 334
Sound:
   and the ear, 3–26
   physical characteristics, 590
Sound (acoustic) pressure, 5, 7, 8
   amplitude, 5, 7, 8, 10, 13
Sound pressure level, 8–11, 13
Spectral density, 122
Spectrometer, 483
Spectrophotometer, 483, 488–495
   detectors, 494
   dual-beam, 498
   light sources, 490–491
   split-beam, 496, 498–500
Spectrophotometry, 481–524
   absorption, 481–500
      flow systems, 495–496
      quantum mechanical basis, 501–524
      role in biology, 481–484
      table of symbols, 489
      units and symbols, 484–489
   infrared, 509–516